Depressive States
and Their Treatment

Depressive States
and Their Treatment

Edited by
Vamık D. Volkan, M.D.

Jason Aronson, Inc.
Northvale, New Jersey and London

Library of Congress Cataloging-in-Publication Data

Main entry under title:

Depressive states and their treatment.

  Includes bibliographies and indexes.
  1. Depression, Mental.   2. Depression, Mental —
Treatment.   3. Psychotherapy.   I. Volkan, Vamık D.,
1932–   . [DNLM: 1. Depression.   2. Depressive
Disorder.   WM 171 D997]
RC537.D96   1985   616.85′27   85-6216
ISBN 0-87668-743-5

Manufactured in the United States of America.

To D. Wilfred Abse, M.D.,
My Teacher, Colleague, and Friend

CONTENTS

CONTRIBUTORS

D. WILFRED ABSE, M.D., is Director of Psychiatric Education at St. Alban's Hospital in Radford, Virginia. He is Clinical Professor of Psychiatry at the University of Virginia and is also a practicing psychoanalyst.

GEORGE S. ALEXOPOLOUS, M.D., is Associate Professor of Psychiatry at Cornell University Medical College in White Plains, New York, and a full-time staff member at New York Hospital.

MAURICE APPREY, M.A.C.P., is Assistant Professor of Behavioral Medicine and Psychiatry at the University of Virginia and a faculty member of the Division of Psychoanalytic Studies at the University of Virginia School of Medicine, where he is also Assistant Dean of Student Affairs.

L. BRYCE BOYER, M.D., is Associate Director of Psychiatric Training at Herrick Hospital in Berkeley, California and a psychoanalyst in private practice in Berkeley.

JOHN BUCKMAN, M.D., is Vice-Chairman and Professor of Psychiatry at the University of Virginia School of Medicine, where he is also Director of Residency Training.

STANLEY H. CATH, M.D., is Associate Clinical Professor of Psychiatry at Tufts University School of Medicine. He is Medical Director of the Family Advisory Service and Treatment Center in Belmont, Massachusetts, and in the private practice of psychotherapy, psychoanalysis, and geriatric psychiatry.

ANDRE P. DERDEYN, M.D., is Professor of Psychiatry at the University of Virginia School of Medicine, where he is also Director of the Division of Child and Family Psychiatry.

ROBERT M. DORN, M.D., is Professor of Psychiatry at the University of California Davis Medical Center in Sacramento and former Training and Supervising Analyst at the Los Angeles Psychoanalytic Society and Institute. He is Chief of the Division of Child, Adolescent, and Family Psychiatry at the University of California.

DAVID R. HAWKINS, M.D., is Director, Consultation-Liaison Service, in the Department of Psychiatry at Michael Reese Hospital and Medical Center. He is Professor of Psychiatry at the Pritzker School of Medicine, University of Chicago.

SHELDON HEATH, M.D., F.R.C.P.(C), is a psychoanalyst in private practice in Toronto. He is past-president of the Toronto Psychoanalytic Society and is on the faculty of the Toronto Institute of Psychoanalysis.

GORDON KIRSCHNER, M.D., is in the private practice of psychoanalysis and psychotherapy with adults and children in Washington, D.C. He is Co-Chairman of the Training Program in Advanced Psychoanalytic Psychotherapy at The Washington School of Psychiatry.

JERRY H. MOREWITZ, M.D., is Director of Psychiatry of the Consultation-Liaison Service, at the Eastern Virginia Medical School, where he is also Assistant Professor of Psychiatry.

BARBARA J. NOVAK, M.D., practices psychiatry as a staff member of the Central Virginia Psychiatric Associates in Charlottesville. She is in psychoanalytic training with the Baltimore-District of Columbia Institute of Psychoanalysis.

HARVEY L. RICH, M.D., is a psychoanalyst in private practice in Washington, D.C. He is a faculty member of the Washington School of Psychiatry and an instructor at the Washington Psychoanalytic Institute.

PERIHAN A. ROSENTHAL, M.D., is Director of the Division of Child/Adolescent Psychiatry, Department of Psychiatry, at Newark Beth Israel Medical Center, Newark, New Jersey, and Associate Professor of Clinical Psychiatry at Rutgers Medical School.

STUART ROSENTHAL, M.D., is Director of Psychiatry and Director of the South Newark/Irvington Community Mental Health Center at Newark Beth Israel Medical Center in Newark, New Jersey. He is Clinical Professor of Psychiatry (Biobehavioral Sciences) at the Boston University School of Medicine, and a Senior Associate of the Levinson Institute in Cambridge, Massachusetts.

STEPHEN B. SHANFIELD, M.D., is Professor of Psychiatry at the University of Texas Health Science Center in San Antonio. University of Texas Health Sciences Center at San Antonio.

CHARLES W. SOCARIDES, M.D., is Attending Psychiatrist at the Bronx Municipal Hospital Center in New York City. He is Clinical Professor of Psychiatry at the Albert Einstein College of Medicine/Montefiore Medical Center in New York and is also in private practice.

VAMIK D. VOLKAN, M.D., is Professor of Psychiatry and Director of the Division of Psychoanalytic Studies at the University of Virginia School of Medicine in Charlottesville. He is Medical Director of Blue Ridge Hospital of the University of Virginia, and Training and Supervising Analyst at The Washington Psychoanalytic Institute in Washington, D.C.

HARRY ZALL, M.D., is Senior Attending Psychiatrist at the Institute of Pennsylvania Hospital and Clinical Instructor in Psychiatry at the University of Pennsylvania Medical School.

STEVEN ZAVODNICK, M.D., is Associate Director, Inpatient Psychiatry, at Pennsylvania Hospital in Philadelphia, and a faculty member of the Department of Psychiatry of the University of Pennsylvania School of Medicine.

ACKNOWLEDGMENTS

The preparation of a book like this is a long and arduous process, so when Dr. Jason Aronson asked me to compile a collection of essays on the subject of depressive states and its treatment I turned to colleagues I know well and whose work I admire. I looked forward to this association with great pleasure and, when I called on some outside my personal acquaintance, was gratified to make new friends as well.

Ms. Joan Langs, the Editorial Director of Jason Aronson Inc., made valuable suggestions and was most helpful in shaping the book's present format. I had the pleasure of working closely once again with my long-time friend and editorial assistant, Mrs. Virginia Kennan, and I thank her for her help.

My receipt of the contributors' essays over many months brought a spirit of friendly relatedness and good fellowship — an excellent antidote for depressed feelings. Perhaps it is not an accident that old and new friends joined in writing about such painful topics, since our intellectual collaboration made me feel that we work against a supportive background.

CHAPTER ONE

The Scope of Depressive States

Vamık D. Volkan, M.D.

This book updates what is known about mourning, depression, and depressive states and brings that knowledge to bear on aspects of psychological practice and medical practice. We will review current knowledge and also take into account the ways, both obvious and subtle, in which any one of these states interacts with another. Although we tend to think of *uncomplicated* mourning as "nature's exercise in loss and restitution" (Volkan 1971, p. 255), and hence somehow benign and even enriching, albeit often painful, we think of depression as being psychopathological. Nonetheless, the two states are often equated in everyday practice when we make formulations about a patient's problems and conflicts. Abraham's (1911, 1916, 1924) and Freud's (1917) classical works on the relationship between the psychodynamics of mourning and melancholia are emphasized in our training, and subsequent clinical experience confirms and reconfirms the views of these two great thinkers despite new findings, emphases, and modifications.

Mourning occurs in reaction to the loss of a loved one without any disturbance of self-regard. Freud noted that in some persons, however, such a loss produces depression rather than mourning. We suspect that these persons have pathological dispositions. We note that there is no one form of melancholia; some forms of it suggest somatic rather than psychogenic affection. Patients to whom Freud ascribed classical depression had a profound sense of dejection, a lack of interest in the environment, and no capacity to love; their activity diminished and and seemed to be inhibited. A crucial difference from mourning is the appearance in depression of reduced self-respect that can culminate in self-reviling, self-reproach, and delusional expectations of punishment. Mania appears when the ego recovers from the loss of the object.

Freud's (1917) *Mourning and Melancholia* is important not only as a paper dealing with clinical issues but also as a milestone in Freud's journey toward his formulation of the theory of the superego and his reassessment of the sense of guilt. In this paper, Freud raised a crucial question about the nature of identification when describing the way in which the mental representation of the object lost in reality or fantasy is introjected and identified with by the mourner. *Mourning and Melancholia* contains the seeds of those psychoanalytic theories of object relations that have attracted such close and systematic study in recent years.

My studies of mourning and related states (Volkan 1981) emphasize what patients do with the mental representation of the person they have lost. After an object is lost, its representation is experienced as an introject for a period of time. Following Abraham's (1924) and Fenichel's (1945) observations, Tähkä (1984) states that such an introject does not represent a regressive transformation of identifications, but it represents "an attempt to protect the self from the experience of a total object loss by preserving the object in the inner world until the working through of the loss gradually makes it superfluous" (p. 16).

In the long run, the mourner develops "remembrance formation". This term, coined by Tähkä (1984) refers to "building and integrating the representation of the lost object into a remembrance of him as he was really experienced during a common period of life. Once it has been established, its later calling back to the mind, reminiscing about it and dismissing it again from the mind, are invariably experienced as activities of the self taking place exclusively on the subject's own conditions" (p. 18).

In remembrance formation, the representation of the dead person is fully differentiated and is experienced as separate from the self representation. As Tähkä also suggests, however, following an object loss other internalizations take place along with and/or besides developing temporary introjects and forming remembrances. Different types of identifications with the representation of the lost person occur and such processes are reflected in the surface clinical picture of the mourner. I described the selective identification with the mental representation of the lost one that is found in uncomplicated mourning and is in the service of healing and growth (Hartmann, Kris, and Loewenstein 1946, Loewald 1962, 1973, Stierlin 1973) and the enrichment of the self-system. Selected aspects of the representation of the one lost continue to live, being to the mourner aspects of an "immortal object" (Schafer 1968), and to promote "generational continuity" (Volkan 1979, 1981) as a sort of psychological gene passed from one generation to the next.

It is profitable to expand the term "loss" beyond its obvious use in connection with such catastrophic events as the death of a spouse. It is also applied appropriately to the need to leave behind (and thus lose) what is familiar and reassuring as we pass from one phase of life to the next, beginning with the stages of childhood development and continuing through the rest of the life cycle. Uncomplicated mourning seen in this context can lead to many different types of selective, growth-producing functions that come from identifications. Psychological genes conveyed from one generation to the next may, however, be disruptive and pathological.

Unlike the person undergoing uncomplicated mourning, a person prone to depression identifies altogether with the representation of the lost one. "In toto" representation (Ritvo and Solnit 1958, Smith 1975, Volkan 1981) is disruptive, preserving within the survivor's self the ambivalent relationship in which the survivor was formerly engaged with the lost one. Aggression turned inward against the self in a nonselective identification fuels a sense of guilt and self-reproach because aggressively tinged aspects of the identification are in conflict with those that are libidinally tinged.

I have found a third type of mourner reaction to the mental representation of someone lost. Here, the patient maintains a stable representation as an unassimilated introject and invests certain inanimate objects with magic (Linking Objects) (Volkan 1972, 1981). This unassimilated introject is different than Tähkä's remembrance formation in three ways: a) it possesses wish-fulfilling functions while remembrance formation "includes the awareness that nothing more can be expected from it and therefore, in its fully-established forms it has chances of becoming the most realistic of all existing object representations" (Tähkä 1984, p. 16); b) it includes elements of regressive transformations from previous identifications with the representation of the dead person; c) it is involved in a constant attempt to become identifications while falling short in these efforts.

Meanwhile, the linking objects provide an external locus for the meeting of the representation of the lost one with the representation of the self. Patients then remain in limbo, entertaining the illusion that they can choose whether to "kill" the one lost or keep this person alive. I have called this state established pathological mourning. The use of the representation of the lost one in this way differentiates this state from one of uncomplicated mourning or (reactive) depression.

Comparison of both uncomplicated and established pathological mourning with the type of depression that occurs after the loss of a loved one points to a basic model for psychological understanding of depression, although one obviously needs to add to this basic model in order to understand more complicated processes. This is so especially in the case of depression that occurs without observable loss as an antecedent. The concept of loss must be expanded to encompass what might be more natural to refer to as change. A change in the organization of which one is a part, for example, may have some symbolic intrapsychic meaning not immediately apparent. The concept of loss may, paradoxically, apply also to the surrender in psychotherapy of a neurotic symptom that had been reassuring to the patient in some way. Often the nature of the "loss" becomes apparent only in the process of psychotherapy. Further complicating the issue is the fact that there are many kinds of depression and, in some of these, as Freud implied, biological factors predominate.

In this volume we do not present a systematic review of psychoanalytic metapsychological understanding of depression and related states. Such reviews can be found in the literature, beginning with the writings of Fenichel (1945, Chapter 17) or of Garma (1947).

Lewin (1950) emphasized the euphoric side of manic-depressive illness in *The Psychoanalysis of Elation* and gave a brief historical survey of what had been written on depression up to that time. Citing the works of Abraham (1911, 1916, 1924), Freud (1917), Rado (1928), Gero (1936), Melanie Klein (1940), Bibring (1953), Edith Jacobson (1957), and Mabel Blake Cohen and her coworkers (1954), Mendelson (1960) offered a comprehensive review of the theoretical models of those psychoanalytic writers who contributed most to the theory of depression. He identified and focused on certain major subjects, including the treatment of depression, that they considered. Mendelson (1960) also has a chapter relating psychodynamic theories to the broader field of clinical psychiatry.

Later, Gaylin collected well-known papers by distinguished psychoanalysts and updated his introduction to the edition of 1984. He included most of those whose work Mendelson had reviewed with the addition of Fenichel (1945), Spitz (1946), Bowlby (1961) and Levine (1965), among others. Although I disagree with some of the emphasis evident in Gaylin's introduction, such as his uncritical acceptance of Bibring's (1953) contributions, I believe that his collection is valuable for its chronological survey of psychoanalytic theories of depression.

Giant steps have been taken in recent decades toward a better understanding of the biological factors in depression and related states, while emphasis on psychological factors seemingly diminished in certain circles. Medicine regards the realm of the mind, which is concerned with meaning, as something apart from the physical brain-body unit that is concerned with matter and energy. This dichotomy is reflected in semantic, conceptual, and methodological differences. In uncomplicated situations, physical growth and the healing of wounds take place in expected ways, and this is paralleled by normal development of the mind (psyche), which progresses through known phases. Furthermore, if one examines the process of mourning, one finds a similarity to the healing of a wound (Engel 1961); healing also follows a predictable course unless what might be called psychological infection occurs.

The interface of the biological and the psychological has received much attention. Despite this, and despite the logical assumption that mind-brain, body-soul, or psyche-soma combine into one unit, we have a tendency in practice to see the patient as being "divided" into mind and body. Only when we insist on the unity of the human organism in respect to a symptom do we use the term "psychosomatic."

Nonetheless, with the influence of high technology and sophisticated laboratory work has come pressure, conscious or unconscious, to enlist the caregiver on the side of "science" to the neglect of appropriate consideration of the patient's psyche. In one sense, every patient represents psychosomatic illness, and I suggest this is especially true in relation to depression. In a recent case presentation at the University of Virginia Medical School, faculty member Kemal Elbirlik told of a middle-aged woman who had lost both limbs to diabetes. Fitted with prostheses, she adjusted mentally to her loss, using the mechanism of denial in an exaggerated way. A subsequent brain infarct led, however, to psychotic behavior. As she began to recover, she had the delusion that she was the father of the Flintstone family in the television cartoon. She wanted to drive a car as he did; this translated into using her feet and legs as motive power. Even in her temporary psychotic state she was preoccupied with the loss of her legs. Clearly, whatever the CT scan and medication could contribute to her care and treatment, it was necessary to take into account how she symbolized her grief at losing her legs, and her mind's attempt to handle it.

I believe it is an oversimplification to classify a depression as being *either* biologically or psychologically caused. The value of the biological approach will be significantly reduced if we fail to consider the intrinsic part played by psychological factors in the etiology of depression. To limit oneself to one view of causation would be to abort the promising and hoped-for collaboration between those exploring the psychological aspects of depression and those whose work focuses on biology.

Basic Concepts

The first part of this volume gives clinical descriptions of mourning, depression, and depressive character, and examines them from current psychoanalytic points of view. D. Wilfred Abse, a scholar of the classical literature of psychology and literature in general, uses psychoanalytic understanding and clinical illustrations to illuminate what we know about depression, introducing his exposition with the simple statement, "Mental depression signifies a sense of ill-being." Psychoanalytic studies of this "ill-being," which brings so much pain and suffering, inevitably involve the psychoanalytic study of affects for which Abse provides a background. (Also see Volkan 1976, Chapter 7). Abse agrees with Rapaport (1942) that the psychoanalytic theory of affects is incomplete and speaks of the relationship between the expression of affect and bodily symptoms.

Bibring (1953), who approaches depression from an ego-psychological point of view, identified four basic ego states: the secure; the elated or triumphant; the anxious; and the depressed. He went on to say that these ego states "cannot be reduced any further" (p. 34). If we were to follow this thinking, we might consider a parallel between anxiety and depression, the former occurring when the ego gives a signal to fight against danger and the latter appearing when the ego is paralyzed by danger.

Abse is not reductionist; acknowledging the usefulness of Bibring's focus on the ego, he criticizes, like Jacobson (1971), Bibring's view of depression as something essentially independent of the vicissitudes of the aggressive drive and orality, neglecting the role of object relations and ambivalence. Mahler (1966) observed that one can see underlying hostility conflicts even in infantile depression. Jacobson (1971) notes that "what Bibring describes as basic ego responses are actually characteristic states of normal or disturbed narcissistic equilibrium, which can be observed in early childhood" (p. 178).

Abse falls back on classical psychological observations (McDougall 1936, Shand 1921), and, citing what the explorer Scott wrote during his polar expedition, he examines mood change from confidence to hope to anxiety to despondency and, finally, to despair. There is much to be learned here about the phenomenology of different affective states. Abse gives a thorough review of depression from depth psychology, comparing it to mourning and not limiting his discussion to the depression that appears in neurotic or psychotic ways.

Abse opens his second chapter on the depressive character by reporting an experiment of the seventeenth century German neuropathologist, Moebius, and continues with an examination of the severe depressive masochistic urges that can explain some fundamental issues involved in recent developments in Iran. He is in general agreement with other psychoanalysts that in most situations a depressive state of mind reproduces to a considerable extent a depression experienced in childhood, and he is in accord with Berliner's (1966) claim that adult patients with depressive character experienced an unhappy childhood during which moral masochism affected their personality. Abse warns, however, that it is difficult to appreciate retrospectively the actual occurrences of early life and the role of fantasy that had no basis in reality.

In the last chapter of Part I, Gordon Kirschner provides a model of depression based on his study of the creative process as well as on his psychoanalytic work with children. His cases indicate the effect of a mother's lack of empathy on the appearance of depression in adult life. He attributes the imbalance we call depression to some *developmental* distortion. In this state one is suspended in time, denying loss and hoping for its reversal. On the other hand, he tells us that creativity is "making a finding new."

Mourning and Depression in the Life Cycle

Gordon Kirschner's chapter in Part I, with its developmental model of depression, leads to a study of depression as it appears in Part II. The chapter "Preschool Age Children," by Perihan and Stuart Rosenthal, reviews depression in children from the viewpoint of psychological, genetic, biological, behavioral, and stress models. The authors describe with case illustrations an eclectic approach to these children.

Andre Derdeyn, whose chapter complements the Rosenthals', offers a discussion of mourning and depression in childhood, approaching the topic by looking at two major causes of childhood depression — parental death and divorce. Current statistics indicate that the latter is an inevitable early experience for many children. In reviewing the literature on childhood depression, Derdeyn notes that investigators differ as to whether we can speak of "true depression" in children before the maturation of the superego. An expert on children's reaction to parental divorce, he gives clinical illustration of how he works with such youngsters as well as with their parents.

Robert Dorn, a child analyst, distinguishes between the psychodynamics of early adolescence and those of adolescence proper, writing with the awareness of the biochemical, neuroendocrinological, neurophysiological, and biopsychosocial aspects of depression that characterizes a growing number of researchers. Adolescents are obliged to regress as a precondition to the reorganization that normally ensues. During this regression, they loosen their ties to the internalized representations of important others that have been theirs throughout childhood. These representations and the corresponding representations of the self are overhauled (A. Freud 1958, Blos 1968). This process is referred to as the second individuation and is included in the list of processes Blos holds necessary for character crystallization. Referring to the process by which ties to internal representations are loosened before the psychic energy thus freed is reinvested in new (or, at least, modified) representations during adolescence, Wolfenstein (1966) stated that it is a normal prerequisite to the ability to grieve in an adult way. Thus, mourning and depression in adolescence need consideration.

A depressed mother is likely to pass her depression onto her newborn child (see Volkan 1982 as well as Heath's contribution to this volume). Maurice Apprey deals in Part II with an even earlier situation, the disturbed relationship of a mother to her unborn child. In this case, clinical experience indicates an unfavorable influence on the child. Apprey emphasizes the difficulties of childbearing women who are not psychologically ready to give life and thus react aggressively toward pregnancy and childbirth.

Aside from a reference to childbearing women, Part II has no chapter on the depressions that occur during adult years; Parts I and III give them adequate consideration. Part II concludes with Stanley Cath's chapter on mourning and depression in the elderly. Cath is highly aware of the biological contribution to depression and speaks of the neuronal changes of later years as well as the need to deal with the imminence of death. He stresses the mind-body connection, and gives clinical data to illustrate his theoretical formulations.

Life Situations

This part gives consideration to the ways in which psychological equilibrium is affected by changes around us and the ways in which we learn to deal with the environment differently than before. Among the countless changes to be considered are those arising from natural or man-made disasters, which may be deeply depressing to survivors. Sometimes such tragedies lead to an attempt to recover the loss; survivors are involved in a form of regeneration to remove the shared depression. An example of regeneration is given by Williams and Parkes (1975), who found that the birthrate in the Welsh village of Aberfan, where 116 children and 28 adults had been lost in an avalanche of coal slurry, increased in the five years after this disaster. When mass trauma is too great, as in the Holocaust, there are no such regenerative consequences. Rangell (1976) notes that, although the unconscious is vast, psychic space is limited and that of the survivors of a massive psychic trauma is overwhelmed. He suggests that "mourning is a model of such an occupation of psychic space" (p. 315). Obviously, he refers not to mourning that is resolved but to that which leads to psychological complications.

In this part we also give examples of life changes starting with a look at military life. Shanfield notes that the major task of the military is to manage violence and that the theme of death is strongly present. A member of the military is immersed in experiences of dehumanization, and relates psychologically to an enemy invested with dehumanized and dangerous qualities. He acknowledges that this situation is essential for survival since it permits smooth psychological functioning associated with minimal guilt, grief, and depression in the performance of duty. Even though few soldiers may be engaged in combat, all share a psychological sense of preparedness for combat. The psychological theme of separation is prominent in psychiatric casualties and resonates with themes of death generated by the organization. Shanfield reminds us also that casualties are subsumed under the label of *military dislocation syndromes*, which addresses the common thematic issues of separation underlying their problems. He concluded that a cohesive sense of self with minimal problems about separation is necessary for membership in the military.

In the next chapter, Stuart Rosenthal, a consultant on psychological well-being within organizations, picks up the theme of mourning and depression as he examines an organization as a living system. One sees here a parallel between an organization and a biological system, since each must maintain equilibrium among its subsystems, and especially with the larger system or systems of which it is a component. It is little wonder that persons placed in a certain spot within an organization may react with depression or mourning to some of the changes taking place within the total system or in its parts.

Self-destructive behavior is discussed by John Buckman in relation to inner and outer life events, to the life cycle, and, most importantly, in its association with depression. Buckman notes that 3,000,000 people in this country attempt suicide each year; this statistic alone justifies the continuing study and reexamination of depression, the most common but far from simplest mental disorder.

Psychotherapy

Part IV deals with psychological treatments from psychoanalysis proper to brief interventions and reports on the presence of depressive states in patients diagnosed initially as having some other mental disturbance.

A patient comes to the psychoanalyst with a depression or a depressive character, but once the psychoanalysis is under way, the surface picture loses its critical significance with the development of therapeutic regression and transference neurosis. The analyst is analyzing, not merely treating symptoms, and the patient's surrender or modification of the depression is, in a sense, a fringe benefit of the analysis. We all know this but tend to forget it much of the time. Therefore, Harvey Rich gives in some detail the total account of the psychoanalysis of a woman who had repetitive symptoms of depression; analysis took the usual route, her underlying conflicts were resolved, and her troubling symptoms disappeared. Rich (personal communication) told me that, when she had initially described herself to him as a frog, he had been tempted to accept her terms in view of her traumatic experiences in early and adult life:

Indeed, there is a tendency in myself—and I fear it is learned from our field of science—to equate early life trauma with impairment in object constancy and thus to exclude such patients from the help they might derive through psychoanalysis. But this patient was not as sick as she "should" have been.

He sensed an insistent internal cry beneath the pathology she exhibited, and recalled a discussion with the late Dr. Lucie Jessner, one of his revered supervisors — and mine, too. He had spoken to her of a boy who made no other sounds than those of a frog during his therapeutic sessions. She commented in reply to this that the boy must have believed that under his pathology lived a prince crying out to be discovered. Dr. Rich's chapter tells of releasing a princess from a frog lost in depression.

Sheldon Heath's paper goes beyond our frequent observation of finding certain people depressing. His many clinical illustrations show that people do indeed select people to make them depressed for their own psychological reasons. When this phenomenon appears in the analytic dyad, one must expect special transference-countertransference problems.

The following chapter reports on work of mine that demonstrated how certain patients suffering from established pathological mourning can benefit from a short-term treatment I call "regrief therapy." I also comment on the analysis of patients with complicated mourning. We need to consider, when making formulations about depression and planning psychological treatment strategies, that depressive conditions also appear in people disposed to other mental disturbances. Dr. Abse's first paper in Part I included statements about depressive states occurring in neuroses in general.

Our clinical observation suggests that no one can live life without experiencing some form of depressive state. This statement is even more appropriate if we view "normal" mourning as occupying the opposite end of the spectrum from severe depression.

A patient may present a conversion symptom, only to reveal in treatment that the symptom conceals a constellation of complicated mourning. Careful investigation of a young man with a weakness in his knees during the early hours of night who was diagnosed as having conversion hysteria showed that his symptom served to identify disruptively with the image of the father who had been killed in an early evening mine collapse (Volkan 1981).

A patient in analysis whose initial diagnosis does not include depression or depressive character may become "depressed" due to therapeutic regression in which the patient reactivates early depressed introjects in order to tame and assimilate them. (When the patient came to treatment, such introjects might have been merged with identifications in which elements without depression were dominant. In this situation, depressed introjects were dormant and shielded by healthier identifications.) But before being tamed and assimilated, they may bring depression.

I recently wrote the entire story of a psychoanalysis that highlighted the appearance of mourning whenever the analysand loosened his hold on (lost) an influential mental representation of his early mother or father. I also emphasized this patient's mourning process in the termination phase of his analysis, when he was about to leave his analyst behind as well as the transference figure that, being resolved, had become more fully a "new object" (Loewald 1960).

The "depressive states" manifested in mental illnesses raise many challenging questions. How do patients with different established mental conditions mourn or get depressed? Searles (1982) wrote about the inability of the borderline individual to grieve unless given therapy. He considered this a major diagnostic criterion for such conditions. We expect mourning in patients with borderline personality organization to occur when they mend their "good" and "bad" self- and object constellations with their accompanying opposing drive derivatives. This occurs because patients "lose" their previously unmended units. My book on the whole story of one analysis gives an example. My patient had almost gained the ability to put together his opposing images of his father.

> He began sobbing and reached for the box of tissues. He had shed tears before but had always avoided this kind of intense display and had never needed to use tissues. As he wept, he described seeing one black and one white wall. "I am keeping the images of my father apart," he said. "But now the walls are becoming liquid, like my imagination. They are turning into oceans, one white and one blue. Moses is walking between them, splitting the white water from the blue. I want to put my father together, but I feel so sad." His weeping increased. (Volkan 1984, p. 186)

If the process does not take place normally, i.e., on a level that makes it possible to tolerate mending, the patient may experience depression.

L. Bryce Boyer here updates his paper on Christmas neuroses 30 years after its first publication. He takes his data from the many patients with severe characterological, borderline, and schizophrenic disorders he has seen in analysis or analytic treatment and from the smaller number who were neurotic. He gives many illustrative vignettes and answers the questions about the depressive response of all these patients to the Yuletide. Here an external event, the coming of Christmas, initiated a reactivation of fantasies pertaining to memories of earlier failure to cope with siblings.

Charles Socarides, widely known for his investigation of sexual deviation, writes about depression in perversion, with special reference to the function of erotic experience in sexual perversion. In this important contribution he explores the centrality of the depressive affect in the formation, meaning, and content of sexual perversion.

He also gives clinical examples and demonstrates that it is not the erotic experience per se (the instinct derivative) but rather the function of the erotic experience that is reanimated and revived in order to restore the self against threats of fragmentation and to gain self-cohesion. This reduces narcissistic injury and diminishes or erases anxiety and depression through the promotion of opposite affective states.

Somatic Issues

Dealing with psychobiological findings and theories as well as somatic treatments, this last section provides a balance between psychological findings and biological theories about depressions, related states, and their treatment.

George Alexopoulos reminds us that one of his ethnic ancestors, Hippocrates (460–355 B.C.), wrote that melan-coli (black bile) was responsible for depression. Hippocrates believed that an excess of black bile reached the brain and made it humid and hot. The notion that black bile was a toxic product of digestion had been considered by Theophrastus (370–286 B.C.), but the emphasis made by Hippocrates was that the brain was thereby made unhealthy (Adams 1939). He also indicated a naturalistic view when he spoke of long-lasting fear and distress as causes of melancholia (Lewis 1934). In any case, the idea that melancholia comes about because something has invaded the brain (body) and made it sicken goes back to ancient times.

Researchers have been busy during the last few decades or so trying to learn the psychobiological reasons for affective disorders. Alexopoulos was asked to give a summary of psychobiological hypotheses concerning depression. Not only does he give a lucid summary, but he provides a bibliography for any reader wanting to delve further into this subject.

Psychoanalysts and psychodynamically oriented therapists will continue to understand and treat their depressed patients in the ways in which they have become expert. Those more at home in psychobiological research may apply their understanding of depression to their clinical work. Both must know, however, what is evolving on either side. Alexopulos speaks of one "notion" that some people evidently have pronounced biological vulnerability to affective disorders and develop symptoms even when the "pressure" of psychological factors is minimal. Conversely, in the absence of biological vulnerability, psychological occurrences that point to depression can be handled in a better way.

David Hawkins expresses a similar view, holding that affective illness, like diabetes mellitus, is now considered to consist of a number of different disorders, the final common pathway of a number of different abnormalities. Hawkins also refers to the time of Hippocrates when sleep disturbance was included among the symptoms of depression. It is not surprising that the advent of sleep and dream research led some researchers to study sleep in affective illness. We are fortunate to have Dr. Hawkins, a psychoanalyst well known for his sleep research, bring up us to date on this field; his list of references can be used as a guide for further reading on this subject. In summarizing, Hawkins identifies "tantalizing" areas, the understanding of which remains elusive at present but which are sure to elicit further study.

In the following chapter, Jerry Morewitz demonstrates how to deal with mourning, depression, and depressive states in patients hospitalized for problems other than mental illness. He refers to several studies that indicate that primary-care physicians tend to diagnose depression too seldom and that misdiagnosis is common. His paper is also designed to illustrate essential features that can be used to diagnose depression in general medical practice. The nosology and classification of diagnosis is included again here to alert general practitioners to look for clues to depression. Morewitz lists medical illnesses that may promote depression, among them pancreatic carcinoma, pernicious anemia, and brain tumor.

It has been reported that 10 percent of the population of the United States experiences or will experience major depression. In fact, this would seem a highly conservative figure since great numbers of patients are being treated for it in different ways. General psychiatry seeks to respond to the enormous problem posed by affective disorders, but we have not yet developed magic pills or instant psychotherapy to deal with our patients. Many therapists are now combining psychodynamic psychotherapy with medication, and we need to be informed about studies conducted by both schools in order not to be turned toward magic — whether "organic" or "psychologic" — by the anxiety of dealing with a difficult patient.

Prange (1983), psychiatrist and biological researcher, has echoed the ideas of Lewis Thomas, the biomedical essayist, concerning three levels of technology: nontechnology, halfway technology, and high technology. Nontechnology refers to what we do when we stand by a patient and lend support. We patch things up with halfway technology, inventing remedies without finding the cause of the illness. Grasping the cause puts us into high technology, which is economical and highly effective. Prange sees the use of psychotropic drugs as a practice of halfway technology. I suspect that the same could be said about our use of antidepressants; while we have psychological theories about depression, as Alexopoulos's paper demonstrates, we also have biological theories about it, and we should not lose sight of the exciting work being done to bring the use of medication in psychiatry to the level of high technology. Perhaps this will be accomplished when the mysteries of the interaction between psychological structures accumulated from childhood and biological processes are better understood.

The last chapter in this volume is by Novak, Zell, and Zavodnick, who were asked to do the impossible, to examine and update the somatic treatments for depression. The literature on this subject is extensive, but these authors have made appropriate selections and link the ideas and findings reported. They have succeeded in telling what is "standard" in the way of medications for affective disorders.

Summary

We have not attempted to narrow the "mysterious gap" that implies a division between mind and body. However, by viewing the human individual as a unit composed of both, we hope we have provided an understanding of mourning, depression, and depressive states from a sufficiently comprehensive viewpoint to allow the critical exploration of established theories (both psychological and biological). These theories take into account the life cycle, relate these conditions to other mental and somatic states, and associate them in a practical way with some of the experiences of life. Aspects of treatment from the psychoanalytic to the somatic are described here in order to acknowledge the wide range of treatment modalities and to encourage exchange and collaboration between the two schools.

This volume can be read as a reference book by mental health professionals interested in a serious study of depression and related states and their treatment and who wish to prepare themselves for closer cooperation between biology and psychology. Anyone wishing to become an effective clinician must probe beneath the surface picture presented by a patient in order to seek multiple factors and their interaction.

REFERENCES

Abraham, K. (1911). Notes on the psycho-analytical investigation and treatment of manic-depressive insanity and allied conditions. In *Selected Papers*, ed. D. Bryan and A. Strachey. pp. 137–56. New York: Basic Books, 1960.
_____ (1916). The first pregenital stage of libido. In *Selected Papers*, ed. D. Bryan and A. Strachey, pp. 248–279. New York: Basic Books, 1960.
_____ (1924). A short study of the development of the libido, viewed in the light

of mental disorders. In *Selected Papers*, ed. D. Bryan and A. Strachey, pp. 418–501. London: Hogarth Press, 1927.

Adams, F., Ed. and trans. (1939). *The Genuine Works of Hippocrates*. Baltimore: Williams and Wilkins.

Benedek, T. (1956). Toward the biology of the depressive constellation. *Journal of the American Psychoanalytic Association* 4:389–427.

Berliner, B. (1966). Psychodynamics of the defensive character. *Psychoanalytic Forum* 1:244–251.

Bibring, E. (1953). The mechanism of depression. In *Affective Disorders*, ed. P. Greenacre, pp. 13–48. New York: International Universities Press.

Blos, P. (1968). Character formation in adolescence. *The Psychoanalytic Study of the Child* 23:245–263. New York: International Universities Press.

Bowlby, J. (1961). Process of mourning. *International Journal of Psycho-Analysis* 42:317–340.

Cohen, M. B., Baker, G., Cohen, R. A., Fromm-Reichmann, F., and Weigert, E. V. (1954). An intensive study of twelve cases of manic-depressive psychosis. *Psychiatry* 17:103–138.

Engel, G. (1961). Is grief a disease? A challenge for medical research. *Psychosomatic Medicine* 23:18–22.

Fenichel, O. (1945). *The Psychoanalytic Theory of Neurosis*. New York: Norton.

Freud, A. (1958). Adolescence. *The Psychoanalytic Study of the Child* 13:255–278. New York: International Universities Press.

Freud, S. (1917). Mourning and melancholia. *Standard Edition* 14:237–258. London: Hogarth Press, 1957.

Garma, A. (1947). Psychoanalytic investigation in melancholia and other types of depression. In *The Yearbook of Psychoanalysis*, Vol. 3. New York: International Universities Press.

Gaylin, W. (1984). *Psychodynamic Understanding of Depression: The Meaning of Despair*. New York: Jason Aronson.

Gero, G. (1936). The construction of depression. *International Journal of Psycho-Analysis* 17:423–461.

Hartmann, H., Kris, E. and Loewenstein, R. (1946). Comments on the formation of psychic structure. *The Psychoanalytic Study of the Child* 2:11–38. New York: International Universities Press.

Jacobson, E. (1957). On normal and pathological moods. *The Psychoanalytic Study of the Child* 12:73–113. New York: International Universities Press.

——— (1971). *Depression: Comparative Studies of Normal, Neurotic, and Psychotic Conditions*. New York: International Universities Press.

Klein, M. (1940). Mourning and the relation to manic-depressive states. *International Journal of Psycho-Analysis* 21:125–153.

Levine, S. (1965). Some suggestions for treating the depressed patient. *Psychoanalytic Quarterly* 34:37–65.

Lewin, B. D. (1950). *The Psychoanalysis of Elation*. New York: Norton.

Lewis, A. J. (1934). Melancholia: a classical survey of depressive states. *Journal of Mental Science* 80:227–378.

Loewald, H. (1960). On the therapeutic action of psychoanalysis. *International Journal of Psycho-Analysis* 41:16–33.

Loewald, H. (1962). Internalization, separation, mourning, and the superego. *Psychoanalytic Quarterly* 31:483–504.

_____ (1973). On internalization. *International Journal of Psycho-Analysis* 54: 9–17.

McDougall, W. (1936). *An Outline of Psychology*. London: Methuen.

Mahler, M. S. (1966). Notes on the development of basic moods: the depressive affect in psychoanalysis. In *Psychoanalysis – A General Psychology*, ed. R. M. Loewenstein, L. M. Newman, M. Schur, and A. J. Solnit, pp. 152–168. New York: International Universities Press.

Mendelson, M. (1960). *Psychoanalytic Concepts of Depression*. Springfield, Ill.: Charles C. Thomas.

Prange, A. J., Jr. (1983). We can't be content with halfway technology. Keynote speech, Mental Health Association of North Carolina, Inc., October 28, 1983.

Rado, S. (1928). The problem of melancholia. *International Journal of Psycho-Analysis* 9:420–438.

Rangell, L. (1976). Discussion of the Buffalo Creek disaster: the cause of psychic trauma. *American Journal of Psychiatry* 133:313–316.

Rapaport, D. (1942). *Emotions and Memory*. New York: International Universities Press.

Ritvo, S. and Solnit, A. (1958). Influences of early mother–child interaction on the identification process. *The Psychoanalytic Study of the Child* 13:64–85. New York: International Universities Press.

Schafer, R. (1968). *Aspects of Internalization*. New York: International Universities Press.

Searles, H. F. (1982). Some aspects of separation and loss in psychoanalytic therapy with borderline patients. In *Technical Factors in the Treatment of the Severely Disturbed Patient*, ed. P. L. Giovacchini and L. B. Boyer, pp. 131–160. New York: Jason Aronson.

Shand, A. F. (1921). *The Foundations of Character*, 2nd ed. London: Methuen, 1929.

Smith, J. H. (1975). On the work of mourning. In *Bereavement – Its Psychological Aspects*, ed. B. Schoenberg, I. Gerber, A. Wiener, A. H. Kutscher, D. Peretz, and A. C. Carr, pp. 18–25. New York: Columbia University Press.

Spitz, R. A. (1946). Anaclitic depression. *The Psychoanalytic Study of the Child* 2:313–342. New York: International Universities Press.

Steirlin, H. (1973). Interpersonal aspects of internalizations. *International Journal of Psycho-Analysis* 54:203–213.

Tähkä, V. (1984). Dealing with object loss. *Scandinavian Psychoanalytic Review* 7:13–33.

Volkan, V. D. (1971). A study of a patient's "re-grief work" through dreams, psychological tests, and psychoanalysis. *Psychiatric Quarterly* 45:255–273.

_____ (1972). The linking objects of pathological mourners. *Archives of General Psychiatry* 27:215–221.

_____ (1976). *Primitive Internalized Object Relations: A Clinical Study of Schizophrenic, Borderline, and Narcissistic Patients*. New York: International Universities Press.

_____ (1979). *Cyprus – War and Adaptation: A Psychoanalytic History of Two Ethnic Groups in Conflict*. Charlottesville: University Press of Virginia.

_____ (1981). *Linking Objects and Linking Phenomena: A Study of the Forms, Symptoms, Metapsychology, and Therapy of Complicated Mourning*. New York: International Universities Press.

_____ (1982). A young woman's inability to say no to needy people and her identification with the frustrator in the analytic situation. In *Technical Factors in the Treatment of the Severely Disturbed Patient*, ed. P. L. Giovacchini and L. B. Boyer pp. 439–465. New York: Jason Aronson.

———— (1984). *What Do You Get When You Cross a Dandelion With a Rose?* New York: Jason Aronson.

Williams, R. M. and Parkes, C. M. (1975). Psychosocial effects of disaster: Birthrate in Aberfan. *British Medical Journal* 2:303–304.

Wolfenstein, M. (1966). How is mourning possible? *The Psychoanalytic Study of the Child* 21:93–123. New York: International Universities Press.

PART I

Basic Concepts

CHAPTER TWO

Affects, Mourning, and Depression

D. Wilfred Abse, M.D., D.P.M.
(Univ. of London), F.R.C. Psych.

Phenomenology

Mental depression signifies a sense of ill-being, as opposed to the sense of well-being which accompanies ego-functioning in health. The very word health has its etymon in common with "whole" and "hale." These words connote, among other things, the comfortable discharge of bodily functions. In the realm of depression, mental and bodily functioning are inextricably intertwined in very complex ways which the several theories of psychophysical parallelism, psychophysical interactionism, and epiphenomenalism do not singly comprehend. The sense of ill-being in depression is suffused with pain, the opposite of pleasure. The causes and occasions of depression are so common that it is hardly possible for anyone to avoid the experience, though some people deploy massive psychic defenses which almost achieve this avoidance for periods of time. Moreover, there is a paradox of importance inasmuch as it is often healthy to experience the ill-being of some forms of depression. Goethe noted that often, in this respect, illness helps preserve health. In his short novel *The Sorrows of Young Werther*, Goethe (1774) reflected in part an experience of his own youth. The novel is the story of an artistically inclined young man gifted with deep, pure sentiment and penetrating intelligence who loses himself in fantastic dreams and undermines himself with speculative thought, until finally, torn by hopeless passions, especially by an infinite love, he shoots himself in the head. Johann Wolfgang von Goethe, after achieving a great popular success with the novel, lived to love again and again into a ripe old age. His novel, however, is reputed to have stimulated a wave of suicides among young German Romantics. Writing the novel may well have facilitated Goethe's own recovery from a depression, whereas the novel created resonances in some which accentuated their own despair. It is indeed not only by means of powerfully persuasive writing that predisposed people can be plunged into depressive mood disorder. As Conrad (1921) wrote of James Wait:

> He seemed to hasten the retreat of departing light by his very presence; the setting sun dipped sharply, as though fleeing before our nigger; a black mist emanated from him; a subtle and dismal influence; a something cold and gloomy that floated out and settled on all the faces like a mourning veil. The circle broke up. The joy of laughter died on stiffened lips. (p. 41)

This dense mortuary imagery signifies the association of gloomy presences with death. Usually, depressed people are avoided, increasing their misery and despair. It is a problem for the psychotherapist who in affectionate and absorbed interest has also to deal with counteridentification in order to preserve therapeutic efficacy. It is also necessary for the psychiatrist to preserve objectivity in order to avoid the use of unnecessary electroshock treatment because of noxious, complex countertransferences.

In 1883, Clouston defined "mere melancholy" as a sense of ill-being and a feeling of mental pain with no real perversion of the normal reasoning power, no morbid loss of self-control, no uncontrollable impulse towards suicide, no destruction of the power to work, and the reduction, not abolition, of the ordinary interests of life. He defined pathological depression or "severe melancholia" as mental pain and sense of ill-being usually more intense than in "mere melancholy," with loss of self-control, or insane delusions, or uncontrollable impulses towards suicide, with no proper capacity to follow ordinary avocations, with most of the ordinary interests of life destroyed, and commonly with marked bodily symptoms such as loss of appetite and constipation. Since he saw "mere melancholy" on a continuum, normative and useful grief would be at one end of his spectrum with severe psychotic depression at the other, whereas the gamut of neurotic depressions would comprise phenomenologically some features of both ends.

In early psychoanalytic work, it soon became clear that anxiety had invariably assumed an important role in the defensive struggle of the individual and in the pathogenesis of neurosis. For both of these reasons the psychoanalytic study of emotions was for a long time focussed especially on the problem of anxiety. Interest in the realm of affects gradually broadened, with respect first to depressive affects — sorrow, grief, despondency and despair — as these were prominently exhibited in borderline and psychotic conditions as well as in neuroses, and then to the nature and functions of affects in general. Rapaport (1942) has contributed one of the few systematic accounts of the psychology of the emotions which includes the avowedly very incomplete psychoanalytic theory of the affects. Within the limits of this chapter, which will include consideration of masked depression and of depressive equivalents manifest in bodily symptoms, the assertions made may appear less dogmatic and less schematic if Rapaport's account is considered as a context. However, it will be apparent that the emphasis here differs in detail from his summarized views.

Depressive equivalents are manifest in bodily symptoms and rival in frequency overt mental depressions. Many depressive syndromes are masked in conversion reactions of a hysterical nature, psychosomatic disorders, hypochondriasis, or in combinations of these. The patients who strenuously avoid the conscious experience of grief and of other dysphoric emotions often present their complaints initially to nonpsychiatric physicians. Lesse (1974) notes that one-third to two-thirds of patients over age 40 who are seen by general practitioners and even by specialists are basically depressed. However, the depressive syndromes are masked by hypochondriacal or psychosomatic disorders. He writes:

> These patients, particularly those in the late middle and older age groups, are extremely prevalent in hospital clinics; they also occupy a sizeable proportion of general hospital beds. Unfortunately, they are usually subjected to a multitude of laboratory examinations and too often are exposed to a variety of organic treatments, even surgery. (p. 325)

Thus, these patients often develop a massive iatrogenic overlay which further complicates treatment.

Affects and Subjective Awareness

McDougall (1936) developed the view that emotions are essentially indicators of the working of derivatives of instinctual impulses. He emphasizes that fear, anger, disgust, tender feelings, lust, feelings of helplessness and hopelessness, elation, loneliness, and other emotions have a cognitive function; they signify to us primarily not the nature of things, but the nature of our impulsive reactions to events. They are the cognitive basis of self-knowledge and self-control. Within the existentialist paradigm, the self is sensitized through emotion to its mode of changing being and interacting in the world. In this sense the emotions are subjective rather than objective in function. With this view, McDougall modified the Lange-James theory of emotions:

> We are now prepared to consider the famous Lange-James theory of the emotions, and to understand in what sense it is true, and in what respects erroneous. The essense of the theory is the assertion that the "emotions" are essentially of the same nature as "sensations"; that "an emotion," as felt or as an

emotional quality, is a mass or complex of confused sensory experience arising from the sensory impressions made by the processes going on in the various
organs of the body, and that each distinguishable quality of emotion, owes
whatever is specific or peculiar in its quality to the specific conjunction of bodily activities, the visceral organs playing a predominant part in this sensory
stimulation. If this statement is modified or supplemented by recognising that,
just as the sensory qualities of the special senses are duplicated in imagery,
the sensory qualities of the visceral or bodily senses are also duplicated in
imagery, we must, I think, accept it as substantially true. (pp. 326–327)

He goes on to criticize severely the overstatement of James which results in the largely false paradox that emotion is always the consequence
of bodily activities, so that, for example, we feel sorry only because we cry,
instead of its being largely the reverse. James (1890) had indeed in his hypothesis ignored the fact that sensational qualities may be centrally excited
in the form of imagery, independent of immediate external stimulation;
or, to quote Spinoza (1677), "A man is as much affected pleasurably or
painfully by the image of a thing past or future as by the image of a thing
present" (p. 143).

Kulovesi (1931) objects to the Lange-James theory on another score,
and modifies it accordingly:

James states that between perception and emotion there lies the bodily expression; we must object to this, since between the perception and the bodily expression unconscious psychic complexes become active [and are] mobilised
when the perception touches upon an object that is in associative connection
with the complex. (Rapaport 1942, p. 30)

Cannon (1929) also amplified the Lange-James theory with his neurophysiologic view based on animal experiments, stating that the peculiar
quality of an emotion is added to simple sensation when thalamic processes
are aroused:

Within and near the thalamus the neurones concerned in an emotional expression lie close to the relay in the sensory path from periphery to cortex. We
may assume that when these neurones discharge in a particular combination,
they not only innervate muscles and viscera but also excite afferent paths to
the cortex by direct connection or by irradiation. (p. 369)

Schematically and in summary: with or without the impact of external perception, for sometimes instinctual excitation is on an autogenic and
periodic basis, there is drive arousal. This drive arousal results in widespread bodily changes, including special neurophysiologic events which al-

ter sensation, the pattern of which is perceived as emotion, or may not be consciously felt because of unconscious defense. In connection with this series of events it is worth pondering a statement by the philosopher Suzanne K. Langer (1967), whose otherwise valuable contribution to the understanding of human feeling is marred by a remarkable underestimation of unconscious processes:

> In the first place, the phenomenon usually described as "a feeling" is really that an organism feels something, i.e., something is felt. What is felt is a process, perhaps a large complex of processes, within the organism. Some vital activities of great complexity and high intensity, usually (perhaps always) involving nervous tissue, are felt; being felt is a phase of the process itself. A phase is a mode of appearance, and not an added factor. Ordinarily we know things in different phases as "the same" — ice, water and steam, for instance — but sometimes a very distinctive phase seems like a product. When iron is heated to a critical degree it becomes red; yet its redness is not a new entity which must have gone somewhere else when it is no longer in the iron . . . But the redness [on cooling] simply disappears; it was a phase of the heated iron. (p. 21)

McDougall (1936), in the wake of Kant's (1870) categorization of knowing, feeling and striving as three aspects of all mental acts, disputes Kant's view of emotion an entirely anoetic. The eighteenth century philosopher had an excessive, one might say obsessional, distrust of emotion, regarding it as destructive to logical thought, as is evident especially in *The Critique of Judgment*. Of course, excessive emotion can be destructive to logical thought, as is dramatically obvious in emotional flooding. On the other hand, Spinoza (1677) had earlier noted the cognitive values of affects, thus affording a seventeenth century philosophical support for McDougall's twentieth century view. At the same time, too, especially in his essay "Of Human Bondage, or the Strength of the Emotions" (Part IV of *The Ethics*), Spinoza expatiated on the theme of human infirmity in moderating and checking the passions. Szymanski (1930) defines affects as expressions of the knowledge (*Erkenntnis*) of "driving-forces," so that his view, too, supports that of McDougall.

Following years of psychoanalytic investigation, Freud (1926) gradually converged on this same view. He came to a turning point in his view of the role of emotion in mental life when he recognized the signal function of anxiety and the capacity of the ego to reduce anxiety for defensive and adaptive purposes. In the early days of psychoanalysis, affect had been equated with the quantity of drive-cathexis. Breuer and Freud wrote in 1893 that therapy "brings to an end the operative force of the idea which was not abreacted in the first instance, by allowing its strangulated affect to find a way out through speech. . . . " (p. 17). Then, Freud (1900) developed this view, regarding affective experience as the psychic reflection of discharge processes of instinctual energies, thereby, as Brierly (1951) indicates, ranging affects more on the efferent than on the afferent pathway of the instinctual arc. However, this was a partial and complementary proposition. *The development, realization and recession of emotional excitement take place in time and comprise from inception circular efferent-afferent bodily processes which become integrated into the complex of perceptual experience.*

As noted, Freud (1926) later laid emphasis on the relation of affective experience to executive, adaptive, and defensive aspects of ego functioning. As early as 1900, he had recognized that one of the concomitants of the development of secondary process and of reality testing was the taming of affects by their transformation into signals, a reduction normally only partially maintained. A quarter of a century later, he elaborated on this signal function.

In reviewing these considerations regarding the taming of affects, Fenichel (1941) points out that children and neurotic persons have more frequent emotional spells than mature adults. A mature adult, of course, does not lack emotion yet does not have overwhelming emotional spells. The ego's increasing strength enables damping of the affects at the moment of arousal. The ego is no longer overwhelmed by something alien to it, but it senses when this alien something begins to develop, and simultaneously upon this recognition it reestablishes its mastery. "To be sure," Fenichel (1941) writes, "even the most adult ego can [only] do this to a certain degree" (p. 217). One must add that the differentiated and more sophisticated ego samples such unwelcome primitive affects as envy and jealousy during a process of mastery.

Fenichel describes a stage of development in which the ego is weak and the affect dominant, followed by another stage in which the ego is stronger and has learned to use the affects for its purposes, one of which is surely and usefully one of self-appraisal. He notes that a third stage is always possible in which once more an elemental affect may overwhelm the organism. The genuinely stronger ego is more open to emotional experience, does not require the rigid checks which detract from the psychobiological value of both signal function and experiencing emotion, and is consequently less brittle and less liable to overwhelming affective experience. In schizophrenic patients, the hyperexic defense against affect breaks down and has far-reaching and protracted effects. In itself, this defense is already pathological inasmuch as experience is impoverished and self-realisation through ensuing integration of felt experience is impeded. In those liable to schizophrenia, the breakdown of rigid defenses results in far-reaching disorganization of executive and adaptive ego functions including perception, memory and thinking. In short, existentially overtaxed, the schizophrenic exhibits and experiences a defective mode of being and interacting in the world.

Sifneos (1967) drew attention to a cluster of cognitive traits found in some patients suffering from a variety of psychosomatic diseases which he named *alexithymia*. Nemiah (1977), who has developed the concept, states that alexithymic characteristics consist essentially of marked difficulty in expressing feelings in words and absence of fantasies appropriate to or expressive of feelings, with thought content being dominated by the details of the events in the immediate external environment (*pensée opératoire*, as Marty and M'Uzan (1963) dub this latter trait). Ruesch (1957) drew attention much earlier to a core problem of somatic reactors: they lacked satisfactory means of self-expression and their higher symbolic functions were undeveloped. He wrote of their limited range of vocabulary and their unimaginative and stereotyped elaborations of fantasy in tests such as the Rorschach and T.A.T. Shands (1975) also has written of this problem. He draws attention to the correlation of the alexithymic cognitive style to Bernstein's (1964) "restricted code" of the working class in England in contrast to the "elaborated code" of the middle class. Shands writes:

> [Bernstein] shows again and again how much the problem is that of 1) developing the kind of code which affirms membership through the unspoken (unconscious) habits which describe a single universe as opposed to 2) the training in adopting and using multiple points of view characteristic of middle-class education. . . . Bernstein has pointed specifically to the difficulty of carrying out the psychotherapeutic "game" with working-class members — and the recent rise of family therapy is presented by some of its proponents as a partial answer to the difficulty in involving working-class persons in the abstract operations of "insight" or "dynamic" psychotherapy. (p. 272)

Sifneos, Nemiah, and Shands, as others, acknowledge, of course, that somatic reactions occur among those who are not alexithymic. Here a case excerpt might indicate clues to a theoretical solution of this apparent paradox.

A middle-aged upper middle-class cultivated woman was in prolonged psychotherapy for severe colitis which improved with medications (antispasmodics, cortisones, etc.) from the gastroenterologist as well as with the psychotherapy. Her illness after this first improvement may be roughly assessed as ranging from severe, when it was life-threatening, to moderate when she found it necessary to visit the toilet about a dozen times a day and was on a special diet. Although ordinarily affectively expressive, she wore a mask of imperturbability whenever she came face-to-face with her divorced husband in social situations in which she could not avoid the confrontation, and was impassive whenever she spoke in treatment of current interaction with him. She carefully nursed an image of herself as a poised and gracious woman, which she was, and rejected any possibility that she entertained any hostile, jealous impulses and feelings. Her narcissistic adherence to this picture of herself and to a posture of well-mannered behavior was always maintained. One day, after two years of psychotherapy, her ex-husband's second wife left him. Her colitis abruptly disappeared (as though a faucet had been turned) when she heard this. The temporal connection and the relationship of her colitis to her hostile jealousy became gradually apparent to her during further interpretive work of the kind that had been quite ineffective previously. Moreover, she was able to explore her feelings about her social reference group, which, she felt, would appreciate from his second wife's defection how "impossibly difficult" her ex-husband was to live with. In this way, she became able to approach guilt feelings and the self-punishing aspects of some of her symptoms, including the colitis, all of which were internal reactions to fierce death wishes.

In regard to the psychotherapy of *alexithymic somatic reactors*, my experience is similar to that of Wolff (1975). In this particular case, however, the patient was *not* alexithymic in general and was usually richly expressive in her fantasy life and emotions. Nor was I bored in the sessions, though admittedly I was perplexed at times by the plateau of improvement reached without adequate symptom abatement before the news of the wreckage of her ex-husband's second marriage. Understanding here led us to a split-off part of her self analogous to that which occurs in dual or multiple personality (Abse 1982).

Often in such cases there is a one-way amnesic situation. The alter ego, or one of the fragmentary personalities, knows about the usual self, but the usual self is oblivious to the split-off fragment or fragments. In other words, the mental barrier is traversible in only one direction. In this case of the woman with ulcerative colitis, the barrier was immediately traversible by certain deeds and could not be breached by words. To be brief, under certain circumstances in some patients who are not alexithymic by definition, psychosomatic disorder occurs as a result of resort under stress to localized but deep splitting, though psychosomatic integration had been achieved previously, and is maintained for the most part between thought and feeling and mind and body, with an important exception developed under stress which leads to bodily symptoms.

The Miscarriage of the Cognitive Function of Affects

Alexander (1950) states:

> A conversion symptom is a *symbolic* expression of an emotionally charged psychological content: it is an attempt to discharge the emotional tension. It takes place in the voluntary neuromuscular or sensory-perceptive systems whose original function is to express and relieve emotional tensions. A vegetative neurosis is not an attempt to express an emotion but is the physiological response of the vegetative organs to constant or to periodically returning emotional states. Elevation of blood pressure, for example, under the influence of rage does not relieve the rage but is a physiological component of the total phenomenon of rage. . . . It is an adaptation of the body to the state of the organism when it prepares to meet an emergency. Similarly, increased gastric secretion under the influence of emotional longing for food is not an expression or relief of these emotions; it is the adaptive preparation of the stomach for the incorporation of food. (p. 42)

In *Hysteria and Related Mental Disorders*, (Abse 1966) I have scrutinized and criticized Alexander's views concerning the differentiation of conversion hysteria from psychosomatic disorder at considerable length, with suitable case illustrations. Here I will confine my remarks to those pertinent to the view that in psychophysiologic disorder the affects have completely or partially failed in their cognitive functions and that patients are alienated from their emotions much more drastically than in conversion hysteria, a view that is a corollary of the notion that alexithymia is pervasive though not invariant in psychosomatic disorder.

In the statement that a vegetative neurosis is not an attempt to express an emotion, Alexander disregards the distinction between instinctual strivings and accompanying affects, a distinction repeated here earlier in connection with discussion of McDougall's psychology of the emotions. It was indicated on the model of the reflex arc that instinctual strivings, like outer perceptions, at first occupy the afferent side of the arc; then, *with affect*, on the efferent side of the arc, they are discharged. The affects are ranged in the efferent side of the arc, that is, they are essentially motoric. Of course, as stated, there is feedback from the motoric events — the efferent paths have their own afferents, and it is these latter which are perceived as emotions, especially those that are of visceral origin. Alexander's statement has the further disadvantage of disregarding the cognitive function of the affects which serve in health to put us in touch with our strivings. His statement may be amended as follows: "A vegetative neurosis attempts a partial discharge of dissociated archaic instinctual strivings, and the accompanying emotions are primarily blocked from perception."

My view is that in psychophysiologic disorder there is dissociation of primitive ego nuclei which represent the frustrated supplicant strivings and rage reactions. This is a piece of drastic psychic autotomy for the purpose of preventing any possible repressive failure on the part of the more organized remainder of the ego. Since the dissociated strivings have access to discharge only through autonomic channels, and these efferent innervations do not lead to integration of emotion with cognition, the autotomy does not result in the prevention of a general state of damming up the organism. The more organized remainder of the ego, with its extensive preconscious system, is thus bound soon and secondarily, to note this damming up, this developing state of emergency, despite attempts at denial and its divorce from the sources of this tension. Typically we thus have primitive ego nuclei with access to discharge only through autonomic channels and the more organized remainder operating with signal anxiety in a state of emergency.

In psychogenic essential hypertension, therefore, the elevation in blood pressure results both from the general state of emergency and from the autonomic discharges appropriate to rage expressing the activity of the sequestrated primitive oral-sadistic nucleus. The rage reaction is also inhibited in its development, for what was sequestrated at the beginning is again blocked off from feedback from the discharges; the visceral sensations are not integrated as emotions in the preconscious ego system where word connection is normatively effected and whereby heightened self-awareness becomes possible. Without aid of the useful term "alexithymia" coined by Sifneos from the Greek language in 1972, I discussed this in 1966.

The essential differentiation from conversion reactions is to be sought dynamically in the divorce of both primitive strivings and their affects from the preconscious ego system. This divorce is much more complete and of a different nature from the simpler repressive defense in conversion reactions. The basic conflicts in psychophysiologic disorder, the defense struggle against primitive strivings, have never reached the level of preconscious word symbolism, whereas in conversion hysteria the preconscious word connections have been made and then secondarily excluded through the process of repression. These word connections in conversion hysteria, as I have shown (Abse 1966, 1971) may be sought in derepression at levels of metaphoric and cryptophoric symbolism. In conversion hysteria the conflicts represented in the symptoms are embedded in experiences when speech was already emergent, whereas in psychophysiologic disorder there is regression to the basic conflicts which belong to the period of preverbal archaic infantile experience. In conversion reactions, as the ideation is recovered through word symbolism, the affects may readily find appropriate connections. In psychophysiologic disorder the affects have more or less completely failed in their cognitive functions, and the patient is alienated from emotions much more drastically.

To be sure, there is global defense against the integration of thought and feeling in neurosis, in obsessional as well as in hysterical neurosis. Allen (1977) notes:

> In short, the hysteric has repressed or dissolved the ideational connections between *feelings* to defend against certain affects; the obsessive-compulsive has repressed or dissolved the feeling connections between *ideas* to defend against certain threatening affects. Curiously, these two styles of thinking, though in a sense opposites, are not mutually exclusive and to some extent can coexist in the same person, and there is a sense in which the obsessive-compulsive and hysteric are similar in that the obsessive-compulsive dwells on the *thought* content without appropriate conclusion of thought and feelings; and the hysterical personality dwells on *feeling* without appropriate conclusion of feeling and thought. (pp. 305–306)

Splitting, though partial and localized, is deeper in psychophysiologic disorder than in hysterical neurosis and more difficult to reach in psychotherapy, as my efforts with the gracious lady with colitis serve to illustrate.

Affect Equivalents

In his discussion of the modes of experience associated with the anticipation of failure or of success of purposive striving, McDougall (1936) considers the emotions categorized by Shand (1921) as "the prospective emotions of desire." These are confidence, hope, anxiety, despondency, and despair. McDougall writes:

> All these [emotions] presuppose the operation of some strong impulse or desire; and, since they presuppose also a certain level of development of intelligence, namely, that level upon which the goal of impulse is more or less clearly imagined and impulse takes the form of desire, we may say that they presuppose desire and arise only in the course of activity prompted and sustained by desire. The desire itself is independent of, and must come into operation before, the rise of these emotions. And during the working of any one strong desire (no matter what may be the nature of the instinctive impulse at work and what the nature of the object or goal to which it is directed) all these five emotions are apt to be experienced. They are, in fact, only so many named points in a scale of feeling or emotion of which confidence and despair are the two extremes. (p. 339)

This statement ignores unconscious factors and would thus require some emendation from a psychoanalytic viewpoint. Yet it deserves our close consideration primarily because of the truth it incorporates, and also because it crystallizes much philosophic and psychological thought through many centuries. McDougall illustrates the series by reference to a party of polar explorers in an arduous expedition as their confidence is gradually disrupted by adverse conditions and the group becomes progressively anxious, then despondent, and despairing.

On his South Polar expedition Robert F. Scott (1912) wrote: "We are already beyond the utmost limit to which man has attained, each footstep will be a fresh conquest of the great unknown. Confident in ourselves, confident in our equipment, and confident in our dog team, we can but feel elated at the prospect before us" (p. 517). The ebullience of this passage contrasts with his disappointment as he contemplates the inevitable agonizing return from Amundsen's cairn at the South Pole: "Well, we have turned our backs on the goal of our ambition and must face over 800 miles of solid dragging—and goodbye to most of the daydreams! Great God! This is an awful place" (pp. 544–45). Deprived of the energizing triumph that being first to the South Pole would have provided, Scott and his companions faced the ordeal of their return, an ordeal which they hoped to endure successfully so that they could return to their homes and loved ones. Adverse winds and threats of snow turned hope to anxiety, and as conditions worsened, with high winds and heavy snow impeding their reaching their next food store, despondency began to dominate the group. A month after reaching the pole, Evans died, and the weakened Oates, realizing that he was another impediment, stepped quietly from the tent into a blizzard and was never seen again. Weakened by the intense cold, the continuous struggle and diminishing supplies, Scott wrote a letter "To My Widow" in which he said that the few survivors disavowed suicide and intended to persevere to the last. Finally, after eight days of impenetrable storm, only 11 miles from the next depot and possible survival, Scott wrote in despair, "It seems a pity, but I do not think I can write more. R. Scott—For God's sake look after our people" (p. 595).

Of the five prospective emotions derived from the interaction of desire and of judgment of probabilities of success or failure, the three beyond confidence and hope, anxiety, despondency and despair, take us into the sphere of dysphoria with which we are here concerned. There are also retrospective emotions in the developed mind and these can be dysphoric, hence, we get regret, remorse and sorrow, with grief allied to the latter. These retrospective emotions are also "derived" in the sense that they are incidental to the evocation in memory of cognitive-affective experiences, rendering these memories painful or reinforcing their painful elements. Like all emotions, these are the result of a differentiation of the fundamental forms of feeling, pain and pleasure, in the differentiated psyche.

In 1895, Freud pointed out that the feeling of anxiety may have linked to it a disturbance of one or more of the bodily functions such as respiration, heart action, vasomotor innervation or glandular activity. He wrote:

> From this combination the patient picks out in particular now one, now another, factor. He complains of "spasms of the heart," "difficulty in breathing," "outbreaks of sweating," "ravenous hunger," and such like; and in his description, the feeling of anxiety often recedes into the background or is referred to quite unrecognizably as "being unwell," "feeling uncomfortable," and so on. (p. 94)

In 1945, Fenichel elaborated upon Freud's notion of anxiety equivalents in the form of sensations as enumerated above, stating:

> It cannot be doubted that all other affects can likewise be replaced in a similar way by equivalents of somatic sensations. It is characteristic of certain compulsive personalities that, when analysis has successfully attacked their affect blocking, they begin to complain of certain changes in body sensations without realizing their psychic significance. Before they can again experience the affects fully, they first find the road to affect equivalents. (p. 167)

Fenichel also notes that Schreber's somatic "basic language" consists of affects reduced to bodily sensations. Alexander (1950) cited many cases of psychosomatic disorder occurring after object-loss when one might have expected depressive feelings to become manifest. Moreover, in this connection, it is to be noted that remission of psychosomatic disorder is occasionally followed by the development of overt psychosis, or vice versa. Grinker and Robins (1954) report both depressive and paranoid schizophrenic disorders in such alternations.

Both in conversion phenomena and in psychophysiologic disorder it might be conceived that one or another physical mode of suffering is sought unconsciously or stumbled upon and held as an evil less pernicious than severe dysphoric affects of anxiety and of a depressive order. In other words, a representation of physical suffering is ultimately the result of defense against becoming conscious of dysphoric feelings. This, however, is an incomplete view because it ignores the inextricable association of these feelings with unconscious strivings and fantasies. The feelings are one part of a Gestalt which includes the strivings, the reality context which may be oppressive, and superego reactions which may be severely punitive.

A Case Report

The following case recently explored and treated illustrates some aspects of the problem of masked depression in a middle-aged woman who had presented to her family physician with frequency of urination and pain in the middle of the lower abdomen.

The patient had been fully investigated physically including CT scans and cystoscopy with negative findings before psychiatric interview. It became apparent that her symptoms replicated those of her sister who had had a surgical operation for tumors of the bladder, followed by thrombophlebitis. The sister then died of heart failure following an embolism. The patient had lost her mother when she was 4 years old, and this sister, two years older than she, had been her closest relationship before marriage; they had sustained a close relationship after they both were married and had children, despite geographical separation for long periods. The patient did not apparently react strongly to the sudden death of her beloved sister. She avoided going to the funeral, though her husband, a pastor in a fundamentalist church, went.

In the psychiatric hospital her symptoms persisted. She continued to complain of pain in the lower abdomen and this prevented her from sleeping soundly at night. At times of complaint she was given a placebo which unfailingly, though temporarily, relieved the pain. This placebo was also effective at night so that the duration of sleep was extended. She was also medicated with a tricyclic with no evident effect. She steadfastly maintained that she was not unduly affected by her sister's demise, though she acknowledged it was a shock since it had been so sudden. She maintained an impatient attitude towards attempts to encourage her to ventilate her feelings during distributive discussions and veered away from the topic of her sister's death, complaining bitterly that she was in the wrong place and that the doctors had made a mistake sending her into the psychiatric hospital to talk with me.

The husband, a minister, had thought that his wife was physically afflicted, but, seen separately from his wife, it was possible to get his cooperation and to show him that her problems could be of nervous origin. In this context, he said that the undertaker had told him that his sister-in-law had died of "a clot in the bladder," a statement he had repeated to his wife when he came from the funeral. His experience of bereaved people in his flock weeping copiously while he attended them was drawn upon, and he remarked that on reflection he was surprised his wife had shown so little emotion, though he knew she loved her sister dearly. In due course, he brought in a photograph of the deceased sister in the casket prior to burial, and in a family session this was shown to the patient who then burst into a flood of tears, a flood which persisted with little decrease for several days. The physical pain abated, however, though with some exacerbations, during which time the patient was afforded considerable emotional support and opportunities to ventilate her feelings and recall her childhood experiences which were associated heavily with her sister. During this time there were no further complaints of urinary frequency. (At the time I thought of Alfred Adler's (1927) saying that some children cry with their eyes and others with their bladders. He was referring to *enuresis nocturna* which he often treated at his clinic in Vienna.)

Later the patient visited her sister's grave with her husband with eventual salutary effects, reinforced in further psychotherapy.

The absence of expectable grief, as Helene Deutsch (1937) noted many years ago, can be an important clinical clue to "masked depression."

Neurosis and Psychosis

Following the *Ego and the Id* (1923), Freud (1924a, 1924b) addressed the complex question of the differential diagnosis of neurosis and psychosis. He elaborated upon the view that neurosis is the result of a conflict between the ego and the id, whereas psychosis is the analogous outcome of a similar disturbance in the relations between the ego and the external world. Regarding the structural neurotic conflict in neurosis, he pointed out that, in undertaking repression of id drives, the ego is under the sway of the superego: "The ego has come into conflict with the id in the service of the superego and reality; and this is the state of affairs in every transference neurosis" (1942a). He noted that a complication entered into this apparently relatively simple situation inasmuch as there are illnesses which are largely based on a conflict between the ego and superego, and he set aside the designation "narcissistic psychoneuroses" for disorders of this kind. It is of course, the failure of repression in neurosis which leads to symptom formation, and it is well known that the symptom is a compromise formation of distorted forbidden wish fulfillment and self-punishment. The neurotic symptom is indeed a masterpiece of condensation, whereas sublimation, which also subserves reduction of drive tensions, is a masterpiece of symbolic transformation to the socially permissible. In the "narcissistic psychoneuroses" as designated by Freud, there is more obvious superego participation in symptom formation and resultant self-punishment, as is evident in a wide array of neurotic depressions. In florid depressive psychoses the ego has also suffered gross disruption of its relation to external reality.

Freud (1917) showed in some forms of melancholia that careful attention to the rebukes and complaints which patients make about themselves logically apply more accurately to the "lost object," lost through rupture of the personal relationship, often through death. Unlike the events in normative grief, as in mourning, the libidinal attachment is rapidly withdrawn. However, the released libido is not free to seek fresh attachments but has returned to the self by means of an intimate identification of the self with the object-representations of the person to whom the patient was attached, albeit very ambivalently. This occurs in a primitive process of introjection. The hatred, exacerbated by fantasized or actual desertion, may not have been formerly so obvious in the ambivalent and dependent attachment but is turned now against the part of the self fused with the introjected lost object. This course of events arises only under certain conditions and in different degrees of intensity. Sometimes, as in psychotic depressions, the ego, overwhelmed by the pathogenic introject and subjected to the fury deposited in the archaic layers of the superego, loses contact with actual social reality. The course of intrapsychic events adumbrated arises only when a strongly dependent ambivalent attachment is readily detachable because of its original choice on a narcissistic basis.

Abraham (1911) showed that in severe depressions there were certain preconditions, namely, fixation at the oral-sadistic level, a severe injury to infantile narcissism brought about by early deprivation by the mother and the occurrence of the first great disappointment in love before the Oedipus wishes were successfully mastered. He showed that, in many cases, repetition of erotic disappointment in later life was a precipitating situation. Freud (1917) had also noted the regression to pregenital fixation in melancholia, attributing importance to the anal-sadistic phase as the basis for many clinical features. A greater or lesser loss of self-esteem is always the resultant of the underlying complex dynamics of depression. This inner loss, in clearly reactive depressions, is due initially to the loss of external supplies of affection. To a greater or lesser extent this becomes complicated by loss of internal supplies from the "protective superego" and/or vilification by the "punitive superego." These disturbances are not as intensive in neurotic depressive reactions as in psychotic depressive disorder.

Orality in Depressive Neuroses

In a footnote to "The Dynamics of the Transference" (1912), Freud wrote:

> Psychoanalysis has talked a lot about the accidental factors in etiology and little about constitutional ones; but that is only because it was able to contribute something fresh to the former, while, to begin with, it knew no more than was commonly known about the latter. We refuse to posit any contrast in principle between the two sets of etiological factors; on the contrary, we assume that the two sets regularly act jointly in bringing about the observed result. [Endowment and chance] determine a man's fate—rarely or never one of these powers alone. The amount of etiological effectiveness to be attributed to each of them can only be arrived at in every individual case separately. (p. 99)

Therese Benedek (1956) explained the dynamic circular processes involved within the primary unit, mother–child, comprising the two sets of multiple factors to which Freud referred. She showed that the feeling of confidence, which we have discussed above, is originally an intrapsychic precipitate of positive libidinal processes of the symbiotic phase of the mother–child relationship. On the other hand, Benedek revealed the transactional processes of ambivalent relationships between mothers and their children which predisposed individuals to depressive or psychosomatic disorder in later life by reducing the stability of confidence and hope. She termed these ambivalent (aggressive and frustrating) events the depressive constellation. The balance between the positive (libidinal, gratifying) and the negative (aggressive, frustrating) symbiotic events influences the ego organization of both the child and the mother, including in the latter the developmental integration of motherliness. The development of the child's confidence depends not only on the mother's capacity to give, but also on the innate and acquired ability of the child to receive, to suck, to assimilate and to thrive. If the infant because of congenital or acquired disability cannot be satisfied, the infant remains frustrated and in turn frustrates the mother. The frustration of the mother manifests itself in anger and discouragement, in the fear of her inefficiency, and in guilt. These attitudes and feelings affect the further course of the emotional symbiosis. Obviously, this course can become a vicious cycle instead of the benign favorable cycle engendered by a loving mother and a thriving infant.

Benedek takes her analysis further toward biological fundaments by emphasizing the dilemma built into the physiology of the female reproductive function. The increment of energy of the receptive-retentive tendencies necessary to maintain pregnancy persists through early mothering though in a lower key as the active, giving, succoring attitude is mobilized and begins to dominate. This duality of function involves the metabolic and emotional challenge which procreative processes represent for women. Each phase of procreative growth, according to Benedek, necessarily brings regression to and consequent increased cathexis of the oral-receptive phase of psychosexual development. Some women, perhaps in a context lacking adequate emotional support, cannot withstand the stress of this normal psychic regression correlated with the physiology of motherhood. Benedek writes:

> The increased charge of incorporative fantasies indicates that during pregnancy and in the post partum period the mother may respond to the increased demands on her with an increased wish to receive. These are exaggerated manifestations of the very emotions which originate in the biological regressions inherent in motherhood. The affect hunger of the mother, her need for love and affection, her wish to reunite with her baby and to overprotect and overpossess him disturb the smooth course of symbiotic events. Although these are pathological exaggerations of the normal process, such manifestations bring our thesis even more sharply into focus: that *the post partum symbiosis is oral, alimentary, for both* infant and mother. (pp. 360–361)

When the frustrated infant frustrates the mother, a regression may be induced in her which intensifies the aggressive components of her receptive needs. This regression stirs up preverbal memories of the oral-dependent phase of her own development. If the recathexis of the infantile relationship with her own mother activates in the mother confidence and hope, she will overcome any actual disappointment and frustration, secure in her wish to love the infant and take care of the infant as she herself was loved and cared for. However, if crying fits or other problems the infant poses stir up not only justified concern but severe anxieties originating in the mother's own early oral phase, her identification with her own mother and with her infant turn negative. She becomes identified with the bad frustrating mother as well as the bad frustrating infant of her own mother. Her conscious intention to be a good mother is thus eroded by these unconscious events. As she experiences through her child that she is not a better mother than her mother, as she had hoped, the infant comes to represent the "bad one" — a projection of her "bad self" — but now the crying, sick baby is actually hostile towards her. Once her mother was the only person who could alleviate frustration and pain. Now her own infant alone, by thriving, can come to do so. Under more favorable circumstances, the libidinal aspects of mothering, satisfied partly by gratification of receptive needs, keep a positive psychoeconomic balance, so that instead of suffering intensification of ambivalence and becoming impounded in depression, the mother is delighted with her motherliness. It is evident that the infant, thought utterly dependent on the mother, wields an immeasurable power over her.

According to Bergler (1950, 1952) depressive neurotics have a rendezvous with orality. He insists that this partial regression does not only involve oral greed and the wish to get, but that this involvement is inextricably intertwined with masochistic elaboration resulting in a dominant wish to be refused. If this elaboration is overlooked, and interpretations offered to the orally regressed masochist point out the aggressive wish to get (also true), this does not reach the basic psychic mechanism of libidinized self-damage. Bergler (1952) writes:

> The masochistic solution preserves infantile megalomania to an outstanding degree. Obviously, the most painful experience of babyhood and infancy — shattering of the grandiose illusion of omnipotence, autarchy, megalomania — cannot be accepted meekly and in toto, and without some recompense. The pleasure-in-pain pattern salvages a few fragments of the original illusion, at the slight cost of some reformulation in the clinical picture. The commentary now reads: "It is not true that the bad mother punishes me: I, through my provocations, *make her* punish me!" (p. 52)

Thus, states Bergler, "the helpless child triumphs over the powerful Giantess!" (p. 52). This kind of masochistic engulfment has at its core, in my opinion, an element which can only be more fully understood by reference to Freud's (1920) concept of the unconscious repetition compulsion which is beyond the pleasure principle. However this may be, there is an imperative urge to repeat actively those experiences one has been forced to endure passively. Certainly the purpose is partly to repair the lesion in self-esteem, a self-esteem which had become impounded in narcissistic omnipotence.

In psychoneurotic forms of depression in general, unlike that which can be expected in florid psychotic disorder of many kinds, working capacity, though diminished, is often the last fortress to be completely overtaken, as Clouston (1904) noted. Bergler (1952) has described some of the vicissitudes of the capacity to work in depressions associated with neurosis. He points out that the person in a self-chosen occupation satisfies in sublimated form deeply motivated desires, whereas for another, work represents little but drudgery, essential for earning a living. For the latter, the punitive quality inherent in the work may also pay a ransom to the archaic superego. Thus a strange incongruity becomes visible when there is neurotic decompensation. The more pleasurable work has been normatively, the more quickly it is absorbed into the neurotic process, whereas the ability to work at a much less interesting job is maintained for a long period. In depressions associated with progredient neuroses, as in "phobic final states," all working activities become blocked.

Whenever working capacity is blocked due to inner unconscious punitive forces or uncontrollable social forces, another considerable blow is dealt to self-esteem with escalation of depression or its visible initiation. On the other hand, as during the course of psychotherapy, when work is resumed, there is usually a considerable shift towards feelings of well-being. Certainly, a major event in psychotherapy occurs when the patient gets over the "work hump," and is thus able to get additional narcissistic supplies.

Rado (1928) classified the connections between depression and self-esteem in his study of melancholia. He unmasked strident self-reproaches as an ambivalent ingratiation with the lost object represented by its introjection in the superego. Blaming himself for the loss, he simultaneously blamed the "bad part" of the lost loved object assimilated in his ego. There is thus a double introjection in severe depressive disorder, which comes to highlight abandonment by the protective superego and surrender to the archaic core of it. There is, in short, regression *in the superego*. Further, Rado's study indicates that in evaluating a depression, the depth and degree and structural type of regression, that is, the fate of the object relationship and, associated with the regression, the extent of instinctual defusion, need to be taken into account. These considerations differentiate psychotic from psychoneurotic forms of depression.

Bibring (1953) focuses on the ego-psychological aspects of depression. However, in his endeavor he neglects totally the role of object relations and of the underlying conflicts of ambivalence, regarding depression as essentially independent of the vicissitudes of aggression and of oral drives. Thus scotomised, he concludes that the oral and aggressive strivings are not as universal in depression as is generally assumed. Yet, he usefully distinguishes four basic ego states: the secure, the elated, the anxious, and the depressed, corresponding to states of balanced narcissism, of exhilarated self-esteem, of threatened narcissism, and of broken-down self-regard. Jacobson (1971) shows that Bibring does not distinguish between moods and emotional responses—pleasurable or unpleasurable, depressive, elated or anxious. She does distinguish, however, between passing emotional responses to specific experiences and moods. The latter are generalized affective ego states that extend over a longer period of time. The guilt feelings in depressive states are generalized, caused by severe ambivalence, and patients condemn themselves. They feel not merely that they have a forbidden impulse, but that they are evil.

Mahler (1966), in her discussion of the rapprochement subphase of separation-individuation, notes that a lack of acceptance and of emotional understanding at this time leads to ambivalence in the mother–child relationship. Such ambivalence results in a turning of aggression against the self and a feeling of helplessness which creates a basic depressive affect comprising a reduction of the child's self-esteem.

The Experience of Depressive Emotions in the Neuroses

MacCurdy (1925) gives a good example of a profound depression occurring during the course of treatment, a depression that was associated with nausea. The patient, a professional nurse, had become sluggish in her responses and could not account for her intense suffering. She stated that she was concerned about a woman for whom she was caring. When pressed, she associated to a woman of the same name to whom she had been rude. The woman apparently did not resent her rudeness, which made her feel as if she had harmed a dead person. Then she slowly came to think of her grandmother who was ill and whom she felt would not live long. Following this, she thought vaguely about how she might have injured her mother. Her mother had died when the patient was 3 years old, or thirty-five years ago. When clarification was sought by Dr. MacCurdy, the patient suddenly became nauseated and was obliged to lie down. MacCurdy (1925) writes:

Continuing in her efforts, she recovered a vague idea of doing something to her mother, who was dying; there was a picture in her mind of a low ceilinged room, fire-light, and her mother sitting up in bed. She has taken something which her mother ought to have, perhaps food, perhaps medicine. Somehow her grandmother was connected with all this. Each effort to remember more, led to a spasm of nausea, and she asked piteously to be helped to remember, but, of course, no suggestions were given to her. Then, suddenly, after a spasm of nausea, she fell into a deep sleep, her body relaxing and her breathing becoming deep and regular. It soon appeared that this was a state of deep somnambulism in which she answered all questions in a monotonous inflexible voice. (p. 352)

Each question asked then elicited a vivid hallucinosis of the events. These were reported in the present tense. She was seated in the dining room eating soup with her mother upstairs in bed. Her aunt tells her she should not eat the soup, for it is meant for her mother. She goes to bed.

> In the morning, my mother is asleep. They show me my mother and tell me she has gone away and is not coming back. I think she has gone away because she could not have the soup.
> ["Did anybody tell you that?" asked Dr. MacCurdy.]
> Before I went to bed my grandmother called me to her room and told me that my mother was sick and needed the soup, and I ought not to eat it. *Every day after that is sad!*" (p. 352)

The suggestion was made that she would remember all this when she awakened. The record of her productions on awakening seemed somehow familiar but not immediately, as if she had been fully involved. In further psychotherapy, the experience was fully realised and integrated, the "pure childishness of this (crime) was apparent to her" (p. 352), and her depression disappeared.

It is clear from this excerpt that this patient's depression was connected with ideas of responsibility for her mother's death and that much inner resistance opposed the recovery of the experience, traumatic for her, which was only reached at first in a hypnoid state. It is also apparent that this concatenation of experience and fantasy persisted as a buried memory for no less than 35 years. As MacCurdy (1925) notes: "As a last struggle, the psychic organism attempted to dispose of the ugly theme by compromise, by a hysterical conversion symptom — the nausea (during the somnambulism the patient explained this as an effort to get rid of the stolen soup)" (p. 353).

The theme of getting rid of her mother in fantasy and stealing her soup — and all that the soup symbolized — condenses, of course, oedipal and preoedipal wishes and remorse, based no doubt on an array of her experiences in childhood and her reactions to them.

In *The Bell Jar*, Sylvia Plath (1971) relates:

> If Mrs. Guinea had given me a ticket to Europe, or a round-the-world cruise, it wouldn't have made one scrap of difference to me, because wherever I sat — on the deck of a ship or at a street cafe in Paris or Bangkok — I would be sitting under the same glass bell jar, stewing in my own sour air. (p. 209)

Caelum non animum mutant qui trans mare currunt, as Horace stated many years ago. Disocciated childhood experiences and conflicts of wishes and guilt feelings are embedded in unconscious fantasy formations connected with these experiences, such as that illustrated here by the case reported by MacCurdy (1925). These experiences and conflicts are revealed time and again in the treatment process and account for the way in which patients with neurotic depression stew in their own sour air *without awareness of the source of their distress*. Of course, they often find a peg on which to hang the coat, and anyway may have elaborate rationalizations.

Melanie Klein (1937) insisted that normatively, under optimal conditions, the infant reaches a "depressive position." Weaning separates the infant from the mother's breast and her milk, all that symbolizes love, goodness and security. The dawning infantile ego, in Klein's view, is bound to develop primitive psychic defenses against the acknowledgement of being bodily separate. As already noted, there is incomplete psychic differentiation from the mother in early infancy. The infant's adaptation to the outer world proceeds, however, beyond this introjective stage of ego development, though with resistance and with difficulty. The earlier incomplete psychic differentiation is suffused with omnipotence, which is only modified with strain and pain. The early absolute dependency, associated with separateness, with its feelings of helplessness, is countermanded by holding onto the phase of shared omnipotence to guarantee survival. Eventually, there is a necessary partial acceptance, but the illusion of omnipotence remains to a varying degree in unconscious fantasy in further psychic development throughout the life cycle as Pumpian-Mindlin (1971) outlined. Ferenczi (1913) endeavored to show that the fixation point of the psychoses occurs at this early stage of narcissistic-omnipotence before a sense of reality is well founded. Here lies buried, no doubt, the psychotic core of every neurosis, in all of us. Helene Deutsch (1937) emphasised the view that the ego of the child is not sufficiently developed to bear the strain of mourning for a lost source of gratification and that it therefore utilizes some mechanism of narcissistic protection to circumvent or avoid the grief of loss. Similarly, she noted that whenever grief in the adult takes an abnormal course, largely due to the intensification of ambivalence towards the lost object, there is, in such cases, an avoidance of necessary grief work.

In the case of MacCurdy's patient, the childhood experiences obviously fell short of optimal mothering. Subsequently, 35 years later, a relatively minor disturbance in a personal relationship of a certain character precipitated a depressive disorder, which could be ameliorated in psychotherapy only by reference to resonating childhood events, a reference heavily resisted by the patient. In her depression, the patient experienced guilt and anxiety which partly satisfied her need for punishment. She experienced the emotional atmosphere which would be more appropriate for a murderer and thief, though she was not conscious of the source of feelings of being wicked. Ideas concerning this source came only with the demolition of dissociative defenses in psychotherapy. In such cases there is gross incompatibility of destructive fantasies and anger with other facets of the personality, including the self-image the patient needs to sustain for self-esteem. Moreover, in depression there is, in greater or lesser measure, recourse to primitive introjective mechanisms of defense whereby relinquishment of the object is replaced by its internalization, and the struggle with it continued in the internal world as part of the self. This is, of course, shown in extreme form in melancholia where, as Freud (1917) first found, the self-reproaches are reproaches against the formerly ambivalently loved one.

In a series of papers (1970, 1971, and 1974) and in his books (1976, 1981) Volkan describes patients who are beset by the polar opposites of yearning to recover the lost object and the dread of doing so. Their symptoms reflect the ambivalent object-relationship before bereavement, a relationship which persists in a distorted form. Thus, one of Volkan's patients who lost his younger brother through drowning kept a representation of the dead boy's face and voice within his bosom and carried on a dyadic dialogue as he drove to work. Some patients in their search and concomitant dread choose a "linking object" which provides an external locus in which part of the patient's projected self-representation may meet with part of the object representation of the deceased. Volkan (1976) states:

> This meeting provides a link in which the ambivalent object relationship is not renounced but "frozen." Although great care may be taken to keep it out of sight, it is important to know where it is at any given moment; the ambivalence of wanting to annihilate the deceased and simultaneously longing for him is condensed in it, and it provides an external reference for the painful and unresolved work of mourning. It makes it possible for internalized object relations with the dead to be maintained externally. (p. 74)

According to Wetmore (1963), "the courage to perceive what has been lost, its symbolic significance, and the ability to examine one's ambivalence about the object are prerequisites for *effective* grief-work" (p. 101). He accords a central place to grief-work in the psychoanalytic situation and regards this as a preeminent ingredient of the psychoanalytic cure. The grief-work which occurs in the unique environs of the psychoanalytic situation and "seals" the cure he refers to as effective grief. He writes:

> It is my hypothesis that the child cannot grieve effectively, and therefore cannot relinquish the earliest essential object-relationships. This means that the repetition-compulsion must continue in full command of the personality until the time when the ego discovers that it can tolerate the postponed separation anxiety and, so strengthened, can face the work of grieving. This mastery of original grief is essentially different from the working through of ordinary day-to-day grief as described by Freud and others. (p. 97)

He explains that simple grief-work results in the transfer of libido from one object to another with the same concomitant intensities and distortions whereas effective grief-work takes place only after the ego has undergone strengthening experiences, including the experience of tolerating anxiety. It results, then, in a deintensification of the original object-relationships. Wetmore believes there is no grief experience to compare with the effectiveness of that in the psychoanalytic situation to free the individual from the neurotic attachments of childhood. If, for by the time there is the potential to grieve effectively, the incorporated objects are largely unknown and the primary external objects displaced, where else, Wetmore asks, can these introjections be made more fully conscious?

Summary

The considerations outlined in this chapter constitute part of the basis for the view that an increased understanding of the complex role of depression in disease requires an ample conceptual framework, one which is currently in a continuing phase of development. The judicious recovery of "lost" affects is an important integrative task in analytic psychotherapy, and eventually issues in augmented integrative capacity. "Only connect" is a maxim especially apt in the psychotherapy of depression when afflicted individuals require to "connect the prose with the passion" to regain their health.

REFERENCES

Abraham, K. (1911). Notes on the psychoanalytical investigation and treatment of manic-depressive insanity and allied conditions. In *Selected Papers*, ed. D. Bryan and A. Strachey, pp. 137–156. New York: Basic Books, 1960.

Abse, D. W. (1966). *Hysteria and Related Mental Disorders: An Approach to Psychological Medicine*. Bristol: John Wright and Sons.

────── (1971). *Speech and Reason: Language Disorder in Mental Disease*. Charlottesville: The University Press of Virginia.

────── (1982). Multiple Personality. In *Hysteria*, ed. A. Roy, pp. 165–184. New York: John Wiley and Sons.

Adler, A. (1927). *Understanding Human Nature*, trans. W. B. Wolfe. New York: Premier Books, 1957.

Alexander, F. (1950). *Psychosomatic Medicine: Its Principles and Applications*. New York: W. W. Norton.

Allen, D. W. (1977). Basic Treatment Issues. In *Hysterical Personality*, ed. Mardi J. Horowitz, pp. 285–328. New York: Jason Aronson.

Benedek, T. (1956). Toward the Biology of the Depressive Constellation. In *Psychoanalytic Investigations, Selected Papers*, pp. 356–376. New York: Quadrangle/New York Times Books, 1973.

Bergler, E. (1950). *The Basic Neurosis*. New York: Grune and Stratton.

────── (1952). *The Superego*. New York: Grune and Stratton.

Bernstein, B. (1964). Social class speech systems and psychotherapy. *British Journal of Sociology* 15:54–64.

Bibring, E. (1953). The mechanism of depression. In *Affective Disorders*, ed. P. Greenacre, pp. 13–48. New York: International Universities Press.

Breuer, J. and Freud, S. (1893). On the psychical mechanism of hysterical phenomena: preliminary communication. *Standard Edition* 2:3–17. London: Hogarth Press, 1953.

Brierly, M. (1951). *Trends in Psychoanalysis*. London: Hogarth Press.

Cannon, W. B. (1929). *Bodily Changes in Pain, Hunger, Fear and Rage*. New York: Appleton–Century–Crofts.

Clouston, T. S. (1904). *Clinical Lectures in Mental Disease*. London: Churchill.

Conrad, Joseph. (1921). *The Nigger of the Narcissus*. New York: Doubleday, Doran.

Deutsch, H. (1937). Absence of grief. *Psychoanalytic Quarterly* 6:12–23.

Fenichel, O. (1941). The ego and the affects. In *Collected Papers*, ed. H. Fenichel and D. Rapaport, pp. 215–227. New York: Norton, 1954.

────── (1945). *The Psychoanalytic Theory of Neurosis*. New York: W. W. Norton.

Ferenczi, S. (1913). Stages in the development of the sense of reality. In *Sex in Psychoanalysis*, pp. 181–203. New York: Dover, 1956.

Freud, S. (1895). On the grounds for detaching a particular syndrome from neurasthenia under the description "anxiety neurosis." *Standard Edition* 3:87–117. London: Hogarth Press, 1962.

────── (1900). The interpretation of dreams. *Standard Edition* 4/5. London: Hogarth Press, 1953.

────── (1912). The dynamics of the transference. *Standard Edition* 12:97–108. London: Hogarth Press, 1958.

_____ (1917). Mourning and melancholia. *Standard Edition* 14:237–258. London: Hogarth Press, 1957.

_____ (1920). Beyond the pleasure principle. *Standard Edition* 18:1–64. London: Hogarth Press, 1955.

_____ (1923). The ego and the id. *Standard Edition* 19:3–59. London: Hogarth Press, 1955.

_____ (1924a). Neurosis and psychosis. *Standard Edition* 19:149–153. London: Hogarth Press, 1953.

_____ (1924b). The loss of reality in neurosis and psychosis. *Standard Edition* 19: 183–187. London: Hogarth Press, 1953.

_____ (1926). Inhibitions, symptoms, and anxiety. *Standard Edition* 20:77–175. London: Hogarth Press, 1959.

Goethe, Johann Wolfgang von (1774). *The Sufferings of Young Werther*, trans. Harry Steinhauer. New York: W. W. Norton, 1970.

Grinker, R. R. and Robbins, F. P. (1954). *Psychosomatic Case Book*. New York: Blakiston.

Jacobson, E. (1971). *Depression*. New York: International Universities Press.

James, W. (1890). *Principles of Psychology*. New York: Dover Publications, 1950.

Kant, I. (1870). The critique of judgement. In *Great Books of the Western World*. Vol. 42. Ed. R. M. Hutchins and M. S. Adler. London: Encyclopedia Britannica, 1952.

Klein, M. and Riviere, J. (1937). *Love, Hate and Reparation*. London: Hogarth Press.

Kulovesi, Y. (1931). Psychoanalytische bemerkungen zur James-Langeschen Affekttheorie. *Imago* 17:392–398.

Langer, S. K. (1967). *Mind: An Essay on Human Feeling*, Vol. I. Baltimore: The Johns Hopkins Press.

Lesse, S. (1974). Masked depression and depressive equivalents. In *American Handbook of Psychiatry*. Vol. 7. Ed. S. Arietti, pp. 317–329. New York: Basic Books.

MacCurdy, J. T. (1925). *The Psychology of Emotion: Morbid and Normal*. New York: Harcourt, Brace & Company, pp. 351–353.

Mahler, M. S. (1966). Notes on the development of basic moods: the depressive affect in psychoanalysis. In *Psychoanalysis — A General Psychology*, ed. R. L. Loewenstein, L. M. Newman, M. Schur, and A. J. Solnit, pp. 152–168. New York: International Universities Press.

Marty, P., & U'Uzan, M. de (1963). La penseé opératoire. *Revue Francaise Psychoanalytique* 27:345–356.

McDougall, W. (1936). *An Outline of Psychology*. London: Methuen.

Nemiah, J. C. (1977). Alexithymia: theoretical considerations. *Psychotherapy and Psychosomatics*. 28:199–206.

Plath, Sylvia (1971). *The Bell Jar*. New York: Harper and Row.

Pumpian-Mindlin (1971). Vicissitudes of Infantile Omnipotence. In *Currents In Psychoanalysis*, ed. I. M. Marcus. pp. 231–245. New York: International Universities Press.

Rado, S. (1928). The problem of melancholia. *International Journal of Psycho-Analysis* 9:420–438.

Rapaport, D. (1942). *Emotions and Memory*. New York: International Universities Press, 1959.

Ruesch, J. *Disturbed Communication*. New York: Norton, 1957.

Scott, R. F. (1912). The diaries of Robert Falcon Scott. In *Scott's Last Expedition*, Vol. 1. Arranged by Leonard Huxley. London: Smith, Elder, 1913.

Shand, A. F. (1921). *The Foundations of Character*, 2nd ed. London: Methuen, 1929.

Shands, H. C. (1975). How are "psychosomatic" patients different from "psychoneurotic" patients? *Psychotherapy and Psychosomatics*. 26:270–285.

Sifneos, P. E. (1967). Clinical observations on some patients suffering from a variety of psychosomatic diseases. *Proceedings 7th European Conference on Psychosomatic Research*. Basel: Karger, 1967.

Spinoza, B. (1677). Ethics. In *The Chief Works of Benedict de Spinoza*. Tran. & introd. by R. H. M. Elwes, pp. 45–271. New York: Dover, 1951.

Szymanski, J. S. (1930). *Psychologie vom Standpunkt der Abhaengiokeit des Erkennens von den Lebensbeduerfuissen*. Leipzig: Barth.

Volkan, V. D. (1970). Typical findings in pathological grief. *Psychiatric Quarterly* 44:231–250.

_____ (1971). A study of a patient's re-grief work through dreams, psychological tests, and psychoanalysis. *Psychiatric Quarterly* 45:255–273.

_____ (1974). Death, divorce and the physician. In *Marital and Sexual Counseling in Medical Practice*, ed. D. W. Abse, E. M. Nash and M. R. Louden, pp. 446–462. New York: Harper & Row.

_____ (1976). *Primitive Internalized Object Relations*. New York: International Universities Press.

_____ (1981). *The Linking Objects and Linking Phenomena*. New York: International Universities Press.

Wetmore, R. J. (1963). The role of grief in psychoanalysis. *International Journal of Psycho-Analysis* 44:97–104.

Wolff, H. H. (1975). The contribution of the interview situation to the restriction of fantasy life and emotional experience in psychosomatic patients. *Psychotherapy and Psychosomatics* 26:58–67.

CHAPTER THREE

The Depressive Character

D. Wilfred Abse, M.D., D.P.M.
(Univ. of London), F.R.C. Psych.

Paul Moebius, the German neuropathologist and alienist of the nineteenth century, introduced medical students to the study of psychology and clinical psychiatry by means of a series of experiments he conducted in his laboratory. He had a huge tank with glass walls in which a pike, caught in a local lake, swam around. The Professor would throw a sturgeon, also caught in the lake, into the tank whereupon the voracious pike would quickly descend upon his natural prey and devour the small fish.

On another occasion, the students would be shown the same tank; this time, however, there was a hefty glass partition dividing it into two sections in one of which the pike swam around. Moebius would throw a sturgeon into the other half of the tank, whereupon the pike, following his natural bent, would rush forth towards the small fish only to collide with the glass and thus get stunned. Following the concussion, the pike would soon revive and once again, spying his prey, rush forth only to collide again. After a number of trials — and Moebius would emphasize the individual differences of pikes to his students — the pike would swim around in his compartment without attempting to make buccal contact with the sturgeon which now swam around unmolested in the other section of the tank.

In a third phase of this experiment, the glass partition was removed and the pike swam around for a lengthy period, a period which varied with different pikes, without attempting to devour the other fish. Of course, after awhile extinction of this learned inhibition took place. Yet Moebius was able to point out to the students that for awhile the pike had internalized the glass barrier.

This excerpt from a series of pike experiments, for which I am indebted to the late Dr. Bernard Glueck, Sr., will suffice to indicate the nature of Moebius's vivid illustrations of the influence of reward and punishment on animal behavior, reward reinforcing the celerity of response, punishment retarding or stopping it. Moebius made it clear to the students, who went on to see some psychiatric patients with him, that this kind of learning applied only partially to human behavior.

This partial view of human nature underlies the currently fashionable behavioral philosophy and accounts for its successes in practical application as well as for its abject failures, too numerous to mention and too important to forget. In no sphere are the failures of behavior therapy more conspicuous than in depressive disorder. In depressive character disorder, par excellence, the voluminous ramifications of human masochism become evident. Here, investigation reveals the inadequacy of a restricted conceptual framework which relies upon variations on the theme of the positive influence of reward and the negative influence of punishment. The revelation is startling when it becomes evident that one motif in the psyche of considerable, albeit unconscious, influence is just the reverse: punishment is sought.

East and West, North and South, cultural systems of value have been influenced enormously by the collective representations embodied in the religions of lament, including Christianity. As Canetti (1978) emphasizes, the common legend around which they form is that of a man or a god who perishes unjustly, the one death that should not have taken place and which arouses grief beyond all measure. He cites the instance of the Muharran Festival of the Shiites, now especially of interest.

Islam, of course, exhibits some traits of a religion of war. However, it has also branched out into the most concentrated and extreme form of a religion of lament in the faith of the Shiites of Iran and Iraq. They believe in a spiritual and temporal leader called the Imam. More elevated, if that is possible, than the Pope, he is the bearer of divine light and is absolutely infallible. Only he who submits to the Imam can be saved; others are consigned to the death of the unbeliever and this includes those other Moslems who adhere to the Sunna of the four kaliphs. The Shiites revere Ali the Fifth, Mohammed's son-in-law, as the first rightful successor of the Prophet. Ali's sons, Hasan and Husain, as grandsons of the Prophet should have inherited his power. Ali was murdered, Hasan retired, but Husain contended valiantly for his inheritance with the son of the deceased ruling fourth kaliph. The devotional literature of the Shiites is concerned mainly with the afflictions of the family of the Prophet. In the battle for succession Husain and his followers were cut off from access to water, and he and his small band, mostly family, were surrounded and attacked and cut down on the plain of Kerbela. Thirty-three lance thrusts were counted on the hero's body and thirty-four gashes from swords. His body was trampled beneath the feet of horses, his head cut off and sent to the new kaliph in Damascus.

From the day of mourning at Kerbela, there evolved a rich literature of martyrology. The tenth day of the month of Muharran is kept as the anniversary of the tragedy of Kerbela. "Our days of remembrance are our

mourning assemblies," states a Shiite poem which sets forth the many afflictions of the Prophet's family. Weeping, lamenting and mourning for
these misfortunes, for the persecution and martyrdom of the Prophet's
family, are the believer's essential concerns.

Canetti (1978) writes, "The frenzy which seizes the mourning crowds
during this Muharran festival is almost inconceivable" (p. 149). He cites
an eyewitness account:

> 500,000 people, seized with madness, cover their heads with ashes and beat
> their foreheads on the ground. They want to give themselves up to torture,
> to commit suicide in groups, or to mutilate themselves with a refined cruelty
> . . . A great silence descends. Men in white shirts advance in hundreds, their
> faces turned ecstatically to heaven. Of these, several will be dead by evening
> and many more mutilated and disfigured; their shirts red with blood will be
> their shrouds . . . With encouraging shouts, and infecting them with their own
> madness, others hand them swords. Their excitement becomes murderous; they
> turn around and around, brandishing over their heads the weapons they have
> been given. Their shouts dominate the shouts of the crowd. To be able to bear
> what they are going to suffer they have to work themselves into a state of
> (anaesthetic) catalepsy. With the steps of automata they advance, retreat and
> move sideways in no apparent order. In time with each step they strike their
> heads with their jagged swords. Blood flows and their shirts become scarlet.
> The sight of the blood brings the confusion in the minds of these voluntary
> martyrs to a climax. Some of them collapse, striking themselves haphazardly
> with their swords. In their frenzy they have cut through veins and arteries
> and they die where they fall before the police have time to carry them to an
> ambulance installed behind the closed shutters of a shop. (pp. 153–154)

The account goes on to describe the escalation of the frenzy of the
surrounding crowd, many of whom mutilate themselves.

It is evident that this form of group hysteria is undergirded by severe
depressive masochistic urges which find their outlet sanctioned and blessed.
The martyrs are offered a mighty acclamation of the frenzied crowd, all
of whom have a core libidinized preoccupation with the humiliation and
suffering and death of Husain. Suffering is thus closely allied with being
loved. The release of derivatives of a powerful masochistic identification
with the mutilated and dead hero is operative in an altered state of consciousness, shared in different degrees by members of the crowd. This kind
of identification is the counterpart of the more familiar unconscious identification with the aggressor and it is clearly in the service of both self-
punishment and the need to be loved.

The plight of Job, a pious and dedicated man afflicted by the Almighty, is described forcefully in the Old Testament. Yahweh has allowed

himself some doubting thoughts following discourse with the devil and agrees to an experiment consisting of the exposure of the righteous Job to a rigorous loyalty test. (Of course, one is permitted to wonder why such a cruel experiment is undertaken at all, and worse, that it involves a wager with the Evil Spirit.) Job is robbed of his herds, his servants are slaughtered, his sons and daughters are killed by a whirlwind and he himself is smitten with disease and brought to the brink of death. For seventy-one verses the Almighty proclaims his world-creating power to the miserable victim who sits in ashes, scratches his sores with potsherds, and attempts to appeal to divine justice. Job has finally no alternative but to withdraw his demand for justice and to answer, "I lay my hand on my mouth" in submission and in fear and trembling. Jung (1954) opines, "Anyone can see how he [Yahweh] unwittingly raises Job by humiliating him in the dust. By doing so he pronounces judgment on himself and gives man the moral satisfaction whose absence we found so painful in the Book of Job" (p. 36).

According to Jung's analysis, Job realizes God's inner antimony, that he is loving if honored and worshipped, and praised as just, but that he cannot tolerate any criticism, overt or implied. On the one hand, he tramples on human life and happiness without regard if there is the faintest suggestion of criticism and on the other, he must have man for an admiring partner. But then the answer to Job comes later. According to Jung, the victory of the oppressed and vanquished Job is in his higher moral achievement. This results ultimately, according to Jung, in the regeneration of Yahweh. Yahweh must become man precisely because he has done man a hideous wrong and in preparation, prefigurations of the Christ occur in the three or four centuries before his advent. Finally Jesus comes to announce the glad tidings of a loving God. Jung acknowledges that "it comes as a nasty shock when this supremely good God only allows the purchase of such an act of grace through a human sacrifice, and, what is worse, through killing of his own son" (p. 111).

Setting aside the metaphysical considerations elaborated upon by Jung (beyond our scope here), an approach anchored in clinical experience suggests that the reciprocal relations between Yahweh and Job may be considered in the light of the possibility that they are an extended representation of an internal dialogue. Though Job is God's creature (as we all are), he created Yahweh, or recreated him, in a complex primitive projection system which includes externalization of parts of Job's self. It also seems possible that Job courted, even invited, some of his terrible afflictions. Others were undoubtedly externally inflicted. In regard to the former, he demonstrates a need for punishment in order to avoid the perception of guilt. As for the latter, he used them to serve his need for punishment and to rationalize his protest against the injustice of his suffering and to buttress his insistence on his innocence.

Nowhere in the Book of Job and nowhere in Jung's (1954) *Answer to Job* is there adequate consideration of the possible sources of Job's deep-seated sense of guilt (or better, his need for punishment to avoid the perception of guilt). In any case, we learn nothing of his childhood, and we are at a loss for a specific psychogenesis.

Yet we must assume that Job as an infant, and as a child, like all of us, traversed in his maturation and development the inevitable sequence of zones of predominant erotogeneity with more or less difficulty, and that in his dependency relationships during this passage there were influential experiences in his primary family, including those of the Oedipus complex. No doubt these molded his fantasies concerning the Almighty.

Jung, like Freud, was impressed with the unconscious legacy of phylogenetic experience. In his view, this was evidenced in a number of dynamic archetypes of the unconscious. Freud was impressed especially with the effects of experience in the prehistoric primal horde, but he also laid emphasis on adverse events (including fantasy-formation) in childhood as determining factors in the genesis of neurosis, including depressive disorder.

There is the inescapable fact of human neoteny — of fetalisation prolonged beyond the womb — and this creates the need for sustained love and protection. When these are not adequately forthcoming there is an aggravation of the inevitable problems and pains of growth and development, including the striving for autonomy attended by the ambivalence of compliance — defiance and a struggle for power, as illustrated in the Book of Job. Job's railings against injustice represent an extreme case of the feelings of the innocent victim who must submit to his fate. We all share such feelings and fantasies in some degree, thrust as we are into the world without exercise of volition, and in thrall in greater or lesser degrees to authority and institution, to appetite and desire. Moreover, there are the changes in ourselves we must welcome or endure (usually both) from infancy through childhood to puberty and adolescence, and then to maturity and middle age; further, there is the difficult adaptation to old age. Along the way, we face all kinds of losses of relatives and friends as well as other possible adverse changes, both social and material, in our environment. There are, in short, the days of gaining strength, the days of strength, and later those of decrescence, as Shakespeare depicted in the seven ages of man in *As You Like It* and in his fine description of senile dementia in the character of King Lear.

In well-integrated societies ostentatious ceremonies accompany an individual's life crises. There is organized community support and participation in crucial events of the life cycle, including the losses of one's relatives and friends. Van Gennep (1960) focused on the *rites de passage* and examined the activities associated with such ceremonies in terms of their order and content. He distinguished three major phases: *séparation* (separation), *marge* (transition) and *aggrégation* (incorporation). Rites of separation are prominent in funeral ceremonies, rites of incorporation at marriages, and transition rites predominate in pregnancy, betrothal and initiation. However, all three elements are present, though not equally developed, in every set of ceremonies and they all may be reduced to a minimum, as in remarriage or adoption. Van Gennep also applied this analysis to the ceremonies associated with changes in natural phenomena, such as those which accompany and assure the change of the seasons. Thus, for example, New Year ceremonies include rites of the expulsion of winter and incorporation of spring. The one dies and the other is reborn.

Chapple and Coon (1942) follow Van Gennep in their analysis of rites of passage and further develop his views. They designate those ceremonies which are entirely group events, "rites of intensification," distinguishing between ceremonies associated with seasons and other regular occurrences which bring about changes in the group activities, and those related to the crises in the individual's life cycle which for the individual do not recur. Chapple and Coon elaborate further upon the function of ritual behavior in maintaining the homeostasis of the group. They show that ritual behavior restores the equilibrium where changes in social interaction are impending or have occurred.

It has indeed become clear that the ritual is a response to an emotional problem which it symbolizes and for which it provides, or attempts to provide, a solution, one which is of communal benefit ensuring continued cohesion and adequate group adaptation. Sometimes the emphasis is upon an individual's disease, especially a disease which may become disruptive for the group if not treated in a healing rite.

A vivid example of this is afforded by Harris (1957) in her description of *Saka*, a "possession hysteria" of women in an East African tribe. Following indications of hysteroid dysphoria a woman becomes convulsive, with jactitations of the shoulders and rhythmic movements of the head from side to side. In an altered state of consciousness the woman then performs repetitive acts, sometimes seizing others' goods. The illness is indeed described as "wanting and wanting" and follows her wanting something belonging to her husband, or something that the husband has refused to buy for her, for example, sugar. The healing is accomplished in a group ceremony when the spirit who possesses the woman is appeased by being given various objects she has craved, usually items associated with men's activities. During the ritual, she wears male garb and carries a walking stick. The husband provides cigarettes and bananas and manufactured cloth in the appeasement ceremony, at which time there is drumbeating and frenzied dancing.

It is notable that in this culture women's rights are sharply limited.

Men have access to work and have cash to spend in the village. As for the mainstays of tribal life, land and cattle, these are inherited by the men. The primitive symbolism in the ceremonial rituals adumbrated above is simple and obvious, affording release for strangulated affects including anger and the fantasy of turning the tables on the privileged men. Bennett Simon (1979) notes that, around the world, the most oppressed group is women and that ecstatic phenomena are more likely to be found in cultures in which there is a rigid division between the sexes and in which men are in the clearly dominant position. He writes:

> While such a formulation hardly constitutes an exhaustive explanation of these phenomena, it is an important component. These group rites can involve men as well, particularly groups of men within the culture who are in marginal and subservient positions. There is no doubt but that these experiences not only provide a release but that they accord importance and dignity to otherwise disenfranchised groups. In the ritual these oppressed groups seem to obtain (symbolically, or in more literal form) something of what the dominant group possesses. Thus, the women in the Bacchae take on male functions and male powers, especially as warriors. They leave their looms and their children, taking up arms and defeating men in the field of combat. They carry the thyrsus which symbolises the disembodied phallus. (pp. 193–194)

Such are the folkways which allow a periodic, though only temporary, switch from masochistic victim to identification with the aggressor.

The description of adult character in terms of childhood experience is one of several basic principles of psychoanalytic characterology. Many anthropological studies lend support to this principle. The observations of anthropologists show relationship of customs of nursing, weaning and toilet training in a preliterate tribe to modal characteristics of the adult community. Conclusions from field studies support the psychogenetic view that generous suckling and later weaning are related to generosity, optimism, and cooperative peaceful behavior, whereas niggardly suckling and early weaning coincide with arrogance, aggression, impatience, quarrelsomeness, retentiveness, suspicion, and nostalgic sadness. Erikson (1945), Mead (1935) and Money-Kyrle (1939) were among the first to supply important corroborative evidence of such a relationship.

Ribble's (1944) work with infants originally showed by direct observation the relationship between nursing experience and the reactions of anxiety, withdrawal, and depression in the infant. Later investigative work, notably that of Spitz (1946) and of Mahler (1968), amplified her findings. These direct observations have fortified theory built upon retrospective studies such as those of Abraham (1924) and Glover (1925), entailed in psychoanalytic therapy of adults. These workers showed the influence of experience in the early oral phase of infancy on later character formation.

Goldman-Eisler (1953) conducted an investigation comprised of quantitative and factorial study of adult character assessed by means of verbal rating scales. The syndromes which emerged were related to the length of breast feeding as determined by interviews with the mothers of the subjects. A bipolar type factor was found, highly saturated with positive and negative manifestations of narcissism and characterized mainly by the traits of pessimism, passivity, aloofness, oral aggression, endocathexis, and autonomy at one end; and optimism, exocathexis, nurturance and sociability at the opposite end of the trait distribution. The composition of this factor showed a striking correspondence to psychoanalytic oral character types as described by Abraham (1924), Glover (1925), Jones (1913) and Bergler (1934).

In any particular community there are many modal personalities within each gender; there are aberrant personalities, too, and phases of aberrance for which the culture provides attempts at resolution and group integration, as already noted. Depressive problems and the means to cope with them vary widely within different societies, but they are always present as part of the condition of being human. There are different degrees of vulnerability to severe depression, and these degrees are heightened by character traits of the orally ungratified type. This type is characterized by a profoundly pessimistic outlook on life, accompanied by moods of depression and attitudes of withdrawal, feelings of insecurity, a passive-receptive attitude, a grudging feeling of injustice and a difficulty in sharing, and sometimes by an impatient importunity. Furthermore, derivatives of oral sadism are often apparent in ambivalence, hostility and envy, in an aggressive use and omnipotent valuation of speech, and in covetousness and maliciousness in social conduct.

In recent decades, social scientists have popularized the notion of alienated man. The diffuse concept of alienation overlaps with that of depression. Seeman (1959) has distinguished five ingredients in alienation, some of which may be more or less dominant: powerlessness, meaninglessness, normlessness, isolation, and self-estrangement. He defines meaninglessness as a low expectancy that satisfactory predictions about future outcomes of behavior can be made. Within the context of a behavioral learning theory this definition is, of course, heavily cognitively biased, and probably represents the kind of rationalization to which a profound pessimism resorts. In any event, it is clear that the dimensions of alienation overlap with those of depression. As Lewis Feuer (1962) insists, the concept "alienation" has a lineage which one can trace back to Calvin, who saw man alienated through all time from God by his original sin. Feuer rightly corrects Fromm (1961) who mistakenly had stated that "the thinker who coined the concept of alienation was Hegel." Like his fellow Hegelians, Karl Marx, in his early writings, regarded man's history as one of increasing alienation, and he depicted aggravation of alienation as the essence of the effect of the capitalist order. He maintained that alienation signified a mode of life in which man was being compelled by adverse social circumstances to act self-destructively. Feuer (1962) writes:

> The economy which men had created presumably to satisfy their needs was finally warping their deepest instincts. Repeatedly the young Marx and Engels characterised the bourgeois society in metaphors and actualities of sexual alienation. . . . In these early writings, Marx and Engels, as Freudian fore-runners, regarded love, not work, as the source of man's sense of reality. (pp. 4–5)

Later, in order, presumably, to dissociate themselves from German idealistic intellectuals, Marx and Engels ceased to emphasize the importance of human divorce from sensuality, that is, to speak more broadly, from nature inside themselves and out. This Feuerbachian emphasis had railed against Christian asceticism but, when it became the property of romantic individualism, it rendered such a concept of alienation politically unacceptable for the foundation of Marxist socialism. They thought of themselves as becoming more scientific by stressing the dynamics of the class struggle as humanity's lever for the achievement of communism. Thus they came to emphasize the role of hate, and wrote disparagingly of the mysticism of the Romantics. Feuer (1962) writes: "This insistence on the primacy of hatred, aggression, for the socialist movement was a reiterated theme in Engels' writing . . . There was a concern always for the maintenance of the masculinity of the movement, a fear that dwelling on concepts such as 'alienation' would indeed masochize the workers' movement as it had the intellectuals" (p. 9).

It is evident in this postindustrial era, that in both communist and capitalist society depressive problems are rampant and that attempts to mitigate them by means of euphoriant substances more often than not create further problems. The mass pursuit of "the good life" has become complicated by the abuse of alcohol, cocaine and other drugs in both the East and the West. Attempts at self-cure in millions of cases become impounded in total or partial self-destruction. It is also notable that reaction to the thermonuclear threat, where it does not lead to protest, results in the despondency of youth, to which the contemporary suicide statistics of the Western world attest.

Today, the cultural opportunities for working through feelings — feelings of protest against adult negligence and feelings about inner change—in natural groups, are not yet as available, or as effective as in traditional societies. Change, of course, always entails some loss of previous sources of satisfaction and some mourning.

Many years ago, Róheim (1923) described celebratory rites in primitive societies. There was much feasting and considerable opportunity for wider instinctual expression. This sometimes included defecation on the graves of departed fathers in bringing to an end a period of mourning. He regarded these rites as a symbolic killing and eating of the father, performed with much pleasure and rejoicing.

Psychodynamics of the Depressive Character

The foregoing considerations concerning the miseries of human existence on this planet make it evident that it is difficult, though not altogether impossible, to avoid such dysphoric emotions as sadness, remorse, and regret about the past, and anxiety, despondency, and despair about the present and future. There are primitive and massive defenses against such emotions, but these are often associated with psychotic distortion of reality, as in manic and paranoid states. Here we are concerned with chronically depressed, pessimistic, and inhibited persons who repeatedly suffer severe frustrations and reversals in their careers, in their social relations, and in their love life. Alexander (1930) viewed these neurotic characters as the victims of unconsciously motivated and self-generated punishment. As he expressed it tersely, the superego in such cases is corruptible by the ego's suffering, so that the ego bribes it by unconsciously self-inflicted punishment. As we have noted, this kind of disorder can be especially widespread in devotees of religions of lament and reach extreme physical limits and is anyway frequent in Western civilization.

Goldman-Eisler (1953), basing a classification on the psychoanalytic findings of Glover (1925) and Abraham (1924), characterizes the depressive character as having a profoundly pessimistic outlook on life, sometimes accompanied by moods of depression and withdrawal; a passive-receptive attitude; intense feelings of insecurity with a need for the assurance of getting a guaranteed livelihood; a vaulting ambition conflated with a feeling of unattainability; a grudging feeling of injustice; much anxiety concerning competition; great dislike of sharing; and an impatient importunity. She groups these character traits together according to the psychogenetic root in early ungratified orality.

Among psychoanalysts there is general agreement that, in most cases, a depressive state of mind in later life is a reproduction in large part of a depression in childhood. Marcovitz (1966) points to some exceptions.

Sometimes patients in analysis remember a generally happy childhood in which they had been the most loved and admired of all their siblings and significant externally produced traumata had not occurred until midlatency or beyond. Such patients, in my experience, belong to the group which Goldman-Eisler designates as possessing character traits of the orally gratified type and an excess of optimism which is at first not appreciably lessened by reality experience. In these patients, as Marcovitz notes, depressive reactions are related to the recurrent disappointment of unconscious expectations and the development of notions of recapture of a very special childhood, only to be regained, perhaps after bitter disappointments, in death.

In general, however, my experience agrees with that of Berliner (1966), who links the unhappy childhood of those of his patients with a depressive character infiltrated with moral masochism. He cites unhappy events, such as disruption of the family or inability of the child to fulfil the expectations of the family; the child was then confronted with critical and punitive attitudes which hampered the development of self-esteem. Some parents, indeed, cannot love their children because they are depressives themselves. Such childhood situations predispose to depression when there is a constitutional vulnerability. As Berliner (1966) notes, "The depressive patient had, or still has, a great need for gratification by way of mouth and body surface. His oral and skin erotisms are constitutionally stronger and more demanding than average" (p. 244).

The fixation resulting from frustrated early oral and skin erotic needs is the basic substratum of the depressive character, as the investigations of Freud (1917) and Abraham (1924) indicated. Berliner (1966) emphasizes, in addition, a point of view which takes into consideration the adaptive functions of the ego and object relations: by demanding and incorporating oral libido the child absorbs — and later unconsciously seeks — displeasure, sadness, and suffering in the place of being loved. The child's suffering is libidinized and takes the place of the absent or inadequate nursing and cuddling. This adaptation of taking suffering for love seems the only way in which a dependent and powerless child can withstand such deprivation and survive.

In the differentiated psyche of later years, the archaic oral disposition outlined lends itself readily to the psychodynamic events discussed by Alexander (1930) and referred to above: the person whose love is needed is later represented in the superego. The superego in the depressive character is malignant because of the strength and durability of the early introjects. It is necessary to realize that these introjects become entangled with the further development of the oral and anal phases including the accumulation of excessive sadistic charges. As Berliner (1966) notes, the experience of hate is added to the picture of early orality, and ambivalence and feelings of guilt appear. Both are prominent in the depressive character, who struggles valiantly with the shadows of the parental imagos which continue to fall upon the ego. Self-esteem regulation in accordance with social realities is thus impaired and a readiness is created for a regressive movement to sadism which becomes turned against the self. When this occurs, further damage to self-esteem results in depressive moodiness compounded of grief, fantasies of vengeance, and guilt.

Berliner (1966) stresses the actual hostility of the parents in the early transactions during the infancy of the depressive character and the libidinal reactions to this experience of hostility. Bergler (1952) emphasizes especially the basic mechanism of libidinized self-damage which, however, he regards as a defense to preserve infantile megalomania. In adult language the commentary is: "It is not true that the bad mother punishes me; I, through my provocations, make her punish me!" Thus, according to Bergler the helpless child is enabled to triumph, to repair the lesion in self-esteem, a self-esteem which had become impounded in narcissistic omnipotence. Children thus learn to repeat actively experiences they had been bound to endure passively.

These considerations advanced by Bergler have been of considerable importance in my own analytic work with depressive characters. However, it has not always been clear that there was actual early predominantly hostile parenting since it has been impossible to extricate memories of actualities from fantasy (and memory of fantasies) especially as the latter infiltrated transference events. In these events, certainly, the accusations which emerge as the introject is projected onto the analyst are those which would be projected against a frustrating and sadistic love-object. At first, the patient expresses feelings of being unloveable and bad, and it is only in later developments that transference projection occurs with sometimes outspoken guilt which for some periods returns the patient to a love-begging, submissive attitude. These transference oscillations illustrate repeatedly the fact that the expression of anger is a temporary antidote to depression but that the patient soon turns the hostility against the self and reestablishes part of the basic psychic condition of the depressive character. These circular transference events are very gradually reduced in intensity with repeated interpretation and working through.

George Devereux (1953) emphasized that the legend of Oedipus consists partly of an element often ignored, namely, that King Laius and Queen Jokasta conspired to murder their newborn son. It is said that the ancient Greeks often resorted to infanticide. In the story the royal couple were warned by the Delphic Oracle that this son would bring disaster upon them. Laius crippled the baby's feet by piercing the ankles and pinning them together and had him thrown on a trackless mountain. The later events which comprise the Oedipus myth are well known, and are, of course, utilized in psychoanalysis to nominate and illustrate the triadic phase of childhood development. However, as Sophocles tells it, Jokasta is the character most gravely incriminated. She had handed her child to a servant with the order to kill him. The servant later appeared as a witness. Berliner (1966) points out that, though our culture no longer allows parents to put a child out to die, some parents behave in a way which threatens the dependent child with annihilation. He regards the deepest meaning of the Oedipus legend, beyond parricide and incest, as infanticide, and this not only in the simple form of killing a child but also in the form of burdening the child with self-destructive guilt. The severe forbidding superego which is a prominent characteristic of Western culture and is exhibited powerfully in the depressive character, is, according to Berliner, more the extension of the experience of the rejected and crippled child than of the murderous rebellious one. He insists, without disputing the universality of the Oedipus complex, that the depressive character originates earlier, and that in the later depressive state the Oedipus complex already bears the stamp of the preoedipal pathology, love-hungry submissiveness toward both parents dominating the child's behavior.

I have mentioned above the difficulties of getting to know retrospectively the actual transactions in the early life of the child. In 1896, Freud advanced the view that many of his patients who suffered hysterical symptoms had been violently abused sexually — mostly women patients seduced by their fathers. His later doubts and partial repudiation of this etiology led to his momentous discoveries of the power of internal wish-fantasy, for the most part unconscious, and of the Oedipus complex. However, a substantial proportion of hysterical and hysteriform disorders, especially frequent in women, reveal an etiological constellation which includes actual sexual seduction in childhood, at any rate in my experience of analytic psychotherapy of severely sick patients. There is, of course, as Freud stated, a complementary series of causative factors which ultimately issue in symptom formation. Similarly, though decision here concerning the nature of the actual traumatic events in the early childhood of depressives is often even more difficult, we should beware of ascribing all events to fantasy formations without any basis in actuality. And, of course, the fantasies regularly also allude to actual experiences of fulfillment and frustration, and of conflict and of trauma.

In our discussion of Van Gennep's *The Rites of Passage*, we considered briefly the cultural mechanisms, the group mournings and celebrations, which are utilized by the members of a society to assuage their grief, diminish their guilt, and express their joy. These cultural mechanisms differ in several ways from those in psychoanalytic therapy including the opportunity such therapy provides for working through. From the analyst's position, a situation is cultivated which enables the analyst to demonstrate again and again to the patient the nature of the patient's resistances. The patient is then led to recognize the more exposed unconscious strivings and fantasies, and to elucidate these fantasies and their connections with past experiences. Of course, even initial recognition often requires interpretation of formidable pathogenic defenses. Freud (1914) noted that working through describes that part of the work which effects the greatest changes in the patient and which distinguishes analytic treatment from any kind of treatment by suggestion. Sedler (1983) has emphasized usefully that working through is accomplished only with the active participation of the patient striving for recovery from neurotic illness; Sedler criticizes the one-sided focus of the considerations in the literature on the analyst's point of view. He quotes Fenichel (1945):

> Systematic and consistent interpretive work, both within and without the framework of the transference, can be described as educating the patient to produce continually less distorted derivatives until his fundamental instinctual conflicts are recognizable. Of course, this is not a single operation resulting in a single act of abreaction; it is, rather, a chronic process of working through, which shows the patient again and again the same conflicts and his usual way of reacting to them, but from new angles and in new connections. (p. 31)

Sedler (1983) stresses that working through is a labor to be accomplished by the patient which the neurosis has, for so long, served to postpone. It is the labor of transformation that makes possible the shedding of the neurotic encumbrance and its symptomatic trappings in favor of a healthier, more rewarding adaptation.

Freud (1893) had discussed working over in the context of the early trauma theory of hysteria. The "Preliminary Communication" maintained that the traumatic situation could have been rendered relatively harmless by an immediate energetic reaction "from tears to acts of revenge." However, when, in the nature of the situation such action was precluded, speech availed to abreact the strangulated affects "almost as effectively." Failing these responses of action and speech, the traumatic event retained its pathogenic power to produce symptoms of illness. In the same year, Freud defined working over as a means to deal with the affects generated by the psychical trauma when adequate motor and speech reactions had been absent. In this early formulation, working over, as Sedler (1983) points out, consists of the production of various associations including contrasting ideas, in the company of which, painful recollections and associations no longer exert so monolithic a pathogenic force. While practicing the investigative psychotherapy of hysterical patients, Freud (1895) elaborated the concept of working over. This concept came to include the gradual exposure of hidden memories of pathogenic events which intensified abreaction instead of diluting the forcefulness of affect. In this second way, by gradually dropping the veil of intermediate associations, a solution to the therapeutic problem of recurrent symptoms was approached more adequately. The concept of working over gradually became absorbed in the concept of working through, comprising both remembering and repeating past experiences, the latter in the service of resistance to the uncovering of pathogenic memories. Sometimes, however, repeating is not altogether oppositional, but is utilizable as in the transference neurosis and in transference manifestations generally.

These considerations of working over and working through, more amply scrutinized by Sedler (1983), are pertinent to the understanding of the usefulness of rites of passage, including mourning ceremonials. These institutionalized rites of passage are adapted for the immediate purpose of working over; this is not to be confused with the full process of working through. The young child's limited capacity to endure the mourning process in order to resolve narcissistic and ambivalence conflicts is well attested to by psychotherapists such as Anna Freud and Dorothy Burlingham (1944). Wetmore (1963) emphasized that the most effective grief experience is possible only within the psychoanalytic situation. There, depressed adult patients can often free themselves from the introjects established during the early ungratified pregenital phase of development. However, when a symptomatic depression is firmly anchored in the matrix of a pronouncedly depressive character disorder, a negative therapeutic reaction can block effective working through. As Jacobson (1971) notes about some of these patients, the profit they derive may be for many months no more than support from a durable transference which may carry them through the depression without fatal consequences. They need the therapist as a patient listener to whom they can address their repetitious complaints and ventilate their feelings in a circular process of working over, thus diminishing the severity of their suffering for part of the time. Some patients, of course, do make slow progress though the process of working through is sluggish and impeded. Much fortitude and patience is required of the therapist, who must deal with problems of counteridentification, including engulfment in gloom. The psychic labor required of the therapist consists of both empathic support and the activities of clarification and interpretation. With all of this effort, tolerance of the considerable hostility which accompanies the deep dependency is necessary in order to preserve the therapeutic situation which is a lifeline for the patient.

These patients evoke the image of the three male nudes who form the group of shades atop August Rodin's Gates of Hell. The shades wearily and with infinite regret prepare to enter while the damned beneath them rise and fall. Some patients periodically expose the limits of psychotherapy without concurrent adjunctive physical measures such as antidepressant medication and, when necessary, shock therapy (Abse and Ewing 1956).

As Sedler (1983) notes, the will to remember, as it becomes part of the determination to follow the path of free association, is the revealed aspect of the will to recovery in psychoanalysis. It is opposed by the repetition compulsion as Freud (1914, 1920) outlined, and this repeating especially in the transference is utilized in a "collaborative counterpoint" (Sedler 1983). In order that therapy progress favorably, remembering must always be favored. Remembering alone makes it possible to both own and distance the past and thereby to curtail its inexpedient distortions of the present. Working through comprises the labor involved in this transformation of repeating to remembering so that adequate distance from the past is achieved.

In Freud's (1920) view, the compulsion to repeat is linked to an inherent conservative instinctual quality he identified as the drive to death, the urge to restore an earlier state of things. Sometimes a desperate poet in an effort at self-cure will illustrate Freud's conception of the human soul as fundamentally, and tragically, conflicted. The writings of Sylvia Plath illuminate the battle in the depths of the mind, with victories along the way, but with a conclusion in the defeat of suicide (Steiner 1973). In dreams, in play, or in art, we may mime the ghosts of traumatic experiences that continue to hold us in thrall and by working over diminish some of their traumatic power, as Plath did in her poetry and in her autobiographical novel *The Bell Jar* (1971). Soon, too soon, she had to acknowledge, "See, the darkness is leaking from the cracks. I cannot contain it. I cannot contain my life" (Stade 1973, p. 29).

We have to acknowledge the paradox of an extraordinary creative power sometimes evident in a severely depressive character disorder. We have also to deplore the fact that adequate treatment is so seldom available for the depressed creative artist.

Depressive Character Disorder and Creativity

Sylvia Plath attempted suicide in 1953 and was then promptly put into a hospital; her treatment included electric shock treatments. In 1961, more than a year before her suicide, she wrote a couple of poems while in the hospital recovering from an appendectomy. One of these, "In Plaster," begins:

> I shall never get out of this! There are two of me now:
> This new absolutely white person and the old yellow one.

The Bell Jar (Plath 1976) gives us a clear notion of the splitting in her personality during her time at Smith College and during a guest editorship in New York City. George Stade (1973) writes of this time:

> "When I was nineteen, pureness was the great issue," says Esther Greenwood. From a poem ("Fever 103°"), old yellow answers: "Pure? What does it mean?" Wedged, for the time, between countervailing forces of equal potency, Esther Greenwood can move neither way: "I wondered why I couldn't go the whole way doing what I should any more. This made me sad and tired. Then I wondered why I couldn't go the whole way doing what I shouldn't . . . and this made me sadder and more tired."
>
> But old yellow begins to break through "yellower than ever," takes charge, decides to seduce a simultaneous interpreter from the U.N., fails, and according to the logic of such things, suffers in return a beating and attempted rape, in a patch of black mud, by a South American play-boy woman hater, who acts as if he knew what secretly she was after. "Slut," he says, "Your dress is black and the dirt is black as well." She leaves New York to return to her home and her mother, but that whole time now seems "vacuous." She goes, for the first time, to her father's grave: "I laid my face to the smooth face of the marble and howled my loss into cold salt rain." The next morning she squeezes into the crawl space beneath her house where a dim undersea light filtered through the slits of the cellar windows. She wraps her black raincoat around her "like my own sweet shadow" and swallows one by one a bottle of sleeping pills. (p. 22)

Thus her first attempted suicide in 1953. Stade (1973) points out that the persona speaking out of any given poem may be either sulphurous old yellow, or plaster saint, "or a consciousness that sometimes contains these two and sometimes lies stretched between them" (p. 9). He points out, too, that works of art, like the wishes incorporated in the apparitions of hallucinosis or of a dream, may be (as Freud [1919] indicated in his essay on the uncanny) "distorted by the disapproving superego into malevolent and sinister shapes that threaten with what they promise, that insinuate the desire beneath the fear" (p. 15). Stade states that "the case of Sylvia Plath is all the more unsettling in that neither the attraction or revulsion is subconscious. She knows perfectly well that what her submerged self wants the plaster saint disapproved of, and she knows why, too" (p. 15).

This particular theme of attraction and revulsion is made particularly explicit in Ibsen's play, *The Lady from the Sea*. In any event, Sylvia Plath's attempts to work over her deepseated and guilt-ridden instinctual conflicts through her art proved insufficient to sustain life for very long.

Along with Proust (see Miller 1957 for a psychoanalytic study) and Joyce (see especially A *Portrait of the Artist as a Young Man* 1916), Virginia Woolf explored new dimensions in the novel. Noble (1980) examines Woolf's creativity. In 1919, Woolf wrote perhaps the fullest early analysis of the need for and the function of the stream-of-consciousness technique. Her view of the task of the novelist surely overlaps with the work of psychoanalysis. It diverges considerably, however, from the working through in the psychoanalytic process emphasized here and from all it entails in the exploration of transference and resistance as well as of ventilation of feelings. In, for example, *To the Lighthouse* (Woolf 1927), frustration of desire, anxiety concerning loss, and feelings concerning the death of the mother are all ventilated. The notion of resolving fantasies about parents is approached and illuminated in an inner voyage by this writer of genius. At this time, Virginia Woolf was attempting, with a measure of success, alleviation of her own depressive suffering. This attempt at stabilizing herself is amply disclosed in passages of A *Writer's Diary* (Woolf 1953).

Sedler (1983) has rightly emphasized the role of resistance of the id in necessitating working through in psychoanalytic therapy. However, as Freud (1923, 1933) has shown, the superego in its archaic core is intimately related to the id, and his diagram of the anatomy of the mental personality in *The New Introductory Lectures* is calculated to represent this. Moreover, Freud (1923) considered that, after sublimation, the erotic instinctual component no longer had the same power of binding destructiveness, and that partial defusion was the source of some of the cruelty against the self exhibited in the ferocity of the archaic core of the superego under conditions of regression. Regression in the superego (Kelly 1965) is indeed the crucial vulnerability of the depressive character, just as severe regression in ego functioning is the crucial vulnerability in schizophrenia. Sometimes in schizoaffective disorder severe regression is evident in both ego and superego. In the case of Virginia Woolf hypomanic and schizoid defense clusters seem evident to me, and she was periodically plunged into schizoaffective disorder.

As already outlined here, the crucial vulnerability of the depressive character is anchored in the persistent need for the affection of a once rejecting mother now introjected.

At times, through critical or popular acclaim, artists may have their self-esteem temporarily boosted. However, in the event of disappointment, and sometimes in reaction to success, regression leads into the characteristic self-deprecating attitude of the depressive. It is acknowledged that creativity is a function of health, as some repeatedly assert, but the intense need to battle with disease is not to be despised (Rickman 1957). In this battle, psychoanalytic psychotherapy has a considerable role, for, after all, there can be no work of art without the artist. Working over in whatever form is ultimately often insufficient to preserve healthy existence.

There is a hazardous dimension to the work of an artist who faces anxiety and guilt and enters into the depths of personal pains and depression. Though the artist may be motivated unconsciously by an attempt to solve conflict and reduce morbid apprehension, the art work does not necessarily become therapeutic. The work may, indeed, also be an attempt at reparation in order to neutralize or offset a strong underlying current of destructiveness. This is often the case when the great strength of creativity is a marker of much-heightened psychic metabolism. Like the notorious sorcerer's apprentice, the artist may call up more than can be handled inwardly and alone without later acting it out self-destructively. Working over in art work thus has its possible dangers as well as its often more immediate benefits for the artist. Sometimes, working through can only be approached in an adequate therapeutic setting. The artist who is closely identified with the creative force within and suffused unconsciously with correlative infantile omnipotent fantasies may not seek help easily. The artist may remain bedevilled by arrogance, which is indeed often part and parcel of the artistic depressive character.

Summary

The considerations here outlined lead to the view that ultimately an adequate psychoanalytic situation must be engendered for the patient with severe depressive character disorder to be decisively relieved of self-destructive behavior, whether this is embedded in interpersonal strife or in substance abuse, or both. It is in psychoanalytic therapy that the opportunity of sufficiently working through is afforded, though other therapies, or activities, may be temporarily ameliorative and useful, and sometimes a necessary prelude. The core problem of suffering being closely allied to being loved, and the resistance of clinging to infantile omnipotence, are formidable barriers to achieving a stable joyful existence by means of any known therapy.

REFERENCES

Abraham, K. (1924). The influence of oral erotism on character formation. In *Selected Papers*, pp. 393–417. London: Hogarth Press, 1942.
Abse, D. W. and Ewing, J. A. (1956). Transference and countertransference in somatic therapies. *Journal of Nervous and Mental Disorders* 123: 32–40.

Alexander, F. (1930). The neurotic character. *International Journal of Psycho-Analysis* 11: 292–311.

Bergler, E. (1934). Zur problematik des oralen pessimisten. *Imago* 20: 330–376.

——— (1952). *The Superego*, New York: Grune and Stratton.

Berliner, B. (1966). Psychodynamics of the depressive character. *Psychoanalytic Forum* 1: 244–251.

Breuer, J. and Freud, S. (1893) On the psychic mechanism of hysterical phenomena: preliminary communication. *Standard Edition* 2: 3–17. London: Hogarth Press, 1953.

Canetti, E. (1978). *Crowds and Power*. Trans. C. Stewart. New York: Seabury Press.

Chapple, E. D. and Coon, C. S. (1942). *Principles of Anthropology*. New York: Henry Holt.

Devereux, G. (1953). Why Oedipus killed Laius. *International Journal of Psycho-Analysis* 34: 132–141.

Erikson, E. H. (1945). Childhood and tradition in two American Indian tribes. *Psychoanalytic Study of the Child* 1: 319–350.

Fenichel, O. (1945). *The Psychoanalytic Theory of Neurosis*. New York: W. W. Norton.

Feuer, L. (1962). What is alienation? In *New Politics*, vol. 2: 116–134.

Freud, A. and Burlingham, D. (1944). *Infants without families*. New York: International Universities Press.

Freud, S. (1895). The psychotherapy of hysteria. In *Studies on Hysteria. Standard Edition* 2: 253–305. London: Hogarth Press, 1955.

——— (1896). The aetiology of hysteria. *Standard Edition* 3: 191–221. London: Hogarth Press, 1962.

——— (1914). Remembering, repeating and working through. *Standard Edition* 12: 145–156. London: Hogarth Press, 1958.

——— (1917). Mourning and melancholia. *Standard Edition* 14: 237–258. London: Hogarth Press, 1957.

——— (1919). The "uncanny." *Standard Edition* 17: 217–251. London: Hogarth Press, 1955.

——— (1920). Beyond the pleasure principle. *Standard Edition* 18: 1–64. London: Hogarth Press, 1958.

——— (1923). The ego and the id. *Standard Edition* 19: 3–59. London: Hogarth Press, 1961.

——— (1933). The dissection of the psychical personality. Lecture 31. In The new introductory lectures on psycho-analysis. *Standard Edition* 22: 57–80, 1964.

Fromm, E. (1961). *Marx's Concept of Man*. New York: Frederick Ungar.

Glover, E. (1925). Notes on character-formation. *International Journal of Psycho-Analysis* 6: 131–153.

Goldman-Eisler, F. (1953). Breast feeding and character formation. In *Personality in Nature, Society and Culture*, ed. C. Kluckhohn and H. A. Murray. New York: Alfred A. Knopf.

Harris, G. (1957). Possession "hysteria" in a Kenya tribe. *American Anthropologist* 59: 1046–1066.

Ibsen, H. (1888). The lady from the sea. In *The Complete Major Prose Plays*, trans. & introd. Rolf Fjelde, pp. 588–688. London: New American Library, 1965.

Jacobson, E. (1971). *Depression*. New York: International Universities Press.

Jones, E. (1913). The god complex. In *Essays in Applied Psychoanalysis*, vol. 2, pp. 244–265. New York: International Universities Press, 1951.

Joyce, James (1916). *A Portrait of the Artist as a Young Man*. New York: Viking Press, 1964.

Jung, C. G. (1952). *Answer to Job*. Trans. R. F. C. Hull. London: Routledge and Kegan Paul, 1954.

Kelly, W. E. (1965). Regression of the superego. *Bulletin Philadelphia Psychoanalytic Association* 15: 224–235.

Mahler, M. (1968). *On Human Symbiosis and the Vicissitudes of Individuation*. Vol 1. New York: International Universities Press.

Marcovitz, E. (1966). Discussion of psychodynamics of the depressive character. *Psychoanalytic Forum* 1: 251–254.

Mead, M. (1935). *Sex and Temperament*. New York: Morrow.

Miller, M. L. (1957). *Nostalgia: A Psychoanalytic Study of Marcel Proust*. London: Victor Gollancz.

Money-Kyrle, R. (1939). *Superstition and Society*. London: Hogarth Press.

Noble, D. (1980). The creativity of Virginia Woolf. Presented at the Washington Psychoanalytic Society, February 1980.

Plath, Sylvia (1961). In plaster. In *Crossing the Water*, pp. 16–17. New York: Harper and Row.

_____ (1971). *The Bell Jar*. New York: Harper & Row.

Ribble, M. A. (1944). Infantile experience in relationship to personality development. In *Personality and the Behavior Disorders*, ed. J. McV. Hunt, pp. 621–651. New York: Ronald Press.

Rickman, J. (1957). On the nature of ugliness and the creative impulse. In *Selected Contributions to Psychoanalysis*, ed. W. C. Scott, pp. 68–89. London: Hogarth Press.

Róheim, G. (1923). Nach dem tode des urvaters. *Imago* 9: 83–121.

Sedler, M. J. (1983). Freud's concept of working through. *Psychoanalytic Quarterly* 52: 73–98.

Seeman, M. (1959). On the measuring of alienation. *American Sociological Review* 24: 783–791.

Simon, B. (1979). Hysteria — the Greek disease. In *The Psychoanalytic Study of Society* 8: 175–215.

Spitz, R. A. (1946). Anaclitic depression. *Psychoanalytic Study of the Child* 2: 313–342.

Stade, George (1973). Introduction. In *A Closer Look at Ariel: A Memory of Sylvia Plath* by N. H. Steiner. New York: Harper Magazine Press, pp. 3–30.

Steiner, N. H. (1973). *A Closer Look at Ariel: A Memory of Sylvia Plath*. New York: Harper Magazine Press.

Van Gennep, A. (1960). *The Rites of Passage*. Trans. M. B. Vizedorn and G. L. Caffee. Chicago: University of Chicago Press.

Wetmore, R. J. (1963). The role of grief in psychoanalysis. *International Journal of Psychoanalysis* 44: 97–104.

Woolf, Virginia. (1927). *To the Lighthouse*. New York: Harcourt Brace.

_____ (1953). *A Writer's Diary*. New York: Harcourt Brace.

CHAPTER FOUR

The Depressive Process Examined in View of Creativity

Gordon Kirschner, M.D.

In Japan a statue was erected to the memory of a faithful dog who refused to stop searching for his deceased master. The dog continued to meet the train on which his master formerly had arrived each day, hunting with determination among all the emerging passengers. Humans have a much greater adaptive capacity, making possible the creation and maintainance of fruitless, frustrating adaptations. Chronic maladaptations based on depression are not unusual. Creativity is blocked by such states. Psychotic and severe, acute depressive preoccupations obviously interfere with creative efforts, but it is seldom noted that chronic depression interferes with creativity in specific ways.

This chapter outlines the creative process and the depressive process, contrasts them and identifies stages where they interact. Mourning is a link between them, as shown in a growing body of literature which explores the connection between grief and creativity (Pollock 1978). Effective mourning makes way for creative developments that arise from a context of loss. Failed mourning becomes pathological grief and its creative products are distorted and repetitious (Volkan 1970, 1972). Depression functions as a defense to avoid awareness of loss (Bibring 1953) and, thus, leads neither to effective mourning nor to the creative accomplishment that consoles for loss or enables the continuation of intentions that loss has defeated.

Chronic depressive states are common. They range from inconspicuous but stultifying avoidance of any potential loss situation to semidisabling mood swings and symptom patterns that severely disrupt ordinary living. Unrecognized depressive patterns interfere with creativity and yet are often not easily recognized as handicaps, leaving observers mystified at the failure of apparently normal people to fully realize promising talents.

Ben, an adolescent arrested for stealing a popular record, had been fighting such impulses for months. At 14, his world was crumbling as his parents, themselves unable to resolve old grief from their childhood, were in a cold war. His extremely tormented mother displaced her rage toward him, denouncing him capriciously for minor infractions. Having moved from a school where discipline had been a support and his success had won respect, he was in a school where his abilities were not being tested or disciplined, thus he had little guidance in his struggle to maintain self-esteem. His chronic depressive disorder was ego syntonic and consisted of minimization of affect and a conviction that losses did not concern him. Thus he was very well defended against any disappointment.

He showed enthusiasm for two seemingly unrelated activities: practical jokes and police or military enforcement of rules and laws. At home, teasing alternated with crude attempts to enforce proper behavior in a younger sibling. Unable to uncover any other ambitions, he suffered severely from boredom in school except when exhilarated by an escapade. Even at the height of his most creative stunts, he preferred to maintain an attitude of cool disdain. In therapy Ben could barely acknowledge problems and almost never complained. He wanted to find a solution to his predicament, but could not get to the step of formulating problems. Thus he had no idea how to proceed except to wish for money. Any less abstract hope presented him with the possibility of disappointment, a risk he could not tolerate. Although quite intelligent, he seemed dull-witted and depended on others to guide and stimulate him. The impulse to steal was the manifestation of his wish or need, but on a concrete, dissociated level where it did not lead to appropriate action. He behaved as though constantly faced by a sadistic authority who could not be pleased.

Pre-conscious, automatic reluctance to risk disappointment is an obstacle to generating motives for creative action. With antisocial aims, Ben could risk failure because he was not hoping to win praise. Where praise might be expected, he could not let himself strive for it. Creativity comes out of a sense of need or wish, and the process is not initiated without awareness of a lack to fill or a problem to solve.

Scientific study of creativity originated in the reports of creative people. A well-known example of 100 years ago comes from the history of organic chemistry. Kekule, who solved the problem of representing the structure of benzene, told how his inspiration for the ring structure came to him as he dozed before his fire:

> Again the atoms were gamboling before my eyes. This time the smaller groups kept modestly in the background. My mental eye, rendered more acute by repeated visions of the kind could now distinguish larger structures, of manifold conformation: long rows, sometimes more closely fitted together; all twining and twisting in snake-like motion. But look! What was that? One of the snakes had seized hold of its own tail and the form whirled mockingly before my eyes. As if by a flash of lightning I awoke, and this time also I spent the rest of the night in working out the consequences of the hypothesis.

Kekule took pains to publish this description and emphasized the two parts of the creative process to which it refers by saying, "Let us dream, gentlemen, and then perhaps we shall learn the truth [but] . . let us beware of publishing our dreams before they have been put to the proof by the waking understanding" (Read 1930, p. 51). The idea that dream thought or dreamlike thinking is characteristically creative is a central concept of Rothenberg's scheme of creativity (1979).

Early in this century, the great French mathematician, Henri Poincaré (1929), presented his classic paper to the Psychological Society in Paris deriving from his own experience the concept that inspiration is guided by aesthetic feeling. From his clear description several important points can be discerned:

> Unconscious thought processes prepare the inspiration;
> inspiration follows a period of intense search,
> it is succeeded by systematic testing.
> The three stages have characteristic states of consciousness.

The twentieth century has seen a revolution in self-knowledge which has focused on what Winnicott called transitional phenomena: the space between inner reality and outer reality. According to Robert Nisbet (1982, p. 138):

> . . . the revolution is traceable as far back as William James whose "view of the interaction of mind and environment breaks for once and all the hateful dualism that Descartes gave to the world. For the empiricist James, mind is no mirror, no circuited receiver, but a function, and in this respect it is like breathing, eating, walking — all functions in which the actor and the environment are in mutual immanence." We are still catching up with James's conception, but it is becoming widespread. At a recent symposium on the brain at The John's Hopkins University the assembled experts all agreed that the mind is a *function* of the brain and body, and not a thing. (Kanigel 1984)

Suzanne Langer (1953, p. 40) encapsulates our aims when she defines art as:

> . . . the creation of forms symbolic of human feeling [and] . . . serves to distinguish a "work of art" from anything else in the world, and at the same time to show why, and how, a utilitarian object may be also a work of art; and how a work of so-called "pure" art may fail of its purpose and be simply bad, just as a shoe that cannot be worn is simply bad by failing of its purpose.

Images of feeling must be avoided by those avoiding feeling.

The Stages of the Creative Process

Three stages of the creative process may be conveniently named study-search, inspiration, and verification-registration. A prior phase, awareness of problems, we have seen already; it is frequently taken for granted.

Awareness of a Need (Stage I)

For an active, motivated attempt to create something new, there must be a wish to find a solution to a problem or fill a void. People employed in creative occupations may be in some phase of the creative process much of the time, and it becomes difficult to assert that one phase follows another in strict order. A kind of play among the phases can be continuous. However, it does seem clear that awareness of a problem sets in motion the mental processes leading to the solution of a particular creative challenge. The awareness of a need or problem is experienced as a wish and a feeling of desire, providing relief from a period of restlessness. Taking notice that a problem exists may be an inspiration itself. Poincaré took for granted his process of discerning a need for a new mathematical formulation. That awareness seemed to grow out of a creative process which for him was continuous over long periods; the awareness may be, on the other hand, a growing search on the basis of growing discomfort which leads a person to recognize a major problem in living.

The state of mind in which awareness of the problem develops varies widely. A comfortable, ordinarily active consciousness may stumble abruptly over a stimulating problem, or a vague sense of unease may escalate to severe discomfort resulting in an active search to identify the problem. The former characterizes a playful attitude exercised in a condition of relative safety while the latter implies a resistance against recognition of the problem.

Study-Search (Stage II)

The search for possible solutions initiates active efforts to review facts and methods. When these efforts fail and motivation is sufficient, they culminate in a period of intense effort and concentration. This concentrated state of mind evolves into a further altered state of consciousness. Poincaré cites an extended midnight siege of study stimulated by drinking strong coffee; Rossini's search for the subject of his opera "La Cenerentola" (Cinderella) was a late night project that included drinking lots of strong tea. Kekule's inspiration for the benzene ring came to him in a doze after an exhausting conscious trial of possible arrangements.

Ehrenzweig (1967) described a change of consciousness allowing contents usually repressed to emerge. He emphasized the search within, realizing that even searching the environment for resources is also a search for inner resources. He characterized this as the stage of "anal" scattering of unconscious contents and speculated that conflict about anality was a characteristic attitude. Milner (1950, p. 150) emphasized the orgasmic quality of the process and the anxiety about loss of control, including loss of sphincter control and loss of body boundaries and individual integrity. She states, " . . . the surrender of the consciously planning deliberative mind to the spontaneous creative force can be felt as a very dangerous undertaking" confronting one with both shame and disillusionment about the "unconscious hankering after a return to the blissful surrender to [the] all-out body giving of infancy." Both she and Ehrenzweig observed anxiety about aggression but are not content with the formulation that creativity is simply an attempt to make restitution for unconscious aggression.

Search both within and outside the self are typical at this stage. As investment in the process intensifies it takes on the emotional quality of an intense relationship with another person. Excitement and elation are characteristic and support the search through difficulties, but the quality of feeling varies with the individual. A manic quality is frequently present and great hopes may appear. The element of pleasure is significant and usually obvious though it may be masked when the individual has conflict about enjoyment and achievement. It seems identical with the joy of free play. As a rule, it is combined with distinct pain where the search is long and must be sustained through difficulties. Elated expectation that one is producing a love-gift is also common; that form of pleasure may carry particular individuals through extremely distressing struggles if not blocked by the conflict Milner describes. Greenacre said, "The artistic product has rather universally the character of a love-gift, to be brought as near perfection as possible and to be presented with pride and misgiving" (1957, p. 58).

Inspiration (Stage III)

The moment of inspiration which is the culmination of Stage II is often ecstatic. However, this may have more to do with the elation of the search and scattering phase than it does with the moment of inspiration. Poincaré describes such a triumph following intense search and contrasts it with the more quiet glow of pleasure when he tells the well-known story of a sudden inspiration occurring on vacation "at the moment my foot touched the step of the omnibus." Poincaré in particular attributed to pleasure a functional role in the creative process. Speculating about the manner in which useful and interesting mathematical combinations reach consciousness, he related his experience that aesthetic pleasure accompanied his inspirations. He attributed to that emotion a decisive role because he noted its presence even with inspirations that turned out to be useless when tested later. He concluded that sensing the aesthetic quality, rather than rational judgement of usefulness, identified the idea to consciousness.

Much of the effort of students of the creative process is aimed at discovering the nature of the process of inspiration itself. As Arieti (1977, p. 20) said, " . . . accumulation of data is not creativity. The creative leap occurs when observed facts are correlated; that is, when by perceiving a heretofore unsuspected identity, a conjunctive path or a new order is discovered." This requires placing elements in a new class, finding for them a new identity as members of the class. Rothenberg (1979) propounds the view that contradictories or opposites are conceived to be indissolubly joined by a mental process he calls "Janusian Thinking." His idea accords with the finding that creative people typically entertain opposing views or paradoxical ideas without an urgent need to resolve them. Rothenberg (1979) also proposed that the creative process is "the mirror image of the dream" implying opposites in opposition. Cohen (1980 ch. 5) argues that existing ideas are transformed, often into virtual opposites, by revolutionary thinkers. He shows that Newton used Kepler's ideas, but transformed the meaning and content, for instance substituting centripetal force, an instance of the force of gravity, for the imaginary centrifugal force, which had been previously believed true. Using existing concepts and sometimes keeping their names, but transforming their content, clearly exemplifies the kind of loosening of mental schema that the creative process requires.

Ehrenzweig argues for the emergence of organization from the unconscious through a process of projection of inner integration onto the externalized elements that have been scattered in the preceding stage. "What appears ambiguous, dubious, multi-evocative or open-ended on a conscious level becomes a single serial structure with quite firm boundaries on an unconscious level" (p. 32).

Verification-Registration (Stage IV)

When the new concept has appeared, and the new class has been conceived, a process of integration occurs which has been compared to secondary revision of dreams (Freud 1900). This step is easily comprehensible in the case of Poincaré who returned prosaically to his desk to test the validity of new mathematical functions conceived on holiday. Ehrenzweig emphasized the painful aspect, a quality of letdown when the manic inspiration has to be viewed "in the cold light of morning" (p. 103) and unworkable parts discarded. He focused particularly on painters and sculptors in whose work elements can be eliminated or strengthened in a single stroke with the whole creation in sight. Writers must reread laboriously if their style involves much revision. The degree of reworking varies greatly from one artist to another. Mozart wrote in final form and revised almost none of his scores whereas Beethoven rewrote everything, starting with sketches only suggesting the concept and sometimes ending with several competing versions.

The conception must at a minimum be put in a form that is either material or memorable, either as an object or an idea. Writing, musical notation, and mathematical symbols combine these qualities. Paintings, photographs, sculpture, models, and other images can serve the purpose. Screen memories perhaps mark and preserve significant steps in personal development. Utilitarian objects can also be works of art and thus serve as memorable images or memorials to a creative idea. Ritual is surely one of the oldest ways to bring an inspiration into a permanent form. It serves to reiterate all sorts of inspired, created experience. For instance, metallurgical insights are recorded by Japanese swordmakers in a ritual performance of actual production, as pointed out by Bronowski in his televised series "The Ascent of Man."

Summary

Recognition of a problem is followed by a loosening of the preceding organization of thought and perception. A new schema becomes possible when an old one is found unsatisfactory. To form a new schema, bold consideration of unknown possibilities is required. All reports describe a state of consciousness in which boundaries are opened and superego vigilance is suspended. This "regression in the service of the ego" (Kris 1953) is similar to the "oceanic state" to which Freud referred in which boundaries melt, distinctions become lost, and ideation is unrestricted. Winnicott (1951) emphasized the playful nature of this process, a process in which the unconscious can control the ordering of the elements in the same way that free association allows the expression of the unconscious in psychoanalysis. Inspiration follows, the conscious representation for the unified structure arising from the primary process. Finally the concept needs to be stated, tested and prepared for presentation.

The Creative Process and the Depressive Process

The concept of the transitional object (Winnicott 1951) has opened a new understanding of the meaning and function of the created object. Modell (1970, p. 249), viewing prehistoric art, concludes " . . . that the creative act consists of the interpenetration of the actual and the inner world" and is thus a transitional phenomenon. Further, he asserts that "the failure of creativity may be related to a failure to accept the separateness of objects" which points to separation problems as obstacles to creativity. Anton Ehrenzweig (1967, p. 102) made the particularly profound remark that a work of art functions as a person, a remark that immediately suggests the corollary that transference reactions are aroused in an artist by the work as it is developed. These transference reactions can have interfering effects similar to those seen in psychoanalysis. A resistance to the creative process can develop, taking the form of thought blocking, feelings of being depreciated, and antagonism to the work. Likewise, affection, protective feeling, and strong attachment can occur. Volkan's concept of the linking object is also a variety of transitional object, a stultified creative product that functions to deny the reality of the loss and yet may serve as a useful bridge to the emotional acceptance of loss (1975).

Artists confirm the idea that the work functions as a person. A poet, in explaining his use of a notebook, made it clear that he enters into dialog with the book, addressing it as "Book," in notes he makes and he announces departures, celebrates inspirations, and explains himself to it, as if it indeed were a beloved companion. Hilda Thorpe, a painter, explaining how a work came alive for her in the process, said that she could tell when a work was finished because at that point "it sings." In discussion with her it also became evident that, for her too, private notebooks were an especially alive part of her work. Historically, the idea of the muse expressed this phenomenon.

Anne had made several attempts to establish a career in art without success. She changed the medium in which she worked and altered her life in many ways, but nothing solved the problem. It appeared that she was unable to nurture her artistic self, provide for it needed work conditions, and protect it in action against distractions. She did not seem to have a friendly muse sponsoring her work. This was a repetition of her childhood experience in which she was not protected in playing out her explorations of competitive and sexual relations. She had been subtly exploited by both men and women who admired her talents and, who, in some awe of her, failed to provide certain needed limits. The stage of "anal" scattering felt to her like destructive rage, and the loosening of ego boundaries felt like suffocating entrapment with a caretaker who was rejecting and controlling at the same time. Thus threatened, she interrupted the playful combination of scattered fragments before she could satisfy her strongest impulses. She barely reached the stage of secondary revision, of confirming the image and accepting its limitations. This interfered with developing her inspirations in serial fashion and exploring them in an extended way.

An exception occurred when an intimate friendship developed with a woman who seemed able to make up for the parents who had failed her. In this period, Anne was able to create a series of images that reached back into her childhood and reinfused memories with loving warmth. Such images of loving sponsorship reinforced a period when one success seemed to lead to another, but competition for vital resources gradually assumed threatening proportions. She did not feel free to push on to the farthest limits of her medium because that seemed too competitive with her childrens' need. Instead, she returned to school to gather more resources, but this turned out to repeat a traumatic history of rivalry with her brother. She entered a field dominated by men, a field, moreover, where competition for scarce resources became a critical issue due to national economic conditions, and just at that time she was displaced by her boss's favored sibling. When her friend was attacked by a fatal illness, she was overwhelmed with depression and disturbances of her self-concept.

As a patient she reproached herself for being a mother unable to care for her loved ones; it seemed to her inevitable that creative urges conflicted with nurturing drives. She felt there were never enough resources to go around. Her problem became clearer when she said that her work would destroy her son. She felt that assertion, aggression, and competitiveness on her part would infuriate her vengeful husband and that he would kill their son. (Anne argued that he had nearly done so in the past.) Underneath we found a fantasy that her own rage was a destructive force that must harm her loved ones. The basis was evident when she recalled her childhood fantasy of destroying her infant brother. She soon produced a drawing of a monster child. She elaborated the image in her work and it led to images of primitive, sexualized aggression. Increased freedom in fantasy made for a rapid interplay of discovery between her work and the analytic treatment.

The rivalry and sexual issues were preoedipal in content, and the symptoms were depressive. She was not inhibited in work or love, but was unable to sustain the play of fantasy. Her creativity was blocked because she felt constantly threatened by the intrusion of reality in the form of needy demands. Arousing her fury, they became transformed into mortal threats to herself or someone dependent on her. Repressed sexuality was not a cause of symptoms; rather, they were caused by repressed longing for nurturance and an unconscious fantasy that her own hungry, raging, oral aggression would destroy what she loved. Her unconscious fantasy and conflict about aggression illustrates the aspect of depression that Katan (1953) described.

Psychoanalytic study of adult patients and observation of normal and disturbed children suggest the model: depressive illness is based on modes of response which are developed or learned in traumatic circumstances and may be valuable and even life-saving but become maladaptive in altered circumstances when new adaptation is blocked by neurotic or characterologic distortions. These distortions occur in reaction to later traumatic emotional experience. The responses are mediated through neurologic, hormonal and biochemical functions. This formulation is not proposed as alternative to "biological" theories, but as a theory of the mental and personality functions which complement the biochemical functions. Thus an infant who suffers an extended loss of mothering care and reacts by withdrawing into the marasmic state described by Spitz (1965) has probably gone beyond the limits of some important physiological parameters in its homeostatic control of neurohumeral functioning. The state becomes a recognizable syndrome and, while reversible with effective care, can result in death. Where the stress to which the child reacts is minor but repeated, the child will have less extreme reactions. A less extreme reaction, not exceeding any or so many neurohumeral limits, will be more dependent on individual variation in biological potentiality. The mother's character will also tend to shape the reaction the child adopts. The studies of children and their mothers by Greenspan (1979, 1982) illustrate this kind of variation. In one child a tendency to withdrawal, a cautiousness, even a mild retreat into apathy, will perhaps be the preliminary to a later depressive tendency in the character. Another child exposed to the same degree of loss may have more of an aggressive reaction, and develop into a more openly hostile character. A third possibility is an anxious style with compliance, appeal through suffering, and decompensation into panic states when these mechanisms fail to ensure contact with the object.

As an adult, Emma showed such a pattern, with constant worry, inhibition, conflict about pleasure and an absence of joy. Not apathetic, she was capable of sustained creative accomplishment, but always required the support of some person who filled the role of guide. She was able to produce works highly admired by a few experts able to appreciate them. She was an effective and creative teacher, especially in small groups. She had been dependent on amphetamines and sedatives for most of her adult life and she benefitted greatly from the use of anti-depressant medication (amitriptyline) to control panic states.

Observing infants separated from their mothers in the second half of the first year, Spitz (1965a, 1965b) was able to define the quality of nurturing essential in the caretaking partner. As did Winnicott (1972), Spitz saw development of the infant occurring via interaction with the mother, in a "stochastic process" in which each step grows out of the preceding one. The loss of mothering care in this model means loss of an interested, interactive partner. The marasmic infants were subjected to reliable, responsible caretaking, but were isolated from interaction of an emotionally involved or playful sort. Solnit's (1966) observations of infants hospitalized with postinfectious diarrhea confirm the need for emotionally involved caretaking, which includes toleration of unavoidable pain the caretaker experiences when dealing with a child who has suffered a severe loss.

Treated in isolation to prevent contagion, thus separated from their mothers, the infants became withdrawn and failed to thrive. Attempts to "mother" them aroused hostile, aggressive rejection of caregiving aid, which had to be endured before a smooth mother infant function could be reinstated. Absence of the modulation of emotion ordinarily provided by a watchful mother resulted in overwhelming aggressive impulses that were life threatening. Depressive withdrawal was a last resort in the infant's struggle with aggressive impulses. Mothering aid was used by the infants to enable toleration of the aggression before they could resume ordinary libidinal behavior, including ordinary physiologic homeostasis.

Engel and Schmale (1972, 1975) made similar findings. Their unique contribution was to emphasize the effort at adaptation behind the infant depression; they called it the "conservation withdrawal syndrome." Engel's patient, Monica, was hospitalized as an infant because of esophageal atresia. She was psychologically abandoned by her depressed mother. Psychiatric intervention with provision of dependable substitute mothering care reversed her nearly fatal marasmic syndrome. The girl's development was followed to adulthood allowing assessment of her character development in detail. She became a cautious, conservative person, showing little willingness to embark on creative adventures. She was effective in moving her life forward and securing what she needed from others. Engel and Schmale concluded that withdrawal from emotional involvement which characterizes the marasmic syndrome has a conserving, even life preserving function. They proposed that it was an adaptive response to a threat of being overwhelmed by powerful emotions which, if unchecked, would be life threatening.

Bibring (1953) concluded that depression in adults was a defense against loss, contrasting it to anxiety, where danger threatens and active efforts to escape or fight are attempted. Brenner (1982) proposes a broadening of the theory of signal affect, with depressive as well as anxious affect serving as a signal for mobilization of defenses. In depression no escape appears possible and psychological escape is attempted through denial and avoidance. The basic affect being avoided is the feeling of helplessness. Action, engaging in fight-flight reactions, tend to confirm helplessness if the threat is inescapable, whereas depression, through apathy, avoidance of libidinal investment, and withdrawal to self-preoccupation, avoids the confirmation of actual helplessness. Bibring proposed that depression is a defense of self-esteem, resorted to where the pain of helplessness is an intolerable threat to self-esteem. The primary method of protection is inhibition. Katan's (1953) contribution to the same discussion put more emphasis on the inhibition of aggression based on unconscious fantasy of destructive omnipotence, as illustrated here by the case of Anne.

Meyersburg, Kotin and Ablon (1974) added a fruitful concept by contemplating a particular kind of relationship with the maternal figure. They specified maternal failure of limit setting accompanied by failure to acknowledge or accept the feeling of helplessness. Caretaker failure to accept this feeling of loss, they said, leads to defense against any of the distressing affects associated with loss; producing characters whose defensive style includes suppression of feeling, active-passive reversals, impulsive aggression and guilt. Failure to set limits and to acknowledge resulting disappointment means failure to provide gradual disillusionment, "the mother's main task (next to providing opportunity for illusion)" according to Winnicott (1951, p. 13). Denial of disappointment in the caretaker can lead to either indulgence or rejection of the child. Either can cause depressive tendencies in the child. "We propose that depression results from the ego's inability to grieve and to accept its helplessness" (Meyersburg 1974, p. 377). By identifying a specific interaction with the developing child, an interaction which repeatedly fails to support a particular developmental step, we can seek confirmation and distinguish between cases. A range of affects are involved in this model: frustration, anger, sadness, rage, and despair. In my experience, cases are seen in which apathy is sought as a substitute for the other affects. Apathy can be an ego syntonic form of chronic depression, seen, interestingly enough, in characters who at other times can be extremely lively. Ben showed this characteristic behavior and his parents demonstrated typical difficulty acknowledging or accepting disappointment or anger over loss.

A mother who does not accept and empathically acknowledge the affect of loss becomes unempathic at that point. Thus, the child experiences loss situations as the cause of the withdrawal of the empathic mother. Grief becomes a cause of object loss and a result of object loss so that a vicious circle is unavoidable. With this model in mind, contemplation of our cultural bias against acknowledging loss and disappointment suggests an explanation of the existential concept of anomie: alienation can be seen as a manifestation of chronic avoidance of feeling.

This model shows that altered states of consciousness are an important aspect of depressive reactions. Apathy is an example, a state that can be observed in infants and young children and can be recognized introspectively by adults. Ben, for example, experienced lengthy periods of apathy during which he felt fatigue and a wish to retire with a book or sit in front of a television set with little interest in the program. The ubiquity of such reactions is marked in language by common expressions such as: "It's all the same to me" or "Who cares?" and described as "spacing out." Such statements are accompanied by feeling states of mild apathy, fatigue, and subdued feeling. If they are challenged, anger arises; if encouragement is offered, pleasurable gratification is often felt but soon may be displaced by guilt since active response is precluded. If the state of consciousness is primarily a dulling of affect or mild, transient apathy there may be no noticeable physiologic disturbance. However, when anxious alertness is combined with denial of helplessness and grandiose intentionality, cyclic augmentation occurs, anxiety leads to hyperarousal which, in turn, intensifies anxiety. Sleep becomes disordered and sleep deprivation further deranges the normal balance. A self-reinforcing cycle develops. A sleep disturbance can occur which is caused by or perhaps causes an abnormal physiologic state.

A synthesis of these models of depression indicates that depression begins as an adaptive response to overwhelming threat of loss occasioned by disruption of empathic nurturance. It evolves into a characteristic pattern of defense aimed to preserve self-esteem in the face of helplessness and object loss. The object loss is a fixation: emotional abandonment, either through actual object loss or narcissistic withdrawal by the object, has deprived the individual of the opportunity to experience affects of distress while receiving object support. Lack of maternal modulation of anxiety during distress leads to functional failure to contain the stress of the affect. The repeated experience of failure threatens self-esteem. The danger that helplessness represents then interferes with normal developmental processes, hampering the creative play which opens the way to learning and discovery. Self-esteem comes to depend more and more on avoidance of feelings of loss, and the attempt to avoid those specific feelings leads to suppression of all feeling. The avoidance of acknowledging feeling leads to a general inhibition of feeling. This model leads to the hypothesis that for depressive persons loss of any kind brings the threat of object loss, a repetition of the infant's experience with unempathic mothering. Caregiver failure to acknowledge the affects of loss leads to the child feeling abandoned as a consequence of having the feelings of loss.

Hostility aroused in the infant or child may be directed inward or outward. The infants considered above directed aggression inward. Beyond a certain point in separation individuation, the aggression is directed outward, against the "bad" object, but if the hostility is rejected while the child is still quite dependent it is again directed inward but in a more specific way. It becomes an internal destructive impulse directed against libidinal investment in objects, in an urge to destroy love. This is a source of profound feelings of loss and helplessness and motivates exaggerated efforts at control, with inhibition and reaction formation; breakthrough of the impulse or frustration of the impulse promote a crescendo of helplessness. Working of the defenses of denial, repression and inhibition interfere with the assessment of the destructive impulse. Recognized but not adequately measured, the quality alone of this impulse determines the response, and it is treated as if infinite in quantity. The experience of transient, murderous rage, perhaps even for an instant, triggers in the unconscious an absolute taboo against action. It could then be argued that the withdrawal seen in depression may be an inhibition of aggression triggered by signal anxiety. Guilt and remorse, however, imply that the damage is already done, (and perhaps in one sense it is) and conveys the sense that destruction of love is part of the depressive withdrawal.

If certain varieties of depression have the structure here outlined, then the hypothesis that affects of loss tend to elicit creativity implies the corollary that conditions limiting the sensation of loss would inhibit creativity. The work of Volkan (1970–1975) delineating states of pathological grief supports this conclusion.

The Effect of Depression on the Phases of the Creative Process

Experiencing a Need or Becoming Aware of a Problem

Where "problem" equals loss, depressive avoidance will tend toward denial of the problem. If the depression is accompanied by partial insight, there may be active efforts to define problems. The form in which the problem is experienced will be shaped by the nature of defensive efforts, and the form will determine what sort of solutions will be found. For instance, if the problem can be posed at all, there may be efforts to seek information, a phase which is consistent with mild depression, and may be considered a search for oral supplies. Solutions will be sought in the form of increasing the inflow of supplies, information, evidence of love, etc; rather than formulating active solutions.

Where the depression is part of a masochistic character structure, the problem will often be posed in terms of wrong and fault finding. As Meyersberg (1974) stated, "The roots of the sense of guilt are set in experiences of deprivation during early infancy. These experiences reinforce primitive omnipotence and bring about passive-active reversals. Failure of help from others is equated with failure of self-help. Self-blame results" (p. 375). The solution implied is submission and repentance of sinful waywardness. This construction denies helplessness and precludes definition of solvable problems through the adherence to the formula which states that there is no helplessness, only disobedience. The same is true where fault is projected and solutions are sought in punishing or abandoning other transgressors because there is no helplessness, only wrongdoing. Frequently, this depressive mode precludes an active, enthusiastic search, and passivity and submission of the subject's ideas to those of the idealized source is observed. The subject's active searching is blocked.

Anton Ehrenzweig led the way in looking at the unconscious meaning of the various stages in the creative process and his viewpoint combined artistic and psychoanalytic knowledge. He described the "anal scattering of inner contents" in the search stage requiring uninhibited production and scattering of unconscious fragments. He considered the intuition stage to have a manic quality, and his description of it recalls the stage of infantile omnipotence. It depends on combinatory play with the fragments in which the unconscious synthesizing capacity is engaged. He suggested that the final stage has a depressive quality, a cool reassessment in which the product is brought into an integrated form that fulfills the creators need for satisfying form and that others can respond to.

Study-Search

Here the depressive inhibition is obstructive. Guilt and emphasis on restitution will interfere with "anal" scattering (Ehrenzweig), an essential aggressive act which brings out the unconscious material with which to work. Weakened self-esteem causing self-contempt makes the scattered content devalued so that it does not provide the stimulus for further work. Guilt, from the formula no helplessness, only wrongdoing, will make "cleaning up the mess" take priority, undoing the necessary scattering before the unconscious reworking is complete. Alternately if unresolved omnipotence and ambivalence impedes the acceptance of reality (Modell), whatever is projected from inside is liable to be contaminated with the rejected "badness." Scattering then leads to loss of good inner content as it is magically transformed into bad, useless dross. Dread of being drained and fear of doing harm paralyze the artist with conflict.

Inspiration

For inspiration to occur, emptiness is required. In the unconscious an existing scheme must be allowed to dissolve to enable a new pattern to form. Cohen's (1980) description of transformation of existing ideas into their contradictories directs us to consideration of the anxiety involved. Loss of the familiar in concept or boundary is potentially terrifying. The manic quality of this stage (Ehrenzweig) is a sign that depression threatens to foreclose on the decoupling before a new unconscious, serial structure can be elaborated. Perhaps a degree of omnipotence always accompanies this experience. If so, it means vulnerability to abrupt disillusionment and collapse into depressive retreat. Conversely, if the manic denial becomes uncontrolled mania, the process is unproductive. There may be generation of some good ideas but they cannot be held for the next stage. In genuine mania there is an attempt to put the grandiose construct into action prematurely in the absence of reality-oriented, persistent work of secondary revision and necessary renunciation.

Verification-Registration

The stage of reworking to put the created product in usable form and make it 'presentable' in Freud's sense of representable (1900, pp. 339–40), is analagous to the process of secondary revision in dreams. In this phase it is necessary to relinquish cherished fragments which do not fit into the structure which has been elaborated. Grandiose feelings which have pushed the process must be surrendered to reality testing which permits assessment of the product and effective self-criticism. These steps are experienced as losses and may trigger depressive moods at this point. Where the effort becomes avoiding loss, the essential acceptance of the loss will be denied. The product may then be left in an unfinished state, abandoned to a limbo where a faint hope for an eventual grandiose triumph is preserved. Or the product may be promoted in an unfinished state with manic, grandiose denial leading to failure. In some cases this step is followed by the product being reworked by another person and made into an effective accomplishment, sometimes with the cooperation and approval of the originator and sometimes without.

The next case illustrates in detail interference with the process of bringing out the unconscious content in order to organize it into an image. Leonard, a man of demonstrated artistic gifts, gave a history of having three careers and told a story of abrupt changes occurring around episodes of loss. He is apparently brilliant and extremely competent in tackling large jobs that involve a wide range of talents and skills, including being an excellent promoter, which enabled him to engage others in his exploits with great success. The careers ended badly in conditions which he experienced as betrayal by those who should have been grateful for his accomplishments on their behalf. He came for treatment because a grave psychosomatic symptom forced a confrontation with his denial and undermined his fantasies of omnipotence. Familiar means of numbing sensation were failing and his life situation was threatened by new loss. He was seriously depressed. He complained of inability to work, to create a piece of art work that would satisfy him. He could initiate and to some extent perform routine work, but he could not lose himself in it in the satisfying fashion that reveals contact with the unconscious. He was movingly distressed by his inability to carry forward any project of an original nature, he could conceive an aim and begin the process but stopped before it reached a satisfying stage. He was able to complete a major job of restoration where creativity was confined to finding a means for conservation of the past. It was apparent that he was filled with rage and grief but was terrified of these affects and unable to let the work proceed to the point where such feelings would surface. It is apparent that any sincere art work he could attempt at this point must include such feelings. He wished to produce a work that would express feelings of love, sensuous pleasure, and supreme mastery. Each of his careers had been successful in outward appearance. He had built up situations and organizations where effective work was done and business transacted, but Leonard himself ended up working for others and not really pursuing his own urge to create something, to make a product or image that would incorporate his own deepest urges.

He suffered from episodes of severe, disabling depression and there were days spent in a withdrawn, numb state of escape. At other times he felt mild elation. The depression was not clearly physiological. A trial with a low dose of amitriptyline, initiated primarily for symptoms of sleeplessness, caused such severe drowsiness that he was reluctant to take the drug.

When he was 8 years old, Leonard's mother died of cancer, remaining at home until the end, treated for increasing pain with morphine. This he administered at midday, when he left school for the purpose. This intimate, comforting, yet ultimately isolating process of easing his mother's pain and easing her completely out of his emotional reach was carried through until she wasted away and died. He was unable to grieve, and when his father remarried he felt unwanted and increasingly rebellious. He broke with his family and departed, the first of the episodes of ending relationships with a sense of betrayal. Hypomanic exercise of his considerable gifts led to a career in an acrobatic and essentially exhibitionistic, powerful, and dangerous medium. Later he became a scholar and finally an artist. He experienced interference with his creative efforts at all stages of the process. He could initiate projects successfully when his sense of omnipotence was sufficiently great; he could carry them forward when he felt that he was encouraged and supported by a nurturing figure to whom he could demonstrate his gifts, performing with a pleased audience. Each time circumstances uncannily reproduced betrayal. His ability to perform was then lost, and his recovery depended on having the strength to defiantly begin in a new territory.

Leonard's need for a partner in reality seemed to interfere with his making of the work itself a satisfactory transitional object. This left him submitting to the aims and needs of others in a subtle conflict with his own. One needs a partner to accept the suffering in order to unmask the kind of wrenching grief that he suppressed. He was unable to use the developing work to be that kind of "partner." His productions were oriented to please others and display success, not to make them aware of his grief, and when dissatisfaction entered the picture in any form, serious conflict always developed, and the partnership was, in reality, broken.

Clark, a professional man with a significant series of accomplishments to his credit was unable to finish work for his degree. His story shows the blockade of the final stage of creativity. His work was essentially complete, but he could not bring himself to present it for acceptance. A brief analytic experience revealed castration anxiety and attendant conflict as well as a significant narcissistic problem. He dreamed that his father was shooting at him from the roof of a tall building. He recalled playing violent games in which companions were injured but he revealed no compassion or remorse for those foolish enough to fail to protect themselves. He felt loved and despised at the same time. The depressive symptoms were exemplified by frequent mood disturbance with hypomanic assertiveness. He broke off the treatment when the therapist relocated and a burdensome commute became necessary. His narcissism could not tolerate that degree of submission, and, rather than find another analyst to continue treatment, he entered a group. Under the influence of a charismatic leader, he was able to complete the necessary steps to graduate. The final steps, requiring recognition of limits, were accomplished when the presence of a new idealized object made the issue of loss temporarily avoidable and provided opportunity for a "transference cure." The issue of triumphing over the departed one is implied also, with projection of the image of a helpless, worthless self that had to submit to limits.

Summary

The tension between depression and creativity involves conserving versus innovating. A developmental distortion causes unbalance that we call depression. To be depressed is to be in a state suspended in time, denying loss and hoping for its reversal. Creativity is making or finding anew. Depression is avoiding change. The creative process is activity toward perception and can be manifested in products, theories, or images. It is natural and constant in the human mind. The association of creativity and genius is a fallacy of idealization disregarding the cultural context and social forces, breeding a star system which relegates the masses to mute adoration. Genius is a combination of talent, opportunity and motivation, driving one to live and work at the limits of human capacity. Depression blocks creativity in the genius just as it does in other persons.

Epochs differ in the degree of individuality they foster. Balinese culture, historically engendering aesthetic sense in all, rewarded enactment and taste, but slight innovation occurred; all learned to dance and move beautifully, but the dances changed little (Mead 1959). Renaissance Italy ushered in our era of reawakening and innovation, leading to modern science and constant change. Innovation was then the province of genius; individuals self-socially selected to lead the finding and making of the new, while the mass of people attempted to remain stable and conserve the basic fabric of life in the midst of upheaval. The process has advanced at an ever-increasing rate because it has not been possible to stabilize our culture at a sufficiently satisfying point. Change is painful but innovation is seen as the solution. Innovation has been rewarded where it can be applied easily and without apparent pain, promoting a culture of dependence and immaturity. Painful and demanding innovation, often imposed ruthlessly in the past, is now resisted. The price of technological exploitation is apparent in pollution and social devastation and we are in a period when pain is unavoidable, whether we change or not; as Toffler (1970) pointed out, costs are high either way.

We are also in the midst of a revolution in creativity where an ever larger portion of mankind is encouraged to live at the limits of human possibility. "Genius" is a term of controversy because it applies to so many, not as a matter of fashion, but of accomplishment. Artists are proliferating faster than opportunities. Change is recognized as the theme of modern life; constant innovation is essential to maintain adaptation at all; at the same time, constant innovation is the source of great misery since change itself is always painful even while it is gratifying and even joyful. This formulation is offered as the basis for the epidemic of depression we suffer. Depression is a primitive, conservative stance adopted in response to intolerable loss. It necessarily interferes with creativity because it is opposed to giving up the old and making new.

REFERENCES

Arieti, S. (1977). New views of creativity. *Creative Psychiatry 10*. Ardsley: Geigy Pharmaceuticals.

Brenner, C. (1982). *The Mind In Conflict*. New York: International Universities Press.

Bibring, E. (1953). The mechanism of depression. In *Affective Disorders*, ed. P. Greenacre, pp. 13–48. New York: International Universities Press.

Cohen, I. B. (1980). *The Newtonian Revolution*. Cambridge: Cambridge University Press.

Ehrenzweig, A. (1967). *The Hidden Order of Art*. Berkeley and Los Angeles: University of California Press, 1971.

Engel, G. L., and Schmale, A. H. (1972). Conservation-withdrawal: a primary regulatory process for organismic homeostasis. In *Physiology, Emotion and*

Psychosomatic Illness, ed. R. Porter and J. Knight. Ciba Foundation Symposium (N.S.), Amsterdam: Elsevier-Excerpta Medica.

Engel, G. L., and Schmale, A. H. (1975). The role of conservation-withdrawal in depressive reactions. In *Depression and Human Existence*, ed. E. J. Anthony and T. Benedek, pp. 183–198. Boston: Little, Brown.

Freud, S. (1900). The interpretation of dreams. *Standard Edition* 5:339–340. London: Hogarth Press.

Gardner, H. (1982). *Art, Mind, and Brain*. New York: Basic Books.

Greenacre, P. (1957). The childhood of the artist. *The Psychoanalytic Study of the Child* 12: 47–72.

Greenspan, S. I. (1979). *Intelligence and Adaptation*. New York: International Universities Press.

———— (1982). Demonstration of videotaped observations of mothers and children to the Washington Psychoanalytic Society.

Kanigel, R. (1984). The brain and the mind. *Johns Hopkins Magazine* 35(1): 34–35.

Katan, M. (1953). Mania and the pleasure principle: primary and secondary symptoms. In *Affective Disorders*, ed. P. Greenacre, pp. 140–209. New York: International Universities Press.

Kris, E. (1953). *Psychoanalytic Explorations in Art*. New York: International Universities Press.

Langer, S. K. (1953). *Feeling and Form*, p. 40. New York: Charles Scribner's Sons.

Mahler, M. (1966). Notes on the development of basic moods: the depressive affect. In *Psychoanalysis — A General Psychology*, ed. R. M. Loewenstein, L. M. Newman, M. Schur, and A. J. Solnit, pp. 152–168. New York: International Universities Press.

Mead, M. (1959). Creativity in cross cultural perspective. In *Creativity and its Cultivation*, ed. H. Anderson, p. 222. New York: Harper and Brothers.

Meyersburg, H. A., Ablon, S. L. and Kotin, J. (1974). A reverberating psychic mechanism in the depressive processes. *Psychiatry* 37:372–386.

Milner, M. (1950). *On Not Being Able to Paint*, 2nd ed. London: Heinemann Educational Books, Ltd., 1971.

Modell, A. H. (1970). The transitional object and the creative act. *The Psychoanalytic Quarterly* 39: 240–250.

Nisbet, Robert (1982). *Prejudices — A Philosophical Dictionary*, p. 138. Cambridge: Harvard University Press.

Poincaré, H. (1929). Mathematical creation. In *The World of Mathematics*, vol. 4, ed. J. R. Newman, pp. 2041–2050. New York: Simon and Schuster, 1956.

Pollock, G. H. (1978). Process and affect: mourning and grief. *International Journal of Psycho-Analysis.*, 59:255–276.

Read, J. (1930). *Textbook of Organic Chemistry*, p. 51. London: Bell.

Rothenberg, A. (1979). *The Emerging Goddess*. Chicago: University of Chicago Press.

Solnit, A. J. (1966). Some adaptive functions of aggressive behavior. In *Psychoanalysis — A General Psychology*, ed. R. M. Loewenstein, L. M., Newman, M. Schur and A. J. Solnit, pp. 169–189. New York: International Universities Press.

Spitz, R. (1965a). *The First Year of Life*. New York: International Universities Press.

———— (1965b). The evolution of dialogue. In *Drives, Affects, Behavior*, ed. M. Schur, pp. 170–190. New York: International Universities Press.

Toffler, A. (1970). *Future Shock*. New York: Random House.

Volkan, V. D. (1970). Typical findings in pathological grief. *Psychiatric Quarterly* 44: 231–250.

_____ (1972). The linking objects of pathological mourners. *Archives of General Psychiatry.* 27: 215–221.

_____ (1975). Re-grief therapy and the function of the linking object as a key to stimulate emotionality. In *Emotional Flooding,* ed. P. Olsen, pp. 179–224. New York: Behavioral Publications.

Winnicott, D. W. (1951). Transitional objects and transitional phenomena. In *Playing and Reality,* pp. 1–25. London: Tavistock Publications 1970.

_____ (1972). *The Maturational Processes and the Facilitating Environment.* London: Hogarth Press.

PART II

Mourning and Depression in the Life Cycle

CHAPTER FIVE

Preschool Age Children

Perihan A. Rosenthal, M.D.
Stuart Rosenthal, M.D.

The existence of affective disorders in adults is widely accepted and has been extensively researched. However, depression in children was ignored until the mid-1970's. DSM-III (1980) groups the essential features of depression under age 6, in older children, and in adolescents in the category of adult depression. However, its clinical picture in children depends upon the child's developmental level, ego structure, cognition, ability to tolerate loss of the state of well being, deprivation, stress and trauma (Toolan 1981).

Theories about the etiology of depression in children abound. Some examples of these theories are the genetic (Puig-Antich et al. 1978, Tsuang 1978, Toolan 1975); psychological (Freud 1917, Abraham 1911, Spitz 1946); biological (Weller et al. 1984, Cytryn and McKnew 1979, Puig-Antich et al. 1979); behavioral (Kashani et al. 1981); learned helplessness (Seligman 1975); cognitive (Kovacs 1981); and stress model (Graham 1974). Various scales assess depressive symptomatology in children 6 and over (Kazdin 1981), but there have been only preliminary efforts to develop scales to assess depressive symptomatology in children age 0 to 3 (Cornell group 1983), and depression and suicide in children age 0 to 5 (Rosenthal and Doherty 1983).

Historical Perspective

As early as the seventeenth century (R. Burton 1621), physicians recognized depression in children. Melancholia was reported in the mid-nineteenth century (Anthony 1975), and described in Dickens' *Oliver Twist* in 1839. Beginning with the twentieth century and until the 1970's, several authors described childhood depression, depressive position, or anaclitic depression in children (Abraham 1911, Klein 1948, Spitz 1946, Bowlby 1961a, Toolan 1962, Mahler 1966). However, until the mid-1960's no major American textbook of child psychiatry (Kanner 1957) or in general psychiatry (Noyes and Kolb 1966) contained a section on childhood depression. Also, the DSM-II (1968) of the American Psychiatric Association did not include childhood depression. Moreover, American psychiatry was influenced by the orthodox Freudian psychoanalytic formulation that childhood depression did not exist (Rochlin 1959, Finch 1960, Rie 1966).

American psychiatry became interested when European clinicians published papers on childhood depression (Hall 1952, Schachter 1952). Barton Hall (1952) reported six cases of affective illness among 1000 patients between the ages of 5 and 16, of whom only two were manic depressive; the others were reactive depressions. Schachter (1952) described a 2-year-old with cyclothymia. Eva Frommer (1968) used antidepressant drugs for children aged 18 months and up. She stated that depression in children accounts for 20 percent of all childhood psychopathology.

The debate among American psychiatrists about the existence of childhood depression comes from a discrepancy between observations and clinical theories. However, some clinicians stayed within the boundaries of psychodynamic theories and modified them to correspond with clinical observations and research. Redlich and Freedman (1966) postulated that adults who become predisposed in childhood to depressive positions due to early chronic losses and deprivation are at high risk to develop depression after a relatively minor traumatic stimulus or stressful life events in adult life. For these authors, depression in children may present as fear, hypochondriasis, or as learning and conduct problems. Noyes and Kolb's (1977) *Modern Clinical Psychiatry* mentioned the existence of childhood depression. A 1975 National Institute of Mental Health conference (Schulterbrandt 1977) explored childhood depression, its etiology, diagnosis, and prognosis. Other American authors began to describe depressive disorders in children and adolescents (Group for the Advancement of Psychiatry 1966, Poznanski and Zrull 1970, McConville and Boag 1973, Cytryn and McKnew 1972). They reported that the expression of depression in children differs widely from adults. Recent studies find that 10 to 25 percent of in and outpatient populations of children have major depressive disorders (Carlson and Cantwell 1979, Petti 1981).

Early Childhood

Early clinical reports of depression in childhood referred specifically to infants and young children. A. Freud and Burlingham (1944) reported severe grief reactions among children separated from their parents, especially children younger than three years. Among the young children they studied, a history of parental loss was more prevalent among the depressed children than the mixed neurotic control group. Spitz (1946) described 6-month-old infants who became withdrawn, listless, developed psychomotor retardation, insomnia, weight loss, and illness following maternal separation. He called this "anaclitic depression." He postulated that the infant's self-directed aggression played a role because the infant lacked an external love object who would both absorb and release its aggression and who would stimulate its libido, which would neutralize aggression. Deprived of a maternal figure, the infant directed this instinctual drive onto itself.

Bowlby (1958) delineates the process of infant attachment by referring to a three-stage separation experience from the mother: protest, when the upset infant tries to reiterate contact with the mother by crying, screaming, and thrashing about; despair, when the infant continues to scream in hope of being reunited with its mother, but gradually becomes silent, decreases its movement, and appears acutely depressed; and detachment, when the infant seems to have overcome his loss and responds to other adults. Bowlby speculated that young children subjected to recurrent separation form progressively tenuous attachments to mother figures, eventually becoming nonfeeling, nonempathic — psychopaths rather than depressed adults.

However, a group of psychoanalysts (Rie 1966, Mahler 1966, Rochlin 1965) thought depression did not exist in children because the child's immature personality structure, superego, and ego did not allow the development of a depressive neurosis. They pointed out that the aspect of the superego responsible for intense, prolonged self-directed aggression is underdeveloped before age 10 or 12.

Mahler (1966) spoke of the toddler's "depressive mood." In her longitudinal observation of the separation–individuation process in the first three years of life, she did not observe actual depressive signs but did note behaviors that seemed to indicate a predisposition to depression in later life. Mahler suggested that children aged 18 to 24 months experience feelings of conquest of their world and begin to relinquish some feelings of omnipotence and the belief in the magic of their wishes and fantasies. If, during this period, the child is uncertain about the emotional availability of the parent, feelings of helplessness may predominate and a basic mood of depression may ensue, becoming the root of later negative mood swings and depressive illness. The "depressive mood" of the toddler may present as severe separation reactions, temper tantrums, and continued attempts to woo the mother, followed by brief periods of despair when unable to prevent separation. The child's mood may be, at various times, one of resignation, discontent, or angry surrender. In other words, the child shows a depletion of "confident expectation" of important others and suffers a lowering of self-esteem, which results in an inability to neutralize the aggression that later causes depressive symptoms.

Poznanski and Zrull (1970) commented on the gap in depressive symptomatology between infancy and middle childhood. In reviewing their outpatient records covering a five-year period, they found only one child under 5 with depressive symptoms. They suggested the need for further study of the development of affect and drives in preschoolers.

Bemporad (1982) noted the lack of depressive symptomatology in the toddler stage. He attributed this to the developmental hallmark of this stage. The toddler is full of curiosity and exuberance, and enjoys exploring and experimenting but is still dependent on caretakers. Bemporad feels that toddlers deal with frustration by active physical movement, loud protest, or by distraction to more pleasant activities. They move from activity to activity. These characteristics are not congruent with the concept of depression. He thinks that the appearance of full affective disorder requires higher cognitive and affective maturation levels.

Anthony (1975) thinks that the paucity of reports on childhood depression derives from the young child's "inability to verbalize his affective state, from the incomplete development of the superego, and from the absence of consistent self-representation." He is concerned that the child's lack of verbal ability may lead to an overdiagnosis of depression. This may lead clinicians to ascribe to the child or infant adult emotions and a more complex psychological makeup than is warranted.

Kovacs and Beck (1977) concluded from their review of the literature that depressive disorders occurring under 5 or 6 years of age are either nonexistent or exceedingly difficult to recognize.

Cantwell (1983) says that depression in preschoolers is difficult to conceptualize because of their lability of emotional expression of fears and their momentary exuberance. The cognitive and affectual limitations of this period prevent the child from understanding future time, anticipating consequences of behavior, or even maintaining mood states for anything but a brief period.

Discussing depression in infancy, Provence (1983) observes that infants and toddlers show fairly immediate responses and that careful observation increases the probability of making reasonable inferences about the feelings and affective state of the child. She was impressed with the high rate of agreement among observers who labeled infants' feelings.

Rosenthal and Rosenthal's (1984a) study of 16 suicidal outpatient preschoolers showed that 56 percent were depressed according to modified Weinberg criteria; 88 percent of nine suicidal inpatient preschoolers were so diagnosed on the Preschool Depression Scale (Rosenthal et al. 1984b).

Toolan (1981) stated that children 12 months old evidence depression differently than at age 5, and that these differences depend on the child's developmental level, ego structure, and ability to tolerate either psychological or biological pain.

Assessment Techniques

Diagnostic interview. During the past 10–15 years, several systemic interview protocols were developed to diagnose childhood depression in children age 6 and older (Cytryn and McKnew 1972, Poznanski and Zrull 1970, Malmquist 1971, Weinberg et. al. 1973). The Kiddie-SADS (K-SADS), developed from the Schedule for Affective Disorders and Schizophrenia for adults (Chamber et. al. 1978), was developed for ages 6–16 years; the Interview Schedule for Children (Kovacs et al. 1977), ages 8–13; the Bellevue Index of Depression (Petti 1978), ages 6–12; the Children's Depression Rating Scale (Poznanski et. al. 1979) follows the same format as the Hamilton Rating Scale (Hamilton 1960) for depression in adults; the Child Assessment Scale (Hodges 1980), ages 7–12 years, is used at times with children as young as 5 years.

Since 1980, DSM-III has provided a unifying framework for the diagnosis of affective disorders in adults as well as children. Its essential diagnostic criteria for major depressive disorders are similar for infants, children, adolescents and adults, but associated features vary according to the child's age. The essential criteria for major depressive disorders are "dysphoric mood or loss of interest or pleasure in all or almost all usual activities and pastimes." The dysphoric mood is characterized by symptoms such as the following: depressed, sad, blue, hopeless, low, down in the dumps, irritable. According to DSM-III, for children under six, "dysphoric mood may have to be inferred from a persistently sad facial expression. . . . At least four of the following symptoms have each been present nearly every day for a period of at least two weeks (in children under six, at least three of the first four).

[1.] Poor appetite or significant weight loss or increased appetite or significant weight gain (in children under 6, consider failure to make expected weight gain);
[2.] Insomnia or hypersomnia;
[3.] Psychomotor agitation or retardation (in children under 6, hypoactivity);
[4.] Loss of interest and pleasure in usual activities, (in children under six, signs of apathy)."

In their pilot project, the Cornell Group (1983) is developing a scale that measures depression-like behavior in infants and toddlers (KIDOS-Kidde Infant Depression Observation Scale). It has two major criteria: the child's affective state and direct observable behavior.

The child's affective state is the primary criterion of depression. It has seven classic Darwinian affect categories as well as distress, flatness, and regulation and modulation of affect. The second criterion is the child's direct observable behavior, such as lack of energy, difficulty being comforted, emotional blunting, and negativism. The Cornell group believes that the predominance of sad affect observed in a child for a period of time does not exclude the simultaneous presence of happiness, anger or fear.

At the University of Massachusetts Medical Center, Rosenthal's group (1983) is developing a Preschool Depression Scale (PDS) from their clinical observations and interviews of preschoolers and infants. This scale uses extrinsic and intrinsic factors to measure the young child's cognition, affect, vegetative symptoms, and interactional patterns. The PDS four major categories contain 36 subcategories. The categories are: cognitive/developmental maturity, tempermental/interactional patterns, affective/behavioral presentation, and vegetative/psycho-physiological symptoms. Each subcategory was given 0 to 4 points according to the severity of the symptoms, affective states and behaviors ("0" = not observed or not present, "1" = normal, "2" = mild, "3" and "4" = severe). Diagnosis of depression and its severity in preschool-age children is based not only on depressed mood and affect, because these were shown by nondepressed children who were temporarily unhappy rather than depressed. The total score of the scale indicates whether the syndrome of depression is present. The scale identifies the child's observable, available emotions and coping skills. In a pilot study of 50 outpatient preschoolers, the PDS had 97 percent interrater reliability and 80 percent concurrent validity; its predictive validity is still being explored.

Self-report inventories. The self-report scales for children aged 6 and older are the Children's Depression Inventory (Kovacs 1981), the Children's Depression Scale (Lang and Tisher 1978), and the Short Children's Depression Inventory (Carlson and Cantwell 1979, 1980).

Projective techniques. This assessment method has been used to uncover unconscious or suppressed material in older children such as the Rorschach, Thematic Apperception Test, and Children's Apperception Test. Drawing tests, such as the Bender-Gestalt, House-Tree-Person, and Draw-a-Person, have also been used, but not in a systematic way to study childhood depression.

Peer and teacher rating. These are used for school-age children, aged 6 and older, e.g. the Peer Nomination Inventory for Depression (Lefkowitz and Tesiny 1980).

Parent rating scale. Several behavioral rating scales completed by parents are employed to screen psychiatric disorders (Rutter et al. 1974), for psychopharmacological research (Conners 1976) and in epidemiological research (Achenbach et al. 1981). Only Achenbach used many items pertaining to the child's mood state. However, he, referring to his behavior check list, pointed out that under age 4, behavior is variable and depends on the organic maturation of the child. Furthermore, he stated that the children's immediate social environment varies so widely that parental reports are of limited value in establishing a baseline for behavioral or other problems.

Biological markers. Carrol et al. (1980, 1981) found a number of analogous changes in the adrenal function of adults with affective disorders. Cortisol secretion and urinary catecholamine metabolites (Puig-Antich et. al. 1979) have been studied as potential markers of depression in children. The observation of Puig-Antich et. al. (1979) that positive responses to tricyclic antidepressants in older children with affective disorders supports the concept of the existence of these disorders in this population. Rosenthal et al. (1984) gave the dexamathesone suppression test to nine suicidal preschool-age inpatients. They found a strong correlation between nonsuppression of cortisol secretion and major depressive disorders.

Causes

Genetic

A growing consensus supports the role of genetic factors in adult affective disorders. The mode of transmission of manic-depressive disorders might be autosomal dominant, x-linked dominant (Perris 1968) polygenic transmission, as well as genetic heterogeneity. Research on monozygotic twins reared apart shows a 67 percent concordance rate (Tsuang 1978). Adoption studies demonstrate increased rates for all psychopathology and an increased incidence of depression in adoptees whose biological parents had an affective disorder. Higher rates of depression were found in the children of depressed inpatients, compared with children of well parents (Welner et. al. 1977) and children of parents with other psychiatric disorders (Cantwell and Baker 1983). Cytryn and McKnew (1980) estimate the lifetime risk of a child of a bipolar parent at about 10 percent and the risk of a unipolar parent at about 15 percent.

Frommer et. al. (1972) reviewed 200 preschool children, 58 percent of whom were diagnosed depressed. Of these, 70 percent of the mothers had serious psychiatric problems (depressive illnesses, alcoholism, other psychopathology). Conners et al. (1979) felt that the effect on a child of parents with unipolar depressions occurs only when the illness adversely affects the child's environment, whereas bipolar illness seems to be genetic, presenting somewhat later in life. Puig-Antich et al., (1979) studied the first degree relatives of children diagnosed as having major depressive disorders. They found major depression, alcoholism, antisocial behavior, and substance abuse.

Psychological

Cytryn and McKnew (1980) think psychosocial stresses may precipitate or accelerate biological affective reactions; lacking a genetic component, they might become the casual agent for the affective illness. They categorized psychosocial stressors as: maternal deprivation; loss of separation from an important object; rejection; and marital discord and family pathology.

Other workers (Abraham 1911, Freud 1917) theorized that depression resulted from the loss of a significant object; in these cases the patient turns the aggression against the self. Freud (1926) postulated that infants have two important defense mechanisms, introjection of the projected attributes to form an internalized mental object and projection of an internal state onto external objects. If the infant's internal state is frustrated by hunger, discomfort, or sleep, the infant reacts with strong protest, i.e. crying, restlessness, fretfulness, whining, clinging, and various visceral dysfunctions — vomiting, diarrhea, or sleep disturbances. On the other hand, lack of warmth, nurturance, stimulation, and security from the caretaker frustrates the infant's introjection of projected attributes. This results in a serious deficiency in need-fulfillment and leads to a developmental delay. If these frustrations are long standing, they have a crippling effect on the child's emotional life.

Bibring (1953) and Sandler and Joffe (1965) viewed depression in children as an emotional state of helplessness and powerlessness of the ego. Bibring sees this as a narcissistic shock; Sandler and Joffe see this as a loss of the feeling of well-being previously experienced by the child along with the loss of a specific object.

Bowlby (1951) concluded that a warm, continued relationship with a mother figure is essential for healthy personality development of the child. For Yarrow (1961), four kinds of noxious experiences, each with a potentially different implication, affect the personality development of the child: institutionalization; multiple mothering; separation from a mother figure; and distortion in the affectual relationship between mother and child. Ribble (1943) described infants with inadequate mothering who developed a pattern of prolonged sleep withdrawal under any condition of frustration. Engel (1956) observed that some babies responded to frustration with inhibition-withdrawal followed by depression-withdrawal, while others become predominantly anxious. In later years, some of these children reacted to frustration with anger, and protested their resentment; others become depressed and helpless. Engel and Schmale (1972) regard this as part of a conservation-withdrawal response that represents the psychological equivalent of the "giving up" attitude of adult depression. They consider conservation-withdrawal a universal mechanism comprised of the behavioral triad of immobility, quiescence, and unresponsiveness that occurs periodically in virtually every species of animal as a primary regulatory process of organismic hemostatis.

Fries and Woolf (1971) described a group of congenitally underactive babies who demonstrated an excessive tendency to inhibition and withdrawal. This inhibition-withdrawal "constitutional complex" remains relatively unchanged throughout development; an apathetic, anergic baby may show a pronounced tendency toward inhibition and depression when stressed during adolescence or later.

Cohen (1954) concluded that some parents make undue demands or unrealistically expect their children to conform to high standards of "good" behavior or to be high achievers. The mother enforces undue dependence of her child but cannot cope with her young child's rebelliousness, so the mother controls the unruly behavior by threats of abandonment. These children came to feel a sense of emptiness and a constant need for support which can only be rectified by external figures. The actual depressive episode is an attempt to win back the mother or attend to the need of others.

Bonime (1976) believes that adult depression derives from a childhood that lacked the needed parental nurturance and respect for the child. The child's true emotional needs were ignored or squelched, and the child grows up feeling cheated, convinced of the right to own the love solicited from others.

Piaget (1952) emphasized that during the sensorimotor stage (18–24 months), mental life consists mainly of innate reactions, habit sequences, and possibly physical discomfort. The mother serves the infant in countless ways; Piaget calls her the primary "ailment" for the infant's budding schemata. Maternal deprivation stunts psychic development. Therefore, according to Piaget, the loss of the mother is equivalent to losing tangible nourishment. Through the mother, the minds of infants develop. They form a sense of self and can begin to anchor themselves in reality.

When the child's substitute caretakers are emotionally unavailable, a chronic depressive state ensues. Goldfarb (1943) compared two groups of children raised in institutions and foster homes. Those in institutions showed an indiscriminate, insatiable demand for affection and attention. Goldfarb characterized their affect hunger as "never had enough." Spitz (1946) described anaclitic depression occurring in infants who established a constant cathexis of a need-satisfying object for the first six months of life and then lost the object and developed a mourning reaction which progressed to a state of depressive withdrawal and debilitation. The syndrome presented as a consistently sad expression on the infant's face. Finally, complete withdrawal and dejection developed, with a frozen rigidity of expression. Spitz considered this syndrome to be the equivalent of the "parathymia" which Abraham (1911) described as the infantile prototype of a later depressive psychosis. Spitz also saw a parallel between anaclitic depression and adult melancholia. In anaclitic depression, the lack of mothering inhibits the neutralization of aggression by the primitive ego.

Biochemical

Sachar et. al. (1970, 1973) found cortisol hypersecretion and a loss of the usual circadian rhythm in a group of depressed adult patients. Subsequently, numerous reports appeared, discussing the changes in some depressed patients in the cortisol dynamic of the hypothalamic-pituitary-adrenal-cortisol system. Puig-Antich et al. (1979) demonstrated cortisol hypersecretion in children with a diagnosis of depressive syndrome. McKnew and Cytryn (1979) compared nine children hospitalized with depressive reactions with a control group, using the parameters of 24-hour urinary excretion of norepinephrine (N.E.), vanylmandelic acid (VMA), and 3-methoxy-4-hydroxyphenyglycol (MHPG). Hospitalized depressed children had a mean MHPG excretion of 753 mg/m² compared with 1092 mg/m² in controls. Poznanski et. al. (1982) administered the dexamethasone suppression test to selected dysphoric prepubertal children and controls in an outpatient population. Of nine children with major depressive disorders, five failed to suppress; eight out of nine nondepressed children had normal test results. Woolston et. al. (1983) reported on matched salivary and plasma cortisol samples in two patients (aged 16 and 40 months) with nonorganic failure-to-thrive in whom post-dexamethasone cortisol levels exceeded 5 μg/dl. They speculated about the relationship between nonorganic failure-to-thrive and major depressive disorder.

Suicide

As with depressive disorders, childhood suicidal attempts and thoughts were ignored in the past. This is because adults deny that suicidal thought and gesture can exist in children, particularly preschoolers. Rosenthal and Rosenthal (1984a) and Rosenthal et al. (1984b) reported on 16 outpatient and nine hospitalized suicidal preschool children. These children had suicidal ideas or made suicidal threats or attempts, e.g., running in front of cars, ingestion of pills, jumping from high places, stabbing. The outpatient group had 56 percent depression, the inpatient group 78 percent.

Case I

This 4½-year-old boy's psychologist-therapist referred him for inpatient evaluation. The parents were concerned about his "aggressive behavior, impulsivity, lack of socialization, his recent trends of self-harm, and his statement that he wants to die." They felt that for the previous six months he was occasionally sad and depressed and cried easily, and at other times was outgoing and entertaining. His psychological tests showed some thought confusion, depressed mood, and morbid ideas.

Developmental history.   The mother drank heavily and abused many drugs during pregnancy. The birth was uncomplicated and his developmental milestones were within normal limits. The mother abused alcohol and drugs until the patient was 15 months old.

Family history.   The maternal and paternal extended families have a strong history of depression, depressive spectrum disorders, and alcoholism which have required hospitalization.

Initial evaluation.   The patient was an attractive, outgoing assertive youngster. During the interview, he insisted on discussing topics of his choice. His speech and language were intact. He was preoccupied with the idea of hurting himself; he poked himself in the face at one point. The patient presented a complex picture of impulsive, hyperactive behavior with underlying depression.

Hospital course.   Because he presented many features of attention deficit disorder, a double-blind trial of methylphenidate was instituted. He worsened on this medication.

The Dexamethasone Suppression Test showed 3.1 ug/dl of cortisol at 4 P.M., indicating cortisol suppression. His EEG and neurological examination were normal.

He scored high (75) on the Preschool Depression Scale and showed the following: irritability, listlessness, and an often sad and tired appearance. His depressed mood was not relieved by his mother or by test-specific stimuli. During temper tantrums, he bit, cut, and injured himself seriously. He fidgeted throughout the testing. He had morbid ideas and wished to kill himself.

The patient was diagnosed by DSM-III criteria as Attentional Deficit Disorder, Dysthymic Disorder, and Parent/Child Problem.

During play therapy sessions, he was agitated, expressed many fears, said he wanted to hurt himself, and wanted his parents to leave and not observe him. He pretended to run in front of a truck and be killed. He said he would not tell his parents if he wanted to harm himself. He felt unloved and "bad because I am a bad boy." In another session, he expressed intense feelings of hunger for nurturance and deprivation. He sought the therapist's acceptance and described himself as a "mad and bad boy." He made the toy dragon hurt himself by "falling from the sky and getting hurt on purpose." The patient could distinguish accidental from purposeful intent.

In another session, the patient made the toy people suicidal and self-destructive. They risked hurting the babies, got into accidents purposely, and hurt themselves by falling off the building instead of flying, which they were capable of doing. They would crash into the ground and the patient would scream and say, "I'm mad at everybody."

During his four-week admission, he responded positively to the structured milieu; his depression subsided.

Case II

The mother and stepfather of this 5-year-old boy brought him to the hospital because his behavior problems increased during the previous eight months. "He beats up on his 14-month-old sister and caused injuries which required medical attention." He behaved wildly and uncontrollably and kicked and bit others during frequent temper tantrums. They had tried several recommended interventions, including making him sit on a chair, hitting his ankles, ignoring him, or locking him in his room. During these incarcerations he "wrecked" his room. Prior to referral, the patient received methylphenidate and behavior therapy without success. His school behavior was disruptive.

Developmental history. The patient was born after a long and difficult labor but without complications. He was a happy baby with a history of poor eating. His motor development was normal but bowel training was difficult. The mother noted that, at times, he was clumsy, accident prone, showed labile mood, and often looked tired. He called himself a "bad boy."

Family history. Psychiatric problems and alcoholism were absent in both sides of the family; the biological father (divorced four years earlier) had problems with his temper.

Initial interview. The patient was active and of small stature. During the interview he was very shy and retreated into the corners or under the chairs or desk.

Hospital course. Most laboratory results were normal. The Dexamethasone Suppression Test revealed 5.1 ug/dl of cortisol at 4 P.M., indicating failure to suppress. His abnormal EEG was not specific for seizure disorder. Psychological tests showed no intellectual impairment.

He scored high (95) on the Preschool Depression Scale and showed the following: problems with articulation, destructive behavior, and shift from activity to activity too quickly. He was aggressive toward siblings, intrusive, and detached from his parents. He did not react when separated or reunited with them. He gave up easily, had blunted affect, was listless, and made sad faces occasionally. His depressed mood was not affected by test-specific stimuli or by his mother's presence. He lacked enjoyment, was slightly agitated, and was also restless at times. During temper tantrums, he pulled his hair and rubbed his skin. He sucked his fist and thumb excessively. He showed vegetative symptoms, i.e., hypersomnia, loss of appetite, and picky eating.

He was diagnosed by DSM-III criteria as Major Depressive Disorder, Intermittent Explosive Disorder, and Conflictual Family Circumstances.

At first, he was difficult to involve in individual therapy. He hid under the desk and made strange noises. Eventually, he settled down and expressed rage and aggression, mostly toward adult figures. He called himself a "bad boy" and said he disliked and wanted to harm himself. He had good symbolic play and eventually was able to emulate some of the staff's ward behavior. His irritable behavior and distractibility gradually abated. He responded to 10 mg. daily of thioridazine. His vegetative symptoms improved.

Case III

This 4½-year-old boy was referred for outpatient evaluation by his mother's therapist because of her intense rage toward her son. Her therapist wanted to protect the boy from the mother's abusive behavior (mother once smacked his face, and on two other occasions hit him on the back, frightening her into seeking help for herself).

Developmental history. The patient was born full term after a difficult and long delivery. Although the umbilical cord encircled his neck his Apgar score and vital signs were normal. He was a calm and quiet baby the first month, but was difficult to handle the rest of the first year because he screamed at night. His developmental milestones, i.e., gross motor and sphincter control and language function, were normal. However, he was very stubborn and did what he wanted despite his mother's efforts to control him. The patient had severe mood swings during the eight months prior to referral. At times he was withdrawn, apathetic, and anergic; at other times he was impulsive, aggressive, hyperactive, and oppositional.

Family history. The parental history revealed that the mother suffered from serious depression, requiring medication at times. Several of mother's relatives suffered from depression and severe alcoholism.

Hospital course. The physical examination was normal. The Dexamethasone Suppression Test showed 6.2 ug/dl of cortisol at 4 P.M., indicating failure to suppress.

His score (70) on the Preschool Depression Scale indicated moderate depression and showed the following: He was very shy and insecure with the therapist. He could not separate himself from his mother, was extremely fearful and anxious and cried easily. He rarely smiled and he looked sad. His depressed mood was not relieved by his mother or by test-specific stimuli. He was very subdued, could not enjoy playing with toys, and was apathetic. He was self-abusive, biting himself and banging his head against a wall.

His DSM-III diagnoses were Major Depressive Disorder and Parent/ Child Problems.

During play therapy he made dolls go to school and talked about nightmares in which animals and witches chased him. He made the baby doll and the mother doll jump from the roof and injure themselves. At times, whenever he was overwhelmed with his aggressive feelings, he insisted upon seeing his mother. Both patient and mother were seen together to help her to understand his underlying depression and to find ways to handle him without force. During the three months of weekly hour-long therapy, he experienced several mood swings. At such times he just sat on the chair, apathetic and withdrawn. At other times he was extremely active and unable to sit still. Each cycle lasted six weeks. His play was filled with morbid talk and ideas. His Preschool Depression Scale score remained moderately depressed during these cycles. The mother increasingly empathized with the patient and was able to set nonpunitive limits, which helped the patient's moods. Eventually, his vegetative symptoms disappeared, he became more animated, and his temper tantrums subsided.

Treatment Methods

Psychopharmacological

During the past 15 years many reports appeared on the usefulness of antidepressants in the treatment of depressed children (Lucas et. al. 1965, Kuhn and Kuhn 1972, and Puig-Antich 1979). These authors found that three-fourths of the children responded positively to medication although none were under 6 years old. Furthermore, these studies have methodological problems, which include lack of explicit diagnostic criteria for childhood depression; absence of structured interviews or protocols; absence of a control group; and variable length of the therapeutic trials.

European psychiatrists are more practiced in the use of antidepressant medication for childhood depression. Frommer (1968) from England has used antidepressants for school-age children since 1962 and for preschoolers over 18 months of age since 1966. She studied over 200 children under 5 and divided them into three groups: aggressive-depressive, depressed, and anxious. Seventy-three to eighty-three percent of these patients responded to antidepressants. This study suffers from over-inclusiveness because of the absence of explicit diagnostic criteria. Puig-Antich and colleagues (1979) found that tricyclic antidepressants achieved a clinical response similar to that in adult depression, with a plasma level of at least 146 ng/ml.

According to White (1979) tricyclic antidepressants are effective in the treatment of depressive symptoms in children, including reactive depression. In most cases, these depressive symptoms were relieved by medication despite noxious environmental conditions.

Except for anecdotal reports, no published clinical papers exist on the use of antidepressants in preschool-age children in the United States.

Behavioral

The behavioral model of treatment of childhood depression taken from Seligman and Maier's (1967) learned helplessness theory consists of learned helplessness; loss of reinforcement against chronic frustration, and lack of control over interpersonal relationships; and a negative cognitive set of helplessness and hopelessness (Petti 1983). Most depressed children treated in inpatient and outpatient settings required intensive behavioral programming, a focus on self-control and on adaptive social interactions, and reprogramming of their perception of their family, peers, and schoolmates. Still, this work involves older children, not infants or preschoolers.

Cognitive Therapy

According to the cognitive model (Beck 1976), depression set a stream of reaction in motion affecting on the person's cognition. The person reacts to stress by activating a set of dysfunctional beliefs and maintains a series of cognitive errors, mishears, misperceives, and misconstrues events to fit this prevailing negative line of thought.

The cognitive method helps children with their subjective feelings and beliefs by closely scrutinizing their faulty beliefs. The method helps them see the evidence, explore alternative explanations and look into the consequences of their faulty beliefs. This method is used for older children only (Emerey 1983).

Psychotherapy

Childhood depression should be taken seriously (Toolan 1981). After diagnosing depression, the therapist has several treatment options, i.e. individual, family, group therapy, and psycho-pharmacologic. Cytryn and McKnew (1980) suggested family therapy as the treatment of choice for the depressed child, although some family therapy must be supplemented with individual therapy. They feel that the former facilitates the child's interactions with family members and increases the family's involvement in the treatment. These authors believe that family therapy fosters the child's self-awareness and decreases feelings of depreciation, rejection, and being scapegoated. Most workers conclude that the younger the child, the more responsive the child is to environmental modification.

In our Center the treatment of choice for all preschoolers (Rosenthal and Rosenthal 1981) is involvement in conjoint therapy with their parents. Conjoint therapy with depressed preschoolers increases the parent's awareness of the child's problem with issues of self-esteem, sadness, and dejection. It provides the therapist with an opportunity to help the child and the parents reestablish a mutually nurturing, caring relationship. We think it is essential in conjoint therapy that the parents be educated about their child's affectomotor behavior, because many parents are aware only of the child's surface behavior, e.g., anger, rage, hyperactivity, sadness, destructiveness, or vegetative difficulties. They see behavior as spiteful, unruly, and uncontrollable (Rosenthal and Rosenthal 1984a). Therapy begins with the therapist's initial interaction with the child while the parents observe. This focuses them on the child's feelings, thoughts, and behavior, thereby facilitating the parents' understanding. In the treatment, play is used to facilitate the child's expression of affectomotor behavior and the symbolic representation of his conflicts. During play therapy, the young child uses the defense mechanism of projection (of primitive destructive impulses), introjects a bad self-image (seeing himself as bad, ugly, unloved), shows a negative identification, introjects bad objects (the destroying and rejecting mother), hungers for the love object, and has suicidal ideas. By developing empathy in the parents, the therapist facilitates interaction between them and the child. In this way, the therapist helps the child to increase self-esteem, trust adults, and verbalize feelings and thoughts, thus decreasing the child's hopelessness and helplessness. If the preschool depressed child is hospitalized, additional treatment modalities — milieu, family, and expressive play therapy — are employed. In our experience many depressed preschoolers show dramatic improvement in their symptoms when they are hospitalized, and sustain this improvement if their home is supportive (Rosenthal et. al. 1984b).

According to Lewis and Lewis (1981), "Psychotherapy of any kind, as long as it involves genuine caring and human interaction, stimulates those neurotransmitters that diminish the subjective feelings of depression and enhances feelings of well-being. Empathic responses to the child may function biologically just as does positive reinforcement of any kind."

Conclusion

At the present time, the etiology of depression (object relations, genetic, biochemical, environmental) in children remains unknown. However, increased research efforts are furthering our knowledge of childhood depressive disorders. Depressive symptomatology in young children must be recognized and treated with appropriate therapy. Failure to identify dysphoric mood (rage, extreme anger, withdrawal), and accompanying behaviors (fussiness, hyperactivity, increased aggressiveness), and vegetative signs (sleeping and eating difficulties) can predispose the child to lasting sadness, depression, and aberrant behaviors.

REFERENCES

Abraham, K. (1911). Notes on psychoanalytic treatment of manic depressive insanity and allied conditions. In *Selected Papers on Psychoanalysis*, pp. 137–156. New York: Basic Books, 1960.

Achenbach, T. M., Edelbrook, C. S. (1981). *Behavioral Problems and Competencies Reported by Parents of Normal and Disturbed Children Aged Four Through Sixteen*. Monograph of the Society for Research in Child Development. Chicago: University Press 188:1.

Anthony, E. J. (1975). Childhood Depression. In *Depression and Human Existence*, ed. E. J. Anthony and T. Benedek, pp. 231–279. Boston: Little, Brown.

Anthony, E. J. (1975). Depression and Children. In *Handbook of Studies on Depression*, ed. G. D. Burrows. New York: Excerpa Medica.

Beck, A. T. (1976). *Cognitive Therapy and the Emotional Disorders*. New York: International Universities Press.

Bemporad, J. R. (1982). Childhood Depression from a Developmental Perspective. Psychiatry 1982 Annual Review of the American Psychiatric Association, ed. Lester Grinspoon. Washington, D.C.: American Psychiatric Association Press, Inc.

Bibring, E. (1953). The mechanism of depression. In *Affective Disorders*, ed. Phyllis Greenacre. New York: International Universities Press.

Bonime, W. (1976). The Psychodynamics of Neurotic Depression. *Journal of the American Academy of Psychoanalysis*. 4:301–326.

Bowlby, J. N. (1951). *Maternal Care and Mental Health*. 2nd ed. Geneva: World Health Organization.

_____ (1958). The nature of the child's tie to his mother. *International Psychoanalysis* 39:350–373.

_____ (1961). Process of mourning. *International Journal of Psycho-Analysis* 42:317–340.

Burton, R. (1621). *The Anatomy of Depression*. 13th ed. London: Thomas Davison, 1827.

Cantwell, D. P. (1983). Depression in childhood: clinical picture and diagnostic criteria. In *Affective Disorders in Childhood and Adolescence: An Update*, ed. Dennis P. Cantwell and Gabrielle A. Carlson. New York: SP Medical and Scientific Books.

Cantwell, D. P., Baker, L. (1983). Parental psychiatric illness and psychiatric disorder in at-risk children. Paper presented at the 30th Annual Meeting of the American Academy of Child Psychiatry, San Francisco.

Carlson, G. A., Cantwell, D. P. (1979). A survey of depressive symptoms in a child and adolescent psychiatric population. *Journal of the American Academy of Child Psychiatry* 18:587–599.

_____ (1980). Unmasking masked depression in children and adolescents. *American Journal of Psychiatry* 137:445-449.

Carroll, B. J., Greden, J. F., Feinberg, M., James, N. McL., et al. (1980). Neuro-endocrine dysfunction in genetic subtypes of primary unipolar depression. *Psychiatry Res.* 2:251-258.

Carroll, B. J., Feinberg, M., Greden, J. F., et al. (1981). A specific laboratory test for the diagnosis of melancholia. *Archives of General Psychiatry* 35:15-22.

Chambers, W., Puig-Antich, J. and Tabriji, M. A. (1978). The ongoing development of the Kiddie-SADS. Read at the Annual Meeting of the American Academy of Child Psychiatry, San Diego, California.

Cohen, M. B., Blake, G., Cohen, R. A., Fromm-Reichman, F., and Weigert, E. V. (1954). An intensive study of twelve cases of manic-depressive psychosis. *Psychiatry* 17:103-138.

Connors, K. C. (1976). Classification and Treatment of Childhood Depression and Depressive Equivalents. In *Depression: Behavioral, Biochemical, Diagnostic, and Treatment Concepts*, ed. D. Gallant and G. Simpson, pp. 181-204. New York: Halsted Press.

Connors, K. C., Himmelhock, J., Goyette, C. H., et al. (1979). Children of parents with affective illness. *Journal of the American Academy of Child Psychiatry* 18:600-607.

Cornell Group. (1983). Measuring depression through the use of specific criteria: the Kiddie Infant Depression Observation Scale. Zero to three. *Bulletin of the National Center for Clinical Infant Programs* 3:8-10.

Cytryn, L. and McKnew, D. H., Jr. (1972). Proposed Classifications of childhood depression. *American Journal of Psychiatry* 129:63-69.

_____ (1979). Affective disorders. In *Disturbances in Development, Basic Handbook of Child Psychiatry*, vol. II, ed. Joseph D. Noshpitz, pp: 321-340. New York: Basic Books.

_____ (1980). Affective disorders. In *Comprehensive Textbook of Psychiatry*, ed. A. M. Freedman and H. G. Kaplan, pp: 2798-2810 Baltimore: Williams and Wilkins Co.

Diagnostic and Statistical Manual of Mental Disorders. 2nd ed. Washington, D.C.: American Psychiatric Association, 1968.

Diagnostic and Statistical Manual of Mental Disorders. 3rd edit. Washington, D.C.: American Psychiatric Association, 1980.

Emery, G., Bedrosian, R., and Garber, J. (1983). Cognitive therapy with depressed children and adolescents. In *Affective Disorders in Childhood and Adolescence: An Update.* ed. Dennis P. Cantwell and Gabrielle A. Carlson. New York: SP Medical and Scientific Books.

Engel, G. and Reichsman, F. (1956). Spontaneous and experimentally induced depression in an infant with gastric fistula. *American Psychoanalytic Association* 4:428-456.

Engel, G. and Schmale, A. (1972). Conservation-withdrawal: a primary regulatory process for organismic homeostasis. In *Physiology, Emotion, and Psychosomatic Illness.* Ciba Foundation Symposium 8. Amsterdam: Elsevier.

Finch, S. M. (1960). *Fundamentals of Child Psychiatry.* New York: W. W. Norton and Co.

Freud, A. and Burlingham, D. (1944). *Infants Without Families.* New York: International Universities Press.

Freud, S. (1917). Mourning and melancholia, In *The Meaning of Despair: Psy-*

choanalytic Contributions to the Understanding of Depression, ed. W. Gaylin. New York: Science House, 1968.

Freud, S. (1926). Inhibitions, symptoms and anxiety. Standard Edition. London: Hogarth Press, 1959.

Fries, M., Woolf, P. (1971). The influence of constitutional complex on developmental phases. In Separation-Individuation: Essays in Honor of Margaret S. Mahler, ed. J. McDevitt and C. Settlage. New York: International Universities Press.

Frommer, E. A. (1968). Depressive illness in childhood. In Recent developments in affective disorders, ed. A. Coppen and Walk. British Journal of Psychiatry, Special Publication 2:117–136.

——— (1972). Indications for antidepressant treatment with special reference to depressed preschool children. In Depressive State in Childhood and Adolescence, ed. A. L. Annell, pp. 449–454. Stockholm: Almquist Wiksell.

Frommer, E. A., Mendelson, W. B., and Reid, M. A. (1972). Differential diagnosis of psychiatric disturbances in preschool children. British Journal of Psychiatry 121:71–74.

Group for the Advancement of Psychiatry (1966). Psycho-Pathological Disorders in Childhood. Group for the Advancement of Psychiatry. New York.

Golfarb, W. (1943). Infant rearing and problem behavior. American Journal of Orthopsychiatry 13:249–265.

Graham, P. (1974). Depression in prepubertal children. Developmental Medicine and Child Psychiatry 16: 340–349.

Hall, M. B. (1952). Our present knowledge about manic-depressive states in childhood. Nervous Child 9:319–325.

Hamilton, M. (1960). A rating scale for depression. Journal of Neurology, Neurosurgery and Psychiatry 23:56–62.

Hodges, K. (1980). Child assessment schedule. Unpublished document. University of Missouri, Columbia School of Medicine.

Joffe, E. G. and Sandler, J. (1965). Notes on pain, depression, and individuation. Psychoanalytic Study of the Child 20:394–424.

Kanner, L. (1957). Child Psychiatry. Springfield: Charles C. Thomas.

Kashani, J. H., Husain, A., Shekim, W. O., et al. (1981). Current perspectives on childhood depression: an overview. American Journal of Psychiatry 138: 143–153.

Kazdin, A. E. (1981). Assessment techniques for childhood depression: a critical appraisal. Journal of American Academy of Child Psychiatry 20:358–376.

Klein, M. (1948). Mourning and its relation to manic-depressive states. In Contribution to Psychoanalysis, 1921–1945, ed. M. Klein. London: Hogarth Press.

Kovacs, M. and Beck, A. T. (1977). An empirical clinical approach towards a definition of childhood depression. In Depression in Children, ed. J. G. Shulterbrandt and A. Ruskin, pp. 1–25. New York: Raven Press.

Kovacs, M. (1981). Rating scale to assess depression in school-aged children. Acta Paedopsychiatry 46:305–315.

Kuhn, V. and Kuhn, R. (1972). Drug therapy for depression in children: indication and methods. In Depressive State in Childhood and Adolescence, ed. A. L. Annell, pp. 455–459. Stockholm: Almquist and Wiksell.

Lang, M. and Tisher, M. (1978). Children's Depression Scale. Victoria: The Australian Council for Educational Research.

Lefkowitz, M. M. and Tesiny, E. P. (1980). Assessment of childhood depression. *Journal of Consultation in Clinical Psychology* 48:43–50.

Lewis, M. and Lewis, D. O. (1981). Depression in childhood: a biopsychosocial perspective. *American Journal of Psychotherapy* 35:323–330.

Lucas, A. R., Lockett, H. J. and Grimm, F. (1965). Amitriptyline in childhood depression. *Diseases of the Nervous System.* 26:105.

Mahler, M. (1966). Notes on the development of basic moods: the depressive affect. In *Psychoanalysis — A General Psychology,* ed. R. M. Lowenstein, L. M. Newman, M. Schur and A. J. Solnit. New York: International Universities Press, pp. 152–160.

Malmquist, C. (1971). Depression in childhood and adolescence. *New England Journal of Medicine* 284:887–893, 955–961.

McCanville, B. J. and Boag, L. C. (1973). Three types of childhood depression. *Canadian Psychiatric Association Journal* 18:133–138.

Noyes, A. P. and Kolb, L. C. (1966). *Clinical Psychiatry.* 6th ed. Philadelphia: W. B. Saunders Company.

————— (1977). Modern Clinical Psychiatry. 9th ed. Philadelphia: W. B. Saunders Company.

Perris, C. (1968). Genetic transmission of depressive psychoses. *Acta Psychiatrica Scandinavica* (supp. 203), 196:45.

Petti, T. A. (1978). Depression in hospitalized child psychiatry patients: approaches to measuring depression. *Journal of the American Academy of Child Psychiatry* 17:49–59.

Petti, T. A. (1983). Imipramine in the treatment of depressed children. In *Affective Disorders in Childhood and Adolescence.* New York: Spectrum Publications.

Petti, T. A. and Davidman, L. (1981). Homicidal school-age children: cognitive style and demographic features. *Child Psychiatry and Human Development* 12:82–89.

Piaget, J. (1952). *The Origin of Intelligence in Children.* New York: International Universities Press.

Poznanski, E. and Zrull, J. P. (1970). Childhood depression: clinical characteristics of overtly depressed children. *Archives of General Psychiatry* 23:8–15.

Poznanski, E., Cook, S., and Carroll, B. J. (1979). A depression rating scale for children. *Pediatrics* 64:442–450.

Poznanski, E. O., Carroll, B. J., Banegas, M. D., et. al. (1982). The Dexamethasone Suppression Test in prepubertal depressed children. *American Journal of Psychiatry* 139:3 321–324.

Provence, S. (1980). Depression in infancy? Zero to three. *Bulletin of the National Center for Clinical Infant Programs* 3:1–4.

Puig-Antich, J., Blan, S., Marx, N., et. al. (1978). Prepubertal major depressive disorder: a pilot study. *Journal of the American Academy of Child Psychiatry* 17:695–707.

Puig-Antich, J., Chambers, W., Halpern, F., et. al. (1979). Cortisol hypersecretion in pre-pubertal depressive illness. *Psychoneuroendocrinology* 4:191–197.

Redlich, C., Freedman, D. X. (1966). *The Theory and Practice of Psychiatry.* Ed. Frederick C. Redlich and Daniel X. Freedman. New York, London: Basic Books.

Ribble, M. (1943). *The Rights of Infants — Early Psychological Needs and Their Satisfaction.* New York: Columbia University Press.

Rie, M. E. (1966). Depression in childhood: a survey of some pertinent contributions. *Journal of the American Academy of Child Psychiatry* 5:653-685.

Rochlin, G. (1959). The loss complex. *American Psychoanalytic Association* 7: 299-316.

———— (1965). *Griefs and Discontents*. Boston: Little, Brown.

Rosenthal, P. A. and Rosenthal, S. (1981). Conjoint treatment of parents and their pre-school children. *International Journal of Offender Therapy and Comparative Criminology* 25:81-90.

Rosenthal, P. A. and Doherty, M. B. (1983). Differentiating primary affective disorders from situational depression and behavioral problems in pre-school children by pre-school depression scale. Presentation American Academy of Child Psychiatry, San Francisco, California.

Rosenthal, P. A. and Rosenthal, S. (1984a). Suicidal behavior by preschool children. *American Journal of Psychiatry* 141:520-525.

Rosenthal, P. A., Rosenthal, S., Doherty, M. B., and Santora, D. (1984b). Suicidal preschool-age psychiatric inpatients. Presented at the Annual Meeting of American Psychiatric Association in Los Angeles, California.

Rutter, M. (1974). Emotional disorder and educational underachievement. *Archives of the Disturbed Child* 49:249-256.

Rutter, M., Tizard, J. and Whitmore, K. (1970). *Education, Health, and Behavior*. London: Langman.

Sachar, E. J., Hellman, L., Fukushima, D. K. and Gallagher, T. F. (1970). Cortisol production in depressive illness. *Archives of General Psychiatry* 23: 289-298.

Sachar, E. J., Roffwarg, H. P., Halpern, F. S., Fukushima, D. K., and Gallagher, T. F. (1973). Disrupted 24-hr. patterns of cortisol secretion in psychotic depression. *Archives of General Psychiatry* 28:19-24.

Sandler, J. and Joffe, W. G. (1965). Notes on childhood depression. *International Journal of Psycho-Analysis* 46:88-96.

Schackter, M. (1952). The cyclothymic states in the pre-pubescent child. *Nervous Child* 9:357-362.

Schulterbrandt, J. G. and Rathkin, A. (1977). *Depression in Childhood: Diagnosis, Treatment and Conceptual Models*. New York: Raven Press.

Seligman, M. (1975). *Helplessness: On Depression, Development, and Death*. San Francisco: W. H. Freeman and Co.

Seligman, M. and Maier, S. (1967). Failure to escape traumatic shock. *Journal of Experimental Psychology*. 74:1-9.

Spitz, R. (1946). Anaclitic depression. *Psychoanalytic Study of the Child* 2:113-117.

Toolan, J. M. (1962). Depression in children and adolescents. *American Journal of Orthopsychiatry* 32:404-415.

———— (1975). Suicide in children and adolescents. *American Journal of Psychotherapy* 29:339-344.

———— (1981). Depression and suicide in children: an overview. *American Journal of Psychotherapy* 35:311-323.

Tsuang, M. T. (1978). Genetic counseling for psychiatric patients and their families. *American Journal of Psychiatry* 135:1465-1475.

Weinberg, W. A., Rutman, J., Sullivan, L., et. al. (1973). Depression in children referred to an educational diagnostic center. *Journal of Pediatrics* 83:1065-1072.

Weller, E. B. and Weller, R. A. (1984). *Major Depressive Disorders in Children*.

Ed. E. B. Weller and R. A. Weller. Washington, D.C.: American Psychiatric Press, Inc.

Welner, L., Welner, A., McCray, M. D., et. al. (1977). Psychopathology in children of inpatients with depression: a controlled study. *Journal of Nervous Mental Disorders* 164:408–413.

White, J. H. and O'Shanick, G. (1979). Juvenile manic-depressive illness. *American Journal of Psychiatry* 134:1035–1036.

Woolston, J. L., Gianfredi, S., Gertner, J. M., et al. (1983). Salivary cortisol: a non-traumatic sampling technique for assaying cortisol dynamics. *Journal of the American Academy of Child Psychiatry* 22(5):474–476.

Yarrow, L. J. (1961). Maternal deprivation: toward an empirical and conceptual reevaluation. *Psychological Bulletin* 58:459.

CHAPTER SIX

Childhood

Andre P. Derdeyn, M.D.

In this chapter, mourning and depression are viewed as adaptive and as incomplete reactions to loss, respectively. While there is a growing consensus that children can indeed be depressed (See Chapter 7), the acceptance of the idea of a mourning process in children is not nearly as widespread. Theoretical issues relating to mourning and depression in children will be discussed and will be followed by a review of empirical research on two of the major causes of childhood depression, parental death and divorce. Clinical issues and examples will be drawn from cases involving parental divorce.

Causes of Childhood Depression

Childhood depression is influenced significantly by the parents: their absence by death, divorce, or other disruption of the family; their lack of interest due to depression or other cause of preoccupation; and their anger. In addition, children with chronic diseases and disabilities are particularly at risk for depression. Even in this group, however, family problems assume great importance. Authors studying children hospitalized for medical illnesses found a high incidence of parental death, desertion, and illness in the families of the depressed children (Kashani et al. 1981a). In the family situations of children who meet strict criteria for depression, there is a very high incidence of parental death, divorce, and depression, and of severely disturbed relationships between these children and their parents (Cytryn and McKnew 1979, Kashani et al. 1981a, Poznanski and Zrull 1970, Poznanski et al. 1976).

Features of Childhood Depression

Symptoms of depression. Dysphoric mood is the central depressive symptom observed in childhood. Negative self-image and self-deprecatory ideation is present in almost all cases (Poznanski and Zrull 1970). Sustained guilt is not a prominent feature of depression in childhood. It may be that, instead of consciously experiencing guilt, the child accepts and incorporates an unconscious judgment of guilt, manifested by feelings of devaluation and poor self-image. Other very common symptoms are decreases in school performance, socialization, and energy level. Children, like adults, also manifest sleep disturbance, somatic complaints, and changes in appetite or weight (Carlson and Cantwell 1979, Cytryn et al. 1980, Kashani et al. 1981b, Petti 1978, Poznanski et al. 1979).

Withdrawal states of early childhood. The withdrawal states of early childhood as described by Spitz (1946) and Engle (1962) would be excluded by some authors from the spectrum of depression. Only after some degree of separation–individuation has occurred and object constancy has been attained can there be a reaction to the loss of the actual person to whom the child has become attached, according to Sandler and Joffee (1965). They consider such an early reaction to be the loss of a state of well-being, constituting a "basic psychobiological reaction to deprivation." While ascribing adult dynamics to infants is surely not justified, investigative work which has established the existence of early reciprocal patterns of interaction between mothers and infants (Ainsworth 1969, Ainsworth et al. 1974, Brody et al. 1959, Escalona 1968, Spitz 1965) suggests that the caretaker is recognized and a loss of that specific person will be experienced.

Hopelessness. Although hopelessness is accepted as part of childhood depression, the child's feelings differ in quality from those of the adolescent and the adult. Children, however severely depressed, do not appear to be able to look to the future with a sense of dread equal to that of their elders. Rie (1966) points out that "an abiding, generalized expectation of failure to gain gratification for all time requires some grasp of what is meant by infinity," a grasp which is very limited before adolescence. A similar view of the child's sense of time is seen in Despert's comment that children tend to regard death as "a kind of deprivation which is unbearable, but seldom as is something definite and final" (Despert 1952). Sullivan (1953) observed that in adolescence "loneliness reaches its full significance . . . and goes on relatively unchanged from thenceforth throughout life," indicating the child's attainment of an adult's sense of time at adolescence. Perhaps the very low incidence of suicide in childhood reflects, in part, the fact that the child does not have a time sense which allows for a pervasive and enduring sense of hopelessness.

Depression and development. Depression in an adult can be destructive in terms of emotional relationships and work productivity or career. Depression in childhood can be quite disastrous due to the critical developmental nature of the years involved. In childhood, a significant depression from any cause can be considered to pose an important threat to the developmental process (Chethik and Kalter 1980). A review of the theoretical understanding of how children react to loss will show how the mourning process is attenuated and why depression so often results.

Mourning in Childhood

In *Mourning and Melancholia*, Freud (1917) described the work of mourning as an adaptive or reparative process occurring in response to the loss of a loved person. The task of mourning is accomplished by the recurrent remembering of the person and finally the painful acceptance of the permanent absence. Later, in *The Ego and the Id*, Freud (1923) added that an identification with the lost person is necessary in order to be complete.

In 1937, Helene Deutsch (1937) wrote a paper entitled "Absence of Grief," in which she related psychopathology in adulthood to the death of a parent in a person's childhood. She held that the unmastered loss in childhood resulted in either recurrent depression or suspension of all feelings. She hypothesized that the ego of the child is insufficient to carry out the work of mourning and instead resorts to mechanisms of self-protection to avoid the process. Furman (1964), while stating that he thought that mourning becomes possible around age 4, agreed that loss which is unmastered stays active in the personality. By means of the defenses utilized to avoid an awareness of loss, all aspects of dealing with feelings and of making lasting relationships are impaired.

Lindeman (1944) pointed out that in adults there is a considerable resistance to mourning the loss of an emotionally meaningful person and that the work of mourning in adults can be greatly facilitated by short-term psychotherapeutic work. Other writers (Loewald 1962, Moriarity 1967) share the impression that death of an emotionally important person tends to be incompletely accepted, resulting in subsequent failure to invest emotionally in new relationships.

Children tend to avoid the acceptance of the reality and the emotional meaning of the loss (Deutsch 1937, Fleming and Altschul 1963, Rochlin 1965, Wolfenstein 1966). This manner of dealing with such losses is analogous to pathological mourning in adults (Miller 1971). When the process of withdrawal of emotional investment in a lost person is avoided, the child can continue to expect the return of that person. Freud gave an example of this phenomenon when he described a 10-year-old boy's remark following the death of his father: "I know father's dead, but what I can't understand is why he doesn't come home for supper" (Freud 1900).

A frequent occurrence in patients described by Wolfenstein (1969) is idealization of the dead parent and hostility toward the surviving parent. Wolfenstein thought that this represented an attempt to undo previous hostile feelings towards the dead parent through displacement onto the survivor. Unconscious hostile wishes directed toward the dead person are thought to constitute a major obstruction to adaptive mourning (Anderson 1949). Children derive guilt from fantasizing that it was their own hostile feelings that caused the death of a parent; such guilt is an almost universal accompaniment of such losses (Rochlin 1965). Lifton (1967) reports an orphan of Hiroshima who said, "We did nothing bad — and still our parents died." This concept of the child's guilt and feeling of responsibility for parental death is quite analogous to feelings about parental divorce.

Mahler (1961) wrote that children's grief is remarkably shortened because mechanisms other than bereavement, such as substitution, denial, and depression, take over. Rochlin (1959, 1961, 1965) has stressed the severe effects of object loss in the realm of self-esteem. Bowlby (1960), on the other hand, feels that children can experience grief and the mourning process. Furman (1964), as stated previously, believes that the child does have the capacity for mourning beginning at around age 4. Nagera (1970) cites Pollack's (1961) conclusion that, for the adult, mourning is a problem of adaptation. In contrast, Nagera feels that, for the child, mourning for a parent constitutes an important developmental interference. The child is in the middle of a number of developmental processes that normally entail and require the presence and the participation of the parent.

Miller (1971) concluded after an extensive study of the literature that children, unlike adults, do not pass through mourning when the latter is defined, following Freud, as entailing the gradual and painful emotional detachment from the inner representation of the person who has died. Miller found wide agreement that children who experience death of a parent exhibit unconscious and sometimes conscious denial of the reality of the parent's death; screen out affective responses connected with the parent's death; increase their identification with and, particularly, their idealization of, the dead parent; experience a decrease in self-esteem; maintain persistent unconscious fantasies of an ongoing relationship or reunion with the dead parent; and suffer powerful feelings of guilt and of anger (Barnes 1964, Birtchnell 1969, Bonapart 1938, Cain et al. 1964, McDonald 1964, Nagera 1970).

Children's limited ability to mourn is thought to be related to the developmental vacuum that acceptance of the loss would entail (Nagera 1970, Wolfenstein 1969). Mahon and Simpson (1977) elaborate that the child's denial is great because the parent is so important to the child. They write that "because the child's dependency on the primary objects is so great, their loss generates affects which threaten to overwhelm the child, but similar, though attenuated, affects can be mastered and studied in the second-ary world of pets, toys, and imagination." That includes, of course, the world of play therapy.

Wolfenstein (1969) describes several cases of bereaved children suffer-ing from these long-term sequelae: persistent quest for the lost parent, rage rather than grief, repetition of disappointments, and a vindictive determi-nation to prove that no one can help. She describes the rage generated by perceived abandonment as being frequently diverted to others, such as the remaining parent and sometimes a therapist.

In wondering why identification with the departed parent is not more effective than it appears to be for these children, Wolfenstein (1969) the-orizes that

> probably the crucial factor here is the phase of development of object rela-tions which has been achieved at the time of the parent's death. To the ex-tent that the parent still serves predominantly as a need-gratifying object, the child feels helpless to assume the parent's role. The child, then, has the per-sistent demand to be taken care of. The image of the self and of the parent remains too disparate for identification to seem feasible. The relationship ap-pears not one of likeness, but a complementary one, of the needy child and the parent as the source of supplies. (p. 456)

Although there is controversy about the ability of children to undergo the mourning process, there is general consensus that the process is in-complete. If in death the child's capacity to mourn is impaired, it would seem to be even more so in divorce. In divorce, the absent parent is liv-ing, and the couple could conceivably come back together. The child's con-tinuing depression and yearning that the family come back together can significantly impede the adaptational process.

Depression in Childhood

The model of melancholia as developed by Abraham and Freud re-quires the presence of a mature superego to turn aggression against the self (Abraham 1924, Freud 1917) manifested by sustained guilt. Pervasive guilt is not thought to be a part of the symptoms presented by depressed chil-dren, and maturation of the superego is not thought to occur until adoles-cence, leading some authors to the opinion that a true depressive syndrome cannot occur in childhood (Beres 1952, Rie 1966, Rochlin 1959).

Depression in childhood is theoretically possible, however, if one ac-cepts the concept of self-esteem developed by Bibring (1953, p. 34–35): "Depression can be defined as the emotional expression . . . of a state of helplessness and powerlessness of the ego, irrespective of what may have caused the breakdown of the mechanisms which established self-esteem." He describes anxiety and depression as representing "diametrically opposed basic ego responses. Anxiety as a reaction to . . . danger indicates the ego's desire to survive. The ego, challenged by the danger . . . prepares for fight or flight. In depression, the opposite takes place. The ego is paralyzed because it finds itself incapable to meet the danger. In extreme situations, the wish to live is replaced by the wish to die."

Bemporad and Wilson (1978), agreeing with Bibring's view of depression as a primary affect, assert there "is no longer a question of whether adultlike depression can occur in childhood but rather how the cognitive and affective limitations at various stages of development modify the experience and expression of emotions in general." Wolfenstein (1969) noted that "reactions to a major loss throughout life precipitate us, at least for a time, back to a very infantile level." Mourning his friend Arthur Hallam in the poem *In Memoriam*, Tennyson (1850) expressed well this level at which loss is felt:

> . . . but what am I?
> An infant crying in the night,
> An infant crying for the light,
> And with no language but a cry.

We will now turn to empirical research on children's reactions to death and to divorce of parents.

Death of a parent. There is considerable literature suggesting a link between adult psychiatric illness, particularly depression, with bereavement in childhood. The writer was able to find, however, only one longitudinal study of normal children who were bereaved. Elizur and Kaffman (1982) followed 22 kibbutz children for 3 and one-half years after their fathers died in the Yom Kippur War of 1973. The percentage of children who were severely affected remained high during the total follow-up—almost half of the children in all phases of the study. In the early months after the loss, there was much crying with expressions of longing, denial, and remembrance of the lost father. Expressions of anger and protest were quite frequent immediately following the deaths. The phenomenon of searching for a substitute father persisted throughout all phases of the study.

One and one-half years after their fathers died, the children's level of anxiety increased significantly, visible in the appearance of various fears among more than half of the children studied. Usually, these were separation types of fears. The increase in the children's level of anxiety was ascribed by the authors to a greater realistic perception of the permanent loss. The most common behaviors were augmented dependency and demandingness, with clinging to the mother and overdependence on teachers. Also, increased aggressive behavior, discipline problems, and restlessness characterized more than a third of the children two to three years after their fathers were killed. Many of the children exhibited overanxious and dependent as well as unsocial-aggressive behavior patterns.

In the third and fourth years, manifestation of overdependence still typified about two-thirds of the sample, but there was a reduction in anxiety level and in separation difficulties. The augmented aggressiveness and concentration difficulties were also reduced.

During the four years of the study, there was a gradual rise in the presence of two other phenomena, general emotional restraint and "exemplary behavior." The authors felt that this pattern was not a rigid or neurotic one but was the child's way of coping with the new situation by accelerated maturation.

In spite of the general trend toward symptomatic improvement during the third and fourth years after their fathers were killed, more than one-third of the children continued to show signs of significant emotional impairment.

Unfortunately, information for this study was gathered from parents and teachers only; the children were not interviewed. How many of them would have been considered clinically depressed cannot be known. What is evident, however, is that children suffer intense grief reactions and continue to exhibit emotional and behavioral sequelae over long periods of time.

Death vs. divorce. A number of years ago, research emphasized father absence rather than more specific divorce-related issues. A number of studies (Anderson 1968, Douglas 1970) showed that coming from a broken home greatly increased the risk for antisocial behavior or delinquency in boys. It was divorce or separation, however, that was most closely associated. Only a slight increase in delinquency followed the death of the father, while divorce or separation resulted in almost double the rate of delinquency (Gregory 1965, Douglas et al. 1966, Gibson 1969).

Hetherington (1966) found disruptions in heterosexual relationships in the adolescent daughters of widows and divorcees who did not remarry. In the presence of males, the daughters of widows exhibited restraint and inhibition while the daughters of divorcees manifested attention-seeking and socially responsive behavior.

Divorce and behavior disorders. Rutter studied whether parental discord was associated with antisocial behavior in intact homes in order to determine whether the parental discord or the divorce itself was the central issue. He found that behavior problems in intact families were very much related to overt conflict between the parents (Rutter 1971, 1981). A number of other investigators have come to the conclusion, as did Rutter, that overt marital hostility correlates with conduct disorders, particularly in boys (Oltmans et al. 1977), Porter and O'Leary 1980). In a large sample of English children, it was shown that negative behavior of both boys and girls was related to marital discord although, again, the relationship appeared greater for boys (Whitehead 1979). Rutter (1981) showed further that the cessation of conflict was helpful to the children. Of the children who had experienced separation as a result of family discord, those whose homes became reasonably harmonious compared to those who were in still severely discordant homes had a significantly diminished rate of psychiatric or behavioral disorder.

Other investigators have contributed to this issue and have shown that delinquency tends to be more common in unhappy, unbroken homes than in harmonious but broken ones (Nye 1957, Jonsson 1967, McCord and McCord 1959). A 1983 paper (Ellison 1983) reporting on parental harmony and its relation to the psychosocial adjustment of school-age children strongly suggested that parental harmony has some predictive significance for the effect of marital disruption on children. Kalter (1977) and Schoettle and Cantwell (1980) have shown children of divorce to be frequent clinic visitors, most often on the basis of behavior problems.

Divorce and adaptation. In a recent article on 133 subjects from 87 middle- and upper-class families followed longitudinally since birth, Chess et al. (1983) found that a high degree of parental conflict when the child was 3 years old was correlated with poor adaptation as young adults when those children had reached the age of 18 to 22. The correlation with the degree of conflict was stronger than with the parents' actual divorce, if it occurred.

On the five-year follow-up of children, Wallerstein and Kelly (1980) found in their study that approximately one-third of the children and adolescents were doing very well and one-third were moderately to severely depressed (often associated with antisocial behavior and intense anger). The remaining third were proceeding satisfactorily through school and appeared to have appropriate social behavior but showed "significant residues of their continuing anger and their persistent emotional neediness, unhappiness, and somewhat diminished self-esteem."

Implications of the Research

The Elizur and Kaffman (1982) and Wallerstein and Kelly (1980) studies document the immense disruption and, for many children, continuing dysfunction following death or divorce of parents. The large epidemiologic studies, however, seem to find only antisocial and other behavioral difficulties in response to divorce and report essentially no findings in response to death of a parent. Similarly, Schoettle and Cantwell (1980) and Kalter (1977) found children of divorce to be over-represented in child treatment clinics, primarily due to behavior problems. The Chess et al. (1983) study correlates impaired functioning in young adults with marital conflict in early childhood. Probably, larger studies can deal only with gross, overt symptoms, such as antisocial or other disruptive behavior, while small studies establish contact with parents, teachers, and, ideally, children and address the less obvious, but just as destructive, phenomena ranging from diminished self-esteem to depression.

The research cited suggests some interesting possibilities. It documents a reaction in children of difficult, disturbing, and even antisocial behavior. Death, on the other hand, as exhibited by the children in the Elizur and Kaffman (1982) study and the adolescent girls of Hetherington's study, may be followed by increased inhibition and restraint (Hetherington 1972).

Perhaps a significant difference between the reactions of children to death and divorce appears in the children's management of anger. In the case of divorce, overt, angry behavior seems to be quite common and is often one of the presenting symptoms. In the case of death, however, children tend not to be overtly angry or disruptive but tend, instead, to engage more in quietly self-defeating behavior.

In the case of death, the dead parent tends to be idealized, and there may be a degree of realization that the abandonment was not intended. Perhaps because of these reasons, guilt predominates over anger, and the anger remains far from consciousness. Generally, a successful therapy will bring forth the anger. Otherwise, the anger may augment superego functions and serve as an impetus to behave better so that such an event does not occur again, or, possibly, the better behavior is hoped to bring the lost parent back.

In the case of divorce, the situation from a realistic point of view was not inevitable and not even necessarily permanent. Perhaps the child's anger at the absent parent or even the custodial parent is more available because these people continue to live and could conceivably act differently or be made to act differently.

Depression and Divorce: Clinical Issues

The remainder of this chapter will be concerned with the management of clinical problems related to divorce. This will include discussions of brief interventions to facilitate mourning, treatment of an older child involved in a loyalty conflict, treatment of an adolescent girl whose rage at a departed father brought her life and development to a standstill, and interventions where parental depression and anger are instrumental in a child's depression.

Brief Intervention with the Child to Facilitate Mourning

The severity of a child's depression may require relatively long-term therapy. In many cases, however, the focus of work may diminish some of the impediments to working through loss so that the mourning process and adaptation to the new life situation are enhanced. The major impediment to working through loss will be the child's feeling of guilt, stemming from distorted ideas regarding the cause of the marital failure.

Working through loss. Younger children tend to work through loss by means of play, drawings, and metaphor. They return repeatedly to memories of the past and make comparisons with the present, grieving over the loss of such objects of the past as homes, automobiles, bedrooms, toys. Speaking directly about a significant loss of the noncustodial parent is fraught with anxiety for many young children.

Children who cannot speak directly of their feelings may be able to express themselves very well in other ways. One 7-year-old boy referred for aggressive behavior first drew a picture of his parents in the front seat of their car driving in the rain. This was followed by a drawing of their old house, also in the rain. In talking about these drawings, he was able to express and acknowledge affects that had been steadfastly avoided previously.

The adolescent will often speak directly about the absent parent and complain openly about the new conditions of life. Work with children of this age is not very different from similar work with adults. Bowlby and Parkes (1970) have characterized the role of the therapist in the working through process as one of "companion and supporter." They point out that it is unnecessary and unhelpful for the therapist to cast himself in the role of representative of reality, "unnecessary because the patient is, in some part of himself, well aware that the world has changed; unhelpful because by disregarding the world as one part of him still sees it, we alienate ourselves from him."

Instead, they say, the therapist's role "should be that of companion and supporter, prepared to explore in our discussions all the hopes and wishes and dim unlikely possibilities that he still cherishes, together with all the regrets and the reproaches and the disappointment that afflict him."

Reducing the impediments to mourning. In some instances, the child's resistance to working through loss may be sufficiently weakened in brief therapy so that adequate mourning and adaptation can resume. The following case histories are examples of this type of work.

Seven-year-old Jane was brought to the therapist because of her problems with poor sleep immediately after her father left the home. With little hesitation, Jane attributed her wakefulness at night to her habit of anxiously listening for the sound of her mother packing her bags and slipping out of the house under cover of darkness.

In the second play session with the therapist, Jane started loading the Playskool children into the cement mixer to be punished for the rest of their lives. They were being punished, she said, because they had been mean. The therapist mentioned that sometimes when bad things happen to people they think they have done something bad to deserve it, and he wondered if Jane, like a lot of other children in her situation, had some idea that her parents divorced because of her. She became tearful and said that she did think that but could not figure out what she had done. The therapist said that he knew enough about her parents' troubles to know that they separated because of themselves and not because of anything important that Jane had done. Jane talked more about this in the session, alternating between saying that she knew she did not do anything wrong and that she knew she did. Jane was seen for two subsequent sessions, with marked reduction in nightmares and fears of abandonment and a return to her interest and participation in peer activities.

Tom was 13 years old, depressed, and uncommunicative. He was referred because of his refusal to go to school and to obey his mother immediately following parental separation. For at least six years, he had been at the center of his parents' conflict.

The scenario, described by both parents, had gone as follows: Tom would frequently return home from school and fail to do his assigned chores; his father would become very angry with him for not attending to duty and would often strike him. Mother would then take issue with the father for being too hard on the boy.

In the fourth hour of contact, the therapist mentioned that he had seen boys Tom's age who sometimes felt that they were responsible for what happened to their parents' marriage. Tom blurted out that he knew he was the cause of the divorce because he used to come home and watch TV instead of doing his chores. He was at first incredulous that the therapist could be suggesting that he might only be feeling that way instead of its being the incontrovertible fact that he knew it to be, but he was willing to consider it as a possibility.

Tom returned to school and became very close to a boy in his class who had recently also sustained a divorce of his parents. Tom soon announced he would rather talk to his friend than to the therapist, and therapy was terminated.

Brief Intervention with Parents

Assuming that the parent is able to cope reasonably well, the therapist can help the parent aid the child with the mourning process. To do this, it will be helpful for the parents to learn about some of the indirect modes of expression that children sometimes use.

Children tend to externalize feelings of loss and anxiety (Solnit 1974). When a child is anxious and fearful that the gratification of dependency needs may not occur, the child is likely to express such feelings in concrete terms in the form of concern about food, clothes, or whether it will be possible to go to college. The parent may need help in not reacting negatively to such apparently mercenary concerns but should be counseled that this is a normal mode of expression for a child in this situation.

Most important of all, the child's externalized and displaced feelings of loss give the parent the opportunity to help the child progress further in resolving and integrating the loss. After a divorce-related move to the home of the maternal grandparents, for example, a boy may complain about his new school. His mother could express interest in what her son brings up but then go on to add that a lot of other things have changed and are difficult because of the separation and divorce. She can then share with him some of the difficulties that she is having as well.

In such a situation the boy may then be able to express further some of his feelings of sadness and anger and his wish that the family could be reunited, thus achieving considerable relief.

Work with a Child in a Loyalty Conflict

Joe was a 12-year-old boy referred initially by his pediatrician for depression. His parents' divorce had occurred two years prior to referral. Mrs. M. described her husband as being increasingly hostile to her but opposed to the divorce which she had initiated. There were many difficulties regarding late support checks and other issues, in spite of the father's high professional earnings and competence.

Upon returning from the summer visit with his father, Joe had been quite hostile to his mother and extremely unhappy. He and mother arranged for him to move his bed into her bedroom because of his complaints that his little brother snored, and because both he and his mother stayed up at night late to study. He related his feelings of anxiety, sadness, and hopelessness to his worries about maintaining good relationships with both his parents and to his preoccupation with what he considered the necessity of having to choose between his parents at a future hearing on custody. The therapist encouraged mother to stop talking with Joe about trial strategy and suggested that they terminate the shared bedroom arrangement on the grounds that she needed more privacy. These changes were followed by an immediate improvement in symptoms.

Joe described his feelings of helplessness and rage when his mother complained of late support payments and expressed anger at his father for mistreating his mother. Joe saw his father, however, as a powerful being whose favor he dared not curry and whose displeasure could bring deprivation of material things. He said that at his father's home he had many fine things, but from the way he was living now, no one would believe him. Joe was worried, among other things, that his father would not fund his education. We identified that he was concerned not only with whom he lived, but also about his father's anger toward him. Joe feared that his father might withhold not only money but also the approval which might help Joe some day feel like a grown-up man.

Joe had resumed his high level of school achievement but continued to be preoccupied with a particular academic rival at school. Just prior to the summer visit with his father, his fears of his father heightened, and he shared a fantasy of saving his little sister from being physically attacked by his father. Prior to visiting his father after seven months of psychotherapy, Joe had a dream of being in a boat fishing on a big lake and he could not get the motor to work when a storm blew up. In a second dream there was a big man attacking him and Joe threw a grenade at him. With the help of the dreams, we were able to establish further that Joe's anger toward his father was making it seem as though father was angry and dangerous to him and that these ideas were related more to Joe's feelings than to reality. While there was no doubt of his parents' anger toward each other, Joe was encouraged to see that their fight was not necessarily his fight.

After enjoying the time with his father that summer, Joe chose to remain with him. Although Joe was a bright and mature adolescent, he needed considerable help in detaching himself emotionally from both parents in the service of maintaining the integrity of his development.

Wallerstein and Kelly (1974) have found a degree of detachment from both parents to be correlated with adolescents' success in coping with their parents' conflicts with each other. The central issue in therapy for many children like Joe is enhancing the developmental process so that they might extricate themselves from the parental conflict.

A Child's Anger as a Central Issue

This case concerns Charity, a 15-year-old girl. Her father had become emotionally involved with a co-worker and had moved out of the family home approximately a year before Charity came to therapy. Three months after that, her brother went off for his first year of boarding school. Charity was seen in April; she had been to school only a few days since the prior September. Extensive history taking with Charity and with both her parents revealed no antecedent history of school phobia, separation anxiety, or any other persistent psychological problems earlier in life. Charity had always been a good student.

Mother was concerned about the school refusal and obvious depression, but also about Charity's occasional violent behavior. There had been some damage to the house and furniture, and mother feared Charity's physical aggression against her. Mother stated, and Charity confirmed, that Charity had been father's favorite, favored over both mother and brother.

Charity talked about everyone — her father and her brother — leaving her and wondered if something were wrong with her. She told about repeatedly telephoning her father; when she started to express any anger at him, he became much more difficult to locate, with his office phone ringing as if it were busy, and there was no answer at his apartment, presumably because he was with his new friend.

Charity talked about looking at old family movies, which indicated clearly her father's interest and concern for her because she appeared in the movies much more frequently than her brother. Part of her current anger was related to the fact that her father was seeing her brother much more often than he was seeing her.

She was soon able to talk about her fury at her father, wishing him dead, wanting to shoot, strangle, or beat him and his girlfriend to death. She said, in fact, the reason she agreed to go to a psychiatrist was to be rid of her intense anger at her father. Charity feared that her anger would send her father further away. She also readily acknowledged the wish that it would be instrumental in bringing him back.

After several weeks' work with Charity, the therapist obtained her permission to see her father. The major goal of seeing him was to help him to acknowledge and tolerate Charity's anger rather than withdrawing from it and from her.

Charity did not return to school that spring, in part because of embarrassment about starting so late in the year. She did obtain a job with a lot of exposure to the public, she was maintaining contact with her father, and she chose to stop seeing the therapist. Later that summer, her father and his friend moved to a new home on the West Coast.

After two successful months of school the next fall, Charity began again to miss school. Although she usually complained of severe stomach pain which made it impossible for her to go to school, she occasionally mentioned to her mother intense fears that her mother would leave her also. Most of the time, Charity, however, was feeling stomach pain and no anxiety. In addition, she felt intense anger at her mother but no great anger at her father. Upon resuming therapy, Charity began to experience very angry feelings towards her therapist. She said she would return to school when her stomach stopped hurting, and she protested that she didn't have anything to talk about to the therapist. She did, however, experience some surprise and curiosity regarding the intensity of her anger at the therapist. We got around to the idea of her needing to work out her relationship with the therapist as she was so afraid of her anger destroying or sending away the other people in her life. That December she began to consider returning to school in January, and she talked at length about her regrets for messing up in school these last two years. She clearly grasped being so powerfully driven by feelings of rage, humiliation, and betrayal because of being abandoned by her father, which was also complicated by the departure of her good friend, her brother. The following month, Charity successfully returned to school, and upon follow-up 18 months later, was continuing to do well.

Charity illustrates the debilitating intensity which anger can reach in reaction to loss. She displayed a great similarity to Wolfenstein's patients who suffered the death of a parent. Wolfenstein wrote that the child demonstrates rage rather than grief and unconsciously demonstrates "what becomes of a fatherless girl [in order] to coerce her father's return." Wolfenstein describes in her patient "the inability to renounce the lost object, the persisting demand to be taken care of, the vindictive rage against the world at large, and the effort to force the lost parent to return by her sufferings." Eventually, the strength of her reaction diminished, and Charity was able to get back to her adolescent tasks.

Parental Affects and the Child

Separation and divorce often profoundly affect children by way of parental depression and anger.

Parental depression. Anna Freud (1965) described infants' achieving a "sense of unity and harmony with the depressed mother not by means of their developmental achievements but by producing the mother's mood in themselves." Malmquist (1971) points out that "a pessimistic mood tone in the parents induces a feeling of failure in the child. It is a combination of feeling that he is somehow responsible for the predicaments of the parent and that he can never please them." He also suggests that children who cannot please their parents perceive an implied threat of abandonment (Malmquist 1977). In addition, as discussed previously, children see themselves much as a reflection of their parents' view of them. Children whose parents are depressed fail to obtain reinforcement for their attachment initiatives and for their achievements (Philips 1979). Attachment becomes an anxious one and the child's explorations are diminished, often related to a constriction of the sphere of the ego that is free of conflict. Such children are likely to see themselves as failing or disappointing their parent and tend to develop a depreciated self-concept.

Szasz (1971) points out that in close human relationships in general

the suffering and unhappiness of one member assumes a signal-function for his partner. This means that his suffering will signify not only that he is hurt or sick, but also that his partner is bad, for he has failed to gratify his needs! Thus arises the more general idea that in all sorts of human relations one's partner's unhappiness or discomfort signifies the badness of the self. Once this step has been taken, its corollary follows, namely that one's self-esteem may be maintained or augmented by means of making one's partner happy.

Adults have significant limitations in discriminating the "ownership" of problems; children, with their immature cognitive abilities and limited experience, are at great risk for assuming that they are somehow the cause of their parents' difficulties.

It is difficult to separate the effects of parental depression from parental anger. In Poznanski and Zrull's (1970) report on a series of depressed children, they called attention to the depression of the children's parents but also noted a high degree of marital discord and of parents treating these children in an angry, punitive, or belittling manner. When some of these children were studied six and one-half years later, a continuation of the depression was highly correlated with continuing parental deprivation and rejection (Poznanski et al. 1976).

Parental anger.   Parental anger probably exerts the most powerful effect of any parental affect. Parental anger may arise in a great variety of situations, may be quite subtle, and is frequently associated with parental depression.

Anger need not be directed primarily at the child in order to have its corrosive effect upon the child's sense of security and self-esteem. Children detect the anger all too easily and apply it to themselves. In addition, in many instances the targeting of an adult's anger may not be very precise if indeed the adult does not actually identify the child with the person for whom the anger is intended (Derdeyn 1980, McDermott 1970, Wallerstein and Kelly 1980, Wylie and Delgado 1959).

A markedly depressed 8-year-old boy had been embroiled for the past three years in the postdivorce struggles of his parents. He said that probably the worst thing was when his mother would angrily announce his father's child support payment was late, which made him feel both angry at his father and also helpless and worthless. On being asked three wishes, he responded he would like to go back in time to make his parents' marriage better. He had no other wishes.

Parental problems of many types — illness, alcoholism, and serious marital conflict — can have similar effects in binding the child to one or both parents in an anxious type of attachment, and in diminishing self-esteem and academic and other achievements in the child's world. One of the basic problems is a lack of buffering or protection so that the child's world comes to include too much of the adult's problems.

Scapegoating is a common manifestation of parental anger and is often a cause of depression (Cytryn and McKnew 1979, Poznanski and Zrull 1970). Parental dynamics include the projection onto the child of undesirable aspects of the self or of aspects of persons from the past, and there is usually a displacement of current marital conflict to the child in the service of maintaining marital homeostasis (Vogel and Bell 1960). The following case is an example of scapegoating leading to serious depression in a child.

Sam, 10 years old, was brought for consultation because he was failing in school (often tearing up completed homework), was withdrawing to his room, and was fearful of his parents' leaving him alone at night. When upset, he would often threaten to kill himself, which prompted his parents to make the consultation. Marital conflict was the inescapable main topic of the first interview with the parents. After several years of marginal performance at his work, the father was going to lose his job. Much of the mother's anger at the father and the father's anger at himself and his wife was focused upon this poorly achieving son, whose conception had precipitated the marriage 10 years earlier. Upon being asked for three wishes, Sam said he just wanted billions and billions of dollars. Some he would burn, some he would let rot, and the rest he would use to purchase all the stores in town. He would double the prices on goods and cut in half the employee's salaries so that all the stores would go out of business.

Intervention with the child.   Direct work with a child may be indicated in those instances where a major loss has occurred, such as death or divorce of parents, or where accident or chronic illness has interfered with sources of satisfaction or self-esteem. In cases involving loss "the interpretation of the defenses against sad feelings, and sense of loss and helplessness will gradually enable the child to re-experience his depressive reactions and work them through" (Solnit 1974). Individual therapy may also be indicated where the child has internalized a poor self-image or a distorted role assignment within the family.

As with adults, depressed children tend to make a good response to the initiation of therapy, as does the family as a whole. One of the immediate benefits of the therapeutic setting is that children cannot fail and do not have to earn acceptance (Malmquist 1976). It is helpful for the therapist to provide situations where the child may be successful, as well as for the therapist to take an interest in the child's achievements in the outside world. Some investigators have been impressed with marked improvement of the depressed child upon hospitalization. While one would be concerned about a negative response due to separation from the family, the removal of the child from noxious family influences plus mobilization of family strengths engendered by the hospitalization appeared to produce a beneficial and often sustained effect in many cases (Cytryn and McKnew 1979, Philips 1979).

Intervention with parents.   In situations where a child's parent suffers from a depressive illness, it is imperative to engage that parent in the appropriate psychiatric treatment. Where excessive parental anger toward and rejection of the child is part of a postdivorce picture, individual therapy of the parent may be in order.

It is accepted theory that once adolescence is traversed, mourning becomes an available mechanism for decathecting a lost love object (A. Freud 1958, Jacobson 1964, Wolfenstein 1966). It is apparent, however, that many adults cannot avail themselves of that device after their marital separations. The postdivorce struggles of adults with which therapists are now so familiar revolve about narcissistic injury and maneuvers to punish or retrieve the lost love object, the former spouse. The hostile feelings for the former spouse are also commonly transferred to a child, often one of the same sex as the lost spouse. Therapeutic work with adults to help them work through the losses of divorce and prior important losses can greatly facilitate their freeing their children from the effects of their anger and perhaps of their depression as well.

For younger children and in those for whom a distorted role assignment is the issue, work with parents becomes an important if not sometimes the exclusive focus of therapeutic work. In scapegoating and other manifestations of excessive parental anger, the therapeutic approach might be family or marital therapy with the focus of unravelling the projections and at least assigning ownership of problems, if not making some progress toward resolving them. In the case example of Sam, the boy who would have used his billion dollars to destroy the local economy, a combination of individual therapy for him and marital therapy for his parents was used. Additionally, occasional family meetings were held as well. In the nine months of work with this family, Sam was much improved, father was able to diligently seek new work, and mother made a firm decision to enter graduate school. In this case, as in many others, the family meetings offered an immediate opportunity for the therapist to model understanding of and an empathic response to the depressed child. In family sessions or in other work, the therapist can also communicate a liking for and an appreciation of the child.

The ultimate goal in intervention in childhood depression is to help children to accept and like themselves. In order to effect this, it is usually necessary to help the parent or parents do exactly the same thing, to appreciate and to like their children. The work with parents may focus upon the issues causing their own depressions, or those distortions that interfere with seeing and accepting their children for what they are. Although the goal sounds a bit mundane, achieving it often requires an extended and complex therapeutic process to help parents see their children as persons rather than as extensions or projections of themselves or of other persons.

Conclusion

Loss in childhood results frequently in significant depression because of the incomplete nature of the mourning process in children. Various types of interventions related to problems raised by the losses in divorce have been discussed. Therapy helps by facilitating the mourning process. In the case of Joe, the boy in the loyalty conflict, therapy facilitated the adolescent process of "object removal" (Katan 1937). The adaptational task is to turn grief into mourning for the past so that the view of self and world can look realistically forward to the future (Marris 1974). There is little distinction between grief work or mourning and psychotherapy (Stewart 1963) since both entail the reviewing of redundant assumptions and the restructuring of the assumptive world (Parkes 1971).

Psychiatric clinicians may not be as aware of the possibility of depression in children as they are of other childhood conditions. Children's affective state and their developmental progress are very sensitive to the familial emotional environment. Marital discord, family psychopathology, and major losses are all importantly implicated in childhood depression. It behooves all psychiatrists to be attuned to the types of situations where childhood depression may be expected to develop and to be ready with strategies of intervention.

REFERENCES

Abraham, K. (1924). A short study of the development of the libido, viewed in the light of mental disorders. In *Selected Papers on Psycho-Analysis*, pp. 418–501. New York: Basic Books.

Ainsworth, M. D. S. (1969). Object relations, dependency and attachment: a theoretical review of the infant-mother relationship. *Child Development* 40:969–
1027.

Ainsworth, M. D. S., Bell, S. M., and Stayton, D. J. (1974). Infant–mother attachment and social development: 'socialization' as a product of reciprocal
responsiveness to signals. In *The Integration of a Child into a Social World*,
ed. M. P. M. Richards, pp. 99–135. Cambridge: Cambridge University Press.

Anderson, C. (1949). Aspects of pathological grief and mourning. *International
Journal of Psycho-Analysis* 30:48–55.

Anderson, R. E. (1968). Where's dad? Parental deprivation and delinquency. *Archives of General Psychiatry* 18:641–649.

Barnes, M. J. (1964). Reactions to the death of a mother. *Psychoanalytic Study
of the Child* 19:334–357.

Bemporad, J. R. and Wilson, A. (1978). A developmental approach to depression
in childhood and adolescence. *Journal of the American Academy of Psycho-
analysis* 6:325–352.

Beres, D. (1952). Clinical notes on aggression in children. *Psychoanalytic Study
of the Child* 7:241–263.

Bibring, E. (1953). The mechanism of depression. In *Affective Disorders*, ed. P.
Greenacre, pp. 13–48. New York: International Universities Press, Inc.

Birtchnell, J. (1969). The possible consequences of early parent death. *British Journal of Medical Psychology* 42:1–12.

Bonaparte, M. (1938). L'identification d'une fille a sa mere morte. *Revue Psycho-
analysis* 2:541–565.

Bowlby, J. (1960). Grief and mourning in infancy and early childhood. *Psychoanalytic Study of the Child* 15:9–52.

Bowlby, J. and Parkes, C. M. (1970). Separation and loss within the family. In
The Child in His Family, ed. E. J. Anthony and C. Koupernik, p. 208. New
York: John Wiley & Sons.

Brody, S., Axelrad, S., and Moroh, M. (1959). Early phases in the development
of object relations. *International Review of Psycho-Analysis* 3:1–31.

Cain, A. C., Fast, I., and Erikson, M. E. (1964). Children's disturbed reactions
to the death of a sibling. *American Journal of Orthopsychiatry* 34:741–752.

Carlson, G. A. and Cantwell, D. P. (1979). A survey of depressive symptoms in
a child and adolescent psychiatric population: interview data. *Journal of the
American Academy of Child Psychiatry* 18:587–599.

Chess, S., Thomas, A., Korn, S., et al. (1983). Early parental attitudes, divorce
and separation, and young adult outcome: findings of a longitudinal study.
Journal of the American Academy of Child Psychiatry 22:47–51.

Chethik, M. and Kalter, N. (1980). Developmental arrest following divorce: the
role of therapist as a developmental facilitator. *Journal of the American Academy of Child Psychiatry* 19:281–288.

Cytryn, L. and McKnew, D. H. (1979). Affective disorders. In *Basic Handbook
of Child Psychiatry*, Vol. 2, *Disturbances of Development*, ed. J. D. Noshpitz,
pp. 321–340. New York: Basic Books.

Cytryn, L., McKnew, D. H., and Bunney, W. E. (1980). Diagnosis of depression
in children: a reassessment. *American Journal of Psychiatry* 137:22–25.

Derdeyn, A. P. (1980). Divorce and children: clinical interventions. *Psychiatric
Annals* 10:145–159.

Despert, L. L. (1952). Suicide and depression in children. *Nervous Child* 9:378–
389.

Deutsch, H. (1937). The absence of grief. In *Neuroses and Character Types*, pp. 225–236. New York: International Universities Press, 1965.

Douglas, J. W. B., Ross, J. M., Hammond, W. A., and Mulligan, D. G. (1966). Delinquency and social class. *British Journal of Criminology* 6:294–302.

Douglas, J. W. B. (1970). Broken families and child behaviors. *Journal of the Royal College of Physicians of London* 4:203–210.

Elizur, E. and Kaffman, M. (1982). Children's bereavement reactions following death of the father: II. *Journal of the American Academy of Child Psychiatry* 21:474–480.

Ellison, E. S. (1983). Issues concerning parental harmony and children's psychosocial adjustment. *American Journal of Orthopsychiatry* 53:73–80.

Engle, G. L. (1962). Anxiety and depression withdrawal: the primary affects of unpleasure. *International Journal of Psycho-Analysis* 43:89–97.

Escalona, S. K. (1968). *The Roots of Individuality*. Chicago: Aldine.

Fleming, J. and Altschul, S. (1963). Activation of mourning and growth by psychoanalysis. *International Journal of Psycho-Analysis* 44:419–432.

Freud, A. (1958). Adolescence. *Psychoanalytic Study of the Child* 13:255–278.

———— (1965). *Normality and Pathology in Childhood*. New York: International Universities Press.

Freud, S. (1900). The interpretation of dreams. *Standard Edition* 4/5. London: Hogarth Press, 1953.

———— (1917). Mourning and melancholia. *Standard Edition* 14:243–260. London: Hogarth Press, 1957.

———— (1923). The ego and the id. *Standard Edition* 19. London: Hogarth Press, 1961.

Furman, R. (1964). Death and the young child: some preliminary considerations. *Psychoanalytic Study of the Child* 19:321–333.

Gibson, H. B. (1969). Early delinquency in relation to broken homes. *Journal of Child Psychology and Psychiatry* 10:195–204.

Gregory, I. (1965). Anterospective data following childhood loss of a parent. *Archives of General Psychiatry* 13:110–120.

Hetherington, E. M. (1966). Effects of paternal absence on sex-typed behaviors in Negro and white pre-adolescent males. *Journal of Personality and Social Psychology* 4:87–91.

———— (1972). Effects of father absence on personality development in adolescent daughters. *Developmental Psychology* 7:313–325.

Jacobson, E. (1964). *The Self and the Object World*. New York: International Universities Press.

Jonsson, G. (1967). Delinquent boys, their parents and grandparents. *Acta Psychiatrica Scandinavica* 43, Suppl. 195.

Kalter, N. (1977). Children of divorce in an outpatient psychiatric population. *American Journal of Orthopsychiatry* 47:40–51.

Katan, A. (1937). The role of displacement in agoraphobia. *International Journal of Psycho-Analysis* 32:41–50.

Kashani, J. H., Barbero, G. J., and Bolander, F. D. (1981a). Depression in hospitalized pediatric patients. *Journal of the American Academy of Child Psychiatry* 20:123–134.

Kashani, J. H., Husain, A., Shekim, W. O., et al. (1981b). Current perspectives on childhood depression: an overview. *American Journal of Psychiatry* 138:143–153.

Lifton, R. J. (1967). *Death in Life: Survivors of Hiroshima*. New York: Random House.

Lindemann, E. (1944). Symptomatology and management of acute grief. In *Death and Identity*, ed. R. Fulton, pp. 186–201. New York: Wiley, 1965.

Loewald, H. W. (1962). Internalization, separation, mourning, and the superego. *Psychoanalytic Quarterly* 31:483–504.

Mahler, M. S. (1961). Sadness and grief in infancy and childhood. *Psychoanalytic Study of the Child* 16:332–351.

Mahon, E. and Simpson, M. A. (1977). The painted guinea pig. *Psychoanalytic Study of the Child* 32:283–303.

Malmquist, C. P. (1971). Depressions in childhood and adolescence. *New England Journal of Medicine* 284:887–893.

———— (1976). The theoretical status of depression in childhood. In *Three Clinical Faces of Childhood*, ed. E. J. Anthony and D. G. Gilpin, pp. 173–204. New York: Spectrum Publications, Inc.

———— (1977). Notes on the psychodynamic treatment of childhood depression. In *Depression: Clinical, Biological and Psychological Perspectives*, ed. G. Usdin, pp. 295–307. New York: Brunner/Mazel.

Marris, P. (1974). *Loss and Change*. London: Routledge and Kegan Paul.

McCord, W. and McCord, J. (1959). *Origins of Crime: A New Evaluation of the Cambridge-Somerville Youth Study*. New York: Columbia University Press.

McDermott, J. F. (1970). Divorce and its psychiatric sequelae in children. *Archives of General Psychiatry* 23:421–427.

McDonald, M. (1964). A study of the reactions of nursery school children to the death of a child's mother. *Psychoanalytic Study of the Child* 19:358–376.

Miller, J. B. M. (1971). Children's reactions to the death of a parent: a review of the psychoanalytic literature. *Journal of the American Psychoanalytic Association* 19:697–719.

Moriarity, D. M. (1967). *The Loss of Loved Ones: The Effects of Death in the Family on Personality Development*. Springfield, Ill.: Charles C. Thomas.

Nagara, H. (1970). Children's reactions to the death of important objects: a developmental approach. *Psychoanalytic Study of the Child* 25:360–400.

Nye, F. I. (1957). Child adjustment in broken and in unhappy unbroken homes. *Marriage and Family Living* 19:356–361.

Oltmanns, T. F., Broderick, J. E., and O'Leary, K. D. (1977). Marital adjustment and the efficacy of behavior therapy with children. *Journal of Consulting and Clinical Psychology* 45:724–729.

Parkes, D. M. (1971). Psycho-social transitions: a field for study. *Social Science and Medicine* 5:101–115.

Petti, T. A. (1978). Depression in hospitalized child psychiatry patients: approaches to measuring depression. *Journal of the American Academy of Child Psychiatry* 17:49–59.

Philips, I. (1979). Childhood depression: interpersonal interactions and depressive phenomena. *American Journal of Psychiatry* 136:511–515.

Pollock, G. H. (1961). Mourning and adaptation. *International Journal of Psycho-Analysis* 42:341–361.

Porter, B. and O'Leary, K. D. (1980). Marital discord and childhood behavior problems. *Journal of Abnormal Child Psychology* 8:287–295.

Poznanski, E. and Zrull, J. P. (1970). Childhood depression: clinical characteristics of overtly depressed children. *Archives of General Psychiatry* 24:8–15.

Poznanski, E., Krahenbuhl, V., and Zrull, J. P. (1976). Childhood depression: a longitudinal perspective. *Journal of the American Academy of Child Psychiatry* 15:491–501.

Poznanski, E., Cook, S. C., and Carroll, B. J. (1979). A depression rating scale for children. *Pediatrics* 64:442–450.

Rie, H. E. (1966). Depression in childhood. *Journal of the American Academy of Child Psychiatry* 5:653–685.

Rochlin, G. (1959). The loss complex. *Journal of the American Psychoanalytic Association* 7:299–316.

_____ (1961). The dread of abandonment: a contribution to the etiology of the loss complex and to depression. *Psychoanalytic Study of the Child* 16:451–470.

_____ (1965). *Griefs and Discontents*. Boston: Little, Brown.

Rutter, M. (1971). Parent–child separation: psychological effects on the children. *Journal of Child Psychology and Psychiatry* 12:233–260.

_____ (1981). Epidemiological/longitudinal strategies and causal research in child psychiatry. *Journal of the American Academy of Child Psychiatry* 20:513–544.

Sandler, J. and Joffee, W. G. (1965). Notes on childhood depression. *International Journal of Psycho-Analysis* 46:88–96.

Schoettle, U. C. and Cantwell, D. P. (1980). Children of divorce: demographic variables, symptoms, and diagnoses. *Journal of the American Academy of Child Psychiatry* 19:453–475.

Solnit, A. J. (1974). Depression and mourning. In *American Handbook of Psychiatry*, Vol. 2, *Child and Adolescent Psychiatry, Sociocultural and Community Psychiatry*, ed. S. Arieti, 2nd ed., pp. 107–115, New York: Basic Books.

Spitz, R. (1946). Anaclitic depression. *Psychoanalytic Study of the Child* 2:113–117.

_____ (1965). *The First Year of Life*. New York: International Universities Press.

Stewart, W. (1963). An inquiry into the concept of working through. *Journal of the American Psychoanalytic Association* 11:474–499.

Sullivan, H. H. (1953). *The Interpersonal Theory of Psychiatry*. New York: W. W. Norton and Company, 1953.

Szasz, T. S. (1971). The communication of distress between child and parent. In *Theory and Practice of Family Psychiatry*, ed. J. G. Howells. New York: Brunner/Mazel, 1971.

Tennyson, A. (1938). *The Poems and Plays of Tennyson*. New York: The Modern Library, p. 323.

Vogel, E. F. and Bell, N. W. (1960). The emotionally disturbed child as the family scapegoat. In *A Modern Introduction to the Family*, pp. 382–397. Glencoe, Ill.: The Free Press.

Wallerstein, J. S. and Kelly, J. B. (1974). The effects of parental divorce: the adolescent experience. In *The Child in His Family: Children at Psychiatric Risk*, Vol. 3, ed. E. J. Anthony and C. Koupernik. New York: John Wiley and Sons.

_____ (1980). *Surviving the Breakup: How Children and Parents Cope with Divorce*. New York: Basic Books.

Whitehead, L. (1979). Sex difference in children's responses to family stress: a reevaluation. *Journal of Child Psychology and Psychiatry* 20:247–254.

Wolfenstein, M. (1966). How is mourning possible? *Psychoanalytic Study of the Child* 21:93–123.

_____ (1969). Loss, rage, and repetition. *Psychoanalytic Study of the Child* 24:432–460.

Wylie, H. L. and Delgado, R. A. (1959). A pattern of mother-son relationships involving the absence of the father. *American Journal of Orthopsychiatry* 29:644–649.

CHAPTER SEVEN

Adolescence

Robert M. Dorn, M.D.

Normal development evokes mourning experiences. A person going from one phase of the life cycle into the next experiences a sense of loss. Latency is a structured stage with clear-cut landmarks, puberty is change. Latency to adolescence is a move from the known (the familiar), to the unknown (the strange). It will be necessary to deal simultaneously with actions in two areas. Janus-like, one focus is looking back "to where I was." Looking in this direction, it represents saying "good-bye." Memories, nostalgia, and idealized recollections prevail. Puberty and adolescenthood present persistent pressures. The more troublesome the passage, the more treasured certain aspects of latency become.

A young man contrasted the shock he felt at puberty with the elementary school period, which he called "prepuberty." Describing the sensations associated with the sixth grade, he said:

> I really had a good time. I enjoyed being a sixth grader. It was like being a big man. I was one of the best dodgeball players in my little world. I didn't come into conflict with other people. School consisted of such lovely things as raising and lowering the flag, and inflating the balls. I had a sense of freedom around school.

The sensations of a troubled puberty were not welcomed by him. In contrast, latency was placid and marked by intellectual superiority and feelings of self-respect. He longed and mourned for the lost, familiar territory and friends of latency. To be a big frog in a little pond evoked enjoyable feelings of pride. Memories of latency experiences represented stable islands, which were held onto in puberty. For example, physical activities in which he excelled and social roles of prominence (being selected by the teacher to carry out symbolic, phallic-related activities in the group setting) were called up from the past and treasured. He mourned over their unavailability as he moved through the passages of his turbulent adolescence. He now felt small (again), no longer "like a big man . . . in my little world."

Loss is a reality for each developmental stage of passage from infancy onward. Dawning awareness of not being in control (big), not omnipotent, and not the center of the universe is a developmental task required of each person. To give up the illusion of being in control, to cope with the disillusionment, requires a capacity to mourn over losses. It is part of the human condition.

The person passing from latency to adolescence will once again feel loss of control and the sensation of being small (not big), outside the center of attention. It is painful to face these feelings and accept the fact that important people upon whom we depend for respect and acknowledgment do not equally reciprocate our wishes and desires. We are not their only interest.

Many budding adolescents have the capacity to cope with these disillusionments. At each stage of development, they have learned to let go of the familiar and to live with the strange, temporarily uncertain of landmarks, anxious, and "at sea." Experiences of aloneness (for them) do not mean "abandonment," for they know that they will trust their coping skills, trust in the world, and trust other people. They know how to make friends, and in the periods without friends, know how to function autonomously. For them, a new crisis may be a creative opportunity.

Passages from infancy to toddlerhood, toddlerhood to nursery school, and nursery school to regular school while simultaneously passing in and out of family life, have, at each stage of development, contributed significantly to a repertoire of mastery. Saying "good-bye" is sad but is part of the human condition. To persistently deny the sadness and pain of loss, and to lose the capacity for autonomous function, is to not develop coping skills essential for healthy functioning. Such people have not learned how to mourn and maintain relationships with others while grieving over losses. They remain potentially vulnerable throughout future stages of their life cycles.

Anna Freud and Dorothy Burlingham (1944) describe the complications evoked in the potential mourner's life when adults try to shield the infant child from this painful reality experience. Essential affects and ego functions are not stimulated and allowed to occur. Part of the human condition is to learn appropriate expressions for these affects and to learn modes of expression acceptable within the given society. Grief expression evokes social responses. Normal adjustment in a normal environment allows for and encourages both expression and response. Distress, pain, and grief are part of essential realities we experience when key people leave us.

Protest and anxiety, as nonverbal aspects of infancy, mature by toddlerhood (rapprochement-individuation). Affects at this age emphasize the "two-world" nature of the preschooler's reality. During affective turbulence, it feels like "you against me," and "I against you." Toddlers have the potential for self control and self-expression. They deal with urges to mess up and spoil the world of the important adult(s). These affective expressions are intrapsychic (fantasies) and interpersonal (action). The toddler is described as "good" (socially adjusted and well behaved) or "bad."

During latency, homeostasis occurs. Reason, understanding, empathy, and compassion gradually heal over old hurts. Speech and cognitive growth afford modes for taming of affects regarding feelings of loss and provide skills for reversing feelings of powerlessness to control others and events. Talking to the "adult(s)" can occur. The verbally secure child, who is not made to feel too anxious, can talk about feelings and describe blows to self-esteem when key persons seem nonsupportive, lacking in understanding, or unavailable. Dialogs can occur.

Jacobson (1964) describes how object representations, established intrapsychically, contribute to a sense of self. Identifications occur with parents and teachers and social goals are shared. Objects, internalized as part of superego (both conscience and ego ideal) work with real parents, teachers, and other authority figures to express approval (praise and encouragement) and disapproval (criticism and shame) when schoolwork is deficient or behavior is socially questionable. Healthy latency children take rules and regulations seriously; socialization wins new recruits to good citizenship.

The Healthy Transition

The healthy, "ideal" child enters puberty and adolescence eager to experience being older and anticipating the acquisition of the skills essential for adulthood. Healthy children are prepared to learn and widen their interests. They feel ready to profit from new adults (teachers, mentors) and new experiences with their peer group. Offer and Offer (1968, 1973) describe adolescents as finding ample ground for self-assertion and growth within the social fields of school, home, and peer group activities. Conflict negotiations and conflict resolution by way of negotiation are characteristics of this style of adolescenthood. In later publications, Offer and Offer (1975) and Offer (1980) confirm this, suggesting that two subgroups, the continuous growth (23 percent) and the surgent growth (35 percent) do relatively well in social-adaptive terms. Only the tumultuous subgroup (21 percent) are felt to be similar to psychiatric, psychoanalytic, and sociologic literature on adolescents. A residual of 21 percent could not be categorized.

While the surgent group manifested conflict, anxiety, and a proclivity to moodiness and depression, especially if there was a wavering of self-esteem, they, too, did relatively well in terms of social adaptation. The following case example probably fits the surgent growth category.

John is 17 years old. His father came to see me because he didn't understand his son. The boy had finished his junior year in high school; he was only doing C work, and according to the school, should be doing at least above-average work. The father described his son as "determined, hardheaded, a boy who shows a great deal of hostility towards me." The father tried to talk with him, the son said, "O.K.," and then walked away to do whatever he wished. The father found John slovenly in both the care of his room and his personal dress. He wore his hair too long and insisted upon going around town barefoot or wearing Marine boots. The father described himself as being a hard driving man who worked his way through college and went from one job to another, always improving himself, while at the same time continuing to help his parents. The father had always set high standards for himself and felt that his older son is a real contrast to this while at the same time, there is a younger son who is very much like the father.

The school counselor pointed out that the father had been "attacking the son on all fronts." He insisted on higher grades, better organization, more neatness, weight reduction, etc. The patient had had about ten months of therapy when he was 9 years old, subsequent to the mother suffering a nervous breakdown and having to be hospitalized. The father's job took him out of town a great deal and the boy had to be left with the housekeeper. He developed symptoms of enuresis, nightmares, and eating problems.

Based on what the father told me, I had a predetermined picture and certain expectations of what John would be like. I was prepared for the kind of independence the father had described. I was not prepared for his main topics: a strong desire not to hurt the father and his concern about the father working too hard, "yet I want him to leave me alone." He described feeling personally neglected and expressed his reproach of the father for not doing things with him when he had been younger but hiring people to take his place. John also described feelings of loss of respect for his father for making threats which he couldn't back up "because they were too fantastic." In other words, he felt that his father had not backed him up when he wanted his support and now resented the amends he was trying to make. In spite of fears about hurting father, John was enjoying his revenge.

For the last year, John has held a part-time job after school with a firm and has done very well. In this contemporary setting, he continued to seek aid and support while he battled his way towards a more independent position. John described an incident where the assistant manager gave him a difficult time, but he stood up for his rights and won the argument. He felt the assistant manager's attitude was both unfair and in poor taste. He was pleased he had won the argument and shared with me fantasies of the assistant manager being put down by the manager. John was pleased and at the same time sorry for his defeat of the assistant manager.

In two or three hours of consulting, John told me a great deal about himself. Above all, he wanted to be heard and listened to. He was not as sure of himself as he would like to be. He needed a great deal of support for his activities. Otherwise, his voice became high pitched and tense as he tried to maintain a logical assertion of his opinion rather than lose control and get angry. He needed approval for what he had accomplished on his own to such a degree that I began to gain insight into an earlier problem in relation to his mother's stay in the hospital, his father's so-called "desertion," and some earlier feelings of competition with the younger brother.

In spite of the evidence of ongoing adolescent conflict, John's choice of dress and manner of speaking, in fact, his whole approach to life, indicated adequate coping with the battle towards identity, autonomy, independence, and success. Even conflict areas were being handled in a fashion which suggested negotiation with authorities, rather than rebellion and overthrow, and intrapsychic authority representations. Father and he, the assistant manager and he, and now he and I represented transitional experiences modeling his character style. He was reality oriented, well accepted by peers (as opposed to a year or two ago) and was successfully holding down a job in a field that he hoped to pursue after graduating college. I felt that at this time I should support him in his individual goals. This would do him more good than trying to deal with evident mourning problems from an earlier period which hadn't been resolved. He planned to check back from time to time. His father was satisfied with our decisions.

Depressive Moods

As scientists, one might contest the accuracy of the Offer (1980) statistics. Epidemiologic studies continue to elicit concern. For example, in the age group 15–24, suicidal deaths have increased from 4 per 100,000 (1957) to 13.6 per 100,000 (1977). Suicide in this age group is second only to accidents as a cause of death. The modes of suicidal death, as reported for 1975, show firearms, poisoning, and hanging to be the major causes of self-inflicted death in the age groups 5–15 and 15–24. (Vital Statistics Report 1979). Therefore, despite the proportion of adolescents and their families who comprise the transactional groups experiencing tumultuous adolescenthood, we must be knowledgeable clinicians able to diagnose, to understand empathically, and must be capable of instituting effective intervention and therapy.

Anthony (1970) believes all adolescents have a propensity for depressive affects as the dawning of a sense of loss breaks through into consciousness. Blos (1962) describes some of the emerging patterns of an adolescent's personality formation. The story of Judy (Blos, pp. 36–51) shows how several factors — biologic, psychologic, and social — contribute to depressive moods. Acne disfigured Judy's face, and she made matters worse by picking at it. She felt ugly and felt her mother lacked understanding. She accused her mother of not even trying to understand her. Overdetermined sibling relationships contributed to persistent mood changes. While possibly making affects especially turbulent, the moods themselves are not unique. Judy experienced feelings of rage and despair alternating with remorse and depression. Headaches made her fear brain illness. She was preoccupied with thoughts of death and suicide; in her daydreams, parents and others suffered remorse as they mourned her death.

She also had no close friends and yearned for at least one good, close girlfriend. When opportunities for a relationship occurred, her growing attachment (demandingness and possessiveness) drove the other person away. She felt deserted. Even though social situations, such as group school activities and summer camp were regular occurrences, she periodically experienced persistent "outsider" feelings (always the "odd one," the "extra member"). She would initiate withdrawal, thus contributing further to her social isolation. During these times, she became depressed and brooding. Suicide thoughts alternated with her fantasies of parents and others who were remorseful and depressed for the pain and depression they caused her.

In a typical way, these depressed moods would lift and be replaced by periods of growing social involvement and brighter feelings. It was evident she had the capacity for playfulness and humor.

Judy's problems were severe enough to require psychotherapy with a skilled woman therapist. Healthy adolescents who do not need help go through similar cyclical spirals, as characteristic of the passage from latency through pre-adolescence, early adolescence, and adolescence proper. Blos (1962) chooses to make these separate categories in order to aid observers in noting and assessing adolescenthood. I, however, prefer two categories, early adolescence and adolescence proper.

Early Adolescence

Early adolescence is the period of repeated attempts at separation from primary love objects (parents, siblings, and family). Usually, one sees an upsurge of idealized, same-sex friendships. These are often abortive and swiftly changing, yet always close and special. Interests also change rapidly, but each interest represents an internal attempt to break away and establish a personal sense of meaning and authenticity. During the lulls between attachments, depressive, lonely moods are prevalent, accompanied by feelings and experiences of isolation and abandonment.

The observer is, it is to be hoped, aware that coping skills are at their lowest point during this period. Attachments to peers are tenuous. Idealized, attachments are vulnerable to disillusionment. One can sense the profound feelings of hurt, feeling misunderstood, unloved, and even empty. Suicidal impulses need to be respected as serious although, most of the time, they are short-lived.

Clinical experience helps to make a strong case for considering and becoming skilled at noting, assessing, and handling this period as a separate entity. The latency period, especially where successful, results in strong attachments to parents and societal values, such as work achievement and belonging to a group. With early adolescence, speaking metapsychologically, object cathexes are removed from family objects. Both agencies of the superego, conscience and ego ideals, are at risk. Self-control threatens to break down, and self-esteem regulation becomes weakened, leaving the early adolescent with an internal sense of lacking certainty and direction. All too often, moral standards become points of contention, evoke argumentativeness, and express disappointment in the adult world. In the past, these were reliable orientation points within the self. They were helpful in working out relationships to other people.

The adolescent's questioning of them, now, contributes to a sense of not knowing where one belongs, in whom to have faith, what to believe and whom to trust. Abandonment sensations and helplessness are common consequences. Searches for new attachments are evidence of potential capacities to move forward to early adolescence. Nonetheless, delinquencies are not uncommon as disillusionment ("in the world"), and narcissistic hurts prevail.

Others have described the need to give up pre-adolescent object ties, their values, and their activities. Katan (1951) called it "object removal." Deutsch (1944) divides puberty into "early puberty" and "puberty and adolescence." The latter she also calls "advanced puberty." Blos (1962, p. 72) helps delineate and define each of these terms, using "object relinquishment," and "object finding". Turning to a friend or mentor initiates the process. In girls, daydreams of attachment to a woman or a man ("a crush") may be the harbinger of early adolescenthood and its idealizations.

Letting go of parent representations is most easily and smoothly accomplished by replacement. Metaphorically speaking, as a parent's hand is let go, there are new hands onto which to hold. There are other people moving into the foreground to relate to and respect. Other adults and peers are felt to afford "better models," worth emulating. They bring "better ideas" worth listening to and respecting. This represents a relatively synchronous mode of letting go of the past (familiar) gracefully, while judiciously selecting from among a wide range of replacements. People, ideas, styles, and values, incorporated over years, will be called into question by many adolescents.

Unfortunately, the ideal is not the norm, at least not in Western cultures. Beginning in preadolescence, object removal (Katan 1951) and object relinquishment (Blos 1962), provide sensations of loss and depression. Idealization of others is prefaced or accompanied by denigration of the formerly respected parents or their internalized representations. Alienation from the superego (estrangement from aspects of its parts) creates significant problems (A. Freud 1936).

Without ego modulations, previously provided by conscience and values, reinstinctualizations occur. Bulimia-anorexia (eating symptoms of food binging and the fight against it) is a private tangible expression of the affective storm raging within. Feeling ravenously hungry, such a person eats extraordinarily quickly and compulsively, consuming massive quantities of food while feeling helpless to stop the forces compelling the eating urges. Guilt and shame occur, followed by urges to force vomiting in order to undo the previous act.

For the anorexic-bulemic adolescent, passions are regressively being expressed and experienced in physical terms. "Emptiness" is a literal, concrete experience, called hunger sensations. The adolescent doesn't feel lonely, isn't missing people, isn't angry with parents or their values, and isn't turning away from them or their ideas. Their replacements aren't other people, conversations, and ideas, nor are they books (conversation "food" and "food for thought"). Evacuated empty spaces are inside "physically," and urges to fill them are literally food, as they probably were initially for the infant who wanted mother (her breast, her smell, her warmth, and the capacity of her milk to comfort).

Anthony (1970, p. 858) suggests a classification for depression based on whether oedipal or preoedipal issues are primary products of adolescent experiences brought into therapy. "The more borderline and psychotic depression stem from the preoedipal *Anlage* possibly reinforced by strong constitutional elements."

Other less regressed adolescents also struggle with primitive emotions. They too feel at the mercy of "storms" of *feelings* (hopelessly in love, hopelessly unattractive, hopelessly alone in a totally alien world, or hopelessly depressed).

Kaufman (1979) describes clearly the wide range of emotions confronting the teenager at risk, the teenager's parents, and the therapist:

> In evaluation sessions with the patient, he appeared sad, distant and lonely. He was irritable, lacked capacity for mutual warmth, and was not responsive to cordial overtures. He acknowledged destructive and self-destructive urges, including suicide, and he talked readily only about topics of violence. The patient was not able to describe his feelings and did not recognize himself as

depressed. There was little capacity to speak about himself, and his remarks about significant figures in his life were usually negative. He could not establish meaning to his feelings.

The most striking feature of this boy's mental life was that from every observation he viewed his parents totally removed from him as comforting, empathizing figures whose love and approval were of no vital interest. This change in representation of his parents was linked by timing with the onset of provocative impulsivity that starkly contrasted the history of composure and self-regulation that before had kept him in harmony with the significant primary figures of his life. Now at age 14½ he frequently endangered himself with alcohol and drug intoxication. The school and juvenile authorities were ready to identify him as irretrievably sociopathic.

While his behavior caused intense concern for his parents, he appeared triumphant and haughty. He was uninterested in their despair, and contemptuously dismissed their expression of distress as "guilt trips" designed to rob him of freedom to master his own destiny. (p. 119)

Kaufman, with great sensitivity, acknowledged it essential for this young man to have a sense of identity, albeit a negative one, that was his own (Erikson 1968). Kaufman similarly acknowledged and accepted the patient's need to remove himself from his parents and their control. As a therapist willing to work with him and his behavior, Kaufman was prepared for the regressive and primitive materials that he and his patient would have to live with, if change and growth were to take place.

Adolescence Proper

Adolescence proper, pushed forward relentlessly by biology's puberty, brings new changes. Heterosexual object finding, or in a minority of instances, homosexual object preference, become more sustained and practiced in masturbation, conscious fantasy life, and reality. Emotional life is richer — wider in scope, more intense, and more sustained. The ability to detach and turn away from enmeshment aspects of parental concerns opens new horizons for exploration, experience, and pleasure. Narcissistic types of early adolescent preoccupations (autoerotism, moodiness, self-sufficiency, self-aggrandizing fantasies, and action) can be, and are given up. No longer are urges to indulge oneself necessary. No longer does one have to fight off these urges. Bulemic sensations and acts, and ascetic practices recede. Fears of being hurt by others and the need to develop narcissistic defenses against anticipated and alleged hurts recede. Isolation ends. Books and defensive hobbies no longer occupy adolescents to the exclusion of social contact. Phobic concerns become less evident. Sexual experiences become less casual and less intermittent. Object hunger and its derivatives diminish.

Identifications with other adults gain significance. Good and bad introjections-projections become quiescent. Selections of friends and lovers emerge. The work of mourning continues, but more quietly. The parents of infancy, childhood and early adolescenthood are slowly relegated to a working through process. The earlier emptiness, grief, sadness and moodiness are overtaken by capacities and experiences of new object relations. Love relationships become realities. Nonetheless, caring adults and therapists should realize the slow nature of working through and dealing with the lost object representations.

Adolescence includes the development of a sense of self (the sense of whom I am). While the two polar positions, merging and alienation, can be observed in the individual and the group, most adolescents initiate a stable identity sense early and use social systems to create shared and differentiating experiences. These groups highlight similarities within the group and differences from others. Such groups provide a safe transitional "turf" between childhood and adulthood. Clubs, sororities, fraternities, athletic teams, secret societies, behavior, hair style, dress, and language are some of the sociocultural modes used to carry out this transition. Inevitably, these modes will provide the adolescent with experiential pasts for the adult nostalgia (a psychic residual as memories of things past are sought after for recapture).

We also need to remind ourselves that adolescenthood can be a very protracted stage in the Western world. Preparation for some professions, e.g., medicine, continues well into the twenties and thirties. Identifications (whom do I want to be like; who are my mentors?) continue, change, and are remodified. Sometimes we discover that lost objects are once again retrieved as identifications.

Identity development takes time. One needs time to develop skills, practice them, and become confident. The drives of sexuality and aggressions are in a new body. Activity and passivity have opportunities to have new meanings. Adolescents need and find time to socialize, to date and court, to go to school and become educated, and to practice vocations. They also need time to practice sharing, intimacy, selfishness, and aloneness. Affect experiences are essential. There is need to "get high" on oneself, on ideas, and about other people.

Cognitive processes are more evident in interests, skills, and sustained expressions of talents. Piaget's (1952, 1967) stage of concrete operations in many, but not all instances, is overtaken by and increasingly superceded by the stage of formal operations. Future planning exists. The adolescent has the ability to abstract, to imagine "what I want to be," and to plan and proceed by learning how to make the future and desires a realizable reality. Contingency plans, relatively free of grandiosity or unreasonable self-sacrifice, are made. Adolescents recruit others to their causes. They enjoy the mutual investment in their own mission and quest.

A 19-year-old girl consulted me for mild symptoms of tension and irritability. She had telephoned her family doctor and asked him for the name of someone with whom she could talk, since she didn't want to talk with him. When she came to see me, she first handled the financial arrangements in a very businesslike manner. She indicated that she would have to pay the fees herself and wanted to have some idea what it would cost her. She explained that she was working and asked if it was alright if she spread out the payments over a period of time; on her salary she could not afford to see me privately otherwise. I told her it was perfectly alright to handle the payments as she requested.

The patient told me that she had a sister five years older and a brother a year and a half younger than she. She described ongoing family difficulties which were caused by rigid religious parental attitudes. The family belongs to a fundamentalist sect and does not believe in movies, radio, television, dancing, alcohol, or smoking. She had been dating two men, one a typical "Joe College" acceptable to her parents, the other a divorced man who had a child by his previous marriage. She was seeing the latter secretly. She found him much too suave and easy with women to be liked by her parents, and he insisted on dating other women. She found she was happiest when she was with him but was unhappy about his insistence on other relationships.

She said to me, "I used to think my father liked my sister better than me, but I don't think this is true anymore." She described how her sister and brother seemed very comfortable with their parents' religious and cultural attitudes. Both siblings had settled down into roles established by this more restrictive culture. She said, "I rebel and do things that people in the world around me like to do."

While in high school, she developed an interest in nursing, spent two years as a student volunteer at the County Hospital, developed a nursing club, and became its first president. Her dating activities were slow in coming, as one might guess from the parental attitudes. With the rebellion against her family, she experienced a loss of confidence in herself, underestimated her actual ability, and decided to get a job in an office rather than attend college. She saw me twice in consultation. I found her to be frank and outspoken and in need only of support. She had almost reached a decision on her own but needed some "advice." After seeing me, she resigned from her job and enrolled in junior college to begin nurse's training. This plan was followed through.

An Adolescent's Depression

Unfortunately, others do not do as well as the girl just described. Sometimes, biologic and psychologic factors seem to conspire against the adolescent. Bob was almost 16 years old when he and his family consulted me. (Actually, his father telephoned initially.) Bob's father stated that Bob had a problem "with his shortness," and went on to say "he also has a real problem with his mother, and sometimes with me." In later meetings with Bob and his parents, it became evident that they had tendencies to be overcontrolling. However, if they relaxed their controls too much, Bob had ways of forcing them back into authority roles.

When Bob and I first sat and talked together, he was clearly unhappy with the move to high school. Most of his friends went to the public school. He felt he should have also switched and maintained those peer contacts which he no longer had. In addition, one student in private school had selected him to be the butt of his sarcasm. (This was confirmed.) Others were old enough to drive; he was not. His grades had begun to fall off seriously in two subjects. By working especially hard, Bob had been able to improve other grades which had been falling also; Spanish went from C to A, English from B − to A, History to B − , and Algebra from C − to B. However, Bob continued to fail Physics. He berated his parents (especially his mother) for being more concerned about school and grades " . . . than about my mental state." As he spoke, he described finding her values and rules inconsistent. For example, if he stayed up after 10 P.M. talking on the telephone to a friend " . . . she'll start in on me. The other night I was watching a program on television about Albert Speer, Hitler's architect. It was 11:15, but that was okay. She resents me for the trouble I've gotten into lately." He went on to describe an impulsive act which caused some problems with a neighbor. He adds " . . . it was dumb."

It became increasingly evident even in the first hour that Bob was a stressed 15-year-old. At times I felt the depression to be serious. The depressive responses seemed to have a "brittle" quality, and Bob seemed to be quite vulnerable. His primary problem, "my unhappiness," was precipitated by the loss of friends when almost all of them left the private school for the public school. When I asked him how serious the primary problem had become, he responded: "Serious; I worry a lot. I dread going back to school each Monday. I cry myself to sleep at night."

Stress seemed both chronic and acute. Appetite was poor. He showed no signs of malnutrition or weight loss but acknowledged losing five to ten pounds over the past six months. He demonstrated irritability, tearfulness, and moodiness. Sleep was restless without evident change in pattern. An appointment was offered for the next day. He demurred, preferring one for the following week. He had specific plans to work on grades whenever he could find the time.

That Sunday evening, Bob's father called me. He expressed concern because Bob had been sitting and watching TV most of the day, not really paying attention to the programs. Upon inquiry from me as to whether or not this clearly depressed mood was something new, Bob's father responded, "It seems brand new. It appeared during the last few days. Since his visit to you, he mentioned something about it to me."

Bob's father shared with me for the first time that he had been hospitalized for depression five years ago. It had responded to ECT. A recurrence had responded to Nortriptylene. He felt empathically in touch with Bob and his behavior throughout the day.

I saw Bob. He told me that he had " . . . been thinking about things, and feeling depressed all day." When I asked if anything specific might have triggered it off, Bob replied that something had happened that weekend: "A person who I thought was one of my few friends had a party. I was not invited. And then last night, a friend had a party, and again I was not invited."

When I asked subsequently about suicidal thoughts, he indicated clearly that he had given specific thought to suicide: "When I will want to do it, I certainly don't want to be stopped. Right now I don't think I want to, but when I want to, I don't want to be stopped."

When asked how he might be thinking of doing it, he responded, " . . . slash my wrists, I guess. I don't know."

It was very clear that Bob had been grievously "injured" by being left out of both parties. I specifically made inquiry about going to school the next day (Monday). He indicated that he definitely did not want to go. An offer to come into the hospital was accepted with alacrity. It was my impression that this provided him with an opportunity to "save face" at a critical time.

The hospital consulting psychiatrist felt it best to treat Bob as a major depression rather than a reactive depression due to family history and growing severity of "hopelessness" and turmoil. He was placed on tricyclics. A complicating tachycardia responded to beta blockers. He continued to see me for psychotherapy. Psychological testing revealed mild disorganization of thinking but no thought disorder. Bob appeared to feel oppressed, rejected, and disappointed by his parents. He tended to respond to feelings and fantasies by resignation, withdrawal, and helplessness. Deeper, less accessible, themes indicated fantasies of revenge and retaliation involving his parents. He was hospitalized for 35 days. It was felt that the first tricyclic (Nortryptylene) helped only with sleep. He was switched to Desipramine. Initially, he went through a marked depression during the change in medication. Subsequently, there appeared to be an evident response, affecting attention, energy, and mood, as well as sleep. Lability appeared to decrease.

After discharge he did well situationally. Bob and his parents worked on modifying rules and regulations (homework, chores, social freedoms, and responsibilities). Bob was able to acknowledge that a part of him was angry, resentful, and negative, although it was painful to pursue this theme. In the fall he enrolled in the school that his old friends attended. By the fourth month following discharge, Bob wanted to stop medication and to talk about stopping therapy. He was increasingly involved with peers, and planned to work after school, weekends, and over the Christmas holidays. He and his father were "negotiating" about a possible car next summer.

Masked Depression

Should the capacity to make friendships not develop, or if those friendships prove to be short-lived due to persistent breaking-off (quarrels with or disappointment in the other), the adolescent is "at risk" for depression. Such adolescents often present as "loners."

Bob's problems and symptoms probably were hidden for more than a year. He was irritable, grumbling, and argumentative with people. They pulled back and began to avoid him. He was actively contributing to experiencing rejection. Bob feared failure and contributed to failure by not seeking appropriate help.

Narcissistic hurts and disillusionments increased while coping abilities decreased. Bob literally aggravated matters. Until suicidal urges and clear-cut depressive apathy evoked parental concerns and "caring," Bob was a sullen, failing teenager. Fortunately, he did not try to "cure" himself with drugs to sedate or to help deny his feelings.

Bob could not ask for help. Depression provided new opportunities to deal with heretofore "neglected" pregenital developmental issues. Angry feelings, disillusionments, lack of trust, and feelings of helplessness began to gain focus. Isolation decreased and therapy initiated a process of greater openness. Empathy was forthcoming from mother, especially from father, and from peers. Bob and his parents began to renegotiate roles and expectations. Accepting his depression, peers responded by including him in their plans and activities. Self-worth increased. Bob continued supportive psychotherapy.

Suicide

As mentioned earlier, suicidal deaths in 1977 in the age group 15–24 were 13.6 per 100,000 (Vital Statistics Report 1979). In 1967, suicide ranked fourth as a cause of death in the 15–19 year old group (Lourie 1967).

In the Vital Statistics report (1979) for this 15–24 year old group, suicide was second only to accidents as a cause of death.

What are some of the characteristics of suicide actions in the adolescent? They tend to show an impulsiveness, a lack of planning, or lack of premeditation. To the outsider, especially to the adult observer, the trigger appears to be "trivial." If one moves back to the preadolescent and early adolescent group, this becomes even more clearly a descriptor.

Why do adolescents commit suicide? Possible reasons are: escape from an intolerable situation; expression of "anger"; expression of a wish to evoke love and admiration from others by sacrificing or hurting themselves; expression of a wish for closeness or attention from others, using a threat of death. These descriptors could well fit the case of Bob as he sat in front of the television that Sunday and caught the attention of his father. The act of suicide in the younger or midrange adolescent is usually impulsive, occurs with a growing sense of helplessness or hopelessness, and very often expresses revenge (spite). Chronic preoccupation with thoughts of suicide is relatively rare. It should be taken very seriously when it is discovered.

By adolescence proper, thoughts of suicide are much more likely to be connected with depressive thinking. Grinker, Miller, Sabshin et al. (1961) provide five groups of characteristics that should be noted as evidence of suicide potential: helplessness, hopelessness, failure, and sadness; concerns about material loss and an inner conviction that this feeling state (or the illness) could be changed if the outside world provided something; guilt over wrongdoing, wishes to make restitution, or feelings that the "illness" has been brought on by the patient or is deserved; "free anxiety"; envy, loneliness, martyred affliction, secondary gain from the illness, attempts to force the world to make redress or to feel guilty for causing the adolescent to commit suicide. Should any combination of these be evident, suicide potential is high.

Biological Aspects of Depression and Therapy

Genetic and biogenic amine studies of endogenous depression in adults are impressive and statistically significant. They highlight such essential features as the x-linked gene in bipolar depressive illness, the value of diagnostic criteria, the use of lithium in bipolar illness, and the benefits of antidepressant medication. Winokur (1973) found that one-third of bipolar manic-depressive patients have at least one manic episode before the age of 20; 10 percent of bipolar manic-depressive patients have a first manic episode between the ages of 15–25; and 10 percent of unipolar depressed patients have a first depressive episode between the ages of 15–25.

Bipolar illness, as a diagnostic entity, clearly exists prior to adulthood. Anthony and Scott (1960) found three cases in the literature and published one of their own. They spelled out specific criteria to be met before this diagnosis can be accepted:

1. Presence of an abnormal psychiatric state approximating the classical clinical descriptions
2. A "positive" family history suggesting a manic-depressive diathesis
3. Early tendency to manic-depressive reactions manifested in cyclothymic tendency with gradually increasing length and amplitude of mood swings, and delirious manic or depressive outbursts during pyrexic illness
4. Evidence of recurrent or periodic illness. There should be at least two episodes lasting months or years
5. Evidence of diphasic illness
6. Evidence of endogenous illness (i.e., minimal reference to environmental events)
7. Evidence of severe illness (i.e. need for inpatient, heavy sedation, or ECT)
8. An abnormal underlying personality of an extraverted type
9. Absence of features that might indicate schizophrenia or organic states
10. Current, not retrospective, judgments

During the 1970s, several authors began longitudinal case studies, some with follow-up into adulthood. Cytryn and McKnew (1974), McKnew, Cytryn, Efron, et al. (1979), and McKnew, Cytryn, Buchsbaum et al. (1981) have contributed cases of children of bipolar parents complete with videotapes following them from childhood into adolescence. These and other researchers continue to gather important data on children and adolescents with probable bipolar and unipolar problems.

Biochemical, lithium, antidepressive medication studies and literature overviews are appearing in rapidly growing numbers (Campbell 1979, Campbell, Schulman, and Rapoport 1978, Jefferson 1982). Biochemical markers, neurophysiologic instrumentation, and non-invasive scan techniques are helping to usher in a new era of knowledge about the brain and brain function. Many clinicians practicing psychotherapy today are sophisticated, knowledgeable, and comfortable with developmental, conflictual, and unresolved archaic issues, reappearing in transference and the second individuation of adolescence. Mourning and depression issues described in this chapter lend themselves to biopsychosocial research and systems exploration (Mandell 1976).

Depression research studies are thus increasingly lending themselves to comprehensive assessment. Contemporary research on adolescence, despite its variables, is encouraging the bringing together of the "circumscribers" and the "generalizers." Even to the untrained eye, biochemical, neuroendocrinologic, neurophysiologic, and biopsychosocial phenomena are evident in the pubertal person. More significant data having to do with diagnostic criteria, classification, morbidity-prevalence, probable etiologies, and treatments (phenomenologic and psychosocial), is now available and recordable.

Biopsychosocial research teams and appropriate treatments of depressions can help to narrow the "mysterious leap" between body and mind. Ongoing and future longitudinal research on depressive illness in children and adolescents can provide opportunities to examine the effect of psychodynamic factors on biological functioning and biological factors on alteration of the mind and behavior. An era of even closer cooperation is at hand.

REFERENCES

Anthony, E. J. (1970). Two contrary types of adolescent depression and their treatment. *Journal of the American Psychoanalytic Association* 18:841–859.

Anthony, E. J. and Scott, P. (1960). Manic-depressive psychosis in childhood. *Journal of Child Psychology and Psychiatry Allied Disciplines* 1:53–72.

Blos, P. (1962). *On Adolescence: A Psychoanalytic Interpretation.* New York: The Free Press.

Campbell, M. (1979). Psychopharmacology. In *Basic Handbook of Child Psychiatry,* vol. III, ed. J. D. Noshpitz. New York: Basic Books.

Campbell, M., Schulman, D., and Rapoport, J. L. (1978). The current status of lithium therapy in child and adolescent psychiatry. *Journal of the American Academy of Child Psychiatry* 17:717–220.

Cytryn, L. and McKnew, D. H. (1974). Factors influencing the changing clinical expression of the depressive process in children. *American Journal of Psychiatry* 13:879–881.

Deutsch, H. (1944). *Psychology of Women.* Vol. I. New York: Grune and Stratton.

Erikson, E. (1968). *Identity, Youth and Crisis.* New York: W. W. Norton.

Freud, A. (1936). *The Ego and the Mechanisms of Defense. The Writings of Anna Freud.* Vol. II. New York: International Universities Press, 1966.

Freud, A. and Burlingham, D. (1944). *Infants Without Families. The Writings of Anna Freud.* Vol. III. New York: International Universities Press.

Grinker, R. R., Miller, Jr., Sabshin, M., Munn, R., and Nunnally, J. (1961). *Phenomena of Depressions.* New York: Paul B. Hoeber.

Jacobson, E. (1964). *The Self and the Object World.* New York: International Universities Press.

Jefferson, J. W. (1982). The use of lithium in childhood and adolescence: an overview. *Journal of Clinical Psychiatry* 43:174–177.

Katan, A. (1951). The role of displacement in agoraphobia. *International Journal of Psycho-Analysis* 31:41–50.

Kaufman, B. (1979). Object removal and adolescent depression. In *Depression in Children and Adolescents,* ed. A. French and I. Berlin, pp. 109–128. New York: Human Sciences Press.

Lourie, R. (1967). Suicide. In *Symposium on Suicide,* ed. L. Yochelson, pp. 93–105. Washington, D.C.: George Washington University.

McKnew, D. H., Cytryn, L., Buchsbaum, M. S. et al. (1981). Lithium in children of lithium responding parents. *Psychiatry Research* 4:171–180.

McKnew, D. H., Cytryn, L., Efron, A. N. et al. (1979). Offspring of patients with affective disorders. *British Journal of Psychiatry* 134:148–152.

Mandell, A. J. (1976). Neurobiological mechanisms of adaption in relation to models of psychobiological development. In *Psychopathology and Child Development*, ed. E. Schopler and R. J. Richter. New York: Plenum Press.

National Center for Health Statistics. (1979). *Vital Statistics Report: Final Mortality Statistics*, 1977. Washington, D.C., 11 May.

Offer, D. (1980). Adolescent development: A normative perspective. In *The Course of Life*. Vol. II, *Latency, Adolescence, and Youth*, ed. S. I. Greenspan and G. H. Pollock. Washington, D.C.: U.S. Government Printing Office.

Offer, D. and Offer, J. B. (1968). Profiles of normal adolescent girls. *Archives of General Psychiatry* 19:513–522.

_____ (1973). *Normal Adolescence in Perspective*. Ed. J. P. Schoolar. New York: Brunner/Mazel.

_____ (1975). *From Teenage to Young Manhood*. New York: Basic Books.

Piaget, J. (1952). *The Origins of Intelligence*. New York: International Universities Press.

_____ (1967). *Six Psychological Studies*. New York: Random House.

Winokur, G. (1973). Diagnostic and genetic aspects of affective illness. *Psychiatric Annals* 3:6–15.

CHAPTER EIGHT

The Primacy of Aggression in the Psychoanalysis of Depressed Childbearing Women

Maurice Apprey, M.A.C.P.

The psychoanalytic observations made in this chapter arose out of intervention research in infant psychiatry, psychotherapy and psychoanalysis of expectant mothers, direct observation of infants and young children and years of self-observation as I lived among people of different cultures. The emphasis in all my observations has been on an attempt to observe conscious and unconscious behavior at all times and to use the appropriate psychoanalytic or theoretical frame to articulate my findings. In addressing the specific problem of aggression in the psychoanalysis of the depressed expectant or new mother, I have come to appreciate three preconditions for the analyst to effect successful treatment: a relative capacity to foster the appropriate therapeutic regression (Winnicott 1954, Balint 1965, 1968); a relative maternal aptitude (Chessaquet-Smirgel 1984); and a relative capacity to conduct superego analysis, i.e., analysis of aggression whether the analyst sees the superego as an early superego or otherwise. In this chapter, I do not intend to examine these preconditions. Further exploration will follow in subsequent publications. I should like instead to explore those intrapsychic issues surrounding aggression and depression that tend to surface when the analyst, equipped to conduct superego analysis, has fostered fertile conditions for the conduct of psychoanalytic treatment.

Intrapsychic Issues

A multitude of intrapsychic tasks confront the expectant mother. Judith Ballou (1978) has written about themes of reconciliation in the psychology of pregnancy. Dinora Pines (1982) has taken up the issue of pregnancy and the developmental task of separation–individuation from the expectant mother's own mother. In these themes of reconciliation, separation–individuation and related themes, aggression plays a significant role. Reconciliation implies reparation and, in the unconscious, separation is experienced as an act of aggression, nondestructive though the process of separation may be. Treatment of pregnant women, thanks to the regression due to analysis itself and also to the regression which accompanies pregnancy, continues to give us insight into areas of anxiety and the negotiation of destructive or non-destructive aggression. Illusions about pregnancies abound:

> We still tend to think that pregnancy should be a state of bliss, and of childbirth as a time of fulfillment and harmony, free from stresses and inner conflicts. For incalculable numbers of women, reality falls short of such expectations. They discover that pregnancy and childbirth are times of crisis, of unexplained fears and forebodings, of self-doubt, disappointment, and depression. The expected blissful moment when the mother holds her baby for the first time is often overshadowed by anxiety and feelings of emptiness, inadequacy, even hostility. (Gordon 1978, p. 201)

Longstanding literary tradition deals with the birth of a child as a triumph, an accomplishment, and a joyous outcome of travail. These sentiments come to us from times in which many women bore child after child in economic hardship and often with failing strength, having no access to birth control methods. In an age of greater candor and resistance to sexual submission, the delivery of a child is no longer necessarily referred to as "a blessing." Indeed, such writings as those of Verity Bargate (*No, Mama, No* 1978) describe the experience as a revolting event that foisted onto the new mother the care of a grotesque bit of humanity. Bargate's protagonist confesses that "the thing that shocked me the most when they gave me my second son to hold was the complete absence of feeling. No love. No anger. Nothing" (p. 5).

To appreciate the depth of such experiences which include depression, disappointment, and hostility, it is necessary to consider early female sexuality in relation to levels of anxiety; separation issues related to the aggressive tearing away from the pre-oedipal mother; and the transformation of aggression into depression that makes mourning and related depressive affect the prototype and basis of the experience of menses, defloration, and childbirth which are subsequent to this early event (Jacobson 1973). It is somewhat simplistic to stress that the separation issue in childbearing accounts for a new mother's disturbance; behind the separation and the reach for autonomy in a depressed mother lie many issues that bring infantile fantasied aggression to the foreground. I highlight the primacy of aggression in depressed mothers and suggest that in the childbearing process women are prone to activate such basic anxieties as those Melanie Klein (1945) identifies in women — those relating to the interior of their bodies —

and the female castration anxiety which Jacobson (1973) considers a pre-oedipal manifestation. I note also the three-way intrapsychic warfare in which the newborn, its mother, and her mother are involved. Such warfare raises a question as to who is delivered when a child is born: the delivery of the newborn or the delivery of its mother from her own.

Some Developmental Antecedents

Before entering into further discussion on some aspects of the intrapsychic issues which relate to aggression and childbearing, it might be useful to observe an 8-year-old in a child psychiatry consultation. Knowing my research interests in child development, a child psychiatrist sought supervision before seeing this 8-year-old child in the epilepsy unit of a university hospital. After the consultation, she wrote up the session for me. I have reproduced the session in full.

Hermione is an 8-year-old girl recently hospitalized in an epilepsy unit for management of an intractable seizure disorder manifest by up to 30 staring spells a day. Psychiatric consultation was requested on a routine basis and revealed Hermione to be a "parental" child, somewhat anxious regarding perceived marital discord, who dealt with her anxiety by compulsive defenses. Initially, intervention was directed at facilitating Hermione's parents' open acknowledgment of their discord with the subsequent recommendation of outpatient marital therapy.

Therapeutic intervention with Hermione was the result of a later unrelated circumstance. During the course of her hospitalization, Hermione developed a small amount of vaginal bleeding. An evaluation of this problem included a referral to obstetrics for pelvic examination. Although accompanied by her mother, Hermione was unable to tolerate this examination, and subsequently reported to staff that she was having "bad dreams" about the event. Staff also noted Hermione seemed verbally preoccupied with the examination to the exclusion of other activities, and so contacted me for further psychiatric evaluation.

I subsequently met with Hermione in the playroom, and after minimal preliminaries Hermione recalled the gynecologic exam. She related that "I had some blood there so I had this exam. They said maybe the bleeding was from some medicine I am taking or maybe from an infection, but it hurt too much to let them look so they said if the new medicine they gave me doesn't help, I'll have to go to the surgery room and they will put me asleep and look." Hermione's recollection was precise; chief indifferential was vaginal bleeding as a side effect of the new anticonvulsant. However, the working diagnosis was excoriation secondary to a monilial infection. Should empiric antifungal treatment not resolve the spotting, a pelvic examination under general anesthesia was planned.

Hermione then went on to say that she had been dreaming since the exam that she was "cut up inside." At this point, she discovered a doctor's bag and a baby doll among the toys on the tabletop. Hermione began playing with the doll, examining her heart with the stethoscope and then declared that something was wrong, that the baby "needs to have surgery." Hermione utilized me as her surgical assistant and together we opened the doll's chest. Hermione became somewhat anxious at this juncture and began searching the playroom shelves for "a needle to sew her up with." I wondered if Hermione had seen something scary inside, and she went to the chalkboard to show me the baby's x-rays. Hermione drew a circle with facial features atop a square body and explained that as these x-rays showed "the baby is messed up inside, you see she is a girl outside and a boy inside here . . . that's why she is bleeding." I questioned Hermione about the x-rays, what was being a boy inside and how does this happen, and Hermione attempted "rational" explanations which seemed increasingly silly to her; she finally laughed and much more calmly returned to the baby doll saying "let's sew her up now." Instead of the surgical assistant, Hermione instructed me to "be her mommy now and hold her hand." After suturing, Hermione drew new x-rays which she explained showed that the baby was better now, and, though she might have to come back in six months for a checkup, things would probably be okay. With this pronouncement, Hermione came over to me and asked me if I was having a baby (I was eight months pregnant at the time). When I said yes, Hermione asked what I planned to name the baby, and when I asked her suggestions, quietly informed me that "Hermione, my name is French, you know." We agreed Hermione was a lovely name and shortly thereafter ended the hour. As we left the room, Hermione reached out and put her hand on my abdomen, and then returned to the waiting room.

In this fascinating session, Hermione works through a traumatic experience which I would postulate reactivated earlier castration anxiety. Hermione's experience of genital bleeding is presented factually at the outset of the session. Her associations through metaphorical play are to a surgical procedure wherein gender identity is unclear — the baby is "girl outside and boy inside." The anxiety this arouses is defended against in part through Hermione's intellectualization of my questions regarding her association. On a much deeper level, though, Hermione is able to master the experience through metaphorical play, the eventual outcome of which is her identification with my femininity and specifically the ability to bear children. She evidences this in turning from play to direct interaction with me in which we speculate on names for the baby and Hermione touches me in identification with the unborn child.

Hermione was subsequently discharged, and follow-up was unfortunately limited. What follow-up was available, however, revealed that Hermione had recovered her normal disposition and sleep was much improved.

The feelings of being "cut up inside" became available to this 8-year-old as a result of a regression precipitated by an organic condition. In a well-conducted session we learned a little about a little girl's perception of her intrapsychic world. In her world we saw castration anxiety which in the context of her family situation translates into fear of loss of love. Unfortunately, we are constrained by the limits of a one-time consultation which for external reasons could not be extended. Nevertheless, we are not entirely at a loss in our quest to learn more from children.

In her study of the little girl, Hertha, observed in analysis from the age of 2 to 5, Edith Jacobson (1973) speaks of her analysand's wish for a child and follows the development of this wish through three phases. In the first phase, from 2 to 3 years of age, she observed in Hertha a strong narcissistic and intensely ambivalent object relationship to the mother, a narcissistic and ambivalent relationship which was the result of both real deprivation and the anxiety that future siblings would bring her further deprivation. Jacobson observed intense oral envy and an identification with the child in her mother's womb.

In the second phase, from 3 to 4 years of age, analysis draws our attention to the child's shift from her powerful oral-incorporative sadism toward the mother to sadistic fantasies which included her desire to rob her father of his penis. We observed her bisexual masturbatory fantasies as well. Jacobson attributed the child's mounting anxiety to her desire to rob the father of his penis, and to her sadistic wishes concerning the mother, whose primacy with the father she greatly envied.

In the third phase, from 4 to 5 years of age, Jacobson observed that the sadistic wish to take in the father's penis in order to have a child and the anal and phallic tendencies towards the mother coalesced into genital oedipal strivings. Now the striving to have a child resulted from the conquest of sadism toward the parents and the consequent disappearance of fear of retaliation.

Melanie Klein (1945) linked the receptive nature of the girl's genitals to her penis strivings, which in turn led her to want to receive the penis and to unconscious fantasies of possessing children. The penis strivings therefore led to the cathexis of the father's penis as the giver of children. This in turn led to a penis-child equation, and the equation of the penis to a gift (or the source of a gift) became combined with and enhanced by the positive cathexis of the mother's good breast. The child balances her conscious awareness that she lacks the ability to bear children by the psychic reality of the magic in mother's breast, since mother is the container of the father's penis and, thus, the container of his children.

The child's desire to ascertain her own fertility and procreativity accounts for her impulse to rob her mother's body of its contents and to rob her father of his penis and its contents, acts for which she fears retaliation from both the internal and external mother. Thus, the predominant oedipal anxieties involve the inner world and inner objects. Melanie Klein sees as the leading feminine anxiety the desire to steal the contents of the mother's body (the father's penis), with the concomitant expectation of attack from the mother. To defend herself against her impulse to rob and its dire consequences, the girl identifies with her mother's maternal role. When the girl identifies with the mother's sexual role vis-à-vis the father, she internalizes the mother as a "good mother" introject, but when she identifies with the mother's maternal role, she strengthens her relationship to the good internalized father by a maternal attitude toward him. This mitigates the persecutory fear of him. The introjection of the good mother who lends her daughter her sexual role and the strengthening of her relationship to the good internalized father are the basis of the feminine superego.

It would thus appear that fear of being inwardly attacked is the girl's predominant anxiety. Her oral sadism, characteristic of the pre-oedipal phase, which envisions aggressive and stealthy incorporation of the contents of her mother's body, leads to anxiety lest she herself undergo the same robbery and destruction.

Beyond Separation and Severance Steps

In view of the rather complicated basis of the girl's negotiation of early sexuality, I hesitate to describe childbearing as a severance step. Although childbearing is a basis for the negotiation of issues of separation–individuation, the psychoanalytic observer must be aware at all times of the complexity of the girl's relationship to her mother while the observer notes her move away from the pre-oedipal object toward differentiation and autonomy. In the unconscious mind separation is perceived as tearing away from the object and thus shedding blood at the site of separation. As a result, there is considerable anxiety regarding the consequence of leaving the self or object lacerated. This unconscious fantasy has important implications as to the role of aggression in the process of separation. Any formulation of the psychic reality of the girl's claim that motherhood will fulfill her early yearnings is only the beginning of our understanding although it is manifest evidence of her movement toward a higher developmental stage in which she becomes like her mother. A mother may believe that her child gives her an opportunity to see herself growing up, but the mother's inability to negotiate hatred of her own mother could cause her to fail to grow along with her child.

Failure to repress and transform negative feelings about her own "bad mother" will undermine the new mother's competence and bring about depression which is manifested in her feeling herself to be an impostor. "I am not really a mother," she says to herself. "I can't even measure two ounces of formula. . . . " An adolescent mother with this impostor feeling may feel like her child's older sibling rather than her mother, and instead of following the cues given by her child as to its needs, she may teasingly and aggressively withhold things from her child as though she were its older sister. An adolescent mother often makes the child a receptacle of her own greed: "I don't want to spoil him. He eats too much. I couldn't breastfeed him. He'll eat everything up. And besides, I'd have to be careful what I eat. Bad gasses from, say a pizza, would be passed on to him. . . . "

In the adult mother the feeling of being ugly, unwanted, and unlovable hides and contains the wish and fear of destroying the new relationship in order to breastfeed. Any suggestion that she do so can only provoke guilt, and bottle feeding may spare a depressed mother intensely conflictual aggressive feelings. If she considers herself helpless in her new role, she cannot be blamed; her lack of skill validates the impostor feelings.

A positive cathexis of one's body in the past and relative success in handling aggression provide a basis for making the childbearing experience a positive one. Bearing a baby requires the loss of one's ideal self, and this must be mourned. When an expectant mother cathects her body as damaged or damaging, she may, consciously or unconsciously, fear she will damage her unborn child. Some women adopt in order to obviate such fantasied aggression. The expectant mother, however, may project her own aggressive fears onto those in her entourage likely, in her view, to blame her for delivering a damaged child, and the aggressive fantasies that seem to threaten her child and yet contain issues of blame and exoneration often lie behind the fear of labor or the fear of being anesthetized at the time of delivery. Feelings of aggression toward her own mother are accompanied in the mind of the depressed new mother by the anticipation of retaliation from her own pre-oedipal mother; such retaliation is both desired and dreaded. The woman's desire for punishment arises from the fear that her new baby would do to her what she once did to her own mother. This is evident in a mother's cry, "If I called my mother to tell her that I had a baby girl, it would kill her."

The depressed expectant mother who fears that she will "make a mess" when she delivers may point to the persistence of anal sadistic feelings she had in early life about her mother. A feeling of castration is not uncommon; one young mother once told me, "It (the fear of labor) is like when

I broke both arms." The young mother's fears are often irrational but none the less real; examinations may be frightening because they might disclose that the subject is "not yet grown up," or reveal "bad things inside." She may identify so closely with her baby that speaking about embarrassment over what happens in labor might be her way of saying that she would make a mess like her baby.

The depressed expectant mother seeking suicide is involved with several dynamic issues. She has a most primitive superego; her identification with her unborn child reminds her that she herself once caused her mother pain and should accordingly be punished; she is intensely ambivalent in the cathexis of her new infant and her own mother; and she perceives herself as a self-lacerated child-mother who is so bad she should be done away with.

Conclusion

Psychoanalytic observation yields useful insights into the state of the pregnant woman and the vulnerable mother with her infant, but sound conclusions about her psychic reality and sound intervention will depend on the analyst's ability to see the activation of basic primitive anxieties and to differentiate one basic anxiety from another. We must articulate more specifically the anxieties that mothers have and their worries about annihilation, separation, fear of loss of object or of love, castration, superego anxiety and dictates of the superego. We must also assess the quality of maternal anxiety and note in what combination those fears appear if we are to discover whether the source lies in the id, the superego, or the external world.

I take the view that aggression is a major issue with the depressed mother. Castration fears may manifestly point to oedipal issues, but it has been my clinical observation that such manifestly oedipal issues have little urgency since the clinical evidence of castration and other aggressive issues is convincing. Like Jacobson, I assign the expectant mother's castration anxiety to the pre-oedipal phase of her life; there, fear has a primitive quality and hence stimulates fantasies of killing of the mother, being killed by the infant, the survival of only one of the dyad, the birth of a damaged "self," damage to the interior of the body, etc. The locus of fantasied catastrophe seems to be inside. But, for the depressed mother, it is an important fact that the delivery of a child is paradoxically delivery from her own mother.

REFERENCES

Ballou, Judith (1978). The significance of reconciliative themes in the psychology of pregnancy. *Bulletin of the Menninger Clinic* 42:383–413.
Balint, M. (1965). The benign and malignant forms of regression. In *New Perspectives in Psychoanalysis*, ed. George E. Daniel. New York: Grune and Stratton.
_____ (1968). *The Basic Fault: Therapeutic Aspects of Regression*. London: Tavistock Publications.
Bargate, Verity (1978). *No, Mama, No*. Glasgow: Fontana/Collins.
Chassaguet-Smirgel, J. (1984). The femininity of the analyst in professional practice. *International Journal of Psychoanalysis* 65:169–178.
Gordon, Bianca (1978). The vulnerable mother and her child. In *The Place of Birth*, ed. Sheila Kitzinger and John A. Davis, pp. 201–215. Oxford: Oxford University Press.
Jacobson, Edith (1936). On the development of the girl's wish for a child. Psihoterapija. *Journal for Psychotherapy and Allied Discipline* 2:99–110.
Jones, Ernest (1975). Early Female Sexuality. In *Papers on Psychoanalysis*, pp. 485–495. London: Maresfield Reprints, 1948.
Klein, Melanie (1945). The Oedipus complex in the light of early anxieties. In *Love, Guilt, Reparation and Other Works 1921–1945*, pp. 370–419. London: Hogarth Press and the Institute of Psychoanalysis, 1975.
Pines, Dinora (1982). The relevance of early psychic development to pregnancy and abortion. *International Journal of Psycho-Analysis* 63:311–319.
Winnicott, D. W. (1954). Metapsychological and clinical aspects of regression within the psychoanalytic set-up. In *Collected Papers: Through Paediatrics to Psychoanalysis*. London: Tavistock Publications, Ltd., 1958.

CHAPTER NINE

The Last Half of Life

Stanley H. Cath, M.D.

The aim of this chapter is to widen the base of conceptual knowledge about affective states in order to lower the barrier to psychoanalysis and psychoanalytic psychotherapy for the elderly. Throughout the various stages of life, there develop more complex and varying cerebral states revolving around psycho-physiological "loss and restitution" phenomena than have ever been described in our books or than can be subsumed under a lifelong diagnostic umbrella of depression. Clinical and drug treatment responses suggest heterogeneity. A composite view of multifaceted heterogeneous depressive states, rather than simplifying the task for therapists already suffering from complexity shock due to the enormous amounts of polarized psychological and biological data, only complicates matters. Nevertheless, I plan to demonstrate that this polarization is contrary to clinical experience and may be inimical to our patients' health. For, in relative ignorance, without attention to the whole person and the multiplicity of adaptive states possible in relation to age-specific stresses within the family system, the potential benefits from psychoanalysis or psychoanalytic psychotherapy may be denied (Cath 1983) and unnecessary relapse is all too likely.

Living long almost inevitably involves increasing contact with health care providers; long-term contact at any age may be associated, more often than not, with disillusionment, despair, disability, and death. Instead of feeling that life stretches interminably into a richer future in which "the best is yet to be", members of a family and caretakers sense, as Shakespeare poignantly reflected, "from hour to hour we ripe and ripe and from hour to hour we rot and rot, and thereby hangs a tale." With this tale in mind, Linden (1953) characterized the first half of life as an evanescent phase, in which life may be regarded in an epigenetic sequence leading to identity consolidation, achievement of intimacy, and various forms of productivity including the "choice" of reproductivity. It is likely that a series of incremental events dominated by hopeful relationships will lead to higher degrees of maturation with peaks of learning, athletic performances, heights of intimacy and intense gratifications.

In the second half of life, Linden's senescent phase, new forms of caring for other generations may emerge with their own particular revitalizing potentials. But losses and depletions in the bio-psycho-social world dominate logorithmically. The varying effects of this shift from evanescent to senescent may be further compounded by ruptures in significant relationships, divorce, the death of dreams, the disability or death of parents, siblings, or even children. When fairly ordinary disillusionment in self, others, and idealized expectations are combined with subtle, ordinary, and less subtle extraordinary organic brain deterioration, the decline and fall of the human empire of personhood may follow.

If one lives long enough, a varied balance will be struck between inevitable changes in "the background of safety," in erosions or shifts in all "basic anchorages" (Cath 1963). With the onset of multiple organic diseases, vicissitudes in the integrity of the total human apparatus appear. In such circumstances, tremendous variations in the capacities to mourn object loss, as well as to simultaneously grieve over decremental losses in the self, are evident. Efforts at restitution also range from inordinate compulsive intellectualization, through frantic object replacement, through "spinning" hyperactivity involving all ego resources to withdrawal and recathexis of stored past introjects. For the rare few I consider gerontocrats, no matter what their fate, ever higher levels of integration, wisdom, and humor seem possible. Such people rarely become our patients. But most of us are less fortunate and fall into the ranks of gerontophobes, experiencing constants of change and depletion, loss and restitution, hope and despair. Such a fate to which even the gods must bend the Greeks called *ananke*.

In this attempt to redefine the vicissitudes of coping with later life affective and affective-organic states, I would include at this point some newly advanced "scientific realities" related to the "psychosomatic interface." For example, widowers at all ages whose wives died of breast cancer, demonstrated a marked decline in lymphocyte (killer cell) function within two months after the loss (Schleifer 1983), leaving the widower more susceptable to disease or death. But those bereaved in advanced years are doubly taxed. Now stress is met by a psycho-physiological apparatus undergoing an age-specific, albeit varying, depletion of many essential resources, including psycho-physiological immunity. This omniconvergence of stress (Cath 1965) and enhanced vulnerability due to decreased immunocompetency may account for seeming late-life lack of resiliency with increased incidence in infectious and neoplastic disease.

Long ago Shock (1960), studying normal physiological aging, advanced the concept of a natural predictable decline (one to one and one-half percent per year) in all cells, tissues, organs, and systems. Cath (1963) expanded this biological concept of lifespan depletion to include in varying degrees all five *basic anchorages*, namely, the body, the home, social-peer relationships, economic security, and meaningful purposes to life. As a result of unique individual vicissitudes, including genetics, e.g., the familial pattern of the mean time to failure of vital tissues or organs, he postulated that the rate of depletion depends on a mysterious condensate of mind-body factors and resistances. In turn, these determine the rate of change in psycho-bio-social integrity heretofore mistakenly judged as "normal aging."

Shock wrote over 20 years ago, long before recent research documented that we do not yet know how far life expectancy may be extended. Mirabile dictu, it seems health-genetic engineers may soon alter the rates of depletion attributed, naively, solely to the passage of time. But whatever the future holds, we can be sure the mind-brain monitors are in tune with various affective charges linked to attempts to integrate, create and compensate for both normal and abnormal losses and decremental changes. From midlife onward, a larger part of the energy of our enteroceptive scanning apparatus, (Cath's "sensor"), is increasingly preoccupied with what it senses and censors but on some level apperceives. These messages may herald an unstable, a declining, a discontinuous physiology, or a diseased organ within. These unwelcome sensory intruders further assault our narcissism when compounded by a benign decline in memory functions which alter our capacities to learn, name, master, or integrate complex new systems. This particularly intense threat to personhood in late life may be countered by denial with enhanced narcissism, e.g., the need to always be right, in order to keep secret the shameful sense of impaired mental alacrity. Benign memory loss intensifies affective states since both memory and affect are related to the integrity and patho-physiology of neurotransmission. Indeed, the synapse is the very site and target of most psychopharmacological therapies for anxiety and depression. So it seems late-life "depression" may be experienced through a changed perceptive apparatus located in a very different body by an ego with altered adaptive potential. There may be relatively minor or major flaws sensed in the feedback systems involved. Characterological defenses add their part. Patients who externalize (paranoids) live longest in nursing homes. Smokers who develop cancer tended to perceive life as more disappointing, feeling "more responsible for bad happenings." Vicissitudes of externalization mark responses of siblings to the same event, i.e., the dementia of a parent or of the self.

The intrapsychic focus of the psychoanalytic therapist should not distract from appreciating that people can best be understood in the specific bio-ego-ecological system (culture and subculture) set in its own time frame. In the second half of life, inventory taking with awarenesss of "normal" depletion-depression may be coped with differently in the Orient. There, the meaning of life and death have other affective valences and depression is much less frequently diagnosed. Cross-cultural aging leads to a redefinition of the meaning of life in terms of time past and time remaining. This is especially so for patient and therapist, should they be involved simultaneously with similar issues. Depressive syndromes treated solely with biochemicals may reflect a mutual silent conspiracy ignoring therapeutically accessible, albeit complex, multiple interacting factors in part to preserve the therapist's theories and narcissistic status quo.

Depletion-Depression

It is likely that one of the greatest challenges to sensed vital continuity in midlife, visibly accelerating the aging process, is the form and quality of long life which children observe either in their parents or in idealized parental substitutes. Consciously and unconsciously, the mode and quality of coping with depression-depletion, dying and death is mentally represented and stored. The impact of such newly experienced proximal "real" destinies upon the middle-aged, self-object world is always modified by particular aspects of the real or fantasied family image (Cath 1957), e.g., "this is how the men or women in this family live, relate, and die." Some, like Freud, are obsessed and predict they can not outlive a particular parent. Others despair over the more subtlely concealed minideaths of idealized expectations in the self-object world. When her mother died, Emily Dickinson wrote:

Her little figure at the gate the angels must have spied
But I could never find her, on the mortal side.

This couplet epitomizes the hope, idealization, regret, disillusion, and despair related to mortal parents, characteristic of repeated self-object inventories midway in the journey through life. In single or married people, such reflections on "the worth of it all" on the human side are never isolated but are mingled and co-identified with seeming successes or failures of significant others, especially children. In the midlife couple about to be presented, the resultant omniconvergance of gratification-depletion imagery related to three generations was especially devastating. After experiencing the real loss of devalued parents and all that implied, to give up on their children's future was equivalent to a series of psychological mini-deaths of their couplehood.

Before I delve into the clinical material, I will expand upon and delineate the complexities of some "normative" biological depletions of mid- to later life. These biological minideaths, while hardly noticeable as single events, combine with the psychological to produce an almost invisible crisis in slow motion. There are those who would stress the creative maturation-potential of such repeated loss and grieving. I do not disagree, and much creativity is forged in the crucible of the family. I would note that the Japanese written character for crisis consist of two ideograms, one for challenge and the other for opportunity. But I would stress how these "normative" combined depletions usually coincide with the aging and death of parents and the adolescing of the young. Their evanescence comes at the time midlifers begin to lose approximately one to one and one-half percent per year of the substance and vitality from all living cells, tissues and organs (Shock 1961). Such long acting, almost invisible summating declinations may seem to act as heralding precursers to that altered, depleted self, self-object, brain-body world observed in the generation past.

Furthermore, to add to this synthesis, it is known that apical dendrites of pyramidal neurons increase exponentially until a person is almost 50 years old. At peak, each of approximately 100 billion neurons makes approximately 40,000–600,000 connections. Long before the actual death of a neuron, terminal dendrites have been observed to break and fall away from the axon. (In animals it has been reported that cyclic AMP may reorborize such neurons.) This early dendritic fragmentation is associated with diurnal hormonal variations which may be some of the reason why the "normal aging process" seems to fluctuate within a span of 24 hours, from day to day, and even from year to year. Certain clusters of brain cells may lie dormant, functioning only when certain hormonal levels are reached, specific motivations are operative, or essential metabolic nutrients are available. These processes of terminal dendritic fragmentation and intermittent cellular integrity accelerate especially after age 70 (Watanabe 1983). I believe a conscious, recognizable impoverishment in associational (synaptic) facility breaks into painful awareness whenever declinations in the richness of thought, in learning new skills, in maintaining performance levels, in naming people at will, in recall of recent events (new imprinting) or in speed of calculations no longer meet expectations, as they almost invariably do in the sixth decade. This normative series of events is considered under the euphemism of benign memory loss.

But it is not memory alone that is changed. Over time, we may become painfully aware that our ears no longer discriminate 300,000 tones (especially the higher frequencies, explaining why female sopranos retire earlier than males); our eyes 8,000,000 subtle differences in color; and our lungs no longer provide 1,000 square feet of surface interchange. At peak, our 600 muscles, if pulling in one direction, can lift 2,545 lbs., our heart pump more than five quarts of blood every minute, (2,000 gallons a day), our blood-forming organs produce one billion red cells, and one cubic inch of bone withstand a two-ton force. Even if some or all of these capacities do not peak at the same time or are not reduced as much (25 to 50 percent by age 70), even if the loss is minimized by excellent self-care and exercise, and despite the original surplus of two of some organs, we would still have to deal with a shrinking depletion in the most crucial and sensitive of all organs, the human brain. So if most other basic anchorages (v.s.) remain intact, starting in midlife, there is a particular loss-depletion in thin fibers of synaptic connections that contribute most to affective stability and to the subjective state that uniquely characterizes human awareness of the aging process. Comparisons with the performance and sharpness of succeeding generations are ongoing.

It is believed that deep sleep, the "D phase," either nocturnal or during daily cat naps, are the major restorative periods for the approximately 30 known chemicals involved in maintaining neurotransmitter and mood integrity. By the sixth decade, not only is there an overall decline in total hours slept, but "D" time is especially reduced. These age-specific changes in the "sleep profile" have an unclear but definitive connection with the altered sleep pattern found in depressed states. Among other things, both share easy arousal and early morning awakening. But it is thought that the integrity of brain function is reflected in the integrity of the sleep profile. In addition, in a 24-hour day, endocrine supplies are ordinarily low if not exhausted by 4 A.M. and 4 P.M. But these lifelong normal variations in hormones, cerebral metabolism, and circulation augment the sleep changes noted. Some of these diurnal factors may be relevant to the normal if intermittant decrements in ordinary cognitive skills and mood which have created the "cocktail hour" syndrome or later have contributed to the more serious personality changes known as "the sundowner syndrome."

With age, there is an increase in the threshold for electrical impulse transmission in the central nervous system while the threshold for chemical transmission decreases. As a result, certain receptor organs are likely to become oversensitive while others less so. Perceived changes in the cerebral rate of reception and processing create their own unique anxieties due to intermittent sensing of the slowed, discontinuous, or contradictory messages. As persons sadly apprehend that the mind does not respond quickly or learn easily, their overriding subjective impression usually consists of a sense of alienation from and disgust with the aging self. This age specific dissociation, "this cannot be me!", is an ego split manifested by the wish to separate the past (best) self from the aged depleted self, a civil war, one never fought with such subtle realities before, all too easily overlooked.

Nathan Schock's investigations of specific changes in organ functions revealed that, with the exception of the BMR and ICW, the functional indices of vital capacity, glomerular filtration rate, renal plasma flow, ulna nerve conduction velocity, and cardiac output increase from a low point at birth to a maximum between 3 and 20 years of age. Robinson (1975), in contrast, discovered that the neurotransmitter enzyme, monoamine oxidase, known to be related to depression, is found in increasing quantities in different parts of the body, including the human brain. It may well be that some marker like this enzyme may be relevant to the fact that the highest incidence of suicide is in elderly, often reasonably intact, males. Most other biological indices peak by age 30 and almost all declined progressively to age 85.

Because the peak of organ function coincides with the period of minimal mortality and maximum fecundity, the curve of organ function across the lifespan may be considered to represent sensed changes in adaptive capacities, if not in the epidemiology of aging health. In more severe depleted, despairing, and depressed elderly without overt dementia, I have observed a process I call the decathexis of life (Cath 1963). Not only are there predictable evanescent and senescent patterns, but we can isolate some other major contributing depleting factors in loss of mental acuity. It has been confirmed that certain diseases, i.e., hypertension, have a significant correlation to intellectual decline from middle to old age. And as if to clinch it, with the diagnosed, hypertensive cerebral vascular or generalized atherosclerotis there is a greater likelihood of stroke and early morbidity and mortality.

It is inconceivable to me that the mind-body connection is not sensitive to these normal and pathological changes. While the subjective effects may be variable, common sense combined with psychoanalytic data seen from this perspective is not. For in the best of life circumstances, with age it has been observed that people become less efficient athletes, and, depending upon the psychological investment in body movement and synthesis, respond accordingly. It is generally believed that most liberal intellectuals become at least a bit more conservative, less spontaneous and, for the most part, less involved if not less creative. There is an increased tendency to hold back, to conserve energy, and stick with the "tried and true." All of this may be seen in the case cited below.

Relevant to this mind-body connection and apperceptions of the declinations in creative output, recent research suggests two forms of intelligence: a crystallized form that continues to develop until about the age of 50, manifest by the ability to use information already learned; and fluid intelligence which is responsible for reconceptualization and the formation of new ideas ("creativity, hot off the griddle"), which seems rare after age 30 (Niederland 1973). Of course the exceptions, like Freud, come immediately to mind. Even the onset of organic disease, (extracerebral, let us assume) did little to impair the outpouring of brilliant work. But there are those (Ater 1983), who see his last works, the *Outline* and *Moses*, as different in quality and very much influenced by his bio-psycho-social-cultural state. Indeed, these works were written in the face of constant threats to his life, to the intactness of his work, to his ego ideals and to Germany itself. In relatively rapid sequence, he fought against cancer, his enhanced lifelong fear of death, the loss of his beloved grandchild "Heinerle," and the rise of Nazism, all converging to destroy everything he held dear. Thus, one must observe how striking it is for such stable and continued creativity to persist through a succession of traumatic later years. Can we assume Freud was just depressed? Does this diagnosis do justice to the complexity of the tasks of his later years?

Clinical Example

When we first met several years ago, my articulate, obviously overweight physician patient, early in his sixth decade, hardly looked like the head of an outstanding department. Intuitively, in this first interview I measured him as defeated, despairing, depressed, and depleted. He had every reason to be disturbed and, as I suspected, suicidal. What was unusual was his train of thought, which made me wonder if he had read some of the above, "I'm in bad shape . . a major regression . . overcommitted . . all I want to do is sleep . . at my age I expected not to remember some things, but I don't think well at all . . I'm convinced my mind is gone . . my I.Q. is down . . I've been depressed before but this is not the same. I feel less than human. I'm lucky no one has uncovered the truth about me and made me retire early. I'm doing a lousy job, no, it's more that I can't keep up with new theories . . it's organic . .I know it . .senile changes . .I'm going to hell in a basket!"

It was some time before I learned my patient's mother, who died when he was in his thirties had become depressed, depleted of all personhood and then completely demented before his eyes. His first serious depression and psychotherapy had followed her death in a nursing home. His father had died of a stroke, when my patient was an adolescent, after years of hypertensive heart disease. And my patient had just started antihypertensive medication. My work with geriatric patients had sensitized me to the possibility that he was in tune with something more going on internally than just depression, despair, and depletion, for all of these may coexist along with early onset dementia. One-third to one-half of the patients with mild to moderate cognitive impairment do manifest depressive symptoms, and depressed older patients are more or less cognitively impaired because of dendritic fragmentation — a 'normal' age-specific breakup of nerve endings (Watenabe 1983).

I learned this brilliant successful professional in his sixties had two children whose passages across the crossroads of adolescence had almost destroyed his marriage. The son, now in his thirties, "a drug addict" in the past had only recently improved sufficiently to try college again. The daughter, having "slept around" for several years, had just returned home to live. The patient required three years of psychoanalytic psychotherapy for the condition he himself described as "halfway between depression and senility." During one critical mid-phase of therapy, his chronically depressed wife had been seen by a social worker "to save the marriage." After a transfer to the Midwest, the patient would take his summer vacation in the East, during which he would have several meetings he called "refueling sessions."

To illustrate the complexities of affective states in midlife and beyond, I've chosen to focus on several of these refueling hours in which the beginning, middle, and end phases of his earlier psychoanalytic psychotherapy were summarized by the patient. His accounting bears directly on and is the clinical base for the theoretical material presented above.

A Major Misery of Discovery

"I know I should have given my children love rather than guidance. Why didn't I? In back of everything I do is a fear of abandonment, of senility, of death, and of failure. I guess that could have had something to do with fearing my children's failures. My son was colicky, had his tonsils out at 4, an appendectomy at 8, and rheumatic fever shortly after that. You know all this. It was I that didn't take it into account. I couldn't understand his fear of me. That didn't stop me from yelling at him. But you shouldn't forget I was the one who took most care of him, mothered him, took his temperature and, I guess, overprotected him. I don't know why I was so afraid of death. Was it his or mine? I think the fear started after my mother died in a nursing home when I was 35 because right after that I truly became a hypochondriac. And my wife was no more sympathetic with me than I was with her or the kids. But long before my son was so sick, I was sure I would die of cancer. Like all good obsessives, the more I worried, the more I tried to put things in order, including my kids.

I don't think I told you, I used to play a game of symmetry with them at night. Fun before bedtime was to hold up our hands and try to make reciprocal images or parallels. I held up my thumb and fingers and would ask them what they thought I see from my side. Instead of fun, the situation gradually degenerated because they didn't seem to sense my need to keep things in harmony, to have fun or to learn. As a teacher, I should have know better. Some children do not understand or master the world in geometric terms. But I would leave angry, defeated and empty. But I was still determined I would succeed the next night. But then my wife got depressed about all this focus on them, and, as we got older, I seemed to lose her along the way.

When Mary [his daughter] began to date, my wife felt morally offended when she and her boyfriend sat too close together, even if only while watching television. I didn't object or support her so we would fight. My wife would cry herself to sleep saying she had never had a mother and that's why she got into trouble as a young girl. Now her daughter was getting into trouble and she felt alone and helpless just as she did then. It was the second time I considered divorce. My wife took to the guest bedroom so I wouldn't see how worried and depressed she was. I felt dirty because somehow my sexual desire always increased when she turned away from me.

That was when my work with you began. It was like a miracle. I gradually felt better and the relationship at home improved. Before that I was impotent in sex and at work. Then my son John told me he had trouble finishing anything because somehow it all was too boring. I remember you told me that boredom sometimes reflects anxiety or depression when I first came and was worried about early senility, losing my memory and had even thought of retiring. But you connected it with my anxiety about the changes I sensed in myself and with competing with younger men. So I screwed up my courage and told my son maybe he didn't finish things because he was afraid of getting out into the world and competing with other bright young men, just as I had been. You could have knocked me over when he said "but I never could beat you at chess." I burned with humiliation when I thought how often I had corrected him on his moves, always thinking I was helping. [He broke into tears.] You talked to me. Most psychiatrists I've had in the past drove me up a wall, they wouldn't talk! And you didn't humiliate me or make me feel my concerns were not important. I despaired of ever being helped. I was through, senile like my mother. Everything I tried for my kids ended up like the chess or our bedtime game of symmetry.

Life has always seemed like that, starting out as a game but ending as a disaster. One thing about being in therapy as you grow older is taking inventories so at least you find out why your good intentions to help people go astray. What I didn't want most was to be a patsy like my father. It seemed to me respect was the most important thing in life, so the obsequious way he acted bothered me. I guess I feared being a patsy with my own kids and worked too hard to overcome it. Even in the office the more I couldn't keep up, the more I felt others were on to me, and if I retired I wouldn't be missed. Now I tell myself I'd rather have built and be a patsy than never to have built at all, or stand aside and be a cynic like my father. I never realized how ashamed I was of him and of me as I aged. But since our last visit I have discovered a new major misery, the misery of knowing he was a better father to me than I was to my children.

This was the end of the hour before his last session at the end of the summer. As he left he asked me to remind him of this thought. Here are some excerpts from that last hour.

T: You ended our last session by saying that the major misery of these years was the discovery that your father was a better father to you than you had been to your kids. You asked me to remind you . . .

P: Especially my son. I still can't understand why he was so frightened of me. I so wanted to help him, to give him a sense of unquestioned love, to grow in more fertile ground, couldn't he sense that?

T: But you talked of your fear of your father who seemed so big when he yelled.

P: And I never appreciated how big I am. God, I'm twice the size of my father, maybe that's why I scared the shit out of him. [tears]

T: Is that what you meant when you called it the worst moment of your life—the major misery to set out intentionally not to repeat when you usually succeed?

P: Sure. I felt so defeated, so through, and so ended. And I keep wondering what my father wanted to or intended to do before he died, and what he felt about having a brilliant son his wife doted on. I can tell you one thing that was different. When he came home as he got older he wanted quiet. I was going to be a more understanding, more involved father than that. I thought anybody could be a better father than he was.

T: Because you would be there and be involved.

P: Because I would be there, I wouldn't be a dull and disinterested old man. I would share a larger part of their lives, not [be] a shadowy threatening person like he was. What originally drove me bananas was my lack of energy despite the urgency I felt to succeed as a father *while there was still time.* Could he have felt that? But this was not just at home, it was just as bad at work. And the truth was in either place the more I tried the more I failed and drove people off.

Even today, the more the angry urgency in something the more I fear I'll fail. When it comes to people, I still fear I won't have what I need. I know it's wrong, but what I'm saying is *I began to fear the limitations I sensed in my resources.* At work on technical problems, I was used to finding out what I was doing wrong and correcting it—or in the lab I'd see what my colleagues were doing wrong and correct them. That's what I was good at. *It terrified me not to be able to think clearly and see what was wrong. That's why I thought I was senile, and they'd find out how long it took me to learn how to use the computer.*

Is that why I keep hoping the kids will see what's wrong in me and correct it? But they caught on. I remember we talked about my early identification with my devalued father and my senile mother. He was always trying to protect himself and did not see the consequences of his withdrawal. I wanted to be a valued father — not the image I had of him. It really was a low point in my life, not like the condition I had when I first came to see you years ago, but like I said, a major misery of discovery, when I realized that I hadn't been the better father. To have a son, even if he is artistic, who cannot study enough to graduate, is stoned three or four times a week, and doesn't enjoy any of the things I do, isn't that enough to make a man like me seem *to have wasted his life*? I have no doubt now mine was the better father by just leaving me to make my own mistakes and not trying to correct me so much.

T: (at the end of the hour, choosing to ignore the transference implications at this point) Possibly the final verdict is not in. As you seem to be doing with your father, your children may feel differently as they age. Perhaps they will revalue what you now think such a misery.

As the patient was leaving my office, he turned to me and said, "Did you know that my father actually taught himself to read English? He read the Jewish paper only. One day when I was a teenager, I said to him 'you're an American, pop, why don't you learn to read English?' He answered 'fourteen hours of work a day, who has time?' Several months later I came home from school and he said 'so why don't you notice?' He was actually reading an English paper. My parents were nothing to be ashamed of, really, but I still developed this tremendous need to be respected and needed. Maybe my children will turn out so I don't have to be ashamed of them, or them of me."

In his next trip East several months later, he continued the themes of previous sessions, e.g., of inordinate need for respect related to the reevaluation of imperfect parents. In this regard, he reported two college dreams from his college days.

I dreamed I had a date with Miss Massachusetts, a typical WASP. I introduced her to all my friends at the frat house but ignored my parents standing on the curb. I knew it was the number one hurt I could inflict on them. Even then I felt the meaning of this dream was clear, and I hated the image of me it implied. I took pride in letting people know selected things about my background, and liked to rub elbows with the high and mighty, especially one brilliant upper-class classmate. When he could not finish his thesis, I tried to help him but he left. He managed to go to another graduate school but could not finish there either. Without his Ph.D. he never got into the field of his choice. The same night as the first dream, I dreamed that I and this man were with a group of apes who were speaking unintelligibly to a professor and this man. I was the interpreter explaining what the apes were saying to the men, but I couldn't explain what the men were saying to the apes. I guess I felt guilty enough about succeeding where he failed and not helping enough to dream I came from the apes and maybe could understand them better than any one else, but didn't understand the people.

As is always the case, a therapist has to decide what to do with such rich, seemingly anachronistic material. Stimulated by a late-life attempt to rework his relationship with both parents and offspring, this patient was in the process of recognizing that he may not need to be ashamed for failing to achieve inordinate respect or of being the perfect brilliant son, husband, parent, or department head. Still his dreams, over 30 years old, revealed aspirations that involved sadistic humiliation of his parents with all the transference implications, and a need to interpret between apes and highly regarded people. This challenged the therapist to synchronize this past material with today's real life and transference manifestations. I chose to focus upon the problems for which he had returned, namely his concerns and disappointment in his children, in his depleting brain power, and with his idealized therapist. While the exact words no longer come to mind, the following is an approximate reproduction of the subsequent several hours' work.

I wondered if, on the one hand, the patient felt that his punishment for snubbing his parents was to have children as unintelligible or as difficult to communicate with as the people in the dream. It might be that he had a special relationship with the apes, reflecting his understanding of what we had been discussing, but all of that was hard to communicate into everyday relationships. Maybe he worried, because of our limited understanding, that his children, like his friend of old, might be deprived of something he felt they desperately needed and that he could not help enough to get them to finish their professional education. It seemed he had needed to shore up his self-esteem with special knowledge which others seemed all too ready to discard, but this had failed him, too. Maybe he saw his children and colleagues turning their backs on him as he felt he had on his parents.

The patient's eyes filled with tears as he said:

When you say that it reaches deep inside. I wanted my kids to confirm I was not from the apes, but they couldn't understand or do that for me. It was selfish on my part to tell them that I know what's good for them, as I did with my father. And I know I want you to do the same thing for me that I did for him, to teach me, to get me to learn a new language, that of relating without teaching my apes or translating for them. No wonder I worried so about my mind. Another connection comes that has special meaning for me and maybe it will have for you in a way I do not see. For the last two weeks, I cared less about being chairman of the department; emotionally, it does not have the grip on me that it had before. You remember I turned the job down two years ago when I thought I was a dement. When I finally took it, I was reluctant because of all the trouble at home. I told myself my sense of ethics would be jeopardized. Then all those things the kids did, I was so ashamed. It was if they were striking at my job too. Then when the department had trouble and some of my friends sided against me, I felt the structure I had built to support me was falling apart, just like me and just like home. My son had failed, my daughter seemed ruined, my colleagues were betraying me and my wife sank more and more into her self, into a real depression. But so was I. God! I felt old. But it was more than that. It seemed like the world had come to an end and I was an empty, depleted shell. At times I thought some one would have to give me or her shock treatments, or that at least one of us would be hospitalized. Now I don't care so much about being the perfect teacher. The job seems to mean less. But I have done better and better. To think I thought I was becoming senile! I'm now more creative than ever before and I attribute that to you. Some of my friends asked, "Why don't you think of doing something else if you don't care about this job anymore?" Others tell me that I'm doing such a great job that I should stay on for another term. I do think of retiring from time to time but it seems by not using the position to shore me up so much, I perform better. I've slowed up but I don't seem to mind it now.

I asked if it was possible to draw a parallel with his children. Might they not be doing better (his son was currently on the Dean's List) if they did not feel such pressure to perform? Maybe they could feel someone was not so disappointed in how they were doing. As the patient became more distant from his children's tasks, they, like he, seemed less constricted and more creative. It was as if the whole family had had a conflict about the secret agenda of hiding daddy's weaknesses, namely, his inordinate need for respect, his fear for the integrity of his mind, and his fear of slowing up. The patient continued:

I've recently wanted to say to my son "Cut it out. Slow down. Have some fun. Enjoy life." And I have. But studying so goddamn hard, he has no time for anything else. It's like my curse, seems built in. In contrast my daughter is still always having fun and has no time for books. I remember you once suggested that having so much fun could be a cover for a feeling of loneliness and maybe she desperately needed the stimulation of contact with people. At first I couldn't see suffering as related to her running around and only could appreciate what you said after her suicide attempt. Maybe I can leave her alone in terms of expectations but how do I know she'll pull herself out of it? I have another worry. I think I've given you a wrong impression. The dream about the apes only strengthens my fear. My daughter, like my wife, is really a loving person. Do I have to make apes out of people to feel special? I remember when she was young she would give all her toys away. If she got dirty she would cry. But if she got a blister working in the garden she would quit and find people to comfort her. I guess she is still doing that, and that's what I fear doing, quitting. But in my own way I have too and maybe I feel like an ape. My son moved to things and she always moved to people. I always wanted to do both but couldn't.

Conclusion

From my theoretical and clinical vantage point, the diagnosis of major depression or major depressive episode (DSM-III) should be reserved for intact individuals problemed by intrapsychic conflict in the first half of life in Western cultures. As in early childhood, there is a need to redefine and refine our understanding of affective responses in those whose intrapsychic structure and basic anchorages and are either unformed, depleted, or diseased. In the first half of life, the evanescent phase, with obvious exceptions, injuries to self-esteem may be primarily infantile fantasies which seem to threaten self-object constancy. To be sure, at any age there are those whose affective equilibrium is inordinately more vulnerable to any disillusion, stress, or trauma. Thus, real or imagined trauma plus a combination of known and unknown factors may activate helplessness, a sense of apocalyptic doom, and unleash either the ravages of a savage superego against a reasonably intact body-ego adversary (depression) or lead to altered levels of consciousness with euphoria (Cath 1983). These emotional upheavals reverberating through the central nervous system may affect hormone levels, hemispheric relationships, and immunological states.

In the senescent phase, threats to body-ego integrity, to ongoingness and stability in relationships may be all too real, challenging not only psychoneuroimmunological processes but activating infantile fantasies of self-world destruction. An omniconvergence of a series of real disappointments in selfobject relationships, actual threats, e.g. hypertension, fantasy admixed with reality feedback of actualized aspirations may summate to present the subjective or objective clinical syndrome often called pseudo-dementia. A clinical vignette has been presented. Some would prefer to consider this case a form of masked depression, an affective state interfering with cognition, memory, and concentration. In my view, this minimizes the more pathologic impact of the multiplicity of subclinical anatomical, physiological, and familial factors involved. These reinforcing factors usually are superimposed upon lifelong neurotic, borderline, or psychotic infrastructures. Thus, some may confuse my concept of depletion-depression in one or more basic anchorages with the intrapsychic sensations of emptiness found in borderline or narcissistic conditions. Others may allege I am minimizing the significance of biological markers which to them suggest a common etiology. But all kinds of people grow old, and they age according to different timetables.

In my clinical experience, whatever the aging personality profile, gerontocratic, with many assets, or gerontophobic with inordinate sensitivity to narcissistic injuries, all of us, including aging analysts, will sooner or later experience an age-specific predictable depletion of reserve, cognitive, mnemonic, immunologic, and psychologic. I submit this combined system-syndrome is a new state of affairs, a unique age specific configuration, even if the manifestations should include biological markers. Indeed, the clinical picture varies in how much it is dominated by biological abberations, characterological traits, narcissistic (self) vulnerabilities, and either transient or more permanent pathological contributions from organic sources. Is there not a different real life problem to be coped with when body mutilation is no longer fantasy, e.g., the death of one's father by a disease which now threatens again, actual mutilation experienced by an amputee, sudden blindness in a habitual reader, deafness in a paranoid personality or cardiac failure with fibrillation in a panic-prone individual? But even without the presence of diagnosable entities, PET research suggests there are metabolic changes in the body which create their own feedback systems. I believe we need to broaden our understanding of the depth and complexity of affective responses in the general setting of the less intact and less resilient body-ego matrix. Our bio-psycho-social state is inventoried at least annually by a birthday mixture of incredulity about the passage of time and by various forms of denial and of protests in the autumn of our lives. Whether we and our patients "ripe or rot" or experience a mixture of both, our concepts of the nature of affective responses to the normal-pathological aging process are bound to color countertransferences. The response of patient and therapist will be unique for each according to creative adaptabilities, residual liveliness, desire for ongoingness and the simultaneous capacities to grieve. In brief, patient and therapist may meet at a time when each is struggling to appreciate what has been, what must be, and what still can be created for both in the therapeutic setting.

REFERENCES

Ater, M. (1983). A new look at *Moses and Monotheism*. *Israeli Journal of Psychiatry* 20:179–191.

Cath, S. H. (1957). Family image. In *The Patient and the Mental Hospital*, ed. M. Greenblatt et. al. pp. 565–576. Glencoe: Free Press.

———— (1963). Some dynamics of middle and later years. *Smith College Studies of Social Work* 33:97–126.

———— (1965). Some dynamics of middle and later years: a study of depletion and restitution. In *Geriatric Psychiatry: Grief, Loss, and Emotional Disorders in the Aging Process*, ed. M. Berzin and S. Cath, pp. 21–72. New York: International Universities Press.

———— (1966). Beyond depression, the depleted state. A study in ego psychology in the aged. *Canadian Psychiatric Association Journal*. Special Supplement 2:329–339.

———— (1982). Psychoanalysis in old age. Presented to the American Psychoanalytic Association, New York, 15 December.

———— (1983). Adolescence and addiction to alternative belief systems: psychoanalytic and physiological insights. *Psychoanalytic Inquiry*, 2.

Linden, M. E. and Courtney, S. D. (1953). The Human life cycle and its interruptions: a psychological hypothesis. Studies in gerontological human relations. *International Journal of Group Psychotherapy* 3:158–170.

Niederland, W. (1973). Psychoanalytic concepts of creativity and aging. *Journal of Geriatric Psychiatry* 6:160–168.

Robinson, D. S. (1975). Changes in monomine oxidase and monomines with human development and aging. *Fed. Proc.* 34:103.

Schleifer, S. J. et al. (1983). Immune system suppression tied to loss of spouse. *American Medical News*: July 22, p. 70.

Shock, N. (1960). Symposium of the American Association for the Advancement of Science, no. 65. Washington, D.C.

Watenabe (1983). Dendritic Fragmentation. *Journal of Tokufuku Hospital*, September.

PART III

Life Situations

CHAPTER TEN

Grief, Depression, and Survival in the Military

Stephen B. Shanfield, M.D.

How does the military function, on a socio-psychological level, to let its members perform its major task of managing violence and weapons of destruction (Huntington 1957, Janowitz 1960)? It is in relating to the task that themes of death are preeminent. These themes are continually renewed and reaffirmed in the daily work of the military member. Early, as a basic trainee, the military member is transformed so that dehumanized experiences are an important part of his military identity. There is much similarity between the soldier and the enemy, who also has such qualities. The actual work of combat is done on something familiar and at the same time "not alive." The continual immersion in death experiences desensitizes the military man to loss and mutes the intensity of the mourning response, so that the job can be done with a minimum of psychological difficulty. These experiences are important for survival.

Themes of death are part of dehumanization experiences. Bernard, Ottenberg, and Redl note that these experiences entail a decrease in a person's sense of individuality and in the perception of the humanness of other people (Bernard et al. 1971). Viewing others as "subhuman," "bad human," or "nonhuman," as if they were inanimate items or "dispensable supplies," are elements of the process of dehumanization. Maltreatment or even destruction of these dehumanized others can be sanctioned or carried out with relative freedom from guilt or grief (Bernard et al. 1971). On a deeper level, Lifton describes inner ideas about death arising in earliest childhood, that articulate around three polarities: connection versus separation, integrity versus disintegration, and movement versus stasis. These form the basis for prototypes of later death imagery. The early imagery formed around death can be reactivated by subsequent suggestions of stasis as well as separation (Lifton 1967, 1976a, 1976b). Separation or loss experiences have been particularly singled out as the earliest paradigm around death (Brown 1959, Reingold 1967).

Mourning, the psychological response to death and separation, is important for the military member, but an intense mourning response can hinder work performance. The mourning response has multiple components (Parkes 1972, Pollock 1977, Bowlby 1980, Shanfield 1981). After a loss there is an initial sense of psychological shock and disbelief. This leads into a period of grief which is characterized by episodic symptoms or a so-called "normal depression," in contrast to the enduring and persistent symptoms of clinically significant depression. Symptoms of grief include episodic crying, anger, and sleep and energy problems. An important aspect of grieving, based on the psychological attachment to the deceased, is sadness, accompanied by the wish that the deceased were still alive, or pining for and thinking about the deceased. These latter symptoms decrease in frequency and magnitude more slowly than the other symptoms (Jacobs et al. 1984) and can be reactivated by internal and external cues associated with memories of the deceased. The actual intensity of the reaction is related to the level of attachment to the deceased. In the military, efforts are made to regulate the level of psychological attachment to the enemy and to a lesser extent to fellow military members. The enemy is portrayed as inanimate and not alive. Thus, mourning related to the potential or actual death of the enemy and even fellow military members is muted.

The general approach of this chapter is one described by Lifton, using shared themes as observed in men and women who have been exposed to particular kinds of collective experiences (Lifton 1976). The method is similar to field research. Data were gathered from a variety of sources while the author was a military psychiatrist in the United States Air Force during the years 1969–1971 and chief of an inpatient unit in a general hospital located on the same base as basic training facilities. A large number of military psychiatric inpatients, who included about eighty basic trainees, were treated by the author. In addition, other cases were supervised and seen in conjunction with psychiatric residents who were assigned to the inpatient unit. The author also visited the basic training school, attended squadron commanders' meetings, discussed basic military training and the military in general with colleagues, basic training personnel, and other military members.

This chapter explores themes of death and mourning in the military. Clinical examples will be drawn from work with patients who were basic trainees; these examples will be used to illustrate the themes of death and grief in the military.

Basic Training and Death Themes

Basic training is an initiation period that acquaints the trainee with the central elements of the military. The trainee learns skills which enable survival in combat, along with basic customs of the military and the art of living in a large group (Bourne 1967, Marlowe 1959). All enlisted men go through basic training although few actually engage in combat (Bourne 1967).

This is the first experience away from home for most military personnel who are in basic training. The previous normal fabric of their lives disintegrates quickly and for many this can be quite upsetting (Marlowe 1959). Trainees are separated from the matrix of previous ties and lose their civilian status — a death, in some part, of the past. Careful attention is brought to bear by the military authorities on that which can be moved from the past into the present. Personal possessions are inspected and those not meeting specific criteria are put in a special place or locked up. Time also takes on new characteristics. Few personnel, at least in the beginning, can imagine the end of basic training and in this sense, the experience has a static quality (Marlowe 1959). Additionally, the basic trainee's future is attenuated into a never-ending series of presents. Life for a number of weeks has a limited future. Moreover, all aspects of the trainee's life, including work and sleep, are carefully regulated and externally controlled. For instance, the order of placement in the foot locker for issued as well as personal items is standardized. If there are deviations, the trainee can be punished. Leisure time is also limited and regulated. In a real sense, the trainee experiences a loss of freedom.

The trainee is viewed as a child who is unable to navigate on his own including making independent decisions and in a sense experiences the loss of individual identity. As an example, during a viral epidemic, the isolation barracks were called "the crib." Military personnel are told exactly how and when to act. The individual self cannot be asserted except in a narrow framework defined by the rigid boundaries of basic training. Whatever real difficulties the trainee experiences in learning about the military are closely associated with the organization's view of military personnel as less than human. Even the names by which the trainee is called point to a less than full person status. Trainees are treated as incompetents who cannot account for themselves; they can at times be called, among other things, an "eight ball," "stupid," "a dumb shit." They are viewed as incomplete and damaged persons who are filled with excrement, something dirty and not alive. For a period of time trainees experience, in some part, the death of the personal self.

Trainees are also told they are parts of a machine; they must act automatically, as if they were machines. Indeed, even some of the language used to describe the trainee is machinelike. For instance, those who are kept back in basic training for further training are spoken of as "recycled." The trainee is learning to be a part of a fighting unit, to become a technological unit which can be an instrument of violence or handle instruments of violence in a disciplined fashion.

Imagery around separation and death is elaborated upon by hospitalized basic trainees. They also articulate themes of disintegration: "I am going to pieces," or "I feel like I am going beserk." There are themes of stasis and stagnation such as "I feel trapped." (There are few, if any, actual opportunities for leaving basic training other than being ill.) Trainees ask, "Why do they treat me like a piece of crap?" "Why do they treat me like nothing?" "They treat cattle better than they do basics."

There is an emphasis on sameness in basic training. Trainees' hair is shaved and each trainee is issued a uniform without a name tag. They are treated as members of a unit; the individual identity is submerged in a group identity. Indeed, basic trainees are often treated as a group. For instance, if something goes awry with one individual, the whole unit is often held accountable. Trainees are immersed in the rigid requirements of obedience and discipline. They are told of the importance of acting in concert with other military members, particularly under the circumstances of combat, to ensure survival. The stage is set for later military membership where the issues of obedience and discipline touch all, regardless of job.

During basic training, trainees become rooted in the group. With their comrades they develop a cohesiveness that is drawn around experiences with sameness. They have no past and are nonpersons without wills, without freedom, without individual identities, and without a past or future. In this sense, trainees become technologized. This transformation is usually complete by the end of the training period. These experiences and membership in the group maximize the potential for survival in combat. Individuals have to act as a unit, to obey immediately, to stereotype and dehumanize, and to be able to kill the enemy (Glass 1961, Huffman 1970, Bourne 1970).

The Military Member and Death Themes

The military member is also continually immersed in themes relating to death. They are subject to the same dehumanized themes as basic trainees. The organization emphasizes the negative aspect of the human being, who is seen as inherently combative and evil, themes that are started in basic training and also used when speaking of the enemy (Huntington 1957). Furthermore, the soldier has to relate to the ethic of obedience and discipline which is linked to a potential combat situation. Soldiers are seen as stereotyped, interchangeable units. The important task of the military is continuously renewed and reaffirmed in all situations where obedience and discipline are encountered in seemingly innocuous transactions. There is also a sense, as with the basic trainee, that one has to be prepared to mobilize instantly for combat. Although most military personnel serve in support functions, the potential exists for all military members to be in direct combat. In a psychological sense, *all* are in combat and share a similar psychological sense of preparedness for combat. Themes of death and survival become institutionalized.

Psychological Issues: Loss and Mourning

What are the psychological issues underlying the themes of death and survival in the military? One strand of data about this psychological substratum comes from hospitalized basic trainees who are unable to tolerate basic training. Other evidence comes from the experiences of psychiatrists who have examined psychiatric casualties. The underlying psychological themes relate to issues of being able to withstand separation and loss, and the resultant mourning response.

Hospitalized Basic Trainees

On admission to the psychiatric inpatient unit, most basic trainees are floridly symptomatic. Whatever the symptomatic coloration, all speak of psychological themes of separation. There is marked anxiety around separation as a central psychological difficulty. All more or less express a desire to go home and to be reunited with a loved one or to return to an unresolved life situation such as taking care of a parent. In a sense, the hospitalized basic trainee is unable to handle the many inevitable losses of being in the military and is unusually sensitive to issues of separation and loss. The trainee experiences an acute stress disorder with a range of symptoms akin to acute grief (Horowitz 1975), including wishes for what was present in civilian life.

George A.

George A. is a 21-year-old airman with two months active duty. He was in a proficiency squadron for reading difficulties, where he had been sent after 11 days of basic training. He was admitted to the hospital following a syncopal episode. He had become symptomatic when he was told he would be set back in training. Along with feelings of panic and anxiety, he was sleepless, anorectic, and had a feeling he would go "beserk." He also had the return of an alarming dream of seeing his dead mother while he stood at the side of her open grave. On admission, he was noted to be anxious, tremulous, and preoccupied with issues related to his mother.

When George A. was 10, his parents separated. His mother, an alcoholic, then began living with another man. He and his three older brothers were shunted from one parent to the other. After high school, for about one and one-half years, the patient worked around the country in carnivals. By this time, his father had become disabled and the patient returned home to support him. Six months later and a year before entering the military, his mother suffered a stroke and he assumed responsibility for her care. Within the next weeks, she had a series of strokes and the patient was unable to continue caring for her by himself. Unable to get help from his brothers, he placed her in a nursing home where she died in his presence within a week of placement. His memories at the time of her death were of her struggling to say something to him that he could not understand.

The patient's symptoms cleared rapidly within a few days, including the dream and his overwhelming preoccupation with his mother. He repeatedly stated that he would not return to basic training—that he would go AWOL and was angry at the threat of being set back. He talked about guilt over his mother's death because of placing her in a nursing home, bitterness over his brothers' inaction, and marked concern about his father's health. He wanted to return home to take care of his ailing father. He was discharged from the hospital with the recommendation for discharge from the service.

This young man experienced profound psychological symptoms during basic training. He experienced the reactivation of prior grief experiences in the context of the prolongation of basic training. This represents a collision of past experiences with military themes, ties to his mother, and the present experience of continuing immersion in basic training with its elaboration of themes of death. What did he lose in basic training? Most likely, he lost a sense of self, of purpose, and of future. Prominent were themes of disintegration (going berserk), inertia and stagnation (inability to control one's fate by being set back), and separation (the wish to return home). His reaction was similar to an acute grief reaction which subsided quickly with support.

Michael B.

Michael B. is a 19-year-old basic trainee with 15 days of military service. He was found running through the barracks screaming uncontrollably and was forcibly restrained and brought to the hospital. Within a day, with supportive treatment, he became much less symptomatic and was able to talk about his difficulties.

He had been receiving calls and letters from his 16-year-old-fiancee stating she would kill herself if he didn't come home immediately— clearly difficult if not impossible for a basic trainee. He spoke with a priest who suggested referring her to a psychiatrist. Her threatening telephone calls and letters continued and became more threatening and insistent. He gradually became symptomatic with sleeplessness and an angry withdrawal. The incident precipitating admission happened after a phone call from his fiancee.

He was ambivalent about returning home since he was not certain what could be settled. He finally did decide to return home and was recommended for an administrative discharge.

This young man joined the military to escape a deeply held ambivalent relationship. His symptoms arose in the context of major problems with separation and connection. As a military member, he was not allowed to reestablish his prior ties and he became symptomatic. In another setting which would have been easier to leave, he may not have been symptomatic. At some other time in his life in the same setting, the issue of separation may not have been so acute. His current problems demonstrate difficulties with separation and loss that are common in this group of young men.

Another common pattern reported by hospitalized basic trainees is that of a "perfect" home without conflict. These individuals describe an unusually close family and idealize their parents. They seem unable to articulate any sense of open conflict in the family nor are they able to deal openly with hostility. They are affectively constricted and seem unable to tolerate the psychological pain associated with the basic training experience, particularly the separation from home, but also the immersion in death and loss experiences. Difficulty in expressing affect has also been noted to be a risk factor leading to problems in other loss experiences, particularly spousal bereavement (Shanfield 1983).

Difficulties are also seen in those who leave home before they are psychologically emancipated from their parents and before they have established a stable identity of their own. They are unable to withstand the separation from their families. Many of these individuals entered the military in response to the pressures of the draft. Perhaps at a later time they would be less vulnerable. They are dependent on being told what to do. They lack the flexibility to be on their own and to withstand the organizational immersion in dehumanization experiences which can result in the loss of self and intense grief.

Other Military Casualties

Other psychiatrists have described core problems with separation in different types of military casualties. Tausk, in World War I, found that deserters all wanted to return to a loved one, usually a mother, occasionally a wife or sweetheart (Tausk 1969, Roazen 1969). Teicher notes anxiety around death as a unifying theme in military psychiatric casualties in World War II (Teicher 1953). Similarly, Fairbairn, during World War II, felt that separation anxiety and infantile dependence were a universal features in the etiology of war neuroses (Fairbairn 1954). Morse as an Air Force psychiatrist in Viet Nam felt the primary vulnerability for psychiatric problems in Viet Nam to be family separation. Most of the patients he saw were career airmen with outstanding records, who had never faced the trauma of family separation (Morse 1967, 1970).

Thus, psychiatric casualties have sensitivities to issues of separation and loss, which are a major paradigm for issues relating to death (Brown 1959, Reingold 1967). They share similar themes with the basic trainee, the deserter, and the career soldier. They have deeply held attachments which they are unable to relinquish, particularly in the context of a concentrated organizational confrontation with loss and separation. Their psychiatric symptoms are akin to those of grief. Their individual themes of separation resonate with organizational themes around death and survival.

Dislocation Syndromes

Military psychiatric casualties are best described by the term military dislocation syndrome (Shanfield 1978). This term addresses the common thematic issues—separation from prior emotional ties—observed in military psychiatric casualties. These dislocations result in a form of grief which has been noted to be important in stress disorders (Horowitz 1975).

Individuals in civilian life experience a type of dislocation syndrome with symptomatic crises around organizational separation and loss. Examples of the latter include professors on sabbatical who experience crises of being on their own without the structure of their work or students who have difficulty separating from their families when they go to college. Many of these individuals experience symptomatic crises in settings which result in separation from their prior ties.

Some individuals, however, have problems that arise as a response to the specific context of the military. The coercive, authoritarian structure in which some military members find themselves contributes to the symptomatic state of many. For instance, the ability to rapidly transfer individuals like "things" to different settings, with little notice or input, which is based on the need to mobilize for combat, can create symptomatic crises. The psychiatric symptoms, in part, are a reflection of the dynamics of the military system. Thus, many military psychiatric problems are environmentally induced and connected to the core organizational task which relates to issues around loss and separation. Moreover, the culture of the military is an important determinant of patienthood as well as psychiatric symptoms. For instance, many patients in the military would not be psychiatric patients in civilian life. One cannot simply quit the military except under the threat of severe punishment. In effect, some individuals who are not functional and working on the job become patients who are on sick leave or in a hospital.

Discussion

In the military's performance of its task of managing violence, psychological themes of death and mourning are pre-eminent. The meaning of the enemy as a human is altered. The enemy is dehumanized and transformed into something not quite alive. This process allows for a suspension of psychological attachments, ambivalences, and the real issues around humanness. Something less than human can be killed.

The military member has a psychological relationship with and a special understanding of the enemy, for the military member, too, at times is treated as a dehumanized machinelike part of a fighting unit, instantly ready for combat. Individual allegiances and even individual identities are suspended in order that military members can be working members of the group. It is as if the military member has repeated loss and death experiences prior to the actual performance of combat, which then allows for a desensitization of these potent issues. In a sense, the military member is continually rehearsing important processes related to issues of death. The transformation of the enemy and the soldier into dehumanized parts affects mourning, the psychological response to loss and death. The intensities of mourning which result from the psychologic response to the real or even the potential death of others is muted, and crippling symptoms of grief are averted. The mourning response is managed so that it does not interfere with the performance of the military task, and psychiatric symptoms are kept within workable bounds. These transformations are important for efficient performance and the ultimate survival of the military member.

The institutionalization of death and the management of grief are incomplete. The object to be killed and the military member, although treated in dehumanized fashion, are human. This accounts for delayed guilt as well as other psychiatric symptoms seen in some Viet Nam combat veterans (Horowitz 1975). Similarly, intense grief about comrades killed in battle can be activated even years after the event.

One could argue that an element of dehumanization is present in any large institution (Goffman 1961). Indeed, dehumanization has been felt to be a general phenomenon of our age (Bernard 1971). It is true that the military is a large bureaucratic organization which contributes to the sense of dehumanization. There are, however, few institutions where issues of death and loss are as concentrated as in the military, institutions that have as a central and primary task the legitimized use of weapons of death and destruction and for which survival is such a direct concern.

The label military dislocation syndrome captures the psychological themes of separation and mourning associated with military psychiatric casualities (Shanfield 1978). Those who lack the capacity to withstand separation from past and present attachments seem to be at risk for not being able to function in the military. Some casualties lack the flexibility to deal with the dehumanization processes of the military or to withstand impersonal treatment. Many are not able to deal with the inevitable losses associated with being a member of the organization. Some are psychologically dependent and unable to withstand the intensities of the feelings of loss and mourning associated with being in the military. Similarly, the older military psychiatric casualty is often depressed and unable to function usually because of real or threatened separation. Necessary for military membership are a cohesive sense of self, minimal problems with separation, and a healthy capacity for change. Additionally, each member must have the capacity to withstand the immersion in the dehumanization process and to tolerate the powerful affects associated with mourning. These transformation experiences around death and dehumanization are an important part of the military identity and are necessary for survival.

REFERENCES

Bernard, V. W., Ottenberg, P., Redl, F. (1971). Dehumanization. In *Sanctions for Evil*, ed. N. Sanford and C. Comstock, pp. 102–124. Boston: Beacon Press.

Bourne, P. (1967). Some observations on the psychosocial phenomena seen in basic training. *Psychiatry* 30:187–196.

_____ (1970). Military psychiatry and the Viet Nam experience. *American Journal of Psychiatry* 127:481.

Bowlby, J. (1980). *Attachment and Loss*. Vol. III, *Loss*. New York: Basic Books.

Brown, N. O. (1959). *Life Against Death: The Psychological Meaning of History*, pp. 110–136. New York: Vintage Books.

Fairbairn, W. R. (1954). The war neuroses—their nature and significance. In *An Object Relations Theory of the Personality*, pp. 256–288. New York: Basic Books.

Glass, A. J., Artiss, K. L., Gibbs, J. J., and Sweeney, V. C. (1961). The current status of army psychiatry. *American Journal of Psychiatry* 117:637–683.

Goffman, E. (1961). *Asylums: Essays on the Social Situation, Mental Patients and Other Inmates*. New York: Anchor Books.

Horowitz, M. J. and Solomon, G. F. (1975). A prediction of delayed stress response syndromes in Viet Nam veterans. *Journal of Social Issues* 31:67–80.

Huffman, R. E. (1970). Which soldiers break down—a survey of 610 psychiatric patients in Viet Nam. *Bulletin of the Menninger Clinic* 34:343–351.

Huntington, S. P. (1951). *The Soldier and the State: The Theory and Politics of Civil-Military Relations*. New York: Vintage Books.

Jacobs, S., Kosten, T., Kasl, S., and Ostfeld, A. (1984). *A New Bereavement Scale*. New Research Abstracts, NR99. American Psychiatric Association Annual Meeting.

Janowitz, M. (1960). *The Professional Soldier: A Social and Political Portrait*. New York: Free Press.

Lifton, R. J. (1967). *Death in Life: Survivors of Hiroshima*, pp. 536–537. New York: Vintage Books.

_____ (1976a). *History and Human Survival*. New York: Vintage Books.

_____ (1976b). *Life of the Self: Towards a New Psychology*, pp. 39–40. New York: Simon and Schuster.

Marlowe, D. H. (1959). The basic training process. In *The Symptom as Communication in Schizophrenia*, ed. K. L. Artiss. New York: Grune and Stratton.

Morse, L. E. (1967). Air force psychiatry in Viet Nam. In *Proceedings of the Fourteenth Annual Conference of Air Force Behavioral Scientists*, January, pp. 149–162.

_____ (1970). Over the hump in Viet Nam. *Bulletin of the Menninger Clinic* 34:352.

Parkes, C. M. (1972). *Bereavement: Studies of Grief In Adult Life*. New York: International Universities Press.

Pollock, G. H. (1977). The mourning process and creative organizational change. *Journal of the American Psychoanalytic Association* 25:3–34.

Reingold, J. C. (1967). *The Mother Anxiety and Death: The Catastrophic Death Complex*. Boston: Little, Brown and Company.

Roazen, P. (1969). Tausk's contribution to psychoanalysis. *Psychoanalytic Quarterly* 38:349–353.

Shanfield, S. B. (1978). The two-year psychiatrist: themes of separation and dislocation. *Psychiatric Annals* 8:5.

_____ (1981). Illness and bereavement: unrecognized implications for prevention. *Arizona Medicine* 37:444–446.

_____ (1983). Predicting bereavement outcome: marital factors. *Family Systems Medicine* 1:30–36.

Tausk, V. (1969). On the psychology of the war deserter. *Psychoanalytic Quarterly* 38:354–381.

Teicher, D. J. (1953). "Combat fatigue" or death anxiety neurosis. *Journal of Nervous Mental Disorders* 117:234–243.

CHAPTER ELEVEN

Mourning and Depression in Organizations

Stuart Rosenthal, M.D.

A discussion of the mourning process, particularly a discussion of the sub-class of bereavement, assumes the real, imagined, or anticipated severing of an attachment to something or somebody psychologically significant. People consistently and persistently underestimate the breadth and intensity of their attachments. Consequently, they are baffled when they lose famil-iar faces, places, routines, and favored ways of perceiving and acting upon their environments. Loss is a cause and a consequence of change. All change produces new demands as well as losses which must be mourned (Levin-son 1973, 1976).

We distinguish here the bereavement reaction following the loss of a significant figure from "the more prevailing universal mourning process [that] . . . is the transformational process that provides for the adaptation to change" (Pollock 1977). "Mourning" describes the psychological processes following loss, while "grief" indicates the subjective states accompanying mourning (Bowlby 1961). References to "depression" in or of organizations include the DSM-III diagnoses of adjustment disorder with depressed mood, with mixed emotional features, or with work (or academic) inhibition.

Employing an organismic-systematic conception of work organizations, our discussion of mourning, depression, and related concepts includes the organization per se as well as individual employees. Bion's comprehensive theory of group working emphasizes the inseparability of individual psy-chology from group psychology: all group members are influenced by the other members; the emotions and irrational feelings of its members affect the rational working of the group; and administrative and managerial problems are simultaneously personal and interpersonal problems expressed in organizational terms (de Board 1978). His conception is consonant with subsequent applications of psychoanalytic theory to work organizations. Levinson's is the most comprehensive.

Along with other workers such as Jaques and Zaleznik, Levinson subscribes to a theory of motivation which emphasizes that

> man is continuously balancing his sexual and aggressive drives, the pressures and demands of his superego or conscience, and the realities of his world in his effort to master himself and it. This view is also environmentalistic because the focus is not with man alone or with organization alone but significantly with the man-organization relationship. (Levinson 1973)

His conception is built around an ego psychology model that defines three broad classes of needs to be met: ministration (for care and support from others), maturation (for growth and development), and mastery (for control of one's fate). Levinson's (1973) "fundamental thesis is that the most powerful motivating force for any human being is his wish to attain his ego ideal."

The workplace is a poignant environment. People enter it carrying their psychological baggage (and garbage) with them and strive to satisfy fundamental existential-psychological needs in the service of psychological balance (Rosenthal 1978). It is a living, open system paralleling biological ones, in that each must maintain equilibrium among its subsystems, between itself and other systems, and between itself and larger system(s) of which it is a part (Harrison 1972, Levinson 1972, Pascale and Athos 1981). An organization has personality or character and developmental phases (Harrison 1972, Greiner 1972, Levinson 1975). It even has cognitive capacity (Jaques 1976, 1979). The clinician's diagnostic frame of reference has been extended to organization, using the clinical case study method (Levinson 1972, 1976).

The Person-Organization Bond

Individuals underestimate the breadth and depth of their attachments. Their attachment to the organization attempts to satisfy therein fundamental existential-psychological needs. Moreover, we discussed briefly the relevance of affection, aggression, dependency, and the ego ideal to job fit, and we reviewed the concept of the organization as an organic system and referred to its character and growth. We can integrate all these elements by considering the concept of "psychological contracts," as Levinson (1962) calls them. Doing so accents the importance of the person-organization bond, thereby making more credible the phenomena of mourning and depression in the organizational context.

People forge psychological bonds to organizations through a variety of implicit and unconscious expectations. Similarly, organizational character, personality, and unconscious expectations contribute to this bonding. When these expectations are for the most part fulfilled, a person-organization fit ensues. Psychological contracts change with time and bind their parties. When they are unilaterally violated, the aggrieved party responds angrily. Organizational change often breaks contracts which must then be renegotiated. The acts that fulfill mutual unconscious expectations may be further conceptualized as forming the rungs connecting the intertwining spirals of the individual life cycle and the organization life cycle that together comprise the "double helix" of the working alliance (Rosenthal 1978). People choose, or elect to remain in, jobs, industries, and organizations whose ways of handling affection, aggression, and dependency and whose ego ideal satisfactions are congruent with that of the individual's. Obviously, we are dealing here with those transference images, whether manifest, implicit, or unconscious, that color an employee's perceptions of the organization as a whole, as well as perceptions of its subdivisions and of co-workers.

Mourning: Process in Context

Discussing mourning, Pollock (1977) says, "I believe what occurs in the individual can also be seen in the group or organization, and this organizational mourning process may be a critical factor in creative change or, conversely, in potentially harmful inertia." Volkan (1979) echoes this view: " . . . it seems to me that groups exhibit a response to loss or change that reflects what we have seen in the mourning of an individual; the pattern seems basically the same." Distilled from the contributions of Bowlby, Parkes, and Freud, Volkan (1979) adds his own observations to summarize this pattern as initial denial of the loss, followed by anger and yearning to recover the deceased (state of disorganization), followed by an acceptance of the loss as irreversible with a marked decrease in preoccupation with the image of the dead person (reorganization). These phases overlap and may fluctuate during progression toward a normal resolution.

Volkan acknowledges that mourning may become fixated at one of these phases (pathological mourning), but he observes that fixation is most likely to occur at the phase of yearning to recover the lost object. Moreover, he asserts (1979) that such yearning "appears simultaneously or alternately with dread of recovering the dead," reflecting the mourner's ambivalence toward the deceased. Furthermore, the fixated mourner continues to have an internal relationship with a part-object representation of the deceased. Volkan (1972, 1979) further notes an external focus of this ambivalent relationship in the form of inanimate objects with magical powers that link the mourner with what has been lost — "linking objects." We can think of these linking objects as psychological halograms. Volkan's formulation is an extension of Pollock's (1961) observation that the mourner may displace psychological investment from the deceased onto mementoes which are reminders of the departed, thereby either keeping the memory alive or denying that the lost object is permanently gone.

Mementoes commemorating instances of significant organizational change are displayed proudly in the offices of managers who were in the vanguard of those changes. Such cherished mementoes may also represent the ambivalent experience of loss in that change, but one does not see the mixture of yearning and dread that characterizes linking objects. This is not surprising given that Volkan (1979) observed this phenomenon in the pathologically bereaved and as an aftermath of war. Even the "losers" in organizational change, their nostalgia evoked by concrete residuals from the "good ol' days," do not show dread. Pollock's (1961) observations come closer to explaining the ambivalent feelings that may be attached to mementoes of organizational change. However, Volkan's observation of frequent fixation at the yearning phase in pathological mourning applies to organizations, especially in chronic manifestations of incomplete mourning.

Hirschowitz's (1973, 1975, 1977) description of the mourning process appears particularly applicable to work organizations. His conception builds on the work of Tyhurst and contains similarities to Pollock's explication. Initially, Hirschowitz (1973, 1977) presented a formulation of crisis theory that outlined a crisis sequence; it delineated a four-step process of the experience of loss: impact, recoil-turmoil, adjustment, and reconstruction. He later (1977) modified and renamed it the grief sequence. The sequence begins with a "period of life disorganization" precipitated by the "impact" of a sudden, unexpected, significant, inescapable life change event. This period can last four to eight weeks. It is followed by an overlapping "period of life reorganization," which may last up to 10 months, that ends with "acceptance" or "coming to terms" with the loss. The length of these periods and the phases within them varies from person to person and is dependent upon the magnitude of loss, coping capacity, and available support.

Our discussion reworks Hirschowitz's early and later formulations of the crisis-grief-transition sequence, as I prefer to call it. The period of disorganization begins with an inciting event that precipitates the impact phase, which lasts from a few hours to a few days. This phase is characterized by shock and incredulity in proportion to the undesirability and unexpectedness of the change, but these may be absent if the change is desired and expected. Psychic numbness accompanies early shock. Pollock

(1977) notes also a shock phase in the acute stage of mourning that occurs "when the ego is narcissistically immobilized by the suddenness and massiveness of the task that confronts it . . . Massive regression with panic can ensue until further restitutive activities take over." Parkes (1970) notes also that numbness in the first phase occurs in the first few days after the death of a loved one.

Hirschowitz (1977) calls the next phase "distraught distress," lasting one to four weeks. It manifests the disorganization implied by the initial numbness. The person's distractibility, disorientation, and impulsivity toward action, according to Hirschowitz, can lead to ineffective busyness and attempts at overcontrol of the environment, resulting in decisions that are poorly conceived, planned, and executed. This phase seems part of the recoil-turmoil stage Hirschowitz (1973, 1975) described in his early formulation.

Recoil is suggested by the denial underlying the impact-shock-numbness experience and by the busyness of the distraught-distress phase. Midway through this phase denial is counterpoised by incipient realization; this produces pangs of grief. This, in turn, triggers avoidance or denial or even numbness. Growing realization drives this approach-avoidance dynamic, which, over the period of disorganization, will be expressed in more subtle forms. Even during the distraught-distress phase, and thereafter, growing realization will surface underlying anger. Here, approach-avoidance takes the form of fight-flight behavior, including numbness. The anger may show as paranoid behavior, self-blame or be displaced. Self-blame may be accompanied by shame and depression. Realization also brings awareness of the permanence of the change-loss, which produces anxiety as well as anger. Anger expressed as restlessness, irritability, or bitterness fits with the protest component of Parkes's second phase of the grief process. Pollock's second phase of the acute mourning stage, the grief reaction, incorporates the hyperactivity described by Darwin (1872), but it emphasizes the intense psychic pain of grief itself (1961).

Concurrent with growing realization and the decrease in denial and avoidance and anger, the distraught-distress phase shades into the phase of grief proper. This phase resembles more closely Pollock's second phase and the yearning component of Parkes's second phase, which Parkes says reaches a peak during the second to fourth week. The grief proper phase is dominated by the feeling of intense sadness and yearning for what has been lost. When denial intervenes, it takes the form of attempts to mitigate the new change demands and their attendant losses by placing the new reality into a better light, by trying to undo some of it, by clinging to old ways, procedures, roles, or relationships threatened with dissolution, or by bargaining with the organization. I propose that, by the end of this grief proper phase, ending the period of disorganization, the clinging dependent attitude begins to yield to budding independence and interdependence as the painful detachment tasks get addressed.

This formulation differs from Parkes' (1970), who described a third phase of grief, disorganization, characterized by apathy, aimlessness, a sense of little purpose in life, and little concern with the future. He studied bereaved widows. The aimlessness and lack of concern for the future he describes may parallel the busyness seen in the distraught-distress phase and the concern with the past seen in the grief proper phase, respectively. However, the apathy and sense of purposelessness Parkes describes would be considered a maladaptive response to organizational change and loss. Pollock (1961) also describes a third phase of acute mourning, separation reaction. "It is regression to this early stage of separation [in infancy] and its defenses that characterize this phase of the mourning process . . . The response to recognizing the separation and its permanence gives rise to anxiety and also to anger. Both these affects are experienced in the acute mourning stage." Discussing this phase, Pollock describes a variety of pathological reactions resulting from unresolved conflicts around the early anxiety experience related to separation. He refers particularly to object relationships where there has not been total assimilation or identification: "In a healthy object relationship, where there has been total assimilation or identification, the mourning process is comparatively short-lived, and comes to a spontaneous end" (1961). It is this latter situation that prevails in reactions to organizational change and loss. Therefore, I propose that Pollock's third phase be folded into the grief proper phase.

While the period of disorganization can last two months, the period of reorganization can take another 10 months depending upon the magnitude of loss, coping capacity, and available support. This period includes the phases of adjustment and reconstruction. During adjustment sadness increases to a peak at around five months after the impact stressor, gradually diminishing thereafter until the change loss is fully accepted. In this phase the grief work continues concurrently with ongoing realization, independence, and interdependence. The detachment tasks are far along by then as the individual explores new relationships and integrates newer reality demands. The person's perspective becomes future oriented and is leavened with hope. The adjustment phase corresponds to Pollock's (1961) chronic stage of mourning. When an individual comes to terms with the new reality and relinquishes the past the individual enters the reconstruction phase of the period of reorganization. This is the "process of attaching himself to the new elements and testing their nature and boundaries. This period may last for a matter of months" (Pollock, 1976).

The anticipatory mourning process may be initiated before actual change loss occurs. This can be seen in persons who anticipate their demise, who face declining health, or who are about to be bereaved. Descriptions of anticipatory mourning often emphasize the negative consequence of the patient's premature withdrawal from loved ones or the withdrawal of loved ones from the patient. However, anticipatory mourning can lead to reconciliation efforts and ameliorate or obviate guilt in survivors. Moreover, survivors can plan for the disruptions that will follow. Similarly, anticipatory mourning occurs in organizations, with negative and positive effects. The announcement of prospective organizational change, whether applicable to an individual or an organizational unit, may initiate premature emotional withdrawal of the parties involved, especially when an employee leaves or when a unit is dissolved or sold. Management must manage the mourning process in these instances in order to maintain productivity in the interim before the change is executed and to ward off "survivor" alienation from perceived managerial insensitivity in the way in which the termination process is handled. Moreover, the manager of a dissolved unit needs help to deal with his or her feelings about leaving and to help subordinates manage the disengagement process. When organizational change does not involve termination or severing the relationship to the organization, those affected by the change adjust by experiencing anticipatory mourning, provided it is managed effectively. It is important to accompany the announcement of prospective change with actions that signal the reality of that change to mitigate denial. Confronting people with the reality of the change and its attendant losses helps. Failure to acknowledge and deal with the breaking of affectional bonds that often accompanies organizational change can lead to resistance to change and depressive reactions.

Mourning and Depression:
Individual Precipitants in Context

The developmental stages and crises of the adult life cycle interact with occupational roles and tasks. The presence of role-stage fit does not inure one to the seismic shifts in the psychological mantle generated by the major transitional periods of adult development. The mid-thirties and the midlife transition encompass a period of maximum vulnerability for one who has achieved a managerial position (Levinson 1973, Levinson et al. 1978). Often, there is a sense one is in an occupational cul-de-sac. The nature of organizational structure, practices, and values stresses upward mobility through an ever-narrowing managerial pyramid. Consequently, a legion of defeated middle-aged managers come to realize that there is a gap between accomplishments and dreams. For some, the ensuing depression subverts initiative and effectiveness, adding to the stockpile of organizational deadwood. Today, this process is happening at an earlier age because top executive rank is attained at a younger age. This, in turn, causes a telescoping of the time allotted to "making it" (Levinson, 1973). As Levinson states, "Crises of executives in turn become crises in organizations for they affect decision making, job performance, morale, and motivation. These crises relate, on the one hand, specifically to changes in the ego ideal with time and, on the other hand, to the nature of work and progress in organizations. . . . Executives must cope with them on behalf of themselves and the organizations for which they have responsibility."

Generally, career and work are related to the way in which one experiences the developmental events and psychosocial stressors of the middle and later years. The aging and mourning processes are intertwined as one comes to terms with inevitable, anxiety producing changes. According to Pollock (1977), "One might describe this process as mourning for former states of the self, as if these states represented lost objects." Aging employees with many years of service who identify strongly with an organization's traditional ideals and values may express their mourning for former states of the self through displacement, evidenced by nostalgic references to products, practices, people, values, and style of management of bygone years in the organization. Alternately, those "old timers" whose self-esteem rests significantly on the old ways of the organization may resist change because they equate its losses with death (Pollock 1977). Effective managers, when initiating organizational change, maintain continuity with the past. This eases the pain so that denial or a collective crisis response is avoided and the mourning process can proceed.

For middle-aged executives whose careers have plateaued or who feel they are on a downward glide path, the lost hope of realizing lifelong dreams and the heartfelt awareness of death's approach makes the task of preparing successors especially poignant (Jaques 1965). Executives who have reached the stage of generativity leaven their grief through vicarious, gratifying service to the next generation of managers. Those unable to acknowledge, bear, and put the losses of aging into perspective experience the organizational expectation to develop successors as rubbing salt into a wound; they may unconsciously sabotage young subordinates in order to deny change and to avoid the pain that looms. This behavior threatens the perpetuation of an organization when it occurs in the founder-leader. Helping these people to deal with the pain of giving up the "baby"—to mourn—is requisite for succession (Levinson 1973).

As mentioned earlier, each of us continuously performs an internal audit. We take the measure of the distance between our current self-image and our ego ideal; the greater that distance, the lower the self-esteem and the more likely is depression. When we feel that we are moving toward that idealized image, self-esteem is maintained (Levinson 1973, 1976). Work is a major vehicle through which one strives toward one's ego ideal. This formulation of motivation implies sources of vulnerability to depressive affect in the organizational context. This formulation is compatible with that of psychological precipitation of affective disorder in biologically predisposed persons.

Person-organization fit is derived from a reciprocal meeting of expectations along the dimensions of affection, aggression, dependency, and ego ideal issues. These dimensions apply also to the behavioral requirements of the job itself. This congruence must be maintained in a variety of assignments for a career to progress if one is to move toward one's ego ideal. People attracted to managerial roles have high ego ideals — (high expectations of themselves). Therefore, feelings of inadequacy are perennial, though usually hidden from others, because achievements will inevitably fall short of these high standards. However, balanced managers accept their own imperfections while striving to achieve high standards and experience gratifications from their successes. In general, conscientious employees, particularly highly skilled and knowledge workers, share the aforementioned characteristics. However, internal and external expectations of career progression into increasingly more responsible and demanding positions that must deal with the vagaries of human behavior increase managers' vulnerability to depression.

Even greater vulnerability awaits those with characteristically low self-image — "I wouldn't join any organization that would have someone like me as a member" — or with a perfectionistic ego ideal. In actuality, perfectionistic strivings may be attempts to compensate for a low self-image or may arise also from an earlier sense of helplessness or from unconscious guilt. Such guilt can cause self-destructive behavior often described as "snatching defeat from the jaws of victory" (Levinson 1979). Alternately, one commonly sees high achievers with astronomically high ego ideals whose unconscious guilt about falling short of their own or their parents' expectations (or both) leads to pathologically compulsive work habits — workaholics (Rosenthal and Rosenthal 1980, Levinson 1981). Enforced lulls in their frenetic pace, especially retirement or its approach, frequently surface depressive affect. In addition to entrepreneurial ventures, jobs that attract and exacerbate the workaholic pattern include those that demand perfectionistic behavior and those that are open-ended in their work-time boundaries, e.g., accounting, engineering, direct sales, and senior management positions.

Salespeople who sell directly to the public, who rely predominantly on commission, or who must meet high performance targets put their self-images on the line daily because they encounter so much rejection. A highly successful salesman confided, "The sale begins when the customer says 'no'." No wonder they look to their sales manager for support. High turnover and career changes are common.

Levinson (1983a) noted, "I have never seen a person make a significant career shift without experiencing a year-long depression. I don't mean that people are down in the dumps for a year but that they feel loss, ambivalence, and fear that things may not work out. Caught in an ambiguous situation in which they are not yet rooted they feel detached from their stable routines." Choosing a second career usually becomes an issue by mid-career or retirement. Conversely, the source of dissatisfaction and unrest leading to career or other life changes may be unacknowledged depressive feelings. Much of the dissatisfaction with and criticism of the quality of work life unearthed by public opinion pollsters originate from other life sectors. Even exciting work cannot cure depression.

Mentoring relationships in business are increasing (Roche 1979). A prominent chief executive officer said, "Everyone who succeeds has had a mentor or mentors" (Collins and Scott 1978). These intense relationships depend upon interpersonal "chemistry." Moreover, they become casualties of developmental tasks of the phase of becoming one's own person in the life cycle of protégés (Levinson et al. 1978). The severing of the bond is often painful and must be mourned by both parties.

We have discussed mainly psychological variables as individual precipitants of mourning or depression in the organizational context. But cognitive variables are important, too. Jaques's ideas about human capacity, mentioned earlier, are critically relevant to person-job fit. Fit includes not only the behavioral dimensions of the job, but also the psychological maturity and the intellectual breadth of the person, both of which are subsumed under Jaques's (Jaques 1976, Evans 1979) concept of work capacity. Vaillant's use of the concept of the hierarchy of defenses to illustrate psychological maturity is particularly applicable to the organizational context (Vaillant 1977, Semrad 1976).

Jaques notes that people vary with respect to the occupational skills and techniques they bring to the workplace and in regard to their capacity to cope with work responsibility. Work-capacity, measured by "the longest time-spans with which an individual can cope" (Jaques 1976), indicates the caliber of that person, the size of the job he or she can carry successfully. "[A] person gets satisfaction from having a level of work consistent with his current work-capacity, and a level of pay which is equitable for that level of work . . . we will use certain findings which appear strongly to relate the sense of fair and equitable differential pay to level of work as measured in time-span" (Jaques 1976).

Even if workers are highly motivated, feel they have chosen the right career, and possess the requisite knowledge and training, self-esteem can fall if they are employed at a level of work above or below their work capacity. In the latter case, boredom and monotony bring restlessness, resentment and, when prolonged, semidepressed resignation and loss of initiative; the self-image suffers and one despairs of achieving the ego ideal. Those who put high demands on themselves for achievement at work may blame themselves irrationally for their situation and become overtly depressed. Where workers are unequal to the work tasks, a lowering of self-esteem and even depression may ensue if workers acknowledge their lack of capacity for the role. Each person needs also to assess a prospective role in terms of its work level. Of course, this can become a catch-22 situation when the role's work level is higher than one's work capacity; often, one must possess that capacity to appreciate the complexities involved. This is why higher management, supposedly possessing higher work capacity, must bear the major responsibility for decisions about promotion.

Organizational Triggers

Organizational structure, process, practices, and change can lower self-esteem by damaging the self-image or by interdicting efforts to attain the ego ideal. The personal meaning and significance of organizational variables and events depend upon past experience. Psychological defenses buffer the impact. The magnitude, frequency, and duration of perceived noxious organizational factors or change that threaten self-esteem are important dimensions. These dimensions apply also to the positive, self-esteem supporting elements of the work climate, dimensions which have countervailing and mitigating effects.

Approval, esteem, and affection from others nourish a positive self-image and provide consensual validation of it. Actually, all work-related attachments that support positive self-image are hostage to organizational factors. When these factors evoke guilt inducing superego conflict by encouraging or requiring unconscionable behavior, self-image becomes a casualty. When circumstances and events arouse a sense of helplessness, a lack of efficacy, or make people feel inadequate or like losers, patsies or fools, self-image suffers.

The loss experience for people working in organizations can be viewed along four dimensions: loss of affection, loss of support, loss of information input, and the loss of the capacity to affect one's situation (Levinson 1973).

The loss of affection occurs when key relationships are severed or disrupted or when events are perceived to signal one's lessened value as a person. Physical disruption of relationships can result from promotion, demotion, transfer, or retirement; reorganization or merger may initiate such change. Organizational change that introduces a power differential in the dyad—when a peer becomes the boss, for example, is disruptive. This may happen even when no direct reporting relationship exists between them, as when their respective functional roles or organizational components are interdependent or are competing for organizational resources. Such changes in power differentials between friends are a source of unrecognized sadness in managerial ranks, often indicated by the recurring lament that climbing the corporate ladder brings some loneliness. The "fraternal" peer relationship, psychologically speaking, becomes a "paternal" one in the boss-subordinate configuration. Nevertheless, feelings of affection exist between bosses and subordinates, leading to a loss experience when paths must diverge.

The mentor-protégé dyad is a poignant example. Another is the departure of a beloved charismatic, often paternalistic, leader. Failure to mourn the leader's departure or failure to acknowledge the anger associated with being left behind may cause displacement of irrational expectations and feeling onto the successor. The loss is felt all the more acutely and the anger toward the old boss repressed when a paternalistic founder of an organization sells out to "hard nosed" professional managers. Idealization of the "old man" and hostile suspiciousness toward the incoming management are common. Massive disruptions of relationships occur with plant closings or when companies go out of business. Here, one sees the tearful response of employees who mourn broken relationships and the loss of the organization itself, as one would mourn a lost friend. Generally, departing leaders should make farewell rounds to facilitate their and subordinates' mourning.

When an organization changes its treatment of people so that they feel less valued, they experience loss of affection. This is illustrated by the previous example of the move from a paternalistic, closely held company to a publicly held one. The dominant ethos of loyalty and being an "obedient" employee must yield to one stressing performance, usually under the aegis of professional managers compensated according to bottom-line considerations. Employees may feel they are merely vehicles to maximize profits. Similarly, pressure tactics to maximize efficiency by treating people as objects to be manipulated and speeded-up arouse the same feelings. So does the shift from a warm, informal management style, where one's input to the decision-making process was sought and appreciated and where one was asked to perform tasks, to a cold and formal style where one is told what to do. This may be seen in a change from oral to written communications.

Besides management style, new strategic planning systems introduced into multiproduct companies have affected people's feelings in different parts of the organization about how it values them. The restructuring of these companies into strategic business units according to the different product markets served has been accompanied by a categorization of these product-units into a multibox matrix (Kiechel 1979). Position in the matrix is determined by relative strength in the marketplace compared to competitors and the prospects for growth in the market for that product or group of products. "Dogs," "stars," and "cash cows" to be milked to nourish fast growing or promising businesses suggest "divest" or "build" strategies and indicate the relative value of each product-unit to the corporation. When those who once made highly valued products in fast-growing units find themselves to be in a backwater of the company, they feel a loss of affection. Similarly, marketplace challenges may demand increasing expertise in new functional areas (less need for engineering and more for marketing expertise), producing a sense of being less valued. This is especially painful when the new emphasis alters the path to senior management positions. When competitive challenges mandate a change in organizational culture, a massive infusion of outsiders with the required experience and spirit may arouse deep feelings of inferiority and devaluation in the "old guard."

Perquisites are the way the organization expresses affection and appreciation to its employes (Levinson 1983). Salespeople are sensitive to changes in the make, model, or luxuriousness of company cars. Managers are sensitive to the size, décor, and privacy of their offices. Having one's own secretary, being party to important information channels, and being selected for prized management development activities inside and outside the company are seen not only as relating to job performance but as relating to the level of regard by the organization as well.

In the workplace, people rely often upon other key people to accomplish tasks. They have favored ways of behaving—handling affection, aggression, and dependency—that they find comfortable and effective, ways which support the self-image. Support for the ego ideal comes from an organizational environment that offers opportunities to better oneself. It comes also from the identification people have with an organization's purposes, goals, and leadership (Levinson 1973). Organizational change threatens self-esteem when it separates one from key people, eliminates favored ways of getting the job done, requires behaviors that are not in one's repertoire or yet mastered, or transforms the character of the organization and what it stands for so that people can no longer identify with it or work toward their ego ideals.

As in the example of a rapidly advancing armored column, success up the corporate ladder may disrupt one's lines of support in a number of ways. Others who joined forces with a corporate fast-tracker and gained a sense of meaning and purpose from this mourn the retirement of that person or that person's departure in the wake of success. Managerial success may become a pitfall. "Getting where you are is not all happiness — it costs a lot in your affective existence. You give up a lot to get what you think you want" (Rako and Mazer 1980). In the rush to become "somebody," to attain some height, some climb the wrong mountain, achieving a pyrrhic victory that does not meet their internalized criterion of personal success, the ego ideal. Moreover, they may realize belatedly that the loss of support of key people will hobble chances for success in the new position. Even those who achieve their heart's desire or reach their peak position in the corporation, may wonder, "Is this all there is?" Here, the loss of support for self-esteem derives from a dependence on opportunities for and success in mastery of greater challenges. Success and contentment notwithstanding, the prospect of having to train one's successors or to relinquish to new blood the organization one built and that supports the self-esteem, creates a loss experience (Levinson 1973).

Shop floor promotion to firstline supervisory responsibilities, the interface between labor and management, can create loss in information input when former co-workers take an adversarial stance toward their erstwhile peer. Auto mechanics who depend on engine sounds and other direct means to troubleshoot problems experience a loss of information input if they must now rely on poorly understood computerized, electronic diagnostic systems to repair microprocessor-regulated vehicles. When organizations institute formal, "scientific," management decision-making systems, in which what counts is what can be counted, managers with an intuitive visceral style of decision making may be at a loss as to how to order numerical data to justify their hunches. Conversely, when in-house data processing specialists had to become sensitive to the service needs of co-workers, some lacked the "marketing" or interpersonal skills to sense these needs. Organizational change that requires a different cognitive style to sense information leads to loss of information input in those with inadequate sensors.

Loss of the capacity to affect one's world evokes feelings of inefficacy and helplessness which lower self-image. This happens when people feel manipulated by economic forces or organizational policies and practices beyond their control, when they are compelled to view themselves as losers because of the pyramidal structure of organizations, or when the job market devalues their skills or age. Loss of mastery occurs when people feel deprived of adaptive skills by age and obsolescence, or when mastery is thwarted because they have responsibility without authority, do not know the boundaries of their functions, how they are to be done, or how well they are performing them.

A conglomerate acquired a small, highly profitable company run by young entrepreneurs accustomed to making multimillion dollar decisions. The parent corporation installed financial controls that required approval for expenditures exceeding one-half million dollars. The founders and their cadre of young dynamic executives resigned, leaving behind a shell of what had been a dynamic enterprise. The bureaucratization of an organization — which centralizes decision making away from the point of implementation and emphasizes rules, regulations, and procedures at the expense of task — reduces managers' capacity to act. Conversely, bureaucrats expert at using the maze of regulations to maintain control of their operations are threatened by a change to more flexible, task-oriented organizational structures and processes. The computerization of the telephone industry workplace, in which telephone operators are allotted a time limit for each call, arouses complaints from operators since "operators often perceive of themselves as having become extensions of the computer instead of human beings" (Serrin 1983). Control systems that assume people must be watched or policed communicate that they are seen as inadequate, incompetent, and untrustworthy. People feel driven by such controls and their self-image suffers (Levinson 1970).

Related Phenomena

Burnout, when people " . . . can't or won't do again what they have been doing," is an example of psychological exhaustion, a sense of futility (Levinson 1981). Managers are among the prime victims of burnout; they are subject to severe pressure in people-oriented jobs for long periods, without adequate support and with limited prospects for gains. Feeling angry, trapped, helpless, and depleted, these managers may appear depressed. Modern organizations have been implicated as breeding grounds for situations that promote burnout.

The term "management by guilt" describes managerial decisions motivated by a desire to avoid irrational guilt stemming from discomfort with feelings of anger in oneself and others (Levinson 1964). Their decisions allow them to deny their anger to themselves, anger that violates their superego standards, and to avoid provoking anger in others that, in turn, will arouse their own hostility. Circumstances in the organization that induce guilt include an unproductive subordinate; concern for long-service employees; obligation to another; younger person put into a position of authority over older ones; having to implement unfair or unwarranted company policy; and giving performance appraisals.

Building on the conceptions of Freud and Melanie Klein, Jaques advances the view "that one of the primary dynamic forces pulling individuals into institutionalized human association is that of defence against paranoid and depressive anxiety; and, conversely, that all institutions are unconsciously used by their members as mechanisms of defence against their psychotic anxieties" (Jaques 1955). Jaques illustrates this from his consulting experience with a small engineering company near London (Jaques 1951). Menzies (1962) explored social defence systems in a general hospital nursing service.

Conclusion

An overwhelming majority of workers in the United States receive a wage or salary in an employment hierarchy with at least one manager and subordinates. This mode of accomplishing work is increasing, compared to the solo provider of services or products or professional partnerships. The workplace has become an increasingly important source of psychosocial stressors and an arena in which people express the effects of nonwork stressors affecting them.

Work organizations are social institutions, the design of which determines the contexts and limits within which individual personality expresses itself. Organizations are central to the social and economic exchange relationships that are essential to societal and species survival, relationships that rest upon the ability for reciprocal or collaborative interaction with others (Jaques 1976). This, in turn, includes an ability to communicate and to establish relationships founded upon trust, confidence, and love. Effective social institutions have structures and processes that fit human nature and the environment and that socially connect people to society by facilitating normal relationships between them.

To the extent that individual and organization needs are congruent and mutual expectations, implicit and unconscious, are fulfilled, an ambience of reciprocity emerges wherein employees invest psychological capital in the enterprise. This can be transduced into more efficient and effective ways of accomplishing tasks.

The process of fulfilling the psychological contract, reciprocation, makes not only the relationship between person and organization a productive one through joint efforts to resolve personal and organizational conflicts that are task related, but it also helps the individual to resolve psychological conflicts related to dependence, distance and change, and occupational identity (Levinson et al. 1962).

Modern organizational life revolves around a hub of change whose adaptive demands must be addressed to perpetuate the organization and to maintain the individual's viability in it. "Sloughing off yesterday" is a prerequisite (Drucker 1980). But this means the ability to mourn: "To be able to mourn is to be able to change. To be unable to mourn, to deny change, carries great risks to the individual and to the organization" (Pollock 1977).

Like the "Big Bang" theory of the creation of the universe, the human life cycle is a story of centrifugal movement that characterizes the scope of an individual's cognition, conceptual capacity, and interpersonal relationships. Successively widening arcs of interpersonal attachments — mother, father, siblings, kin, kith, schoolmates, workmates, institutions and other collectivities — weave a psychosocial safety net integral to individual health and the commonweal. The biopsychosocial perspective of illness accents the importance of a systems approach to medical practice. Workplace factors need to be considered in the evaluation of patients. Such factors include psychological "toxicity" in addition to chemical and physical ones. Mental health professionals can cast a wider diagnostic net by expanding their ecological perspective.

REFERENCES

de Board, R. (1978). *The Psychoanalysis of Organizations*. London: Tavistock Publications.

Bowlby, J. (1961). Process of mourning. *International Journal of Psycho-Analysis* 42:317–340.

Collins, E. G. C., and Scott, P. (1978). Everyone who makes it has a mentor. *Harvard Business Review* 56:89–101.

Darwin, C. (1872). *The Expression of the Emotions in Man and Animals*. London: Murray.

Drucker, P. F. (1980). *Managing in Turbulent Times*. New York: Harper & Row.

Evans, J. S. (1979). *The Management of Human Capacity*. West Yorkshire: MCB Publications.

Greiner, L. (1972). Evolution and revolution as organizations grow. *Harvard Business Review* 50:37–46.

Harrison, R. (1972). Understanding your organization's character. *Harvard Business Review* 50:119–129.

Hirschowitz, R. G. (1973). Crisis theory: a formulation. *Psychiatric Annals* 3:33–49.

_____ (1975). Psychological cost-accounting. *The Levinson Letter*, Addendum. Cambridge: The Levinson Institute.

_____ (1977). *Managing Termination: I. The Levinson Letter*, Addendum. Cambridge: The Levinson Institute.

Jaques, E. (1951). *The Changing Culture of a Factory*. London: Tavistock Publications.

_____ (1955). Social systems as a defense against persecutory and depressive anxiety. In *New Directions in Psychoanalysis*, ed. Klein, M., Hermann, P., Money-Kryle, R. E., London: Tavistock Publications.

_____ (1965). Death and the mid-life crisis. *International Journal of Psycho-Analysis* 46:502–514.

_____ (1976). *A General Theory of Bureaucracy*. New York: Halsted Press.

_____ (1979). Taking time seriously in evaluating jobs. *Harvard Business Review* 57:124–132.

Kiechel, Walter. "Playing by the Rules of the Corporate Strategy Game." *Fortune*, 24 September 1979, p. 110–118.

Levinson, H. (1964). *Emotional Health in the World of Work*. Cambridge: The Levinson Institute.

_____ (1970). A psychologist diagnoses merger failures. *Harvard Business Review* 48:139–147.

_____ (1972). *Organizational Diagnosis*. Cambridge: Harvard University Press.

_____ (1973). *The Great Jackass Fallacy*. Cambridge: Harvard University Press.

_____ (1975). The conceptual context for compensation. In *Man and Work in Society*, ed. Cass, E. and Zimmer, F. New York: Van Nostrand Reinhold Company.

_____ (1976). *Psychological Man*. Cambridge: The Levinson Institute.

_____ (1979). *The Levinson Letter*. Cambridge: The Levinson Institute, 1 October.

_____ (1981a). *Executive*. Cambridge and London: Harvard University Press.

_____ (1981b). When executives burn out. *Harvard Business Review* 59:73–81.

_____ (1983a). A second career: the possible dream. *Harvard Business Review* 61(3):122–129.

_____ (1983b). *The Levinson Letter*. Cambridge: The Levinson Institute, 3 October.

Levinson, D. J., Darrow, C. N., Klein, E. B. et al. (1978). *The Seasons of a Man's Life*. New York: Alfred A. Knopf.

Levinson, H., Price, C. R., Munden, K. J. et al. (1962). *Men, Management and Mental Health*. Cambridge: Harvard University Press.

Menzies, I. E. P. (1967). *The Functioning of Social Systems as a Defense Against Anxiety: A Report on the Study of Nursing Services of a General Hospital*. Tavistock Pamphlet no. 3. London: Tavistock Institute.

Parkes, C. M. (1970). The first year of bereavement. *Psychiatry* 33:344.

Pascale, R. T. and Athos, A. G. (1981). *The Art of Japanese Management*. New York: Simon and Schuster.

Pollock, G. H. (1961). Mourning and adaptation. *International Journal of Psycho-Analysis* 42:341–361.

_____ (1977). The mourning process and creative organizational change. *Journal of the American Psychoanalytic Association* 25:3–34.

Rako, S. and Mazer, H. (1980). *Semrad, The Heart of a Therapist*. New York and London: Jason Aronson.

Roche, G. R. (1979). Much ado about mentors. *Harvard Business Review* 57:14–28.

Rosenthal, S. (1978a). A clinical perspective of work organizations. *Psychiatric Opinion* 15:19–23.

_____ (1978b). Expression of the emotions in the world of work. *Psychiatric Opinion* 15:24–28.

Rosenthal, S. and Rosenthal, P. A. (1980). Effect of career obsessions on marriage. *Medical Aspects of Human Sexuality* 14:16–31.

Semrad, E. (1967). The organization of ego defenses and object loss. In *The Loss of Loved Ones*, ed. Moriarty, D. M. Springfield: Charles C. Thomas.

Serrin, W. (1983). *The New York Times*, p. 1. 18 November.

Vaillant, G. E. (1977). *Adaptation to Life*. Boston and Toronto: Little, Brown and Company.

Volkan, V. D. (1972). The linking objects of pathological mourners. *Archives of General Psychiatry* 27:215–221.

_____ (1979). *Cyprus – War and Adaptation*. Charlottesville: University Press of Virginia.

CHAPTER TWELVE

Self-destructive Behaviors

John Buckman, M.D.

Self-destructive Behaviors

Only persons wished dead by others kill themselves. This was suggested by Federn (1952) and explains the dynamics behind some suicides. However, for other reasons we will have to turn to Freud (1920a) who postulated the death instinct and self-murder (Freud 1920b), implying that the aggressive energy at first directed against another person is ultimately turned against oneself. Fenichel (1945) describes suicide as an attempt by the ego to appease the superego by submissiveness. This attempt, he said, is doomed to failure because the superego has become inordinately cruel and has lost its ability to forgive. Stekel (1910) describes suicide thus: "No one kills himself who has never wanted to kill another or at least wishes the death of another. The secret court of the unconscious follows the principle of an eye for an eye and a tooth for a tooth. It declares itself guilty of the death wish and condemns itself to death." Menninger (1933) observed in the suicidal person the wish to kill and to be killed, as well as the wish to die. He said that one has the impression that, for such people, the suicidal act is sometimes a kind of insecure playacting and that the capacity for dealing with reality is so poorly developed that they perceived that they could actually kill themselves and not die. Menninger felt that this wish could have had its origin in childhood when the child acts as though death were reversible. Zilboorg (1936) suggested that suicide was an attempt to thwart frustrating external forces, to gain immortality, and to maintain the ego rather than to destroy it. At times it seems that suicide is an endeavor to injure someone else through an aggressive retaliation. Stengel (1964) gradually came to the conclusion that those who attempt suicide and those who commit suicide are not exactly the same group, but an overlapping population.

Indirect self-destructive behavior.   Among these behaviors could be included drinking, drugs, smoking, overeating, difficulties in accepting chronic illness (punishing the body), neglect of health, excessive stress-seeking, self-mutilation, hunger strikes, asceticism, martyrdom, constant breaking of norms, and seeking repeated operations. Motivation may be to receive care or correction, to receive recognition and to be rid of a sense of helplessness, unworthiness and hopelessness. Many "accidents" are probably suicides.

Suicidal Thinking, Gestures, and Attempt

A number of studies estimate that 10 percent of the population have had suicidal thoughts during the previous year, women twice as often as men. According to Beck and Rush (1978) early childhood experiences form a basis for their negative view of the external world. Suicides tend to be rigid, more present-oriented, and poor in imaginative resources.

Attempts are more common in young persons and women. In the United States the number of attempts is estimated between 200 and 600 per 100,000 persons. Thus, attempts are 20 times as frequent as completed suicides. Some of the reasons are increasingly complex society, changing attitudes towards suicides, use of drugs, lower threshold to use of tranquilizers, less family interaction, more divorce, increasing character pathology leading to behavior changes other than neurosis. One interpretation holds that people are more dejected and experience life as less meaningful. On the other hand, the fact that suicide has not increased substantially in the recent decades points to the ambivalence in the mind of the suicidal person.

Recently, more attention has been paid to the indirect self-destructive behavior exhibited by the so-called "character disorder" patients. Menninger (1933) developed the concept of death instinct to the fullest, including the indirect self-destructive behavior, by postulating the change in the balance between opposing instincts toward life and death. Under the influence of patterns containing guilt, aggression, and neuroticism, instincts might produce a number of self-injurious or self-limiting behaviors. Menninger's classification would include focal suicide with self-mutilation, malingering, polysurgery, purposeful accidents, impotency and frigidity, chronic suicide including asceticism and martyrdom, neurotic invalidism, alcohol addiction, drug addiction, antisocial behavior, psychosis, and organic suicides. We should add to this list forgetting or omitting medication, ignoring dietary restrictions, gambling, excessive risk-taking, drug experimentation, and a host of stress-seeking behaviors. Farberow (1978), in comparing the indirect self-destructive patient with some psychosomatic and chronically ill patients, noted certain characteristics. The indirectly self-destructive patient tended to be younger, to be ill longer, to have a number of other illnesses, to deny, neglect, or disregard the illness, to choose the hospital as a major source of support, to have more overt suicidal behavior, to show disregard of other illnesses, to have drunken driving records, to be complaining, demanding, aggressive, hostile, suspicious, with poor impulse control and few outside supports. Indirectly self-destructive patients are highly present-oriented, have poor work histories, are manipulative, possibly aggressive, dependent, insist that the illness is the hospital's responsibility, and use the indirect self-destructive behavior as an outlet for feelings of inadequacy. These patients feel that life has little to offer and show no frustration tolerance coupled with poor impulse control.

While suicidal thinking is very common and suicide attempts numerous, actual suicide is not very common, even though it ranks as the ninth or tenth most frequent cause of death. Paykel (1974) and his collaborators estimated that nine percent of American adults reported suicidal thoughts during the preceding year. In women this occurs twice as often as in men. Suicidal thoughts correlated strongly with psychic disturbance and psychic symptoms, particularly with depression. There was also a correlation with social isolation, somatic disease, and stressful life events. A study of female office workers in Helsinki showed that 12 percent had suicidal thoughts during the preceding year. According to Beck and Rush (1978), suicidal thoughts are common in states of grave dejection. The cognitive failure of depression formulated by Beck offers a hypothesis about the forming of a predisposition to suicidal thinking. Early experiences constitute a basis for forming a negative view about one's self and a tendency to interpret one's ongoing experiences and the future in a negative way. These negative concepts are formulated in terms of schemas and, although different persons may conceptualize the same situation in different ways, any one person tends to be consistent in the response to similar types of events.

According to Lonnqvist (1978), suicide attempts have increased in recent years. The author also points out that we mistakenly exclude indirect self-destructive behavior from the statistics. He poses the question of whether the frequency of suicide attempts reflects the community's well being and changes in it. Obviously, our constantly changing and complex society challenges our adaptive ability and increases the prevalence of crisis reactions and suicide attempts. Attitudes towards self-destructive behavior have grown increasingly liberal. There is less interaction within the family than in the past; emotional relationships are less intense and marriages are dissolved more often and more easily. All of these factors are conducive to increased character pathology. We now tend to identify more often the borderline and narcissistic personality; one wonders whether there is a statistically significant increase in these conditions. Are we justified in suggesting that people today are actually more dejected and do not experience life as meaningful? Suicide rates have remained fairly constant and this may suggest that the intention is not to die. Stengel (1964) noted that in the last measure of the suicidal act there is a degree of uncertainty of outcome. Most people who commit suicidal acts want neither to die nor to live, but to do both at the same time.

Estimating increased risk. There are some behaviors or behavioral changes which should alert one to the greater likelihood of suicide in a patient. Among these are psychotic depression, hypochondriasis, sleep disturbance, alcohol and drug addiction, previous attempts, family history of suicide (especially as a consequence of depression and alcoholism), a sudden relaxation of symptoms, a bout of drinking following a period of abstinence, a rapid swing between mania and depression, and hallucinations with voices either denigrating or persuading the patient to commit suicide. A severe deterioration of a chronic physical condition, a sudden major loss of narcissistic supplies and the rejecting attitude towards helpers may also be contributing factors. Durkheim (1951) stressed the importance of alienation and anomie in the genesis of suicide.

Epidemiology of Suicide

In the United States, suicide is the ninth or tenth major cause of death. About 30,000 deaths are certified as suicides each year. Attempted suicides number about 300,000. The United States rate for suicides is 12 per 100,000 persons, male suicides numbering 18 and females 6. The rate increases with age and peaks in middle years, preceded by a slight peak in late adolescence and early adult years. In successful suicides, men outnumber females by 3 or 4 to one. This ratio is reversed in attempted suicides. There is a rise of suicide in the involutional period, which occurs somewhat later in males than in females. In the United States, high rates of suicide are recorded in Alaska, Wyoming, Montana; somewhat lower rates are shown for California, Florida and Virginia. The lowest rates are found in Louisiana, Alabama, Mississippi, and New York. For the 15–24 age group, suicide is the second or third most frequent cause of death, the others being cancer and accidents. The most vulnerable population is white, middle-aged or elderly males; persons who are single, divorced, or separated; persons who live alone without family; persons who use alcohol; persons with somatic complications; persons with prior attempts or family history of suicide; alcohol and drug addicts; and especially those persons who can be labeled psychotic depressives. Marital, economic, religious, and cultural factors play a role. Suicide is higher in the divorced, the unemployed, higher in Protestants than in Catholics and Jews. The suicide rate among immigrants is equal to that in their country of origin. Most suicides occur early in the morning and the days chosen are, for the most part, Mondays and Tuesdays. Of the group of previous attempters, two-thirds make repeated attempts, the second attempt occurring within three months of the first. Twenty percent have a family history of suicide. One out of 10 attempters will succeed within 10 years; five to 10 percent of medical admissions are for overdose. Methods of suicide depend on age, sex, tradition, and availability of the method. In the United States, the highest rate of suicide is among males who use firearms to commit suicide. In the United States suicide by firearms is 80% for males and 20% for females. Males generally use more violent, and therefore more effective, methods of suicide. Poison accounts for 60 percent of female suicides and 40 percent of suicide among males.

The Sex Bias

Some research has been done on the association between sex hormones, aggression, and suicidal behavior. Mood and behavioral changes in relation to the menstrual cycle have been investigated. In most species the male is more aggressive than the female although any given obstruction to goal-directed behavior in either sex may result in deprivation. However, men generally have a stronger aggressive response to frustrating stimuli. The fact that suicidal girls communicate their suicidal intent more often than boys suggests that girls use suicidal behavior more often than boys as a means of manipulating their environment. Men may have stronger aggressive drives and women may have stronger inhibitions against aggression. Young males who cannot find meaning in life and who cannot resolve their aggressive drive may turn to suicide as a solution to their depression and anger. The pattern frequently involves lack of a strong masculine figure at home.

Retirement in our achievement-oriented society weighs heavily on those who are emotionally unprepared. Work is an esteemed social role, the loss of which is highly correlated with suicidal potential even in primitive societies. The retired male may perceive himself as finished, useless, rejected, with accompanying feelings of despair, resentment, and rage. Living alone in social isolation plays a large role, as does chronic disease. The elderly make few suicide attempts and these attempts are more successful than those of younger persons.

Therapy

Main (1957) pointed out that only the most mature therapists are able to encounter frustration without some ambivalence towards patients who do not get better or who get worse despite long and devoted care. We all have rather ambivalent and complex attitudes towards death and self-inflicted injury, and our education does not equip us to deal realistically with these issues. On the basis of interviews with therapists about 7,200 suicides, Litman (1965) noted that the therapists reacted to dead patients in a personal manner. These therapists felt emotions such as grief, guilt, depression, personal inadequacy, and sometimes anger. Some of the therapists noted partial identification with the dead person in their dreams. One frequent psychological maneuver was to review the case and present it to their colleagues.

Our difficulties in dealing with the suicidal patient should be recognized rather than minimized. As physicians we are not taught to recognize that some patients, by their behavior, provoke in us some very negative and bizzare responses, obviously the same responses they provoke in their own families, friends, and peers. Rosenbaum and Richman (1970) found that the families of suicidal patients experienced more hostility and offered less support towards patients than the families of nonsuicidal patients. Successful suicide is probably the result of intimacy, hostility, and the victim's inability to retaliate.

Individual interviews with the suicidal group indicated a mutual feeling of discontent among patients and their own families. Family members expressed anger at patients much more often than patients expressed anger at them. Several of the relatives did not acknowledge their own role in the event when interviewed privately and rarely, if ever, did so in the family session without a large measure of therapeutic intervention. Death wishes toward the patient were implicit or explicit in many statements made by relatives and were voiced with unexpected frequency.

Many therapists view suicidal patients as depressed, rather dependent, and of low self-esteem. Most therapists favor extending themselves in order to provide support for the patient and contact those who might assist a patient's progress. Those who view the patient as primarily manipulative would tend not to worry about the number of suicide attempts. This may indicate an unwillingness to recognize the seriousness of suicidal communication. In some therapists the suicidal patient may produce feelings of malice and aversion and the resulting hostile countertransference may produce a major obstacle to treatment. Maltsberger and Buie (1974) pointed out that countertransference is inevitable in all psychotherapy and that it is likely to be particularly intense in the treatment of borderline and psychotic patients, many of whom are prone to suicide. These patients have great difficulties with their loneliness, hostility, and sadism. The authors pointed out that transference operates against the therapist continuously preconsciously and unconsciously. To support and justify, as well as to bear it, the patient employs a reciprocating system of provoking and projecting. Hate in itself when intense is difficult to bear. When felt towards the therapist, it gives rise to a severe sense of worthlessness and primitive guilt.

Suicidal patients may employ indirect means to provoke a countertransference hate to substantiate their projections. They are surprisingly quick to recognize in a therapist any lingering magical expectations that the therapist could provide a panacea. The patient would be strongly motivated not to improve in order to convince the physician that the physician is worthless. The initial period of work with the suicidal patient, especially if the patient is a woman and the therapist is a man, may be marked by the patient explicitly declaring in a neurotic way that she is convinced that only the physician and no one else can help, that she thinks the physician will understand what others have not. If therapists attempt to view themselves as this omnipotent, both patients and therapists will soon feel hopeless. Successful treatment of such patients requires recognition of magical expectations as burdensome problems that lead to inevitable disappointment.

Our hostile countertransference can be well illustrated in our responses toward patients who chronically self-inflict wounds. These patients exhibit symptoms indicative of the category of factitious disorders, one of which is termed the Munchausen's syndrome. The term was coined by Asher (1951), who described a category of dramatic and untruthful patients showing numerous admissions to hospitals. These patients underwent many serious operations. They nearly always discharged themselves against medical advice after quarrelling violently with doctors and nurses. Spiro (1968) tried to elucidate the motivation for this type of behavior. He identified early deprivation, confused self-image, the need to re-enact an original dramatic situation, and the wandering in search of a lost love object. These patients harbored hostility and provoked it in the treating team. Schwartz et al. (1974) and Schwartz (1979) formulated a concept of "suicidal character." He said:

> In certain patients suicidality is not a symptom of another psychiatric disorder but a central element of character structure [and stated further that] suicidal behavior is generally taken to be symptomatic in nature rather than ego-syntonic, however, any behavior which comes to be used as a means of adaptation to the world long enough, tends to become ego-syntonic. There are some suicidal people for whom suicidality has become a means of securing nurturance from the interpersonal world. The usual crisis response to suicidality reinforces such patients in their suicidal styles. The increasing long-time risk becomes the price of short-time nurturance.

Schwartz further stressed that suicidal ideas or impulses are generally experienced as alien events which arise in response to great anguish or dread as final desperate ways of escape from an unbearable situation, and that suicidal impulses are generally thought to be acute and limited by time. Approaches to suicide prevention are organized for the most part as crisis responses. Schwartz's thesis is that chronic suicidality necessitates therapeutic response vastly different from crisis intervention. He states, "In fact it may well be that the suicidal character is an iatrogenic condition produced by such inappropriate responses towards what was initially symptomatic suicidality." He stresses that treatment of this suicidal character is a long-term undertaking. It is unique only in that the consequences of neglecting it are more likely to be fatal than neglecting other characterological conditions. Hospitalization, he says, should be as brief as possible, because prolonged hospitalization fosters precisely the kind of dependence that promotes suicidal character formation. It is necessary to remind the patient constantly that others cannot guarantee the patient's life; they can only be supports. The emphasis in psychotherapy should be on seeking internal motivations for life rather than attempting to replace them with external ones. A similar point is made by Olin (1976):

> A major issue in the psychotherapy of the chronically suicidal person is the patient's avoidance of his responsibility. If the patient is not helped to reorganize this avoidance the therapist's effort may be consigned to future attempts to either assume responsibility for the patient or to rescue him.

Beck stressed that suicide-prone individuals have a particular disposition to overestimate the magnitude and insolubility of their problems. He talked of the cognitive triad and the exaggerated negative view patients hold of the outside world, themselves, and of the future. Beck advocated that in psychotherapy, suicide-proneness should be a major target and stated that the most promising approach is to train patients to think of solutions to problems and to divert attention from suicidal wishes. Beck also recognized that suicidal wishes fluctuate during psychotherapy and that patients must frequently be encouraged not to view the emergence of suicidal wishes as a sign of failure of their treatment. In addition, Beck stressed the importance of being continuously alert to the effects of traumatic experiences outside of therapy that may exacerbate suicidal wishes. He said that the therapist's stance should be that the reemergence of suicidal wishes should present an opportunity rather than a setback.

Suicide in Children and Adolescents

Suicidal behavior in children is much less common than in adults and is expressed in different ways. There are differences in frequency and sex distribution. Many children who want to kill themselves do not actually wish to die. Children under 5 conceive of death as a temporary reversible state. Between 5 and 9 the child begins to appreciate death as a fearful state in which one is separated from loved ones. Death is personified as a skeleton and identified with physical changes, such as the person becoming all bones, rather than the possible obliteration or transformation of consciousness. After 9, children begin to exhibit an adult view of death as the termination of life and as universal. These characteristics are well described by Arietti and Bemporad (1978).

Motives for childhood suicides were thought to be fear of impending punishment, an attempt to punish the parents, or a wish to join dead relatives. A different picture is presented by adolescents. Attempts and gestures are frequent, and suicide ranks as one of the leading causes of death in the 15–19 group. Twelve percent of all suicidal attempts are made by teenagers, of whom 90 percent are female. Arietti and Bemporad quote Mattson et al. (1978) who distinguish six groups of child and adolescent suicidal attemptors. Their motivations were: loss of love object; self-hatred as "the bad me"; a final cry for help; the revengeful angry teenager; the psychotic adolescent; and the suicide game (flirting with death in order to get peer approval and experience a thrill).

The college student maybe singled out as a subgroup which deserves special attention. College students have a higher rate of suicide than non-college persons of the same age. Investigations of the differences between suicidal and nonsuicidal classmates revealed that suicidal students were older, did better academically, showed more emotional disturbance, and were more likely to be foreign. Hendin (1975) quoted by Arietti and Bemporad writing of the college student said:

> They are so inhibited and tied to past familial atmosphere of gloom and despair that they cannot tolerate the opportunity for pleasure and involvement which college life offers them. These students see the relationships with their parents as dependent on their emotional, if not physical death, and become tied to their parents in a death knot. Coming to college, graduating, becoming seriously involved with other persons and enjoying an independent existence have the power to free them. In fact the meaning of suicide and depression lies in their encounter with the forces that might unleash their own possibilities for freedom.

For such individuals, according to Arietti and Bemporad, "numbness is a sort of protection and from the possibility of gratification arose guilt over betraying the secret bond with the parents." The guilt and the understanding that it blocks pleasure leave individuals frozen in a state of inhibition. They cannot break through the old sanctions and yet cannot endure living with them. Suicide becomes a possible solution. Death has always held special fascination for these individuals. Their own self-destruction appears to fulfill the parental command not to dare to live. Hendin's work, according to Arietti and Bemporad, draws attention to some of the potent forces for suicide in all age groups:

> A lack of being appreciated for what one is, a failure of parents to instill a sense of joy and approval of life in the child, and finally a prevailing sense in the individual that his enjoyment of other relationships, or other activities is a guilty betrayal. Suicide and depression may be the result of self-induced elimination of satisfactory, and satisfying life alternatives that are not tied to omnipotent others or dominating goals.

Various attempts have been made to document the predictability of suicidal potential. A number of useful rating scales have been designed to identify the suicide-prone individual. Tuckman and Youngman (1968) designed the high risk factor list in attempted suicides. Weissman and Worden (1972) devised a risk rescue scale. Kovacs, Beck, and Weissman (1975) compiled a list of hopelessness items such as "I might as well give up, I can't imagine my future, I don't expect to get what I want, there is no use in trying." Ringel (1976) talked about the presuicidal syndrome. He suggested that one can identify a suicide-prone individual by several alerting factors during the time prior to suicide. Keith-Spiegel and Spiegel (1967) wrote about affective states of patients immediately preceding suicide. Comstock (1973) designed an impulsivity scale and uses that together with intentionality and lethality scales in order to evaluate suicidal potential and the need for psychotherapy.

Hospitalization is required for the severely suicidal patient. This often has to be accompanied by the use of antidepressants and antipsychotics and, in some cases, the use of electroshock treatment. Shein and Stone (1969) have pointed out that therapists often fail to recognize potential suicidal patients. At other times therapists, while recognizing the dangers, fail to discuss them with patients. Too often, patients are not asked directly whether they find their life situations intolerable and whether they are thinking of suicide. This failure to assign crucial priority may thereby unwittingly encourage patients to incorporate suicidal preoccupations in a negative aspect of the transference relationship with the therapist. Shein and Stone (1969) also suggest some guidelines for working with the suicidal patient. The therapist must express concerns frankly and discuss them explicitly with the patient. The therapist should consider suicide to be a maladaptive action and do everything that can be done to prevent it. The therapist must label all suicidal thoughts as crucial to any psychotherapeutic endeavor. The therapist and the patient together must communicate the suicidal potential to important figures in the patient's professional and family environments. The therapist must explore in detail whether or not the patient believes that current relationships and situations have become intolerable. The therapist must accept the fact that the transference produced will be distorted by the previously defined role of the therapist as someone involved in preventing dangerous or destructive acts. Both Shein and Stone believe that for the borderline or psychotic patient such committment is essential. The authors recognized that the patient may test the therapist's investment. Auxiliary personnel are therefore often essential. There are also difficult issues of countertransference with this type of patient and the therapist will have to consult freely and often with professional colleagues and supervisors. As mentioned before, this type of active approach has been criticized by those therapists who insist that eventually patients must take responsibility for their actions.

Physical Illness and Suicide

Physical illness and physical pain are highly correlated with suicide. Emotionally disturbed individuals also develop physical illnesses for which they are admitted to general hospitals. A recent study by Shapiro and Waltzer (1980) looked at successful suicides and serious attempts in general hospitals over a 15-year period. They noted that attempts and successful suicides are not random or impulsive acts and that, in the vast majority of cases on retrospective review, there was a reasonable degree of predictability. Each episode occurred over a discernable stress related to an almost overwhelming affect, stemming from either a recent abandonment or severe physical impairment. There was also apparent evidence of another set of clinical circumstances that heralded the onset of a crisis leading to suicidal behavior. These were associated with the withdrawal states secondary to alcohol intoxication, episodes of disorganization, and hallucinations or delusional ideas leading to suicidal acts in schizophrenic patients. They found a bimodal age distribution: older patients had a history of chronic obstructive pulmonary disease and malignancy; younger patients had a history of alcoholism or schizophrenic illness. They noted a distressing frequency of lack of request for psychiatric consultation in the presence of an aberrant or unusual behavior of medically ill patients. They suggested the routine inclusion of psychiatric personnel in ward rounds on medical and surgical floors.

Conclusion

To this point we have talked about issues of life and death, aggression, violence and murder. Suicide has to be viewed as murder and in German the word for suicide is indeed "Selbstmord," self-murder. Unless we understand this we cannot understand the vicissitudes of transference and countertransference in the therapy of the suicidal patient. We cannot understand the patient's rage or torment; we cannot understand our own reactions, rescue fantasies, omnipotence, hopelessness, and angry feelings toward patients who insist on destroying themselves. Fenichel (1945) describes suicide as an attempt by the ego to appease the superego by submissiveness. This attempt, he said, is doomed to failure because the superego has become inordinately cruel and has lost its ability to forgive. If we view suicide as turning of sadism against the person, then we can understand the aggressive and sadistic wishes towards the suicidal patient that are held by family, peers, and also by therapists, physicians, nurses, psychologists, social workers, counselors, and all others who see themselves in the rescuing role. For some patients, suicide may be seen as an escape from an intolerable situation, as a means of reunion, or as an attempt to magically control death itself.

The Therapist's Suicide

Our world, of course, is not divided into patients and therapists. Sometimes therapists themselves are potential patients, and we know that the suicide rate among psychiatrists and health professionals is high. Each year, the equivalent of one graduating class from medical school will kill themselves. Sensitive patients often verbalize their concern about the therapist's well-being and mental health, and wonder if therapists might be unable to protect patients and themselves from the patients' excessive demands and attacks. When therapists kill themselves, their patients grieve. Ables (1974), Chiles (1974), and Ballenger (1978) have enumerated some of the reactions of patients whose therapists committed suicide. They identified feelings of omnipotent responsibility for the death, questions about the continuance of therapy, concerns about the fallibility of the therapist and their own sense of abandonment. They often found the event incredible and found themselves demoralized as well as angry. Ballenger pointed to the importance of instituting as soon as possible another therapeutic relationship which would see as its first task the working through and resolution of the feelings that this apparent abandonment provoked in the patients.

Postscript

We are seeing these days an epidemic of violent behavior on the personal, interpersonal, or intermotional level. The aggressive instinct seems to appear more unbound, freer of libidinal cathexis, and more unmodified by the superego. We know that suicide and homicide are not mutually exclusive. The increase in destructive behavior may be the result of failure of superego formation and regression prompted by increased feelings of helplessness and narcissistic rage experienced by modern man.

REFERENCES

Ables, B. (1974). The loss of a therapist through suicide. *Journal of the American Academy of Child Psychiatry* 13:143–152.

Arietti, S. and Bemporad, J. (1978). *Severe and Mild Depression*, pp. 185–207. New York: Basic Books, Inc.

Asher, R. (1951). Munchausen's syndrome. *Lancet.* J:339–341.

Ballenger, J. (1978). Patients' reactions to the suicide of their psychiatrist. *Journal of Nervous Mental Disorders* 166:859–867.

Beck, A. and Rush, J. (1978). Cognitive therapy of depression and suicide. *American Journal of Psychotherapy* 32:252–269.

Chiles, J. (1974). Patient reactions to the suicide of a therapist. *American Journal of Psychiatry* 28:115–121.

Comstock, B. (1973). Selection for Psychotherapy of Suicidal Patients Presenting in an Emergency Area. Seventh International Congress for Suicide Prevention, Amsterdam.

Durkheim, E. (1951). *Suicide.* New York: McMillan.

Farberow, N. (1978). Research in indirect self-destructive behavior. *Psychiatry Fenn Suppl.* Helsinki. 21–35.

Federn, P. (1952). *Ego Psychology and the Psychoses.* New York: Basic Books.

Fenichel, O. (1945). *The Psychoanalytic Theory of Neurosis*, p. 400. New York: W. W. Norton, Inc., 1972.

Freud, S. (1920a). Beyond the pleasure principle. *Standard Edition* 18:3–66. Hogarth Press, London, 1957.

———— (1920b). A case of homosexuality in a woman. *Standard Edition* 18:145–175.

Hendin, P. (1975). Growing up dead: student suicide. *American Journal of Psychotherapy* 29:327–338.

Keith-Speigel, P. and Speigel, D. (1967). Affective states of patients immediately preceding suicide. *Journal of Psychiatric Research* 89–93.

Kovacs, M., Beck, A., Weissman, A. (1975). Hopelessness: an indicator of suicidal risk. *Suicide* 5:98–103.

Litman, R. (1965). When patients commit suicide. *American Journal of Psychotherapy* 19:570.

Lonnqvist, J. (1978). Self-destructive behavior. *Psychiatry Fenn Suppl.* Helsinki. 11–21.

Main, T. (1957). The ailment. *British Journal of Medical Psychology* 30:129–145.

Maltsberger, J. and Buie, D. (1974). Counter-transference hate in the treatment of suicidal patients. *Archives of General Psychiatry* 30:625–633.

Mattson, A., Seese, L., Hawkins, J. (1978). Suicidal behavior as a child psychiatric emergency. *Archives of General Psychiatry* 20:100–109.

Menninger, K. (1983). Psychoanalytic aspects of suicide. *International Journal of Psychoanalysis* 14:376–390.

Olin, H. (1976). Psychotherapy of the chronically suicidal patient. *American Journal of Psychotherapy* 30:570–575.

Paykel, E., Myers, J., Lindenthal, J., Tanner, J. (1974). Suicidal feelings in general population: prevalence study. *British Journal of Psychiatry* 124:460–469.

Ringel, E. (1976). The presuicidal syndrome: suicide and life-threat. *Behavior* 6:131–149.

Rosenbaum, M. and Richman, J. (1970). Suicide: the role of hostility and death wishes from the family and significant others. *American Journal of Psychiatry* 126:1652–1655.

Schwartz, D., Flinn, D., Slawson, P. (1974). Treatment of the suicidal character. *American Journal of Psychotherapy* 28:194–207.

Schwartz, D. (1979). The suicidal character. *Psychiatric Quarterly* 51:64–70.

Shein, H. and Stone, A. (1969). Psychotherapy designed to detect and treat suicidal potential. *American Journal of Psychiatry* 125:141–153.

Shapiro, S. and Waltzer, H. (1980). Successful suicides and serious attempts in a general hospital over a 15-year period. *General Hospital Psychiatry* 2:118–126.

Spiro, H. (1968). Chronic factitious illness: Munchausen's Syndrome. *Archives of General Psychiatry* 18:569–579.

Stekel, W. (1967). *On Suicide: Discussion of the Vienna Psychoanalytic Society*, p. 87. New York: International Universities Press.

Stengel, E. (1964). *Suicide and Attempted Suicide*. Baltimore: Penguin Books.

Tuckman, J. and Youngman, W. (1968). A scale for assessing suicidal risk of attempted suicide. *Journal of Clinical Psychology* 24:17–29.

Weisman, A. and Worden, J. (1972). Risk-rescue rating in suicide assessment. *Archives of General Psychiatry* 26:553–560.

Zilboorg, G. (1936). Differential diagnostic types of suicide. *Archives of Neurological Psychiatry* 35:270–291.

PART IV

Psychotherapy

CHAPTER THIRTEEN

Psychoanalysis of a Depressed Woman

Harvey L. Rich, M.D.

Mrs. F., 29 years old, sought consultation because of a repetitive symptom of depression. She observed that her episodes of depression were precipitated by separation from people important to her and characterized by a loss of interest and enjoyment in mothering, sex, her personal appearance, and the management of her household. She became irritable and angry toward her husband and her child and had spells of weeping over the hopelessness of her life. She saw no future for herself in or out of her marriage.

Although she was well dressed on her first visit, she was conspicuously without any adornment. Her anxiety was evident in her stuttering and in the agitated movement of her arms and hands. At times, she seemed unable to answer the simplest question but readily described the pervasive depressive quality of her life, which was constant even when she exhibited no overt depressive symptoms. The depression was most severe in the context of her marriage to a man she found insensitive and driven, both in respect to his work and his family relationships. Although she had experienced orgasm in premarital sex with him, she was no longer interested in him sexually and found herself frigid.

Married for seven years when she first came to see me, Mrs. F. had a 5-year-old son whose twin had died a day after birth. She had lost another child in the fifth month of pregnancy. She had been very happy during her pregnancy and her son's infancy and, although she now spoke with pride of her conscientious mothering, it seemed as though she protested too much, in order to conceal misgivings. The child's moves away from the closeness she had so enjoyed during the early months of his life upset her. She felt she could not do justice to another child and decided not to have another; it would take too much energy and would interfere with her graduate studies at the local university.

Analysis

Early in her analysis Mrs. F. elaborated on three aspects of her history. First, when she was 14 months old, her mother had had a "nervous breakdown" that necessitated the infant's placement in foster care, where she remained until age 5. Second, her father, having divorced her mother and remarried, refused to take the infant during the five years she was in foster care. Third, when, at 15, she was ordered out of her mother's house, Mrs. F. went to live with her father. At her own request, the girl attended boarding school while in her father's custody.

Mrs. F. described her mother, with whom she had lived for 10 years, as a brilliant and capable woman. She was a librarian who expressed disdain for "silly women" preoccupied with cosmetics and fashion, and her daughter identified with this view. She gave the details of her parents' divorce and spoke of her own bout with polio at age 4 that left some weakness in the muscles of her right leg with such flat affect that I thought her history sounded as though it was being read by a court reporter.

When I noted the rigid control she held over her feelings, she commented that having to lie on the couch made her feel humiliated and vulnerable. She then spoke of having "a silly thought," which I encouraged her to express. Laughing nervously, she said it concerned her having failed to remove some meat from the freezer for that night's dinner. When I asked for free associations, she said quickly that she thought of her mother as a frozen piece of meat. Then, as she began to reevaluate her history, she exhibited affect and was surprised by the affect-laden thoughts and memories that surfaced. She said her mother grew fatter and uglier each year, that she wore ugly shoes, and was asexual, scorning women who sought sensual enjoyment instead of concentrating, as she did, on life's necessities. "She liked sick women like Judy Garland, who were damaged and saw themselves as damaged." The mother's mental illness had depressive and hypomanic phases, becoming ultimately more paranoid and delusional, particularly in respect to her perceptions of her body.

As Mrs. F. reexamined her life with her mother, she also discussed her father, who had been given a medical discharge from the military for "psychaesthenia." He claimed that his daughter had been conceived "against his will" just when he had decided to abandon his 10-year marriage to his wife. When the child's mother was hospitalized, he arranged for relatives to care for her until a foster home could be found; he did not want the 14-month-old girl "even for one night." Mrs. F. acknowledged that this was a bitter memory, but it was one she could not let overwhelm her; she consoled herself by recalling that her father had always comforted her when she was sick. This came into the transference when she spoke of being fragile and requiring careful handling lest she break.

I interpreted this transference, noting that she was once more freezing the affect of her associations. She disagreed, at first gently, but then vociferously. She became very defensive about my comments, the bulk of which she rejected. She thought my taking notes was a rude invasion that suggested my weakness as an analyst. As I listened, loneliness seemed the predominant affect, and I made the interpretation that she felt that I abandoned her in my notetaking and failed to rush to her bedside to comfort and help her. I noted that she saw me this way to protect us both from her repressed feelings about her early abandonment. She cried, and screamed, "He didn't give a shit about me, whether I lived or died!" She cried that I was "pompous and classical" and cared nothing about her. She began to enjoy fantasies of grinding me up in her new food processor as she would like to grind her father for his indifference to her.

Mrs. F. recalled that her mother had visited her from time to time in the foster home and had taken her out for the day. She had "looked so strange" and yet was "nice," although she never offered to take her child back.

Although these were productive hours with my patient, she still felt obliged to argue; her positive cooperation would suddenly give way to angry outbursts about what she considered my pompous detachment and my forcing my ideas on her. After several hours of hostile carping, she would recall some memory or dream about her early life in which she confused the damage her mother represented with her own sense of self. "I was afraid mother would make me and my children crazy," she said. I interpreted that she may have been afraid of being damaged by her mother's illness. She then recalled a fierce battle — over how to get the ketchup out of a bottle — she had had with her mother at puberty. She had screamed, "You will not interfere or have a word to say about my having a baby or how I get ketchup out of a bottle!" Mrs. F. explained, "I was afraid of her delusions," recalling her fears over puberty and her unwillingness to share them with her mother.

It was clear that Mrs. F. had incorporated the damaged mother in her self-image, and that this sense of self and related affect had been carried over into the genital phase of her development and her subsequent depressive episodes. She did not approach genital issues at first, lingering on separation–individuation. Issues remained to be resolved. She derepressed a screen memory, recalling how, while at the zoo with her mother, she had objected furiously to returning to her foster home. This was reenacted in the transference in her tenacious refusal to proceed or to let me say anything about her emotional or genital life.

She began reacting with greater heat to my comments. She spoke of a neighbor's remark that her having only one child and planning to return to work seemed an indication that she did not care much about being a mother. She spoke angrily and, when I commented, blew up in a fit of rage: "How could you give any credit to such a remark?" I was obviously too young and inexperienced to be the right analyst for her. Announcing that she was through, she marched out of the office. I was successful in encouraging her subsequent return, and our alliance seemed undamaged although she was still negative toward me. That I had thought for a moment that she was a bad mother pained her deeply. She had left no stone unturned to be a perfect mother, and she had succeeded. I interpreted that the construction she put on my remarks was a projection of her own unconscious judgment of unconscious urges to harm her child and that these must frighten her so badly that she exhausted herself with scrupulous attention to being a perfect mother. She objected weakly through her tears.

At the next session she was more collected and cooperative. She had pondered my interpretation and acknowledged that she had known this about herself for a long time, but had believed that if nothing were said it would not, by some magic, be true. Then she launched into an account of her damaging mothering, speaking of her miscarriage and the death of her son's twin immediately after birth. She derepressed the memory of wishing one twin would die because she felt unable to cope with more than one infant. She recalled that when her son was 14 months old, he had been nagging her for attention but rejected all her efforts. She picked him up and thrust him away so violently that she was afraid she had hurt him. She had guarded against this fear until now; she was full of remorse and thought of leaving her son and husband for the good of all. I made the interpretation that this frightening breakthrough of aggressive feelings toward the child related to their shared conflict over separation and individuation, and that her part of this conflict contained a sense of being incomplete and possibly damaged if left to herself. She made no objection but began a long process of working through current experiences with her son as he sought more autonomy and independence from her, while also working through her own history.

As vacation approached, Mrs. F. began to get negativistic and withholding in the transference. She noted that she wanted to be disagreeable and say no to everything because she resented my approaching departure:

> I don't like this in myself one bit. I want you to stop me. Once you commented on my rigidity. I got very compulsive yesterday, yelled at my son for being messy. I remember terrible fights with my mother over being messy. It's like I want to be messy and have to clean up instead. Father was a mess. His of-

fice was mess—not like yours. Wanting to be messy is like being bad. I want to connect this anger with my polio. But it was before I was sick that my foster sister and I cut up all our clothes. After having polio I was good. This anger is connected with someone; you must help me get closer to this anger because if you leave me unsettled I'll wander in circles and hopeless darkness.

I said she was reexperiencing a feeling from her early life.

"It's like trying to walk in physical therapy when I was paralyzed— impossible," she said. "It's something physical I can't do. I want to scream with fury and say, 'Shit, I just won't do it. Screw you and goddamn it!'" At her next session she connected this affective memory to my departure. Her husband had gone on a business trip and, as she noted how sad her son was over his father's departure, she realized that my departure was of great significance. "It was like my childhood with my mother; I'd get close and she'd be gone."

Then she moved farther into the transference neurosis saying, "Something that happened with my husband in the weeks before our wedding is now happening with you. It coincided with my being bothered by your taking notes—it was as though I felt you withdrawing from me. I remember my great uncle would take a pen and write a check rather than communicate an emotion. Father was the same—no emotions. Just the money the court ordered." I noted an association between marriage, notetaking, and separations, and she agreed. "They all have to do with detachments. It's strange that I should see marriage as a separation. Separation is a part of me. It's not that I really want to be so bad you won't want me back. I can't face saying that I don't want you to go. It reminds me of part of myself that is gone."

She spoke of my notetaking as recordkeeping and said that looking back at her life was like being picked up in pieces, "like existing in brief discrete disconnected intervals. Like a train with cars missing, like the pages fall out of a book with a broken spine." This association recalled polio and her notion that everyone was attacking her with spinal taps and physical therapy. There must have been something wrong with her, something twisted and distorted. "They were hiding what was wrong with all of us. I would be guilty if I knew about me. No one made it clear why I spent four years in a foster home without parents."

On the day when she came down with polio she had had her earliest experience with masturbation, fondling herself while bathing and thinking that her clitoris must be connected with something inside that produced babies. She had feared that her fondling might affect her ability to have babies. Later that day she fell paralyzed to the floor.

Following her recovery from polio, she went to live with her mother.

During a visit to her father and step-mother, she was rebuked for sitting on her father's lap. She was told that young girls "didn't do such things." Her mother and stepmother conveyed the message that sensuality was "silly." Any sexual reference I made in her associations was vigorously rejected by Mrs. F. When not angry at me, she saw me as orthodox and aloof. She had repeated dreams of waiting for her father at the train station and riding with him to his weekend home.

She began to speak of her husband who, like her father, was a "take charge" person. She complained that his "obsessionalism" gave him the same affective remoteness as her father. They had greatly enjoyed their college courtship; she was highly pleased with her first experience of sexual intercourse, and was orgastic during their premarital union.

A turning point in her life came on her wedding day. The wedding was elaborate, at her father's request, and she wore a gown purchased on a wonderful day spent with him and her stepmother during which her father had, in an exceptional gesture, taken a great interest in her gown. She remembered that just before the ceremony took place her father left her side for a minute and she felt so "horribly alone" that she wept. She sobbed again while telling me about this. She had not wanted to invite her mother because of mother's mental state. But her mother did come, in a wheelchair she claimed to need because her legs were weak. After the ceremony, mother ranted at everyone and had to be removed. At the end of the evening Mrs. F. was calm, happy — and frigid.

One day she laughed at a "silly thought" and asked if I could lend her a spoon since she had forgotten to bring one to eat her yogurt lunch with. This prompted an association that she rejected, insisting that she refused to be "brainwashed by my Freudian propaganda." Her "silly thought" about borrowing a spoon arose from her sense of my dogma. She turned cold and assailed me with invective but was much calmer the next day when she acknowledged the importance of her thought; the spoon represented my penis and expressed her desire for it.

She reported that she enjoyed foreplay with her husband, but that a moment would come "when, as if a switch had been turned," she repelled him and froze. After this, she would not want him to touch her, thinking, "This is for him, not for me — I would be better off alone and divorced." She was able to receive my interpretation that this was what was being enacted in the transference to me, in that she could associate freely along a broad range of levels and ideas until I would make an interpretation, at which point she repelled me and froze.

She remembered thinking as a child that her own conception had deprived her father of his penis, and that was why he displayed no sensual interest in her and had no children in his second marriage. Interpretation of the enactment of her frigidity in the transference let her speak more freely about her current and early sexual fantasies. Her husband's "pushiness" in sex was related to his large penis, which she feared would tear her apart if she failed to control it. She returned to the screen memory of the ketchup bottle, which recalled the alarm she had felt at her menarche. The issue of blood confirmed inner damage. She hated her breasts, and envied the flatchested and angular girls in her dancing class. Her own curves made her feel ugly and awkward. Well-endowed girls who were beautiful and sexy must be "loose women." When I interpreted that she envied the well-endowed girls, she responded with a flood of memories of sexy thoughts and wishes. She had wanted to dance the "Dance of the Seven Veils" for her father, but he never came to see her dance.

She immediately associated to a perceptual error of the previous day when her husband cut his arm badly while gardening. When she answered his cry she thought he had amputated his arm, but she soon grasped what had happened and gave the needed aid. She was disturbed by the association. It was uncomfortable to have such thoughts in the midst of such sexy longings. I made the interpretation that she was afraid of her longings because she felt that to want the penis was to have to wrest it violently from its owner. In her reply, she gave evidence of synthesis. Many loose ends about her negativism and withholding and rejecting came together — her chopping and grinding and messing fantasies were all in the service of her terrible urge to have the penis by damaging the man. Her scrupulosity served to control the pregenital fantasies and to defend against the aggressive genital wishes.

Mrs. F. began to be overtly coquettish, a contrast to her behavior when dominated by depressive symptoms. She began to use makeup and to wear jewelry and soft feminine dresses. Soon she reported having occasional orgasms and began considering what she wanted sexually from her husband, who had not felt free to gratify her desires without her help. She began to enjoy the job she had formerly found dull.

One day she announced that she had given me and the analysis much thought and had realized the analysis would not be complete until she was comfortable with her desire to be a lusty lady. She saw me now as cute, charming, brilliant, and funny, though still orthodox. Orthodoxy now was simply a feature of my strong personality, which had withstood so much abuse from her. She had come to realize I was not aloof. Her husband's great strength of character was rigid in a way that suggested inner weakness. She had laughed at first at the thought of having sexual longings toward me or anyone else. I interpreted this ridicule as being like that of her three parents, and she stopped laughing. She was meeting me in her dreams in romantic places and thinking of a romance meant to be. But her stepmother brought her grotesque gifts of dead chickens in these dreams; they represented what she was able to give her husband in their childless marriage. Mrs. F. could offer me much more. In her dreams, there was an understanding that one day we would be together.

She spent hours with me talking about her son's entry into manhood as his latency and autonomy progressed. She also discussed her husband's progress in his analysis, which he had undertaken a few years after she began hers. He was resisting introspection. Often an hour spent on her "lusty lady" feelings led to hopelessness over her husband's inability to be as sensitive as I was. I was able to interpret how she encouraged his defensive isolation and depression to defend herself against her lusty, sharing feelings. Wouldn't it be nice to have lusty feelings only with a neat analyst with a neat office and nothing messy to worry about? I said how proud she must be of her fine young son, and how she had not only managed to let him separate but had also come to enjoy his phallic strivings that had caused her such conflict in the past. She resisted sharing this joy with her husband because it represented to her her wish for his penis.

We continued to share the problems of her home, her work, and her father and stepmother, her mother having died of cancer shortly after the analysis began. Her mood was now gay and light, and she wanted to dance about the room sometimes. She said her only problem was her rigid husband.

One day she had a "silly impulse" to sit up to share a piece of gossip about one of my colleagues. I asked for her free association, and, lying down, she said she wanted to separate "what she could share with me" from her "analysis of the unconscious." She repeated this so often that I commented that she was replacing some meaningful wish to share her life with me. I was the perfect mate for her, but I was taken!

During the following weeks she was lighthearted and had exhibitionistic wishes in the transference. She wanted to swirl her sexy dress before me, to dance, and stretch her arms to the ceiling as in a dance class. These luxurious moments were interrupted from time to time with displays of negativism toward me. I made the interpretation that she was disappointed in my lack of enthusiastic response to her seductive manner, just as she had been disappointed with her father. She agreed:

> The weather changes. Everything changes but me. If I change, I will have to be a consistently light and happy woman. I should stop now on an up moment. Why must I be consistent because you expect it? My husband is upset that he can't run faster as he ages; he expects to get better with age. He's depressed about it, and I'm sorry for him. No, I'm not. I think I enjoy his depression. You can stop me any time you want. I'm not doing this on my own.

I think I'm nearly finished. I almost cut my finger off yesterday. I have nothing to say, really. You do what I can't — get serious and down to business. I'm not being serious and doing what I have to do. This puts you in a funny position — you lose. I'm castrating you, making you impotent. You haven't done enough, so I'm being vengeful. I can't win, so you can't either.

I commented that I didn't think it would be harmful for us both to play to win. She became flippant and anxious:

I can't play to win with you because we'd have to be equal, and I'm not, so I must play for you to lose. The gap is narrow now, but I'm still not equal. I feel on a par with other women, but never with men like my father. I felt superior to my mother. This notion is getting more vague . . . it's sad. I'll never be your equal, but I'm not your inferior, either. One way I can make you lose is to refuse to play. You can't show off your prowess then.

The notion of our inequality became less symbolic as she returned to the fantasy of being damaged that underlay her desire for my penis to repair and complete herself. Her fear of damaging me in such interaction was lessened by my readiness to work with her without fearing her fantasy. She was sad about this; she knew the analysis had affected her life positively but it had not brought the solution she was unconsciously seeking.

The fifth year of her analysis was now nearing its close, and when I returned from summer vacation she greeted me by recounting how she had continued her analysis without me, self-analyzing her reaction to her son's fierce show of independence as her own separation anxiety. She had had "an anxiety attack" over his insistence on returning home and caring for himself after school rather than going to a daycare establishment to await his mother's return from work. She had been able to analyze that he was indeed separate from her and did not have her history or anxieties. She had accomplished what she had hoped to do: she had reared an independent son with good judgment who wanted to prove this to himself and to his parents. It was time to let go.

That evening she dreamed that she was rushing to leave the house for work, which she anticipated with excitement. She was late and fearful of being too late at work. Her analysis of the dream and the discussion with her son was that day care represented her analysis and her attachment to me. She had identified with her son's wish to give it up and was anxious to get on with her work, where she was gaining great respect for herself as a therapist. She asked what I thought of her analysis, and I replied that it was indeed time to give me up. She cried over surrendering the always available magical father. How did I know she was ready? I asked how she knew.

Mrs. F. then told of having had "dreadful negative feelings" over an event at the zoo on her vacation; she was able to accept help from her husband and recovered. She was able to see that this was a reexperiencing of the outing with her mother while she was in foster care as a child, which also involved separating from mother. She was proud, not only of her self-analysis, but of her ability to accept help from her husband, who was seeming much more compassionate and tender. She realized that she had been able to tell him of her needs, and that he had become a wise and calming influence.

In following sessions she insisted that she was not ready to end and that I was rushing her for my own purposes. She did not yet have all she needed for the future. Her husband would be upset because she was not yet a finished product. I reminded her how helpful he had been at the zoo and that it was she who considered herself not finished. She wished she had had a different mother. She reminded me that there had been a time when she felt competent outside analysis, and incompetent within it, but this was now reversed. She bickered with her husband over the way he had regressed in analysis. I made the interpretation that she was angry at me for "abandoning" her and displaced this anger onto her husband.

She was conflicted over being her own good mother. The feebler her husband seemed, the angrier she became. He would "end up all right," but she would "go down the tubes." She was on the bottom of the totem pole. I said, "And you want to be on the top!" She replied that I sought to replace her with a patient so important that I would feel puffed up over the connection. She was not important enough to feed my ego. I told her that remark was addressed to her father. She deplored being a girl. "If only I were a boy!" Her father telephoned her son and had his picture on his desk. I interpreted this exchange as evidence of her wish to gain in analysis the completeness she lacked as a birthright. Her desire for a penis was symbolic of a deeper sense of being incomplete which itself stemmed from her pregenital experiences with a depressed mother, the breakup of her home, and her early abandonment. This sense of not being whole was now being projected onto the termination process. She worried aloud about what our relationship would become after she left analysis: "When you go off, how can you come back?" One of us would be defeated, perhaps both of us. I interpreted the separation–individuation fear that to return to mother and "bury the hatchet" might entail burying it in her. She feared it now must be buried in me.

Mrs. F.'s protests about not being ready to terminate gave way to sadness over her inadequacies. She reexperienced sadness that her mother was so damaged that she wasted some fine talents. She expressed sorrow over her father's reticence and her own inability earlier to develop the rapport with her stepmother she had established recently. She reported that her husband said he was not disappointed with her termination after all, spoke of his sensitivity, and began to plan how she would now invest the time and money she had been spending in analysis. She knew she was done because when her son awoke coughing one night, she was able to send him back to bed instead of becoming conflicted over doubts of her mothering instincts.

On her final day she brought me a fresh yellow rose, saying that she had lacked time to buy a silk rose that would be a permanent reminder of her hours with me. I suggested she might feel this one to be more appropriate to the occasion — we had shared an important experience, but were now done, none the worse for it, but better. She spoke of fearing her temptation to idealize me in order to avoid the anger and sadness of our separation. She hugged me as we said goodbye. Ten days later she asked for one more hour, afraid that she had succumbed to the idealization she dreaded.

When she came she reported having dreamed on the previous night that she was busy at home trying to leave to catch a ferryboat. Knowing she was late, she kept trying to do more at home before leaving, and when she finally got to the dock "the ferry was gone." I told her she need not worry about idealizing me. She was busy at home with the strong man to whom she was married and with her life there. The "fairy" was indeed gone.

Discussion

Mrs. F.'s history includes separation trauma, loss, and the development of psychological readiness for a pervasive depressive mood and repeated episodes of depression. Her mother's hospitalization, her father's refusal to give her a home, and her rejection by her mother when a teenager were only the tip of the iceberg of the losses through separation she had suffered, although these were her conscious focus. Her first year of life had seen the departure of her father when she was 6 months old, the death of her maternal grandmother during the six months she and her mother lived with the grandparents, and the hospitalization of the mother soon after the return to Mrs. F.'s birthplace. We could describe this patient's condition as depression following repeated separations in her life, but we should not stop with the clinical picture as it appeared on the surface. Beneath her chief complaint was a general sense of joylessness of the sort Dr. Abse describes as depressive character. Moreover, she was frigid although at the same time she had made some generally good adaptations to her life.

She presented herself to me as a very plain woman and, while her history might have put me off, it did not because something else was being communicated. Loewald (1960) speaks of that "something else" as a perception of the patient's core undistorted by neurosis which the analyst and the patient share. Although that sense of a core may be vague and rudimentary, according to Loewald it is transferred from the patient's unconscious to the analyst, who, in the role of an early parental object, can in true neutrality perceive it both consciously and unconsciously. The analyst also has a sense of that potential (p. 20). Mrs. F.'s presentation of herself as a very plain woman also communicated unconscious recognition of the "princess" inside. What was being communicated was not that something was missing, as she believed, but that something that once had been whole was later distorted by neuroses and was recoverable. For, as a youngster Mrs. F. was not a wallflower, and had tried to make dance a career in spite of residual damage from polio. Her reaching out to others and her dancing meant that somewhere hidden in her was a view of herself fighting to contradict the distortion of her perceived reality.

Moreover, she had lifelong experience of seeking and getting help from important others. From foster caretakers, orthopedic surgeons, physical therapists, the headmaster and nurse of her boarding school, she had asked for help and received it. She also had memories of her mother's exercising her leg and of her father coming to her bedside when she was ill. Loewald notes that the sense of oneself as "central" develops from such ministrations.

Mrs. F. did not need to retreat into love of self as object, to defend against too great a trauma in object relationships. She was capable of object relations, approaching objects of her desire with an organized sense of self that included the damaged identifications with her early love objects. Loewald (1969) makes an important distinction between these two tracks, comparing secondary with primary narcissism, which involves powerful preobject identifications.

> Primary narcissism must be understood without reference to what we call libido attachment or distribution with the ego — as well as without speaking of libido attachments to objects. There is as yet neither ego nor object. We may speak of an undifferentiated force field which later becomes differentiated into ego and objects. From here we can understand how our love life develops in such a way that one main current desires and longs for other persons as objects, while the other, more ancient current remains "narcissistic" in the sense that it does not recognize boundaries between ego and object, it creates identity of ego and object . . . in early childhood this process plays a prominent part in ego formation and consolidation; but it continues, in far more complex ways, in later developmental stages as well, especially in superego development. (p. 39)

One should not judge a patient's inner structure by that which appears on the surface. Mrs. F.'s analysis showed that she had many positive characteristics along with her repeated episodes of depression and her depressive character. It also disclosed the reason for her having good adaptive capabilities: her psychic experience of the environment included enough rapport to permit ego-differentiation and the attainment of a sense of separateness in an object-constant world. At the same time, it revealed that this rapport contained the psychic and affective conflicts of herself and her mother (or mothering figures).

Mrs. F.'s first affective association to her mother was in her first "silly thought" in which mother was seen as "a frozen piece of meat." Therapeutic analysis began with the first of her "silly thoughts," of which there were at least three. Each "silly thought" heralded a step in the emergence of her sexual interest with a corresponding definition of her symbols. The first symbol was a formless "shape" that attained the shape of a spoon and finally of her own body sitting erect. This is a good example of the progression of ego differentiation or repair during the course of analysis.

Her use of the word "silly" is also a good example of the adaptive use of identification that troubled her on unconscious levels. Father and the two women he married shared this condescending and disparaging view of sexuality. Although this must have been disappointing to Mrs. F., who had so little of their attention anyway, she made the best of things by falling in with their view enough to apply the term "silly" to herself at times. It is interesting that the first "silly thought" was about food. The moments she had shared with family were mostly those at the table. She had sensuous memories of enjoying lobster with her mother and father on separate occasions, and as an adult she allowed herself a fleeting sense of exhibitionism when putting on a dinner party. Her other memory of a shared moment was that of travel to her father's weekend home with him and going out on his boat. This memory yielded residue for important dreams throughout her analysis.

Mother was first affectively symbolized as frozen and associated to as disparaging, and depriving her of sensuality. Mrs. F. clearly felt that something had been taken or kept from her that would have significantly altered the joy of her life. Her thought of having forgotten to thaw the meat for dinner betrayed a hesitant first wish to thaw her genital sexual object libido which had survived this disparagement. Her father's shortcomings had disappointed her as a child and enraged her as an adult. He had failed her in terms of caring for her when she was small and later he failed as the object of her sexual longings. This seemed to confirm unconsciously her feeling that something was wrong, "twisted and distorted," and that it was her fault.

Loewald (1978) refers to consciousness as the state of self-reflection that represents the internalization of the interplay originally occurring between the infant and the primary caretaker, mostly the mother, and then recurring in many other relationships. The infant–mother psychic unit is seen as a mirror in which infants gradually begin to recognize and know themselves by being recognized by the mother. Loewald notes that whatever conflicts or affective disturbances the mother brings into this unitary sense is shared (p. 13).

Mrs. F. had shared her mother's affectively disturbed sense of self. In recounting her early memories of her parents, she felt the need to control her bitterness. Whether the bitterness and rage were part of the original sense of self or reaction to initial affective memories of parents, Mrs. F. was afraid of being overwhelmed. Not yet sufficiently secure in the transference relationship to risk the frightening affect, Mrs. F. resisted interpretation of her defensiveness, and here we hear the first of the genital imagery in her sense of self. She rejected "the bulk" of me, taking only bits of my interpretation. The bulk and the "rude invasion" of my notetaking threatened to disrupt her as her earliest "self" awareness had obviously done, but her fear represented also defense against the desire to complete herself and the fantasy that, to do so, she must wrest back what was missing and thus damage the object of her love. In that sense she feared the weakness demonstrated in my notetaking, and she tested it for months. She offered fantasies of sadistic revenge for my orthodoxy that represented my lack of sensual sharing, hesitantly at first but later with enjoyment. It must have been a relief for her to do this after years of defending against her impulses.

I turn to Loewald (1960) again to make sense of a mutually frustrating period in which Mrs. F. seemed stuck on testing, proving, fearing my weakness, my "orthodoxy." What controlled her willingness or unwillingness to move along? According to Loewald:

> . . . the transference neurosis, in the sense of reactivation of the childhood neurosis, is set in motion not simply by the technical skill of the analyst, but by the fact that the analyst makes himself available for the development of a new "object-relationship" between the patient and the analyst. The patient tends to make this potentially new object-relationship into an old one. On the other hand, to the extent to which the patient develops a "positive transference" (not in the sense of transference as resistance, but in the sense in which "transference" carries the whole process of an analysis) he keeps this potentiality of a new object-relationship, represented by the analyst. (p. 17)

Mrs. F. was not yet ready. She had hoped that I was new and different, but the risk was great and the positive transference not yet secure enough.

She had to deal with her fear that I wanted to damage her ability to bear children, as she feared her mother had wanted and indeed, had done already through this shared identification. At this time in her analysis the wish that I father her babies, in a reparative stroke of genius, had yet to surface.

She was not finished with the uncovering of frightful urges. These broke through when she thought I was thinking of her as a bad mother. It took much time to uncover and work through her aggressive urges toward those she loved. Her thrusting away her 14-month-old son and then fearing that she had hurt him was a replay of the separation–individuation crisis she had experienced at that age, one that was repeated and resolved only in the last phase of her analysis.

The conflict over a damaged self and fantasies of repair emerged through layers of development during her associations to being "messy" and to her insistence that I "give an inch" lest she be doomed to disorganization. Besides being a reference to the organizing influence of the penis, this association refers to earlier development. Loewald (1978) writes: "The totality or coherent organization is to begin with merely in the mother's foreseeing eye (the caring environment's active mirroring), as a kind of unperceived plan. And so the infant's uniform mental acts thus acquire differentiation" (p. 17). Without this inch, this organizer, she would feel as though trying to walk while paralyzed and being unable to do so, though she had once known how. Her rage arose from having a sense of being capable but not performing. My impending departure was connected with the removal of her organizing part. Her sense of her father's withdrawal before the wedding and her husband's aloofness all represented "departures." Mrs. F. was shocked at her lack of control over this other half of what should be a unit. She couldn't say that she needed me in a most fundamental way, and connected this feeling with the sense that pieces were missing from her as a result of some attack. As soon as she had fantasized her ability to make babies, polio had struck her down. Immediately after exploring her genitals she realized her worst unconscious fear — she now had damaged parts and always would have.

One wonders why polio and its effects did not constitute a greater trauma; perhaps it was merely symbolic confirmation of some earlier damage to her self-image and hence could not bring greater trauma than the original events.

Although she rejected my sexual interpretations, she began bringing in dreams of longing for her father. The train and train station were symbols of shared genital joy; her unconscious was moving faster than her consciousness was willing to go. Consciously, she entered the area of penis envy through being frigid.

Again, the theme of separations beyond her control was the hallmark. When she found herself "horribly alone" at her wedding with her crazy mother raving in the background, all the elements of unconscious conflict were present, and the symptom was formed. She had reestablished that glorious early unity in her courtship, and her father had given more interest and time to her wedding than she had expected, but then she was faced with the wedding ceremony and the work of setting up a house. (Work on their house had already begun and was probably accountable for her sense that her husband was withdrawing from their idyllic relationship.) Her father would not be at her side for life; her husband would be only a second best stand-in. Her mother's background raving reminded her of the guilty secret that she herself was damaged. She could not control and hold onto that part of her self, embodied by her departing father, which would complete her.

The desire for that part, now specifically a penis, was ready for derepression. Her associations took her from borrowing my spoon to taking my penis, to that moment in foreplay when she thought that this was *his* penis, not *hers*, a thought that froze her excitement. She turned her aggression against herself in fantasy and recalled bad feelings associated with her puberty. The intensity of her anger at her mother over the incident with the ketchup bottle indicated condensation of blame for her "castration" and the more subtle affect of being damaged in her identificatory love for her mother.

When her reenactment of frigidity in transference and her envy of sexy women were interpreted, it became possible for her to derepress further childhood fantasies about having or missing a penis. She could no longer defend against her sexy, exhibitionistic urges, and no longer saw her curves as ugly. She really didn't wish them away, and what, after all, was so bad about being a little loose like the well-endowed girls she had scoffed at? The potential for a "new object-relationship" in the transference now overwhelmed the forces of repression and resistance.

The results of working through were dramatically evident in her becoming sexy and orgasmic. We could now be lovers in her dreams; she would be "the other woman" like her stepmother. The issue of sharing and not owning or controlling my penis again became a problem. At first she envisioned an asexual connection with which we could live happily forever. This would be good for father, but why would she suppose, I asked, it would be good enough for me? She wished to have my babies, a process which would be perfect and perfecting. The awakening of these longings also aroused their disappointment. Now the negativism was in defense of genital libidinal wishes and urges. Although the struggle was colored by tones from earlier conflicts, the more genital issues stood out sharply. The issue was now more clearly one of our inequality and her penis envy.

Kestenberg (1968) has discussed the female's envy of the male's penis. The female child envies the male his ability to organize the environment around a visible sense of his genital life. This makes his fantasies of activity and passivity less frightening than those of the female, who must use the unseen and the "potential" for a baby as this organizing influence. Kestenberg makes the point that, until the female has dealt with her unconscious fantasies and conflicts regarding her activity and passivity genitally in relationship to the male, she will be partially or wholly frigid (p. 486).

It was now my penis, which still was not separated from the issue of her damaged self, rather than just my presence that would make us equal. Her husband's penis would make him more successful in his psychoanalysis than she, since his ego could organize the experience better because of his having a penis. He would not have to settle, nor would I. But she would "go down the tubes," her expression being an obvious reference to her female hollowness.

She did settle and soon had a consolation prize. She dreamed of having to rush out into the busy world before it was too late, and she analyzed this dream as evidence that she and her son no longer *needed* day care though it might be nice to have it. Unconscious demands had been replaced by the freedom to choose.

Termination was quite traditional. Longings to "stretch" to take me in and defenses against these longings were fleetingly evident, as were sadness and grief over the lost magical other who would complete her. The crucial separation–individuation issue was prominent, and there was underlying fantasied fear of damage if she took from me what she had gained. How could I feel kindly toward her if she were to return?

Her final hour provided a good example of unconscious repair already slipping away from the working observing ego that had accomplished it. Although she consciously wanted the flower she gave me to be a lasting memorial to our work, there was no unconscious necessity for this. A fresh flower simply saying "thank you" was enough. I felt that in her posttermination hour she was tying up a loose end; it seemed important that she tell me and herself that her strong husband was her real choice of a love object, not the diminutive and antiseptic father-analyst.

We can only speculate about what was missing in the unitary preobject identificatory love with her depressed mother, who must have communicated anxiety about a future plan for her child's life. Her day-to-day ministrations had obviously been adequate, but the sense of the future was troubled. I think Mrs. F. would say that ideal mothering made a child confident about the future. Her mother had not done this, and, unfortunately, her own experiences in early life had added to her sense of insecurity. When asked before her analysis was over how she knew she was done, she cited the incident in which she had let her husband rescue her from great discomfort on the visit to the zoo. Faced with a moment of disorganization, but bolstered by her successful experience with me, she had risked a "new object relationship" with her husband. She had let him help organize her experience, and it worked. There was ego growth. The very plain woman allowed, even encouraged, her prince to kiss her, and the princess began to emerge.

Summary

In this chapter, the entire analysis of a woman who suffered recurrent depressive episodes is presented. The case illustrates how intrapsychic conflicts appear in surface symptomatology. Through the analytic process and the resolution of intrapsychic conflicts, the patient's depressive symptoms were alleviated.

REFERENCES

Kestenberg, J. S. (1968). Outside and inside, male and female. *Psychoanalytic Association* 16.
Loewald, H. (1960). On the therapeutic action of psychoanalysis. *International Journal of Psycho-Analysis* 41.
_____ (1978) *Psychoanalysis and the History of the Individual*. New Haven: Yale University Press.

CHAPTER FOURTEEN

Depression Caused by Others: The Patient and the Therapist

Sheldon Heath, M.D., F.R.C.P.(C)

Much attention is given to better understanding therapists' reactions to their patients. In some cases, it is regarded as a therapeutic necessity to be caught up in a patient's psychosis or turbulence. Searles (1965) does so in his work in the psychotherapy of schizophrenia. To respond to a patient with a conscious or unconscious countertransference reaction is part of the ongoing therapeutic process. To have sexual or violent fantasies evoked by the patient is understood to be part of the therapist's working life. Presumably, these feelings and fantasies are conscious or made to be so by self-analysis, and self-analysis is a continuous part of our therapeutic work.

To respond to seduction or provocation without action in the therapeutic setting suggests an intuitive and understanding therapist. To be depressed, however, seems to be a far less desirable response. Yet people remark how depressing certain individuals are; depressing persons are avoided through the usual defenses of avoidance, disavowal, repression, denial and the manic defenses of triumph, control, and contempt (Segal 1973). Such behaviors include reinforcing the depressed person's omnipotent defenses by reassuring that there will be a replacement for the lost loved one, that the person who did the abandoning was not really worth it and so on. Persons who cannot cope with their depression are met with contempt.

Why then do therapists not deal with this response to depression in the consulting room? Further, how much do we overlook concerning the ways in which patients are made depressed by others around them?

Projective Identification

Melanie Klein developed the concept of projective identification (Segal 1973, pp. 27–28) which is becoming one of the most useful concepts in psychoanalytic understanding of both patient and social systems. Projective identification means that part of the psyche is unconsciously put into another person. The mother dressing her daughter for the wedding thus "puts part of herself" into her daughter and vicariously enjoys and lives out the role of the bride. The daughter unconsciously introjects or takes in parts of her mother and allows this. As one can see from this brief example, the element of control is present. The bride feels that part of herself is in her mother under her direct guidance or, perhaps, control. Of course, this is generally unconscious.

Turquet (1975) in a brilliant paper on the psychodynamics of the large group has moved this concept into the role of reality testing. He suggests that projective identification occurs in all situations. When individuals meet other persons, they put part of themselves into the other persons and then take it back to get a feel of what the other persons are really about. This is done rapidly, spontaneously, and unconsciously. In small groups, we instantly put parts of ourselves into the other members and then take these back, so we get a feel for those with whom we are dealing in the small groups in both clinical and social situations.

Projection, on the other hand, involves externalizing an internal part of oneself, usually a thought or feeling, then putting it into the other and then perceiving it coming back at oneself. A different kind of projection, projective identification, involves putting a part of the self into the other person and, consequently, feeling it to be in the other person's psyche in various ways.

Bion (1962) has emphasized that therapists, too, are containers for the projective identificatory bits and that it is very important for therapists to recognize what is being done to them. This is invaluable in the understanding of patients. We must deal with the nonverbal aspects of patients from the moment they come into the consulting room, transmitting in a nonverbal, unconscious way that which is going on within themselves.

Projective identification explains the phenomena seen with scapegoating in a family and groups. A particular individual in a family is "selected" unconsciously to "carry," for example, the delinquency of all the others, to act out their rebellion and so on. Sometimes the scapegoat is made into the family failure and usually at the same time, the family member who is depressed. Likewise in groups, particular individuals are selected quite unconsciously to play particular roles or object relationships. Group failures "carry" the failure and the depression for themselves and for the other group members as well.

The "Selected" Patient

Susan, a 30-year-old Australian woman married but was unsuccessful in getting pregnant and experienced subsequent depressive crises. She was the older daughter of a prominent family of lawyers who placed much evidence upon success and had proven their own competence in their selected fields. Father was reputed to be a brilliant criminal lawyer and mother a brilliant corporate one. While high achievers, both were reported at times to be hypochondrical; mother was reported to be depressed.

Susan seemed to be regarded as a particular failure as both had wished a boy. They rejoiced at the birth of their second child, Harold, their long-sought male offspring, who was endowed with all the capabilities for success which he subsequently fulfilled, at least on the surface.

Susan reported that she had been periodically depressed all her life. In adolescence, she handled this by overeating, which only made the family regard her as more of a failure within their social system. In her treatment, of course, it appeared that her overeating had an appeal function for love and nurture, accompanied by certain provocative aspects. Nevertheless, she was constantly regarded in a derisory way by both her father and mother. Susan chose to study history. Her intellectual brilliance came forth and was supported by her peer group and the rest of the family since academia was considered an alternative route to the professions.

Harold, her younger brother, chose law, to his parents' joy, and succeeded brilliantly, while admitting to his sister that he hated this work. However, Harold felt his negative feelings were unacceptable and, accordingly, minimized these about his work to his parents.

Within the family, one can see how Susan had been brought up to be an unwanted object. In her treatment she longed for a penis and was narcissistically vulnerable to attacks upon her body image, her intellectual competence. As a result, Susan came to regard herself as a failure. With the conscious help of her family, she chose to marry a man she did not love and her husband, in turn, regarded her as an adjunct to his own professional development, constantly berating her for her inability to cope and for recurring depressions in contrast to his own "normality."

I remember well seeing her for the first time in consultation. She was regressed, crying, complaining of being depressed, hopeless, unable to cope, unable to bear a child, the only role open for her and for her own disgrace to her family and to her husband over her chronic failure. As she had been referred by a colleague in another country, I remember well after the session feeling angry and depressed and wondering how I could possibly help her in any way. The history, nevertheless, did indicate that her previous analysis was of significant help in getting her through her reactions to the miscarriages and helping her to function despite many suicidal fantasies.

It is important to emphasize how Susan put part of her depression and feelings of helplessness into the analyst during both consultation and in the early stages of her analysis. This process was an externalization of what had been done to her within her family and was now being done by her husband.

Through analysis four times per week, she came to see that the process of projective identification had occurred repeatedly within her nuclear family since childhood. The analyst's perception of her depression was diagnostic of Susan's own internal processes.

Susan came to recognize that she had "chosen" her husband unconsciously so that she could repeat her family role. Similarly, he in turn "chose" her unconsciously as a masochistic adjunct into whom he could put his depression and fears in a projective identificatory way. Also, Susan had a series of female friends whose problems she listened to and absorbed, which depressed her while her friends were relieved. Interpretations were directed to the "carrying nature" as well as the "caring nature" of her ego. She learned to distinguish those depressions reactive to life events from those put into her, especially by her husband.

There were of course, other factors involved. She needed to fail in a relationship with a man and subordinate herself to her female friends on an oedipal basis. Her "dumping" of feelings had an anal form. Her oral fixation lead to a swallowing or taking in of the depressive symptoms of others.

She and her husband were intertwined in a relationship where he provided total direction for her life. He would, however, become angry and restrict her food and finances for everyday living, just as her mother had done.

The therapeutic work was quite successful. She did conceive a child and was able to separate herself from her husband and what he was doing to her psychologically. She filed for separation and, then, divorce. She was able to relate in a more significant way to her family, recognizing what they were doing to her and as a consequence, as would be expected, they had to learn to deal with their own depression over retirement and old age. Susan's brother, Harold, was helped by her and in turn, entered therapy to deal with his own emerging depression and repeated failures in his relationships with women and with his profession. She was, so to speak, no longer the scapegoat for a number of other people.

The Scapegoat Phenomenon

From the above, it can be seen that certain individuals are selected as scapegoats in families. This is not a new phenomenon. In the case of Susan, a particular individual who was of the "wrong" sex, was selected by her family quite unconsciously to carry their failure and depression. The family had an underlying sense of failure and depression about themselves. Further, one can see how Susan responded with the angry provocation of obesity in adolescence, denial that it was a problem, and with her determination to get pregnant at all costs. Her family and husband encouraged Susan's responses. She, in turn, was caught up in their manic defenses as the object of their contempt for being such a weakling. By identification with them, she had at times a narcissistic sense of omnipotence, which had to be worked on in the treatment. She introjected their depressive projective identifications easily and had done so since early childhood.

Her depressions were over real or fantasied losses, but these were aggrandized by the family pouncing upon them while they minimized their own sense of failure and personal losses within their own marriage, friendships, and professional failures. Susan's own angry, depressed sense of futility was also revealed in the analysis. Her tendency to accept the scapegoat role came up again in the social and professional groups in which she moved, and she learned to deal with these quite successfully.

Depressing the Therapist

It is exciting to work with extremely disturbed, schizophrenic, or borderline patients, and therapists as well as theorists find this fascinating work. The understanding that comes from working with such patients is extremely valuable in contacting their primitive psychic functioning and the crude forms of primitive defense. There is a sense of acceptable omnipotence which comes from the successful treatment and understanding of these very difficult patients.

To work with extremely depressed patients is not as exciting. The slow, methodical work is tedious with the chronically complaining, hypochondrical, and depressed patient. Even the most psychologically minded therapist must refer severely depressed patients for treament by organic methods. Thus, the therapist backs away from depression within clinical settings as much as in everyday settings.

Is it possible that depressed patients with suicidal fantasies and the persecutory aspects of hypochondriasis threaten all of us? We all get depressed, but this has really resulted in a theoretical homily, a statement which is acknowledged but then dismissed by clinicians. Of course, we all get depressed, but how we become depressed by our patients is discussed only rarely.

> Charles is a 67-year-old man, whose career was coming to an end. He desperately negotiated with his company to allow him to extend his work years in order to provide for himself financially. His wife was a provocative alcoholic. Charles felt a sense of total alienation. All of the factors could be attributed to a childhood psychological pattern extending throughout his life, where he coped by turning to his work. I was reminded of the demands of my own profession and conjured up fantasies about my own future.

Sessions with Charles were laborious and depressing, and I found myself wondering where I could dispatch or dump him. I needed to work on my own reactions to him, the burden that he was "inflicting" upon me, my anger at my colleague who had made the referral, and myself for having taken him on.

What was his life all about? Charles was depressing and he depressed me. At first, I preferred to ignore this with all the usual therapist's rationalizations about the needs for empathy in the therapeutic situation. However, he also evoked questions about the meaning of my own professional life, a life which would be paralleled by his at times and by what was in store possibly for me at retirement (fortunately some years away). The patient seemed better after the sessions, but I was much worse. I began to understand that he was putting part of his depression into me as the container for it, and I was becoming afraid of being overwhelmed.

Characteristically, my defenses were originally a denial of this event, accompanied by omnipotent fantasies about what I could do for him, and for that matter, for myself. I resorted to the manic defenses described so well by the Kleinian school (Segal 1973), developed a sense of contempt for Charles, and came to feel that I could control the situation and triumph in an omnipotent way because my capabilities were greater than his. Even a falling out of the therapeutic role into a directive form of therapy was of no help to Charles.

As I was working hard to deal with Charles, I came to understand how other people reacted to him. They avoided him as much as I did. His wife coped by talking of divorce; his daughters avoided him. I, too, wished to find some way of "divorcing" and dumping him into another therapeutic institution.

Recognition is, of course, the first step in reversing this reaction. I realized that Charles did not need to depress me, nor did I need to use my coping ineffectual defense patterns. One does not have to be overwhelmed by the patient's projective identifications. Showing Charles what he did to his wife and others was extremely helpful to him, and it also helped him to negotiate an extension of his contract at work; this, in turn, lessened his depressive effect on others. They no longer backed away from him in an angry, depressed way. He was able to convince his wife to seek help for her alcoholism. She stopped threatening to divorce him, which in turn eased the pressure upon him.

This is not to diminish the problem of dealing with the psychology of Charles' old age. Yet it illustrates very clearly how patients stir up in us that with which we have to deal in our heavy professional duties, and our own fantasies about mortality and even about our own aging, fantasies which we deny. Of course, patients like Charles also prompt us to think about our own death.

The Depressive Creator

While we deal routinely with patients who are depressed due to various causes, we hear indirectly about persons who make them so. On occasion, we get patients who are the instigators of depression by projective identification into others.

Collin, a 45-year-old senior executive, was referred after he got my name from his ex-wife, who was in psychotherapy with a colleague for suicidal and depressive behavior, apparently over the breakup of their marriage two years earlier. The precipitating event in Collin's case, however, was, on the surface, a second severe loss of job status.

The first loss occurred four years before he came to me, when he learned to his horror that he had been passed over for a very senior position in an industrial corporation. The bad news, which was a severe blow to his narcissism, came not directly, but in the morning newspaper. His wife, Ellen, was very supportive at that time. Competent and socially well connected, Collin was able to move to another firm where the same pattern repeated itself. Difficulties with very senior executives represented a hidden, unresolved oedipal problem.

By the time he arrived for analysis, Collin was in the process of final negotiations for an honorary position on a contract basis with a high salary and severance pay. He had left his wife because of her alleged neurotic difficulties which he claimed were aggravated by his rise to success.

Analytic work dictated that we had to look at his identifications with his father and mother, who were enormously successful people, the former, a businessman, and the latter, a socialite. They were, so to speak, without any psychological problems. One suspects that they projected their own failures and difficulties into particular individuals and their own respective families as each one seemed to have a "casualty" in it.

The patient was unable to compete directly with his father, but they worked in a related line. Collin functioned well under his father's tutelage, but difficulties began to arise due to Collin's underlying dislike of authority. Within the family atmosphere, failure was never allowed. Even a bout of tuberculosis in late adolescence, which almost ruined his academic career, was handled in the family with an almost "manic" collusion, extolling the benefits of such an illness. True to form, he read extensively and argued that his euphoria at the time was due only to the tubercular infection.

Collin married Ellen 12 years before I met him, and they had three children. He complained about her constant preoccupation with social climbing and her scheming and maneuvering to aid him. At the same time, he complained of her own inability to cope in the same firm and believed she was having an affair with his superior. This caused him no end of chagrin in his fantasies and feelings about Ellen, but he triumphed in his conquest of her, winning her away from his oedipal rival in the firm. Their marriage was not a happy one. He blamed all of this upon her and her inability to find a role as a female executive, so much so that she had taken marriage to him as a way out of having to face her failure to climb the corporate ladder.

Their marriage was stormy. Collin described himself as quite normal, despite repeated affairs. Ellen found out about some of these and raised a furor. She complained constantly about his derisory ways and about being undercut whenever she made efforts within the community women's associations. They seemed to be caught up in a masochistic-sadistic relationship. Although separated, they could not stay apart from each other since they were hurt and hurting constantly.

It is easy to see the possibility that Ellen was, in fact, the depressive carrier for the failure of this hitherto "normal" man. He attributed his working failures to her and she became depressed over this. Of course, she may have had a personality for this since she had been a deprived child and was unable to cope with this until her adult years when rejection led to feelings of deprivation and intense depressions. Collin was not much help. Ellen would feel suicidal when he had suffered a setback. She dreaded constantly that she would be deserted by him. She had been deserted by her father, and Collin deserted her by having affairs. The main point, however, was that Collin suffered only temporary feelings of depression in his business setbacks. Even the major one, four years earlier, led to the most anguish within Collin's wife. The current setback was the first time that Collin had really experienced depression. He had rationalized even the marital breakup, two years previously, as being due to his wife's severe character disorder.

The therapeutic work functioned well at first because he regarded both of us as superior men, having to manage as executives in a difficult world. Interpretations about how he unconsciously used Ellen began to take their effect and the patient became very depressed. We reviewed his life, and he had to reexperience depressions that he had not before, including a concealed reaction to his adolescent illness and his hitherto denied depressions over certain academic failures. Some of these had been glossed over, such as his not gaining a higher degree and his grief over the breakup of his marriage.

He had used his ex-wife as a container for his own failures and got her to wonder about his own future. As might be expected, he tended to put some of this into me and I began to wonder about him. Recognizing what was going on meant conveying to the patient what he was doing and what he had done to Ellen.

A casualty developed in the form of his older son who became a school dropout and, in turn, entered treatment for depression. The son's depression was labelled by his therapist as a depression over the loss of his parents through the marriage breakup. This was alleviated to a certain extent by the reunion of the parents who benefitted from their treatment, so much so that they reunited permanently. A follow-up interview three years later suggested a good marital readjustment, with each partner taking responsibility for their own psychological problems. Ellen did not return to the executive world, but was reported to function well as a person in her own right.

Depressing the Clinical Team

Depressive patients are depressing and they, in turn, depress not only the therapist, but also those in the psychiatric unit. This is usually dealt with in the all-important team conference where reactions to the patient are aired.

A common pattern, which we all have observed, is manifested when staff fall into a derisory attitude towards certain depressed patients because of the patient's apparent difficulty to cope with the loss of objects and the entanglements of interpersonal relationships in which the patient engineers repeated rejections. Such patients stir up the internal personal and private difficulties of the nursing staff, support staff, and the therapist. Attempts to cope with the depressions privately may be aroused in each member of the staff, but it is important also to consider fully how depressed individuals can depress other patients and the clinical team.

Bion (1961) has talked about "conglomeration." Patients will project parts of themselves into a number of other individuals in a group. This projective identification can be of confusion, a sense of futility or simply depressed feelings. Then, the patient finds himself in a group of individuals that he has disturbed. The individuals will next react to him in a depressed or confused manner and in turn depress or confuse him further.

Just as psychotic patients may make a psychiatric team psychotic for periods of time, one can observe that depressed patients, particularly the more severe ones, can evoke similar responses within those individuals who care for them. This is due in part to the sense of identification with the patient, but also may have to deal with introjection of patients' projective identifications of depressive parts that they take in and become depressed themselves. Being cared for by depressed staff only depresses the depressed patient further, even when the patient has created the situation. Recognition by staff of projective identification can reverse the process.

The Disguised Depression

Chronic fatigue, insomnia, and hypochondrical preoccupation suggest manifestations of a depressive pattern or the way in which a particular individual expresses the underlying psychodynamics of his own personality and life circumstances. These disguised depressive aspects can also be projected. Also, the persecutory aspects of such hypochondriasis (Rosenfeld 1965) can be detected in the recipient, for example in the therapist, into whom these projections are made and introjected.

Louise, a 35-year-old, married woman in therapy was preoccupied with bodily complaints which throughout her life had necessitated multiple visits to her family practitioner for a variety of reasons. She had been given a large number of medical and surgical remedies. She complained of chronic fatigue and pestered me for pills as oral gratification to alleviate her symptoms. Her clinging behavior disturbed members of the general medical and surgical units on a number of her admissions which ultimately led to a psychiatric referral.

It is of interest that her hypochondriasis was noted to stir up similar symptomatology in a number of the nursing staff. In the course of her therapy, the therapist observed that he also became preoccupied about his health. Her symptoms reflected a sophisticated knowledge of various medical conditions and the therapist began to worry about his own health until he recognized that Louise was evoking in him, in his countertransference, similar fantasies and preoccupations about cancer and heart disease, fantasies which were particularly intense during psychotherapy sessions with her. Recognition of the therapeutic reactions led to an alleviation of the therapist's anxiety, since he could focus upon what Louise's actions and the chronic tormenting aspects of her psychosomatic symptomatology.

As Louise was involved in a number of hospitalizations for investigation, during the early part of the therapy, part of the case management meant use of an intermediary psychiatric consultant to convey to the medical and surgical teams some of the aspects of what she evoked in those around her, including how she handled her depression. The consultant emphasized the way in which Louise handled depression in terms of making others depressed and arousing fatigue and hypochondriacal worries in nursing and support staff.

What Kinds of Depression Are Involved?

Depression has been discussed in this chapter from a number of etiological bases. These will be defined in other chapters and the focus here has been upon how others, including therapists and support staff, are made depressed by patients. Let us take a brief look at how the variety of forms of depressive symptoms can be projected.

Fairbairn (1952) differentiated the schizoid sense of futility, which is very similar to depression, from depression. The former is the inability to relate to an internal object (the representations of this are then projected upon an external object or person). This leads to a sense of futility in an individual about the inability to relate to others. This state may be chronic and as such is often confused with chronic depression.

Depression has many forms. The most common form stems from a sense of rejection, the inability to deal with the angry feelings, and an identification and introjection of the lost object with an internal attack upon the object. Chronic depressions over repeated rejections and fantasy rejections or anticipated rejections look very similar to the chronic sense of futility.

The sense of futility can also be projected in a projective identificatory way. Patients who suffer from a constant inability to relate to people make up a large portion of long-term psychotherapy and psychoanalytic cases. They, in turn, evoke a sense of futility in therapists about their own lives and about life in general. The whole question of existential anxiety comes into therapeutic focus. Even the most well-adjusted therapist will be roused by powerful questions about the patient's real nature, ways of existence and the meaning of life. Such sessions are painful for both therapist and patient. It is, of course, the prerogative of both patients and therapists to look at the meaning of life, a function performed by the patient in therapy and by the therapist away from the therapeutic setting. Most of us can function, recognizing the limitations and difficulties of interpersonal relationships which reflect some of the difficulties of our internal world; we then bring the internal world into our relationships with the external. Life, for most of us, has great meaning.

Depression as a result of guilt is also commonplace. Experience shows that patients need to keep depression an internal problem. They let their superegos torment them for what they have done, whether real or imagined. There is much less of this put into other people since it is important for the patient to maintain an internal sense of suffering and torment.

Depressive patients are depressing, with depressions ranging from the reactive depression (due to real or fantasied object-loss) to supposedly endogenous depressions. It is easy for a therapist to introject this and to attempt to cope with it without recognizing what has occurred. The denial of what the patient evokes in oneself is, in itself, diagnostic. Manic defenses of triumph, control, derision, and a sense of omnipotence about oneself as a therapist and the handling of one's therapeutic work are also valuable diagnostic signs of what is occurring in the patient.

Therapist Variables

Are certain therapists more vulnerable to being affected or even over-whelmed by depressing patients? Under what circumstances are therapists vulnerable?

Obviously, a range of therapeutic personalities deal with a range of patients, who, in turn, express a range of variables. The extent to which one is affected by a particular patient depends upon a variety of circumstances (including the results of one's personal therapy or analysis) but these may be reactivated by particular patients.

In the analysis of a professional, Arthur, who was himself involved in marital therapy, we had to work with the depressing aspects of his own potential marital breakup, including how he came to be married to a particular female, how they interrelated and how they did not. The therapist — the patient — could not, of course, suspend his own professional work until he had worked out a solution to his external and internal problems but had to continue in his hospital and private practices.

Much of Arthur's professional work resonated with his own problems. The marital couples he dealt with were struggling with problems and often overwhelmed by feelings about them. Some of these problems struck areas within his own internal world, which further depressed him. Sometimes, Arthur would come to his sessions and report his own therapeutic work: he dealt with highly depressed people who made him more depressed but seemed better themselves after sessions with him. This seemed to involve the mechanisms discussed, and part of our analytic work dealt with his introjection of other's depressions. Therefore, we worked with elements related to Arthur's childhood, his current situation, and with those elements that were "put into him" by his patients.

At times, he was involved in long-term psychotherapy with patients who had life histories very similar to his own: ambitious, hard-driving professionals, with immigrant parents who had great expectations for their sons. We worked on his intolerance of his own failure and the failures of others and his close identification with certain patients. At times, he lived part of his life vicariously through them. Blows to their narcissism became blows to his. In his projective identification, Arthur almost literally put himself into particular patients.

Arthur's therapeutic vulnerability was not constant. With the resolution of his own marital difficulties, Arthur became more tolerant of the marital difficulties of others and less affected and depressed by them. With his own analytic work, examining and working with his own narcissistic vulnerability and his overidentification with certain others led to a lessening of the overinvolvement with certain patients and, therefore, a lessening of his vulnerability to the depressive aspects of their lives.

Empathy And Vulnerability

We return to the traditional therapeutic stance. Empathy is part of one's humanness and understanding, compared with sympathy, an identification. The former is therapeutic, the latter, overinvolvement.

This leads to the position that all of us are, nevertheless, vulnerable to the processes described in this chapter. Therapeutic effectiveness requires a therapist to be attentive, empathic, sensitive, and attuned. At the same time, the therapist must remain an individual. In my view, the therapist must be vulnerable and invulnerable at the same time. This means receiving all the patient's projective identifications in an ego-functioning way as a receiving organ or container, while, at the same time, not letting these introjects overwhelm one internally, nor become part of one's own personality. These psychic parts belong to others.

The recognition that these are part of the patient's life, not the therapist's, is crucial. Overinvolvement by the therapist occurs when this is not recognized. The catastrophes and horrors in which patients get caught up and live through belong to them, even though they remind us of our own experiences. Patients "do things" to us but it is only *their* "doing" which we recognize by our self-analysis of the ongoing countertransference.

Regardless of theoretical conceptual scheme, the therapist has to be a recipient of what the patient infuses. This is the essence of "therapeutic listening," which involves the therapeutic resonance to the patient's problems.

Guntrip (1960) has stressed that we, as therapists, tolerate badly what he terms "ego weakness": the helpless, dependent parts of ourselves, covered by layers of ego and ego defenses, always denied, never recognized, which we in turn despise in others, including our patients. This term "ego weakness" while only a metaphor, may be useful.

Guntrip emphasizes that we would prefer the "mighty instincts," particularly about aggressiveness, to the utter helplessness that we feel about ourselves at certain times. We prefer to feel tough and aggressive and, indeed, prefer this in others. Depression in others and ourselves is a threat. We prefer our formulations about internally directed hostility about lost objects rather than formulations of how we constantly experience a series of losses which threaten our omnipotent defenses, our control of others, and our control of ourselves.

In the same way, we prefer our patients to have a mastery of their own lives. When patients cannot cope, we feel the inner urge to render them whole, even at the risk of pushing them, consciously or unconsciously, to regain the sense of self, and thereby overcome their vulnerability. By our identification with them, we hope to overcome our own sense of vulnerability as well.

Concluding Remarks

That depressive patients are depressed and depressing is common knowledge. Yet this is minimized in the literature on the supervision and training of psychotherapists. The therapist, in his therapeutic role, is vulnerable because he has to be attuned to what the patient is saying or sending in a conscious or unconscious way. Depression, particularly on the basis of real or fantasied object loss is not a "respectable illness." The threats to self-esteem and the ego ideal are also depressions.

Through projective identification, depressive patients put their depression into others, including therapists. Those surrounding depressed people, including therapists, introject these depressive feelings or psychic parts. They, in turn, become depressed. Nevertheless, these depressive bits are alien to the therapist and can be recognized as such, with immediate relief for the therapist from the temporary and hopefully transitory depressions which are created by patients. Other depressive symptoms in therapists are resonated by personal experiences and can be worked at by self-analysis in the ongoing therapeutic process.

Patients are depressed by others. Certain patients are chosen in families or in groups as the scapegoat to carry the depressive aspects of the others. This continues when people choose partners or get involved in situations where they carry as part of their unconscious roles, the depressive feelings which are put into them by other people. Sometimes the projective identification parts, which are, of course, unconscious, evoke fatigue and hypochondriasis in others who are the recipients. This may be done to the therapist.

Patients will react to others in ways which have to be interpreted. They deny what is being done to them psychologically or become derisory when there are threats to their loss of self-control. They, when depressed, do things to those of us who care for them. We react by denial, disavowal, contempt, develop a sense of mastery or control and a sense of triumph since they, not us, are involved. Our manic defenses (Melanie Klein) have to be worked with, just as we have to interpret theirs.

Depression threatens our narcissism and self-esteem. Yet, our patients are made to be depressed by others in varying degrees and they, in turn, do this to us, as therapists. The genius of Freud was that he was willing to look at in detail what others had known but had chosen to deny before, for example, infantile sexuality and the meaning of dreams. The next years of our clinical and theoretical work will follow this pathway of looking at that which we now choose not to see. We may focus on the depressing aspects of depression which affect both patient and therapist.

REFERENCES

Bion, W. R. (1961). *Experiences in Groups*. London: Tavistock Publications.
_____ (1962). *Learning from Experience*. London: William Heinemann, Ltd.
Fairbairn, W. R. D. (1952). *Psychoanalytic Studies of the Personality*. London: Tavistock Publications.
Guntrip, H. (1960). *Schizoid Phenomena, Object Relations and the Self*. New York: International Universities Press.
Rosenfeld, H. (1965). *Psychotic States*. New York: International Universities Press.
Searles, H. F. (1965). *Collected Papers on Schizophrenic and Related Subjects*. New York: International Universities Press.
Segal, H. (1973). *Introduction to the Work of Melanie Klein*. London: Hogarth Press.
Turquet, P. M. (1975). *The Large Group: Dynamics and Therapy*, pp. 87–144. Ed. L. Kreeger. London: Constable.

CHAPTER FIFTEEN

Psychotherapy of Complicated Mourning

Vamık D. Volkan, M.D.

The Course of Mourning

It has been demonstrated (Bowlby 1961, Bowlby and Parkes 1970, Engel 1962, Pollock 1961, Volkan 1980) that the course of mourning has predictable sequential phases through which anyone who has lost someone important can be expected to pass. It can be divided into two stages.

The *initial stage* begins with numbness and shock accompanied by denial of the death. This is followed quickly by the splitting of ego functions concerning the perception of the death, the bereaved perceiving that death has occurred but acting though it had not happened; the activation of certain images of the dead person; exaggerated inner relatedness to the deceased; and painful emotions accompanied by weeping with frustration over the absence (Pollock 1961). This stage concludes with anger toward the deceased, indicating the ego's attempt to accept the loss and all of its pychological implications. This narcissistic response to separation initiates integration under the reality principle of the initially split ego functions pertaining to the death. The different constellations involved may appear serially or simultaneously and may disappear only to reappear. Finally, however, anger — sometimes displaced onto others — marks the conclusion of the initial stage, which usually lasts for a period of from a few weeks to a few months.

The *work of mourning* (the second stage) involves a slow-motion review of the mourner's relationship to the one mourned; a struggle between keeping or rejecting a close tie with representation of the deceased; a painful awareness that no longer will the deceased be able to justify the mourner; and regressive disorganization, which is ultimately followed by a new inner organization able to test reality more fully for confirmation that the death, with all its psychological implications, has indeed taken place. The work of mourning usually takes from one to two years.

In the absence of complications, the mourner will identify during and at the end of mourning with selected aspects of the one mourned. Such aspects are depersonified and changed into functions; the mourner will assume some functions of the departed. When the work of mourning is successful, the mourner's ego can be expected to manifest enrichment due to the internalization of such new functions. Mourning thus ends with a new inner adaptation to the external loss. The psychological process of mourning can be compared to the organic process involved in the healing of a wound or the mending of a broken bone, the return to health of an organism that has suffered some damaging blow (Engel 1961, Bowlby 1961, Volkan 1981).

But just as a wound can become infected, so can the process of mourning run into complications, some of which may respond well enough to social support provided by family, friends, and, perhaps, religous resources. Some complications may, however, be serious enough to require attention from a professional trained to treat complicated psychological problems.

Factors Affecting the Course of Mourning

Certain general factors affect the way a mourner deals with death and determine the kind of pattern to be expected in the initial response and in the work of mourning.

The mourning process may be initiated not only by an actual death but in some cases by an anticipated or even fantasied death. *Anticipatory grief* (Lindemann 1944), which is based on a belief, realistic or not, that death impends, accustoms the mourner gradually to imminent loss. The mourner has been vaccinated, so to speak, so when finally exposed to the "illness" itself, the mourner experiences it in attenuated form.

However, anticipatory grief can also have negative results, especially when the death that has been anticipated does not, in fact, occur. For example, a bride fantasized that her husband would not return from his assignment to the war zone, and when he did return uninjured she perceived him as a "ghost," someone quite other than the man she had married, and soon divorced him (Volkan 1981).

Sudden exposure to a death provides an experience contrary to that undergone when death has been anticipated. The sudden and altogether unexpected death of someone important (Volkan 1970) in one's life evokes a response quite different from that evoked by the demise of someone whose age and physical condition have suggested for some time a frail hold on life. When the mourner's psychological makeup was unprepared for the death, its occurrence may trigger something like traumatic neurosis, and the trauma will be responded to according to the maturity of the mourner's psychic organization.

The *amount and nature of psychological business* involving the two parties that was left "unfinished" by the death of one of them will have its effect. The term "unfinished psychological business" refers to the way in which the mourner depends on the person who died for psychological equilibrium and the hope of advancing psychological growth. The death of anyone the mourner idealized to enhance own self-esteem by the connection with a "superior" other will bring marked consequences; if the mourner "kills" the idealized dead, the mourner's psychological equilibrium suffers. With such a strong psychological need to keep the dead person's image "alive," the process of mourning becomes complicated, just as it does when the bereavement impedes the mourner's efforts to grow psychologically. An example is provided by the case of a young man who lost to death an elderly man who represented for him the oedipal father. When he died, the young man was involved in a *reactivated* oedipal struggle with him in which he was seeking to identify with him in order to grow psychologically.

Unfinished psychological business with an important other is usually accompanied by ambivalence, conscious or not. This need for the other is congruent with hate toward the other, and ambivalence about "keeping" the representation or "letting it go" produces conflict.

The *degree to which reactions to past loss are reactivated* (Klein 1940) will help determine whether the death of someone important in one's life will reawaken the trauma of past loss. Loss is considered here in sufficiently general terms to include the surrender of dependence on others as we individuate, form a new identity, and move through the life cycle. When one's response to past loss, due either to real separation or to psychological detachment in the course of development, has been stormy but repressed, the death of an important other may trigger its unconscious return and complicate the mourning process.

The *degree to which the death involved violence* can be a determinant. Empirical findings (Volkan 1972, 1981) suggest that mourning is often complicated when the death was a violent one—a suicide, perhaps, or an accident involving mutilation. This is because the mourner's natural anger toward the dead, a response to being rejected (left behind) and thus damaged narcissistically, must take into account recognition of the violence. In this situation the mourner feels more than the usual guilt, thus becoming unable to pass smoothly through the mourning process.

Changes in the real world brought about by the death of someone close must be taken into account. A death may bring not only its own emotional trauma but wrenching changes in the mourner's circumstances. For example, the unexpected death of the family head sometimes presents the family with a serious reduction of its living standard. It may be necessary to give up the family home or the mother may have to go to work for the first time.

All of these factors are considered here in connection with the mourning reactions of adults. There remains considerable controversy in the literature as to when children are capable of mourning in the adult sense. The child's mental apparatus must be sufficiently mature to permit an internal maintenance of a representation of the other — to develop object constancy — before he can come close to grieving as adults do (A. Freud 1960). Still, children use the adults in their environment for their own psychic functions and as resources for the mastery of anxiety. For example, a mother performs functions necessary for the child's psychological well being. The loss of a mother with actual executive functions for the child cannot be mourned properly unless there is a good enough substitute for her. Otherwise, the child will take into adulthood a search for persons to perform the functions of his lost mother. Passage through adolescence, the period in which the youth modifies and/or surrenders the images of the parents of childhood and experiences a mourning model as part of this developmental milestone, is a necessary precondition for "normal" adult mourning (Wolfenstein 1966).

The professional faced with a patient whose mourning is severely complicated will do well to keep all the above factors in mind and to assess their role in keeping the mourning process from resolution.

Complications in the Initial Stage of Mourning

Exaggerated Response to Death

The signs and symptoms expectable in the initial stage of response to death may be exaggerated. This does not necessarily mean that the mourner will not be able to avoid complications in the initial stage of dealing with the death if help is rendered by family members, religious beliefs, and adequate inner strength; only time will tell whether the exaggerated responses will persist. For example, a woman who sobs with narcissistic hurt, "How could my husband leave me! I want him back!" may abandon this dramatic response within a few weeks and settle down into a quiet course of mourning that will ultimately be resolved without intervention. However, the continued exaggeration of two special responses is alarming to those in the mourner's circle, and usually leads to the mourner's entry into therapy. The two most symptomatic behavior patterns are denial and anger.

Denial. Although it is "normal" for one bereaved to deny the death initially, exaggerated and dominant denial lasting for more than a few days will be considered "pathological" since it is so clearly at odds with reality. The family or religious advisor of the denier may be able to help, but if their efforts fail, psychiatric help may be sought, although the psychiatrist is seldom faced with a patient able to maintain total denial into chronicity. Of the 150 mourners I studied (Volkan 1980), only two exhibited denial of death long enough to be brought in for psychiatric treatment. One was a man who had been summoned to a hospital to identify the body of a brother killed in a car accident but who did not attend the funeral, continuing to believe that his brother's death was nothing but a dream.

Anger. It is usual for the mourner to be angry at a doctor, a relative, the funeral director, or someone else during the initial phase of grief. Even when there is an objective cause for such anger, this emotion absorbs the "normal" anger one expects will be unconsciously directed toward the deceased. There may even be open, direct anger. However, when such anger is greatly exaggerated because of some associated negative reaction, the mourner is likely to be brought to psychiatric attention. This will almost certainly be the case if the mourner obtains a gun and threatens to kill strangers with it, although such behavior, however alarming, may be simply a storm that will subside, allowing the patient to resume an orderly course of mourning. I (Volkan 1970) describe elsewhere a man who threatened to kill others with a gun as a response to his grandfather's death. After being treated during a brief confinement in a protective hospital environment, he resumed a "normal" sort of mourning, and a five-year follow-up showed that his complications and his bizarre behavior never returned.

Absent or Minimal Response to Death

Signs and symptoms expectable in the initial stage may may be absent or minimal. Denial of a death is not the same response as the acceptance of it with apparent equanimity. Sometimes a patient who does not deny that an important death has occurred fails to show shock or to weep; the patient is neither angry nor preoccupied with the image of the dead. Deutsch (1937) demonstrated that this negative response points to the presence of complications and indicates that sooner or later, in one form or another, a complicated reaction will become evident.

One young man who failed to manifest the usual signs and symptoms of the initial response to a death was enabled by professional help to express his grief 10 years later. He had been in his late teens when, as he sat with his mother and sister in their home one evening, they were told by a messenger that my patient's father had been killed in a mine accident. Stoically, he then became "the man of the house" himself. In his late twenties, he entered the neurological ward of a hospital because he had trouble standing up, especially in the early evening. The first attack of this disability had come on the ninth anniversary of his father's death, and he had suffered from it for a year. An insurance policy that had been supporting the family was terminated when the youngest child turned 18, nine years after her father's death. This put a heavy financial burden on the patient, who had been able to establish himself as a professional man without having to support his mother and sister. He then developed the symptoms that identified him with the father's collapse in the mine, symptoms that yielded the secondary gain of disqualifying him as the family wage earner. It took psychotherapy to induce in this patient the responses characteristic of the initial response to death, whereupon he went into a forward-moving process of mourning.

Protracted Mourning

Signs and symptoms of the initial stage may fail to disappear after a few months, but become chronic. A protracted course (Wahl 1970) indicates the presence of complications. One sometimes sees a person bereaved five or even 10 years earlier who bursts into tears at any reminder of the lost one and manifests intense pain, appearing "normal" in every way except for such episodes. When such signs and symptoms occur often enough to disturb daily adjustment and reduce productivity, the complication has become chronic although such chronicity in a pure form is rare; it is more usual for the persistent initial reactions to be combined with the complications of the work of mourning.

Unusual New Symptoms

In speaking of "unusual new symptoms" here, I refer to recognizable psychological or psychosomatic illnesses, both of which need professional treatment. Such illnesses appear in this context for different reasons in different persons and must be formulated in psychodynamic terms with appropriate individualized treatment plans.

A young physician with a hysterical personality organization continually competed anxiously with other men, especially with those older than himself, and often seduced women in an attempt at oedipal victory. His "victories" were illusory ones, however, and he would repeat this behavior often. One evening, when called to the home of an ailing uncle, he seduced his uncle's wife, a woman considerably younger than her husband, and had intercourse with her in a room not far from the sickroom. After going to sleep that night in his own apartment he was awakened by the news that his uncle had just died. On the following day he manifested a severe obsessive-compulsive neurosis, entertaining obsessional thoughts about having a fungal infection of the penis and spending hours washing it. He prescribed medication for himself to use on the skin that was supposedly infected. He saw several dermatologists about his problem, but they all agreed that he had no infection, so he sought psychiatric help. The psychiatric formulation was that guilt over "killing" the father figure and sleeping with his uncle's wife had led him to regress. The "infection" of his penis was punishment, while washing it was his attempt to repent and cleanse his incestuous feelings for his mother and his murderous feelings for his father although other condensed psychological constellations could also be discerned.

The following vignette exemplifies initial grief reactions giving way to psychosomatic response. A teenager's father was dying slowly of multiple sclerosis while his son, caring for his physical needs, began some preparatory mourning. The boy was highly ambivalent toward the dying man, who had been at times very harsh to him. As the boy carried his father's wasting body to the bathroom he began to think of flushing him down the toilet even as he nursed him more and more faithfully. When at last the man died, his son began to grieve in the usual way. He was Jewish and conformed to the appropriate Jewish customs, but before the ritual was completed his mother insisted that he be sent to a relative who lived in the country in order to escape the grieving household and get some rest. He caught a small snake in the country, killed it, and put it in a bottle of acid, watching it being eaten away slowly. His later psychotherapy indicated that this was an act of "killing" his father, an effort made prematurely to complete the initial stage of grieving that had been interrupted, with the snake representing the dead man. The boy himself developed a severe dermatitis, associated with his disruptive identification with the snake's rotting skin.

Complications in the Second Stage of Mourning

Volkan (1981) suggests that in the long run complications in the work of mourning result either in reactive depression or established pathological mourning. Similarities and dissimilarities of mourning and "melancholia" (the term "reactive depression" is used interchangeably with melancholia) have been noted since the work of Abraham (1911, 1916, 1924) and Freud (1917). However, the concept of established pathological mourning, which more directly reflects fixation in the work of mourning, is a relatively original contribution of Volkan (1974, 1981).

It is further suggested that complications in the initial response to death may condense in either reactive depression or established pathological mourning if they become chronic. Although one sometimes sees other unusual clinical pictures associated with complications in the work of mourning, they are psychodynamically akin to the two cited here.

Reactive Depression

Freud (1917) indicated that mourning is a typical and expectable reaction to the loss of someone loved, whereas "melancholia" may be a more selectively determined response to such an event. The phenomenology of the latter state involves profoundly painful dejection, a loss of interest in the outside world, a loss of the ability to love, and the inhibition of any activity not concerned with thoughts of the lost one. These also occur in mourning, but mourning is distinguished from reactive depression by the marked lowering of self-regard characteristic of the latter state. One hears from the depressed individual statements full of self-reproach and self-revelations that culminate "in a delusional expectation of punishment" (Freud 1917, p. 244).

As a result of the work of mourning, the mourner identifies with selected aspects of the one mourned, which are depersonified and turned into functions. This process leaves the mourner's ego enriched. In depression provoked by a death, however, internalization results in a "total" sort of identification, and hated and dreaded traits of the deceased are internalized along with the loved and admired ones. The ambivalence with which the dead had been regarded then becomes an internal conflict; the love for the deceased promotes "keeping" the deceased within the self, while hate toward the former promotes "destruction" (Fenichel 1945). The mourner's self-system thus becomes a battleground; aggression preserved in oneself through identification contributes guilt and self-reproach.

Suicide in reactive depression.   One possible outcome of the complication of the work of mourning that goes into depressive reaction is the "melancholic" suicide. The mourner, having taken on the conflict between the thrust to "keep" the dead person's representation and the thrust to "destroy" it, is likely to attempt self-destruction. People in this state obviously require professional care.

Established Pathological Mourning

The individual in established pathological mourning, like the individual depressed after a death, is faced with some complications in the work of mourning. However, the person in pathological mourning has not developed a disruptive total identification with the dead person's representation; it is kept instead as an unassimilated introject, which is a special kind of object representation not entirely absorbed into or identified with the self-representation (Volkan 1976). It strongly influences the self-representation but leads to no structural change and does not influence ego organization as identification does. The mourner describes the introject as an "inner presence" (Schafer 1968) living inside where contact with it can be maintained. The ambivalent relationship of the past continues in the mourner's involvement with the introject; the mourner is torn between a strong yearning for the restored presence of the one mourned and an equally deep dread that the deceased might be confronted. The presence of the introject provides an illusion of choice, and in this way it reduces anxiety.

An interest in reincarnation and impulses to search for the lost one on earth sometimes give evidence of such ambivalent yearning. A glimpse of some stranger who resembles the dead person often leads the individual in established pathological mourning to anxious pursuit and scrutiny to establish or rule out the possibility that the one mourned continues to live. The compulsive reading of obituary notices, rather common in this state, betrays not only anxiety about one's own death but a hope of denying the death that has occurred by finding no current mention of it. The person in established pathological mourning continues to use the present tense when speaking of the one lost: "My father likes to walk" — "My mother has blue eyes," etc. The daily life of such mourners seems focused on death, their conversation on graveyards and tombs. They refer to people who are about to die or who have just died, and one gets the impression that the dead person and other figures representing that person by displacement populate the mourner's mind.

People with established pathological mourning have typical dreams the manifest content of which can be classified under three headings: "frozen" dreams, dreams of a life-and-death struggle, and dreams of death as an illusion. Such dreams provide important diagnostic clues.

Frozen dreams.   This term is often used spontaneously by patients themselves to describe dreams composed of one tableau after another with no action. One patient likened his dreams to a slide series, and another compared his to slices of bread slipping out of their wrapping (Volkan 1981). "Frozen" also indicates "lifeless." Associations to such dreams reflect fixation in the work of mourning, a defensive situation in which the patient tries to deny aggression toward the dead person while at the same time finding a way to bring the latter back to life. The conflict between the wish to do so and the dread of success is handled by "freezing" the conflict and averting resolution.

Dreams of a life-and-death struggle.   In this kind of dream, the dreamer sees the dead person as living but engaged in a life-and-death struggle, for example, on the point of drowning. The dreamer tries to save the person, but usually awakens with anxiety before succeeding. Such a dream leaves the mourner again in the indeterminate position of being faced with "killing" or "saving" the one mourned.

Dreams of death as an illusion. The dreamer dreams of seeing the mourned one dead, but the dead person exhibits signs of life such as sweating and twitching, so that doubt about the person being dead persists.

All of these three kinds of dreams often repeat for years after the death being mourned.

Linking objects and phenomena. Another diagnostic clue to established pathological mourning is the presence of linking objects and phenomena (Volkan 1972, 1981). The individual in this state not only maintains internal contact with the representation of the one mourned through the introject but maintains also the illusion of external contact by means of a linking object. This object is used in a magical way to be, in metapsychological terms, a locus for meeting with the representation of the dead individual. Its employment facilitates the illusion that the mourner has full control of the choice between "killing" or "not killing" the one mourned, and thus need never resolve the dilemma of grief. I describe elsewhere (Volkan 1972, 1981) the relationship between a linking object, the fetish, and a reactivated transitional object (Winnicott 1953).

A linking object may be a personal possession of the deceased, perhaps an article of clothing or a watch; a gift from the deceased; something the deceased had used to extend senses or bodily functions, such as a camera (an extension of sight); a realistic representation of the deceased such as a photograph; or something that was at hand when the mourner first learned of the death or saw the dead body.

Linking phenomena are fantasies, sensations, or behavior patterns that perpetuate the possibility of contact between the mourner and the one mourned without reference to any tangible object. Religious belief in an afterlife may be an example of this although in any culture that fosters this belief, only an exaggerated application of it should be considered suggestive of pathology. Something with sensory impact, like a song, could be a linking phenomenon. One patient who had attended her father's funeral in the rain used the song "Raindrops Are Falling on my Head" as a linking phenomenon; even after many years it would induce eerie feelings in her, helping to perpetuate the illusion that through this song she could choose to be in contact with her father or to bury him. Linking objects and linking phenomena can be advantageously used in "re-grief" therapy, as will be shown.

Suicide in established pathological mourning. The risk of suicide is not as great in established pathological mourning as it is in reactive depression since the individual in the former condition is protected from the impulse to self-destruction by a stable linking object or introject. The mourner maintains the illusion of contact with a representation of the dead, an illusion that is not included in self-representation but remains exterior to it. When the mourner is aggressive toward the introject or the linking object, the aggression is not addressed toward the self. More importantly, the illusion maintained manages feelings of guilt since through the illusion the mourner can, if so chosen, "bring the dead back."

It is rather rare for a person in established pathological mourning to attempt suicide. The effort is not of the "melancholic" type, but reflects the wish for magical reunion with the representation of the dead. The anniversary reaction of persons in established pathological mourning may initiate such a strong desire to merge with the representation of the dead (which exists independently of the self-representation) that suicide seems a compelling prospect.

We have noted that the signs and symptoms of the initial stage of mourning may give way to unusual psychological or psychosomatic manifestations. Some complications in the work of mourning (the second stage) may also initiate unusual symptoms, the appearance of which is influenced by the individual's personality organization, the nature of object relations, the severity of the structural conflicts reactivated by the death, the points of fixation, and the tendency to (re) somatization. Accordingly, the treatment of such conditions, especially when they become chronic, may be time consuming and require highly developed professional skills, such as the ability to conduct psychoanalysis or psychoanalytic therapy.

Even a brief review of the psychiatric and psychoanalytic literature (Brown and Epps 1966, Cobb, Bauer, and Whiting 1939, Crisp and Priest 1972, Evans and Liggett 1971, Greene and Miller 1958, Hill 1972, Lehrman 1956, Lidz 1949, McDermott and Cobb 1939, Parkes 1964a, 1964b, Parkes and Brown 1972, Peck 1939, Schmale 1958, Volkan 1965) shows widespread awareness of the number of psychiatric and psychosomatic illnesses associated with, triggered by, or condensed with complications in the work of mourning. This phenomenon has, as a matter of fact, long been known to poets and novelists or at least used by them for dramatic effect, as when a character whose lover dies declines physically from grief. Reference to creative artists underlines the possibility that some complications in the work of mourning have positive rather than negative outcomes since such writers as Hamilton (1969, 1973, 1975, 1979) believe that the creativity of many artists is the end result of their inability to pass smoothly through the mourning process. It is also suggested that complications in mourning can lead certain persons into political leadership (Pollock 1975, Volkan and Itzkowitz 1984) or archeological activity (Niederland 1965).

I wish to emphasize here my finding (Volkan 1981) that some complications of the work of mourning, when condensed with complications stemming from the initial stage of response to death, can lead to a clinical picture like that of psychosis. I stress the importance of giving close attention to events related to a death and the psychological consequences of those events when making a diagnosis. The condition brought on by complications in the mourning process is not a true psychosis, in spite of the resemblance, but one that can be treated successfully in even brief psychotherapy.

I have described elsewhere (Volkan, Cillufo, and Sarvay 1975) the successful "re-griefing" of a man who had the delusion that his wife was trying to poison him. Here I report another case, that of a woman in her fifties who seemed psychotic but was put back on the course of "normal" mourning by the briefest of psychotherapeutic experiences, one which offered nothing beyond one significant clarification-interpretation. Such technique is reminiscent of that which Socarides (1954) used when he applied psychoanalytic explanations and interpretations to a patient's symptoms and history.

> My patient had had two married sons, the younger of which had been killed flying his own airplane. His wife, in the plane with him, escaped without a scratch, and my patient could not dismiss the notion that she had been responsible for the accident, which was officially attributed to pilot error. My patient often spoke of "foul play" in connection with the accident. She had "delusions" about her daughter-in-law's poisoning her husband. She spent a year, and much of her energy, trying to understand the nature of the foul play in which she believed so firmly. She even employed a detective to investigate her daughter-in-law and to review the autopsy findings and official report connected with the plane crash. Unable to sleep because of her suspicions, she seemed greatly disturbed. Her husband, a mild and loving man, comforted her with assurances that the daughter-in-law would not have gone with her husband on any flight she knew would crash. He said there was no reason to suspect the survivor of any malign intent, since everything indicated the daughter-in-law's marriage had been happy. My patient had persisted in adhering to her conviction of foul play in the absence of any justification and had been diagnosed as paranoid before I saw her.
>
> During our diagnostic interview the patient freely discussed her theory of foul play. When I probed for background information, I realized that her son's death had reactivated some past concerns about death. She was one of six siblings, some older and some younger than she, and the only girl. Her childhood had been spent in a home oriented to boys, but parental kindness made it tolerable. When she was 13, one of her brothers died suddenly from a ruptured appendix, and the mother's reaction to this loss was extreme. It seemed that the mother had been

deeply involved in established pathological mourning, withdrawing from the family and centering all her thoughts on her dead son. The patient had felt victimized by "foul play" when it was assumed that, as a girl, she was responsible for looking after the family, including her grieving mother. Her own needs were disregarded, and her mother did not even attend her high school graduation. Her reaction formation led her to become a "do-gooder," working throughout her early twenties to make money and to help a brother who needed surgery for a brain tumor. Then she met and married an undemanding man by whom she had two sons. Her altruistic devotion persisted; anger over her mother's withdrawal was repressed until the mother died three years before the plane crash.

The mother was still suffering from established pathological mourning at the time of her death. On her deathbed she summoned her children and their families and told them about her "secret objects," linking objects she had kept over the years to bind her to her dead son. Aware that she was dying, she wanted her remaining children to treasure them after she died. Obliged to humor her, my patient had felt angry, reviewing the death-related "foul play" that had kept her bound for so long, and the way in which her mother had seemed "uncaring" and had deprived her of the maternal warmth that was her birthright. She subsequently re-repressed this anger.

Her recital led my patient to say how "uncaring" her daughter-in-law had seemed during her husband's funeral. This perception stimulated thoughts of "foul play" and the displacement onto the daughter-in-law of the image of the mother whose complicated grief had made life so difficult. The one basic understanding given the patient during this interview was that the treatment she thought she was getting from her daughter-in-law reflected the earlier experience with her mother. It was, in fact, established that the bereaved wife had been sedated by her physician before the funeral and this accounted for her apparent composure.

A week later my patient said that, on the way home from this interview, she had decided to visit her daughter-in-law. As it turned out, the visit was in the service of testing reality, and the two women stayed up all night talking and weeping together about their common loss. My patient then saw the younger woman as a deeply caring widow, one no longer contaminated with the mother's image; this revelation directed her mourning process into a more productive avenue. I saw this patient eight times in the next six months to check on the progress of her work of mourning, which was now showing the expected manifestations. Although I neither encouraged her to report childhood conflicts nor explored defensive-adaptive aspects of her personality, she spontaneously reported a childhood memory that I felt needed limited attention to connnect it to the theme of "foul play." My patient, while in early latency, had been teased by her brothers and had seized a toy airplane belonging to the brother who was soon to die, throwing it from the stairs to crash on the floor below. This memory and the accompanying feelings of guilt had stayed in her mind for years. She even thought that she had encouraged her dead son to become a pilot in response to her unconscious guilt over crushing her younger brother's toy aircraft. We dealt with this notion without pushing her to reveal any symbolic meaning connected with planes or any psychosexual fantasies. She remains "symptom free" in respect to her "paranoid condition," and on the second anniversary of her son's death her whole family, including her son's widow, gathered in a public park to unveil a picnic shelter dedicated to the dead pilot's memory. This "memorialization" marked the end of her work of mourning, and she no longer needed my services.

Treatment

Since the mourning process is nature's exercise in loss and restitution, it seldom needs special professional attention unless it becomes complicated. Indeed, uncomplicated grief is seldom handled by a psychiatrist. Clayton et al. (1968) showed that 98 percent of those who suffer from bereavement sought no psychiatric assistance, and of that 98 percent, 81 percent began to improve from six to 10 weeks after the death. Four percent did not improve.

I believe that "improvement" is hard to assess statistically without an intensive study of the inner adaptation to death made by the individuals in question. Also, as I have shown, some people whose initial reactions were absent or minimal may appear healthy enough to be included among those who mourn without difficulty, whereas we know that the state of some of these may eventually reflect complications of the initial stage. Thus, when the absence of initial reaction is striking, professional help should be sought if only because such a move is good preventive medicine. The professional should then search for psychological reasons for the negative response and help the mutely bereaved to initiate mourning. If short-term therapy is not beneficial, at least it gives the patient the option to seek more intensive therapy and encourages the patient to think of professional help if the need arises.

I generally consider the use of drugs to suppress the symptoms and signs of the initial stage of grief contraindicated. In fact, one should support rather than suppress the initial responses. This is an economic move since it prevents the need of further grieving at some later time when it is likely also to be less socially acceptable. The development of a variety of religious rituals to deal with death and the emotions it generates is no accident; we should advise mourners to indulge fully in them, for they will find these rituals beneficial.

The grief-stricken person is distant from others and, at times, hostile. Hostility may be "projected" onto the professional caregiver, who, being familiar with this symptom, is able to "absorb" the patient's hostility without returning it. Whenever the anger is highly exaggerated, however, it should be taken seriously although I still prefer to refrain from the use of drugs if possible in such cases. The professional should, however, set limits, perhaps insisting that the patient be hospitalized. After the patient is placed in the protective environment of a hospital, the therapist can respond to the patient's anger by assuming a role in which the patient's narcissistic hurt can be borne. The therapist must reject drastic measures in response to the patient's behavior patterns and must allow the patient to experience pain, anger, and other emotions. The therapist should help the patient empathically to heal the "wound," always remembering that the patient is responding to a process of nature. Some mourners may even be relieved by little more than an educational and therapeutic effort to assure them that anger is an expectable initial reaction to the death of someone close.

I would like to state once again that the appearance of severe signs and symptoms in the initial stage does not necessarily mean that the patient will have complications in the second stage, the work of mourning. An individual is prone to reactive depression as a complication of the work of mourning if the individual is fixated at the oral stage in which self-esteem depends on external supplies (Fenichel 1945) since, with the loss of such supplies, self-esteem is reduced. Thus, the treatment of the depressed requires work on characterological makeup to forestall a depressive reaction when future important losses occur. The psychotherapy recommended for the depressed patient is a long-term, intensive, insight-oriented treatment dealing with the underlying matrix of the individual. I will describe later the "re-grief" therapy that may be suitable for some patients with reactive depression caused by a death and which may put a complicated mourning process back onto its "normal" track, one that works toward an appropriate resolution and restoration of the mourner's ability to reinvest the libido and take up life once again.

The individual who develops an established pathological mourning may benefit greatly also from insight psychotherapy on a long-term basis. The short-term therapy called "re-grief therapy" was originally developed in response to the need to care for patients hospitalized for a short time for established pathological mourning and reactive depression (Volkan 1971, 1981, Volkan, Cillufo, and Sarvay 1975, Volkan and Josephthal 1979, Volkan and Showalter 1968). I will briefly outline its technique; a detailed explanation of this procedure, with case examples, appears in the references cited. In the case of psychosomatic involvements, it is essential to combine medical or surgical assessment and treatment plans with the psychological.

Re-grief Therapy

The patients chosen for this therapy had in the course of mourning, met with complications that resulted in either established pathological mourning or reactive depression. It should be noted that these two states may coexist and that some symptoms indicative of complications in the initial stage may appear in both. Although the clinical picture may be mixed, one identifies established pathological mourning more clearly in the patient who uses a linking object and is preoccupied with longing for, yet dreads, the return of the one mourned, although the mourner may also have some degree of disruptive identification with the one mourned.

Since the patient taken into re-grief therapy has a strong and persistent hope of seeing the deceased alive again, but still has a desire to "kill" the deceased in order to complete mourning, the mourner places a high value on psychological contact with the deceased's representation, which may be perceived as an introject. Those able to externalize the representation onto their linking objects may not report an introject but, in any event the patient is clearly trying to relate ambivalently to an unassimilated representation of the one lost.

During the initial phase of re-grief therapy the therapist helps the patient to grasp the distinction between what is the patient's and what belongs to the dead person's representation. In first conceptualizing re-grief therapy, I considered using rather mechanical means, which we called demarcation exercises (Volkan and Showalter 1968). For example, one patient was preoccupied with a letter written by his father just before he died in which the father had expressed criticism of his son. The therapist saw that the patient's feelings of guilt kept him from being upset by this criticism, and that he was, in fact, presenting it as though he had made the statement himself. The mechanical nature of the demarcation exercise was to encourage the patient's recognition that the criticism appeared in his father's handwriting, not his, so that his secondary-process thinking was directed toward acknowledging that two entirely different people were involved. I no longer use such "mechanical" methods since I have discovered that the detailed and empathic uncovering of the patient's history can serve the same purpose.

The therapist is well advised not to question the patient directly when taking the history, but to develop nondirective exchange. In this the therapist can help the patient to begin differentiating thoughts, attitudes, and feelings from those influenced by the introject. The patient in established pathological mourning will surely broach the subject of death and the lost one. A focus on the history and the associations pertaining to the relationship between the patient and the one mourned enables the therapist to help the patient see what has been taken in and, thus, what is felt about the introject or representation of the other and which of its aspects bother the patient so much that he wants to reject them.

One must realize that, although the patient may use the kind of physical terminology we have used in referring to an introject, an affective-dynamic process is actually involved. The therapist treating patients of this sort should be sufficiently experienced to refrain from treatment based on mere intellectual gymnastics. The manifest content of the patient's dreams helps to show how the mourning process became arrested and why the patient feels that he carries a special representation of the one mourned. The dream can, in short, help the patient to understand the fixation. However, the therapist who shares too quickly the formulation of the reasons for the patient's fixation may find that affective-cognitive process involved in the activation of a forward-moving mourning process has been slowed. In the "demarcation" which may take several weeks, the therapist does not encourage an outpouring of great emotions but helps the patient prepare for it. The patient may feel unable to accommodate the rising flood of emotion, to which the therapist may respond, "What is your hurry? We are still trying to learn about the circumstances of the death and the reasons why you can't grieve. When the time comes, you may allow yourself to grieve."

Meanwhile, the therapist has expanded the formulation that will guide later clarifications and interpretations. The therapist has learned more about the reasons for the patient's arrest and inability to grieve. The patient is encouraged to go over reminiscences of the deceased, the circumstances of the final illness or the accident, the conditions in which news of the death arrived, reactions to seeing the body, and the particulars of the funeral. Again, direct questioning of the patient is far less productive than encouraging the patient to offer such topics himself while displaying appropriate feelings.

The ambivalence felt toward the dead person is clarified. Instead of commenting that such ambivalence is normal, the wise therapist conveys the appropriate message through therapeutic neutrality and empathy. The therapist promotes the patient's curiosity about this ambivalence and the insight that the ambivalence is largely responsible for the patient's quandary over wanting to "save" the deceased as opposed to "killing" the deceased once and for all. As soon as the patient can readily alternate between negative and positive aspects of the ambivalence, the patient is apt to become angry. Such anger may be diffused and directed toward others, but it authenticates the reality of the death as though the patient had gone back to the initial stage of the dilemma. Understanding the patient's need to keep the dead "alive," the therapist then slowly clarifies the relationship between the two and interprets it, along with the reasons for the normal, angry feelings. Abreaction — "emotional reliving" (Bibring 1954) — concerning certain past experiences connected with the deceased or the death may occur at this point if everything is going well. Such abreactions reflect the (re)visiting of the initial response to death and the (re) commencement of the work of mourning. The patient has begun to "re-grieve." It can be assumed that certain impulses such as death wishes are now surfacing, and the patient's readiness to have them interpreted and to reduce guilt feelings can be assessed.

The patient with established pathological mourning typically uses the mechanism of splitting the ego functions, an action experienced in the initial reaction to the death. The therapist calls attention to this by helping the patient to focus at an appropriate time on the way in which the deceased was perceived as dead. This focus will obtain good results if it is made at an emotionally suitable time and not as an intellectual exercise. The patient may show real surprise and blurt out something like: "I thought he was not breathing any more. But I didn't really look!" The therapist has helped the patient to revisit the point where splitting began and to re-evaluate reality.

Our patients often report that there had been problems at the funeral and that they did not actually see the coffin lowered into the grave. When the therapist asks at an appropriate time, "How do you know that the dead person is buried?" the patient is likely to be surprised that one part of the self never did believe that the burial had been accomplished. The patient is then likely to feel anger at those who stood in the way of the patient's participation at the funeral ritual. It has been made clear that, although the patient felt and even knew that death had occurred, the patient paradoxically continued to behave as though nothing had happened.

The most important part of this phase of confrontation, clarification and interpretation of death-related impulses, fantasies, and wishes, and of the defenses the patient has been using against them, is the focus on the linking object. Because it has physical existence, with properties that reach the senses, it has greater "magic" than the introject. Once the patient grasps how the linking object has been used to maintain absolutely controlled contact with the image of the dead person, as well as to postpone mourning and keep it frozen, the patient will use it to activate mourning. It is suggested that the patient bring the linking object to a therapy session, where it will usually be avoided at first. The therapist then asks permission to keep it and points out that its magic exists only in the patient's perception of it. When it is finally introduced into a therapy session, it is placed between patient and therapist long enough for the former to feel its "spell." The patient may then be asked to touch it and to report what comes to mind. I am even now astonished at what intense emotion is congealed in the object, and warn others about this. This emotion serves to unlock the psychological processes that until then were contained in the linking object itself. Emotional storms so triggered may continue for weeks; at first diffuse, they become differentiated, and therapist and patient can then together identify such emotions as anger, guilt, and sadness. The linking object finally loses its power whether or not the patient chooses to dispose of it.

Clarifications and interpretations concerned with death and the deceased and the sharper focus on these subjects made possible by the use of the linking object lead to the final phase of the treatment—disorganization. This is then followed by organization and the appearance of sadness. A sort of graft of secondary-process thinking then is required to help heal the wound that this experience has torn open; patients who had never visited the grave of the one they mourn do so now, as if to say goodbye, and those who had been unable to arrange for the tombstone make arrangements to have one put in place. The mourner can feel sad but no longer need feel guilty. Many patients at this point plan some memorial ritual, and many consult priests, ministers, or rabbis for religious consolation as they begin accepting the death.

I have been able to use the manifest content of the serial dreams of suitable patients coming to the end of their therapy to indicate at what point they were in their re-griefing. These patients seem to feel that their introject has departed, leaving them in peace, and they feel free, even excited, at the lifting of their burden, beginning to look for new objects for their love. My experience has been that the re-griefing that so liberates the patient can be completed within two to four months with sessions three or four times a week.

The elucidation of some of the important meanings of the patient's loss would benefit little if emotions and ideation were not blended. Throughout the treatment, patients experience a variety of emotions as they gain insight into their inability to let the dead person die. This insight is reached by the clarifications and interpretations given, the therapy being designed to loosen up and reactivate the arrest of the mourning process. The patient's resistance to acknowledging the fixation in the work of mourning is interpreted so that interpretations do not necessarily effect resolution of the infantile conflicts underlying the fixation. One must assume that the patient may indeed further repress such conflicts even as the patient loosens those condensations into such conflicts that have been made on a higher level. The use of the linking object brings about special emotional storms that are not curative without interpretation that engages the close scrutiny of the patient's observing ego. Thus the link to the representation of the dead, externalized into the linking object, is brought into the realm of the patient's inner experience.

In spite of the use of a special device, the linking object, in re-grief therapy, the transference relationship becomes the vehicle whereby insight into ambivalence and the conflict between longing and dread may be gained and resolution accomplished. The therapist is a new object, a healer, for the patient's consideration, aiming, as in psychoanalytic therapy, to develop a therapeutic alliance without encouraging an infantile transference neurosis. Rado (1956) uses the term "interceptive interpretations," which I have modified to describe my interception of the development of infantile transference neurosis by premature interpretation of the transference phenomena whenever I think it could lead to a ripened infantile transference neurosis. For example, one interferes with full displacement of the dead person's representation onto the therapist so the patient is kept aware of complications in mourning the original lost one. However, the patient's reactions to parallel situations of loss involving the therapist — separations at weekends, for example — are interpreted in due time, and such interpretation makes it possible to work through past conflicts with the dead person in a focal way. (Also, the fresh grief caused by separation from the therapist when therapy is terminated can be put to appropriate use.) Transference reactions are inevitable but infantile transference neurosis is not; selected reference to and interpretations of the transference reactions may be therapeutic by providing close and intimate contact within the therapeutic setting as the patient's conflicts are understood. Thus, although re-grief therapy is brief, lasting for months rather than years, it is intense, intimate, and certainly not superficial.

Established Pathological Mourning and Psychoanalysis

The therapeutic spectrum in our research ranged from what we regarded as "re-griefing" to psychoanalytic psychotherapy, or, beyond that, to psychoanalysis proper (Volkan 1981). There are established ways of conducting proper Freudian analysis with suitable patients, whether the initial diagnosis is hysterical neurosis, character disorder of a high level, or established pathological mourning. The patient's conflicts are addressed by interpretations during the working through of the transference neurosis. The patient in established pathological mourning will at some point become aware of the reasons for unconsciously and symbolically defending against "killing" the one mourned. Different patients have different reasons for keeping the dead "alive." A patient may narcissistically need the deceased's representation in order to maintain the sense of self, or his need may be oedipal, the presence of the dead necessary for developmental advancement. These needs clash with derivatives of, for example, the wish to deny dependency or to gain oedipal triumph by "killing."

We should also consider the influence of infantile pathogenic fantasies still available in the complicated mourning process, especially when the dead person's representation is an external depository of a character dominant in the fantasies. For example, one young woman fell into established pathological mourning after the death of a boyfriend younger than she. Her analysis showed that some of her dominant behavior patterns were affected by a pathogenic infantile fantasy and by her defense against the wishes to which it gave expression. At two years of age the birth of a brother had been traumatic for her due to external attendant circumstances. She fantasized ridding herself of the baby (the cause of her unhappiness) by consuming him as she would ice cream. We reconstructed this fantasy in her analysis from her dreams, her transference constellations, and the reappearance of the fantasy in a current version: thoughts of cannibalism that had come when, during a train ride, she had been physically close to a mother and her crying baby.

Her analysis further revealed that the boyfriend she had lost represented her younger sibling; as long as she controlled their relationship and "adored" him she could defend against her murderous wishes. She was jolted by his death as the gratification of her aggressive drive and the loss of a character featured in her infantile pathogenic fantasy.

Although I suggest that it is not necessary in treatment of established pathological mourning to modify basic rules of psychoanalysis, two issues do need consideration:

The clinical picture of established pathological mourning may appear in persons of different personality makeup. A person with low-level character organization who presents characteristics of established pathological mourning is probably not a good candidate for re-grief therapy or for psychoanalysis proper. This sort of person may, however, benefit from long-term treatment with modified psychoanalytic techniques. I point out elsewhere (Volkan 1981) how the results of psychological testing may identify those for whom re-grief therapy is suitable; one may also consider them good candidates for psychoanalysis. The choice may depend on external factors such as the higher cost of the latter, but the evaluation of internal considerations is more important. Do the underlying pathologies need resolution *now*? Can the patient's ego adaptively contain the underlying pathologies once the complicated mourning is resolved? I have reported how some patients elect to undergo psychoanalysis after completing "re-griefing."

The presence of established pathological mourning, even in the patient suitable for psychoanalysis, interferes with effective resolution of the other psychopathologies, especially when linking objects are used secretly. A seeming paradox here needs attention: although preexistent psychopathologies such as dependence and aggression have caused the patient to react to loss in a pathological way, the complicated mourning must be ameliorated before the antecedent pathologies can be analyzed.

One young man I treated cherished as a linking object a gold chain with a St. Christopher medal he had, although not a Catholic, felt compelled to buy after the death of the "good father" figure who had met all his narcissistic needs and nourished his self-esteem. The patient's narcissistic personality organization stemmed from a traumatic early relationship with his mother. The meaning of the dead man's representation became clear once the patient was in analysis. It was something he continued to depend on to supply his narcissistic needs. He gradually became aware during analysis of his need to keep the older man "alive" and his dread of having to acknowledge his dependence. This was all reflected in the transference. There had been little change during the first two years of analysis in this patient's personality organization, but he then disclosed the secret of his golden linking object he always wore, even when making love or taking a shower. In previous sessions it had been concealed beneath his shirt, but once its part in the drama of his object relation was analyzed, he was able to "let go" and to disclose much anal matter connected with gold and secrecy and to work through in the transference neurosis reactivated early trauma.

Summary

This chapter is designed to acquaint the reader with what can be expected from a bereaved individual when the mourning process becomes complicated, either in initial reactions to the death or during the course of accomplishing the work of mourning. It is necessary to identify the nature of the complications and the course they are taking if one is to assess the degree of the disturbance and the patient's need for professional help.

REFERENCES

Abraham, K. (1911). Notes on the psycho-analytical investigation and treatment of manic-depressive insanity and allied conditions. In *Selected Papers*, ed. D. Bryan and A. Strachey, pp. 137–156. New York: Basic Books, 1960.

_____ (1916). The first pregenital stage of the libido. In *Selected Papers*, ed. D. Bryan and A. Strachey, pp. 248–279. New York: Basic Books, 1960.

_____ (1924). A short study of the development of the libido, viewed in the light of mental disorders. In *Selected Papers*, pp. 418–501. London: Hogarth Press, 1927.

Bibring, E. (1954). Psychoanalysis and the dynamic psychotherapies. *Journal of the American Psychoanalytic Association* 2:745–770.

Bowlby, J. (1961). Process of mourning. *International Journal of Psycho-Analysis* 42:317–340.

Bowlby, J., and Parkes, C. M. (1970). Separation and loss within the family. In *The Child in His Family*, vol. 1, ed. E. J. Anthony and C. Koupirnik, pp. 197–216. New York: Wiley Interscience.

Brown, F., and Epps, P. (1966). Childhood bereavement and subsequent crime. *British Journal of Psychiatry* 112:1043–1048.

Clayton, P., Desmarais, L., and Winokur, G. (1968). A study of normal bereavement. *American Journal of Psychiatry* 125:168–178.

Cobb, S., Bauer, W., and Whiting, I. (1939). Environmental factors in rheumatoid arthritis. *Journal of the American Medical Association* 113:668–670.

Crisp, A. H., and Priest, R. G. (1972). Psychoneurotic status during the year following bereavement. *Journal of Psychosomatic Research* 16:351–355.

Deutsch, H. (1937). Absence of grief. *Psychoanalytic Quarterly* 6:12–23.

Engel, G. L. (1961). Is grief a disease? A challenge for medical research. *Psychosomatic Medicine* 23:18–22.

———— (1962). *Psychological Development in Health and Disease*. Philadelphia: W. B. Saunders.

Evans, P., and Liggett, J. (1971). Loss and bereavement as factors in agoraphobia: implications for therapy. *British Journal of Medical Psychology* 44:149–154.

Fenichel, O. (1945). *The Psychoanalytic Theory of Neurosis*. New York: Norton.

Freud, A. (1960). Discussion of Dr. John Bowlby's paper. *The Psychoanalytic Study of the Child* 15:53–62, New York: International Universities Press.

Freud, S. (1917). Mourning and melancholia. *Standard Edition* 14:237–258. London: Hogarth Press, 1957.

Greene, W. A., and Miller, G. (1958). Psychological factors and reticuloendothelial disease. *Psychosomatic Medicine* 24:124–144.

Hamilton, J. W. (1969). Object loss, dreaming and creativity: the poetry of John Keats. *The Psychoanalytic Study of the Child* 24:488–531. New York: International Universities Press.

———— (1973). Jensen's *Gravida*: a further interpretation. *American Imago* 30:380–412.

———— (1975). The significance of depersonalization in the life and writings of Joseph Conrad. *Psychoanalytic Quarterly* 44:612–630.

———— (1979). Joseph Conrad: his development as an artist, 1889–1910. *The Psychoanalytic Study of Society* 8:277–329.

Hill, O. W. (1972). Child bereavement and adult psychiatric disturbance. *Journal of Psychosomatic Research* 16:357–360.

Klein, M. (1940). Mourning and its relation to manic-depressive states. *International Journal of Psycho-Analysis* 21:125–153.

Lehrman, S. R. (1956). Reactions to untimely death. *Psychiatric Quarterly* 30:565–579.

Lidz, I. (1949). Emotional factors in the etiology of hyperthyroidism. *Psychosomatic Medicine* 11:2–9.

Lindemann, E. (1944). Symptomatology and management of acute grief. *American Journal of Psychiatry* 101:141–148.

McDermott, N. T., and Cobb, S. (1939). A psychiatric survey of fifty cases of bronchial asthma. *Psychosomatic Medicine* 1:203–245.

Niederland, W. G. (1965). An analytic inquiry into the life and work of Heinrich Schliemann. In *Drives, Affects, Behaviour*, vol. II, ed. M. Schur, pp. 369–396. New York: International Universities Press.

Parkes, C. M. (1964a). The effects of bereavement on physical and mental health: a study of the case records of widows. *British Medical Journal* 2:274–279.

_____ (1964b). Recent bereavement as a cause of mental illness. *British Journal of Psychiatry* 110:198–204.

Parkes, C. M., and Brown, R. J. (1972). Health after bereavement, a controlled study of young Boston widows and widowers. *Psychosomatic Medicine* 34:449–461.

Peck, M. W. (1939). Notes on identification in a case of depressive reaction to the death of a love object. *Psychoanalytic Quarterly* 8:1–18.

Pollock, G. H. (1961). Mourning and adaptation. *International Journal of Psycho-Analysis* 42:341–361.

_____ (1975). On mourning, immortality and Utopia. *Journal of the American Psychoanalytic Association* 23:334–362.

Rado, S. (1956). Adaptational development of psychoanalytic therapy. In *Changing Concepts of Psychoanalytic Medicine*, ed. S. Rado & G. E. Daniels, pp. 89–100. New York: Grune & Stratton.

Schafer, R. (1968). *Aspects of Internationalization*. New York: International Universities Press.

Schmale, A. H. (1958). Relationship of separation and depression to disease. A report on a hospitalized medical population. *Psychosomatic Medicine* 20:259–277.

Socarides, C. W. (1954). On the usefulness of extremely brief psychoanalytic contact. *Psychoanalytic Review* 41:340–346.

Volkan, V. D. (1965). The observation of the "little man" phenomenon in a case of "anorexia nervosa." *British Journal of Medical Psychology* 38:299–311.

_____ (1970). Typical findings in pathological grief. *Psychiatric Quarterly* 44:231–250.

_____ (1971). A study of a patient's re-grief work through dreams, psychological tests, and psychoanalysis. *Psychiatric Quarterly* 45:255–273.

_____ (1972). The linking objects of pathological mourners. *Archives of General Psychiatry* 27:215–221.

_____ (1974). Death, divorce and the physician. In *Marital and Sexual Counseling in Medical Practice*, ed. D. W. Abse, L. M. Nash, and L. M. Louden, pp. 446–462. New York: Harper & Row.

_____ (1976). *Primitive Internalized Object Relations: A Clinical Study of Schizophrenic, Borderline, and Narcissistic Patients*. New York: International Universities Press.

_____ (1981). *Linking Objects and Linking Phenomena*. New York: International Universities Press.

Volkan, V. D., Cillufo, A. F., and Sarvay, T. L. (1975). Re-grief therapy and the function of the linking objects as a key to stimulate emotionality. In *Emotional Flooding*, ed. P. T. Olsen, pp. 179–224. New York: Human Sciences Press.

Volkan, V. D. and Itzkowitz, N. (1984). *Immortal Atatürk, a Psychobiography*. Chicago: University of Chicago Press.

Volkan, V. D., and Josephthal, D. (1979). The treatment of established pathological mourners. In *Specialized Techniques and Psychotherapy*, ed. T. B. Karasu & L. Bellak, pp. 118–142, New York: Jason Aronson.

Volkan, V. D., and Showalter, C. R. (1968). Known object loss, disturbance in reality testing, and "re-grief work" as a method of brief psychotherapy. *Psychiatric Quarterly* 42:358–374.

Wahl, C. W. (1970). The differential diagnosis of normal and neurotic grief following bereavement. *Psychosomatics* 11:104–106.

Winnicott, D. W. (1953). Transitional objects and transitional phenomena. *International Journal of Psycho-analysis* 34:89–97.

Wolfenstein, M. (1966). How is mourning possible? *The Psychoanalytic Study of the Child* 21:93–123. New York: International Universities Press.

CHAPTER SIXTEEN

Christmas "Neurosis" Reconsidered

L. Bryce Boyer, M.D.

In "Christmas 'Neurosis'," material from 17 patients who suffered from severe characterological, borderline, or schizophrenic disorders and from four neurotics who had been treated either by psychoanalytically oriented psychotherapy or psychoanalysis, revealed that all suffered from Yuletide depressions which stemmed from unresolved sibling rivalries (Boyer 1955). It was suggested tentatively that the birth of Christ, a fantasied rival against whom they were unable to compete, reawakened in them memories of earlier real or imagined failures to cope with siblings, thus causing the loss of self-esteem which regularly precedes depression (Abraham 1924, Fenichel 1945, Freud, 1917, Garma and Rascovsky 1948, Jacobson 1971, Lewin 1950). Oral conflicts were stimulated and repressed cravings and frustrations were rearoused. In their attempts to undo the resultant narcissistic loss and to recover from their depression, those patients sought to obtain phalluses with which they could woo their mothers in order to give them the love that they felt had been unequally showered on their siblings.

Jekels (1936) suggested that Christmas had been introduced as a holiday in a culturally supported effort to deny inequalities between the Father and the Son, that is, in oedipal terms. My female patients, like those of Eisenbud (1941), sought to obtain penises with which they could influence their parents, but especially their mothers, to give them the love they desired. The male patients tried to obtain bigger, more effective penises. Some men viewed their competition with their fathers in terms of a triadic relationship. However, others saw both brothers and fathers as siblings and imagined that owning a bigger and more potent phallus would enable them to sexually gratify their mothers who would, in turn, eschew all others and permit their male children to symbolically nurse forever. One man fantasized a "perfect circle" consisting of his sucking endlessly on his mother's breast as her vagina nursed on his phallus. These patients' solutions to the problem only appeared to be oedipal in nature. Others also sought to recover from their depressions through an identification with Christ, attempting thereby to deny their own relative inferiority and to obtain the limitless favoritism accorded to Him. The issue of father's favoritism toward siblings arose rarely and then only with little emotional investment.

In the 30 years which have intervened since the writing of "Christmas 'Neurosis'," my practice has continued to involve, for the most part, those patients who have suffered from disorders near the psychotic end of the continuum of psychopathological states (Boyer 1961, 1976, 1983, Boyer and Giovacchini 1980, Giovacchini and Boyer 1982). For this reconsideration of the themes of the original paper, material is used from 40 further seriously disturbed and 10 more neurotic patients who have been analyzed or are now in analysis. Each patient has regressed at various times during the holiday season. Their reactions were almost always initially depressive in nature, but in some cases, they deepened into blatant psychotic episodes which were confined almost totally to the consultation room. The Christmas"neuroses" of two patients began with hypomanic symptomatology. The great majority of the regressions were precipitated by reawakened, unresolved sibling rivalries. The means used by this series of patients in an attempt to recover were the same as those employed by the group 30 years earlier. Occasionally, depressive reactions were stimulated in other ways, for example, by monetary problems or the failure of a family reunion to establish harmony (E. Jones 1951). Two holiday regressions were anniversary reactions to early deaths of relatives (Hilgard 1953, 1969, Hilgard and Newman 1959).

Unexpectedly, those patients who focused on data pertaining to Christmas or Easter at other times of the year almost always did so while attempting to deal with unresolved sibling rivalry problems. In a similar fashion, their introduction of Christmas- or Easter-related material heralded such an attempt.

The clinical abstracts which follow show varieties of regression which were stimulated by unresolved sibling rivalry problems at Christmastime. Events in two of the case histories illustrate also that actions and thoughts pertaining to Christmas or Easter at other periods of the year often occur while the patient seeks to deal with such problems.

Clinical Material

Mrs. A.

Mrs. A. was a 35-year-old architect, the mother of two unwanted sons who had been conceived in an effort to cleave her husband to her. She competed with them for his maternal concern. [Mrs. A. resembled Mrs. W. (Boyer 1955, pp. 469–471] in every way. The case of Mrs. W. is not discussed in this chapter.) A lapsed Anglican, she had attended religious services from earliest childhood until she left home to attend college. Her wealthy, self-professed atheistic parents did not go to church or speak of religion; Mrs. A.'s church going resulted from her mother's concern about the neighbors' opinions. An only child, she was accompanied during girlhood by a nursemaid and later went alone. She always enjoyed the pomp and the opportunity to exhibit her immense wardrobe but never listened to Sunday School lessons or sermons. From early on, she "spaced out" when her asocial parents talked of anything but her and in church she spent her time daydreaming of others' admiration of her or fantasizing that she was a lost princess who would eventually be found by her true parents.

Tremendously vain, she suffered from a severe narcissistic personality disorder with "as-if" qualities (Kernberg 1975, Deutsch 1934, 1942). She was a dependent, orally aggressive, exhibitionistic woman who manifested various hysterical and psychosomatic complaints. During the course of her analysis (when she achieved a capacity for meaningful object relations), she developed transient conversion symptoms: globus hystericus, tunnel vision, and clitoral anesthesia. In her preschool years she came to believe that her parents had previously lost a son and that she was supposed to replace him. She raised pigeons and rabbits and was intensely interested in their anatomy and sexual activities and the birth process. She dreamed then, and again during her analysis, that baby birds and rabbits turned into phalluses which she acquired by eating them; in other dreams, as she stood erect, she became a huge rigid phallus. Always believing herself to be unwanted except as a showpiece for her parents, she had ascribed her undesirability to being female. Physically beautiful and highly intelligent, she first became a professional model, unconsciously believing in the body-phallus equation (Lewin 1933), and later studied subjects usually especially interesting to men, believing that the acquisition of such knowledge would magically change her clitoris into a penis.

During the first two years of her analysis, her capacity for true object relations remained most tenuous. She was quite unable to believe that she was not the center of her parents', husband's and analyst's thoughts, and she could not empathize with the needs of others. She did not manifest affectual reactions to the holidays although her dreams included Christmas trees and ornaments in their manifest contents and she associated phalluses to them. In the third year, she reacted to my Thanksgiving weekend absence with transient depression and a fear that I had been killed while enjoying the company of one of my sons. Following a dream of the "dream screen" variety (Boyer 1960, Lewin 1946, 1948, 1950, Rycroft 1951), she became depressed to a degree previously unexperienced. Her appetite flagged, she was insomniac, her movements were slowed, she could not concentrate, and her capacity to perceive brightness of colors diminished. A fortnight before Christmas she talked for the first time of her unhappiness during childhood Yuletides and remembered that she had always felt she had lost something which would be restored to her at Christmas. It became clear that she had wanted Santa Clause to bring her the missing penis. If I would somehow give her a penis, either by having intercourse with her or permitting fellatio, or by giving her a piece of jewelry in the shape of a Christmas tree which she could then wear on the front of a sporran, she would deserve to be my only child. For the first time in her memory, she became preoccupied with religious thoughts, thinking that if she turned to religion and believed in the reality of God, He would give her a penis or He would restore her to her fantasied royal parents as their only child, a prince (Deutsch 1930, Ferreira 1963, Jacobson 1965, Kris 1956, Lehrman 1927). She said that if one couldn't *be* a Christchild, worshipped "by all mankind," one could "make it into a religion." She remembered that childhood family Christmases had seemed to her to be celebrations for her father. Just after Christmas, she dreamed that I brought her a magnificently wrapped package in which was a beautiful baby boy. She then was able for the first time to enjoy her sons' pleasure in using their Christmas toys and her anxious depression lifted.

Subsequent Yuletides stimulated depressions, each with the revival of unresolved rivalry with a baby boy who had died, as she believed, before her birth. The depressive episodes she experienced during the fourth and fifth Christmas seasons of her analysis were severe and lifted after she once again came to believe she was valuable to me both in my role of mother surrogate and as an actual love object (Loewald 1960). The sixth and last Yuletide depression was brief and mild. By then, dyadic relationship and pregenital aspects of her problems had been largely resolved, and her analysis had progressed to involving predominantly triadic relationship, oedipal material.

Mrs. A. was one of approximately a dozen patients who spoke of Christmas or Easter while dealing with sibling rivalry problems at other times of the year. One day about six weeks following Easter in the third year of her analysis, she began talking first of disappointing early Christmas experiences and then for the first time spoke of Easter and her confusion in childhood about its historical events and their meanings. She became depressed until she remembered that as a young girl she had come to believe that the alleged brother who had died before her birth had either been born, or died — perhaps both — on the May date when she had begun to think again of Christmas.

Mr. B.

Mr. B. was a childless junior business executive in his middle thirties, religiously inactive, although his childhood had been steeped in fundamentalist Protestantism (see also Boyer 1955, pp. 475–477). He suffered from a borderline disorder characterized by impulsivity, antisocial, obsessional and paranoid traits, and psychosomatic problems. Initially, he projected idealized internalized good objects indiscriminately onto caretakers whom he then provoked to disappoint him and projected "unqualifiedly bad" parts of himself equally indiscriminately onto authority figures whom he induced to persecute him. During the first year of his analysis, he quickly came to view me uncritically as an idealized father figure whose traits, however, were predominantly nurturing (Shapiro 1978, Volkan 1976). As he did so, his initial severe free-floating anxiety, migraine, peptic ulcer symptoms and intractable constipation were alleviated. He began to trust women enough to allow himself to have tenuous, fearful social relationships with them for the first time since his wife had left him three years previously. In order to maintain such an idyllic picture of me, he simultaneously pictured his business superior as totally hostile and persecutory and lived in constant fear that his veiled hatred of his superior (whom he had previously seen as totally benevolent) would lead to his termination. (See Boyer 1971 for a description of my earlier technical maneuver applied to a similar case.) During the period when these split transference relationships were unquestionably maintained by the patient, his initial troublesome symptomatology remained in abeyance.

His mother had wanted a girl to replace a sister she had lost in early childhood (Volkan 1982). From a reconstruction derived from data provided by Mr. B., she had held herself responsible for her sister's death and wanted to rid herself of guilt by being totally giving to a child of her own. She dressed Mr. B. as a girl and kept his hair in long curls until he was 6 years old. Then his mother was required to dress him as a boy for his admission to grammar school. His mother rewarded him for "cute" or passively obedient behavior by cuddling and cooing which often occurred when she took him to bed with her while his salesman father was "on the road" or carousing. She did not object to his enuresis while he slept in her arms. He especially enjoyed being held close to her as they knelt by the bedside during her impassioned nightly prayers in which she pled with God to punish her husband for his lewd, thieving, lying behavior and to keep Mr. B. "saintly." He was ridiculed by his father throughout his childhood and when, in his latency years, he sought to be included on his father's fishing and hunting trips, he was rejected scornfully.

A sister was born when Mr. B. was 7. Thereafter, he was ignored or abused by his mother who now lavished her full loving attention on her daughter. An orphaned boy of 5, a relative of the mother's, was adopted when Mr. B. was 8 or 9. He was treated like a little prince by both of Mr. B.'s parents. His aggressive boyishness was overtly encouraged and his sexual curiosity was treated with laughing approval. Previously, Mr. B. had been ashamed to have a penis and now he felt inferior because he compared his penis unfavorably to that of his foster brother. He no longer felt rivalry toward his sister but found competition with his foster brother in masculine ways to be most frustrating. He later turned to various parental surrogates whom he sought, with transient success, to please through overt homosexual and criminal behavior.

During the first Christmas season of his analysis, while he still viewed me as totally benevolent, he hired a prostitute and entered a blissful trance-like state while they engaged in simultaneous fellatio and cunnilingus; he repressed the fantasies which accompanied the activity. He then dreamed that he was a baby in a crèche. He remained happy throughout the Yuletide.

During the ensuing years, inroads were made on his split transference and he sometimes viewed me as a hostile persecutor. While I had been the all-good father–mother, his recountings of sibling rivalry failures were recited with scant affect. As my transference aspects changed, his similar recollections included increasing anger and, at times, fury. Early in December, his initial symptomatology returned: anxiety, headaches, indigestion, and constipation. He quickly became depressed and the sibling rivalry data were accompanied by insomnia, anorexia, weight loss, and suicidal thoughts.

A week before the third Christmas he dreamed that as he slept, his flaccid penis grew into a magnificent, tall, decorated Christmas tree, its top surrounded by light. Although I conjecture that he had in very early childhood observed his father's erection and added to his observation a halo, no such memory was recovered during his analysis (Boyer 1971, Greenacre 1947). Many beautifully wrapped presents lay around its base, all for him. In the corner of the room appeared a crèche; the Christ child had Mr. B.'s early boyhood face. He now related for the first time having suffered Christmas depressions from childhood, dating their onset to his sister's birth. Following the addition of his foster brother to the family, Mr. B. always felt the gifts and attention he received to be inferior to those accorded the new rival; he always wanted "something else." On that third Christmas Eve he suckled at his girlfriend's breasts and ejaculated without erection. In the interview following Christmas he recalled his childhood nocturnal wetting of his mother, but it was not until a year later that he came to understand that the action was his enactment of a fantasy that he could replace his father as his mother's sexual satisfier, with her vagina nursing on his penis as he suckled at her breast. Previously, he had imagined that his girlfriend was attracted to him solely because of his swashbuckling facade and sexual athletics. Now he found her to be pleased by his dependency and tenderness. On Christmas Day, she told him she no longer wanted to see other men; his depression lifted almost immediately.

During each of the following two Yuletide periods, he reexperienced depression with diminished intensity; the content of his memories, dreams, and fantasies varied little. Some years after his analysis was successfully completed, he sent me a totem pole which looked very much like an erection saying he "owed it" to me. In the accompanying letter, he wrote he'd learned that I was interested in religious aspects of anthropology, that he'd been reading about phallic worship cults, that his new marriage was successful, and that he had a "fine, boyish son."

Mrs. C.

Mrs. C. was one of two manic patients who have been treated psychoanalytically by me. There was no record of mental disorder in her parental families nor any record of cyclic or other psychotic disorder in her extended family. A 45-year-old Jewish woman, she was the mother of several children, all of whom had done well. Before the sudden death 13 years previously of her husband, a hyperactive, outgoing, somewhat paranoid and immensely successful dealer in antiques, she had been a retiring, bookish woman, happily devoted to being a good wife and mother and to keeping a kosher household. She had studied the humanities in college and become knowledgeable in art history and art appreciation. When her husband died, she grieved for some weeks while simultaneously taking over his business, discovering previously unknown commercial capabilities. She gradually replaced the antiques with paintings and sculptures and within a year or so was almost as successful as her husband had been. Her identification with him was even more profound. She soon became aggressive, hyperactive, and suspicious. After a couple of years, she began to suffer from overt manic episodes which led to her brief hospitalization at least 10 times during the ensuing years. She became very curious about the origins and mechanisms of her disorder and read much psychiatric and psychoanalytic literature. When she read *Mourning and Melancholia* (Freud 1917), she believed she understood the dynamics of her personality change and was surprised that her intellectual understanding did not cure her. Her various psychiatrists tried unsuccessfully to keep her on a maintenance dose of lithium carbonate. She believed she should receive psychoanalytic treatment but it was refused to her several times before analysis was begun with me on an experimental basis (Boyer 1961).

Her analysis began when she was emerging from an episode which had required hospitalization. She claimed she was taking a recommended dosage of lithium carbonate and agreed to continue to consult with her hospitalizing psychiatrist about her medication.

Mrs. C. was the second youngest of many children of deeply religious Sephardim, her birth followed by that of a brother when she was 3 years old. Her immigrant parents settled in a ghetto in a large Eastern city when she was 5. She spoke no English until she was 6 and began attendance at a public school where the majority of her classmates were black or of Italian descent. After school, she attended classes with her brothers so that she could learn Hebrew to prepare for her bas mitzvah.

Unexpectedly, her analysis proceeded smoothly. Immediately upon its inception, her hypomanic tendencies diminished drastically. Although she spoke rapidly and denied connections between successive thoughts and was at all times hostilely vigilant, she, nevertheless, made every effort to be a "good patient." During the first seven months, she occasionally mentioned in passing that she had felt that her parents preferred their sons to their daughters. She said she had always been surprised that she had reacted blandly to the accidental death of her younger brother when she was 17, inasmuch as she had loved him very much and spent much time looking after him. During those months of treatment, the dominant theme was her handling of intense oral-sadistic hatred of her mother through denial and projection onto her mother and various maternal surrogates. Periodically, it was superposed by her tearful grieving for her beloved, all-good "nana" whom she had lost at 7 and her idealized father who died when she was 10. She had read all of my writings, knew of my interest in anthropology, and viewed me as a totally benevolent omnipotent and omniscient shaman.

Channukah preceded Christmas by about two weeks during the first year of her analysis. As had been the custom of her husband's family and then of her family with him, its celebration was both deeply religious and joyous. Every child received lavish gifts each night. At its end, she suddenly became hyperactive and intensely paranoid and, for the first time, became critical of and directly hostile toward me. Previously comfortable on the couch, she now paced the room, shouted, and threatened to kill me by smashing my head with heavy books. Typical manic speech prevailed and its contents symbolized, among other things, her wish to destroy my brain and eat it. For her, brain power was equated with phallic power; my intelligence-masculinity made it possible for me to have become a shaman-rabbi. With infinite hatred she revealed her conviction that I was anti-Semitic and enamored of and favored by male patients, particularly admiring their intellectual capacities.

I finally learned that she had stopped taking lithium immediately after beginning her treatment with me despite her statements to the contrary. Following a tirade, she became expectantly silent and could listen to my interpretation that her regression was in the service of defending herself against anxiety engendered by cannibalistic fantasies. I also told her that she was not treating me as she had earlier stated that she wished to treat her mother and was ascribing to me qualities she had stated previously belonged to her mother. Then she returned to the hospitalizing psychiatrist and resumed lithium treatment. Her gross hypomanic symptomatology disappeared within hours of her ingesting her first dose of lithium carbonate, long before its chemical effect would have been expected to cause such an amelioration.

The following day she brought me as a Christmas present a painting of an Easter egg. Although it is my policy to refuse gifts from patients, I chose to accept this one, believing that to refuse it would hurt her unnecessarily. She did not mention the gift subsequently nor did I press for an understanding either of her giving it or my accepting it.

Immediately following her improvement, she revealed that just prior to her regression she had found herself to be very angry with one of her sons because he enjoyed his Channukah presents. She was envious of his capacity to enjoy receiving. She unwittingly called him by the name of her dead younger brother. The night before, she dreamed that one twin crocodile fetus had eaten its sib while they were inside the egg. The dream had been succeeded by a transient flood of heavily cathected memories of her having been glad her younger brother had died and her guilty conviction that she had induced him to have taken the risk which had resulted in his having been killed. Those recollections had been concurrent with others pertaining to her childhood reactions to Jewish and Christian holidays.

For the first time, she revealed that her parents, especially her father, wanted their sons to become rabbis and, as she felt, belittled the intellectual capacities of women whose role it was to efface themselves, unstintingly support their husbands and children, and focus all of their activities and interests in the home. Now she said that the Jewish holidays were celebrated with great solemnity and comparative frugality by her childhood family. During the Feast of Lights, the children received Channukah gelt but once and then only a small coin. In Iberia, she believed such an observance to be universal among Jews, and knew nothing of Christians except that there were colorful public performances during the holiday season. When she attended grammar school in this country, she was very envious of her classmates' reception of gifts at Christmastime, of their stated belief in Santa Claus, and of their having Christmas trees. Like Mrs. Y. (Boyer 1955, pp. 474–475), she became interested in Christ and His teachings and composed prizewinning essays about the Yuletide and Easter in school competitions. Those writings and her envy of her classmates' Christmas experiences had been concealed from her family.

For some weeks, she continued to deal with the vicissitudes of her unresolved rivalry with her younger brother. Periodically she returned to her wish that her family had celebrated Christmas and that she could have had a Christmas tree. It was clear that on one level she equated the tree with a penis and hoped that if she could magically obtain a penis, she would finally feel complete and be happy. Her envy of her son's pleasure at receiving a present resulted from her dissatisfaction with what she got at Channukah. However, the reasons for the crocodile egg dream and the Easter egg Christmas present selection remained unexplained.

As Easter approached, she underwent another milder hypomanic episode. Once again, its onset was precipitous. Its content mirrored that of the regression which preceded Christmastime and my similar statements were followed by her prompt improvement, this time without resumption of the lithium therapy which had once again been abandoned secretly some weeks after her recovery from the pre-Christmas regression. Soon she talked of Easter and its symbolic meanings to her. Christ's death was an altruistic act aimed at making happy the lives of little children. He allowed His crucifixion to absolve Him of guilt from two sources. He was tormented because He lusted after his virgin mother who had been deprived by God and Joseph of sexual pleasures and He had oral sadistic wishes toward boys who were His peers because he envied the freedom of action that was forbidden to Him. Using the body-phallus equation, she viewed His crucifixion as both castration and execution. She thought of the cave within which He was interred as His mother's womb. The two women who awaited Him outside the cave, the virgin Mary and the reformed prostitute Magdalene, represented two aspects of one mother. Had He chosen to do so, He could have gratified Magdalene sexually for the privilege of having permanent infantile access to Mary. However, since, while in the cave, His good part had overcome His bad part, He was all good after His rebirth and could thereafter be with, care for, and be cared for by both Mary and Magdalene in a loving, guilt-free relationship.

Having spun this story, Mrs. C. laughed, saying she had identified herself with Christ and ended up in a permanent fantasied relationship with two representatives of a totally good mother, a relationship exclusive of any male figure at all, whether father- or brother-surrogate. Then she recalled the dream in which the crocodile fetus had devoured its twin, now saying it later emerged as its mother's only child. Finally she talked of her thoughts about the Easter egg Christmas present she had made to me some years before. She said at the time she had actually believed herself to have been inside the egg and to have thought that she might emerge as the infant Christ.

A few patients who suffered from Christmas regressions had consciously or unconsciously identified themselves with Jesus earlier in their lives.

Mr. D.

Mr. D., an unmarried man, held a professional position which enabled him to take care of young children. He perceived Christ to have been castrated and "feminine-masochistic." Like Lubin's (1959) patient, he preferred homosexual to heterosexual physical gratifications and, like Van Gogh, who also identified himself with Christ (Lubin 1961), ambivalently enjoyed self-mutilation, partly in the service of revenge against his mother and as a bid for her exclusive love.

Mr. D.'s family called him "Jesus Baby" because of his religious preoccupation, his depicting himself as Christ in his drawings, and because, when he played "dress-up," he costumed himself alternately in Christ's or his mother's clothes. During much of his latency period, he chose to play in and around cemetery vaults, imagining that the corpses were alive and trapped in confining coffins as probable punishment for their murderous wishes toward their siblings. They could only be released after God or their parents had forgiven them. He simultaneously suffered intensely from nightmares in which he was similarly confined forever in a tight coffin, and could only be solaced, when he awoke screaming, by his mother's leaving "father's bed" to come to his.

Greatly interested from early childhood in esthetic phenomena and pageantry, Mr. D. insisted on attending Catholic religious services although his parents, atheists who had been reared as Protestants, ridiculed him for that activity. He was preoccupied with Christ allowing His symbolic castration which Mr. D. believed was done to succeed in having His mother all to himself. From early boyhood, Mr. D. collected exotic Easter eggs and from the age of 6 or 7, he constructed beautiful ones to give at Eastertime to almost everyone whose love he sought. They eventually evolved into artistic objects which could be opened and emptied like Fabergé's Easter eggs and then closed again, beautiful and undamaged. However, his Easter eggs were not filled with jewels or other valuables as additional gifts but with candy, which he identified as parts of himself or parts of Christ to be eaten in a kind of sacramental service.

During his analysis, his Christmas depressions were twice terminated when he dreamed that the confining coffin of his childhood nightmare turned into an Easter egg which was opened for him by a doting mother; he emerged as Christ whose "wounds-symbolic castrations" were healed and was thenceforth her exclusive favorite. They would have a "pure" relationship in which each would take care of the other and he, as Christ, would atone for childhood murderous wishes toward his siblings by devoting his life to the care of children. At other times his regressions would be lifted when he had fantasies in which I had eaten him and he had become an intrinsic part of my body so that we would live indistinguishably united forever.

In February of one year, Mr. D. became preoccupied with Easter themes; this was followed by depression and a return to the theme of his unsuccessful competition with his siblings. He awoke one night from a forgotten dream and found himself compelled to make Easter eggs although that holiday was two months away. He brought one to me the next morning, laughed, said he must be seeking to get inside me once again. Then, for the first time, he recalled his rage at the age of 4 when mother came home from the hospital with a new baby.

Discussion

The holiday reactions of the current group of patients differed from those of the former group only because some of the regressions which occurred in the second sample progressed to deeper levels and then became transiently schizoaffective in nature. In two cases, the holiday reaction began with hypomanic symptomatology. However, the major stimulus which precipitated the regressions, regardless of their nature, remained the same: reawakened conflicts related to unresolved sibling rivalries. In the earlier paper it was suggested tentatively that "partly because the holiday celebrates the birth of a Child so favored that competition with Him is futile, earlier memories, especially of oral frustration, are rekindled" (Boyer 1955, p. 467). The present data strongly support that suggestion.

The means employed by both groups of my patients to undo the loss of self-esteem which set off their regressions were the same: either they sought to acquire penises with which they could court their mothers and give them permanent, exclusive union or they sought to identify with Christ, becoming the favorite child of all mankind, a maternal surrogate.

Eisenbud (1941) wrote of the regressive reactions of two women during their analyses. Each suffered from intense penis envy and a belief that she could not compete successfully with a brother for her mother's love. They were depressed at Christmastime because their renewed childhood hope that Santa Claus would bring them phalluses was once again dashed. All of my female patients who underwent Yuletide regressions also sought to obtain phalluses. While most similarly hoped to receive a penis as a gift, almost every woman also imagined obtaining it through aggressive, oral means, either through eating a man's penis with vaginal teeth or while performing fellatio. Others, as in the cases of Mrs. A. and Mrs. C., imagined getting or becoming a phallus through ingesting symbolic sibling surrogates in the form of little animals or birds. The intensity of the hypomanic woman's oral aggression was represented by her choice of crocodiles as symbolic siblings.

Eisenbud did not spell out how his patients imagined they would use their newly acquired or reacquired penises. My female patients fantasized two means of becoming mother's favorite. When they imagined phalluses to have replaced their clitorides, they fantasized that they could satisfy their mothers sexually and make any male rival unnecessary to them. When they used the body-phallus equation, they had the same fantasy or imagined that they could get into their mothers' wombs and live in an idyllic, pre-birth, symbiotic relationship. A very few alternately used the phallus-breast equation and thought of establishing a symbiotic union through imagining their mothers performing fellatio on them while they either did cunnilingus or suckled at their mothers' breasts. My male patients regularly sought to obtain bigger and better penises to be used in similar manners and to achieve similar ends. Their displacement of fathers and siblings for their mothers' favoritism was in the service of dyadic, not triadic, relations.

Of the patients who supplied the data for the earlier paper, only three fantasized themselves to be in direct competition with Christ for maternal favoritism at Christmastime and no one had identified himself or herself with Jesus in childhood although some briefly imagined they were Christ at the Yuletide. Several patients in the latter series had believed with delusional intensity at different periods of time during their lives that they were Christ or could become Him. All of these patients included Easter in their Christmas fantasies or were preoccupied with Easter and Christ's rebirth at other times of the year.

However, we cannot assume that there is a high correlation between identification with Christ and Christmas "neurosis." The clinical experience of everyone who works with psychotics reveals that many psychotics delusionally identify themselves with Jesus, but the literature does not speak of their also undergoing Christmas "neurosis" (Lubin 1959). My informal suvery of 35 psychiatrists and psychoanalysts who are aware of the "neurosis" as a clinical phenomenon indicates no significant statistical correlation.

Discussants of the first paper were surprised that Jewish as well as Christian patients suffered from Christmas "neurosis." My practice has involved more Jewish than Christian patients and all of the approximately 50 analysands who are being discussed here underwent holiday regressions. However, all of the Jews were reared largely in areas in which Christianity was the dominant religion and Christians constituted a majority. We know from analyses of the cargo cults (LaBarre 1970) and the diffusion of folklore data (Boyer 1979) that members of the subordinate social groups tend to incorporate and use the religion and other expressive cultural elements of the dominant group in the service of the minority group and its individuals.

Various analysts who have practiced abroad present contradictory data regarding the incidence of Christmas "neurosis" in Europe. Siegfried Bernfeld (1953) found that his patients in Austria suffered less depression at the Yuletide than patients in America. Bernhard Berliner (1954), on the other hand, emphasized a sharp rise in the incidence of suicide in Germany on

Christmas Eve. In Europe, religious aspects of Christmas are generally more important than in the United States. Thus, one would think that since Christ's birth is an important stimulus for the revival of sibling rivalries, regressions would be observed more prominently in Europe. However, in the United States, Christmas has become associated more with gift-giving in a family setting, and this probably leads to a focalizing of oral conflicts. The elements of favoritism probably become more important. Also, for many patients Santa Claus is a symbol for parents, and frustration resulting from his apportionment of presents plays an important role in the precipitation of regressive responses. We may remember at this point that Santa Claus is depicted as a woman in Italy despite his historical representation elsewhere as a man (C. Jones 1954, 1978, pp. 324–370, Lalanne 1847).

Clearly, Christmas "neurosis" is not a clinical entity. The regressive reactions that occur at this time of the year are phenomenologically and dynamically the same as those observed at other times. The cultural and emotional constellation surrounding Christmas makes it a more important holiday and a more powerful trigger for reactions in the predisposed. It is interesting to consider, nevertheless, the problem of whether there may be a phylogenetical vulnerability to regressive reactions at the period of the year when darkness predominates, as has been suggested to me by some Scandinavians. The celebrations and folklore of Western and Near Eastern worlds are replete with evidences of uneasy, manicoid reactions to the yearly threatened disappearance of the sun. Notwithstanding our psychologically deduced knowledge that darkness symbolizes separation from the mother and death, we know that darkness and cold produce physiological changes in animals and men (Berliner 1914).

Twenty years ago, a research group comprised of Drs. Philip Evans, Felix H. Ocko, Earl J. Simburg and I sought to determine the worldwide incidence and dynamics of Christmas regressions among psychoanalysands. Too few analysts answered our questionnaire to permit statistical confidence. However, we found a tendency toward a higher incidence of such regressions in countries in which Christianity predominated, regardless of climate. We also found that reawakened sibling rivalry problems were mentioned fairly regularly by those clinicians who had observed and analyzed holiday regressions. The northern Europeans who responded were more impressed with climatic causes of winter depressions and had not noticed regressive reactions to Christmas *per se*.

Jekels (1936) surmised that the introduction of the festival of Christ's nativity indicated a growing tendency to regard the Son as coequal with the Father. He could see a wish, born of a "grandiose identification" with Jesus, that if the Son be the equal of the Father, there would be neither supremacy nor subordination and, therefore, because all was unity, equality and harmony, guilt would cease to exist. He wondered whether this sort of psychological usefulness of Christmas partly led to its adoption as a major holiday.

Winter solstice celebrations have existed throughout recorded history. Men have always attributed the success of their crops to the existence of the sun. In widespread areas of the world, they have feared that because of their misdeeds, the sun would not reappear. Hence, their crops would fail to grow again and they would starve. To assure themselves of a returning sun and a replenishment of food supplies, they have felt the necessity of atoning for their sins and pleading for divine forgiveness.

According to official Christian doctrine, Jesus had no earthly father and no siblings. Wherever Christianity has come to be accepted, and recent trends indicate it has begun to make significantly more inroads even in the Orient since World War II, the masses have chosen to believe that there must have been a son so fortunate as to have been the permanently primary object of his asexual mother's love. If we turn our attention briefly to artistic productions, we find that before the birth of Christ, the mother-child theme was very rarely portrayed in Western art (Bodkin 1949). Subsequently, however, that symbol of unity is a frequent theme in religious art (Belvianes 1951). The popularity of the Madonna paintings which very rarely include any suggestion of father or sibling, illustrates man's preoccupations with that dynamic idea.

The philosophical tenets of Mithraism and Christianity contain wide areas of agreement (Leach and Fried 1950, Reinach 1930, Taraporewala 1928, 1945). Although the development of the Christian religion out of Judaism has been traced from many standpoints (Ferm 1951), one must wonder whether Christianity has succeeded in becoming the popular religion of at least the Western world partly because of the unconscious dream in all of us to retain the early belief in the unity of mother and child. This would supplement but not contradict Jekel's (1936) idea.

Christmas stemmed originally from festivals such as the Saturnalia (Goethe 1789) onto which Christian coloring was superposed. In recent centuries, man has mastered the preservation of his crops and learned enough about the movements of celestial bodies that worries concerning the reappearance of the sun have been determined to be unrealistic. Nevertheless, his infantile anxieties about emotional and physical starvation persist. It would seem that the celebration of Christmas as a children's holiday is still an acceptable medium through which man can express those fears and seek to deny their existence. He is able to give his children food (gifts), and through his identification with them, feel that he himself is fed by a beneficent mother. Perhaps this explains to some extent why it has been possible for Santa Claus to displace God temporarily as the figure to be worshipped.

Yet Christmas anxieties continue. In America, physicians in all specialties note a significant increase of all symptomatologies during the holiday season. Popular literature depicts the hostilities which appear at that season (Christie 1952). Families convene with the hope that old conflicts of various natures can be resolved (E. Jones 1951). The angers usually revolve around the theme of who will get the most and whether monetary sacrifices can be tolerated without harm to the givers. "It is more blessed to give than to receive" is an admonition which is necessary only because the wish to receive predominates over the wish to give.

The Use of Christmas "Regressions" in Treatment

When I observed in the late 1940s and early 1950s that many of my patients underwent Christmas regressions and that the analyses of those reactions provided useful insights, it occurred to me that other patients might not experience similar regressions because the latter group were able to successfully use denial or isolation as a defense against dealing with material related to possible conflicts pertaining to the holiday season. Thus, I began to put up simple Christmas decorations early in December: a holly wreath on the door to my consultation room, a lighted candle on a shelf in the room, perhaps a colorful Christmas tree ball hanging from a limb of one of the bonsai trees which I customarily use for greenery. When patients ignored the decorations, I confronted them. At times, the decorations have been more elaborate, but I have noted that the degree of complexity or specificity is unimportant.

I customarily use a technical device which helps patients to get in contact more rapidly with repressed material. Thinking about that which has been repressed follows regressed patterns; preverbal thinking employs visual images (Freud 1900). When patients make equivocal or otherwise indefinite statements, I sometimes ask them whether they have a mental picture which would illustrate what they mean. Frequently, when the patient remembers such a picture or conjures it, the imagery leads to either a clearer exposition of a conflict, a significant memory, or both. Occasionally, the device has helped patients recover conflicts and memories pertaining to Christmas.

Mrs. E. is a case in point. Although a lighted candle and Christmas ball had been displayed for three weeks, she neither mentioned them or anything pertaining to the holidays. Finally, I commented that she had not spoken of Christmas and I wondered why. She could then tell me that she was very angry that I had so imposed my personal life on her, reminding her through the decorations that I was a patriarch who reveled in my grandchildren's adoration at Christmastime while I consigned the women in my "tribe" to "inferior, scutwork roles." She could not elaborate until I inquired whether she had seen a mental picture. She was surprised to become aware that she saw me in Biblical garb, on a throne, with a chained woman washing my feet. This led to memories of how her mother complained on holidays that she got no help and had to do all the "scutwork." For the first time, Mrs. E. remembered that her mother had been incapable of permitting anyone to be happy on any holiday and always complained about the debased role of women. Eventually, she recalled her childhood belief, long since proved erroneous, that a brother whom she believed to have been favored had stolen from her a prized Christmas present, a "magical" pen which could be used to write in three different colors, one of which matched the hue of my Christmas candle. The magical, beautiful candle and pen were both viewed as erect in her mind and led in another way (Arieti 1948, Von Domarus 1925) to fantasies within the framework of sibling rivalry that she had been born with a penis which had been stolen from her subsequently.

Much has been written about the necessary and beneficial role of periods of regression in normal processes of maturation and in psychoanalysis (Boyer 1983, Loewald 1960, 1982). Nevertheless, the majority of therapists who treat patients suffering from severe personality disorders and psychoses are reluctant to permit patients to experience transient psychotic episodes during treatment, even though such episodes may be limited to the consultation room. Along with Giovacchini (1979), Volkan (1976), Winnicott (1971) and a growing number of others, it is my conviction that such regressions facilitate beneficial structural change. The surprisingly primary process dominated associations that have been included here often occurred during periods of regression that I believe to have been deeper than most of my colleagues would have permitted. Thus, while they would have become aware of the depth of the patients' motivation by dyadic, not triadic, conflicts, they might not have permitted the emergence of fantasies and memories of fantasies involving such predicate-dominated logic. The fantasies that led to my patients' previously unconscious desires for "perfect circle" relationships led subsequently to Hermann's (1936) "dual-union" concept that has now become popularized as Mahler's (1968) "symbiosis."

Summary

In "Christmas 'Neurosis'" (Boyer 1955), clinical data revealed that Yuletide depressions usually stem from unresolved sibling rivalries. It was tentatively suggested that the birth of Christ, a fantasized rival against whom patients were unable to compete, reawakened in them memories of earlier failures, real or imagined, to cope with siblings, and that oral conflicts were stimulated and repressed cravings and frustrations were rearoused. The depressions were alleviated when the patients imagined that they had found means of achieving their mother's unqualified favoritism, or the favoritism of their analyst as the mother-surrogate; their fantasies often involved the establishing of a variant of a symbiotic union with their mothers.

Review of case material obtained from 50 patients who have been analyzed during the intervening 30 years affirms the observations and conclusions of the prior publication. Additionally it was learned that when patients become preoccupied with Christmas or Easter at times of the year other than the Yuletide or the Paschal seasons, they do so while attempting to deal with unresolved sibling rivalry problems.

REFERENCES

Abraham, K. (1924). A short study of the development of the libido, viewed in the light of mental disorders. *Selected Papers*, pp. 418–501. London: Hogarth Press.

Arieti, S. (1948). Special logic of schizophrenia and other types of autistic thought. *Psychiatry* 11:325–338.

Belvianes, M. (1951). *La Vierge par les Peintres*. Paris: Editions de Varenne.

Berliner, B. (1914). Der einfluss von klima, wetter and jahrzeit auf das nerven- und seelenleben auf physiologischer grundlage dargestellt. In *Grenzfragen des Nerven- und Seelenlebens*. Vol. 99. Wiesbaden: J. F. Bergman.

_____ (1954). Discussion of "Christmas "Neurosis" by L. Bryce Boyer at the (Biannual) Meeting of the West Coast Psychoanalytic Societies, Coronado, California, October.

Bernfeld, S. (1953). Personal communication.

Bodkin, T. (1949). *The Virgin and Child*. New York: Pitman.

Boyer, L. B. (1955). Christmas "neurosis." *Journal of the American Psychoanalytic Association* 3:467–488.

_____ (1960). A hypothesis concerning the time of appearance of the dream screen. *International Journal of Psycho-Analysis* 41:114–122.

_____ (1961). Provisional evaluation of psycho-analysis with few parameters employed in the treatment of schizophrenia. *International Journal of Psycho-Analysis* 42:389–403.

_____ (1971). Psychoanalytic technique in the treatment of certain characterological and schizophrenic disorders. *International Journal of Psycho-Analysis* 52:67–86.

_____ (1976). *Die Psychoanalytische Behandlung Schizophrener*. Munich: Kindler Verlag.

_____ (1979). *Childhood and Folklore. A Psychoanalytic Study of Apache Personality*. New York: Library of Psychological Anthropology.

_____ (1983). *The Regressed Patient*. New York: Jason Aronson.

Boyer, L. B., and Giovacchini, P. L. (1980). *Psychoanalytic Treatment of Schizo-*

phrenic, Borderline and Characterological Disorders. 2nd rev. ed. New York: Jason Aronson.

Christie, A. (1952). A Holiday for Murder. New York: Avon.

Deutsch, H. (1930). Zur genese des familienromans. Internationale Zeitschrift für ärtzliche Psychoanalyse 16:249–253.

———— (1934). Über einen typus des pseudoaffectivität ("als ob"). International Zeitschrift für Psychoanalyse 20:323–335.

———— (1942). Some forms of emotional disturbance and their relationship to schizophrenia. Psychoanalytic Quarterly 11:301–321.

Eisenbud, J. (1941). Negative reactions to christmas. Psychoanalytic Quarterly 10:939–945.

Fenichel, O. (1945). The Psychoanalytic Theory of Neurosis. New York: W. W. Norton.

Ferm, V., ed. (1951). Encyclopedia of Religion. New York: Philosophical Library.

Ferreira, A. J. (1963). Family myth and homeostasis. Archives of General Psychiatry 9:457–463.

Freud, S. (1900). The interpretation of dreams. Standard Edition 4:549–553. London: Hogarth Press, 1953.

———— (1913). Totem and taboo. Standard Edition 13:100–161. London: Hogarth Press, 1955.

———— (1917). Mourning and melancholia. Standard Edition 14:237–258. London: Hogarth Press, 1957.

Garma, Á. and Rascovsky, A. (1948). Psicoanalisis de la Melancolía. Buenos Aires: Editorial "El Araneo."

Giovacchini, P. L. (1979). Treatment of Primitive Mental States. New York: Jason Aronson.

Giovacchini, P. L., and Boyer, L. B., eds. (1982). Technical Factors in the Treatment of the Seriously Disturbed Patient. New York: Jason Aronson.

Goethe, J. W. von. (1789). Das Roemische Carneval. Weimar: Carl Wilhelm Ettinger.

Greenacre, P. (1947). Vision, the headache and the halo. In Trauma, Growth and Personality, pp. 132–148. New York: W. W. Norton, 1952.

Hermann, I. (1936). Clinging — Going-in-Search. Psychoanalytic Quarterly 45: 5–36.

Hilgard, J. R. (1953). Anniversary reactions in parents precipitated by children. Psychiatry 16:73–80.

———— (1969). Depressive and psychotic states as anniversaries to sibling death in childhood. In Aspects of Depression , ed. E. Shneidman and M. Ortega, pp. 197–212. Boston: Little, Brown.

Hilgard, J. R., and Newman, M. F. (1959). Anniversaries in Mental Illness. Psychiatry 22:113–122.

Jacobson, E. (1965). The return of the lost parent. In Drives, Affects and Behavior. Essays in Honor of Marie Bonaparte, vol. 2, ed. Max Schur, pp. 193–211. New York: International Universities Press.

———— (1971). Depression. New York: International Universities Press.

Jekels, L. (1936). The psychology of the festival of Christmas. Selected Papers, pp. 142–158. New York: International Universities Press, 1952.

Jones, C. W. (1954). Knickerbocker Santa Claus. The New York Historical Society Quarterly 38:357–384.

———— (1978). Saint Nicholas of Myra, Bari and Manhattan. Biography of a Legend. Chicago: University of Chicago Press.

Jones, E. (1951). The significance of Christmas. *Essays in Applied Psycho-Analysis* 2:212–224. London: Hogarth Press.

Kernberg, O. F. (1975). Borderline Conditions and Pathological Narcissism. New York: Jason Aronson.

Kris, E. (1956). The personal myth: a problem in psychoanalytic technique. *Journal of the American Psychoanalytic Association* 4:654–681.

LaBarre, W. (1970). *The Ghost Dance. The Origins of Religion.* New York: Dell.

Lalanne, L. (1847). *Curiosités des Traditions, des Moeurs et des Legendes.* Paris.

Leach, M. and Fried, J., ed. (1950). *Standard Dictionary of Folklore, Mythology and Legend.* 2 vols. New York: Funk and Wagnalls.

Lehrman, R. P. (1927). The fantasy of not belonging to one's family. *Archives of Neurology and Psychiatry* 18:1015–1023.

Lewin, B. D. (1933). The body as phallus. *Psychoanalytic Quarterly* 2:24–47.

———— (1946). Sleep, the mouth and the dream screen. *Psychoanalytic Quarterly* 15:419–434.

———— (1948). Inferences from the dream screen. *Psychoanalytic Quarterly* 29: 234–241.

———— (1950). *The Psychoanalysis of Elation.* New York: W. W. Norton.

Loewald, H. (1960). On the therapeutic action of psychoanalysis. *International Journal of Psychoanalysis* 41:16–33.

———— (1982). Regression: some general considerations. In *Technical Factors in the Treatment of the Severely Disturbed Patient*, eds. P. L. Giovacchini and L. B. Boyer, pp. 107–130. New York: Jason Aronson.

Lubin, A. J. (1959). A boy's view of Jesus. *Psychoanalytic Study of the Child* 14: 155–168.

———— (1961). Vincent Van Gogh's ear. *Psychoanalytic Quarterly* 30:351–384.

Mahler, M. S. (1968). *On Human Symbiosis and the Vicissitudes of Individuation.* New York: International Universities Press.

Reinach, S. (1930). *Orpheus.* New York: Liveright.

Rycroft, C. (1951). A contribution to the study of the dream screen. *International Journal of Psycho-Analysis* 32:178–184.

Shapiro, E. R. (1978). The psychodynamics and developmental psychology of the borderline patient: a review of the literature. *American Journal of Psychiatry* 135:1305–1315.

Taraporewala, I. (1928). Some aspects of the history of Zoroastrianism. *Journal of the K. R. Cama Oriental Institute*, no. 2. Bombay.

———— (1945). Mithraism. In *Forgotten Religions*, ed. V. Ferm, pp. 205–214. New York: Philosophical Library.

Volkan, V. D. (1976). *Primitive Internalized Object Relations. A Clinical Study of Schizophrenic, Borderline and Narcissistic Patients.* New York: International Universities Press.

———— (1982). A young woman's inability to say no to needy people and her identification with the frustrator in the analytic situation. In *Technical Factors in the Treatment of the Severely Disturbed Patient*, eds. P. L. Giovacchini and L. B. Boyer, pp. 439–466. New York: Jason Aronson.

Von Domarus, E. (1925). The specific laws of logic and schizophrenia. In *Language and Thought in Schizophrenia*, ed. J. Kasanin, pp. 104–114. Berkeley: University of California Press.

Wallace, E. R. IV. (1982). *Freud and Anthropology. A History and Reappraisal*, pp. 5–112. New York: International Universities Press.

Winnicott, D. W. (1971). *Playing and Reality.* New York: Tavistock Publications, 1982.

CHAPTER SEVENTEEN

Depression in Perversion: With Special Reference to the Function of Erotic Experience in Sexual Perversion

Charles W. Socarides, M.D.

From the analysis over several decades of patients with various forms of perversion, it is my belief that both the depressive affect and anxiety are of central importance to the formation, meaning, content, and expression of sexual perversion. While frequently alluded to in clinical studies of perversion, the depressive affect has not been systematically studied or elucidated in relation to perversion, nor has it yet been integrated into an emergent comprehensive theory of perversion (Socarides 1979).

The affect of anxiety has primacy over all other affects (Freud 1926) in the causation of psychiatric disorders. The scientific observer had at first to delineate and describe the function and content of various forms of anxiety, i.e., separation anxiety, engulfment anxiety, fragmentation anxiety, castration anxiety. These have received considerable attention from psychoanalysts in the past two or three decades. These anxieties have been associatively connected with deficits in the body ego, fears of bodily disintegration, unusual sensitivity to threats of bodily damage, the increase in primary and secondary aggression leading to threats to the object and the self, threats to the loss of the object, and to the loss of the object's love.

Our understanding of the contribution of the affect of depression to perversion, in contrast to that of anxiety, had to await further theoretical contributions and infant observational studies, studies which were never as advanced as those in the area of the affect of anxiety. In part, this lack of knowledge resulted from the difficulty in defining the precise nature of infant and child depression.

In the following chapter, I shall review briefly the work of several analysts who have investigated the infantile genetic matrix of the depressive affect in order to better comprehend the psychopathology of well-structured cases of sexual perversion. These are relatively pronounced cases in which the perverse development is clear and definite. In these patients, nonengagement in perverse practices induces severe anxiety. Because the perverse acts were usually the only avenue for the attainment of sexual gratification and were obligatory for the alleviation of intense anxieties and because the intensity of the need for such gratification was relatively pronounced, I refer to these cases as the "well-structured perversion."

Analytic reconstruction is enriched by utilizing our expanding knowledge of primary psychic development as it pertains to separation–individuation phases and by articulating our current knowledge of development with earlier traumatic experiences which have caused developmental interferences. Focusing my attention on the clinical phenomenon of the depressive affect in perversion, I suggest that the matrix out of which perversions arise is one in which there is a negative affective predisposition characterized by the sense of helplessness, hopelessness, narcissistic deflation,and a consequent disturbance in gender-defined self identity. This occurs concomitantly and is intimately interwoven with the affect of anxiety.

Perverse acts reduce the suffering produced not only by anxiety but by the painful affect of depressive states. The relief of the depressive affect through perverse acts helps fortify the self against threats of fragmentation, diminishes separation anxiety, and compensates for narcissistic injury. It constitutes an erotized flight from despair and helplessness, perceived in the unconscious as the threat of starvation found commonly in depressed patients. Furthermore, I hope to show that it is not the fixated erotic experience per se, i.e., the instinct derivative that is regressively reanimated in the perversion, but rather that the early function of the erotic experience is retained and regressively relied upon (Socarides 1978, Stolorow 1979). Through erotization, the pervert attempts to diminish or erase anxiety and depression (both "basic ego responses") (Bibring 1953) and maintain "the structural cohesion and stability of crumbling, fragmenting, and disintegrating self and object representations" (Lachman and Stolorow 1980, p. 149).

I shall illustrate these findings by clinical examples of depressive moods and depression in transvestitism, pedophilia, and homosexuality.

Preliminary to reviewing advances in the comprehension of these early depressive reactions which have special relevance to the development of sexual perversions, I shall briefly touch upon my theoretical and clinical position on the psychopathology found in all "well-structured perversion." In previous publications (Socarides 1968, 1978, 1979) I described the psychopathology found in all preoedipal perverts and classified them according to the degree of pathology of internal object relations. The patient suffers from a lifelong persistence of the original primary feminine identification with the mother, resulting in a pervasive conscious-unconscious feeling of femininity and/or deficient sense of masculinity. The patient is symbiotically attached to the mother, has fantasies of fusing with her, but is also intensely ambivalent toward her. Narcissistic vulnerability is manifest, especially in relations with the mother, to whose attitudes and behavior the patient is unduly sensitive. There is a failure to successfully construct intrapsychic representations of the self and object, especially of the mother as a stable, need-satisfying, trustworthy object of symbolic value.

Pre-oedipal perverts of Type I have developed sufficient ego structure and differentiation between self and object and possess enough capacity for object relations to indicate that they have successfully traversed the earlier phases — symbiotic, differentiating — and practicing subphases of the separation–individuation process. They have been less able, however, to resolve the challenges of rapprochement, the subphase of separation–individuation leading to the successful development of object relations. The Pre-oedipal Type I pervert cannot, because of the absence of successful internalization, accept someone else as a substitute for the mother in her absence or in the context of a threat of her loss. Pre-oedipal Type I perversion serves to repress a pivotal nuclear conflict, the urge to regress to a pre-oedipal fixation in which there is both the desire for and dread of merging with the mother in order to reinstate the primitive mother–child unity. Having been unsuccessful at traversing the separation–individuation phase, the patient has a fear of reengulfment that continually threatens a differentiation that is insufficient, unstable, and impermanent under the severe stress engendered by attempts at autonomy and total differentiation.

Both Pre-oedipal Type I and II patients suffer from an object relations class of conflict (in contrast to structural conflict in those who have reached the oedipal phase) due to an insufficient structuralization of the psychic apparatus (Dorpat 1976). Their anxiety and guilt are associated with the failure of development in the phase of self-object differentiation. In Pre-oedipal Type 2 patients, self-object differentiation is much more severely impaired, as the self is just emerging as autonomous; its cohesiveness is greatly damaged with resultant "identity diffusion." The predominant anxiety is of fragmentation related to an imperiled self-representation in contrast to separation anxiety seen in Pre-oedipal Type I patients (Socarides 1982). This anxiety all but obscures the separation anxiety and separation "guilt" (Modell 1965) arising from the unresolved mother–infant tie.

Theoretical Contributions on Depression in Infancy and Childhood

In 1953, Bibring made an outstanding contribution to our understanding of depression in children by applying our then-expanding knowledge of primary psychic development. He introduced the concept of "basic depressive affect," and proposed that anxiety and depression are both basic ego reactions representing opposing basic ego responses. Anxiety is a reaction to external or internal danger which indicates the ego's desire to survive; the ego responds with signals of anxiety. In depression, however, the ego becomes paralyzed, finds itself incapable of meeting the danger, and in extreme situations "the wish to live is replaced by the wish to die" (Bibring 1953, p. 35). Rene Spitz (1946) had already described a potentially lethal form of depression in infants, "anaclitic depression," a product of severe maternal deprivation and neglect in the first 12 months of life. Bibring's theoretical concepts provided a bridge to the understanding and relationships between adult clinical depressions and their ontogenesis in earliest infancy and childhood. It should be noted that, as early as 1946, Edith Jacobson predicted the impact of early disappointments in parental omnipotence and the subsequent devaluation of the parental images on the little child's ego formation, i.e., a devaluation and destruction of the infantile self, and a "primary childhood depression" which, if repeated in later years, produced a similar "disillusionment" (Jacobson 1946). These writers laid the groundwork for later infant observational studies, especially those made by Mahler and her associates (1961, 1966, 1975).

Bibring contended that frequent frustrations of the infant's oral needs may at first mobilize anxiety and then anger, which then leads to exhaustion, helplessness, and depression. This is an "early self-experience of the infantile ego's helplessness, of its lack of power to provide the vital supplies," and is "probably the most frequent factor predisposing to depression" (p. 37). He noted that it is not the oral frustration and fixation per se, but the "infant's or little child's shock-like experience of and fixation to the feelings of *helplessness*" (p. 37) that is pathogenic. Bibring wrote not only of the child's need for affection and need to be loved but also of the opposite defensive need "to be independent and self-supporting." In this way he antedated Mahler's concept of separation–individuation phases leading to object constancy. He noted furthermore that certain of the child's strivings and cherished sources of gratification fight against interferences by the object (the rapprochement struggle of Mahler). In a different context, Bibring describes the helplessness of the anal phase: "The child struggles to independent ego strength, to control his body through defiance and mobilization of forms of aggression, and he may attempt separation from the mother. Intense aggression may lead to remorse and guilt, fear of punishment, and corresponding aspirations . . . to be good, not to be resentful, hostile, defiant" (p. 38).

Mahler's Infant Observational Studies

The major contributions of Mahler and her co-workers in the area of sadness, grief, and depression in infancy and early childhood span two decades. Three articles are of central importance: "On Sadness and Grief in Infancy and Childhood: Loss and Restoration of the Symbiotic Love Object" (1961); "Notes on the Development of Basic Mood: The Depressive Affect" (1966); and "The Epigenesis of Separation Anxiety, Basic Mood and Primitive Identity" (1975). In her first paper Mahler agrees with Bibring that anxiety and depression are indeed basic affective reactions, and that such "depressions" at this early age, since sufficient structuralization of the mental apparatus has not occurred, express a state of helplessness and not a clinical depression as we know it in adults. Such frustrations lead to anxiety and anger, and if they continue are replaced by feelings of exhaustion, helplessness, and larval states of depression.

Synchronous with the advances of the rapprochement phase, e.g., acquisition of primitive skills, cognitive faculties, clearer differentiation, and the formation of intrapsychic representation of the love object, is the realization of a large number of obstacles standing in the way of magic omnipotent wishes and fantasies. The world is no longer the "child's oyster," and the child must cope as a relatively helpless, small, and lonesome individual. The child begins to find that parents withhold omnipotence, no longer permit the child to share in everything, and deny emotional needs and supplies. Disturbances in separation due to faulty mother–child interaction in the context of an "abdicating father" (Socarides 1982b) lead not only to sadness, grief, and helplessness, but to increased ambivalence, loss of self-esteem, an increase in unneutralized aggression, and a disturbance in the child's progress toward object constancy.

In the rapprochement phase one can clearly discern a basic depressive mood in those whose self-representation is imperiled (Mahler 1966). Unneutralized aggression may be handled by splitting and projection, and potentially pathological combinations of defenses are employed to ward off the child's hostility and the fear of annihilating the love object. The child may begin to feel an acute deflation of the omnipotence which was formerly used to ward off injuries to self-esteem. The resultant critical "negative depressive affective response" (Mahler 1966) may take the following forms: separation and grief reactions following dramatic struggles with the love object, marked by temper tantrums and giving up in despair; impotent resignation and surrender; masochistic reactions; discontented anger; and increased clinging to the mother. These are formidable obstacles to the attainment of object constancy.

In 1975 Mahler and her associates included the disturbance in "gender-defined self-identity" (a central finding in all sexual perverts I have analyzed) as one of the developmental issues which is seriously affected by the "negative depressive affective state." She commented: "Our data indicate that the boy's active aggressive strivings, his gender-determined motor-mindedness seems to help him maintain (with many ups and downs, to be sure) the buoyancy of his body ego feelings, his belief in his body strength, and his pleasure in functioning" (p. 13). Under normal conditions the momentum of the body's motor functions counteracts excessively abrupt deflation of the practicing grandeur and omnipotence and helps the child overcome increasing hypersensitivity about separation from the mother during the rapprochement phase.

Appropriate gender-defined self-identity occurs under the following conditions, conditions which are never met by mothers of boys who later develop perversions: The mother respects and enjoys the boy's masculinity and phallicity, especially in the second half of the third year; she encourages an identification with the father or possibly with an older brother, thereby facilitating the boy's gender-defined self-identity; and she happily and willingly relinquishes the son's body and ownership of his penis to himself (Mahler 1973).

In contrast to those mothers who set the stage for perverse formation in their male children, favorable mothering leads the boy to cope with the anxiety feelings of helplessness, loss of sources of infantile gratification associated with symbiosis and separation; and to disidentify with the mother and make a counteridentification with the father (Greenson 1968). Mother must not be intrusive and interfere with the boy's phallic strivings, and the boy must not give in with passive surrender. This is particularly harmful if the father does not lend himself to idealization and identification so that his son may find comfort and joy in his sense of masculinity.

Clinical Examples

A Transvestite Patient

Alfred, a 39-year-old, highly successful professional man, had practiced a transvestite perversion since the age of 13 when he first began to wear his mother's clothes. Although able to perform sexually on some occasions without the use of women's underclothes, he usually found them an absolute necessity for achieving orgasm. Whenever he was unable to secure women for sexual relations, he experienced anxiety, depression, feelings of emptiness. He wore the underclothing especially when angry, upset, or felt "picked on" by associates, when he was lonely or bored, and on occasion inserted "feminine articles," such as diaphragms and vaginal douche syringes, into his anus in order to reduce severe states of tension. Throughout the early and middle phases of the analysis he verbalized intense oral demands, needs to suck everyone dry, especially women. Women had a responsibility to provide him with things that they possessed, and they had no right to retaliate if he exploited them. When they were unavailable for sexual relations, clothing was a substitute for their presence, providing erotic arousal and a feeling of security. Transvestite acts made up for maternal coldness, neglect, and deprivation of childhood and provided him with a sense of power and control, dissipating his sense of emptiness, making him feel "alive" emotionally, and reducing feelings of sadness and melancholy.

He frequently searched the trash baskets at his apartment house in order to find discarded women's pantyhose; Albert then put them on and masturbated. "The boredom and depression I feel then leaves me. I want to be filled up. I feel I could get an erection if I could fill myself up with a fountain syringe . . . if I had a bra on my thighs my emptiness would be overcome. My hunger is so great and my loneliness for other people so overwhelming. I want women to cry for me, feed me, fill me up. I want them to cry even after I leave them."

He sought revenge and restitution for the suffering he experienced during his early years: a tonsillectomy at age 2; frequent enemas administered by a "kooky," chronically depressed mother who never touched him except when she bottle-fed him (he was told); a weak, passive, and compliant father who abdicated his responsibility as a father in protecting him from his mother; feelings of personal physical ugliness ("big lips, short stature, too much hair"). "She couldn't handle me, forced me to eat, then gave me enemas, and I remember my screaming. She couldn't get me to move my bowels, and she caused me to cry. I picture myself at maybe 2 years of age not being in control of my own destiny. And then I was sent away. I would argue with her, talk back. And she never held or hugged me."

Alfred's temper tantrums made him unmanageable in his mother's eyes and resulted in his being sent away to a home for "difficult boys" for six months at the age of 4 and one-half. "I recall saying goodbye to my parents. It is so upsetting now. I didn't want to leave them. I always felt embarrassed by mother. I wonder why she was so mean to me. My cries were filled with loneliness and rage. I could not bear to be separated from her, and I could not bear to go to school. I would just cry and cry, and my mother just wouldn't listen to me." He recalls recurrent dreams in late childhood of being in a war, coming out of a trench, and as he lifted his head he gets shot in the heart and is dying or dead — a "toddler over the top."

Whenever he feels rejected by a woman or is forced to be alone with his thoughts, he fears that he will experience "a loss of self," often represented in his dreams as "being lost in space or falling long distances and awakening in great fear." On such occasions he suffers an acute dislocation of mood downward, can hardly move, is unable to keep appointments, and suffers a severe drop in self-esteem. He describes these states as a form of emptiness, and were they to continue they would make him feel that "no one would recognize me," "pay attention to me," "that I will cease to exist and that I am empty and rotten, and that no one really cares." These depressive periods are abruptly and magically relieved through fantasies of wearing female clothing, especially underclothing, masturbating while holding or wearing female clothing, or by having sexual relations with a woman while partially dressed as a woman. He then feels restored to himself, feels whole and complete, comforted, and "filled up." The abrupt alteration of mood, the change in the affective coloration of the self, is enhanced by the pleasurable effect of sexual orgasm, produces a sharp rise in self-regard, and an elevation in mood, in effect, a euphoria bordering on elation. These experiences are repeatedly sought after whenever the ego is faced with a similar intrapsychic crisis.

He describes himself as an "empty dirigible or a shell of a dirigible." The becoming empty, or the fear of becoming empty and depressed, also the falling, is the key to my problem. What happens if I fall being upside down, loss of control, lost in space, without relatedness?" My patient suffered from "empty depression" or "depletion depressions," terms introduced by self-psychology (Tolpin and Kohut 1980) to differentiate this state clearly from the syndrome of "guilt-depression" which is due to a structural conflict. The former is "characterized by a specific endopsychic state, a self-perception of emptiness, depletion, and hopelessness. . . ." (p. 436). Feelings of emptiness are experienced as sensations "of not being anchored, grounded, or being unplugged" (p. 435–436).

If for some external reason Alfred is unable to practice his perversion, he feels agitated and depressed, while its successful enactment wards off feelings of dissolution, helps create object relationship through merger with the symbiotic image of the mother, and temporarily succeeds in eliminating depressive affects. When he is traveling alone, he becomes upset unless he brings along women's clothing. "When I get anxious I feel I'm losing myself, and I also have a déjà vu feeling and I experience fear." (Déjà vu feelings are common temporal distortion experiences in depression.) The patient was prone to these déjà vu experiences when the torment of separation from anyone grew too intense. They represented a perceptual experience of returning to the mother when the ego was severely inundated by danger through a hypercathexis of the primal love object (Pacella 1975).

This patient regularly had manifest dreams of engaging in transvestite acts. This type of dreaming constituted a prophylactic device against the enactment of a perversion as well as diminished overwhelming affective states and tension crises faced by an archaic ego during sleep (Socarides 1980b). On some occasions even the manifest dreams of the transvestite perversion had to be followed by the enactment of the perversion in real life. When he struggled against the perversion, Alfred experienced emotional flooding in the form of fits of despair, crying, anxiety, often suicidal preoccupation, and the fear that he was "going crazy." Through dreaming or acting out, he stabilized his sense of self, reinforced object relations, overcame depressive anxiety, eliminated destructive aggression and feelings of vulnerability, and brought pleasure both to an external object and to himself.

A Pedophiliac Perversion

Jenkins, was a 38-year-old pedophile with associated severe narcissistic personality disorder, whose symptoms at times verged on borderline psychopathology. (The introjective-projective anxieties and splitting phenomena in this patient were briefly described by me in an article entitled "Meaning and Content of a Pedophiliac Perversion" (1959).) He was the second oldest of a large number of children in a disturbed, quarreling, financially borderline family. He often went hungry and continuously felt mistreated as far back as he could remember. His father was often cruel and vicious to his mother, and he remembers his father's angry outbursts and his intense wishes that he could protect what he later felt was a "cold and heartless woman." When the patient was 5 years old, he and four older siblings were placed in an orphanage with the promise that the mother would return for them the next day. "I just waited and waited, the nights led to days, the days to weeks, the weeks to months and then to years." On his mother's occasional Sunday visits he would beg her to allow him to return home, promising that he would not be any trouble. Since his placement in the orphanage he has felt that there was no love in the world. In the orphanage a brother, two years older, was often harsh with him, making him carry out delinquent activities, frightening him, and then holding him close to his body and kissing him. At the age of 12, he was told by his mother that she had wanted to abort him, and he felt "lucky and happy to be alive." Shortly thereafter, while attending a father-son dinner as a guest from the orphanage, he fell into a depression lasting several years upon seeing a young boy engaged in an animated conversation with a loving father.

He ceased imploring his mother to take him home at about 11 years of age, but shortly thereafter developed fears of death, often attempting to approximate this condition by becoming immobile and holding his breath. In early adolescence he responded to the growth of pubic hair with disgust and shame and a feeling that the appearance of pubic hair meant a step closer to death. By 15, a sense of personal dissolution and fragmentation of his ego appeared. At those times he would gaze intently at himself in the mirror in order to help control a threatened loss of ego boundaries and fragmentation. "I have the overwhelming fear I'll vanish, break apart, dissolve, be no more. I can only stop it by calling my brother's name over and over again, and then I regain myself."

Although the most dramatic episode in his life was his abandonment at age 5, the first five years were filled with feelings of helplessness, loneliness, and despair, events which produced a profoundly negative mood predisposition affecting and coloring all early phases of ego development: self-object differentiation, separation/individuation, affect control, and the development of healthy narcissism. He suffered from a profound increase in primary and secondary aggression, a disturbance in gender-defined self-identity, and a pathological and split-off grandiose self. The patient lived with two personalities, "personality A" and "personality B," which allowed him to perform guiltlessly his perversion with prepubertal children, dissociated from the world around him.

Between 9 and 10 he had his first sexual experience with a brother, three years older. From 12 to 14 he was seduced by older boys, his older brother, and a counselor; fellatio and mutual masturbation were practiced. Until the age of 14, the patient had not actively engaged in any sexual practices initiated by himself with boys younger than he. His first act of pedophilia (sexual activity with prepubertal boys) occurred after he reached adolescence and denoted a change from passivity to activity. The important organizing experience for the later expression of his pedophilia occurred on a day on which he was roaming through the "tremendous halls of the orphan asylum," unable to go home for the day because he was punished and did not have the subway fare:

> I had a terrible feeling, a painful, depressive, lonely feeling which is painful to me, terribly painful, a vacuum that I even now feel when I don't have a boy. It's hard to describe that feeling, that "no purpose," that "nowhere to go," that "nothing to do." On that day I had that feeling of helplessness. There was this kid sitting on the window, a 10-year-old. That was the first time I actually ever had sex with him. It was the same feeling that I have coming back over and over again, a purposelessness of life, a helplessness, a bleak view of everything, and with nothing to do, a complete blank, a vacuum. I was lost, no one to talk to, an awful feeling, a horror feeling. I don't know what it was. And then I saw that kid. Somehow or other I seemed to know somebody else had "used" the kid. He had sucked somebody off. Suddenly when I saw the kid there, I felt different. All the bad feelings were gone, the depression, the loneliness. I didn't have the hollow feeling any more. I took him someplace and had sex with him. I knew every nook and corner of the place. He was very docile, and a sexy kind of kid, like I knew he wouldn't refuse me.

Sexual activities with younger children continued while he was in the orphanage, especially when depressed, lonely, or dejected. He kept them secret, had some feelings of mild guilt and shame, feared the authorities, and that he might become "unpopular" in the orphanage where he now was a "student leader." After leaving the orphanage at age 18, he completed college and obtained a master's degree in an area of social service to the community and to children (reparative tendencies) where he was considered to be a thoughtful, concerned, and brilliant leader. He resolved to control his sexual activities but was unable to do so. Depressive attacks, threats of fragmentation, and unendurable anxiety began to trigger intense pedophiliac needs. In the following episode he relates the absolute necessity for sexual contact with the narcissistic object, the child, an idealized version of himself, one who was well treated, youthful, not approaching death; masculine, not feminine, i.e., with a penis; loved and protected. In later phases of the analysis the prepubertal child was revealed to be the good maternal breast, free of any connection with the mother, which allowed him to express his needs for loving and being loved and promoted the eradication of destructive aggression against mother, father, and himself.

In an almost lyrical vein he narrates:

At 18 a very important thing happened. I was sharing an apartment with my brother. I am an opera lover and I was listening to La Boheme, and the main theme had a tremendous depression and nostalgia which overwhelmed me. "Your tiny hand is frozen. . . . " She pretends she can't find her key, and his hand touches hers. He notices it's cold and sings the aria, "Your tiny hand is frozen." One of the doors of the courtyard opened, and a little boy entered, dressed in a navy blue suit with old-fashioned knickerbockers. He was brown-complexioned, and I figured he was going to the street. Suddenly an impulse came to run down, to look at this child. I looked in the store. He was about 8 or 9. I looked at him and something was gripping me inside. I kept looking at him, I felt like I was in love with him. I wanted to pick him up and hug him in my arms. He seemed untouchable and unattainable, beyond me . . . an awe about it, and yet just looking at him was not enough. . . . I can't recall wanting my penis between his legs or any of those things at the time. I feel I only woke up then. The renaissance of Mr. X. I began to develop a philosophy. "If I am not for myself, who will be for me? I am all alone and helpless. And if not now, when?"

Shortly thereafter, the full-scale pedophiliac acts increased in frequency so that when he entered psychoanalysis he had had several hundred sexual contacts with prepubertal boys.

The depressive episodes were part of a symptom complex which included fears of ego dissolution, grandiosity, and flight from fragmentation anxiety and depression through erotization:

A hollow empty feeling tears me up and destroys me, incapacitates me so that I can't do anything to stop it. Also I don't want to do anything else. It makes me feel restless, unwanted, alone, and helpless, and there's nothing in me. There's no purpose to my thought, to my work, or anything I might do. Things pile up on my desk and I can't deal with work. Everything is meaningless, including words. . . . Things don't matter, as if all the goals I had are gone and I have no reality. I cannot stand it for perhaps maybe a day or less. . . . The happiest moments, the moments that lift me into joy, that make this terror and depression leave me are, when I see a boy, a feeling of power when I see him. I decide I'm going to have sex with him. *The sex itself is just a sexual release, and what is important is I suddenly feel powerful and alive.* It's going to keep me living and it's a challenge that keeps me occupied. It tries my wits and ability. . . . The feeling is, I want him, I want to hold him in my arms, control him, and dominate him, and make him do my bidding."

It is not the erotic experience, but the function of the erotic experience that is regressively reenacted in his perversion.

Homosexual Pre-oedipal Type 2 Patient with Associated Narcissistic Personality Disorder

Willard was a 50-year-old, attractive, highly articulate and intelligent man who suffered from both a homosexual perversion and narcissistic personality disorder proper. When first seen, he was living with his severely ill father upon whom he had always been financially dependent. He entered treatment because he did not want to endanger a sizeable inheritance which would come to him after his father's death. Only later in treatment did it become apparent that this rather unusual aspect of his motivation for analysis was an expression of his basic core disturbance: a need for self-objects to guide and control his behavior. Among his important symptoms were severe periods of depression, lethargy, feelings of exhaustion, and the need to engage in intense homosexual activity. One of his worst symptoms was that he had been unable to complete actions which he felt were normal for adult human beings, and that attempts to do so left him exhausted and depleted (depletion depression). He capsulized his position by stating that "there is a terrible negative force of energy in me which puts me in thrall. I'm continually putting reality on hold. Keeping reality not so far away, but just far enough so that I cannot be touched by it. I am a cipher with an incapacity to act at all."

Throughout his early life, Willard felt effeminate, terrified of his peers, and unattractive. He engaged in secret fantasies of being "beautiful, superbly intelligent, and endlessly rich." He felt that he might become "impure through growth and aging," and in midadolescence he engaged in what he felt was ideal behavior, ideal values, ideal virtues. He feared that by making an adjustment to the external world he would "compromise the very sacred essence, the integrity of my being." Homosexual desires were present ever since he could remember, and he had had several homosexual "romances" with idealized older men since the age of 19. He was now engaged in active homosexual life with a series of casual partners, including male prostitutes.

The rich and variegated symptomatology of Willard's narcissistic personality disorder cannot be fully related within the limits of this chapter. Briefly stated, the guiding principle of his behavior revolved around the status of his self-cohesion: to protect it when it was threatened, to minister to it when it was damaged, and to recapture it when it was lost. In narcissistic compensation, Willard was comfortable in his environment of fine hotels, servants, and restaurants (paid for by his father and through his mother's alimony). They helped create a "perfect world," as he put it, in which he felt safe, provided with emotional supplies and narcissistic enhancement, and all but removed his sense of inadequacy. When the "bombardment of reality" interfered with his "tranquil integrity," grandiose exhibitionistic demands came out of repression and collided with reality, leading to regressive fragmentation and a depletion depression. In this state of decompensation he often retreated to his bed, depressed, lethargic, unable to move, often defecated on the floor, put clamps on his nipples during masturbation or in homosexual relations to heighten his sense of self by direct erotic stimulation. These actions made him feel alive, restored him to his former self, and tended to decrease the strong depressive affect and his inability to act which permeated these regressive periods.

Willard's insatiable and voracious homosexuality functioned as a substitute for action in the external world. It relieved his depression and helped him to fill a void created by an inability to take part in life. He did everything possible to create an emotional response in his partner in order to "feel alive" himself. "I'm trying to put something right in myself . . . something that I didn't get as a child. I'm trying to get back my relationship with my mother and father, and also with some other people." The desire is to produce a "big involvement" in order to find "a place to put emotions which I don't know where to place." The homosexual act served to partially and temporarily correct a basic disturbance. It "undoes splitting by putting together the self-representation with the appropriate object representation, combining both with suitable affective discharge." As Volkan (1976) notes correctly, splitting keeps apart "contrasting ego states which included self-representation, object representations, *and their affects*" (emphasis added). The "undoing" of splitting via the sexual act is, in a very primitive manner, achieved by producing pleasurable excitement and thrills in the partner so that he finds himself in the reflection of the partner's responses. At that moment he feels emotion, even elation, and feels alive. "I will support him with my financial ability and he will spoil me with his beauty, charms, weakness, easiness to relate, and his desire to compensate me for what I give him. This quest will temporarily satisfy me."

The lack of emotional sustenance and depth, the feeling of helplessness and grief which pervaded his psyche was the reason not only for his homosexuality, but for his maladjustment throughout life. This patient's fixation was in the early practicing and differentiating subphases, with findings suggestive of early developmental arrest of that period. These findings consisted of disruption in the emergence of the autonomous self; an impairment in self-object differentiation; deficiencies in the self-representation with a tendency to develop grandiosity; a marked freedom from internal conflict, since sufficient structuralization of the psychic apparatus had not taken place; and defenses that were at a primitive stage of development with splitting and denial paramount (Kernberg 1980). All these pointed to an early fixation to the practicing and, to some extent, to the differentiation subphase (Socarides 1982a), in contrast to Pre-oedipal Type I perverts in whom the fixation occurs at the rapprochement subphase (Socarides 1978). When such a patient loses his sexual partner, it is not the loss of the object nor the loss of the object's love for which he grieves. He feels the anguish of the undernourished child (Tolpin and Kohut 1979).

Narrating the loss of a lover to the analyst one day, he was immediately reduced to tears and sobbing in response to the analyst's empathic comment:

> When I came back to my room following my session, I got to thinking about P, and I started to cry. I wept disconsolately for about an hour and a half, and I kept saying, "My baby, my baby." I was in a lamentation. I really don't know of what this great profundity of emotion was apropos. I'm not sure I would have had it at all if you hadn't said this morning that it was a pity he was going. . . . Whether you were sympathizing with me for losing my friend for a time, or whether you meant that he was a constructive or beneficient influence upon me, something that I *needed*, I can't tell. I have a feeling that it was the latter, that I was somehow bereft because his good presence for me was gone, and you noticed. My sexual feelings for him have not been so urgent lately, but my tears were absolutely unstoppable. I was shouting with *grief*, shouting with grief. And it went on for at least half an hour, and I couldn't believe it was some sort of ideal representation of myself in him, and that all the things he does for me are ways for me to complete myself and to feel alive and in reality.

Willard's homosexuality was a consequence of disturbance belonging to the early infancy-childhood developmental stage in which self and body ego boundaries are in the process of being established through maternal care and management. He tries to remedy the result of a disturbance in object differentiation and integration through perverse activity, through the use of self objects. The homosexual contact allowed him to participate in a sense of maternal calmness and composure and to overcome feelings of grief and helplessness. Through acting out and mobilizing interest on the part of the partner with imaginative sharing and play-acting activities (Khan 1979), the deadness of Willard's internal world is ameliorated and his fragmented self is temporarily healed. Conversely, the loss of the homosexual object leaves him bereft, in inconsolable grief, with a resurgence of helplessness, apathy, weakness, and empty depression.

Discussion

I have noted the significance of the depressive affect for the success or failure in traversing separation–individuation phases of development and have described how a developmentally arrested ego seeks out perverse activities in an erotized flight from feelings of helplessness, deadness, and grief.

Through acting out, an intrapsychic crisis is averted and passivity, guilt, and anxiety are reversed by an erotized flight to reality and toward an external object; there is a denial of sensations of depression, heaviness, and sadness by specifically opposite sensations (Sachs 1923). Winnicott (1935), in a different theoretical frame of reference, has defined this function of perverse acting out as a "sexual variant of manic defense" in which there is a "reassurance against death, chaos and mystery . . . a flight to external reality from internal reality" (p. 132). Superego strictures are side-stepped, depression and psychic pain are eliminated through the exploitation of every possible aspect of sexuality, bodily sensations, in order to deny stillness, slowness, seriousness, discord, failure, and boredom. It is tempting to note here that the word "gay," commonly and currently used to refer to homosexuals and homosexuality, with its connotation of liveliness, gladness, joy, and merriment, represents a wholesale flight from the opposite sensations, namely sadness, misery, and despair. These emotions are a defensive position against the depressive affects in order to escape the deadness of an internal world, the futility and ego depletion secondary to the inability to establish sustained and permanent object relations. The inhibitions or lack of feelings of which perverse individuals complain in analysis, the complaint that they have "lost their ego," a common feature in all depressions, is magically remedied.

Affects require passage through certain developmental stages before their "maturation." The depressive pattern in a sexual pervert who has reached the oedipal phase with full structuralization of the mental apparatus is clinically different from that found in perverts fixated in the practicing and differentiating phases of the separation–individuation process, e.g., the Pre-oedipal Type II pervert with associated narcissistic personality disorder proper (Socarides 1982a). The former is characterized by classical symptoms of a cyclothymia: dislocation of mood downward; vegetative imbalance; psychomotor retardation; associated feelings of guilt and sense of unworthiness; and resentment that life has not given one a "fair deal." In the latter, there is a pronounced absence of guilt, and mood regulation is exceedingly dependent on external circumstances with many ups and downs. The mood swings of the narcissist differ from those of the classical cyclothymia because they follow a narcissistic loss or defeat, have a primary quality of apathy, and show a predominance of shame over guilt. However, the patient fears he may overshoot the mark and become "too excited," lose contact, and be unable to stop, be consumed and die. This hyperarousal is associated with physical transcendency, grandiosity and megalomania (Bach 1977, p. 224).

In those perverts who are also schizophrenic, rare psychotic forms of depression may occur with total adaptive incompetence rather than adaptive impairment, with the presence of self-accusatory delusions and hypochondriacal convictions that their gastrointestinal system has been destroyed or that they are being poisoned. In those perverts who are borderline narcissistic schizoid, the absence of neutralization leads to a lack of fusion between libidinal and aggressive drives, producing intense affective states. "When rage is felt, it is felt as murderous, when hypomania is experienced, it is often exhilerating, and when depression is experienced, it is profound, shattering in its intense feelings of despicable worthlessness, emptiness, diminishment of self-esteem, self-depreciation, profound negative self-appraisal, and an almost total inability to function" (Bach 1977). Such depressions in the pervert are marked by regressive, psychoticlike transferences, loss of executive functioning, hollowness, inferiority, and other profound incapacities. (See the case of Sumner in *Homosexuality*, Socarides 1978, pp. 307–341.)

The pervert attempts to regain his capacity for pleasure and the enjoyment of life by spurious means, bringing about the illusion of control through the magical powers of seduction and sensuality. His triumph lifts him to a state of intoxication, euphoria, and even elation. Elsewhere I have termed the homosexual's reintegration through incorporation of another man's body and his phallus as the "optimal fix" (Socarides 1968), resembling the experience following the intake of opium derivatives, restoring body ego boundaries, and producing a sense of well being and temporary integration. In other circumstances, the pervert may forestall depression by a spell of preventive sexual enactment with associated euphoria, a euphoria short-lived because it reinforces dependence and ensures future reenactments.

REFERENCES

Bach, S. (1977). On the narcissistic state of consciousness. *International Journal of Psycho-Analysis* 58:209–233.

Bibring, E. (1953). The mechanism of depression. In *Affective Disorders*, ed. P. Greenacre. New York: International Universities Press.

Dorpat, T. L. (1976). Structural conflicts and object relations conflicts. *Journal of the American Psychoanalytic Association* 24:855–875.

Freud, S. (1914). On narcissism: an introduction. *Standard Edition* 14:69–102.

——— (1926). Inhibitions, symptoms and anxiety. *Standard Edition* 20:77–175.

Greenson, R. R. (1968). Disidentifying from mother. *International Journal of Psycho-Analysis* 49:370–374.

Jacobson, E. (1946). The effect of disappointment on ego and superego function in normal and depressive development. *Psychoanalytic Review* 33:255–262.

Kernberg, O. (1980). *Internal World and External Reality: Object Relations Theory Applied*. New York: Jason Aronson.

Khan, M. M. R. (1979). *Alienation in Perversions*, pp. 1–245. New York: International Universities Press.

Lachmann, F., and Stolorow, R. D. (1980). The developmental significance of affective states: implications for psychoanalytic treatment. In *The Annual of Psychoanalysis*, 1980. New York: International Universities Press.

Mahler, M. S. (1961). On sadness and grief in infancy and childhood: loss and restoration of the symbiotic love object. In *The Selected Papers of Margaret S. Mahler*. Vol. 1, *Infantile Psychosis, Early Contributions*, pp. 261–279. New York: Jason Aronson, 1979.

——— (1966). Notes on the development of basic moods: the depressive affect. In *The Selected Papers of Margaret S. Mahler*. Vol. II, *Separation–Individuation*, pp. 59–75. New York: Jason Aronson, 1979.

——— (1973). Discussion of R. J. Stoller's article: healthy parental influences on the earliest development of masculinity in baby boys. *Psychoanalytic Forum*, vol. 5, pp. 244–247. New York: International Universities Press.

Mahler, M. S., Pine, F., and Bergman, A. (1975). The epigenesis of separation anxiety, basic mood and primitive identity. In *The Psychological Birth of the Human Infant*, pp. 210–220. New York: Basic Books.

Modell, A. H. (1965). On having a right to a life: an aspect of the super-ego's development. *International Journal of Psycho-Analysis* 46:323–351.

Pacella, B. L. (1975). Early development and the déjà vu. *Journal of the American Psychoanalytic Association* 23:300–317.

Sachs, H. (1923). On the genesis of sexual perversion. *International Zeitschrift für Psychoanalyse*, Vol. 9, pp. 177–182. Reprinted in *Homosexuality*, C. W. Socarides, trans. by H. F. Bernays, Appendix B. New York: Jacon Aronson, 1978.

Socarides, C. W. (1959). Meaning and content of a pedophiliac perversion. *Journal of the American Psychoanalytic Association* 7:84–94.

_____ (1968). *The Overt Homosexual*. New York: Grune and Stratton.

_____ (1978). *Homosexuality*. New York: Jason Aronson.

_____ (1979). A unitary theory of sexual perversion. In *Sexuality: Psychoanalytic Observations*, ed. T. B. Karasu and C. W. Socarides, pp. 161–188. New York: International Universities Press.

_____ (1980a). Homosexuality and the rapprochement subphase. In *Rapprochement: The Critical Subphase of Separation–Individuation*, ed. R. F. Lax, S. Bach, and J. A. Burland, pp. 331–352. New York: Jason Aronson.

_____ (1980b). Perverse symptoms and the manifest dream of perversion. In *The Dream in Clinical Practice*, ed. J. M. Natterson, pp. 237–256. New York: Jason Aronson.

_____ (1982a). Considerations on the psychoanalytic treatment of male homosexuality: the preoedipal homosexual with associated narcissistic personality disorder.

_____ Abdicating fathers, homosexual sons: psychoanalytic observations on the contribution of the father to the development of male homosexuality. In *Father and Child: Developmental and Clinical Perspectives*, ed. Cath, S. H., Gurwith, A. R., and Ross, J. M. pp. 509–521. Boston: Little, Brown. (in press).

Spitz, R. (1946). Anaclitic depression — an inquiry into the genesis of psychiatric conditions in early childhood, Part II. *Psychoanalytic Study of the Child* 2:313–342.

Stolorow, R. D. (1979). Psychosexuality and the representational world. *International Journal of Psycho-Analysis* 60:39–46.

Stolorow, R. D., and Lachmann, F. M. (1980). *The Psychoanalysis of Developmental Arrest: Theory and Treatment*. New York: International Universities Press.

Tolpin, M. and Kohut, H. (1980). The disorders of the self: the psychopathology of the first years of life. In *The Course of Life: Psychoanalytic Contributions Toward Understanding Personality Development*. Vol. 1, *Infancy and Early Childhood*, ed. S. I. Greenspan and G. H. Pollack. National Institute of Mental Health.

Volkan, V. D. (1976). *Primitive Internalized Object Relations: A Clinical Study of Schizophrenic, Borderline, and Narcissistic Patients*. New York: International Universities Press.

Winnicott, D. W. (1935). The manic defense. In *Collected Papers: Through Pediatrics to Psychoanalysis*, pp. 129–144. New York: Basic Books, 1958.

PART V

Somatic Issues

CHAPTER EIGHTEEN

Psychobiology of Affective Disorders

George S. Alexopoulos, M.D.

The notion of an underlying biological disturbance in affective disorders is very old. Hippocrates theorized that a humoral disturbance (melan-choli means black bile) was responsible for the pathogenesis of depression (Lewis 1967). In 1896 Kraepelin wrote that manic depressive psychosis has innate causes and is by and large independent of environmental factors (Kraepelin 1921). Freud assumed the presence of a physiological disturbance in depression; he developed his theory as an attempt to explain and understand the psychological development of depressive symptoms since the science of his time was unable to deal with it directly (Freud 1953).

Recent studies (Nurnberger and Gershon 1982, Cadout 1978) suggest strongly that genetic factors predispose to affective disorders. Genetic vulnerability must be mediated through a biological substrate. However, this does not mean that all affective syndromes result from an underlying biological abnormality. It is helpful to conceptualize the relationship of biological predisposition to affective disorders and psychosocial factors by assuming a synergism between the two (Fig. 18-1). According to this notion an individual with pronounced biological vulnerability to affective disorders may develop symptoms even when little psychological stress is present. Conversely, a person with minimal biological predisposition may survive an enormous psychosocial catastrophe without developing an affective syndrome.

Traditionally, patients with affective disorders are thought to lack anatomic brain abnormalities detectable through autopsy. However, organic factors are capable of leading to a mood disturbance and other affective symptoms. Manic symptomatology has been described in patients with brain tumors, neurosyphilis, viral or microbial infections, or in patients who received drugs such as isoniazid, adrenal hormones, l-dopa, and bromides (Winokur 1981, Goodwin and Guze 1979). Patients with preexisting medical problems prior to development of mania have age of illness onset 15 years later than the average age of onset in patients who spontaneously develop a bipolar disorder (Winokur 1981). Also, patients with medical problems do not as a rule have family history of affective disorders unlike patients with a bipolar disorder (Winokur 1981). These clinical differences suggest that the etiology of manias induced by medical conditions is different from that of bipolar disorder. However, it further supports the notion that physical factors are capable of leading to mania. Depression can be caused by an even larger variety of structural, infectious, metabolic, and toxic factors than mania, suggesting that this syndrome may have a less specific etiology (Winokur 1981, Goodwin and Guze 1979, Klerman 1976). While the development of depression in response to these factors is not well understood, some pharmacological observations have provided information implicating brain biogenic amines in the mechanisms underlying affective disorders.

The Biogenic Amine Hypothesis

Extracts of the plant rauwolfia serpentina have been used for centuries, particularly in India, as a treatment for cardiovascular disorders and behavioral excitement (Kline and Stanley 1955, Hoffman and Konchegul 1955). Since 1952, reserpine has been used in hypertension and in various psychiatric disorders. Approximately 20 percent of the patients treated with reserpine develop feelings of sadness and discouragement with lack of ambition and energy, crying spells, lack of interest in usual activities and anxious preoccupation over trivial problems (Goodwin and Bunney 1971). The most prominent symptoms in these patients are sedation and retardation. Although the clinical presentation of the reserpine-induced depressive syndrome is not identical to that of primary depressive disorders, the best prediction of depression developing in a reserpine-treated patient has been past history of depression (Goodwin and Bunney 1971). The observation that reserpine causes depression more frequently in predisposed individuals suggests that its action is related to the pathogenetic mechanism of affective disorders.

As early as 1955 Shore et al. observed that reserpine depletes serotonin from storage sites in the brain (Shore et al. 1955). Later, it was shown that reserpine would also deplete the catecholamines norepinephrine and dopamine (Carlson et al. 1957). Clarification of the biological action of reserpine as well as the clinical observation that this drug may cause depression at least in predisposed individuals led to the development of hypotheses implicating biogenic amine dysfunctions in affective disorders (Schildkraut 1965). Initially, two hypotheses were proposed. The first was the catecholamine hypothesis which was advanced primarily by American investigators; this hypothesis postulated that a functional deficiency in brain norepinephrine is responsible for depression (Schildkraut 1965, Goodwin and Sack 1973, Medical Research Council 1972). The second hypothesis was the indoleamine hypothesis which postulated a dysfunction of brain serotonin in affective disorders. The indoleamine hypothesis was initially proposed by Coppen and other British and Scandinavian investigators (Zis and Goodwin 1982). Soon it became clear that more than one amine dysfunction could lead to an affective syndrome and the biogenic amine hypothesis took the following form: depression is associated with a functional deficit of one or more neurotransmitter amines at critical brain synapses while mania is associated with a functional excess of these amines.

The biogenic amine hypothesis has been supported by several pharmacological findings (Zis and Goodwin 1982). Drugs like dextroamphetamine, cocaine, monoamine oxidase inhibitors, and tricyclics that enhance the function of norepinephrine and serotonin in the brain have a stimulating or antidepressant action and may precipitate mania. Agents like lithium and neuroleptics which reduce brain monoamine neurotransmission are sedatives or antimanics. However, not all pharmacological studies support the biogenic amine hypothesis. The new antidepressant iprindole has a weak effect on biogenic amines (Roslow 1974). Lithium inhibits the release of norepinephrine and enhances norepinephrine reuptake in in vitro experiments (Davis et al. 1979). However, it prevents development of depression and in some cases it even acts as an antidepressant.

Although most research has focused on disturbances of norepinephrine and serotonin neurotransmission several studies suggest a role of the dopamine system in affective disorders. Reserpine decreases not only the norepinephrine and serotonin output but also that of dopamine (Shore et al. 1955). This drug has been used successfully in the treatment of manic excitement (Kline and Stanley 1955, Hoffman and Konchegul 1955). Neuroleptics act rapidly and are particularly efficacious in controlling psychomotor agitation and psychotic symptoms in manic patients but have been less powerful in correcting elated mood (Goodwin and Zis 1979). These drugs act primarily by blocking brain dopaminergic receptors (Snyder 1976). Pimozide, a more selective dopamine receptor blocker, appears to control rapidly agitation and psychosis of manic patients (Post et al. 1980). Although lithium has probably little if any effect on dopamine turnover in the brain (Schubert 1973) when administered chronically seems to prevent neuroleptic induced supersensitivity of dopamine receptors (Bunney et al. 1979). Alpha-methyl-paratyrosine, an inhibitor of the rate limiting synthetic enzyme of both norepinephrine and dopamine, ameliorates manic symptoms (Brodie et al. 1971). Finally, inhibition of dopamine conversion to norepinephrine with fusaric acid does not reduce manic symptomatology but rather leads to development of more psychotic symptoms (Goodwin and Sack 1974). These findings suggest that disturbance in dopamine neurotransmission occurs at least during some stage of mania and is associated with certain symptoms of the disorder (Zis and Goodwin 1982).

The biogenic amine hypothesis is compatible with the nature of affective disorders. The biogenic amine systems are widely distributed in the brain and have an important role in regulating emotional, cognitive, motor, and appetitive behavior (Dahlstrom and Fuxe 1965; Fuxe, Hamberger, and Hokfeld 1968). Only disruption of biological systems with diversive action can explain the complex symptomatology of affective disorders.

The introduction of techniques such as stereotaxic lesioning and electrical stimulation through implanted electrodes helped to elucidate the role of biogenic amines in modifying behavior. The norepinephrine system has cell bodies lying in the brain stem projecting to many brain areas (Loizou 1969). The locus coeruleus, a stem nucleus with high concentration of norepinephrine cell bodies projects to the ipsilateral cortex in the rat (Loizou 1969). The norepinephrine system has been implicated in excitation and in exploratory behavior (Everitt and Keverne 1979). The main dopaminergic neurons arise in the substantia nigra and project to the corpus striatum (Faull and Carman 1968). In animals, stimulation of dopaminergic receptors with apomorphine leads to stereotyped behavior such as sniffing, licking and biting (Anden et al. 1967) Lesions of the substantia nigra result in hypokinesia in rats, reminding the clinical presentation of parkinsonism (Ungerstedt 1971). However, ablation of the cortex and striatum leads to hyperactivity and stereotypes (Everitt and Keverne 1979, Mettler 1964). It is possible that the brain dopaminergic system is related to the general arousal level that is essential for several functions.

Experiments using implanted electrodes have shown that animals will self-stimulate when electrodes are placed in the locus coeruleus and the substantia nigra (Crow 1971, 1972). These findings suggest an involvement of both the norepinephrine and dopamine systems in reward-related behavior, a function which may be impaired in affective disorders. Administration of amphetamine leads to hyperactivity and stereotyped behavior in rats (Iversen 1971). Lesions of either the substantia nigra or bilateral lesions of the locus coeruleus modify this effect (Medical Research Council 1972). It appears that both norepinephrine and dopamine are involved in these aspects of behavior.

The serotoninergic system has its cell bodies primarily in the raphe nuclei of the brain stem and projects widely in the brain and spinal cord. Serotonin mediates several aspects of behavior. There is evidence that serotonin participates in the regulation of sleep. Lesion of the raphe nuclei leads to insomnia in cats (Jouvet 1968). Stimulation of the raphe nuclei reduces habituation to repeated stimuli, suggesting that these serotoninergic centers control sensory input from the brain (Sheard and Aghajanian 1968). It has been suggested that the serotoninergic system antagonizes the behavioral effects of the nonadrenergic and dopaminergic system (Medical

Research Council 1972). All of these experiments were able to study simple patterns of behavior that are unlike those observed when animals are in their typical environment. However, these simple behavioral changes may represent building blocks to more complex adaptive behavior.

The common problem of all animal experiments is that there is no satisfactory animal model for depression or mania. Various clinical research strategies have been developed to test the biogenic amine hypothesis in patients with affective disorders. All these methods use indirect measurements of brain neurotransmitter function.

Metabolites of Biogenic Amines

Five hydroxyindoloacetic acid (5 HIAA), homovanillic acid (HVA), and 3-methoxy-4-hydroxyphenylglycol (MHPG) are the main cerebrospinal fluid (CSF) metabolites of brain serotonin, dopamine and norepinephrine respectively. The majority of studies agree that depressives have approximately 25 percent lower 24-hour urine MHPG concentration compared to normal control subjects (Zis and Goodwin 1982, Maas 1976). Reduction of urine MHPG occurs primarily when patients are symptomatic and usually MHPG rises when symptoms remit (Maas 1976, Schildkraut et al. 1978). Bipolar depressed patients have lower 24-hour urine MHPG levels than unipolar depressed patients or normal subjects (Maas 1976, Schildkraut et al. 1978). Among the unipolar patients, those with endogenous depression have 24-hour urine MHPG levels in the range found in bipolar patients. Bipolar patients with low urine MHPG have more frequent and longer manic or hypomanic episodes during treatment with tricyclic antidepressants, compared to bipolar patients with higher MHPG (Maas et al. 1972). It has been suggested that depressed patients with low 24-hour urine MHPG levels respond preferentially to imipramine (Maas et al. 1972, Fawcett et al. 1972).

Urinary MHPG is a peripheral measure. A large amount of urinary MHPG originates in the spinal cord (Post and Goodwin 1978). However, many of the norepinephrine axons and terminals have their origin in the locus coeruleus (Loizou 1969) and, therefore, urine MHPG can still give information about brain norepinephrine. Some of the urinary MHPG is produced in the peripheral sympathetic system and the adrenals (Maas et al. 1973). Another problem is that MHPG is converted to vanillylmandelic acid (VMA) (Blombery et al. 1979) and it is unknown whether the rate of this reaction is stable in each individual. Finally, stimulation of peripheral nerves has been shown to activate brain noradrenergic neurotransmission (Cedarbaum and Aghajanian 1977) and stimulation of the brain norepinephrine system leads to an increase in plasma MHPG probably due to an increase in peripheral sympathetic activity (Crowley et al. 1978). All of these factors contribute to variation in urine MHPG levels. Although it cannot be safely ascertained that 24-hour urine MHPG reflects necessarily brain norepinephrine output, most MHPG studies have consistently shown differences between depressed patients and psychiatrically normal subjects (Zis and Goodwin 1982, Maas 1976).

Several investigators have reported that both depressed and manic patients have low CSF 5HIAA levels compared to normal controls (Coppen et al. 1972, Asberg et al. 1976) although negative reports also exist (Goodwin et al. 1973, Bowers et al. 1969). Others have found that depressives are divided into two groups: one with a low and another with a high CSF 5HIAA level (Asberg et al. 1976, Van Praag, 1977). Similar findings have been reported when CSF 5HIAA has been assayed 24 hours after probenecid administration (Goodwin et al. 1973, Van Praag 1977, Goodwin et al. 1977). Probenecid inhibits the transport of 5HIAA through the blood brain barrier and allows measurement of the accumulation of 5HIAA over time (Goodwin et al. 1973). CSF 5HIAA remains relatively stable even when symptoms remit constituting a trait related characteristic in patients with affective disorders (Goodwin et al. 1973, Asberg et al. 1976). Recently, Asberg et al. (1976) have demonstrated that patients with history of suicidal attempts have lower CSF 5HIAA.

It appears that low CSF 5HIAA levels correspond to normal levels of 24-hour urine MHPG and correlate with selective treatment response to serotonin-enhancing drugs such as chlorimipramine and amitriptyline (Van Praag 1977). Depressed patients with normal or high CSF 5HIAA and low 24-hour urine MHPG level may constitute a group who respond preferentially to drugs that predominantly enhance norepinephrine transmission, for example, imipramine, desipramine (Maas et al. 1972, Beckman and Goodwin 1975).

Most of 5HIAA obtained by lumbar puncture is derived from serotonin neurons of the spinal cord (Bulat and Zivkovic 1971) which, however, may be controlled by vital stem centers. Another problem is that a significant quantity of CSF 5HIAA is removed by the blood (Meek and Neff 1973), which may contribute to differences of CSF 5HIAA level. Finally, brain serotonin synthesis is sensitive to changes in the concentration of tryptophan (Goodwin et al. 1973).

The CSF concentration of the dopamine metabolite HVA in depressives is similar to that of normal control subjects (Goodwin et al. 1973, Berger et al. 1980). However, CSF HVA after probenecid administration has been found reduced in depressed and manic patients (Goodwin et al. 1973, Berger et al. 1980), suggesting a role of the dopaminergic system in affective disorders.

Despite its limitations, monoamine metabolite research supports a dysfunction of brain catecholamines and serotonin in affective disorders. This strategy has provided evidence suggesting that affective syndromes are biologically heterogeneous. Furthermore, it has become clear that neither depression nor mania can be attributed to a single neurotransmitter dysfunction. Instead, they seem to be related to reciprocal neurotransmitter dysfunctions which may even change during the various phases of the disorder.

Neurotransmitter Receptors

Although changes in monoamine availability in brain synapses have been associated with affective disorders, several findings suggest that other factors play a role in the development of these syndromes. The time course of the clinical effect of antidepressant drugs does not coincide with their effect on monoamine output. Tricyclic antidepressants block monoamine presynaptic reuptake (Banki 1957) and monoamine oxidase inhibitors interfere with the catabolism of monoamines, thus increasing the concentration of brain monoamines within a few hours after a single dose (Goodman et al. 1980). However, the antidepressant effect of these drugs usually occurs within two to three weeks. Nontricyclic antidepressant drugs like iprindole and mianserin do not substantially inhibit presynaptic reuptake of norepinephrine and serotonin (Roslow 1974, Gluckman and Baum 1969, Leonard 1974, Goodlet et al. 1977), while drugs that increase the synaptic availability of monoamines in the brain like cocaine and amphetamine have no antidepressant action (Post et al. 1974, Overall et al. 1962, Ghose et al. 1977). These observations suggest that alterations in monoamine output in the brain are neither a necessary nor sufficient condition for the development of affective disorders.

Monoamine neurotransmitters convey their chemical signals through specific membrane surface receptors to the inside of the cells. Recently, research on affective disorders has focused on neurotransmitter receptor function. A method of assessing the sensitivity of postsynaptic receptors to neurotransmitters is by measuring the production of cyclic adenosine 3',5'-monophosphate (cAMP) in brain slices of experimental animals. The nucleotide cAMP has been considered a "second messenger" at the postsynaptic level, mediating the action of brain neurotransmitters (Greengard 1976). Therefore, the production of cAMP after stimulation by a particular neurotransmitter reflects the sensitivity of postsynaptic receptors to this transmitter (Sulser 1979, Baudry et al. 1976). Chronic administration of tricyclic antidepressants (Schultz 1976, Mishra and Sulser 1978), atypical antidepressants like mianserin (Mishra et al. 1980) and iprindole (Wolfe et al. 1978), monoamine oxidase inhibitors (Vetulani et al. 1976), and electroconvulsive therapy (Vetulani and Sulser 1975, Gillespie et al. 1979) decrease the production of norepinephrine stimulated cAMP in brain slices. The fact that such variable antidepressant treatments can change the receptor sensitivity function suggests that this effect may be related to their antidepressant action (Charney et al. 1981).

Another basic research strategy for assessing brain receptor function is to determine their binding characteristics to neurotransmitters. Prolonged exposure to tricyclic antidepressants (Bergstrom and Keller 1979, Peroutka and Snyder 1980a, 1980b, Sellinger-Barnette et al. 1980), monoamine oxidase inhibitors (Sellinger-Barnette et al. 1980, Campbell et al. 1979), or electroconvulsive therapy (Gillespie et al. 1979) decrease the density of beta adrenergic and 5-HT$_2$ serotoninergic receptors in several brain areas of experimental animals. Even deprivation of rapid eye movement sleep, a non-pharmacological antidepressant treatment, has been found to decrease beta andrenergic receptor binding (Mogilnicka et al. 1980). Antidepressant treatments change the density of alpha$_1$ and alpha$_2$ adrenergic receptors but not in a systematic fashion (Peroutka and Snyder 1980, Johnson et al. 1980, Campbell et al. 1979, Vetulani et al. 1980). It appears that decrease in beta adrenergic and 5-HT$_2$ serotoninergic receptor density is a specific common property of several antidepressant treatments that may be related to their therapeutic action.

An electrophysiological approach has added to the information contributed by biochemical research on neurotransmitter receptors. Single unit electrophysiological studies of the neuronal response to iontophoretic application of neurotransmitters provides a measure of receptor function. In brain areas with predominantly alpha adrenergic postsynaptic and serotoninergic receptors the response to norepinephrine stimulation has been reported to increase after chronic treatment with antidepressants (Menkes and Aghajanian 1981, Wang and Aghajanian 1980) or electroconvulsive therapy (De Montigny 1980). A reduction in the sensitivity of beta adrenergic postsynaptic receptors has been reported after long term treatment with tricyclic antidepressants (Diller et al. 1978, Hoffer et al. 1971), but negative findings also exist (De Montigny and Aghajanian 1978). Although electrophysiological findings on beta adrenergic receptor changes have not been as consistent, they complement the observation that chronically applied antidepressant treatments reduce the density of beta receptors in the brain. Treatment with tricyclic antidepressants has been reported to induce subsensitivity of the presynaptic noraderenergic alpha$_2$ receptors in the locus coeruleus (Svensson and Usdin 1978, Svensson 1980). Reduced sensitivity of these inhibitory presynaptic receptors may increase the norepinephrine release in the synapse. This effect may be related to the therapeutic action of tricyclic antidepressants and suggests a down regulation of presynaptic adrenergic autoreceptors in depression.

In addition to animal experiments, clinical studies suggest that changes in the function of brain neurotransmitter receptors may be implicated in affective disorders. Most clinical studies focused on changes in neuroendocrine function in patients with affective disorders. Since neurotransmitters participate in endocrine regulation, hormonal secretion has been considered to reflect some aspects of brain neurotransmitter function (Carroll et al. 1976a). Hyperactivity of the hypothalamic pituitary-adrenal axis (HPA) has been reported in some depressed patients (Carroll et al. 1976a, 1976b). HPA dysfunction is manifested as elevated 24-hour urine-free cortisol, abnormal circadian cortisol secretion, early escape from dexamethasone suppression, and impaired cortisol response to amphetamine stimulation (Carroll et al. 1976a, 1976b, Checkley 1978, Sachas et al. 1980, Brown and Shuey 1980). The regulation of HPA is complex. One hypothesis proposes that depressed patients have decreased sensitivity of the noradrenergic postsynaptic receptors. Since norepinephrine tonically inhibits neurons controlling the production of corticotropin releasing factor, decreased sensitivity of norepinephrine receptors may result in hyperactivity of HPA.

Blunted growth hormone response to challenge with clonidine, has been reported in depressed patients (Matussek et al. 1980, Checkley et al. 1981). Since growth hormone release in response to clonidine is mediated by alpha adrenergic postsynaptic receptors, these findings suggest a diminished sensitivity of postsynaptic noradrenergic receptors in depression (Matussek et al. 1980, Checkley et al. 1981). The growth hormone response to challenge with hypoglycemia (Sachar et al. 1971, Gruen et al. 1975, Mueller et al. 1969) or amphetamine (Checkley 1979) is also blunted in a subgroup of depressives. However, the interpretation of these findings has been less clear because other neurotransmitters participate in the regulation of these responses.

Studies of cortisol and prolactin response to hypoglycemia performed in the morning and in the evening have demonstrated that depressives have abnormal diurnal hormonal responses (Sachar et al. 1980). The regulation of diurnal levels of cortisol (Cavagnini et al. 1976) and prolactin (Krulich 1976) is probably controlled by the serotoninergic system. Therefore, circadian abnormalities in cortisol and prolactin response to hypoglycemia may result from a dysfunction of the serotoninergic system in depression. Electroconvulsive therapy has been reported to augment prolactin's response to thyrotropin releasing hormone (TRH) in depressed patients (Coppen et al. 1980). This response is probably mediated by serotonin (Ettigi and Brown 1977) and suggests that electroconvulsive therapy increases the sensitivity of postsynaptic serotoninergic receptors.

Clinical studies investigating biological changes during the course of long-term treatment with antidepressants suggest that the time table of therapeutic response correlates with receptor changes. Monoamine oxidase inhibitors lead to orthostatic hypotension which is probably mediated by adrenergic receptors (Murphy et al. 1983). Hypotension induced by mono-amine oxidase inhibitors reaches its maximum at the fourth week of treatment and its time course tends to parallel that of the antidepressant effect (Murphy et al. 1981, 1983). In patients receiving the monoamine oxidase inhibitor clorgyline, blood pressure reduction had a positive correlation with reduction in depressive symptomatology (Murphy et al. 1983). Symptoms of depression reappeared and blood pressure returned toward pre-treatment levels 7–10 days after discontinuation of clorgyline.

A more direct approach to the clinical assessment of noradrenergic receptor alterations during antidepressant treatment uses a biological challenge with the drug clonidine. This agent lowers blood pressure by stimulating the alpha$_2$ presynaptic inhibitory autoreceptors leading to an inhibition of noradrenergic activity (Zandberg et al. 1979). In a recent study depressed patients received a single dose of clonidine once when they were free of antidepressants and again after treatment with clorgyline (Siever et al. 1982). Clonidine initially led to a transient drop of blood pressure. Three day treatment with clorgyline did not influence the blood pressure response to clonidine. However, the clonidine hypotensive response was almost completely attenuated after four weeks of treatment with clorgyline. Diminution of the hypotensive response to clonidine has also been reported after chronic administration of the tricyclic antidepressant desipramine (Siever et al. 1981). The antagonism of clonidine response by long term antidepressant treatment may represent decreased sensitivity of brain alpha$_2$ adrenergic receptors and its appearance seems to correspond with the onset of antidepressant action. These findings suggest that the clinical effect in some antidepressants may be mediated by desensitization of the alpha$_2$ adrenergic receptor in the brain.

A review of findings derived from various research strategies suggests that several receptor abnormalities may occur in affective disorders. Sulser et al. (1978) have proposed that supersensitivity of beta postsynaptic adrenergic receptors is one of the pathogenetic factors in depression. They based this hypothesis on animal studies demonstrating that antidepressant treatments decrease both cAMP synthesis following norepinephrine stimulation and the density of beta adrenergic receptors. Electrophysiological studies in animals (Menkes and Aghajanian 1981, Wang and Aghajanian 1980), and clinical neuroendocrine studies in depressed patients (Carroll et al. 1976a, 1976b, Checkley 1978, Sachar et al. 1980, Brown and Shuey 1980, Matussek et al. 1980, Checkley et al. 1981) support a decreased sensitivity of postsynaptic alpha noradrenergic receptors in depression. Long-term antidepressant treatments increase the neuronal electrophysiologic response to serotonin (Wang and Aghajanian 1980, De Montigny 1980), suggesting a subsensitivity of serotonin receptors in depression. This notion is further supported by neuroendocrine clinical studies (Browne and Shuey 1980).

There are several problems in neurotransmitter receptor research. Most findings are derived from in vitro or animal experiments focusing on the action of antidepressant drugs or electroconvulsive therapy. Direct application of these findings to man is not possible since there may be species differences in brain receptors. The integration of receptor changes in response to antidepressant treatments is not simple since findings are derived from studies involving different experimental strategies. The physiological role of some brain receptors in humans, i.e., beta adrenergic, HT_2 serotoninergic, is not well understood. Finally, clinical studies attempting to demonstrate receptor changes in affective disorders use indirect measures of receptor function which lack specificity and are difficult to interpret.

Despite these problems, neurotransmitter receptor research has contributed new information and concepts on the pathogenesis of affective disorders. It complemented the studies of neurotransmitter output with measures of specific receptor function and elucidated several aspects of the complex neurotransmitter regulation in depression and mania. Changes in reciprocal regulation of alpha and beta adrenergic receptors or in the balance of adrenergic and serotoninergic function may be at least partly responsible for the therapeutic action of antidepressant treatments. Even if neurotransmitter disturbances are involved in the pathogenesis of affective disorders, output or receptor function abnormalities seem to be only a few steps of a series of events which by themselves can hardly account for the whole illness process.

Cholinergic Hypothesis

Although most biological research has focused on the role of brain catecholamines and serotonin in affective disorders, Janowsky et al. (1972) proposed that a cholinergic disturbance may contribute to the pathogenesis of depression. The cholinergic hypothesis postulates that an imbalance between adrenergic and cholinergic neurotransmitter activity exists in brain areas responsible for the regulation of affect. Depression has been proposed to be a disorder with central cholinergic preponderance, relative to norepinephrine and/or dopamine while the converse imbalance is associated with mania. The role of neurotransmitter balance in regulating biological functions has been long recognized. Specifically, balance between the adrenergic and cholinergic systems regulates several diverse functions such as heart rate, blood pressure, gastrointestinal mobility, and pupillary size. Imbalance between dopaminergic and cholinergic systems is implicated in Parkinson's disease (Yahr and Clough 1983). The concept of a disturbance in neurotransmitter balance in affective disorders has heuristic value and has led to several basic and clinical studies.

In animals, drugs increasing central cholinergic activity suppress locomotion and self-stimulating behavior and antagonize methylphenidate-induced stereotypes (Janowsky et al. 1972). Similar effects have been observed when animals were treated with reserpine which decreases the availability of monoamines in the brain (Janowsky et al. 1972, 1973).

Antiadrenergic drugs such as alphamethyldopa and propranolol lead to an increase in parasympathetic activity (Goodman et al. 1970). The behavioral effects of these drugs could be explained by their central cholinomimetic action as well as by their adrenergic action. Conversely, tricyclic antidepressants have central and peripheral anticholinergic action (Goodman et al. 1970). However, there is no association between the degree of anticholinergic activity of tricyclic antidepressants and their clinical efficacy (Janowsky et al. 1972, 1973). Moreoever, atropine, a strong anticholinergic agent, has no obvious antidepressant affect (Goodman et al. 1970).

Cholinesterase inhibitors that increase brain cholinergic activity have been reported to alter affective symptomatology. In an early study, the cholinesterase inhibitor DFP was observed to increase symptoms of depression and ameliorate symptoms of mania in patients with affective disorders (Rowntree et al. 1950). Depression has been reported to develop in patients poisoned with cholinesterase inhibitor insecticides (Gershon and Shaw 1961). Also, increased incidence of depression has been observed in orchardists exposed to such insecticides. Controlled studies of manic or hypomanic patients show that intravenous administration of the cholinomimetic agent physostigmine exerts an antimanic effect and often leads to apathy, lack of energy and psychomotor retardation (Janowsky et al. 1972, 1973a, 1973b, Carroll et al. 1973, Davis et al. 1978). In a small number of subjects, relatively high doses of physostigmine led initially to energy loss but later to an increase of manic symptomatology (Shopsin et al. 1975). The rebound increase of manic symptoms to levels higher than baseline has been interpreted as a result of adrenergic overcompensation for the initial cholinergic overactivity induced by physostigmine (Shopsin et al. 1975). Physostigmine has been observed to intensify depressive symptoms in manic and depressed patients (Davis et al. 1980, Modestin et al. 1973). Although the antimanic and depressant effect of physostigmine precede the onset of side effects such as nausea and vomiting (Janowsky 1980), it remains unclear whether its action on affective symptoms is specific.

There is evidence that patients with affective disorders are more sensitive to the effects of cholinomimetics than subjects without affective disorders. In a study of patients with tardive dyskinesia the cholinergic drug deanol led to depressive symptoms only in patients with history of affective disorders (Casey 1979). Controlled and uncontrolled studies of intravenous physostigmine administration suggest that symptoms of dysphoria, anxiety, anger, fatigue and tension develop more frequently in patients with affective disorders than in other psychiatric patients (Janowsky 1980, Janowsky et al. 1980, Janowsky et al. 1982, Davis and Davis 1979).

Neuroendocrine studies using physostigmine as a biological probe have been used to assess brain cholinergic activity in patients with affective disorders. In a placebo controlled study Janowsky (1980) and Janowsky et al. (1980) observed that physostigmine led to an acute elevation of serum prolactin, cortisol and growth hormone. Dysphoric and depressed mood correlated positively with the rise in serum prolactin. However, increase in serum growth hormone after physostigmine administration had a weak correlation with physostigmine induced dysphoria, while the serum cortisol elevation did not correlate with any of the physostigmine induced behavioral changes. Patients with affective disorders had significantly more energy, less dysphoria, and a higher prolactin rise than psychiatric patients without affective disorders (Janowsky 1980, Janowsky et al. 1980).

Janowsky et al. (1980) speculated that the prolactin response may be a marker for patients with affective disorders since it correlates with physostigmine's behavioral responses. However, it remains unclear whether neuroendocrine responses to physostigmine reflect changes in the cholinergic regulatory system or represent non-specific stress responses (Davis 1979).

A recently developed investigative strategy of the brain cholinergic system function uses cholinergic stimulation to precipitate onset of rapid eye movement (REM) sleep (Sitaram et al. 1976, Sitaram et al. 1978, Sitaram 1983). Animal studies have suggested that cholinergic mechanisms mediate the cycles of REM and non-REM sleep. Injections of the cholinomimetics carbachol or physostigmine into the brain stem of cats induce REM sleep (Amatruda et al. 1975). Anticholinergic agents on the other hand suppress REM sleep in animals (Domino and Stavinski 1971). Single-cell recording experiments in cats suggest that the neurons of the fastigial tegmental gigantocellular field (FTG) mediate REM sleep (Sitaram 1983). Bilateral FTG lesions have been reported to eliminate REM sleep in cats (Jones 1979). FTG cells have cholinergic receptors and are possibly cholinergic too since minute amounts of carbachol administered into FTG induce prolonged REM sleep (Amatruda et al. 1975). FTG neurons interact reciprocally with locus coeruleus and raphe nuclei neurons (Sitaram 1983). Since REM sleep appears to be regulated by cholinergic neurons interacting with adrenergic and serotonergic centers investigation of this function has been useful in testing the cholinergic hypothesis which postulates an imbalance of these neurotransmitters in affective disorders.

In a placebo controlled study Sitaram (1983) infused intravenously arecholine at the end of the first REM sleep period. The subjects were pretreated with methscopolamine to minimize peripheral anticholinergic side effects of arecholine. Arecholine induced REM sleep occurred significantly more rapidly in remitted and in depressed patients compared to normal control subjects. Fast induction of REM sleep after arecholine infusion was observed also in subjects with personal or family history of affective disorders (Sitaram 1983).

It has been reported that remitted bipolar patients have significantly higher density of the first REM period than normals (Sitaram 1983, Sitaram et al. 1982). Increased REM sleep density during the first REM period correlated significantly with rapid induction of REM sleep after arecholine administration (Sitaram 1983). This finding suggests a supersensitivity of the cholinergic system in patients with affective disorders.

In a preliminary study, Nurnberg et al. found a negative correlation between arecholine REM sleep induction and amphetamine-induced behavioral excitation in patients with affective disorders and normal control subjects (Sitaram 1983). Behavioral changes after amphetamine administration are presumably mediated by release of catecholamines in the synapse. Therefore, the presence of subsensitivity to amphetamine in subjects who are supersensitive to cholinergic challenge suggests a balance between cholinergic and catecholaminergic systems.

Conclusion

Review of recent research in affective disorders supports that several biological abnormalities are associated with these syndromes. This notion is consistent with the heterogeneous clinical presentation of affective disorders and their variable response to treatment. The early biological theories that proposed a single biochemical disturbance as a causative factor in affective disorders have not been validated. Sophisticated basic and clinical strategies of the last decade have provided new findings and also new concepts in affective disorders, i.e., biological heterogeneity of affective syndromes, abnormalities in reciprocal regulation of brain neurotransmitters, disturbances in pre- and postsynaptic receptor function. A new generation of antidepressants with a different mode of action has been introduced and new research is expected to follow. Increased awareness of the complexity of the biology, clinical presentation, and treatment of affective disorders have made the traditional debate between psychodynamic and biologic psychiatrists anachronistic and have led to a more comprehensive clinical approach.

REFERENCES

Amatruda, T. T. et al. (1975). Sleep cycle control and cholinergic mechanisms: Differential effects of carbachol at pontine brain stem sites. *Brain Research* 98: 501–515.

Anden, N. E., Rubensson, A., Fuxe, K., and Hokfelt, T. (1967). Evidence for dopamine receptor stimulation by apomorphine. *Journal of Pharmacy and Pharmacology* 19:627–629.

Asberg, M., Thoren, P., Traskman, I. et al. (1976). "Serotonin depression": a biochemical subgroup within the affective disorders? *Science* 191: 478–480.

Asberg, M., Traskinan, I., and Thoren, P. (1976). 5HIAA in the cerebrospinal fluid. *Archives of General Psychiatry* 33:1193–1197.

Banki, C. M. (1957). Correlation between cerebrospinal fluid amine metabolites and psychomotor activity in affective disorders. *Journal of Neurochemistry* 29:255–257.

Baudry, M., Martres, M. P., and Schwartz, J. C. (1976). Modulation in the sensitivity of noradrenergic receptors in the CNS studied by the responsiveness of the cyclic AMP system. *Brain Research* 116:111–124.

Beckmann, H. and Goodwin, F. K. (1975). Central norepinephrine metabolism and the prediction of antidepressant response to imipramine or amitriptyline; studies with urinary MHPG in unipolar depressed patients. *Archives of General Psychiatry* 32:17–21.

Berger, P. A., Faull, K. E., Kilkowski, J. et al. (1980). CSF monoamine metabolites in depression and schizophrenia. *American Journal of Psychiatry* 137:174–180.

Bergstrom, D. A., and Keller, K. J. (1979). Adrenergic and serotonergic receptor binding in rat brain after chronic desmethylimipramine treatment. *Journal of Pharmacology and Experimental Therapeutics* 209:256–261.

Blombery, P., Kopin, I. J., Gordon, E. K. et al. (1979). In *Catecholamines: Basic and Clinical Frontiers*. Vol. 2, ed. E. Usdin, I. J. Kopin, and J. Barchas, pp. 1875–1877. New York: Pergamon Press.

Bowers, M. B., Jr., Heninger, G. R., and Gerbode, F. A. (1969). Cerebrospinal fluid 5-hydroxyindoloacetic acid and homovanillic acid in psychiatric patients. *International Journal of Neuropharmacology* 8:255–262.

Brodie, H. K. H., Murphy, D. L., Goodwin, F. K., et al. (1971). Catecholamines and mania: the effect of alpha-methyl-paratyrosine on manic behavior and catecholamine metabolism. *Clinical Pharmacology and Therapeutics* 12:218–224.

Browne, W. A., and Shuey, I. (1980). Response to dexamethasone and subtype of depression. *Archives of General Psychiatry* 37:747–751.

Bulat, M., and Zivkovic, B. (1971). Origin of 5-hyroxyindoleacetic acid in the spinal fluid. *Science* 173:738–740.

Bunney, W. E. Jr., Pert, A., Rosenblatt, J. et al. (1979). In *Lithium Controversies and Unresolved Issues*. International Congress Series 478, ed. T. B. Cooper, S. Gershon, N. S. Kline, and M. Schou, pp. 675–685. Amsterdam: Excerpta Medica.

Cadoret, R. J. (1978). Evidence of genetic inheritance of primary affective disorders in adoptees. 135:463–466.

Campbell, I. C., Murphy, D. L., Gallagher, D. W. et al. (1979). Neurotransmitter-related adaptation in the central nervous system following chronic monoamine oxidase inhibition. In *Monoamine Oxidase: Structure, Function, and Altered Functions*, ed. T. P. Singer, R. W. Von Korff, D. L. Murphy, pp. 517–530. New York: Academic Press.

Carlsson, A., Rosengren, E., Bertler, A., and Nilsson, J. (1957). Effects of reserpine on the metabolism of catecholamines. In *Psychotropic Drugs*, ed. S. Garatini and V. Ghetti. Amsterdam: Elsevier.

Carroll, B. J., Curtis, G. C., and Mendels, J. (1976a). Neuroendocrine regulation in depression: limbic system-adrenocortical dysfunction. *Archives of General Psychiatry* 33:1039–1044.

_____ (1976b). Neuroendocrine regulation in depression: discrimination of depressed from nondepressed patients. *Archives of General Psychiatry* 33:1051–1058.

Carroll, B. J., Frazer, A., Schlesser, A. et al. (1973). Cholinergic reversal of manic symptoms. *Lancet* 1:427.

Casey, D. E. (1979). Mood alterations during deanol therapy. *Psychopharmacology* 62:187–191.

Cavagnini, F., Raggi, V., Micossi, P. et al. (1976). Effect of an antiserotonergic drug metergoline on the ACTH and cortisol response to insulin hypoglycemia and lysine vasopressin in man. *Journal of Clinical Endocrinology and Metabolism* 43:306–312.

Cedarbaum, J. M., and Aghajanian, G. K. (1977). Activation of locus coeruleus noradrenergic neurons by peripheral nerve stimulation. Abstract of Seventh Annual Meeting of Society for Neuroscience. Anaheim, California.

Charney, D. J., Menkes, D. B., and Heninger, G. R. (1981). Receptor sensitivity and the mechanism of action of antidepressant treatment. *Archives of General Psychiatry* 38:1160–1180.

Checkley, S. A. (1978). Corticosteroid and growth hormone responses to methylamphetamine in depressive illness. *Psychological Medicine* 8:1–9.

_____ (1979). Corticosteroid and growth hormone responses to methylamphetamine in depressive illness. *Psychological Medicine* 9:107–115.

Checkley, S. A., Slade, A. P., and Shur, E. (1981). Growth hormone and other responses to clonidine in patients with endogenous depression. *British Journal of Psychiatry* 138:51–55.

Coppen, A. J., Prange, A. J., Whybrow, P. C. et al. (1972). Abnormalities of indoleamines in affective disorders. *Archives of General Psychiatry* 26:474–478.

Coppen, A., Rao, Rama, V. A., Bishop, M., et al. (1980). Neuroendocrine studies in affective disorders: effect of ECT. *Journal of Affective Disorders* 2:311–315.

Crow, T. J. (1971). The relation between electrical self-stimulation sites and catecholamine-containing neurons in the rat mesencephalon. *Experientia* 27:662.

Crow, T. J., Spear, P. J., and Arbuthnott, G. W. (1972). Intracranial self-stimulation with electrodes in the region of the locus coeruleus. *Brain Research* 36:275–287.

Crowley, J. N., Hattox, J. W., Maas, J. W., Roth, R. H. (1978). 3-methoxy-4-hydroxy-phenyl ethylene glycol increase in plasma after stimulation of the nucleus locus coeruleus. *Brain Research* 141:380–384.

Dahlstrom, A., and Fuxe, K. (1965). Evidence for the existence of monoamine containing neurons in the central nervous system. I. Demonstration of monoamines in the cell bodies of brainstem neurons. *Acta Physiologica Scandinavica Supplement* 232:1–55.

Davis, J. M., Colburn, R., Murphy, D., and Robinson, D. S. (1979). Lithium: controversies and unresolved issues. International Congress Series 478, ed. T. D. Cooper, S. Gershon, N. S. Kline, and M. Schou, pp. 834–840. Amsterdam: Excerpta Medica.

Davis, K. L., Berger, P. A., Hollister, I. E. et al. (1978). Physostigmine in mania. *Archives of General Psychiatry* 35:119–122.

Davis, K. L., and Davis, B. M. (1979). Acetylcholine and anterior pituitary hormone secretion. In *Brain Acetylcholine and Neuropsychiatric Disease*, ed. K. L. Davis, and D. A. Berger, pp. 445–458. New York: Plenum Press.

DeMontigny, C. (1980). Electroconvulsive shock treatment increases responsiveness of forebrain neurons to serotonin: a microiontophoretic study in the rat. *Neuroscience Abstracts* 6:453.

DeMontigny, C., and Aghajanian, G. K. (1978). Tricyclic antidepressants. Long-term treatment increases responsivity of rat forebrain neurons to serotonin. *Science* 202:1303–1306.

Diller, N., Laszlo, J., Muller, B. et al. (1978). Activation of an inhibitory noradrenergic pathway projecting from the locus coeruleus to the cingulate cortex of the rat. *Brain Research* 154:61–68.

Domino, E. F., and Stawinski, M. (1971). Modification of the cat sleep cycle by hemicholinium-3, a cholinergic antisynthetic agent. *Research Communications in Chemical Pathology and Pharmacology* 2:461–465.

Ettigi, P. G., and Brown, G. M. (1977). Psychoneuroendocrinology of affective disorders: an overview. *American Journal of Psychiatry* 134:493–501.

Everitt, B. J., and Keverne, E. B. (1979). Models of depression based on behavioral observations of experimental animals. In *Psychopharmacology of Affective Disorders*, ed. E. S. Paykel, and A. Coppen, pp. 41–59. New York: Oxford University Press.

Faull, R. L. M., and Carman, J. B. (1968). Ascending projections of the substantia nigra. *Journal of Dairy Science* 132:73–92.

Fawcett, J. A., Mass, J. W., and Dekirmenjian, H. (1972). Depression and MHPG excretion. 26:246–251.

Freud, S. (1893). Studies in hysteria. *Standard Edition*. London: Hogarth Press, 1953.

Fuxe, K., Hamberger, B., and Hokfeld, T. (1968). Distribution of noradrenaline nerve terminals in cortical areas of the rat brain. *Brain Research* 8:125–131.

Gershon, S., and Shaw, F. H. (1961). Psychiatric sequelae of chronic exposure to organophosphorous insecticides. *Lancet* 1:1371–1374.

Ghose, K., Gupta, R., Coppen, A. et al. (1977). Antidepressant evaluation and the pharmacological actions of FG-4963 in depressive patients. *European Journal of Pharmacology* 42:31–37.

Gillespie, D. D., Manier, D. H., and Sulser, F. (1979). Electroconvulsive treatment: rapid subsensitivity of the norepinephrine receptor coupled adenylate cyclase system in brain linked to down regulation of B-adrenergic receptors. *Community Psychopharmacology* 3:191–194.

Gluckman, M. I., and Baum, T. (1969). The pharmacology of iprindole, a new antidepressant. *Psychopharmacologia* 15:169–185.

Goodlet, F., Mireylees, S. E., and Sugrue, M. F. (1977). Effects of mianserin, a new antidepressant, on the in vitro and in vivo uptake of monoamines. *British Journal of Pharmacology* 61:307–313.

Goodman, Gilman A., Goodman, L. S., and Gilman A. (1970). *The Pharmacolog-*

ical Basis of Therapeutics. 6th ed., pp. 418–427. Toronto: MacMillan Publishing Company.

_____ (1980). *The Pharmacological Basis of Therapeutics.* 6th ed., pp. 427–430. New York: MacMillan Publishing Company.

Goodwin, D. W., and Guze, S. B. (1979). Psychiatric Diagnosis. 2nd ed., pp. 3–27. New York: Oxford University Press.

Goodwin, F. K., and Bunney, W. E., Jr. (1971). Depressions following reserpine: a reevaluation. *Sem. Psych* 3:435–448.

Goodwin, F. K., Rubinovits, R., Jimerson, D. C., and Post, R. M. (1977). Serotonin and norepinephrine "subgroups" in depression: metabolite findings and clinical pharmacological-correlations. *Scientific Proceedings of the American Psychiatric Association* 130:108.

Goodwin, F. K., and Sack, R. I. (1973). Affective disorders: the catecholamine hypothesis revisited. In *Frontiers in Catecholamine Research*, pp. 1157–1164. London: Pergamon Press.

Goodwin, F. K., Post, R. M., Dunner, D. L. et al. (1973). Cerebrospinal fluid metabolites in affective illness: the probenecid technique. *American Journal of Psychiatry* 130:73–79.

Goodwin, F. K., and Sack, R. L. (1974). Behavioral effects of new dopamine-beta-hydroxylase inhibitor (fusaric acid) in man. *Journal of Psychiatric Research* 11:211–217.

Goodwin, F. K., and Zis, A. P. (1979). Lithium in the treatment of mania. *Archives of General Psychiatry* 36:840–844.

Greengard, P. (1976). Possible role for cyclic nuleotides and phosphorylated membrane proteins in postsynaptic actions of neurotransmitters. *Nature* 260:101–108.

Gruen, P. H., Sachar, E. J., Altman, N. et al. (1975). Growth hormone responses to hypoglycemia in postmenopausal depressed women. *Archives of General Psychiatry* 32:31–33.

Hoffer, B. J., Siggins, G. R., and Bloom, F. E. (1971). Studies on norepinephrine containing afferents to Purkinje cells of rat cerebellum: sensitivity of Purkinje cells to norepinephrine and related substances administered by microiontophoresis. *Brain Research* 25:523–534.

Hoffman, J. L., and Konchegul, L. (1955). Clinical and psychological observations on psychiatric patients treated with reserpine: a preliminary report. In *Reserpine in the Treatment of Neuropsychiatric, Neurological and Related Clinical Problems. Annals of the New York Academy of Science* 61:144–149.

Iversen, S. D. (1971). The effect of surgical lesions to frontal cortex and substantia nigra on amphetamine responses in rats. *Brain Research* 31:295–311.

Janowsky, D. S. (1980). The cholinergic nervous system and depression. In *The Psychobiology of Affective Disorders*, pp. 83–98. Boca Raton, Karger, Basel.

Janowsky, D. S., El-Yousef, M. K., Davis, J. M. et al. (1972a). A cholinergic-adrenergic hypothesis of mania and depression. *Lancet* 2:632–635.

_____ (1972b). Cholinergic antagonism of methylphenidate-induced stereotyped behavior. *Psychopharmacologia* 27:295–303.

_____ (1973a). Parasympathetic suppression of manic symptoms by physostigmine. *Archives of General Psychiatry* 28:542–547.

_____ (1973b). Acetylcholine and depression. *Psychosomatic Medicine* 35:568.

Janowsky, E. S., Risch, S. C., Judd, L. L. et al. (1980). Acetylcholine in affective disorders. Annual Meeting of the American Psychiatric Association, San Francisco.

Janowsky, D. S., Risch, C., Parker, D., and Judd, L. L. (1982). Potential behavioral, neuroendocrine, and cardiovascular markers of central cholinergic function. In *Alzheimer's Disease: A Report of Progress*. Vol. 19, *Aging*. ed. S. Corkin, D. L. Davis, J. H. Growdon, J. H. Usdin, R. Wurtman, pp. 49–53. New York: Raven Press.

Johnson, R. W., Reisine, T., Spotnitz, S. et al. (1980). Effects of desipramine and yohimbine on a_2 and B-adrenoceptor sensitivity. *European Journal of Pharmacology* 67:123–127.

Jones, B. E. (1979). Elimination of paradoxical sleep by lesions of the pontine gigantocellular tegmental field in the cat. *Neuroscience Letters* 13:285.

Jouvet, M. (1968). Insomnia and decrease of cerebral 5-hydroxytryptamine after destruction of the raph system in the cat. *Adv Pharmac*, Suppl 6B: 265–279.

Klerman, G. L. (1976). Overview of depression. In *Comprehensive Textbook of Psychiatry*. II. ed. A. M. Freedman, H. Kaplan, and B. J. Sadock, pp. 1003–1012. Baltimore: The Williams and Wilkins Company.

Kline, N. S., and Stanley, A. M. (1955). Use of reserpine in a neuropsychiatric hospital. In *Reserpine in the Treatment of Neuropsychiatric Neurological and Related Clinical Problems. Annals of the New York Academy of Science* 61: 85–91.

Kraepelin, E. (1921). *Manic-Depressive Insanity and Paranoia*. Edinburgh: E. S. Livingstone.

Krulich, L. (1976). The role of central monoamines in stress-related changes of the secretion of prolactin and TSH. *Psychopharmacology Bulletin* 12:22–24.

Leonard, B. E. (1974). Some effects of a new tetracyclic antidepressant compound, Org GB94, on the metabolism of monoamines in the rat brain. *Psychopharmacology* 36:221–236.

Lewis, A. (1967). Melancholia: a historical review. In *The State of Psychiatry: Essays and Addresses*. New York: Science House.

Loizou, L. A. (1969). Projections of the nucleus locus coeruleus in the albino rat. *Brain Research* 15:563–566.

Maas, J. W., Dekirmenjian, H., and DeLeon-Jones, F. In *Frontiers in Catecholamine Research*, ed. E. Usdin, and S. Snyder, pp. 1091–1096. New York: Pergamon Press.

Maas, J. W., Fawcett, J. A., and Dekirmenjian, H. (1972). Catecholamine metabolism, depressive illness, and drug response. *Archives of General Psychiatry* 26:252–262.

Maas, J. W. (1976). Biogenic amines in depression. *Archives of General Psychiatry* 32:1357–1361.

Matussek, N., Ackenheil, M., Hippius, H. et al. (1980). Effect of clonidine on growth hormone release in psychiatric patients and controls. *Psychiatry Research* 2:25–36.

Medical Research Council. (1972). Modified amine hypothesis for the aetiology of affective disorders. *Lancet* 1:573–577.

Meek, J. L., and Neff, N. H. (1973). Is cerebrospinal fluid the major avenue for the removal of 5-hydroxyindoloacetic acid from the brain? *Neuropharmacology* 12:497–499.

Menkes, D. B., and Aghajanian, G. K. (1981). Alpha-l-adrenoceptor-mediated responses in the lateral geniculate nucleus are enhanced by chronic antidepressant treatment. *European Journal of Pharmacology* 74:27–35.

Mettler, L. A. (1964). Substantia nigra and parkinsonism. *Archives of Neurology* 11:529–542.

Mishra, R., Janowsky, A., and Sulser, F. (1980). Action of mianserin and zimelidine on the norepinephrine receptor coupled adenylate cyclase system in brain: subsensitivity without reduction in B-adrenergic receptor binding. *Neuropharmacology* 19:983–987.

Mishra, R., and Sulser, F. (1978). Role of serotonin reuptake inhibition in the development of subsensitivity of the norepinephrine (NE) receptor coupled adenylate cyclase system. *Common Psychopharmacology* 2:365–370.

Mogilnicka, E., Arbilla, S., and Depoortere, H. et al. Rapid-eye movement sleep deprivation increases the density of ^{3}H-dihydroalprenolol and ^{3}H-imipramine biding sites in the rat cerebral cortex. *European Journal of Pharmacology* 65: 289–292.

Modestin, J. J., Hunger,, R. B., and Schwartz, R. B. V. (1973). Uber die depressogene wirkung von physostigmin. *Archiv Fuer Psychiatrie Und Nerven-Krankheiten* 218:67.

Mueller, P. S., Heninger, G. R., and McDonald, R. K. (1969). Insulin tolerance test in depression. *Archives of General Psychiatry* 21:587–594.

Murphy, D. L. et al. (1981). Cardiovascular changes accompanying monoamine oxidase inhibition in man. In *Function and Regulation of Monoamine Enzymes: Basic and Clinical Aspects*, ed. E. Usdin, N. Weiner, and C. Creveling, pp. 549–560. Hampshire, England: MacMillan.

Murphy, D. L., Siver, L. J., Cohen, R. M., Roy, B. F., Pickar, D. (1983). Some clinical evidence supporting the possible involvement of neurotransmitter receptor sensitivity changes in the action of antidepressant drugs during longer term treatment. In *The Affective Disorders*, ed. J. M. Davis, and J. W. Maas, pp. 125–134. Washington, DC: American Psychiatric Press.

Nurnberger, F. I. and Gershon, E. S. (1982). Genetics. In *Handbook of Affective Disorders*, ed. E. S. Paykel, pp. 126–145. New York: The Guilford Press.

Overall, J. E., Hollister, L. E. Pokorny, A. D. et al. (1962). Drug therapy in depressions. Controlled of imipramine, isocarboxazid, dextroamphetamine, amobarbitall, and placebo. *Clinical Pharmacology and Therapeutics* 3:16–22.

Peroutka, S. J., and Snyder, S. H. (1980a). Regulation of serotonin$_2$ (5-HT$_2$) receptors labeled with H-spiroperidol by chronic treatment with the antidepressant amitriptyline. *Journal of Pharmacology and Experimental Therapeutics* 215:582-587.

Peroutka, S. J., and Snyder, S. H. (1980b). Chronic antidepressant treatment decreases spiroperidol-labeled serotonin receptor binding. *Science* 210:88–90.

Post, R. M., and Goodwin, F. K. (1978). Handbook of Psychopharmacology. Vol. 13, ed. L. I. Iversen, S. D. Iversen, and S. H. Snyder, pp. 147–185. New York: Plenum Press.

Post, R. M., Kopin, J., and Goodwin, F. K. (1974). The effects of cocaine on depressed patients. *American Journal of Psychiatry* 131:511–517.

Post, R. M., Zimerson, D. C., Bunney, W. E., Jr. et al. (1980). Dopamine and mania: behavioral and biochemical effects of the dopamine receptor blocker pimozide. *Psychopharmacology* 67:297–305.

Rauwolfia Story, The (1954). Summit, N.J.: Ciba Pharmaceutical Products.

Rosloff, B. N., and Davis, J. M. (1974). Effect of iprindol on norepinephrine turnover and transport. *Psychopharmacologia* 40:53–64.

Rowntree, D. W., Neven, S., and Wilson, A. (1950). The effects of diisopropylfluorophosphonate in schizophrenia and manic depressive psychosis. *Journal of Neurology, Neurosurgery, and Psychiatry* 13:47–62.

Sachar, E. J., Asnis, G., Nathan, S. et al. (1980). Dextroamphetamine and cortisol in depression: Morning plasma cortisol levels suppressed. *Archives of General Psychiatry* 37:755-757.

Sachar, F. J., Finkelstein, J., Hellman, L. (1971). Growth hormone responses in depressive illness: response to insulin tolerance test. *Archives of General Psychiatry* 25:263-269.

Sachar, E. J., Nathan, R. S., Asnis, G. et al. (1980). Neuroendocrine studies of major depressive disorder. *Acta Psychiatrica Scandinavica* (Suppl. 260):201-210.

Schildkraut, J. J. (1965). The catecholamine hypothesis of affective disorders: a review of supporting evidence. *American Journal of Psychiatry* 122:509-522.

Schildkraut, J. J., Orsulak,P. J., Schatzberg, A. F. et al. (1978). Towards a biochemical classification of depressive disorders: differences in urinary excretion of MHPG and other catecholamine metabolites in clinically defined subtypes of depressions. *Archives of General Psychiatry* 35:1427-1433.

Schubert, J. (1973). Effect of chronic lithium treatment on monoamine metabolism in rat brain. *Psychopharmacologia* 32:301-311.

Schultz, J. (1976). Psychoactive drug effects on a system which generates cyclic AMP in brain. *Nature* 261:417-418.

Sellinger-Barnette, M. M., Mendels, J., and Frazer, A. (1980). The effect of psychoactive drugs on beta-adrenergic receptor binding sites in rat brain. *Neuropharmacology* 19:447-454.

Sheard, M. H., and Aghajanian, G. K. (1968). Stimulation of midbrain raphe neurons: behavioral effects of serotonin release. *Life Sciences* 7:19-25.

Shopsin, B., Janowsky, D. S., Davis, J. M. et al. (1975). Rebound phenomena in manic patients following physostigmine. *Neuropsychobiology* I:180-187.

Shore, P. A., Silver, S. L., and Brodie, B. B. (1955). Interaction of reserpine, serotonin, and lysergic acid diethylamide in brain. *Science* 122:284-285.

Siever, L. J., Cohen, R. M., and Murphy, D. L. (1981). Antidepressants and a_2-adrenergic autoreceptor desensitization. *American Journal of Psychiatry* 138:681-682.

Siever, L. J., Uhde, T. W., and Murphy, D. L. (1982). Possible subsensitization of a_2-adrenergic receptors by chronic monoamine oxidase inhibitor treatment in psychiatric patients. *Psychiatry Research* 6:293-302.

Sitaram, N. (1983). Faster cholinergic REM sleep induction as a possible trait marker of affective illness. In *The Affective Disorders*, ed. J. M. Davis and J. W. Maas, pp. 125-133. Washington, DC: American Psychiatric Press.

Sitaram, N. et al. (1982). Cholinergic regulation of mood and REM sleep: potential model and marker of vulnerability to affective disorder. *American Journal of Psychiatry* 139:571-576.

Sitaram, N., Moore, A. M., Gillin, J. C. (1978). The cholinergic induction of dreaming in man. *Archives of General Psychiatry* 35:1239-1243.

Sitaram, N., Wyatt, R. J., Dowson, S. et al. (1976). REM sleep induction by physostigmine infusion during sleep. *Science* 191:1281-1283.

Snyder, S. H. (1976). The dopamine hypothesis of schizophrenia: focus on the dopamine receptor. *American Journal of Psychiatry* 133:197-202.

Sulser, F. (1979). New perspectives on the mode of action of antidepressant drugs. *Trends in Pharmacological Science* 1:92-94.

Sulser, F., Vetulani, J., and Mobley, P. L. (1978). Mode of action of antidepressant drugs. *Biochemical Pharmacology* 27:257-261.

Svensson, T. H. (1980). Effect of chronic treatment with tricyclic antidepressant drugs on identified brain noradrenergic and serotonergic neurons. *Acta Psychiatrica Scandinavica* 61 (Suppl. 280):121–131.

Svensson, T. H., and Usdin, T. (1978). Feedback inhibition of brain noradrenaline neurons by tricyclic antidepressants: a-Receptor mediation. *Science* 202:1089–1091.

Ungerstedt, U. (1971). Stereotaxic mapping of the monoamine pathways in the rat brain. *Acta Physiologica Scandinavica* (Suppl. 367):1–48.

Van Praag. (1977). Significance in biochemical parameters in the diagnosis, treatment and prevention of affective disorders. *Biological Psychiatry* 12:101–131.

Vetulani, J., Pik, A., and Nikitin, K. (1980). The effect of chronic imipramine treatment of rats on ^{3}H-clonidine binding in the brain. *Progress in Neuropsychopharmacology* 12 (Suppl. 1):349.

Vetulani, J., Stawarz, R. J., and Sulser, F. (1976). Adaptive mechanisms of the noradrenergic cyclic AMP generating system in the limbic forebrain of the rat: adaptation to persistent changes in the availability of norepinephrine (NE). *Journal of Neurochemistry* 27:661–666.

Vetulani, J., and Sulser, F. (1975). Action of various antidepressant treatments reduce reactivity of noradrenergic cyclic AMP-generating system in limbic forebrain. *Nature* 257:495–496.

Wang, R. Y., and Aghajanian, G. K. (1980). Enhanced sensitivity of amygdaloid neurons to serotonin and norepinephrine after chronic antidepressant treatment. *Common Psychopharmacology* 4:83–90.

Winokur, G. (1981). *Depression. The Facts*, pp. 86–99. New York: Oxford University Press.

Wolfe, B. B., Harden, T. K., Sporn, J. R. et al. (1978). Presynaptic modulation of beta-adrenergic receptors in rat cerebral cortex after treatment with antidepressants. *Journal of Pharmacology and Experimental Therapeutics* 207:446–457.

Yahr, M. D., and Clough, C. G. (1983). Parkinson's disease. In *H. Houston Merritt Memorial Volume*, ed. M. D. Yahr, pp. 1–26. New York: Raven Press.

Zandberg, P., DeJong, W., and deWeid, D. (1979). Effect of catecholamine receptor stimulating agents on blood pressure after local application in the nucleus tractus solitarii of the medulla oblongata. *European Journal of Pharmacology* 55:43–56.

Zis, A. P., Cowdry,, R. W., and Wehr, T. A. et al. (1979). Tricyclic induced mania and MHPG excretion. *Psychiatry Research* 1:93–99.

Zis, A. P., and Goodwin, F. K. (1982). The amine hypothesis. In *Handbook of Affective Disorders*, ed. E. S. Paykel, pp. 175–190. New York: The Guilford Press.

CHAPTER NINETEEN

Sleep and Depression

David R. Hawkins, M.D.

Since at least the time of Hippocrates, sleep disturbances have been a hallmark of depression. In more modern times, clinical experience has underscored the finding that early morning awakening is particularly characteristic of depression in contrast to sleep disturbances associated with other types of mental illness.

Poets and other writers have been aware of the link between sleep (or its absence) to mental distress, especially links to guilt which is, of course, a major issue in the psychology of the depressed individual. Shakespeare was particularly aware of this to which many passages in "Hamlet" and "Macbeth" attest. After his murders, guilt-ridden Macbeth continues to see Banquo's ghost. Lady Macbeth says to him, "You lack the season of all natures, sleep" (III, iv, 141). In Coleridge's "The Rhyme of the Ancient Mariner," sleep comes finally as restitution when the Mariner has suffered countless sleepless days after killing the albatross. He says:

"Oh sleep! it is a gentle thing,
Beloved from pole to pole!
To Mary Queen the praise be given!
She sent the gentle sleep from Heaven,
That slid into my soul." (lines 292–296)

It is part of cultural knowledge that guilt interferes with sleep. Witness the German saying, "Ein Gutes Gewissen ist ein sanftes Ruhkissen" — "A good conscience is a soft pillow."

Relationship of Sleep and Depression

Good clinicians have identified changes in the diurnal rhythm of many depressed patients, changes linked presumably to early morning waking. These patients typically feel most unhappy and lacking in drive early in the morning and feel somewhat better as the day goes on. Manic patients typically sleep very little (or not at all, in some extreme cases), but subjectively are not troubled by lack of sleep. They regard sleep as a waste of time. We had no clear objective evidence for the abnormal sleep pattern of those with affective disease until, in recent years, the electroencephalogram (EEG) has been applied to the study of sleep in depressed patients.

Prior to the upsurge of scientific interest in sleep which followed the discovery by Aserinsky and Kleitman (1953) of the rapid eye movement (REM) sleep state, only one group of investigators had utilized the EEG to study the sleep patterns of depressed patients. Diaz-Guerrero et al. (1946) utilized the EEG to study the sleep throughout the entire night of six manic-depressive, depressed type patients under the age of 40. The team was able to eludicate the principle characteristics of sleep in depressed patients, but since they did not know of the REM phase, they did not identify it. Diaz-Guerrero et al. did say: "The disturbed sleep of patients with manic-depressive psychosis, depressed type, is not only characterized by difficulty in falling asleep and/or by early or frequent awakenings, but by both a greater proportion of sleep which is light and more frequent oscillations from one level of sleep to another than normally occurs."

Sleep Psychophysiology

It is suggested that the reader who is not familiar with modern sleep psychophysiology refer to a comprehensive treatise such as "Human Sleep and Its Disorders" (Mendelson, Gillin and Wyatt 1977) or "Sleep Disorders: Diagnosis and Treatment (Williams and Karacan 1978). We present here only a brief statement of the subject.

Normal sleep consists of two phases which are profoundly different physiologically. The first phase, now usually referred to as non-rapid eye movement (NREM) sleep, has also been termed quiet sleep, slow wave sleep (SWS), and synchronized sleep (S sleep). Following its onset, the sleeper enters a state of unconsciousness characterized by relaxed musculature and slow regular heart and respiratory rates. As measured by the electromyograph, there is a residual continuing muscle tonus.

Cerebral activity during NREM sleep decreases shortly after onset and the threshhold for arousal becomes increasingly great. By convention, four stages of NREM sleep can be detected by the EEG. Stage 4 consists almost entirely of large slow regular waves called delta activity. It is the stage of the lowest level of body and cerebral activity; most of delta wave sleep is found in the first third of the night. Starting usually in the fifth decade, delta activity, which in the young occupies close to 20 percent of the sleep period, begins to decrease and is thought to be practically absent in later life. During delta sleep, the most growth hormone is released into the blood stream. When a normal young individual has been totally deprived of sleep for several nights, the percentage of delta sleep increases on the recovery night, suggesting a special need for this stage of sleep.

After about 90 minutes of NREM sleep, the normal adult sleeper enters the phase of rapid eye movement (REM) sleep. Other names which have been used for this phase or state include paradoxical, activated or desynchronized (D) sleep. This phase, which recurs cyclically about every 90 minutes for four to six episodes during a typical night's sleep, is unique neurophysiologically and has been termed by Snyder (1963) the third organismic state. It is perhaps unfortunate for terminology that the discovery of the REM phase was based on the bursts of synchronized rapid eye movements, since there are many other activities which characterize it, for example, bursts of activity in the small muscles attached to the small bones in the inner ear. A center in the pons known as the nucleus ceruleus, which contains the most actively norepinephrine secreting neurons in the central nervous system, seems to control many of the activities which occur in this phase of sleep.

Probably the most striking and important feature of REM sleep is the enormous activity of the central nervous system which at that time equals or exceeds that of the waking state. This is true whether the activity is measured by the amount of neuronal firing or overall metabolic activity. The autonomic nervous system is at a high state of arousal as indicated by irregular heart and respiratory rate and by the phasic bursts of rapid eye movement and movements of the ossicles of the inner ear. These latter events are spoken of as the phasic events of the REM period.

REM sleep seems to be controlled by centers in the pons including the nucleus ceruleus. The increase in CNS acitivity and inhibition of motor activity and penile erection are termed the tonic aspects of this period which, under normal circumstances, never occurs until more than 45 minutes (typically 90 minutes) after onset of NREM sleep.

When subjects are wakened from the REM period, they recall vividly remembered, usually long and detailed dreams, as contrasted with rare reports from NREM periods. Most recall, if any from NREM, consists of short fragments of logical thought.

If a subject is selectively deprived of REM sleep in the sleep laboratory for several nights and the sleep pattern of the recovery night is studied, the percentage of sleep occupied by REM has increased. If, however, a subject is totally deprived of sleep for several days, stage 4 sleep on the recovery night is found to have increased considerably. The implication of these studies is that stage 4 and REM sleep are needed more urgently than the other stages, the need for stage 4 being most compelling.

Sleep Laboratory Studies of Affective Illness

With this hasty review of sleep psychophysiology as a background, let us return to an examination of the sleep of those with affective disorders. We shall see that there is great variation: in the young and mildly depressed individual sleep may be increased, while in the other depressed patient it is decreased and fragmented.

Not long after the significance of REM sleep began to become known, a number of sleep laboratories including our own began to systematically study the sleep of depressed patients. Initially, these were cross-sectional studies. The early findings confirmed the clinical impression that sleep in depression is indeed disturbed. While there is usually some increase in sleep onset latency, the striking disturbance is in what Kupfer (1975) later termed sleep continuity. Patients awaken frequently, particularly in the latter portion of the night. The classic early morning wakening described in psychiatric texts is not as impressive in the sleep laboratory, but we think that is an artifact of the sound, light, and temperature control of the sleep laboratory. Certainly, there is some earlier wakening, but the sleep for several hours often is very near waking and is punctuated by many actual brief wakenings. The most consistent finding is a marked diminution to absence of delta sleep. Moreover, unlike most other dimensions of sleep abnormality in the depressed patient, delta sleep does not return to normal immediately on clearing of the depression. This finding proved not to be specific for depression being seen in hypothyroidism, mental retardation, and the aged.

There were many more stage shifts than normal and wave forms of the EEG ordinarily not seen together, such as Alpha-Delta Sleep (Hauri and Hawkins 1971) were frequently seen in juxtaposition. In severe depression other than depression among the young, the sleep mechanisms are severely affected.

Zung et al. (1964) demonstrated that the threshold of stimuli which would cause wakefulness was decreased in every stage of sleep in depressed patients as compared with normal controls. In our first studies (Hawkins and Mendels 1966, Mendels and Hawkins 1967) we found that the mean percentage of REM time during a night's sleep was approximately normal but there was much greater variability with some depressed patients having a distinctly increased amount of REM sleep. Our assessment of this finding was congruent with that of Snyder (1974), who also emphasized that this probably represented a rebound phenomenon after some period of relative REM deprivation in the poor sleep of patients with depression. In our first report to the Association for the Psychophysiological Study of Sleep (APSS) in 1961, we reported finding that the initial REM period, instead of being foreshortened as in normals, was about the same length as the other periods in depressed patients. This finding was later established by Vogel et al. (1980).

Initially there seemed to be more NREM than REM abnormalities in depression, but then it became apparent that the amount and patterning of eye movements within an REM period were different in depressives. The depressives had bursts of increased eye movement activity intermixed with relatively long periods of eye movement quiescence. We showed that a measure called percent phasic REM activity correlated inversely with degree of depressed mood in depressed patients, i.e., the more depressed, the less percent phasic REM (Hauri and Hawkins 1971).

Possible Biological Markers?

Others have demonstrated that there is an increase of the number of actual eye movements and call this increased REM density. Kupfer (1976) demonstrated that REM onset latency was decreased in depressed patients. He termed this finding a psychobiologic marker for depression, and he and Foster (1975) reported that the more severe the depression, the shorter the mean REM latency. Other investigators (Mendelson et al. 1977) have confirmed this finding, and there seems little doubt that any group of biologically depressed patients will have a mean REM latency shorter than normal, or shorter than their matched controls. (Rush et al. 1982) studied a group of depressed patients separated into endogenous (E) vs. nonendogenous (NE) types utilizing both sleep studies and the dexamethasone suppression test (DST). The DST in this study was a clear marker of E but only 41 percent of the Es were nonsuppressors. REM latency decrease was more sensitive as a discriminator but less specific. Short REM latency was found in virtually all nonsuppressors. However, many patients with low REM latency had a normal DST. When both tests were used they discriminated better than when either test was given alone. However, over 40 percent of the patients showed neither biological derangement. The authors inferred that major depressions are biologically heterogeneous.

It has been the fond hope of those who talk of biological markers that they might prove effective clinical tests for primary depression. However, at best a significant percent of depressives do not show a shortened REM latency. (Most studies report only mean and standard deviations, hence it is not possible to know how many subjects individually would have been found to have an abnormally low REM latency). Speaking pragmatically, the time and expense involved in a sleep laboratory study would preclude its clinical diagnostic use unless it were much more sensitive and reliable than other means of diagnosing depression.

Schulz et al. (1979) studied the frequency distribution of REM latency in depressed patients and found two peaks of REM sleep onset rather than a unimodal distribution. They concluded that depressed patients experience an abnormality in regulation of REM/NREM sleep cycles with many sleep onset REM phases.

Are Sleep Changes State- or Trait-Related?

Recent studies question whether the sleep changes found in severely depressed patients are entirely state-related, that is, whether they come and go with the depressive episode or are to an extent trait-related. Our study (Hauri et al. 1974) of 14 patients who had previously been hospitalized for a major primary depression but who had been in a clinical remission for at least six months suggests that there are trait-related sleep disturbances in patients who have had a serious depression. The sleep abnormalities were not great in those previous patients but were statistically significant when compared to carefully matched controls. The remitted depressives showed mild continuity disturbances and decreased delta sleep. Surprisingly, they showed fewer interruptions in the REM periods. There were both intra- and inter-subject variabilities within the depressed group. (Schulz and Trojan 1979, Sitaram et al. 1982) have demonstrated increased REM density in remitted bipolar patients.

Puig-Antich et al. have made the interesting observation that prepubertal children with depression show no REM sleep changes when compared with normals and neurotic nondepressed controls. However, the same depressed children when in clinical remission showed a distinct decrease in REM latency time (Puig-Antich et al. 1983).

Remitted depressed patients studied to date have some sleep abnormalities. Whether or not these antedate an initial clinical episode of depression remains at present unknown. It seems plausible that the sleep abnormalities are a reflection of genetic factors predisposing to affective illness. There, of course, remains the possibility that an episode of depression (or perhaps mania) leads to a more or less permanent alteration in the complex systems that control the sleep mechanisms.

The seemingly paradoxical findings in the childhood depressives of less decrease in REM latency during the actual depression are difficult to understand. They should certainly be studied as should the whole area of the sleep of remitted patients. While it seems unlikely that sleep studies will be used clinically to diagnose affective illness, the use of sleep studies to identify subjects at risk for affective illness for research purposes seems a distinct possibility after we learn more about sleep between episodes of affective illness.

Sleep Manipulation as Therapy

There have been several differing types of manipulation of sleep which have had some therapeutic efficacy for depression. Reasoning from the observation that all successful antidepressant drugs, with the exception of lithium, have REM suppressing properties, Vogel et al. (1975) decided to try selective REM deprivation to treat depressed patients. They found that 17 out of 34 endogenously depressed patients had a satisfactory therapeutic response, a ratio close to that which might have been expected had imipramine been used. Because it is so costly and arduous, this method will never be used clinically but it is of great research interest.

Pflug and Tolle (1971) pioneered the use of total sleep deprivation for one night as a means of treating depression. This seemingly paradoxical means of treatment has produced striking temporary improvement in a significant number of patients. In many clinics, especially in Europe, it is used in combination with antidepressant drugs, leading in successful cases to an earlier amelioration of the depression. More recently Schilgen and Tolle (1980) have demonstrated that deprivation of sleep in the second half of the night is even more efficacious in endogenously depressed patients and especially in those with major vital or vegetative symptoms. They postulate, as have others, that it is critical for the patient to be awake at the time when there is a change in the direction of vital functions which fluctuate with the diurnal cycle. They mention blood pressure and pulse rate which reach a low point sometime after 2 A.M. in a typical night's sleep (with bedtime at 9 P.M.) and then start to rise. Perhaps more crucial is body temperature, which reaches a low point in the latter part of the night. Of course, other functions vary, too, and the important issue may be in changing the diurnal rhythm. It is a possibility, since the majority of REM sleep occurs in the second half of the night, that REM deprivation helps to ameliorate depression. At this point we can't do more than speculate, but the disruption of the diurnal cycle seems the most attractive hypothesis and perhaps the results of Vogel et al. (1980) utilizing REM deprivation in depression were actually more related to the disruption than the REM deprivation per se.

Another piece of evidence in favor of the latter hypothesis, also fascinating in itself, is the demonstration by Wehr et al. (1979) that some rapidly cycling bipolar patients can be improved by inducing a phase shift in the subjects' sleep-wake cycle. In their successful use of this technique, they advanced the time of going to sleep and awakening by six hours in a 57-year-old woman who cycled rapidly and was relatively unresponsive to other modes of treatment. As a result of the first phase advance from an 11 P.M.–7 A.M. sleep period to one from 5 P.M.–1 A.M., she shifted in two days from a depressed to a normal or slightly hypomanic state which lasted two weeks. Another advance of six hours was again temporarily successful. Two subsequent advances were without systematic change. On the first two successful advances, the patients' circadian temperature rhythm advanced. In the case of the other two advances, the temperature rhythm delayed. In two other depressed patients there were improvements gained from this technique. Others did not respond. The similarity to the previous partial sleep deprivation is obvious. The question then arises as to what the critical issue is: sleep deprivation, phase advance, or being in a waking state at the time of change from fall to rise in certain vital functions? It should be noted that the phase shift in these few subjects lasted longer than the remission usually brought about by sleep deprivation. Phase shifting also differs from treatment with antidepressant drugs or REM deprivation; when successful, the effect is very prompt.

Biochemical Links Between Sleep and Depression

At first intuitively and later by systematic clinical observation activities, we have noted and demonstrated connections between sleep and depression. It is now exciting to note that basic biochemical links are being established. The broad strokes are worth painting here. Increasingly, it is becoming apparent that key neurohumoral transmitters, such as norepinephrine, serotonin, and acetylcholine play a major role in the mechanisms of affective illness even though the catecholamine hypothesis as such no longer stands. As the biochemical mechanisms involved in the regulation and switching from one phase of sleep to the other and to the waking state are studied, we see that the same neurotransmitters involved in affective illness are crucial for sleep regulation. With extirpation of the serotonin secreting neurones of the median raphe, sleep is no longer possible (Jouvet 1969). The neurones of the nucleus ceruleus which Jouvet early demonstrated as being a key center in the control of REM sleep are the greatest norepinephrine secretors in the central nervous system. Gillin and his colleagues (Gillin 1983) have demonstrated that a change in the level of acetyl choline can lead to an earlier onset of REM sleep. These tantalizing basic links cry for better explication.

Chronobiological Changes

There have been other earlier observations which suggested a link between affective illness and circadian rhythm changes. Before discussing them, let us review some of the things already known about circadian rhythms.

In both the animal and vegetable kingdoms organisms undergo complicated biochemical changes in a rhythmic fashion every 24 hours. Evidence indicates that the changes are under endogenous control. Each species has a periodic rhythm that approaches but does not span precisely 24 hours. The cycle of the human being is approximately 25 hours and under normal conditions is entrained to a 24-hour rhythm by *Zeitgebers*, (a German neologism for timegivers), light-dark being the usual one. There is evidence that there are two principle human pacemakers, an "x" pacemaker which controls body temperature rhythm, REM sleep cycles, and cortisol secretion and a "y" pacemaker which controls the rest activity cycle, slow wave sleep, and secretion of growth hormone. The "y" pacemaker is in the suprachiasmatic nuclei of the ventral hypothalamus. The "x" pacemaker seems to reside elsewhere. Under certain free-running conditions where all *Zeitgebers* are excluded: for example, living in a cave without clocks, the two rhythms may become desynchronized, the rest activity cycle having a period of about 33 hours and the body temperature rhythm a period of 24.5 hours.

It has long been known that affective illness is characterized by changes that have been proven to involve circadian rhythm. The tendency to phase advance in depression is reflected in early morning wakening and in mood changes from early morning to night. The recent discovery of reduced REM latency is probably also a reflection of this. The manic patient probably is phase-delayed.

If the sleep pattern is reversed by 180°, alterations occur in the sleep pattern (as measured in the sleep laboratory) which are very similar to those found in patients with primary depression (Weitzman et al. 1970). Moreover, shifts in the timing of sleep lead to dysphoric mood and poor performance (Kripke et al. 1978), symptoms that are similar to those of retarded depression.

Another link in the connection between circadian rhythms and affective illness is the discovery that, of the very few substances which have the ability to alter circadian rhythms, all are pharmacologic agents which have proven effective in the treatment of affective illness. Lithium salts have been reported to lengthen the period of body temperature rhythm in healthy subjects (Johnson et al. 1979, Wirz-Justice et al. 1982).

Doerr et al. (1979) conducted a study of a 66-year-old male patient with 48-hour unipolar depressive cycles in an isolation unit without *Zeitgebers*. The man alternated between good and bad days and revealed that he switched regularly from a normal to a depressive mood during sleep between 10 P.M. and 2:30 A.M. The more variable time of switch to a good mood generally occurred in the afternoon or evening.

As already discussed, complete or partial sleep deprivation is effective in the temporary improvement of many depressed patients. This almost certainly works by influencing the circadian rhythms and is a further indication of the connection between affective illness and circadian rhythm.

Chronobiology is the term applied to the rapidly growing study of biological rhythms. It has not only great promise for better understanding basic mechanisms but already has demonstrated that there are many clinical and public health applications beyond those which apply to affective illness.

We must deal here with these questions: In what fashion are affective illness and altered rhythms linked? What are the biological implications? Are the alterations in the biologic clock fundamental or are they just a manifestation of some more basic process? If the rhythm alterations are basic, what triggers them? What are the connections to psychological and sociological factors? Certainly early morning awakening, one of the hallmarks of endogenomorphic depression is seen without the full clinical syndrome. It seems to represent the response to our awareness of a need to get ready to meet potentially overwhelming problems of the coming day. If prolonged, this leads to sleep loss and an urge to go to bed earlier. Could this be a link? What is the biological meaning of a major connection between affective illness and fundamental rhythm?

Age and Depression

As Post (1962) pointed out, it has long been held that with increasing age affective illnesses tend to become increasingly severe, that they become more protracted, and that they recur with increasing frequency. Post's own studies have borne this out.

In our original sleep study of 22 depressed patients (Mendels and Hawkins 1967), we found that patients over the age of 50 had more disturbed sleep, including greater fragmentation, decreased REM sleep, and essentially absent delta sleep. The latter was not due solely to aging, for the carefully matched over-fifty control group had diminished, but nonetheless present, delta sleep. At that time, unfortunately, we did not measure REM latency in all of our subjects.

More recently (Hawkins et al. 1985, Taub et al. 1978), we studied a group of 20 young depressives under the age of 26 who were severely depressed as measured by the Beck Depression Inventory and the Hamilton Observer Rating Scale. When rigorous criterion for depression were applied, few clinically diagnosed young depressives met the standards which have been met by older depressives. The 20 who did meet the standards, while clearly showing typical signs and symptoms of depression, were different clinically from older patients. The younger group was more labile in mood and more susceptible to changes related to external psychosocial forces.

Their sleep showed relatively little abnormality. When carefully compared with controls, there were some significant changes, including more waking, more stage shifts, and less delta sleep. The under-26 group did not show a decreased REM latency. One of the purposes of the study was to test the clinical impression that young people have hypersomnia rather than hyposomnia or insomnia when depressed. On the fifth night of the study in the sleep laboratory, the subjects were permitted to sleep as long as they wanted. All subjects extended their sleep over baseline values, the controls by a mean of 87 minutes and the depressives by a mean of 169 minutes. Thus, the study bore out the clinical impression of oversleeping in the young depressed patient.

The only published systematic study of a series of depressed patients of varying ages comes from investigators at the National Institutes of Mental Health (Gillin et al. 1981). They reported on 69 patients separated into cells divided by decades ending at ages 24, 34, 44, 54, and 64 respectively. Unfortunately, the cells at either end of the spectrum each contained only 8 patients. They pointed out that most of the sleep abnormalities reported in depressed patients also occur in aging individuals. It might be said that the sleep of a depressed patient looks like that of a much older person. However, the under-25 depressives did not show any increase in REM density in the initial REM period and the over-55 group did not show any increase in the initial REM period when compared with matched controls. As contrasted with our findings, the NIMH group did find a significant decrease in REM latency in the under-25 group. (However, there were only a few patients in this group.) They emphasize that abnormalities in sleep continuity, such as waking, lack of delta sleep, and early morning wakening are particularly noticeable in the older age groups. The only variable in which they found a statistically meaningful age by group interaction was in early morning wakening; this actually reflects the fact that the group found no increase in this variable in the nondepressed elderly individual but found marked change in the elderly depressed patient.

We had previously emphasized that there was an age-depression interaction as far as sleep is concerned: the older the depressive, the worse the sleep. Of course, it may be significant that the more aging has already interfered with smooth sleep, the more susceptible the individual is to depression. Can sleep, when its control mechanisms are working very well in the young, protect against depression? Certainly in the history of many of those who have recurring unipolar or bipolar affective disorder, there appear to be episodes early in life which are relatively mild and don't as a rule come to medical attention. In retrospect those attacks were clearly initial mild episodes of illness.

Psychological Influences on Sleep

New discoveries which increasingly link organic problems with sleep and affective disorder lead to an attitude which tends to view the origin of sleep abnormalities and other vegetative accompaniments of affective illness as internal and biochemically based. Is there any evidence of psychological forces not only precipitating depression at times but having an influence on sleep parameters?

Greenberg et al. (1972) found reduced REM latency in patients with traumatic war neuroses. In 1975, Greenberg et al. found that, for a patient in psychoanalysis, the REM latency was lower on nights following especially stress-producing treatment sessions. This view was similar to previous suggestions by Hawkins (1966, 1969) and Breger (1967) which stated that a possible function of REM sleep may be that of solving affective problems.

In a thoughtful and ingenious study, Cartwright (1983) attempted to test a psychological model in order to explain the decrease in REM latency usually found in primary depression. She proposed to find a situation where there would be important waking dysphoric states without possibility of an easy solution. She also wished to show that REM abnormalities occurred in subjects without previous depressive illness and that subjects with high levels of new information not affectively disturbing did not have REM changes. Finally, Cartwright hoped to show that under the dysphoric conditions only REM sleep and not sleep in general was altered.

She decided that the reaction to divorce represented the optimum situation and for six nights in the sleep laboratory studied 29 women undergoing divorce. She was able to do follow-up studies one to two years later on 13 of these women. Women who had a more "traditional view" compared to those measured as "liberated" scored higher on depression inventories. Twenty-four had or had had a major depressive episode by DSM III criteria. All the women also had shortened REM latencies and increased REM density. At follow-up, REM latency had increased but was still lower than expected for the subject's age. Delta sleep was decreased in the high depression groups but not in a statistically significantly manner. Delta sleep time had increased by nearly 50 percent at follow-up. Traditionality and depression inventory scores were correlated in the recently divorced women but not in a group of married normal women.

Cartwright's study strongly suggests the validity of the original hypothesis that the function of REM sleep is to solve affective problems is correct. However, one could still conclude that lowered REM latency and increased REM density are part of depression and that the stress related to divorce is not directly related to the REM changes. It is not clear from this study whether these REM changes are both state and trait or only trait disturbances.

Whether the sleep changes are a direct result of psychological forces or are secondary to a depression mechanism which is put into operation as a result of the divorce-related stress remains moot. What is clear, however, is that the process including sleep abnormalities has been triggered by a psychological stress.

Sleep Changes in Other Illness

Another study (Insel et al. 1982) has raised further questions about the specificity to depressive illness of the constellation of sleep abnormalities described in connection with depression. Fourteen patients with obsessive-compulsive disorder (OCD) were studied in the sleep laboratory and their sleep patterns compared to those of normals and depressed patients studied in the same laboratory. Seven of the patients did have affective symptoms but the symptoms were judged to be secondary to the OCD and not indicative of a primary affective disorder. Both subgroups demonstrated sleep abnormalities consisting of decreased total sleep time with more wakefulness, less stage 4 sleep, decreased REM efficiency, and shortened REM latencies. There were a few minor sleep differences between the OCD patients and those with primary depression, but the striking finding was the similarities. The authors understandably emphasize a possible biological link between OCD and affective illness. There remains the possibility of a psychological problem leading to a common organic abnormality. This raises the question of the specificity to that disorder of the various sleep abnormalities seen in affective illness.

At one time, Kupfer (1976) called shortened REM latency a biological marker for primary depression. Carroll et al. (1981) also called the Dexamethasone Suppression Test, a biological marker for primary depression. However, as already illustrated by some of the examples given for REM latency, the findings are not specific or universal for primary depression. When they are present, we don't know whether they are state- or trait-dependent. Some of the factors behind the premature claims represent an understandable wish to find a certain indicator for a condition with amorphous presentations, whose etiology and pathophysiology are only dimly perceived. Finally and particularly, part of the motive is to make psychiatry "scientific" and "physical" as the rest of medicine strives to be. However, a biological marker should either be invariable or play a clearly understandable role in the genesis or pathophysiology of the disorder. Currently, psychiatry deals with measurable organic changes which are related in some fashion to "functional" illnesses. It is premature to term them biological markers.

As Gillin (1983) points out, the more we learn about sleep in a variety of conditions, the less specific some of the sleep abnormalities characteristic of affective illness become, even though they are relatively sensitive measures of affective illness. Given a patient with significant affective illness, one can fairly accurately predict what the sleep patterns are particularly if age is taken into account. However, even such a finding as short REM latency, which has been touted as a biological marker for affective illness, has been shown to occur in normal morning nappers, in individuals in time-free environments ("free-running"), in the elderly, and in anyone else who has been REM deprived. It has also been demonstrated in other pathological states, such as narcolepsy, anorexia nervosa, acute schizophrenia, chronic schizophrenia, schizoaffective disease, atypical or secondary depression, obsessive-compulsive neurosis; it has also been observed in divorced women. There may be some reservations about the findings for reasons of questionable diagnoses in some studies and because, in many instances, the conclusions are derived from unreplicated findings.

Research Problems

Although in the past quarter century enormous amounts of time, money and energy have gone into a study of affective illness and sleep psychophysiology, there are huge gaps in our knowledge and big problems of methodology. The early sleep studies did not measure some of the indices now thought to be crucial in depression, such as REM period lengths and densities. Many of the studies do not have proper controls. Some studies lack them altogether. Despite great improvements in standardization of terminology and definition of criteria for scoring sleep records, big differences remain in scoring such crucial variables as REM latency and REM density. As we pointed out (Hawkins and Mendels 1966, Mendels and Hawkins 1967) in our earliest reports, the more severely depressed the subject, the more difficult it is to accurately score the sleep record. When there are intrusions of NREM sleep or frequent waking within REM periods, how does one score that? Certainly, this must continue to be problematic for the comparison of findings from different laboratories.

Another related but somewhat different issue which received a lot of attention is that of diagnosis. At the moment, I believe, we are victims of our own success. Feighner et al. (1972) recognized the great difficulties in comparing results of studies of affective and other major psychiatric disorders due to different diagnostic criteria. Therefore, they established a more precise classification; Spiker et al. (1978) then established what are known as research diagnostic criteria (RDC) which, however, are not precisely the same as the later, more widely used DSM-III. Now every study includes a statement that the subjects were diagnosed according to one of these schemes, generally without further qualification or description. However, one wonders how vigorously these criteria are really applied. We are probably missing many important findings by assuming that all patients who fit into one of these categories are all the same. There is a tendency for investigators to stop thinking about clinical differences among the patient population and readers are therefore deprived of the opportunity to get clinical leads from the work of others.

Sleep and Depressive Pathophysiology

Finally, we should ask if the sleep studies shed any light on the pathophysiology of depression and if the findings make any sense from a broad biological point of view. From the latter stance we might ask why there should be any relationship between strong affective states or disorders and sleep.

Common sense and clinical judgement would suggest that sleep and affective states can influence each other. Sleep deprivation (despite its seemingly paradoxical efficacy as a temporary cure for depressive illness in some) and acute sleep inversion (reversal of day and night sleeping) both lead to dysphoria though not to full-blown disease. Moreover, acute sleep inversion leads temporarily to a sleep pattern resembling that of depression. Sleep disturbance, as has already been documented, clearly accompanies depressive illness, at least in middle-aged or older depressives and especially influences early morning awaking. What about situations of stress in presumably normal individuals who don't develop a full-blown depressive illness? Sleeplessness is certainly present frequently in the case of major acute bereavement. It is part of folklore that guilt, among other things, has the capacity to interfere with sleep. Most readers of this chapter (who probably were ambitious, compulsive students) have experienced sleeplessness and particularly early morning waking and dysphoria before major examinations.

Sleeping difficulty is indicative that an individual is hyperaroused. From a variety of other studies, we know that the depressed patient is hyperaroused in many dimensions, even in the face of seeming lethargy and withdrawal. For purposes of this discussion it is useful to emphasize Zung's (1964) findings of a lowered threshold for arousal in the depressive at all sleep stages, as compared with the same sleep stages in normal controls. Our contention is that in the depressed individual there is a substantial increase in pressure for arousal; after the depression has been in effect for a while, the pressure for sleep is heightened. The resulting imbalance hinders a well-regulated ebb and flow of sleep and arousal. The two systems are competing and aspects of NREM, REM, and waking intrude into each other. We believe that the phenomenon of alpha-delta sleep (Hauri and Hawkins 1973) is an example of this.

This conceptualization may explain why depressive illness generally tends to get more frequent and more severe with aging. The older the depressed patient, the worse the sleep. We think that the complex sleep regulatory mechanisms become less efficient with aging. The young person is able to sleep relatively normally and in fact sleep longer than usual in the face of the hyperarousal in depression. We postulate that the ability to maintain a relatively good sleep architecture and quantity may help keep the depressive illness from becoming as severe in later life; as Shakespeare said, sleep may be the "balm of hurt minds." However, sleep alone will not cure depression and, as already described, one of the treatments for depression is sleep deprivation.

In an excellent review, Gillin (1983) discussed a number of attempts to understand the sleep abnormalities and the pathophysiology of depressions as indicated below. Snyder (1969), a pioneer in sleep research, proposed that some of the REM phenomena seen late in the course of depression could result from relative REM deprivation in the early (waxing) phase of depression. These phenomena include the short REM latency and enhanced REM density. Early in the formulation of Snyder's hypothesis, he was attempting to deal with the finding of variation in the amount or proportions of REM sleep. As was true in our initial study (Hawkins and Mendels 1966), some depressed patients in cross-sectional studies showed a definite decrease in REM sleep while others had more REM than controls. These issues were discussed by Hawkins, Snyder, and others at a NIMH-sponsored workshop in 1969 on the depressive illnesses (Williams et al. 1972). Subsequent studies do not seem to have borne out the ideas of partial but prolonged REM deprivation as a likely explanation of abnormal REM findings in depressive illness. We still don't know what happens in the early stages of a depressive illness, particularly with regard to sleep processes.

The chronobiologic models suggest intriguingly that depression may be related to abnormalities in various rhythms or improper synchrony. The blame might be laid upon alterations in oscillators which control the timing of events. Phase changes or internal desynchronization could be instrumental in the development of affective illness.

Voget et al. (1980) have pointed out that in some respects depressed patients resemble normal subjects who are sleeping on an extended sleep regime. He proposes that endogenously depressed patients could have defective mechanisms for inhibiting REM sleep. Gillin and his colleagues have undertaken a series of studies (Gillin et al. 1978, 1979, 1981) which indicate that REM sleep can be induced during NREM sleep by a preponderance of cholinergic substances. They can produce REM sleep either by an anticholinesterase, physostigmine, or arecoline, a muscarine agonist. Conversely, the use of a muscarinic antagonist, scopolamine, can block the effects of arecoline and delay REM sleep. By giving scopolamine for three consecutive mornings to normal volunteers, Gillin and his co-workers were able to induce sleep changes which resemble those typically seen in a depressed patient.

These workers then developed what they call the Cholinergic REM Induction Test (CRIT). They administer an intravenous dose of placebo or arecoline during NREM sleep to a subject pretreated with a peripherally active anticholinergic substance. They find that patients with major affective illness, both when ill and when in remission, enter REM sleep more rapidly following arecoline than controls do. There is no difference following the placebo. The mechanisms by which arecoline works are unknown.

In essence these results suggest an inherited supersensitivity to cholinergic, muscarinic stimulation in patients with major affective disorders. Gillin et al. (1983) point out the relationships to an earlier hypothesis of Janowsky et al. (1972) which proposed an increased ratio of cholinergic to noradrenergic functional activity in depression. Moreover, Gillin and his colleagues point out that the evidence suggests the following: patients prone to depression have a state-independent sensitivity to cholinergic influence which may be brought out by a state-dependent shift in aminergic influences leading to the depressed condition.

Some of the different conceptual schemes are not necessarily mutually exclusive. They may represent different aspects of control systems; different models often address themselves to different levels of function or integration. When systems are changed by "floods" of a neurotransmitter, the primary problem is not necessarily at the same level. A more specific group of neurones may be over- or underactive, and the extra neurotransmitter may be counterbalancing the specific neurone group.

Affective illness will, in my opinion, turn out to be the final common pathway of a number of different basic abnormalities. As an example, diabetes mellitus is turning out to be a number of different disorders, all of which lead to ineffective functioning of the carbohydrate metabolism system and in some fashion have to do with improper insulin function. So, too, in depression it seems almost certain that there may be a variety of pathways or abnormalities leading to the final common denominator which we term affective illness. In some, it would seem that flaws in the circadian rhythm control mechanisms are the problem. In others, the problem is likely to be an abnormality in the dysphoria control system; in still others, we may see the problem as constant pressure on the control systems exerted by psychosocial issues.

Summary

Changes in sleep accompany most cases of affective illness. In general, sleep is curtailed and fragmented. However, in young people, those with mild depression, and probably in some patients with bipolar illness, excessive sleep may be seen instead.

In general, the more severe the depression and the older the patient, the more abnormal is the sleep record obtained in the laboratory. Usually there is marked reduction in sleep, especially in the delta-wave stages and fragmentation with early morning waking is prominent. These findings, while most typically seen in affective illness, occur in other states as well and may in large part be an indication of the degree of emotional distress. Changes in REM patterning, especially decreased latency, increased duration of the initial REM period, and increased REM density have been proposed as "biological markers" or specific abnormalities found in primary depression. As more studies are performed, it becomes obvious that these abnormalities are not limited to affective illness, at least as we now define it.

It is clear that there is a very close tie between sleep and affective illness. We can study and conceptualize the connections at a variety of levels of integration. The connection may be quite close since the neurotransmitters which are of crucial relevance to the control of shifting sleep and awake phases are somehow implicated in the pathogenesis of affective illness. The exact mechanisms involved, however, remain elusive. Eventually we must understand the significance of sleep biologically as well as the adaptive mechanism of which affective illness is an aberrant form. Much work remains to be done to elucidate the biopsychosocial mechanisms and interrelationships.

REFERENCES

Aserinsky, E., and Kleitman, N. (1953). Regularly occurring periods of eye motility, and concomitant phenomena during sleep. *Science* 118:273–274.
Breger, L. (1967). Function of dreams. *Journal of Abnormal Psychology* 72:1–28.
Carroll, B. J., Feinberg, M., Greden, J. F. et al. (1981). A specific laboratory test for the diagnosis of melancholia: standardization, validation and clinical utility. *Archives of General Psychiatry* 38:15.
Cartwright, R. D. (1983). Rapid eye movement sleep characteristics during and after mood-disturbing events. *Archives of General Psychiatry* 40:197–201.
Diaz-Guerrero, R., Gottlieb, J. S., and Knott, J. R. (1946). The sleep of patients with manic-depressive psychosis, depressive type. *Psychosomatic Medicine* 8: 339–404.
Doerr, P., Von Zerssen, D., Fischler, M. et al. (1979). Relationship between mood changes and adrenal cortical activity in a patient with 48 hour unipolar-depressive cycles. *Journal of Affective Disorders* 1:93–104.
Feighner, J. P., Robins, E., Guze, S. B. et al. (1972). Diagnostic criteria for use in psychiatric research. *Archives of General Psychiatry* 26:57–63.
Gillin, J. C. (1983). Sleep studies in affective illness: diagnostic, therapeutic, and pathophysiological implications. *Psychiatric Annals* 13:367–384.

Gillin, J. C., Duncan, W., Murphy, D. L. et al. (1981). Age related changes in sleep in depressed and normal subjects. *Psychiatry Research* 4:73–78.

Gillin, J. C., Mendelson, W. B., Sitaram, N. et al. (1978). The neuropharmacology of sleep and wakefulness. *Annual Review of Pharmacology & Toxicology* 18: 563–569.

Gillin, J. C., Sitaram, N., and Duncan, W. C. (1979). Muscarinic supersensitivity: a possible model for the sleep disturbances of primary depression? *Psychiatric Research* 1:17–22.

Greenberg, R. and Pearlman, C. (1975). REM sleep and the analytic process. A psychophysiologic bridge. *Psychoanalytic Quarterly* 44:392–402.

Greenberg, R., Pearlman, C., and Ganipel, D. (1972). War neuroses and the adaptive function of REM sleep. *British Journal of Medical Psychology* 45: 27–33.

Hauri, P. and Hawkins, D. R. (1973). Alpha-delta sleep. *Electroencephalographic Clinical Neurophysiology* 34:233–237.

——— (1971). Phasic REM, depression and the relationship between sleeping and waking. *Archives of General Psychiatry* 25:56–63.

Hauri, R., Chernik, D., Hawkins, D. R. et al. (1974). Sleep of depressed patients in remission. *Archives of General Psychiatry* 31:386–391.

Hawkins, D. R.(1980). Sleep and Circadian Rhythm Disturbances in Depression. In *The Psychobiology of Affective Disorders*, ed. Joseph Mendels and Jay D. Amsterdam. Pfizer Symposium on Depression, Boca Raton, Florida, 28–29 February. Karger-Basel.

——— (1969). A Freudian view. In *Dream Psychology and the New Biology of Dreaming*, ed. M. Kramer, pp. 39–56. Springfield: Charles C. Thomas Company.

——— (1966). A review of psychoanalytic dream theory in the light of recent psycho-physiological studies of sleep and dreaming. *British Journal of Medical Psychology* 39:85–104.

Hawkins, D. R. and Mendels, J. (1966). Sleep disturbance in depressive syndromes. *American Journal of Psychiatry* 123:682–690.

Hawkins, D. R., Taub, J., and Van de Castle, R. L. (1978). Extended sleep (Hypersomnia) in young depressed patients. Accepted for publication by *The American Journal of Psychiatry*.

Insel, R. T., Gillin, J. C., Moore, A. et al. (1982). The sleep of patients with obsessive-compulsive disorder. *Archives of General Psychiatry* 39:1372–1377.

Janowsky, D. I., El-Yousef, M. D., and Davis, J. M. (1972). A cholinergic adrenergic hypothesis of mania and depression. *Lancet* 2:632–635.

Johnson, A., Pflug, B., Engelmann, W. et al. (1979). Effect of lithium carbonate on circadian periodicity in humans. *Pharmakopsychiatrie Neuropsychopharmacology* 12:423–425.

Jouvet, M. (1969). Biogenic amines in states of sleep. *Science* 163:32–36.

Kripke, D. F., Mullaney, D. J., Atkinson, M. et al. (1978). Circadian rhythm disorder in manic-depressives. *Biological Psychiatry* 13:335–351.

Kupfer, D. J. (1976). REM latency: a psychobiologic marker for primary depressive disease. *Biological Psychiatry* 11:159–165.

Kupfer, D. J., and Foster, F. G. (1975). The sleep of psychotic patients. Does it all look alike? In *The Biology of the Major Psychoses. A Comparative Analysis*, ed. Freedman. New York: Raven Press.

Mendels, J., and Hawkins, D. R. (1967). Sleep and depression. A controlled EEG study. *Archives of General Psychiatry* 16:344–354.

Mendelson, W. B., Gillin, J. C., and Wyatt, R. J. (1977). *Human Sleep and Its Disorders*. New York: Plenum Press.

Pflug, B., and Tolle, R. (1971). Disturbance of the 24-hour rhythm in endogenous depression and the treatment of endogenous depression by sleep deprivation. *International Pharmacopsychiatry* 6:187–196.

Post, F. (1962). *The Significance of Affective Symptoms in Old Age*. Maudsley Monograph no. 10. London: Oxford University Press.

Puig-Antich, J., Goetz, R., Hanlon, C. et al. (1983). Sleep architecture and REM sleep measures in prepubertal major depressives. *Archives of General Psychiatry* 40:187–192.

Rush, A. J., Giles, D. E., Roffwarg, H. P. et al. (1982). Sleep EEG and dexamethasone suppression test findings in outpatients with unipolar major depressive disorders. *Biological Psychiatry* 17:327–341.

Schilgen, B., and Tolle, R. (1980). Partial sleep deprivation as therapy for depression. *Archives of General Psychiatry* 37:267–271.

Schulz, H., Hurd, R., Cording, C. et al. (1979). Bimodal distribution of REM sleep latencies in depression. *Biological Psychiatry* 14:595–600.

Schulz, H., and Trojan, B. (1979). A comparison of eye movement density in normal subjects and in depressed patients before and after remission. *Sleep Research* 8:49.

Shakespeare, W. *Macbeth*. Act III, Scene 4. *Oxford Standard Edition of Shakespeare's Works*. London: Oxford University Press, 1963.

Sitaram, N., and Gillin, J. C. (1980). Development and use of pharmacological probes of the CNS in man: evidence of cholinergic abnormality in primary affective illness. *Biological Psychiatry* 15:925–955.

Sitaram, N., Nurnberger, J. I., Gershon, E. S. et al. (1982). Cholinergic regulation of mood and REM sleep: potential model and marker of vulnerability to affective disorder. *American Journal of Psychiatry* 139:571–576.

——— (1980). Faster cholinergic REM sleep induction in euthymic patients with primary affective illness. *Science* 208:200–202.

Snyder, F. (1974). NIH studies of EEG sleep in affective illness, In *Recent Advances in the Psychobiology of the Depressive Illnesses*, ed. Williams, Katz, and Shields. Washington, D.C.: Department of Health, Education and Welfare.

——— (1969). Dynamic aspects of sleep disturbance in relation to mental illness. *Biological Psychiatry* 1:119–130.

——— (1963). The new biology of dreaming. *Archives of General Psychiatry* 8:381–391.

Spiker, D. G., Coble, P., Cofsky et al. (1978). EEG sleep and severity of depression. *Biological Psychiatry* 13:485–488.

Taub, J. M., Hawkins, D. R., and Van de Castle, R. L. (1978). Electrographic analysis of the sleep cycle in young depressed patients. *Psychology* 7:203–214.

Vogel, G. W., Thurmond, A., Gibbons, P. et al. (1975). REM sleep reduction effects on depression syndromes. *Archives of General Psychiatry* 32:765–777.

Vogel, G. W., Vogel, R., McAbee, R. S. et al. (1980). Improvement of depression by REM sleep deprivation. *Archives of General Psychiatry* 37:247–253.

Wehr, T. A., Wirz-Justice, A., Goodwin, F. K. et al. (1979). Phase advance of the circadian sleep-wake cycle as an antidepressant. *Science* 206:710–713.

Weitzman, E. G., Kripke, D. F., Goldmacher, D. et al. (1970). Acute reversal of the sleep-waking cycle in man. *Archives of Neurology* 22:483–489.

Williams, R. L., and Karacan, I. (1978). *Sleep Disorders. Diagnosis and Treatment*. New York: John Wiley and Sons.

Williams, R. L., Karacan, I. and Hursch, C. J. (1974). *Electroencephalography (EEG) of Human Sleep. Clinical Applications.* New York: John Wiley and Sons.

Williams, T. A., Katz, M. M., and Shield, J. A. (1972). *Recent Advances in the Psychobiology of the Depressive Illnesses.* Washington, D. C.: Government Printing Office.

Wirz-Justice, A., Groos, G. A., and Wehr, T. A. (1982). The neuropharmacology of circadian timekeeping in mammals. In *Mammalian Circadian Rhythms,* ed. J. Ashoff, S. Daan, and G. A. Groos, pp. 183–193. New York: Springer-Verlag.

Zung, W. W., Wilson, W. P., and Dodson, W. E. (1964). Effect of depressive disorders on sleep EEG responses. *Archives of General Psychiatry* 10:439–445.

CHAPTER TWENTY

Assessment of Depression in the General Medical Patient

Jerry H. Morewitz, M.D.

Given the increased prevalence and incidence of depression in general medical practice and the ubiquitous nature of the personally evoked depressive experience, one might imagine that its diagnosis in the general medical patient would be a reasonably straightforward and rational procedure (Moffic and Paykel 1975). Unfortunately, this is not always the case. Studies by Nielson (1980), Rawnsky (1968), and Moffic and Paykel (1975) have documented the low rate of correct diagnosis of depression by primary care physicians. Although the etiology of this problem remains uncertain, several contributory factors are considered. Katon (1982) has suggested that patients in primary care often focus selectively on the somatic manifestations of major depressive disorder with denial or minimalization of the affective and cognitive components. He maintains that the main difficulty lies in the inability of some physicians to believe depression exists in the absence of the patient recognizing and reporting an abnormal affective state. Another aspect undoubtedly lies in the often ill-defined, diverse, and unnecessarily complex diagnostic schemes that have been used over the years to define the depressive state. This is true not only for the primary care physician, but also for many specialists in psychiatry who remain uncomfortable with the ambiguities and contradictions that persist even with our present usage.

Thus, three major areas of concern need to be addressed by the psychiatrist consultant or nonpsychiatrist physician in the assessment and treatment of depression. First, feelings of despondency or demoralization, the normal grief process, and a pathological depressive state must be distinguished from each other. Second, symptomatology of an abnormal depressive state that is a manifestation of another underlying medical illness must be recognized. Third, a depressive disorder masquerading as a somatic illness must be recognized. This chapter will briefly consider aspects from each of these general areas. A proposal for a modified and parsimonious classification scheme for depression, suitable for usage in the general medical setting as well as the general psychiatric setting, will also be made.

Nosology and Classification of Depression

Although the presence of depression has been noted and described since the time of Hippocrates and Aretaeus of Cappadocia, much dispute has persisted regarding its terminology and classification (Altschule 1977). Two of the more traditional, commonly used classifications that have distinguished psychotic-neurotic and endogenous-reactive forms of depression have undergone recent criticism because they have made assumptions about etiology that are deficient in current research backing (Woods 1982). Thus, as the Meyerian unitary concept of illness has given way to a more pluralistic view of causality in more recent years, these earlier dichotomous classifications have also undergone revision (Klerman 1978). Instead of a primarily psychological view of depression that stresses the importance of early experiences and life events as causal agents, or of a singular neurobiological view of depression that postulates a primary abnormality in neurotransmitter physiology as etiologically significant, the more recently derived pluralistic view maintains that the pathogenesis of depression arises out of a complicated interaction between environmental stressors, psychodynamic forces, personality, and a variety of genetic-endocrine-biochemical factors. The final "titration point" for a given individual appears to be a locus, determined by complex factors, along a psychological-neurobiological continuum based on a particular mix of the pathogenic variables stated above.

A similar conceptualization can be found in Leigh and Reiser's (1980) hypothetical integrated model of depression, where environmental, symbolic, and genetic-chemical factors influence a final common pathway made up of diencephalic neuronal systems concerned with pleasure and reinforcement. These authors proposed a hypothesized threshold related to vulnerability to depression in the central nervous system. Given a large genetic loading or a low threshold for depression, only minimal environmental or symbolic stimuli would be necessary to trigger a severe depression. In individuals with minimal genetic loading or a high threshold, even significant environmental or symbolic stimuli might not be sufficient to trigger a depression.

Given the complexity of these variables, the question arises whether such an endeavor is worth all the effort, or indeed whether such a complicated assessment is possible! The question of effort can certainly be answered in the affirmative given the increased sophistication and effectiveness of treatments presently available to clinicians for the treatment of depression. A possible solution to the latter problem can be accomplished by adapting and integrating the DSM-III classification for depressive disorders with the diagnostic scheme originally elaborated by Robins and Guze (1969), distinguishing primary and secondary affective disorders. The

DSM-III classification is based on observable, descriptive operational criteria rather than on etiological considerations. Essential features of a significant depression in this scheme include:

I. Dysphoric mood or loss of interest or pleasure in all or almost all usual activities
II. The additional significant presence of at least four of the associated symptoms for a period of at least two weeks:
   1. Diminished or increased appetite or significant weight fluctuation from the norm for a given individual
   2. Sleep disturbance
   3. Psychomotor retardation or agitation
   4. Decreased sexual drive
   5. Excessive fatigue or loss of energy
   6. Feelings of worthlessness or inappropriate guilt
   7. Decreased concentration and indecisiveness
   8. Recurrent thoughts of death or suicide
   9. Positive history of depression or alcoholism in first-degree relatives
III. The exclusion of individuals with significant organic mental disorder or uncomplicated bereavement

Although the classification outlined above fails to maximally satisfy the official DSM-III criteria, the scheme is sufficiently objective and flexible for use by the primary care practitioner in general medical practice as well by the general psychiatrist. Such a system allows treatment specificity and comprehensiveness. As noted earlier, Robins and Guze (1969) made a useful distinction in their proposal, differentiating primary and secondary affective disorders. However, their initial conceptualization of secondary affective disorder applies only to disorders secondary to psychiatric illness, such as schizophrenia or somatization disorder. Klerman and Barrett (1973) and other investigators have expanded this concept subsequently to include affective disorders secondary to general medical illnesses or drug reactions. The major distinction is in the timing of the depressive event (Cassem 1978). A depression is classified as primary if it precedes any other psychiatric or serious medical illness or if preceding episodes were also affective (depressive or manic) in nature. A depression is classified as secondary when there is a preexisting psychiatric diagnosis or a preceding life-threatening illness or one which significantly changes a life-style. Since this primary-secondary classification scheme does not make necessary for inclusion the presence or absence of precipitating life events or the degree of illness, etiological issues posed by endogenous-reactive and psychotic-neurotic distinctions can be circumvented (Klerman 1983).

In summary, I propose that a classification scheme integrating core

DSM-III depressive criteria within a modified primary-secondary disorder framework would be reasonably comprehensive and yet of sufficient practical utility to allow increased use in both general medicine and psychiatry settings for the diagnosis of significant depressive illness.

Despondency, Grief, and Depression

One major problem still associated with the diagnostic classification described above is its failure to distinguish among depondency, grief, and the syndrome of depression as responses to medical illness (See Fig. 20-1). Dysphoric mood, or sadness, is a universal part of the human experience. Arieti (1978) defines normal sadness as "the emotional effect on a human being when he apprehends a situation that he would have preferred not to occur, and which he considers adverse to his well-being." Despondency, an intensification or accentuation of these normal feelings of sadness, can occur as a consequence of a severe or incapacitating medical illness. Cassem considers despondency in serious illness to be a natural response to the narcissistic injury inflicted upon the patient's self-esteem by the disease process (Cassem 1978). The results of such an assault on the individual's self-esteem, described as a "mixture of dread, bitterness, and despair," presenting "the self as broken, scarred, ruined," certainly implies a more pathological process or state along the depressive continuum than normal feelings of sadness.

A quite similar concept, demoralization, has been utilized by Hall (1980) to describe a process analogous to the use of despondency. Key elements include an alteration in self-image, a sense of decreased effectiveness in controlling one's life, increased feelings of helplessness, and a decreased ability to interact spontaneously with one's environment. In contrast to the depressed medical patient, the demoralized patient maintains vegetative functions such as sleep and appetite within the normal range. Hall adds that this form of despair is generally unmodified by antidepressive medication but responsive to supportive interventions. Although a specific etiologic mechanism is not postulated, the demoralization is particularly likely to occur in conjunction with certain types of incapacitating physical illnesses, such as cancer, myocardial infarction in a younger person, and burns. It is also thought to occur with increased frequency in those individuals with chronic, socially debilitating diseases such as epilepsy, diabetes, ulcerative colitis, regional enteritis, renal failure, stroke, and spinal cord injury.

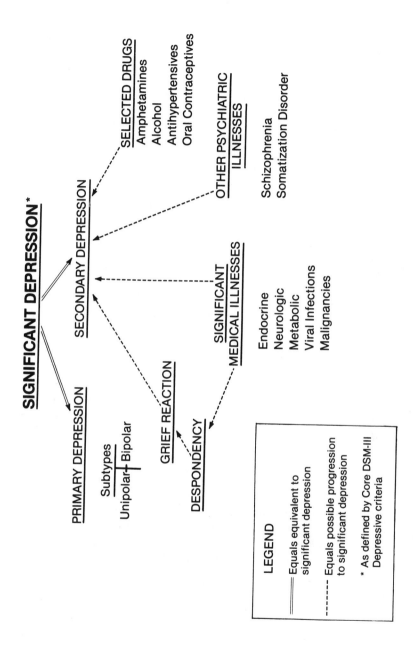

Figure 20-1. Outline of Depression (Adapted from Klerman, 1983, p. 377).

Depression Following Myocardial Infarction

A 42-year-old married investment broker was seen in psychiatric consultation for evaluation of depression three weeks following post-hospital discharge from a relatively uneventful recovery from a myocardial infarction. Since his return home, this premorbidly active, hard-driving individual had been reporting persistent feelings of weakness and sadness and had been declining to participate in anything other than completely sedentary activities, claiming that he did not want to risk having another MI by "overexerting" himself. The patient had not made any attempt to recontact his employer regarding the status of his position which was being held awaiting his recovery and return to work. The wife noted the patient's markedly different manner of relating to her and their two young daughters, with little demonstration of the spontaneous, playfully affectionate behaviors characteristic of his preinfarction interpersonal style. Other than a mild sleep disturbance, no vegetative signs of depression were noted to be present. There were no previous depressive episodes reported. The overall clinical impression was that of a post-MI despondency. A stepped-up rehabilitation program that included supportive psychotherapy, educational counselling related to common post-MI issues and concerns, and a graduated, highly structured physical conditioning component were initiated. The patient responded fairly well to these intensified efforts, returning to his premorbid level of functioning over the next nine weeks.

Finally, both Cassem (1978) and Hall (1980) seemed to place emphasis on the maintenance and restoration of self-esteem as a key factor in working with medically ill individuals experiencing despondency or demoralization. This was believed to be accomplished through involvement in a vigorous individualized rehabilitation program that included the use of early mobilization and opportunities to explore alternative life-styles and a supportive continuing relationship with a physician or medical staff.

The term "normal grief" will be utilized to represent the next more intensive level on the depressive continuum. The reaction of grief to the loss of a significant loved person has been described as a universal experience in the classic works of Lindemann (1945), Bowlby (1961), and Parkes (1970). This conceptualization holds up quite well when considering the reaction of patients to the losses of function and sense of health that accompany significant medical illness. Peretz (1970) suggests that a loss of health is usually experienced as a change in some aspect of the self. This may be felt as a loss of a positive feeling state as the disease results in feelings of pain, weakness, or other symptoms. There may also be total or partial loss of important body functions such as breathing, vision, hearing, coordination, or bowel function. Decreased libidinal and appetitive drives as well as loss of body integrity, attractiveness, independence, and even control over one's daily activities may constitute critical losses for a given individual. The loss of one's occupational or family roles may also adversely affect a person's life. Even improvement in a disease symptom can be felt as a loss if there is an associated decrease in the amount of secondary gain obtained vis-a-vis the interpersonal environment. Finally, a patient's perception of own impending death can be understood as an ultimate loss, anticipating the loss of self.

A given individual's reaction to one or more of these losses can be determined by different factors, including early life experiences, premorbid personality, previous capacity to deal with losses, the nature and severity of the loss, and the interplay between the patient's personality and the disease process associated with the loss (Blacher 1970, Broden 1970). For purposes of this chapter our focus is limited to the consideration of normal grief in the medical patient and its differentiation from clinical depression.

Considered by Peretz (1970) as the most common and adaptive reaction to serious loss, grief is described as a predictable phasic process characterized by intense psychic suffering, sorrow, and regret (Parkes 1970, Bowlby 1961). The stages described below should be considered generally applicable to all of the significant types of losses noted previously and not restricted to the loss of significant persons. Initially, shock and denial dominate the bereavement state. This phase gives way to a period of disorganization and bewilderment that includes heightened somatic distress, agitation, an increased preoccupation with and yearning for the image of the decreased or the actual loss involved, feelings of guilt, feelings of unreality, and despair. Finally, a psychic reorganization takes place in relation to the experienced loss, with eventual completion of the grief work occurring, for the most part, in one to two months (Huston 1975).

Can the process of grieving be differentiated from a true clinical depression? Peretz has noted that a number of the common features in normal grief are also commonly considered features in depression: insomnia, anorexia, weight loss, poor concentration, sadness, weeping, and self-reproach (Peretz, 1970). However, grieving and depression were also found to be significantly different processes as determined by a number of qualitative and quantitative variables.

In contrast to the grief-stricken individual, the depressed person will be more persistently disheartened and pessimistic, will be relatively unresponsive affectively to most interpersonal or environmental stimuli, will have a more pervasive restriction of pleasure, will often have more intense and persistent self-destructive ideation, and will likely be much more preoccupied with the self than with the deceased or the nature of the loss. The depressed individual will also have a much more negativistic and self-reproachful attitude, will tend to feel a more intense inner emptiness, and will be more likely to develop psychotic-level delusional thought content related to themes of guilt or hypochondriacal concerns. It is also critical to remember that an actual clinical depression might follow, either immediately or several months after a normal grief process. The importance in being able to make a clinical distinction between these two processes lies in the recognition that the pathological depressive presentation requires and, in most cases, benefits from treatment with psychotherapy and either antidepressant medication or ECT.

Depression in a Rheumatoid Arthritic

Psychiatric consultation was requested to assess the level of depression in a 46-year-old divorced dentist with a 12-year history of progressive rheumatoid arthritis. The patient had built up a very busy private practice over the years, experiencing relatively little impairment from his disease until 16 months prior to evaluation since which time there had been a significant intensification of the illness. Pain, stiffness and swelling in the joints of his wrists and fingers had progressed to the point that he had been forced to cut back his work schedule to somewhat less than 50 percent of his previous patient load. His internist noted that the patient had become increasingly despairing of the possibility of ever returning to full productivity in his dental practice. The patient was not even sure he would not undergo further loss of functioning in his hands or in his overall sense of health. The patient also reported a 15 pound weight loss and increasing feelings of malaise over the past month as well as intermittent periods of sudden weeping. During the assessment, the psychiatric consultant noted the absence of psychomotor slowing, sleep disturbance, self-destructive ideations or of any true sense of hopelessness or helplessness. The patient acknowledged to her that he continued to be an avid civic booster and fan of the local professional baseball team and still attended almost all of the home games with a couple of his friends. The consultant's overall impression was that the patient was undergoing a type of grief reaction in response to the significant progressive losses that were vitally affecting his life. A supportive, short-term psychotherapy process was initiated, focusing on the nature of these losses as well as the life-style and occupational changes that were being made necessary by the progressive, debilitating illness.

Medical Illnesses Presenting with Depression

Excluding depressive presentations that are characterological in nature, reactive to, or coincidental with medical illnesses, certain illnesses and drugs appear to be specifically associated with a major depressive syndrome (Jefferson and Marchall 1981a). The precise mechanism by which these depressions are produced in association with these conditions remains undetermined although individuals with enhanced predispositions for depression or with previous depressive episodes appear to be at increased risk (Sachar 1975a; Whitlock 1978). Although the vast majority of depressions are not associated with these specific medical illnesses or medications, it is necessary to be aware of these possibilities when considering the differential diagnostic aspects of depressive symptomatology. If the presence of one of these secondary depressions can be established through the use of comprehensive medical history, a thorough physical examination, and selected laboratory tests, the treatment of the underlying disorder can be carried out in a timely fashion, positively affecting morbidity and mortality. Treatment of the underlying disease also seems to be the key step in the resolution of the presenting depressive symptomatology for many of these patients (Leigh and Reiser 1980).

Given the formidable number of medical illnesses, syndromes, and medications known to be associated, at one time or another, with depressive symptomatology (Hall 1980), an attempt will be made here to highlight only those illnesses and drugs known to have a specific frequent relationship with a significant depressive syndrome.

Endocrine Disorders

Significant depressive illness can be found frequently in association with a number of the endocrinopathies. Both hyperadrenalism and hypoadrenalism have been found to have depression as a common clinical feature. Although there is as yet no specific psychiatric outcome reported with Cushing's syndrome, one of the more comprehensive reviews of published clinical reports by Fawcett and Bunney (1967) noted the presence of severe depression as a significant feature in over half of 94 patients with hyperadrenalism. Suicide attempts have been found to occur in about 10 percent of the individuals with Cushing's syndrome. Sachar (1975b) and others have also noted an association between Addison's disease and depressive illness. Much of the depressive symptomatology in both Addison's disease and Cushing's syndrome is thought to be due to the effects of ACTH and corticosteroids on the central nervous system, although the specific mechanisms of action remain uncertain.

Significant depressive affect has also been an almost universal finding in association with hypothyroidism (Whybrown et al. 1969, Gold and Pearsall 1983). Research evidence has suggested that the underlying mechanism involves decreased neuroreceptor sensitivity to catecholamines and diminished catecholamine metabolism in the presence of low thyroid hormone levels (Jefferson and Marshall 1981b, Whybrow and Prange 1981). This latter finding has resulted in the use of thyroid hormone supplementation along with tricyclic antidepressants in the treatment of certain resistant depressions; there is evidence of enhanced antidepressant response in selected cases. Regarding the management of the affective disturbance found in hypothyroid individuals, Jain (1972) noted the persistence of significant depression even after successful treatment of the patients' physical conditions. He concluded that it was important to supplement such physical treatment with psychiatric treament when there is evidence of affective disturbance, instead of assuming the mental state will have a one-to-one correspondence with the physical state.

A specific link has also been found between depression and hyperparathyroidism. In one of the more recent comprehensive studies focusing on this association, Peterson (1968) noted that more than 50 percent of his patients with hyperparathyroidism suffered from a listless, apathetic depression also characterized by a lack of initiative and loss of drive. This affective state was believed to be directly associated with a calcium level in the 12 to 16mg./100ml. range. The higher the serum calcium in this range, the more severe the depressive symptomatology. The affective symptoms were completely reversible when the serum calcium returned to a normal level. In addition to the above postulated mechanism of action involving calcium metabolism, the role of hypomagnesemia in the etiology of depressive changes in hyperparathyroidism remains to be explored.

Pancreatic Carcinoma

A number of investigators have noted the frequent, specific finding of severe depression in carcinoma of the pancreas (Fras et al. 1967). In fact, the incidence of depression in this disorder is significantly higher than the incidence of depression that occurs with other types of cancer. The reason for this finding is unknown. Characteristic early findings in nearly half of these patients included symptoms of depression with an associated loss of ambition and feelings of premonition of serious illness. Most of these patients have no previous history of depression, no significant family history of psychiatric illness and no obvious environmental or interpersonal precipitating events. Psychiatric symptoms, most commonly those of depression, preceded the appearance of physical symptoms of pancreatic carcinoma by an average of six months (Fras et al. 1968). This latter finding has led to the suggestion that signs of first-time nonpsychotic depression without psychomotor retardation in a male aged 50–70 be considered a possible aid in the early detection of pancreatic carcinoma.

Metabolic Disorders: Pernicious Anemia

A consistently strong relationship has been noted between depression and pernicious anemia (Vitamin B-12 deficiency) (Roos, 1978; Martin, 1979). Although there is no pathognomonic psychiatric presentation of

Vitamin B-12 deficiency, when depression presents as part of the initial clinical picture it can be quite intense, with a marked dysphoria, feelings of guilt and worthlessness, diminished concentration, and irritability. Although this may be in addition to symptoms of anemia — fatigue, weakness, and lethargy — the affective manifestations can occur in the presence of a normal blood picture and a normal neurological examination. Vitamin B-12 replacement is an effective treatment for both the neurologic and psychiatric manifestations of pernicious anemia if instituted early enough in the clinical course of the disorder (Jefferson and Marshall 1981d).

Neurologic Diseases: Parkinson's Disease

Clinically significant depression occurs with greater frequency in Parkinson's disease than in other neurologic disorders, with prominent symptomatology appearing in one-third to one-half of all patients (Wells and Duncan 1980). Current clinical evidence supports the notion that this depression is an integral part of the disease process itself and not predominantly a psychological reaction to the disease. Recognition of a true depressive illness associated with Parkinson's disease is important because of its positive response to tricyclic antidepressants and the relative lack of response to Levodopa alone (Marsh and Markham 1973).

Brain Tumors

Psychiatric symptoms, including those of depression, can often be the earliest or occasionally the only symptoms of an intracranial tumor (Martin 1979). The specific behavioral and affective changes resulting from a brain tumor are a reflection of numerous dynamic forces including altered CNS functioning, the patient's response to these changes, and the rate of tumor growth. Tumor location also seems to be an important factor, with studies of intracranial tumors presenting with depressive and other psychiatric symptomatology revealing a predilection for involvement of the temporal and frontal lobes (Hall 1980). The depressive illness found in these patients is often associated with a marked lability with frequent episodes of crying and agitation. Increasing evidence of cognitive deterioration and memory impairment can be seen along with the depressive symptoms as the course of the illness progresses.

Viral Illnesses

Depressions have been noted to occur often in patients with, or following, infectious hepatitis, mononucleosis, or viral pneumonia (Schwab 1969). These depressive syndromes are characterized by dysphoria and mood lability, easy fatigability, anorexia, sleep disturbance, decreased libido, and multiple somatic complaints such as headache and GI disturbance. The etiology of these depressive episodes remains uncertain although

Sachar has postulated that the symptomatology might be linked to sequelae of the original disease process, may represent a reaction to feeling weak and tired, or may reflect a virally induced set of neurochemical changes (Sachar 1975a).

Drug-Related Depressions

In their comprehensive review of this area, Whitlock and Evans (1978) noted that, although over 200 drugs have been claimed as causative agents for depression in certain individuals, only relatively few have been noted to precipitate significant depressive symptoms with any frequency. Those most commonly implicated include amphetamines, ethanol, the antihypertensives, and oral contraceptives. As noted earlier, these drug-induced depressions are far more likely to occur in individuals who are genetically predisposed, those with a history of previous depressive illness, or the elderly, whose responsiveness to drugs might be altered secondary to alterations in tissue metabolism or in drug disposition. Environmental stressors might also play a role in determining vulnerability to the development of depression. These authors suggested that the common mechanism underlying these depressions involved a possible drug-stimulated depletion of dopamine, norepinephrine, or serotonin or an augmentation of acetylcholine in the CNS, the specific mechanism being determined by the particular drug involved. Finally, a number of authors have emphasized the importance of distinguishing the physical and psychological symptoms of depression from the anergia, sedation and alteration in physiological functions which occur with a wide variety of medications (Ayd 1975, Jefferson and Marshall 1981a).

Among the antihypertensive agents, reserpine, methyldopa, guanethidine, propranolol, and colonidine have all been implicated as causative agents for at least moderately significant depressive episodes (Whitlock 1978). Reserpine and methyldopa in particular appear to be frequently associated with depression (Goodwin et al. 1972). At least 15 percent of patients receiving reserpine have been noted to develop significant depressive phenomena, and a substantial number of these individuals have had previous episodes of depression. Consistent with the clinical implications of this latter finding, discontinuance of reserpine in these patients did not often result in remission of the depression, necessitating a formal course of treatment including antidepressant medication.

There is significant clinical evidence of an association between alcoholism and depression (Woods 1982). Suicide rates of heavy drinkers have also been found to be significantly higher than those found in the general population, ostensibly as a reflection of increased depressive illness in this group. Winokur (1973), utilizing the concept of depressive spectrum disease, has suggested a genetic linkage between depression in females and sociopathy or alcoholism in males. The controversial area related to causality, whether depression precedes alcoholism or vice versa, has undergone some resolution through the accumulating of research that demonstrates alcohol's adverse impact on biogenic amine metabolism (Walsh 1973).

Although a preponderance of clinical research evidence has noted a significant relationship between oral contraceptive use and depression, this is not a controversy-free conclusion (Whitlock 1978). Findings by Kutner and Brown (1972) and others have concluded that there is no significant evidence that oral contraceptives cause depression. As noted earlier with certain other drugs, some women with previous histories of depressive illness may be at increased risk for recurrence following oral contraceptive administration. The question of whether predominantly estrogenic or progestogenic medications are more likely to induce dysphoric symptoms remains unsettled (Jefferson and Marshall 1981c). Finally, Rose (1969) has hypothesized that depressive illness that is induced by oral contraceptives might be caused by a decreased availability of pyridoxine (Vitamin B-6), with a subsequent negative impact on serotonin production. However, attempts to utilize Vitamin B-6 supplementation to treat depressive symptoms in patients taking oral contraceptives have remained inconclusive (Stokes 1972).

Finally, abrupt discontinuation of high dose amphetamines can precipitate the onset of severe depressive symptomatology, including apathy, psychomotor retardation and sleep disturbance, that may last for months (Wesson 1973). Treatment recommendations include gradual tapering withdrawal of 5mg. per day in a controlled environment like a hospital to minimize the risk of suicide. Tricyclic antidepressants have also been utilized to combat postamphetamine depression.

Depression and Somatization: Selective Considerations

Earlier in this chapter, I noted Katon's (1982) belief that patients in primary care often selectively focused on the somatic manifestations of major depressive disorder to the exclusion (through denial or minimalization) of affective or cognitive components. These somatic manifestations included insomnia, fatigue, anorexia, weight loss, impaired concentration, constipation, headaches, and backaches. Katon further noted that the underrecognition of depression in this population could be traced to this excessively selective focus on the part of patients and primary care physicians alike. Goldberg and Blackwell (1970) referred to this group of psychiatrically disturbed patients who present with a physical complaint and who do not have the underlying psychiatric impairment identified as the "hidden psychiatric morbidity of medical practice." Goldberg and Blackwell found that the majority of these patients formulated their concerns in somatic terms not only to the physician but also to themselves. Direct inquiry through the use of a self-administered questionnaire was necessary to detect depression in the absence of volunteered affective symptoms. The authors suggested three reasons why these patients presented with somatic complaints. The first reason can be understood in terms of a social learning paradigm: the patients might have learned that, since physicians deal with physical illnesses, the physician expects them to produce physical symptoms. Second, the patients might have undergone increased emotional distress with concurrent exacerbation of their somatic symptomatology. It is the somatic symptom that seems worse to the patient and so it is the somatic symptom that gets presented to the physician. Finally, these patients might have felt that it was more socially acceptable and less stigmatizing to be physically ill than emotionally ill.

Stoeckle and Davidson (1962) also noted the usual tendency of depressed patients in their general medical clinic to present with somatic symptoms in lieu of overt depressive signs. The two most common somatic symptoms were those of an overwhelming fatigue and insomnia. These authors also indicated that depressed patients in their population with known medical disease reported a worsening of their symptomatology in the absence of any increase in objective clinical findings. They further suggested the correct diagnosis of the underlying affective disorder depended upon the identification, through a careful clinical interview, of associated depressive symptomatology (such as dysphoric mood, injured self-esteem, helplessness, loss of pleasure in social relationships, withdrawal and irritability) plus positive evidence that these symptoms followed a traumatic event that involved a loss of personal security or an important person, or a change in self-image.

A similar trend was found in the Widmer and Cadoret study of 154 depressed family practice patients. When compared with matched controls in the seven months prior to diagnosis of depression, the depressed patients showed a significantly increased number who presented complaints of three types: ill-defined "functional" complaints such as fatigue, weight loss, or dizziness; "nervous" complaints such as increased tension; and feelings of anxiety and pain of undetermined etiology in a variety of sites: head, chest, abdomen and extremities (Widmer and Cadoret 1978).

Many others, including Lindsay and Wyckoff (1981), Von Knorring (1965), and Blumer et al. (1980) have also noted a significantly increased association between chronic somatic pain complaints and depression. Sternbach (1978) and Sternbach et al. (1976) put forward the idea that this close relationship between chronic pain and depression suggested a common underlying mechanism, later postulating this mechanism involved diminished brain serotonin. Blumer and Heilbronn (1982) identified within their chronic pain patient population a psychobiological syndrome with distinctive clinical psychodynamic, genetic, and biographic features. The paper poses an intriguing suggestion: the overt denial of an affective component of depression in the pain patients of Blumer and Heilbronn could be understood in terms of the concept of alexithymia, the inability to recognize and verbalize one's feelings. This idea was similar to the earlier finding of Nemiah and Sifneos (1976) who also showed that many of their psychosomatic patients were alexithymic and therefore left to react somatically to stressors and conflicts. The psychobiological syndrome was felt to be applicable to chronic pain patients without discernible somatic disease as well as to patients with the physical disease who suffer out of proportion to the actual disease process. The authors term this syndrome the pain-prone disorder, conceptualizing it as a depressive disease variant.

Finally, Lindsay and Wyckoff (1981), Blumer and Heilbronn (1982), and others have found the use of antidepressant medications significantly effective in providing analgesic relief in chronic pain and depression states. Although the precise relationship between biogenicamines and enkephalins remains to be clarified, the response of these depression-pain syndromes to antidepressant medication seems to involve the mechanism of action that restores serotonin, norepinephrine, and encephalin levels to normal via mutually interacting feedback loops at midbrain, medullary, and spinal cord levels (Basbaum and Fields 1978).

Summary

Several factors contributing to the underdiagnosis of depression in the general medical patient population are noted. These include the inability by some physicians to conceptualize the existence of depression in the absence of a patient-reported affective state and the poorly defined, unnecessarily complex classification schemes proposed in the past. The more recently derived pluralistic concept of depression is presented, maintaining that its pathogenesis results from a complex interaction between genetic-neurochemical factors, early life experiences, personality factors, environmental stressors, and cognitive percepts.

A proposal is made for a reformulated classification scheme integrating core DSM-III depressive criteria within a modified primary-secondary disorder framework. It is thought to be sufficiently comprehensive and practical to allow increased utilization in the general medical care and psychiatric consultation settings.

Distinctions are made between despondency or demoralization (a normal grief process) and a pathological depressive state as a response to medical illness. Despondency is an accentuation of normal feelings of sadness in response to narcissistic injury to the patient's self-esteem. A grief reaction can be said to represent a more intensive level along the depressive continuum. It is a predictable phasic process characterized by intense psychic suffering and despair in response to a significant loss.

Medical illnesses and drugs known to have a specific, frequent relationship with a significant depressive syndrome are highlighted. Timely recognition and treatment of the underlying disorder can have often have a considerable positive impact on morbidity and mortality for these patients.

Finally, consideration is given to the concept of depression manifesting as somatic illness, the "hidden psychiatric morbidity of medical practice." The significant association between chronic pain and depression is also explored within this context.

REFERENCES

Altschule, M. D. (1977). Depression as seen by the internist. In *Disease-A-Month* ed. H. F. Dowling, vol. 24, pp. 3–47. Chicago: Yearbook Medical Publishers.

American Psychiatric Association. (1980). Diagnostic and Statistical Manual of Mental Disorders. 3rd ed. Washington, D.C., pp. 205–224.

Arieti, S. (1978). The psychobiology of sadness. In *Severe and Mild Depression — The Psychotherapeutic Approach*, eds. S. Arieti, J. Bemporad, pp. 109–128. New York: Basic Books.

Ayd, F. J. (1975). The depot fluphenazines: a reappraisal after ten years clinical experience. *American Journal of Psychiatry* 132:491–500.

Basbaum, A., and Fields, H. L. (1978). Endogenous pain control mechanism: review and hypothesis. *Annals of Neurology* 4:451–462.

Blacher, R. S. (1970). Reaction to chronic illness. In *Loss and Grief: Psychological Management in Medical Practice*. eds. B. Schoenberg, A. C. Carr, D. Peretz, and A. H. Kutscher, pp. 189–198. New York: CIBA — Columbia University Press.

Blumer, D., Heilbronn, W., Pedraza, E., and Pope, G. (1980). Systematic treatment of chronic pain with antidepressants. *Henry Ford Hospital Medical Journal* 28:15–21.

Blumer, D., and Heilbronn, W. (1982). Chronic pain as a variant of depressive disease: the pain prone disorder. *Journal of Nervous Mental Disease* 170:381–394.

Bowlby, J. (1961). Process of mourning. *International Journal of Psychoanalysis* 42:317–340.

Broden, A. R. (1970). Reaction to loss in the aged. In *Loss and Grief: Psychologi-*

cal Management in Medical Practice, ed. B. Schoenberg, A. Carr, D. Pertez, A. H. Kutscher, pp. 199–217. New York: CIBA and Columbia University Press.

Cassem, N. (1978). Depression. In *Massachusetts General Hospital Handbook of General Hospital Psychiatry,* ed. T. P. Hackett, and N. Cassem, pp. 209–225. St. Louis: C. V. Mosby Company.

Fawcett, J. A., and Bunney, W. E. (1967). Pituitary adrenal function and depression. *Archives of General Psychiatry* 16:517–535.

Fras, I., Litin, E. M., and Pearson, J. S. (1967). Comparison of psychiatric symptoms of carcinoma of the pancreas with those in some other intraabdominal neoplasms. *American Journal of Psychiatry* 123:1553–1562.

Fras, I., Litin, E. M., and Bartholomew, L. G. (1968). Mental symptoms as an aid in the early diagnosis of carcinoma of the pancreas. *Gastroenterology* 55: 191–198.

Gold, M. S., and Pearsall, H. R. (1983). Hypothyroidism – or is it depression? *Psychosomatics* 24:646–656.

Goldberg, D., and Blackwell, B. (1970). Psychiatric illness in general medical practice. *British Medical Journal* 2:439–443.

Goodwin, F. K., Ebert, M. H., and Bunney, W. E. (1972). Mental effects of reserpine in man: a review. In *Psychiatric Complications of Medical Drugs,* ed. R. I. Shader, pp. 73–101. New York: Raven Press.

Hall, R. (1980). Depression. In *Psychiatric Presentation of Medical Illness,* ed. R. Hall, pp. 37–63. New York: Spectrum Publications.

Huston, P. E. (1975). Psychotic depressive reaction. In *Comprehensive Textbook of Psychiatry,* vol. 2, 2nd ed., ed. A. M. Freedman, H. I. Kaplan, and B. J. Saddock, pp. 1043–1055. New York: Spectrum Publications.

Jain, V. K. (1972). A psychiatric study of hypothyroidism. *Psychiat. Clin* 5:121–130.

Jefferson, J. W., and Marshall, J. R. (1981a). Physical illness and psychiatric symptoms. In *Neuropsychiatric Features of Medical Disorders,* pp. 1–12. New York: Plenum Publishing Corporation.

_____ (1981b). Endocrine disorders. In *Neuropsychiatric Features of Medical Disorders,* pp. 133–178. New York: Plenum Publishing Corp.

_____ (1981c). Reproductive and sexual function disorders. In *Neuropsychiatric Features of Medical Disorders,* pp. 303–327. New York: Plenum Publishing Corp.

_____ (1981d). Vitamin disorders. In *Neuropsychiatric Features of Medical Disorders,* pp. 231–257. New York: Plenum Publishing Corp.

Katon, W. (1982). Depression: somatic symptoms and medical disorders in primary care. *Comprehensive Psychiatry* 23:274–287.

Klerman, G. L. (1983). The nosology and diagnosis of depressive disorders. In *Psychiatry Update,* Vol. 2. *The APA Annual Review,* ed. L. Grinspoon, pp. 356–382. Washington, D.C.: American Psychiatric Press.

_____ G. L. (1978). Affective disorders. In *The Harvard Guide to Modern Psychiatry,* ed. A. M. Nicholi, pp. 253–281. Cambridge: Harvard University Press.

Klerman, G. L., and Barrett, J. (1973). Clinical and epidemiologic aspects of affective disorders. In *Lithium: Its Role in Psychiatric Research and Treatment,* ed. S. Gershon, and B. Shopsin, pp. 201–236. New York: Plenum Press.

Kutner, S. J., and Brown, W. L. (1972). Types of oral contraceptives, depression, and premenstrual symptoms. *Journal of Nervous Mental Disorders* 155:153–169.

Leigh, H., and Reiser, M. F. (1980). Depression. In *The Patient: Biological, Psychological, and Social Dimensions of Medical Practice*, pp. 91–127. New York: Plenum Book Company.

Lindemann, E. (1945). Symptomatology and management of acute grief. *American Journal of Psychiatry* 101:141–148.

Lindsay, P. G., and Wyckoff, M. (1981). The depression-pain syndrome and its response to antidepressants. *Psychosomatics* 22:571–577.

Marsh, G. G., and Markham, C. H. (1973). Does levodopa alter depression and psychopathology in parkinsonism patients? *J. Neurol. Neurosurg. Psychiatry* 36:925–935.

Martin, M. J. (1979). Physical disease manifesting as psychiatric disorders. In *Psychiatry in General Medical Practice*, ed. G. Usdin, and J. M. Lewis, pp. 337–351. New York: McGraw-Hill.

Moffic, H. S., and Paykel, E. S. (1975). Depression in medical inpatients. *British Journal of Psychiatry* 126:346–353.

Nemiah, J. C., Freyberger, H., and Sifneos, P. E. (1976). Alexithymia: a view of the psychosomatic process. In *Modern Trends in Psychosomatic Medicine.* Vol. 3, ed. O. Hill, pp. 430–439. Boston: Butterworths.

Nielson, A. C., and Williams, T. A. (1980). Depression in ambulatory medical patients. *Archives of General Psychiatry* 37:999–1004.

Parkes, C. M. (1970). The first year of bereavement. *Psychiatry* 33:444–467.

Peretz, D. (1970a). Development, object-relationships, and loss. In *Loss and Grief: Psychological Management in Medical Practice*, ed. B. Schoenberg, A. C. Carr, D. Peretz, and A. H. Kutscher, pp. 20–85. New York: CIBA and Columbia University Press.

———— (1970b). Reaction to loss. In. *Loss and Grief*: pp. 3–19. New York: CIBA and Columbia University Press.

Peterson, P. (1968). Psychiatric disorders and primary hyperparathyroidism. *Journal of Clinical Endocrinology* 28:1491–1495.

Rawnsky, K. (1968). Epidemiology of affective disorders. *British Journal of Psychiatry*, Special Supplement 2:27–36.

Robins, E., and Guze, S. B. (1969). Classification of affective disorders: the primary-secondary, the endogenous-reactive, and the neurotic-psychotic concepts. In *Recent Advances in the Psychobiology of the Depressive Illnesses*, ed. T. A. Williams, M. M. Katz, T. A. Shield, pp. 283–293. Washington, D.C.: NIMH-HEW.

Roos, D. (1978). Neurological complications in patients with impaired Vitamin B-12 absorption following partial gastrectomy. *Acta Neurologica Scandinavica* 59 (Suppl 69):1–7.

Rose, D. P. (1969). Oral contraceptives and depression. *Lancet* 2:321.

Sachar, E. J. (1975a). Evaluating depression in the medical patient. In *Psychological Care of the Medically Ill: A Primary in Liaison Psychiatry*, ed. J. J. Strain, S. Grossman, pp. 64–75. New York: Appleton-Century-Crofts.

———— (1975b). Psychiatric disturbances associated with endocrine disorders. In *The American Handbook of Psychiatry*. Vol. 4, 2nd ed., ed. S. Arieti, pp. 299–313. New York: Basic Books.

Schwab, J. J. (1969). Psychiatric illness produced by infections. *Hospital Medicine* 5:98–108.

Sternbach, R. A. (1978). Clinical aspects of pain. In *The Psychology of Pain*. New York: Raven Press, pp. 241–264.

Sternbach, R. A., Janowsky, D. S., and Huey, L. Y. (1976). Effects of altering brain serotonin activity on human chronic pain. In *Advances in Pain Research and Therapy*. Vol. 1, ed. J. J. Bonica, pp. 601–606. New York: Raven Press.

Stoeckle, J. D., and Davidson, G. E. (1962). Bodily complaints and other symptoms of depressive reaction. *Journal of the American Medical Association* 180:134–139.

Stokes, J., and Mendels, J. (1972). Pyridoxine and premenstrual tension. *Lancet* 1:1177–1178.

Von Knorring, L. (1965). The experience of pain in depressed patients. *Neuropsychobiology* 1:155–165.

Walsh, M. J. (1973). The biochemical aspects of alcoholism. In *Alcoholism: Progress in Research and Treatment*, ed. P. G. Bourne, pp. 43–61. New York: Academic Press.

Wells, C. E., and Duncan, G. W. (1980). *Neurology for Psychiatrists*. Philadelphia: F. A. Davis, Company.

Wesson, D. R., and Smith, D. E. (1973). Recognizing and treating amphetamine abuse. *Hospital Physician* 8:22–25.

Whitlock, F. A., and Evans, L. E. J. (1978). Drugs and depression. *Drugs* 15:53–71.

Whybrow, P. C., Prange, A. J., and Treadway, C. R. (1969). Mental changes accompanying thyroid gland dysfunction. *Archives of General Psychiatry* 20:48–63.

Whybrow, P. C., and Prange, A. J. (1981). A hypothesis of thyroid-catecholamine receptor interaction. *Archives of General Psychiatry* 38:106–113.

Widmer, R. B., and Cadoret, R. J. (1978). Depression in primary care: changes in pattern of patient visits and complaints during a developing depression. *Journal of Family Practice* 7:293–302.

Winokur, G. (1973). The types of affective disorder. *Journal of Nervous Mental Disorders* 156:82–96.

Woods, B. T. (1982). Medical and neurological aspects of depression. In *Update III: Harrison's Principles of Internal Medicine*, ed. K. J. Isselbacher, et al., pp. 167–183. New York: McGraw-Hill.

CHAPTER 21

Somatic Treatment of Depression

Barbara J. Novak, M.D.
Harry Zall, M.D.
Steven Zavodnick, M.D.

This chapter is a review of specific somatic treatments for depressive disorder. The three standard therapies currently used in clinical practice, TCAs, MAOIs, and ECT, are discussed first, followed by a discussion of less conventional treatments including lithium and carbamazepine. For each treatment modality there is an overview of its pharmacological action, associated side effects and their management, and treatment applications including indicators, pretreatment steps, guidelines for dosaging and duration of treatment, and a discussion of strategies for those patients who respond minimally or not at all to a single modality.

We begin with a discussion of biological tests developed on the basis of specific neuroendocrine and neurochemical abnormalities observed to accompany affective illnesses. Clinical use of the dexamethasone suppression test (DST) and the thyrotropin-releasing hormone (TRH) test is described in detail as these tests may be helpful to the clinician in confirming a diagnosis of depression. At the present time, the neurochemical markers are essentially of heuristic rather than clinical importance and are not useful in routine practice. They have been included here as an indication of the potential for objective diagnostic tests in this rapidly developing area.

Biological Markers of Depression

A number of biological abnormalities have been identified in patients with affective disorders. Although testing for these does not purport to replace the careful clinical examination of a patient in order to arrive at a diagnosis, certain laboratory tests may assist the physician in confirming a clinical impression. Since depression, which is sometimes masked clinically, is likely to be a highly treatable psychiatric disorder with as much as an 80–90 percent positive response to somatic treatment (Avery and Winokur 1977), proper diagnosis is especially important. The biological deviations to be discussed here involve a presumptive dysfunction in the limbic-hypothalamic structures, the phylogenetically older areas of the brain which have been implicated as likely neuroanatomical sites for regulation of emotions and affective states.

Neuroendocrine Markers

In neuroendocrine tests, exogenous hormone administration should activate a homeostatic reaction in an interconnected system which includes parts of the limbic system, the hypothalamus, the pituitary, and peripheral endocrine glands. Abnormal responses to the exogenous challenge have been observed in patients with major depressions, suggesting a neuroendocrine dysregulation in these patients. Such deviations do not commonly accompany nondepressive psychiatric disorders. The dexamethasone suppression test (DST) is currently the most popular of these challenge studies; the recommended protocol (Carroll et al. 1981) involves giving 1 mg. of dexamethasone, a synthetic glucocorticoid, orally at 11:00 P.M. The following day, blood samples to be tested for plasma cortisol levels are drawn at 4:00 P.M. and 11:00 P.M. For outpatients, only the 4:00 P.M. sample is drawn as a convenience. Normally, dexamethasone stimulates a negative feedback response to the hypothalamus which secretes less corticotropin releasing factor, and, consequently less ACTH is released by the anterior pituitary. This in turn results in diminished cortisol release by the adrenals. In patients with major depression, especially those with the melancholic subtype, this normal cortisol suppression is impaired. These patients exhibit a nonsuppressive response to dexamethasone resulting in relatively high plasma cortisol levels. They break through the suppression which normally prevails for 24 hours. A cortisol level above a criterion of 5 μg/dl (50 ng/ml) with competitive protein binding (CPB) cortisol assays or 4 μg/dl with the more specific radioimmunoassay method is considered a positive or abnormal DST. The laboratory must employ highly discriminative tests in the lower concentration range in order for a value of 6, for example, to be validly distinguished from one of 4 or 3. Using the above protocol, the sensitivity of the DST for endogenous depressions ("true"-positive rate among those suspected of diagnosis) is 40–67 percent, and the specificity ("true"-negative rate in a control population) is 96–100 percent (Brown et al. 1979, Carroll et al. 1981). A loss in sensitivity of 18 percent can result from obtaining a 4:00 P.M. sample alone as compared with obtaining both afternoon and evening samples (Carroll et al. 1981). An abnormal DST carries a high predictive value for endogenous depression, but a negative result does not exclude the diagnosis.

A second neuroendocrine marker, the thyrotropin-releasing hormone (TRH) stimulation test, measures the response of the anterior pituitary in releasing thyrotropin (TSH) following exogenous TRH stimulation. It is performed after an overnight fast and the $\triangle$max TSH value is measured as the largest difference between the baseline TSH and levels obtained at 15, 30, 45 and 60 minutes following an injection of TRH (IV dose of 0.5 mg. protireline injected over 30 seconds). Normally, the $\triangle$max is from 10–20 μU/ml. A blunting of $\triangle$max to less than 7 μU/ml has been discovered as an accompaniment to endogenous depression but not usually to other psychiatric disorders (Gold et al. 1980a, Extein et al. 1981a).Test sensitivity is 50 percent with a specificity of about 90 percent (Loosen and Prange 1982, Extein et al. 1981, 1982).

The underlying neuroendocrine abnormality manifested by a blunted TSH response appears different than the dysfunction associated with a positive DST since only a minority of patients with major depression simultaneously exhibit both abnormalities (Loosen and Prange 1982, Rush et al. 1983). Therefore, by combining the tests serially, with the TRH followed by the DST, the results will likely increase the total sensitivity to endogenous depression to approximately 80 percent (Extein et al. 1981a, Rubin et al. 1982).

Other neuroendocrine disturbances which research has uncovered as possible markers for endogenous depression are a blunted response of growth hormone (GH) secretion to several challenges, including amphetamine, desmethylimipramine, clonidine and insulin-induced hypoglycemia (Checkley, 1980); reduced nocturnal and diurnal secretion of leutinizing hormone (LH) (Rubin and Marder 1983); a decreased response of prolactin (PRL) release to TRH stimulation (Winokur et al. 1983) and to infusion of an opiate (Gold et al. 1980). Before the clinical utility of these several tests can be established, their validity, standardization, sensitivity and specificity must first be determined using large groups of subjects.

Neurochemical Markers

For more than 15 years, the catecholamine and indoleamine hypotheses of depression have been promulgated as models by which the presumed biochemical bases of depression could be understood. For example, measurements of urinary 3-methoxy-4-hydroxyphenylglycol (MHPG), a possible major metabolite of central nervous system norepinephrine (NE) (Maas and Landis 1968), have been made in order to uncover a noradrenergic pathophysiological cause of depressions and to define subgroups of depression which would respond differentially to various antidepressant drugs. Schildkraut and his co-workers (1983) have suggested the existence of three subtypes of unipolar depressions distinguished by differences in their respective urinary MHPG levels. According to Schildkraut, depressed patients with low pretreatment levels of urinary MHPG ($\leq$ 1950 μg/24 hours) may have low central nervous system (CNS) NE output as a result of decreased synthesis or release from NE neurons. This noradrenergic group of patients is reportedly responsive to imipramine or maprotiline, antidepressant drugs which have relatively strong noradrenergic potentiating effects at synapses. A second group with pretreatment high urinary MHPG levels (>2500 $\mu g/24$ hours) may have high CNS NE output due to alterations in noradrenergic receptors and/or an increase in cholinergic activity and are responsive to only very high doses of maprotiline (perhaps required to offset the cholinergic excess state). An intermediate group with urinary MHPG levels between 1951–2500 ug/24 hours may have normal CNS NE output in association with abnormalities in other non-noradrenergic biochemical systems. This group may be more responsive to agents that are relative potent serotonergic potentiators (e.g., clomipramine or amitriptyline) (Goodwin et al. 1978).

Studies of indoleamine metabolism utilizing CSF levels of 5-hydroxyindole acetic acid (5-HIAA), the major CNS metabolite of serotonin, suggest a subgroup of depressed patients (either unipolar or bipolar) as defined by low CSF levels of 5-HIAA (Post and Goodwin 1978). Further work by Maas, Goodwin, and their co-workers indicates that a group of depressed patients with low CSF levels of 5-HIAA, suggesting a serotonin deficiency disorder, selectively respond to serotonin-enhancing agents such as precursor amino acids (e.g., 5-hydroxytryptophan) or antidepressants which block serotonin uptake (e.g., clomipramine and amitriptyline). A second group which has normal CSF levels of 5-HIAA but low levels of urinary MHPG may respond preferentially to antidepressants that selectively enhance noradrenergic transmission (e.g., desipramine, imipramine) (Goodwin et al. 1978). These latter patients also show an improvement in mood when given a test dose of dextroamphetamine (Maas 1975). A 4–5 day trial of a bidaily dextroamphetamine dose of 10–15 mg. (Fawcett and Siompoulos 1971) or methylphenidate dose of 20–30 mg. (Sabelli et al. 1983) has been suggested as an aid in deciding whether to initiate treatment with a noradrenergic or serotonergic agent; a euphoric response predicts a positive clinical response to the noradrenergic agents.

Unfortunately, these measurements of noradrenergic and serotonergic metabolites are not applicable for routine clinical use due to the wide variation among individuals in MHPG and 5-HIAA levels (about 30 percent) as well as the impracticality of routine lumbar punctures (Post and Goodwin 1978). Also, not all research reports agree that there are well-defined correlations between levels of these metabolites and changes in affective states. The dextroamphetamine and methylphenidate stimulation tests are the exception; they are easily carried out and may be useful to the clinician.

Tricyclic Antidepressants

The tricyclic antidepressants (TCAs) have been in widespread use for more than 20 years and their efficacy in the treatment of depression has been well documented in the psychiatric literature (Klein et al. 1980). Imipramine, the prototype TCA, is chemically related to chlorpromazine and was originally investigated in the search of more effective antipsychotic drugs. More recently, other drugs have been employed as antidepressants. Some of these are tetracyclic in structure but resemble the tricyclic drugs in their pharmacological properties; others are quite novel and differ from the tricyclic drugs in many ways. These new antidepressants will be discussed following a review of the tricyclic antidepressants which remain the mainstay of the pharmacological treatment of depressive illness.

Pharmacological Action

Soon after the discovery of the usefulness of TCAs in treating depression, it was discovered that they are potent inhibitors of the presynaptic uptake of the biogenic amine neurotransmitters norepinephrine and serotonin (Glowinski and Axelrod 1964). Removing a methyl group on the terminal nitrogen of the TCA produced a change in action on the metabolism of these central nervous system neurotransmitters. Traditionally, it was thought that the monomethylated secondary amines (desipramine, nortriptyline, protriptyline) primarily block reuptake of norepinephrine (NE), whereas dimethylated tertiary amines (imipramine, amitriptyline, doxepin, trimipramine) exert a major inhibitory effect on the reuptake of serotonin (5-HT) (Schubert et al. 1970). Current thinking, based on more recent studies, indicates that all TCAs predominantly inhibit NE reuptake and, to a lesser extent, inhibit 5-HT reuptake. The exceptions are desipramine and protriptyline which exert relatively pure NE reuptake blockade (Baldessarini 1983). Since inhibition of reuptake occurs within hours of administration (Glowinski and Axelrod 1964), this mechanism may not account for the clinical efficacy of antidepressants which develops over two or more weeks.

The most consistent neurochemical effect observed after chronic administration of TCAs is a reduction in the functional activity and number of beta-adrenergic receptors in the cerebral cortex of laboratory animals (Banerjee et al. 1977; Charney et al. 1981). This desensitization or "down regulation" of beta-adrenergic receptors is believed to result from an increase in the intrasynaptic concentration and turnover of NE. This antidepressant-induced phenomenon occurs with all TCAs and requires a lag time of from one to several weeks which is similar to the clinical response time seen with antidepressants. It has been proposed as the basis on which the alleviation of depression occurs (Mobley and Sulser 1981).

In addition, chronic, but not acute, treatment with many TCAs reduces the density of serotonergic (5-HT$_2$) receptors ([H^3]-spiroperidol labeled receptors) in cerebral cortical areas. Amitriptyline, a tertiary amine with strong but not exclusive selectivity for blocking serotonin reuptake, preferentially desensitizes these receptors. Conversely, desipramine, a secondary amine which blocks NE reuptake, is more effective than amitriptyline in desensitizing the beta-adrenergic receptor (Peroutka and Snyder 1980). These results support the notion that a single biochemical "mechanism" may be insufficient to explain the clinical effects of all antidepressants.

Recent evidence also suggests a functional linkage between the serotonergic and noradrenergic systems in mediating the neurochemical effects of antidepressants. In animal studies where the serotonergic system is destroyed by specific lesioning with the serotonin neurotoxin 5,7-dihydroxytryptamine, administration of TCAs fails to reduce the density of beta-adrenergic receptors or the sensitivity of beta-adrenergic receptor-coupled adenylate cyclase. Thus the serotonergic system plays a "permissive" role in the desensitization of beta-adrenergic receptors by TCAs (Janowsky et al. 1982). This functional linkage between the two neuronal systems may provide a basis for unifying the two major hypotheses of affective disorders, the "serotonin" and "norepinephrine" hypotheses.

Hormones can also induce modifications in the effects of antidepressants. Studies in rats of the effects of ovariectomy (eliminates the desensitization of 5-HT$_2$ receptors produced by imipramine) and estradiol or progesterone administration (restores "down regulation") suggest that hormonal changes that occur in postmenopausal women may profoundly influence the efficacy of TCAs (Hauger and Paul 1983). Although the effect of thyroid hormone on brain neurotransmitter receptors has not been fully elucidated, a lack of circulating thyroid hormones has been shown to decrease the number of cerebral cortex beta-adrenergic receptors in rats (Gross et al. 1980). Conversely, administration of thyroid hormone increases the density of these receptors in rat heart (Williams et al. 1979). A similar phenomenon in the brain could help explain the finding that triiodothyronine (T$_3$) can rapidly convert TCA nonresponders to responders (Goodwin et al. 1982).

Clinical Indications for TCA Use

Depressive illnesses are the most prevalent of psychiatric disorders. The lifetime risk of clinically significant depression in the general population is greater than 1 in 10. Multiple causes, a variety of symptoms and a wide range of severity, disability, and duration characterize these disorders.

Depressive symptoms may signify the presence of a "primary" affective disorder or may accompany other psychiatric or medical conditions as a "secondary" process. In the general psychiatric literature depression characteristically is portrayed as a phasic disorder with illness episodes separated by months or years of normal functioning. In addition to pervasive dysphoric mood, which may be expressed as sadness, tearfulness or irritability, behavioral and cognitive changes are usually reported. These include loss of interest in usual activities, inability to respond, even transiently, to pleasant events and situations (referred to as mood autonomy), distinct changes in sleep, eating, energy level, and motor activity, and feelings of guilt, worthlessness, recurrent thoughts of death, and impaired concentration.

These characteristics have supported the use of such terms as "endogenous," "endogenomorphic," "vital," or "melancholic" in recent diagnostic attempts to subdivide severe depressions. Most systems also recognize a difference between illnesses that are relatively minor ("neurotic," "reactive") and others that are currently referred to in DSM-III (1980) as major and include the subgroup of severe illnesses described above. Patients within this subgroup of severe depressive illness are most likely to respond favorably to TCAs.

No clinical subtype is clearly responsive to one particular TCA over another. There is evidence that the presence of delusions in patients with endogenous depression responds to a combination of antipsychotics with TCAs (Nelson and Bowers 1978) or to ECT (Glassman et al. 1975) in preference to treatment with TCAs alone. It is not unusual to encounter the situation of so-called "double depression," that is, patients in whom episodes of acute major depression are superimposed upon a chronic, milder depressed state. These patients may get some relief from their acute symptomatology with antidepressant treatment although typically the chronic symptoms are not completely ameliorated by drug therapy (Keller and Shapiro 1982).

In general, it is appropriate to consider TCA treatment for patients whose symptoms have persisted unabated for at least three weeks, whose social, familial or occupational functioning is impaired by these symptoms, and who meet DSM-III diagnostic criteria for some form of depressive disorder. Although TCAs are generally considered the treatment of choice only for patients with major depression, others with moderate or even mild depression may be suitable candidates either initially or after other therapeutic approaches have failed (Rabkin et al. 1983).

Dosage and Duration of Treatment

In general, it is wise to institute outpatient treatment with antidepressant medication by administering the drug in divided doses during the day, starting with a dose of 25 mg. a day and increasing in increments of 25 mg. until the desired clinical effect is achieved. Because of differences in rates of metabolism, a smaller initial dose and therapeutic dose is usually indicated for the elderly and for children. By using this strategem, patients can gradually accommodate to adverse side effects and the drug can be more easily titrated until the optimal therapeutic dosage is reached. At that time, either a single bedtime dose can be given or smaller divided doses during the day can be continued. The latter regimen is especially helpful for the anxious patient who may benefit from the anxiolytic effects of the drug and for the elderly patient who may better tolerate the anticholinergic effects of the antidepressant in small divided doses. Inpatients may be started at 75–100 mg. daily and increased to the usual effective range as rapidly as tolerated.

The dosage range of the currently available antidepressants is wide. The usual adult dose for amitriptyline, imipramine, trimipramine, desipramine, and doxepin is 150–200 mg/day with a range of 50–300 mg/day; protriptyline daily dose is 30–40 mg. with a range of 15–60 mg.; and nortriptyline dose is 75–100 mg/day with a range of 30–150 mg/day (therapeutic window effect for these last two drugs implies the possibility of reduced therapeutic effect with higher dosages). It is important to note that elderly patients may attain two-fold higher blood levels as compared with younger patients at comparable dosages of tricyclic antidepressants (Nies et al. 1977).

Klein and his coauthors (1980) suggest that no patient be considered refractory until he has received a dose of 300 mg/day of the TCA. Some patients will require even higher doses and some may respond to unusually low amounts of antidepressants. The wide individual differences in drug plasma levels among patients given uniform oral doses of an antidepressant probably reflect differences in rates of metabolism, differences in the blood brain barrier, and possible insufficient sites for drug action. As important as adequate antidepressant dosage in evaluating clinical response is continuing treatment long enough to allow the patient to recover from the immediate depressive symptoms; this provides a period of prophylaxis to guard against recurrences of depression (Klerman 1978). A therapeutic response may require from one to two weeks of treatment and may not be maximal until the fourth or fifth week (Klein et al. 1980). A recent study (Quitkin et al. 1984) reports that 20 percent of a group of depressed patients who did not respond to four weeks of antidepressant therapy did respond when the drug was continued for six weeks.

The duration of treatment is a subject of much interest and discussion. Bernstein (1983) recommends a three-month course of treatment for the individual with no prior history and no family history of depressive illness. For the patient with a history of recurrent depressive episodes or with a positive family history, a six-to-twelve-month course of antidepressant medication is recommended. Still others with a chronic or lifelong depressive illness may require maintenance therapy for years and possibly throughout the lifetime of the patient. When the antidepressant is discontinued, it should be done gradually, since symptoms of nausea, vomiting, malaise, and muscular pains occasionally occur as part of a mild withdrawal response. As the dose is slowly tapered, careful observation of the patient's reactions can be monitored with close attention to the recurrence of depressive symptoms and the need to reinstitute maintenance treatment. Davis (1976) has reviewed studies demonstrating that more than twice as many patients relapse when antidepressants are not continued after treatment of an acute depression than do so when maintenance drugs are prescribed.

Therapeutic Blood Levels

For patients who have not responded to the recommended upper limit of antidepressant after several weeks of treatment, it may be useful to obtain a plasma level of the drug to determine if the patient is receiving an adequate drug dosage. At the present time, therapeutic plasma levels have only been clearly established by extensive, consistent data for imipramine and nortriptyline. Nortriptyline has a therapeutic window, which is between 50 and 150 ng/ml, above which the therapeutic response diminishes (Asberg et al. 1971, Kragh-Sorenson et al. 1976). In contrast to the data for nortriptyline, there appears to be a sigmoidal relationship between plasma concentrations and clinical response for imipramine with a maximal effect above 200 ng/ml of imipramine plus its major metabolite, desipramine (Glassman et al. 1977, Matuzas et al. 1982).

For the most part, the reported relationships between antidepressant plasma levels and therapeutic response have been determined in patients with endogenous depression and are therefore most valid for this population of depressed patients. It is important when collecting the blood sample that it be drawn 10–12 hours after the last dose and that measurement is of a steady-state level which is achieved when the patient has been on the same antidepressant dose for at least five days. Finally, it is wise to carefully check the quality of the laboratory used and to ask for data regarding the validation and reliability of the assay employed since few laboratories offer specific, well validated tricyclic determination.

In the case of a patient who is receiving adequate drug dosage but has not responded to treatment, obtaining plasma levels for imipramine and nortriptyline can readily determine whether a change in dosage is necessary to achieve therapeutic levels. Occasional plasma level measurements may also be useful in young and elderly patients for whom there are reported differences in pharmacokinetics of antidepressants (Friedel 1982). Monitoring antidepressant plasma levels may help to identify the noncompliant patient who can then be encouraged to discuss the reasons for not taking the medication and the difficulties worked through. Furthermore, drug-drug interactions can significantly effect the TCA plasma levels. Neuroleptics, methylphenidate, propranolol, cimitidine, sodium bicarbonate, and acute alcohol intake all tend to increase TCA plasma levels. By inducing liver enzymes and increasing the rate of metabolic breakdown of the TCAs, the following drugs tend to lower plasma levels: barbiturates, carbamazepine, phenytoin, oral contraceptives, chronic alcohol use, and tobacco smoking. Antidepressant plasma levels can help prevent over- or under-medication in these situations.

Side Effects

Most of the side effects of TCAs are due to their anticholinergic and adrenergic effects (Klein et al. 1980). The various antidepressant agents differ in their side effect profiles and individual patients may vary considerably in their vulnerability to these side effects as well as in their level of tolerance to the annoying nature of these effects Usually the side effects subside within one to two weeks of treatment as the patient adapts, either physiologically or psychologically, to them. The clinician can further minimize these bothersome side effects by careful choice of agent, proper dosaging, and the addition of another pharmacological agent to counteract the effects, if needed.

Dry mouth is perhaps the most frequent complaint by patients on TCAs. Blurry vision, especially near vision, is the other most common anticholinergic complaint associated with TCA usage. Frequently, adaptation occurs over several weeks and the patient should not be advised to purchase new glasses in the meantime. Local cholinergic compounds, such as 1 percent pilocarpine eye drops, may be of some benefit. A less frequent but potentially more serious ophthalmological complication of TCAs is aggravation of glaucoma, in particular of the narrow-angle type. Patients with narrow-angle glaucoma may be safely treated with TCAs if they are maintained on their antiglaucoma medications and are closely followed by an ophthalmologist with frequent tonometric exams.

Another anticholinergic side effect of tricyclic agents is constipation. Ordinarily, this can be managed conservatively with water-retaining laxatives, but at its worst can lead to paralytic ileus. The elderly and patients receiving combinations of strongly anticholinergic drugs are most susceptible to this very rare complication. When paralytic ileus does occur, it is life threatening and requires hospitalization.

Another important peripheral anticholinergic TCA side effect is urinary retention. This is more likely to happen in older patients, particularly men who have enlargement of the prostate. A lowering of the TCA dosage or concurrent treatment with bethanechol chloride may be helpful. Caution should be used in cases of significant urinary retention where urinary tract obstruction must be considered and ruled out. Anticholinergic-based difficulties with erections may also happen occasionally.

Central anticholinergic effects can lead to sedation or drowsiness. In patients who experience insomnia or anxiety, it can be advantageous to utilize a more strongly sedating antidepressant in a single bedtime dose (e.g., doxepin, amitriptyline). If the patient tends to be excessively drowsy during the day, one of the antidepressants with lower sedative potential (e.g., desipramine) may be given in divided doses throughout the day with good tolerance. Drowsiness and sedation may occur during TCA treatment through inhibition of the histamine H_1 receptor. Blockade of these receptors may also result in weight gain and hypotension (Richelson 1982).

Patients who are particularly sensitive to anticholinergic activity or patients who have taken excessive doses of antidepressants may experience a toxic organic delirium with disorientation, stupor, agitation, anxiety, and hallucinations. Vulnerability to anticholinergic psychosis increases with age. It most typically occurs when patients are being treated with a combination of anticholinergic medications (such as neuroleptics, antiparkinsonian agents, and antidepressants). Stopping medications and use of physostigmine salicylate are important aspects of treating this emergency. The use of an antidepressant with low anticholinergic activity (e.g., desipramine, nortriptyline) is advisable for patients with a prior history of sensitivity to anticholinergic effects and for elderly patients.

Other effects of the TCAs are thought to be mediated on the basis of their antialpha-adrenergic properties. The most common and notable of these effects is orthostatic hypotension (Glassman and Bigger 1981). Although not limited to the elderly, orthostatic hypotension is a major concern in the geriatric population because of the increased risk of complications from falls, transient ischemic attacks, strokes and myocardial infarctions. One predictor of drug-induced postural hypotension has been found to be the degree of lying-to-standing drop in systolic pressure before starting treatment; a value greater than 15 mm Hg. suggests a significantly greater drop will occur with the tricyclic (Cassem 1982). A pretreatment systolic orthostatic blood pressure change of 10 mm Hg. or more may also predict positive treatment response to TCAs in elderly patients (Jarvik et al. 1983). Often it is necessary to change the TCA to avoid or minimize orthostatic hypotension. Nortriptyline has been noted to increase pretreatment orthostatic hypotension by approximately half that observed with imipramine (Roose et al. 1981) and is probably the drug of choice where this side effect is of special concern.

Interference with cardiac conduction is another area of concern with regard to TCA treatment. TCA-induced delay of cardiac conduction can be revealed on an electrocardiogram (EKG) as a prolongation of the PR interval or a widening of the QRS complex. A 20 percent increase in the duration of either the PR interval or the QRS complex is an indication not to raise the TCA dose further. Patients with sick-sinus syndrome or bundle branch block should be closely monitored in the early stages of TCA treatment in the event that aggravation of these defects necessitates cardiac pacemaker placement. First-degree heart block is a contraindication to TCA therapy unless a pacemaker is inserted to allow for antidepressant treatment. Tachycardia frequently occurs as a side effect. A greater increase in heart rate may occur with amitriptyline or nortriptyline than with imipramine or desipramine. TCAs also appear to have antiarrhythmic properties similar to those of quinidine in that they are antiarrhythmic in lower (therapeutic) concentrations and arrhythmogenic in higher (toxic/overdose) concentrations. This antiarrhythmic capacity raises a caution in the treatment of patients with chronic atrial fibrillation who may convert to normal sinus rhythm with the addition of the TCA, creating the risk of embolization. Pretreatment anticoagulants are advisable for these patients (Siris and Rifkin 1983).

In addition to those effects discussed above, there are several other adverse effects of note. The TCAs tend to lower the seizure threshold (with the exception of doxepin which may be antiepileptic); they infrequently cause paresthesias, fatigue, weakness, and ataxia; extrapyramidal syndromes are rarely seen; allergic skin rashes may occur; cholestatic jaundice in the absence of other abnormal liver function tests has been reported; agranulocytosis is a very rare hematological reaction. It has also been suggested that TCAs may accelerate the biological rhythmicity of affective disorders. The induction of "rapid cycling" and an increase in manic episodes during maintenance TCA treatment has been observed in affectively disordered patients (Wehr and Goodwin 1979).

Drug interactions are known to occur between the TCAs and anticholinergics, barbiturates, digoxin, nitroglycerine, and others. TCAs block the antihypertensive effects of quanethidine, clonidine and alpha-methyldopa and potentiate the antihypertensive effect of Prazosin (Richelson 1982). The use of marijuana during TCA treatment can lead to increased heart rate on the basis of beta-adrenergic stimulation. Nortriptyline increases the half-life of coumarin anticoagulants and prolongs and intensifies the anticoagulant effect. In treating the depressed patient with insulin-dependent diabetes mellitus, serum glucose levels should be monitored until a steady state of antidepressant is reached as the TCAs can either raise or lower the glucose level.

Treatment-Resistant Depression

If the depressed individual has not responded after attaining adequate blood levels for several weeks, a number of considerations may guide the clinician in making systematic decisions for further treatment. A patient who has not responded to several norepinephrine active drugs (e.g., desmethylimipramine, nortriptyline) should be given a trial of serotonin active antidepressant (e.g., imipramine, amitriptyline). The addition of 25 to 50 mg. of cytomel (25 μg L-triiodothyronine, T_3) to imipramine or amitriptyline treatment, especially in depressed women, may enhance or speed the magnitude of response to the antidepressant (Goodwin et al. 1982).

It has been observed that an adjunctive dose of 5 to 20 mg/day of amphetamine can convert a partial response to a complete response. A positive response should occur within 10 days and the amphetamine can be continued at a fixed dose for four to six weeks and then slowly withdrawn (Rabkin et al. 1983). The use of a MAOI alone or in combination with a TCA, the addition of lithium carbonate or carbamazepine to the tricyclic regimen, or a course of ECT may be necessary to achieve the desired therapeutic response. In particular, several groups have recently described augmented clinical response after adding lithium carbonate to the treatment of patients who were unresponsive to antidepressants alone (dé Montigny et al. 1983, Heninger et al. 1983). Combined treatments will be discussed further in the following sections.

New Antidepressants

There are three new nontricyclic antidepressants available in the United States: amoxapine, a demethylated derivative of the antipsychotic drug loxapine; maprotiline, the first tetracyclic compound released in the U.S.; and trazadone, a triazolopyridine derivative. These drugs are heralded as advantageous in providing faster onset of action, a lower cardiovascular side effect profile, or fewer anticholinergic effects. Despite earlier optimistic views, all of these new agents have proven capable of producing undesirable cardiac effects and each is associated with troublesome side effects not usually seen with the traditional tricyclics. These newer antidepressants have not proved to be more effective than older agents in mild or severe depression, but may offer some advantages for particular patient populations as discussed.

Pharmacologically, amoxapine has the mixed properties of an antidepressant and an antipsychotic. The major active antidepressant metabolite is 8-hydroxyamoxapine, a potent norepinephrine reuptake inhibitor and a milder inhibitor of serotonin reuptake. Amoxapine's 7-hydroxy derivatives are dopamine antagonists and produce neurological side effects typical of antipsychotic drugs. Dystonia, akathisia and parkinsonism are all possible. Galactorrea, increased prolactin, and impaired sexual functioning have also been observed with this drug. More important, after long-term administration, amoxapine also carries the potential for tardive dyskinesia (Blackwell 1982). Clinical use of amoxapine has also failed to demonstrate a decisive advantage over standard tricyclics in incidence of sedation or anticholinergic effects. Several cases of seizures have been reported and amoxapine may increase the likelihood of seizures as compared with other antidepressants.

The dosage range of amoxapine is generally from 200–400 mg/day but it may be necessary to raise this as high as 600 mg. Most clinicians remain unconvinced that amoxapine is faster acting or any more efficacious than older agents. A potential advantage of amoxapine may be in the treatment of patients with agitated or psychotic depression, but further studies in this area are needed.

Despite the different tetracyclic structure of maprotiline, double-blind placebo-controlled studies have not consistently reported a decisive advantage over other antidepressants in overall efficacy or more rapid onset of action (Singh et al. 1976). Pharmacologically, maprotiline is a specific norepinephrine reuptake blocker with no apparent effect on serotonin uptake. It has moderate anticholinergic and histamine H_1 blocking activity, similar to amoxapine. The overall side effect profile of maprotiline is generally similar to the other TCAs, although there is an increased hazard for lowering seizure threshold and causing skin rashes (Blackwell 1982). Due to its reduced atropine effect, this agent may be more useful in geriatric depression and in patients with cardiovascular disease. The dosage range is from 50–300 mg/day and may be given in divided doses or as a single bedtime dose.

Trazadone is atypical in both its structure and pharmacology. It is a selective inhibitor of serotonin reuptake with virtually no effect on dopamine or norepinephrine, and no atropine effect (Riblet and Taylor 1981). Its hypnotic effect is therapeutically useful, especially for depressed patients with agitation, anxiety, and insomnia. Because of fewer anticholinergic side effects, there is a higher rate of acceptance among the elderly population. In addition, since trazadone has minimal effects on the dopamine system, theoretically it would not exacerbate manic symptoms although proof of this lies in the test of time.

Compared with the TCAs, trazadone has a short half-life, with a steady state being reached within 2 to 4 days of regular administration. The dosage range is 50–600 mg. Because of its short half-life, trazadone should be administered in divided doses although a major portion of the dose should be prescribed at night because of associated drowsiness. Negative side effects include lethargy, drowsiness, headaches, nausea and mild gastrointestinal distress. In addition, eleven cases of priapism, five requiring surgical procedures, have been reported since March 1982, when trazadone became available in the United States (Scher et al. 1983).

A number of other antidepressants are currently undergoing extensive research and may become available in the future. These include mianserin, a selective norepinephrine-enhancing tetracyclic, and several agents which affect the serotonin reuptake mechanisms, such as zimelidine, fluvoxamine and viloxazine. Another category, which interacts with dopamine mechanisms, includes bupropion and nomifensine.

A new anxiolytic drug reported to have antidepressant effects is alprazolam, whose action as a benzodiazepine is mainly on gamma-aminobutyric acid (GABA) mechanisms and whose antidepressant effects may be mediated via beta-adrenergic receptors (Sethy and Hodges 1982). Alprazolam, in doses ranging from 1.5–5 mg/day, has been effective in alleviating depression in outpatients with moderate degrees of primary major depressive disorder (Fabre 1976) and in severely depressed hospitalized patients (Feighner 1983). In the latter study patients with predominantly anxious-agitated depression responded best and the antidepressant effect was evident within the first week of treatment. A potential drawback to the use of alprazolam in the treatment of depression is its addictive potential and risk of withdrawal syndrome once discontinued.

Monoamine Oxidase Inhibitors

In the early 1950s, a fortuitous observation of the mood-elevating effects of iproniazid was made by nonpsychiatric physicians utilizing this investigational drug in the treatment of tuberculosis. The recognition that iproniazid was a potent inhibitor of the enzyme monoamine oxidase (MAO) (Zeller et al. 1952), the growing awareness of the importance of this enzyme in the catabolism of the central nervous system monoamine neurotransmitters, and observations of the antidepressant effects of iproniazid led researchers to further study the monoamine oxidase inhibitor (MAOI) drugs and their clinical applications.

Although early clinical trials of iproniazid in the treatment of depression were encouraging, subsequent double-blind control studies failed to confirm its therapeutic efficacy (British Medical Research Council 1965). In addition to a growing reputation for lack of effectiveness, reports of iproniazid-induced hepatotoxicity and the occurrence of hypertensive crises led to a sharp decline in the popularity of the MAOIs in the early 1960s. Despite the removal from the market of the more hepatotoxic MAOIs, including iproniazid and the subsequent elucidation of the mechanism of the hypertensive response to concomitant use of MAOIs with tyramine-rich foods and stimulant drugs (Blackwell et al. 1967), the fears generated by these early clinical mishaps have persisted and have resulted in many physicians avoiding this class of drugs.

In the 1970s, critical reviews of the earlier studies of efficacy revealed frequent use of subtherapeutic MAOI dosages and failure to use strict diagnostic criteria (Robinson et al. 1973). More carefully designed controlled trials have correlated clinical efficacy with adequate dosage of MAOIs (Robinson et al. 1973) as well as with degree of platelet MAO inhibition (Ravaris et al. 1976).

Pharmacological Action

These drugs all share the common property of inhibiting MAO, an enzyme which catalyses the oxidative deamination of norepinephrine, epinephrine, dopamine, phenylethylamine, serotonin, and other biogenic amines. Treatment with MAOIs can result in elevation of brain levels of neurotransmitters, such as norepinephrine and serotonin (Koplin and Axelrod 1963). These agents may also block amine reuptake or act indirectly by discharging amines from storage sites (Knoll and Magyar 1972). Although overall amine levels may not be changed, there may be altered turnover with a subsequent increase in "functional" levels of amines. Although the clinical effectiveness of these agents is roughly parallel to their *in vitro* potency as MAO inhibitors, their efficacy as antidepressant and antianxiety agents has not yet been directly related to their MAO inhibiting activity (Nies and Robinson 1982). Charney et al. (1981) have suggested that "down regulation" of postsynaptic beta-adrenergic receptors with varying presynaptic effects may be a common mechanism of action for many antidepressants, including the MAOIs.

Two MAO subtypes, A and B, have been distinguished on the basis of differences in substrate activity and inhibitor specificities (Johnston 1968). Clorgyline and deprenyl are investigational selective MAO inhibitors of types A and B respectively. With the exception of pargyline, which is a relatively selective inhibitor of MAO-B, conventional MAOIs are nonselective, exerting significant effects on both types A and B MAO. Centrally, it appears that phenelzine (inhibition of MAO type A and B) reduces beta-NE binding sites, whereas clorgyline (selective inhibition of type A) primarily affects reduction of the $alpha_2$-NE receptors in rat cortex (Cohen et al. 1982). With the exception of phenelzine, which competitively inhibits MAO, the clinically available MAOIs act irreversibly by binding near active sites on the enzyme molecule, thus requiring at least a ten-day synthesis period before MAO activity begins to return to pretreatment levels.

Clinical Indications for MAOI Use

The available literature suggests that the MAOIs may be more effective in neurotic or reactive depressions while TCAs are more likely to be effective for the endogenous depressions. MAOIs seem to have fairly specific antianxiety effects as well. Further research is necessary to clarify the role of MAOIs in the treatment of patients with endogenous depression and should certainly be given a trial in patients with more typical depressive symptoms who fail to respond to TCAs. Klein and his coauthors (1980) recommend that the MAOIs be the first antidepressant prescribed for depressed patients with atypical features such as hypersomnolence, lethargy, hyperphagia, reactivity of mood, and rejection sensitivity. Well-documented studies (West and Dally 1959, Robinson et al. 1973, 1978, Ravaris et al. 1976, Sheehan et al. 1980) confirm the utility of MAOIs in atypical neurotic depressions characterized by initial insomnia, hypersomnia, fatigue, hyperphagia, weight gain, P.M. worsening, tremulousness (i.e., vegetative symptoms not associated with endogenous depression or a reverse pattern), and with psychopathological symptoms including retained mood reactivity, irritability, panic episodes, agoraphobia and social phobias, and hypochondriacal and obsessive preoccupations. Such patients may have had a prior poor response to ECT or a dysphoric TCA response and may abuse alcohol or sedatives. MAOI treatment may also be indicated for a group of patients with histrionic personalities who react with intensification of anxiety, depression and episodes of depersonalization in response to loss or to interpersonal rejection (King 1962, Quitkin et al. 1979). Potter et al. (1982) also recently reported that low dose (2.5–10 mg/day) clorgyline was effective in five female bipolar patients defined as "rapid cyclers" who had been refractory to several conventional treatments, including lithium.

The patient selected for MAOI treatment should be intelligent and cooperative in order to understand and follow the dietary and medication restrictions. The individual with medical conditions requiring use of nasal decongestants, bronchodilators, thiazide, and centrally active antihypertensives will require special consideration as these medications may result in hypertensive complications. Conjoint MAOI treatment may retard phenothiazine metabolism and potentiate hypotension or extrapyramidal side effects or prolong the effects of central anticholinergics, barbiturates, narcotics, and ethanol. The patient should be given both verbal and written instructions prior to instituting MAOI treatment with emphasis on the avoidance of most cheeses, herring, liver, aged unpasteurized meats and sausages, red wine, beer, fava beans, decongestants in the form of nose drops, cough and cold remedies, and stimulant drugs. McCabe and Tsuang (1982) discuss the relative risks of various foods which are to be restricted or which have been erroneously forbidden in the past. While caution is necessary, it is not in the patient's interest to make the MAOI diet so restrictive as to be unacceptable. If the patient should experience any symptoms of a sympathomimetic crisis characterized by headache, diaphoresis, mydriasis, hypertension, neuromuscular excitation, and potential cardiac dysrhythmia, the patient should be instructed to go to an emergency room immediately for treatment. Gerner (1983) recommends giving patients 50 mg. of chlorpromazine or 50 mg. of phentolamine, both of which antagonize MAOI-associated hypertension, with instructions to utilize it if they develop a severe headache as a result of breaking dietary restrictions.

Caution should also be used in prescribing MAOIs for the patient prone to impulsive suicide attempts since that patient could combine various foods or other medication in addition to taking an overdose of the MAOI with a theoretically greater chance at a successful suicide. Suicidal ideation does not necessarily preclude treatment with an MAOI, but ongoing evaluation of the patient's suicidal status would be imperative as with any antidepressant treatment.

Dosage and Duration of Treatment

The available MAOIs can be divided into two main categories: hydrazines (isocarboxazid and phenelzine) and nonhydrazines (tranylcypromine, pargyline, deprenyl, and clorgyline). The hydrazine derivatives have the potential (though rarely) for producing a lupus-like syndrome and chemical hepatotoxicity. Phenelzine, the MAOI for which there is presently the most substantial evidence of efficacy, has been associated with very little hepatotoxicity.

Hydrazine derivatives. Clinically, phenelzine has been shown to be superior to TCAs in controlling agoraphobia and is probably the most effective MAOI in alleviating phobic and obsessive symptoms (Ravaris et al. 1976, Sheehan et al. 1980). Early attempts (Johnstone and Marsh 1973) to establish a relationship between clinical response to phenelzine and the genetically determined ability to acetylate sulphadimidine have not proven useful clinically. On the other hand, percentage of platelet monoamine oxidase inhibition does seem to correlate with both antidepressant efficacy (Ravaris et al. 1976) and phenelzine dosage (mg/kg body weight) with an optimal dose of 1 mg/kg body weight (i.e., phenelzine doses of between 60 and 75 mg/day for most patients). In studies by Robinson et al. (1978a, 1978b), patients with greater than 80 percent inhibition showed significantly better improvement than patients with less inhibition, and inhibition of at least 80 percent at two weeks predicted a more favorable response at six weeks.

One should begin treatment with a low dose of 15 mg/day gradually working up to a divided dose regimen of 15 mg qid up to 90 mg a day for three to six weeks before assessing success or failure of a therapeutic response. A larger single dose often produces more postural hypotension and occasionally increased drowsiness. In the patient who does not respond to conventional doses, measurement of platelet MAO inhibition may be helpful, but in general it is best to use the patient's weight as a guide to dosage in determining adequate treatment. As with other antidepressants, a lower dose is recommended initially in geriatric patients.

Isocarboxazid, the other available hydrazine derivative, is somewhat more hepatotoxic, but has the advantage of possibly producing less postural hypotension than phenelzine (Klein et al. 1980). A low dose of 10 mg. a day initially and increasing to approximately 0.5 mg/kg of body weight or 20 to 40 mg/day is recommended. Preliminary data suggest therapeutic dosage also correlates with greater than 80 percent inhibition of platelet MAO (Giller 1980).

Nonhydrazine derivatives. Tranylcypromine differs from amphetamine by its cyclopropyl side chain and seems to have greater stimulant properties than phenelzine (Klein et al. 1980). At subtherapeutic doses (≤ 10 mg) tranylcypromine achieved greater than 90 percent inhibition of platelet MAO (Giller 1980) suggesting at least some of its antidepressant activity may be through another mechanism, such as a direct stimulant effect or inhibition of MAO reuptake. It is especially useful in withdrawn, anergic, depressed patients and may have a more rapid onset of action than other MAOIs with some patients experiencing improvement in mood within the first several days (Bernstein 1983). Optimal therapeutic dosage is approximately 0.5 mg/kg of body weight or 30 to 60 mg/day. Since tranylcypromine can cause insomnia if taken late in the day, a divided dose regimen of 10 to 20 mg. two to three times daily may be used with the last dose given around 4:00 P.M. if sleep disturbance occurs. Perhaps because of its direct stimulant action, it has less tendency to cause postural hypotension than phenelzine, but may have potential for abuse and/or physical dependency states similar to other psychostimulants (Tollefson 1983).

Pargyline, approved for use in the United States as an antihypertensive agent only, has also been shown to have antidepressant effects (Klein et al. 1980) and may be especially useful in treating depressed hypertensive patients. A starting dose of 10 mg. twice a day can be employed with gradual increase in dosage until a suitable improvement in blood pressure and mood is observed. The recommended therapeutic dose is 75 to 125 mg/day. It may be combined with thiazide diuretics or propranolol, but should not be used along with reserpine or methyldopa (possible worsening of depression) or with guanethidine and clonidine (possible hypertensive reaction) (Bernstein 1983).

As with TCA treatment, patients with a chronic or recurrent course of depression often require prolonged maintenance for months or years with MAOIs. Abrupt discontinuation of MAOIs is associated with rebound effects, including exacerbation of myoclonic movements and unpleasant nightmares. A useful procedure for gradual discontinuation of MAOIs is reduction by one dosage unit per week.

Partial Responders to MAOIs

For patients whose response to MAOI is either partial or temporary, the clinician may consider a number of strategies. If side effects are not severe in a partial responder, very high doses (e.g., phenelzine dose up to 120 mg/day or tranylcypromine to 75 mg/day) may be effective. L-Tryptophan, a naturally occurring amino acid and precursor to 5-hydroxytryptophan, may enhance the efficacy of MAOIs (Stern and Mendels 1981). Some depressed patients show evidence of a vitamin B_6 deficiency and those patients with low B_6 levels and only a partial response to MAOI may benefit with an adjunctive trial of pyridoxine (Rabkin et al. 1983). Two reports have suggested a combination of MAOIs and lithium may be effective in some cases of severe depression (Zall 1971, Himmelhoch et al. 1972). This combination may be useful in bipolar patients since an MAOI by itself may precipitate a manic episode.

The combined use of MAOIs and TCAs has been reported to be effective and feasible after nonresponse to other treatments (White and Simpson 1981). The risk of dangerous adverse reactions, including convulsions, cerebral hemorrhage, and death are greatest if a TCA is introduced *after* an MAOI has already been administered. For this reason, the recommended procedure is simultaneous initiation of both drugs at low doses after a drug-free interval of one to two weeks or starting with a TCA such as imipramine (50 mg/day) and, after one or two days, adding 15 mg. of phenelzine. The dose of each drug is increased by one dosage unit every several days until a maximum of 200 mg. imipramine and 60 mg of phenelzine is reached (Rabkin et al. 1983). Development of side effects warrants discontinuation of dosage increments. Tranylcypromine poses substantially greater risk in combination therapy than does phenelzine. Imipramine, amitriptyline, doxepin, or maprotiline are the recommended TCAs for this combination.

Side Effects and Toxicity of MAOIs

While much attention has been given to the possibility of a hypertensive crisis, a systematic study of dietary noncompliance showed that although nearly 40 percent of the 98 patients taking tranylcypromine acknowledged "cheating" on their restrictions, no serious complications ensued (Neil et al. 1979). Due to the irreversible inhibition of MAO, dietary restrictions should be followed for three weeks following discontinuation of the MAOI.

More common and potentially troublesome side effects include insomnia, increased appetite and weight gain, postural hypotension, and anorgasmia in both men and women. Insomnia can usually be controlled by adjusting dosage schedule as described above or one can add a benzodiazepine or tryptophan to the bedtime MAOI dose. In most cases, the difficulties with weight gain can be controlled by diet during treatment or following recovery and after discontinuation of the MAOI. The degree of postural hypotension can be predicted by pretreatment postural fall in blood pressure. If the hypotension becomes symptomatic, the physician can consider concomittant use of a mineralocorticoid such as fludrocortisone 0.1 mg/day, which will reduce the severity of the postural hypotension in most cases. Unfortunately, failure of ejaculation in men and inability to experience orgasm in women may persist at therapeutic doses, but often patients can tolerate this when assured that the symptom is temporary and will disappear on discontinuation of the medication.

One of the advantages of the MAOIs over the TCA-like drugs is the essential lack of anticholinergic side effects. The occasional occurrence of dry mouth, urinary hesitancy and retention, and constipation are less severe than with the TCAs and tend to remit during the second week of treatment. Presumably, this is due to a mild degree of adrenergic predominance of the peripheral autonomic system rather than a direct anticholinergic effect. Another distinct advantage of these agents is an absence of direct cardiotoxic effects. A recent report of tranylcypromine-induced atrial flutter-fibrillation has been related to amphetaminelike properties (Gorelick et al. 1981). These properties of low cardiotoxicity and absence of anticholinergic effects give the MAOIs an advantage in treating depression in the elderly.

Less frequently encountered reactions include hypomania, psychosis, unsustained clonus, and MAOIs rarely cause fever, rash, a reversible lupus-like reaction (positive LE prep), and chemical hepatotoxicity. The major contraindications include known sensitivity to the drug, pheochromocytoma, congestive heart failure, and significant compromise of hepatic function.

Electroconvulsive Therapy

In the 1920s, it was widely believed that schizophrenia and epilepsy were mutually antagonistic (Krapf 1928). Although this observation was not supported by later research, it did give rise to the use of a number of chemicals including camphor, pentamethyline tetrazol (Cardiazol), and hexafluorodiethyl ether (Indoklon) to induce seizures initially in schizophrenic patients (Meduna 1935). Cerletti and Bini (1938) first described the technique of inducing seizures electrically, a technique of greater reliability and faster action than chemical convulsants. Although the early work with convulsive therapy was introduced for the treatment of schizophrenia, its main value has proved to be in depression, and depression has become the primary indication for electroconvulsive therapy (ECT).

Despite its acknowledged efficacy in alleviating severe depression, ECT remains highly controversial in the public's mind. In November, 1982 voters in Berkeley, California banned its use (Bower 1982) though the ordinance has been overturned in court. Whatever the public's opinion, clinicians recognize that ECT is sometimes the only treatment that will break through a deep depression or thwart a suicide. As such, it remains an important somatic treatment of endogenous depression, especially in those refractory to pharmacotherapy (Klein et al. 1980).

Mechanisms of Action

Although the mechanism by which ECT leads to improvement remains uncertain, the only finding that appears absolutely necessary for therapeutic efficacy is the development of a generalized electrical discharge within the brain (APA Task Force on ECT 1978). Since manic patients and some schizophrenic patients also respond favorably to ECT, its mechanism of action seems all the more puzzling. Our knowledge of the various neurotransmitters, however, remains rudimentary and there are probably a large number which are still unknown. The sometimes contradictory effects on neurotransmitters may account for what appear to be opposite results when ECT improves either depression or mania (Ilaria and Prange 1975). Animal studies suggest that ECT exerts its effects in a similar manner to antidepressant drugs by increasing the functional activity of serotonin, dopamine, and perhaps norepinephrine (Grahame-Smith et al. 1978). There is also weak evidence that ECT may lower levels of 5-HIAA in human CSF (Goodwin and Post 1978), a finding that accords well in theory with recent evidence that antidepressants may increase the functional sensitivity of central 5-HT receptors (Wang and Aghajanian 1980). In addition, chronic, but not acute, ECT in animals "down regulates" cerebral cortical beta-adrenergic receptors in a similar fashion to the chemical antidepressant therapies (Bergstrom and Kellar 1979).

Clinical Indications for ECT

Although a number of other psychiatric conditions have been treated with ECT (APA Task Force on ECT 1978), there is little evidence to suggest it is superior to other forms of treatment except in the patient with refractory endogenous depression who has been unresponsive to intensive pharmacotherapy or who presents an immediate risk of suicide. Evidence indicates that ECT is slightly more effective than antidepressants in producing a positive therapeutic response on a short-term basis.

In a significant number of severely depressed patients, the risk of giving an ineffective treatment for perhaps three weeks cannot be accepted. For these, ECT remains the treatment of choice. The indications are similar to those governing need for hospitalization and include delusions of guilt or nihilism, marked retardation or agitation, strong suicidal ideation and life-threatening weight loss. Prior good response to ECT may be another indication to prefer this treatment over pharmacotherapy, particularly if adequate drug trials have failed in the past. However, following a favorable response to ECT, all patients will require maintenance therapy for six months to prevent relapse. To avoid exposure to both treatments, Klein and coauthors (1980) recommend reservation of ECT for depressions resistant to medication. Maintenance ECT performed as an outpatient on a weekly, biweekly, or monthly basis, is an alternative strategy which may be employed. The clinician may need to exercise his own judgment, depending on the clinical situation, the economic resources for length of hospital stay, and the feelings of the patient or family members.

Preliminary Medical Work-Up

Proper administration of ECT must begin with a thorough clinical evaluation of the patient, both psychiatrically and medically. A thorough medical evaluation includes a complete blood count, a serum chemistry profile, urinalysis, and baseline electrolyte and creatinine determinations in a patient receiving diuretics. These studies may elucidate an underlying physical condition contributing to the patient's depressive illness or that may potentially complicate anesthesia. An EKG and chest x-ray are necessary to the preliminary work-up as are spine x-rays to rule out or document the presence of compression fractures so that their later appearance is not seen as a complication of ECT. To optimize safety, one may also obtain an EEG and CT scan of the brain. The EEG will identify any previous seizure focus which may lead to an extended series of seizures in response to ECT; the presence of a prior seizure focus does not necessarily contraindicate ECT. However, the presence of a brain tumor is the primary contraindication to this treatment since increased intracranial pressure may lead to herniation during the course of treatment (APA Task Force on ECT 1978). Therefore, obtaining a CT scan is an added safety measure. In addition to a brain tumor, contraindications to ECT include infections, recent cerebrovascular accident or myocardial infarction.

Patients with cardiac pacemakers can be safely treated with ECT and in pregnancy there is no particular danger, either to mother or fetus. Since the presence of organic brain dysfunction, especially in the elderly, can lead to an increased confusional response to ECT, consultation by a neurologist to clarify potential concerns may be useful for these patients. On the other hand, cases of apparent dementia in the elderly may, at times, be recognized as the "pseudodementia" of depression when a dramatic improvement is seen after successful ECT treatment.

Method, Frequency, and Duration of Treatment

Electrode placement must be considered in treating patients with ECT. There is still considerable disagreement as to whether bilateral (bitemporal) or unilateral (dominant or nondominant hemisphere) placement is more effective. Although the bitemporal placement may be slightly more effective, it also seems to be associated with greater confusion and memory difficulties than the unilateral electrode placement (APA Task Force on ECT 1978). The d'Elia electrode placement technique utilizes the placement of one electrode in the temporal region and another on the vertex of the skull over the nondominant hemisphere (instead of on the forehead in the more traditional unilateral placement). This method appears to produce far less cognitive dysfunction than bilateral ECT with equal efficacy in most patients (d'Elia 1970). In order to minimize the potential memory dysfunction, especially in elderly patients, one might begin with unilateral electrode placement and switch to bilateral placement for the remaining series if no response is observed after the third treatment (Bernstein 1983).

It is customary to give ECT two or three times a week, but now that the memory disturbance has been minimized, more frequent treatments may prove as effective and reduce the length of hospitalization. Strömgren (1975) has shown that ECT is as effective given four times or twice a week. However, there does seem to be an upper limit to the frequency with which effective seizures can be induced as attempts to complete the whole course in one day's session have met with little success (Abrams and Fink 1972).

The total number of treatments required varies greatly from patient to patient and, although many respond after five to eight seizures, a substantial number require more. If the patient is judged to have endogenous depression justifying ECT, the treatment should be continued beyond 20 sessions, if necessary, before considering treatment failure (Kiloh 1982). However, once a patient's symptoms have been alleviated, there does not seem to be any advantage in the common practice of giving one or two extra treatments (Barton et al. 1973).

Side Effects and Morbidity

The most troublesome aftermath of ECT is temporary loss of memory and confusion secondary to the production of an acute organic brain syndrome. The degree and duration of memory disturbance that may persist after full recovery of consciousness depends on a number of factors including electrode placement and age, older patients tending to show a greater degree of impairment. Recently, a group of 231 psychiatric patients were evaluated with the Wechsler Adult Intelligence Scale and the Halstead-Reitan Neuropsychological Test Battery prior to and following ECT, utilizing either unilateral (71 percent) or bilateral placement (29 percent). Statistically significant ($p < 0.05$) improvement was noted in 37.5 percent of measurements of cognition and memory with some improvement in 96 percent of all measures, indicating generally improved functioning following ECT (Malloy et al. 1982).

The question of permanent brain damage resulting from ECT remains a debatable matter. Transient neurological abnormalities, including asymmetry of reflexes, slight hemipareses, tactile and visual inattention, and homonymous hemianopias can sometimes be demonstrated, but these abnormalities disappear within 20 minutes after treatment (Kriss et al. 1978). Although temporary, minor and reversible memory deficits may be noted in many patients treated with short courses (6 to 12 treatments) of ECT, there is some evidence suggesting that those individuals who have had extensive ECT (more than 50 treatments) may develop long-lasting or permanent impairment in memory or cognitive function (APA Task Force on ECT 1978). However, systematic controlled evidence of such an effect is largely lacking (Klein et al. 1980).

Transient episodes of cardiac arrhythmias such as bradycardia, sinus arrhythmia, atrial flutter or fibrillation, ventricular tachycardia, and varieties of heart block sometimes occur. Rarely, a period of apnea may occur, usually related to an unduly prolonged effect of the muscle relaxant in individuals with a genetically determined deficiency of plasma psuedocholinesterase. The use of muscle relaxants (e.g., succinylcholine) has virtually eliminated vertebral and long-bone fractures and dislocations. The rare cases of pseudocholinesterase deficiency require the presence of a medical team equipped to do artificial pulmonary ventilation and endotracheal intubation.

Minor complaints on recovery from a seizure include headache, nausea, stiffness, and aching of muscles. A few patients complain of anxiety which may increase with successive treatments and may lead to early termination of the ECT course. Occasionally, ECT may precipitate a manic phase and must be discontinued for this reason.

In competent hands, ECT is a very safe form of treatment. The mortality risk of a course of ECT has been estimated at 0.03 percent (Heshe and Roeder 1976), well below the mortality risk of suicide in such patients. In this study of 22,210 ECT treatments given in a year in Denmark, there was one death and one fracture without any other serious complications. The death was not clearly related to ECT. These data suggest that, with modern technique, mortality and severe morbidity are extremely rare.

Combined ECT and Pharmacotherapy

Antipsychotic medication may be needed prior to and during the course of ECT in patients who are agitated or psychotic at the outset of treatment (APA Task Force on ECT 1978). A low dose (2 to 20 mg. daily) of haloperidol is a good choice of antipsychotic drug in that it can be conveniently administered intramuscularly, has little anticholinergic effect and very little ability to provoke hypotension. Benzodiazepines may be necessary to relieve anxiety in ECT patients, but the sedative and respiratory depressant effects may be additive with any anesthesia agent administered and they should be used with caution (Bernstein 1978). More importantly, benzodiazepines may raise the seizure threshold complicating ECT induction.

Coadministration of tricyclic antidepressants with ECT is generally safe and may enhance the response to ECT (APA Task Force on ECT 1978). They should perhaps be avoided during ECT in patients with preexisting cardiovascular disease and in patients with hemodynamic instability since the hypotensive and antiarrhythmic effects of the TCAs will add to the risks of anesthesia. The more anticholinergic TCAs may enhance confusional problems and interact with other anticholinergic agents administered prior to ECT. Coadministration of monoamine oxidase inhibitors should be avoided because of their ability to potentiate barbiturate anesthetics, to enhance hypotensive responses to anesthesia, and to potentiate the hypertensive response generally observed during the course of ECT (Bernstein 1978). Lithium carbonate should be discontinued several days prior to starting ECT since coadministration appears to enhance and prolong memory deficits and confusional states associated with ECT (Small 1980). Lithium may also increase the paralytic effect of succinylcholine so that spontaneous breathing following the metabolic breakdown of this muscle relaxant may be more difficult (Packman et al. 1978). Following the completion of ECT, however, either lithium or a TCA should be started and maintained for at least six months in order to prevent recurrence of the depressive illness which necessitated electroconvulsive therapy (Klein et al. 1980). Prophylactic ECT has also been used as an alternative maintenance treatment.

Lithium

Despite the discovery of the efficacy of the lithium ion as a treatment for mania in Australia in 1949 (Cade 1949), lithium was not introduced into the market in the United States until 1970. The unfortunate lag between its discovery and application may have been due in part to fatalities associated with the use of lithium as a salt substitute in hypertensive patients on salt-restricted diets in the 1940s and early 1950s, prior to the advent of effective antihypertensive drugs (Baldessarini 1980). An understanding of the physiology and pharmacology of lithium salts has since made its administration quite safe, and extensive clinical trials have demonstrated that lithium is effective in reducing the morbidity associated with cyclical affective disorders.

Pharmacological Action

Extensive research has not yet clearly elucidated lithium's crucial mechanism(s) of action in affective disorders. Several theories involving the effects of lithium on the functional activity of neurotransmitters, norepinephrine (NE), dopamine (DA), and serotonin (5-HT), have been postulated to explain lithium's antimanic effect, its reasonably well-established antidepressant properties, and its prophylactic action against both phases of bipolar illness. Theories of pharmacological action relating to the effects on depression and prophylaxis are emphasized here.

Lithium may cause an augmented release of norepinephrine intraneuronally, which, together with a lithium-induced increase in monoamine oxidase (MAO) activity, could augment intraneuronal turnover. Lithium may also block the response of beta-adrenergic receptors to norepinephrine by diminishing the activity of adenylate cyclase (Gerbino et al. 1978). In addition, administration of lithium to animals decreases the number of cerebral cortical beta-adrenergic receptors, an effect which corresponds temporally with its antidepressant effects (Rosenblatt et al. 1979).

Serotonin is believed to play a "permissive" role in both mania and depression; any action of a drug that might stabilize the serotonin system might lead to mood stabilization. Lithium both stimulates serotonin release and decreases the number of postsynaptic serotonin receptors in the hippocampus (Treiser et al. 1981). Stabilization of serotonin receptor alterations and increased functional activity of serotonin may be one mechanism whereby lithium prevents recurrence in bipolar illness. It is also possible that dysfunction in any of the neurotransmitter systems contributes to altered biorhythms that are increasingly documented in severe depression and mania (Wehr et al. 1980).

Electrolyte and water abnormalities have also been described as possible pathophysiologic mechanisms in both phases of manic-depressive illness. Lithium is distributed more evenly in body water than is sodium or potassium, and it may substitute for either cation. During depression, cell sodium is elevated and its flow out of the cell is restricted. Lithium in the extracellular fluid acts similarly to potassium and stimulates sodium efflux, either by cation exchange or stimulation of a pump mechanism (Glen and Reading 1973).

Finally, the frequently postulated "membrane stabilization" effect of lithium may provide the common link in the diversity of theories to explain its mode of action. Both calcium and magnesium are required for stabilization of cell membranes, tending to make them less fluid. Lithium may interact with calcium due to a similar charge density or with magnesium due to a similar ionic radius. The substitution of lithium for either calcium or magnesium might increase membrane permeability. The interaction with magnesium may also affect its function as a cofactor in many enzyme systems, such as magnesium-dependent sodium-potassium ATPase of the ionic pump (Birch 1973).

Clinical Indications

Currently, lithium carbonate is approved by the FDA for two uses only: in the treatment of manic episodes of manic depressive illness and in the prophylactic treatment of patients with a history of mania wherein it may prevent or diminish the severity of recurrent manic episodes (Jefferson and Griest 1977). In addition, there is a strong suggestion that lithium carbonate exerts some prophylactic benefit in regard to the recurrence of depression in bipolar patients (Prien et al. 1973, Quitkin et al. 1981). Prevention of recurrent illnesses is usually not complete, but a majority of patients will experience a reduction in the frequency, intensity and duration of episodes. Such benefits have enabled many patients previously incapacitated to lead productive lives.

There is also evidence to support the prophylactic value of lithium in patients with recurrent depressive disorders without mania, i.e., in unipolar depressive disorders. Large scale studies comparing lithium and TCAs as prophylactic agents in unipolar depressive disorders have found them about equally effective (Prien et al. 1973, Glen et al. 1981). Disadvantages with lithium are the repeated plasma level determinations needed and the unclear risks of renal structural damage (Ayd 1983). Lithium's efficacy in the treatment of acute depressive episodes has been more controversial (Goodwin et al. 1972, Worral et al. 1979). Although it is doubtful that lithium is as generally effective as other available antidepressant treatments, some bipolar and, to a lesser extent, unipolar depressives, achieve an adequate therapeutic response without the need to add other agents (Ramsey and Mendels 1981). Of particular interest and clinical importance is the ability of lithium to increase the efficacy of tricyclics (dé Montigny et al. 1981, 1983, Heninger et al. 1983) and MAOIs (Zall 1971, Himmelhoch et al. 1972) in previously intractable depressions.

New depressive illnesses during lithium prophylaxis are more common than manic recurrences. Approximately 25–35 percent of patients will require concomitant antidepressant therapy (tricyclics, MAOIs, or ECT) for the treatment of a depressive episode not adequately prevented by lithium maintenance alone (Dunner et al. 1976). A liability of using antidepressants alone or even with lithium in bipolar patients is the risk of their inducing a manic episode (Prien et al. 1973, Quitkin et al. 1981). In addition, there is evidence suggesting that the use of TCAs in bipolar patients can have a negative effect on the long-term course of the illness by shortening the cycle length (Wehr and Goodwin 1979). Kukopolus and co-workers (1980) found 13 percent of bipolar patients treated with TCAs converted from a classical bipolar course (i.e., a manic episode, a free interval, a depressive episode) to a continuously circular course, which is analogous to "rapid cyclers." Rapid cyclers characteristically have a history of four or more mood swings per year and generally have a less favorable prognosis with respect to lithium response. These patients may respond better to carbamazepine or a combination of lithium and carbamazepine. Some preliminary data indicates that treatment resistant rapid cyclers may be responsive to a combination of lithium and clorgyline, a selective MAO-A inhibitor (Potter et al. 1982).

Lithium has also been advocated as a treatment of schizoaffective illness. This group of disorders is characterized by a mixture of schizophrenic and affective symptoms with manic or depressive features. The possibility has been raised that, in this disorder, concurrent lithium treatment may be superior to antipsychotic drugs alone (Biederman et al. 1979). Satisfactory research studies regarding the best treatment for schizoaffective disorders, depressed type, are lacking (Pope and Lipinski 1978).

Following the clearing of an acute affective episode, persistent use of medication for six to eight months is termed continuation (or maintenance) treatment. Research findings strongly support the need for continuation therapy to reduce the likelihood of relapse. Ideally, continuation therapy should be maintained for as long as the episode is expected to last. However, if treatment is effective, it may be difficult to determine when the episode is over. Preliminary findings from a National Institute of Mental Health (NIMH) collaboration study suggest that every effort should be made to continue treatment until symptoms have been absent for two or three months (Prien et al. 1980). The results also indicate the need for focusing upon mild, as well as moderate and severe, symptomatology in determining continued need for medication.

Sustained drug use beyond eight months is called prophylactic treatment. The indications for this are less clear than with continuation therapy. Angst and Grof (1979) have suggested that such treatment be considered after the second episode in patients with bipolar and schizoaffective illness and after the third episode in those with unipolar illness, especially if the patient is over 40 years old and if the two or more episodes occurred within the last two years. Clinically, the physician must consider the likelihood of a recurrence in the near future; the potential impact of the recurrence on the patient, family, job, and therapeutic relationship; the patient's willingness to commit to a program of indefinite maintenance treatment; and the presence of possible medical contraindications to long-term treatment (Prien 1983).

Some patients must continue prophylactic treatment for many years or risk serious recurrence, perhaps even hospitalization. However, others, especially among the unipolar group, may discontinue treatment after a shorter period. Following three to four years of relapse-free prophylactic treatment, the patient and physician may together consider discontinuing this regimen under close supervision so that treatment can be restarted early if relapse should occur.

Initiating Lithium Treatment

Prior to the initiation of lithium therapy, a detailed medical history should be obtained, along with a physical and laboratory examinations, to uncover any medical contraindications to using lithium. Laboratory tests should include a complete blood count with differential, fasting blood sugar, blood urea nitrogen, serum creatinine, serum electrolytes, thyroid function tests (T_3, T_4 and TSH), and a urinalysis with microscopic examination of sediment. For patients with screening evidence suggesting renal disease, a 24-hour creatinine clearance determination, and a urine concentration test should be obtained. If abnormal, consultation with a nephrologist prior to starting lithium is indicated. A 12-lead EKG should be obtained for patients over 35 and others with a history of cardiac disorders. Some clinicians obtain EKG's for all lithium candidates. If there is evidence of organic brain damage, cautious dosing regime with lithium is in order, since coexisting dementia is frequently associated with a poor response to lithium and a heightened risk of lithium-induced neurotoxicity (Himmelhoch et al. 1980).

Lithium Preparations, Dosages, and Therapeutic Blood Levels

Lithium is a monovalent cation and exists in nature as a salt. The standard pharmaceutical preparation is lithium carbonate, available as a tablet or capsule. Lithium citrate, prepared as a liquid, may be useful for patients who complain of epigastric distress with the carbonate salt. Ordinarily, 300 mg. of lithium carbonate contains 56 mg. or 8 mEq. of the lithium ion. Generally, within one to two hours after standard preparations of lithium are ingested, there is a peak in blood level. This postabsorptive peak can contribute to a transient worsening of side effects, including nausea, diarrhea, and tremors of the hands. Slow release tablets are available which have the advantage of avoiding the sharp absorption peaks in serum lithium levels, and therefore may be better tolerated by certain patients. However, these slow release tablets may worsen diarrhea which lessens their desirability.

For individual patients, it is preferable to prescribe a particular form of lithium and utilize it uniformly to preserve the correlation between dosage, blood level, and therapeutic response. Similarly, it is important to utilize a proven reliable laboratory to insure the validity of the plasma level determinations. For proper results, blood samples should be drawn 11–12 hours after the last dose and after at least 5–6 days on the same dose. The latter is the time it takes to reach steady-state serum levels, i.e., 5–6 half-lives of the drug. Lithium has a half-life of approximately 24 hours, but it can be 30–36 hours in elderly patients and as little as 18 hours in adolescents.

Lithium treatment should be instituted utilizing a schedule of gradual dosage increments in order to minimize unpleasant side effects. Using large loading doses does not usually hasten the onset of therapeutic action and often creates great distress for the patient.

Klein and coauthors (1980) suggest a starting regimen of lithium carbonate, 300 mg. BID, for the first 2–3 days and increasing this dose to 300 mg. TID if there are no significant side effects. After five days at this dose, the serum lithium concentration is determined. For acute treatment, a therapeutic plasma level of 0.8–1.2 mEq/L is desirable. For maintenance purposes, a range of 0.5–1.0 mEq/L is acceptable. A rough rule of thumb is that each additional 300 mg. of lithium carbonate increases the lithium blood level by 0.2–0.3 mEq/liter. Most acutely ill patients require at least 900 mg. of lithium a day. However, some will require less, such as: elderly patients; those with impaired renal functioning; those on diuretic therapy; or those receiving other drugs which interfere with lithium's clearance, such as tetracycline, cimetadine, or the prostaglandin synthetase inhibiting analgesics.

Until plasma stabilization on a given dose has been achieved, blood levels should be drawn every 5–7 days. As soon as two successive determinations at the same dose achieve approximately the same values, levels can be checked less frequently. During follow-up, monthly determinations for two to three months are sufficient, and if the concentration remains in the therapeutic range, subsequent tests can be done every 2–3 months. Although an increase in serum lithium concentration with unaltered dosage may be a benign, transient phenomenon, tests for impaired renal function should be initiated.

Side Effects and Toxicity

In starting lithium treatment, it is important for the clinician to educate the patient as to what unwanted effects might occur. Generally, the adverse reactions to lithium are mild and transient, but occasionally they can become intolerable and may prohibit further treatment. Side effects involving thyroid, cardiovascular, and renal abnormalities are discussed here.

Therapeutic plasma levels of lithium have a rapid inhibiting effect on thyroid hormone release which can lead to decrease of plasma free thyroxine (T4) and triiodothyronine (T_3) during the first several weeks of treatment. Thereafter, a new equilibrium is established via a compensatory increase in basal TSH which results in normal levels of circulating thyroid hormone. The added stimulation of the thyroid gland resulting from the increased pituitary secretion of TSH may occasionally lead to the development of a goiter in the presence of normal thyroid function tests. Serial testing for plasma T_3, T_4 and TSH are indicated every six months. If a patient is clinically hypothyroid, or if a goiter is present, or if circulating thyroid hormone levels remain depressed, replacement treatment with thyroid hormone may be necessary in conjunction with lithium therapy. Rapid cyclers seem to be particularly vulnerable to the anti-thyroid effects of lithium, a finding which may relate to the relatively low efficacy of lithium in these patients (Goodwin 1983).

A variety of cardiovascular effects may be seen in association with lithium. Since lithium displaces intracellular potassium, the most common EKG changes resemble those of hypokalemia, namely T-wave flattening or inversion without associated cardiovascular symptoms (Tilkian et al. 1976). These changes are associated with therapeutic plasma levels. Much less common are various conduction disturbances which are more likely to occur at toxic levels (Jefferson and Griest 1977). Nonetheless, patients with preexisting cardiac conduction abnormalities should probably be given continuous cardiac monitoring during initiation of lithium therapy to ensure that rhythm control has not worsened after therapeutic lithium levels are reached (Cassem 1982).

Although most patients have some degree of increased urine excretion, about 10 percent develop actual diabetes insipidus accompanied by severe loss of fluid. This vasopressin-resistant diabetes insipidus may respond favorably to thiazide diuretics which, under such circumstances, exert a paradoxical antidiuretic effect (Levy et al. 1973). The combination of lithium with thiazides requires close clinical observation of the patient for early signs of toxicity, along with frequent monitoring of serum lithium levels. A reduction in the dose of lithium by one-third to one-half may be necessary. Interestingly, there is some evidence to suggest that thiazides may actually synergize with lithium to produce improved mood in some lithium-refractory manic-depressive patients (Himmelhoch et al. 1977).

Initially, polyuria, polydipsia and nephrogenic diabetes insipidus were viewed as reversible pharmacological effects of lithium on renal tubule function. This view began to be modified in 1977, following a report by Hestbech and associates. This group discovered irreversible structural damage to kidney tubules and, to a lesser extent, the glomeruli in fourteen long-term lithium patients. These findings aroused great concern among clinicians using lithium, especially on a long-term basis. Further investigation by several groups found little difference in either histological changes (Kincaid-Smith et al. 1979) or renal function (Coppen et al. 1980) of lithium-treated patients with affective disorders when compared to control groups who were not treated with lithium. However, there have been several reports of persistent nephrogenic diabetes insipidus lasting for months to years after discontinuation of lithium (Rabin et al. 1979, Bucht and Whalin 1980). The matter of lithium-induced renal structural damage remains unsettled. At this time, it appears that 5–10 percent of lithium-maintenance patients are at risk for permanent nephrotoxic effects. Careful evaluation of the patient and the need for prophylactic lithium treatment can reduce unnecessary risk for permanent renal damage. It may add somewhat to the safety of long-term lithium management to measure urine osmolality following a 12-hour period of fasting once or twice yearly. Routine use of creatinine clearance measurements during treatment is not necessary unless specific indications of renal disease or severe polyuria are present. The periodic measurement of serum creatinine is likewise not generally indicated.

Lithium poisoning does not develop suddenly. Paying attention to signs of impending toxicity, especially in high risk patients, will enhance treatment safety. Risk conditions leading to dangerous levels of lithium retention are primarily those that involve negative fluid and sodium balance or impaired kidney function. Although the difference between the toxic and therapeutic dose is small, generally one sees an exacerbation of relatively innocuous side effects before the more serious ones occur. That is, before lithium would cause renal shutdown and stupor the patient would likely have very bothersome nausea or diarrhea which would be a clue to evaluate the blood level. Treatment of lithium toxicity consists of the correction of fluid and electrolyte imbalance and general supportive measures. Since diuretics, water loading, and high sodium diet do not rapidly increase renal clearance, dialysis is now recommended for all patients whose lithium level is above 4 mEq/liter and for those debilitated individuals whose lithium level is 2–4 mEq/liter (Thomsen and Schou 1975).

Carbamazepine

Carbamazepine (Tegretol), a tricyclic compound chemically related to imipramine, has been extensively used in the treatment of seizure disorders and various neurological conditions. Recent preliminary investigations have shown carbamazepine to have specific antimanic, as well as prophylactic, efficacy in the treatment of bipolar disorders (Okuma 1983). Although the antidepressant effects of this drug are less well documented at this time, as compared to its antimanic efficacy, carbamazepine may have antidepressant effects when used alone (Ballenger and Post 1978, 1980), or in combination with lithium or conventional antidepressants (Okuma et al. 1973, Folks 1982). Its usefulness in the treatment and prophylaxis of bipolar disorders may rank with lithium treatment, and it is recommended particularly in cases which do not respond to lithium (Ballenger and Post 1980). It may have special prophylactic value in patients with early onset of illness (below twenty years of age) and in "rapid cyclers" (Okuma 1983). Another potential patient population who may be considered for treatment with carbamazepine are those patients who are unable to tolerate lithium side effects (e.g., patients with nephrogenic diabetes insipidus).

Advantages of carbamazepine over lithium include a more rapid antimanic effect, usually within the first week of treatment, a wider safety range between therapeutic and toxic dosage, and, therefore, less need to measure blood concentrations. As with other antidepressants, however, the therapeutic effects of carbamazepine in depression have not been evident until after several weeks (Ballenger and Post 1980). Therapeutic effects occur without notable signs of oversedation and with low incidence of adverse reactions.

For prophylactic treatment, carbamazepine may be given during the symptom-free period with gradual increments over a two to three week period to 600 mg. daily. If any adverse reaction occurs at this dose, the patient may be maintained at a daily dose of 400 mg. or 200 mg. Prophylactic effect may be achieved at a blood level around 6 μg/ml. Antidepressant effect is less clear but may require blood levels of 8 to 12 μg/ml (up to 1200 mg. a day).

Side effects most commonly reported, especially during the initial phases of treatment, are drowsiness, dizziness, unsteadiness, lassitude, headache, exanthema, nausea, and vomiting. Most untoward effects subside spontaneously within a week or after a reduction in dosage. Carbamazepine does have mild anticholinergic action requiring close observation of patients with increased intraocular pressure. Less commonly, various dermatological reactions may occur, usually benign rashes, but sometimes severe enough reactions to warrant discontinuation of the drug. Stevens-Johnson syndrome has been reported.

Cardiovascular, genitourinary, metabolic, hepatic, and miscellaneous reactions have also been reported but are very uncommon. Caution should be used in patients with cardiovascular, liver, renal, or urinary tract disease. Prior to starting carbamazepine, a complete blood cell count with differential white blood cell count, platelet count, and liver function tests should be done. These laboratory tests should be repeated at the end of the first and second weeks of therapy and, subsequently, monthly and, eventually, every two to four months during the course of treatment. Although carbamazepine has been reported to produce transitory leukopenia, agranulocytosis, aplastic anemia, and thrombocytopenia, these and other hematological reactions are exceedingly rare. The drug can be administered quite safely with judicious use of the laboratory studies listed above and with careful screening of patients to exclude from treatment patients with a history of previous bone marrow suppression, an adverse hematological reaction to any drug, or hypersensitivity to carbamazepine or any tricyclic. Patients should be advised to discontinue the drug and notify their physician if any signs of hematologic toxicity appear (e.g., fever, sore throat, easy bruising, petechial or purpuric hemorrhage).

Few interactions between carbamazepine and other drugs have been reported. Phenobarbital is said to enhance the metabolism of carbamazepine, and the biotransformation of phenytoin may be enhanced by carbamazepine. Interaction between carbamazepine and antipsychotic drugs has not been thoroughly studied but appears not to have associated adverse effects. The use with MAOIs is not recommended (Okuma 1983).

The mechanism of therapeutic and prophylactic action of carbamazepine is still at the conjectural stage. It is possible that carbamazepine alters the action of monoamine metabolism in such a way as to modify transmission in the central nervous system, especially in the diencephalic and limbic structures, in a manner similar to lithium. This is supported by studies of behavioral effects in rats whereby carbamazepine produced changes in response to amphetamines and tetrabenazine (Yogi 1977) in a similar manner to the central effects of lithium salts (Furukawa et al. 1975). Ballenger and Post (1980) have postulated a kindling model of affective illness in which cumulative bioelectrical changes, particularly in the limbic area, secondary to repeated biochemical or psychological stress, could result in abnormal limbic neuronal sensitization and major psychiatric disturbance. They suggest that carbamazepine's neurophysiologic properties as a limbic anticonvulsant and anti-kindling agent might be able to usefully modify this type of postulated disorder.

At the present time, while it is clear that carbamazepine has psychoactive properties that are beneficial to some patients, it is by no means obvious just which patients these are. In light of the absence of data defining this target population, a therapeutic trial of carbamazepine for patients with affective disturbances and, perhaps, other psychoses which do not respond to more conventional management, seems warranted.

REFERENCES

Abrams, R., and Fink, M. (1972). Clinical experiences with multiple electroconvulsive treatments. *Comprehensive Psychiatry* 13: 115–121.

American Psychiatric Association. (1980). *Diagnostic and Statistical Manual of Mental Disorders*. Washington, D.C.: American Psychiatric Assoc.

American Psychiatric Association Task Force on ECT. (1978). *Electroconvulsive Therapy*. Washington, D.C.: American Psychiatric Association.

Angst, J., and Grof, P. (1979). Selection of patients with recurrent affective illness for a long-term study: testing research criteria on prospective follow-up data. In *Lithium: Controversies and Unresolved Issues*, ed. T. B. Cooper, S. Gershon, N. S. Kline, et al. pp. 355–369. Amsterdam: Excerpta Medica.

Asberg, M., Cronholm, B., Sjoquist, F., et al. (1971). Relationships between plasma level and therapeutic effect of nortriptyline. *British Medical Journal* 3: 331–334.

Avery, D., and Winokur, G. (1977). The efficacy of electroconvulsive therapy and antidepressants in depression. *Biological Psychiatry* 12: 507–521.

Ayd, F. J. (1983). Continuation and maintenance antidepressant therapy. In *Affective Disorders Reassessed*, ed. F. J. Ayd, I. J. Taylor, and B. T. Taylor. Baltimore: Ayd Medical Communications.

Baldessarini, R. J. (1980). Drugs and the treatment of psychiatric disorders. In *Goodman & Gilman's: The Pharmacological Basis of Therapeutics*, ed. A. G. Gilman, L. S. Goodman, A. Gilman. pp. 391–447. New York: Macmillan.

———— (1983). *Biomedical Aspects of Depression and its Treatment*. Washington, D.C.: American Psychiatric Press.

Ballenger, J. C. and Post, R. M. (1978). Therapeutic effects of carbamazepine in affective illness: a preliminary report. *Communications in Psychopharmacology* 2: 159–175.

———— (1980). Carbamazepine in manic-depressive illness: a new treatment. *American Journal of Psychiatry* 137: 782–790.

Banerjee, S. P., Kung, L. S., Riggs, S. J., et al. (1977). Development of β-adrenergic receptor subsensitivity by antidepressants. *Nature* 268: 455–456.

Barton, J. L., Mehta, S., and Snaith, R. P. (1973). The prophylactic value of extra ECT in depressive illness. *Acta Psychiatrica Scandinavica* 49: 386–392.

Bergstrom, D. A., and Kellar, K. J. (1979). Effect of electroconvulsive shock on monoaminergic receptor binding sites in rat brain. *Nature* 278: 464–466.

Bernstein, J. G. (1983). *Handbook of Drug Therapy in Psychiatry*. Boston: John Wright PSG.

———— (1978). Medical psychiatric drug interactions. In *Massachusetts General Hospital Handbook of General Psychiatry*, ed. T. P. Hackett, N. H. Cassem. pp. 483–507. St. Louis: C. V. Mosby Company.

Biederman, J., Lerner, Y., and Belmaker, R. H. (1979). Combination of lithium carbonate and haloperidol in schizoaffective disorders. *Archives of General Psychiatry* 36: 327–333.

Birch, N. J. (1973). The role of magnesium and calcium in the pharmacology of lithium. *Biological Psychiatry* 7: 269–272.

Blackwell, B. (1982). Antidepressant drugs: side effects and compliance. *Journal of Clinical Psychiatry* 43: 14–18.

Blackwell, B., Marley, E., Price, J., et al. (1967). Hypertensive interactions between monoamine oxidase inhibitors and foodstuffs. *British Journal of Psychiatry* 113: 349–365.

Bower, B. Berkeley passes ECT ban: APA may challenge move. *Psychiatric News*, 19 November 1982.

British Medical Research Council (1965). Clinical trial of the treatment of depressive illness. *British Medical Journal* 1: 881–886.

Brown, W. A., Johnston, R., and Mayfield, D. (1979). The 24-hour dexamethasone suppression test in a clinical setting: relationship to diagnosis, symptoms, and response to treatment. *American Journal of Psychiatry* 136: 543–547.

Bucht, G., and Wahlin, A. (1980). Renal concentrating capacity in long term lithium treatment and after withdrawal of lithium. *Acta Medica Scandinavica* 207: 309–314.

Cade, F. J. J. (1949). Lithium salts in the treatment of psychotic excitement. *Medical Journal of Australia* 2: 349–353.

Carroll, B. J., Feinberg, M., Greden, J. F. et al. (1981). A specific laboratory test for the diagnosis of melancholia: standardization, validation and clinical utility. *Archives of General Psychiatry* 38: 15–22.

Cassem, N. (1982). Cardiovascular effects of antidepressants. *Journal of Clinical Psychiatry* 43: 22–28.

Charney, D. S., Menkes, D. B., and Heninger, A. R. (1981). Receptor sensitivity and the mechanism of action of antidepressant treatment. *Archives of General Psychiatry* 38: 1160–1180.

Cerletti, U., and Bini, L. (1938). L'elettroshock. *Archivio Generale di Neurologia Psychiatria e Psychoanalisi* 19: 266–268.

Checkley, S. A. (1980). Neuroendocrine tests of monoamine function in man: a review of basic theory and its application to the study of depressive illness. *Psychological Medicine* 10: 35–53.

Cohen, R. M., Campbell, I. C., Dauphin, M. et al. (1982). Changes in alpha and beta receptor densities in rat brain as a result of treatment with monoamine oxidase inhibiting antidepressants. *Neuropharmacology* 21: 293–298.

Coppen, A., Bishop, M. E., Bailey, J. E. et al. (1980). Renal function in lithium and non-lithium treated patients with affective disorders. *Acta Psychiatrica Scandinavica* 62: 343–355.

Davis, J. M. (1976). Overview: maintenance therapy in psychiatry: II. Affective disorders. *American Journal of Psychiatry* 133: 1–13.

d'Elia, G. (1970). Comparison of electroconvulsive therapy with unilateral and bilateral stimulation. *Acta Psychiatrica Scandinavica* (Supplement 215) 46: 30–43.

dé Montigny, C., Cournoyer, G., Mousiette, R. et al. (1983). Lithium carbonate addition in tricyclic antidepressant-resistant unipolar depression. *Archives of General Psychiatry* 40: 1327–1334.

dé Montigny, C., Grunberg, R., Mayer, A. et al. (1981). Lithium induces rapid relief of depression in tricyclic antidepressant drug non-responders. *British Journal of Psychiatry* 138: 252–256.

Dunner, D., Stallone, F., and Fieve, R. R. (1976). Lithium carbonate and affective disorders. *Archives of General Psychiatry* 33: 117–121.

Extein, I., Pottash, A. L. C., and Gold, M. S. (1981). The thyrotropin-releasing hormone test in the diagnosis of unipolar depression. *Psychiatry Research* 5: 311–316.

———— (1981a). Relationship of thyrotropin releasing hormone test and dexamethasone suppression abnormalities in unipolar depression. *Psychiatry Research* 4: 49–53.

Extein, I., Pottash, A. L. C., Gold, M. S., et al. (1982). Using the protirelin test to distinguish mania from schizophrenia. *Archives of General Psychiatry* 39: 77–81.

Fabre, L. F. (1976). Pilot open label study with alprazolam (U-31, 889) in outpatients with neurotic depression. *Current Therapeutic Research, Clinical and Experimental* 19: 661–668.

Fawcett, J., and Siomopoulos, V. (1971). Dextroamphetamine response as a possible predictor of improvement with tricyclic therapy in depression. *Archives of General Psychiatry* 25: 247–255.

Feighner, J. P. (1983). Open label study of alprazolam in severely depressed inpatients. *Journal of Clinical Psychiatry* 44: 332–334.

Folks, D. G., King, L. D., Dowdy, S. B. et al. (1982). Carbamazepine treatment of selected affectively disordered inpatients. *American Journal of Psychiatry* 139: 115–117.

Friedel, R. O. (1982). The relationship of therapeutic response to antidepressant plasma levels: an update. *Journal of Clinical Psychiatry* 43: 37–42.

Furukawa, T., Ushizima, I., and Ono, N. (1975). Modification by lithium of behavioral responses to methamphetamine and tetrabenazine. *Psychopharmacologia* 42: 243–248.

Gerbino, L., Oleshansky, M., and Gershon, S. (1978). Clinical use and mode of action in lithium. In *Psychopharmacology. A Generation of Progress*, ed. M. A. Lipton, A. DiMascio, & K. Killam. pp. 1261–1276. New York: Raven Press.

Gerner, R. H. (1983). Systematic treatment approach to depression and treatment resistant depression. *Psychiatric Annals* 13: 37–49.

Giller, E. G. (1980). Monoamine oxidase inhibitors and platelet monoamine oxidase inhibition. *Communication in Psychopharmacology* 4: 79–82.

Glassman, A. H., and Bigger, J. T. (1981). Cardiovascular effects of therapeutic doses of tricyclic antidepressants. *Archives of General Psychiatry* 38: 815–820.

Glassman, A., Kantor, S., and Shostak, M. (1975). Depressions, delusions, and drug response. *American Journal of Psychiatry* 132: 716–719.

Glassman, A. H., Perel, J. M., Shostak, M., et al. (1977). Clinical implications of imipramine plasma levels for depressive illness. *Archives of General Psychiatry* 34: 197–204.

Glen, A. I. M., and Reading, H. W. (1973). Regulatory action of lithium in manic-depressive illness. *Lancet* 2: 1239–1241.

Glen, A. I. M., Johnson, A. L., and Shepherd, M. (1981). Continuation therapy with lithium and amitriptyline in unipolar depressive illness: a controlled clinical trial. *Psychological Medicine* 11: 409–416.

Glowinski, J., and Axelrod, J. (1964). Inhibition of uptake of tritiated noradrenaline in the intact rat brain by imipramine and structurally related compounds. *Nature* 204: 1318–1319.

Gold, M. S., Pottash, A. L. C., Martin, D. A., et al. (1980). Opiate—endorphin test dysfunction in major depression. *Neuroscience Abstracts* 6: 759.

Gold, M. S., Pottash, A. L. C., Ryan, N., et al. (1980a). TRH induced TSH response in unipolar, bipolar and secondary depressions: possible utility in clinical assessment and differential diagnosis. *Psychoneuroendocrinology* 5: 147–156.

Goodwin, F. K. (1983). Special issues in the treatment of recurrent affective illness. Presented at the Twentieth Institute of Pennsylvania Hospital Award Lecture in Memory of Edward A. Strecker, M.D. Philadelphia: 17 November.

Goodwin, F. K., and Post, R. M. (1978). Spinal fluid amine metabolites following electroconvulsive therapy. Paper read at 11th CINP Congress, Collegium Internationale Neuro-Psychopharmacologicum, Vienna, 9–14 July 1978.

Goodwin, F. K., Cowdry, R. W., and Webster, M. H. (1978). Predictors of drug response in the affective disorders: toward an integrated approach. In *Psychopharmacology: A Generation of Progress*, ed. M. A. Lipton, A. DiMascio, K. F. Killam, pp. 1277–1288. New York: Raven Press.

Goodwin, F., Murphy, D., Dunner, D., et al. (1972). Lithium response of unipolar versus bipolar depression. *American Journal of Psychiatry* 129: 44–47.

Goodwin, F. K., Prange, A. J., Jr., Post, R. M. et al. (1982). Potentiation of antidepressant effects by L-triiodothyronine in tricyclic non-responders. *American Journal of Psychiatry* 139: 34–38.

Gorelick, D. A., Marder, S. R., Sack, D., et al. (1981). Atrial flutter/fibrillation associated with tranylcypromine treatment. *Journal of Clinical Psychopharmacology* 1: 402–404.

Grahame-Smith, D. G., Green, A. R., and Costain, D. W. (1978). Mechanism of the antidepressant action of electroconvulsive therapy. *Lancet* 1: 254–256.

Gross, G., Brodde, O-E., and Schumann, H. J. (1980). Decreased number of β-adrenoreceptors in cerebral cortex of hypothyroid rats. *European Journal of Pharmacology* 61: 191–194.

Hauger, R. L., and Paul, S. M. (1983). Neurotransmitter receptor plasticity: alterations by antidepressants and antipsychotics. *Psychiatric Annals* 13: 399–407.

Heninger, G. R., Charney, D. S., and Sternberg, D. E. (1983). Lithium carbonate augmentation of antidepressant treatment. *Archives of General Psychiatry* 40: 1335–1342.

Heshe, J., and Roeder, E. (1976). Electroconvulsive therapy in Denmark. *British Journal of Psychiatry* 128: 241–245.

Hestbech, J., Hansen, H. E., Amdisen, A. et al. (1977). Chronic renal lesions following long-term treatment with lithium. *Kidney International* 12: 205–213.

Himmelhoch, J. M., Detre, T., Kupfer, D. J. et al. (1972). Treatment of previously intractable depressions with tranylcypromine and lithium. *Journal of Nervous and Mental Disease* 155: 216–220.

Himmelhoch, J. M., Forrest, J., Neil, J. F. et al. (1977). Thiazide-lithium synergy in refractory mood swings. *Journal of American Psychiatry* 134: 149–152.

Himmelhoch, J. M., Neil, J. F., May, S. J., et al. (1980). Age, dementia, dyskinesias, and lithium response. *American Journal of Psychiatry* 137: 941–945.

Ilaria, R., and Prange, A. J., Jr. (1975). Convulsive therapy and other biological treatments. In *The Nature and Treatment of Depression*, ed. F. F. Flach, S. C. Draghi, pp. 271–308. New York: John Wiley and Sons.

Janowsky, A., Okada, F., Manier, D. H. et al. (1982). Role of serotonergic input in the regulation of the β-adrenergic receptor-coupled adenylate cyclase systems. *Science* 218: 900–901.

Jarvik, L. F., Read, S. L., Mintz, J. et al. (1983). Pretreatment orthostatic hypotension in geriatric depression: predictor of response to imipramine and doxepin. *Journal of Clinical Psychopharmacology* 3: 368–372.

Jefferson, J. W., and Griest, J. H. (1977). *Primer of Lithium Therapy*. Baltimore: Williams and Wilkins.

Johnston, J. P. (1968). Some observations upon a new inhibitor of monoamine oxidase in brain tissue. *Biochemical Pharmacology* 17: 1285–1297.

Johnstone, E. C., and Marsh, W. (1973). Acetylator status and response to phenelzane in depressed patients. *Lancet* 1: 567–570.

Keller, M. B., and Shapiro, R. W. (1982). "Double depression": superimposition of acute depressive episodes on chronic depressive disorders. *American Journal of Psychiatry* 139: 438–442.

Kiloh, L. G. (1982). Electroconvulsive therapy. In *Handbook of Affective Disorders*, ed. E. S. Paykel, pp. 262–275. New York: The Guilford Press.

Kincaid-Smith, P., Burrows, G. D., Davies, B. M., et al. (1979). Renal biopsy findings in lithium and pre-lithium patients. *Lancet* 2: 700–701.

King, A. (1962). Phenelzine treatment of Roth's calamity syndrome. *Medical Journal of Australia* 1: 879–883.

Klein, D. F., Gittelman, R., Quitkin, F. et al. (1980). *Diagnosis and Drug Treatment of Psychiatric Disorders: Adults and Children*. Baltimore: Williams and Williams.

Klerman, G. L. (1978). Psychopharmacologic treatment of depression. In *Clinical Psychopharmacology*, ed. J. G. Berstein, pp. 63–79. Littleton, MA: PSG Publishing Co.

Knoll, J., and Magyar, K. (1972). Some puzzling pharmacological effects of monoamine oxidase inhibitors. In *Advances in Biochemical Psychopharmacology*, Vol. 5, pp. 393–408. New York: Raven Press.

Koplin, J., and Axelrod, J. (1963). The role of MAO inhibitors in biogenic amine metabolism. *Annals of the New York Academy of Science* 107: 848.

Kragh-Sorensen, P., Hansen, C., Baastrup, P. et al. (1976). Self-inhibiting action of nortriptyline's antidepressive effect at high plasma levels. *Psychopharmacology* 45: 305–312.

Krapf, E. (1928). Epilepsie and schizophrenie. cit. in *Clinical Psychiatry*, ed. E. Slater & M. Roth, p. 470. London: Bailliere, Tindall and Cassell.

Kriss, A., Blumhardt, L. D., Halliday, A. M. et al. (1978). Neurological asymmetries immediately after unilateral ECT. *Journal of Neurology, Neurosurgery and Psychiatry* 41: 1135–1144.

Kukopulos, A., Reginaldi, D., Laddomada, P. et al. (1980). Course of the manic depressive cycle and changes caused by treatment. *Pharmakopsychiatrie Neuropsychopharmakologie* 13: 156–167.

Levy, S. T., Forrest, J. N., Jr., and Heninger, G. R. (1973). Lithium-induced diabetes insipidus: Manic symptoms, brain, and electrolyte correlates and chlorothiazide treatment. *American Journal of Psychiatry* 130: 1014–1018.

Loosen, P. T., and Prange, A. J., Jr. (1982). Serum thyrotropin response to thyrotropin-releasing hormone in psychiatric patients: a review. *American Journal of Psychiatry* 139: 405–416.

Maas, J. (1975). Biogenic amines and depression: biochemical and pharmacological separation of two types of depression. *Archives of General Psychiatry* 32: 1357–1361.

Maas, J. W., and Landis, D. H. (1968). *In vivo* studies of metabolism of nonepinephrine in central nervous system. *Journal of Pharmacology and Experimental Therapeutics* 163: 147–162.

Malloy, F. W., Small, I. F., Miller, M. J. et al. (1982). Changes in neuropsychological test performance after electroconvulsive therapy. *Biological Psychiatry* 17: 61–67.

Matuzas, W., Javaid, J. I., Glass, R. et al. (1982). Plasma concentration of imipramine and clinical response among depressed outpatients. *Journal of Clinical Pharmacology* 2: 140–142.

McCabe, B., and Tsuang, M. T. (1982). Dietary consideration in MAO inhibitor regimens. *Journal of Clinical Psychiatry* 43: 178–181.

Mobley, P. L., and Sulser, F. (1981). Down-regulation of the central noradrenergic receptor system by antidepressant therapies: biochemical and clinical aspects. In *Antidepressants: Neurochemical, Behavioral, and Clinical Perspectives*, ed. S. T. Enna, J. B., Malick, E. Richelson. New York: Raven Press.

Neil, J. F., Licata, S. M., May, S. J. et al. (1979). Dietary noncompliance during treatment with tranylcypromine. *Journal of Clinical Psychiatry* 40: 33–37.

Nelson, J., and Bowers, M. (1978). Delusional unipolar depression description and drug response. *Archives of General Psychiatry* 35: 1321–1328.

Nies, A., and Robinson, D. S. (1982). Monoamine oxidase inhibitors. In *Handbook of Affective Disorders*, ed. E. S. Paykel, pp. 246–261. New York: The Guilford Press.

Nies, A., Robinson, D. S., Friedman, M. J. et al. (1977). Relationship between age and tricyclic plasma levels. *American Journal of Psychiatry* 134: 790–793.

Okuma, T. (1983). Therapeutic and prophylactic effects of carbamazepine in bipolar disorders. In *Psychiatric Clinics of North America: Recent Advances in the Diagnosis and Treatment of Affective Disorders*, Vol. 6, ed. H. S. Akisol, pp. 157–173. Philadelphia: W. B. Saunders Company.

Okuma, T., Kishimolo, A., Inoue, K. et al. (1973). Anti-manic and prophylactic affects of carbamazepine on manic depressive psychosis. *Folia Psychiatrica Neurologica Japonica* 27: 283–297.

Packman, P. M., Meyer, D. A., and Verdun, R. M. (1978). Hazards of succinylcholine administration during electrotherapy. *Archives of General Psychiatry* 35: 1137–1141.

Peroutka, S. J., and Snyder, S. H. (1980). Long-term antidepressant treatment decreases spiroperidol-labeled serotonin receptor binding. *Science* 210: 88–90.

Pope, H. G., Jr., and Lipinski, J. T. (1978). Diagnosis in schizophrenia and manic-depressive illness. *Archives of General Psychiatry* 35: 811–828.

Post, R. M., and Goodwin, F. K. (1978). Approaches to brain amines in psychiatric patients: a reevaluation of cerebrospinal fluid studies. In *Handbook of Psychopharmacology*, Vol. 3, ed. L. L. Iverson, S. D. Iverson, S. H. Snyder, pp. 147–185. New York: Plenum Press.

Potter, W. Z., Murphy, D. L., Wehr, T. A. et al. (1982). Clorgyline: a new treatment for refractory rapid cycling patients? *Archives of General Psychiatry* 39: 505–510.

Prien, R. F. (1983). Long-term maintenance therapy in affective disorders. In *Schizophrenia and Affective Disorders. Biology and Drug Treatment*, ed. A. Rifkin, pp. 95–115. Boston: John Wright PSG, Inc.

Prien, R. F., Klett, C. J., and Caffey, E. M., Jr. (1973). Lithium carbonate and imipramine in prevention of affective episodes. *Archives of General Psychiatry* 29: 420–425.

Prien, R. K., Kupfer, D. J., Mansky, P. M. et al. (1980). Continuation therapy in depression: preliminary findings from the National Institute of Mental Health — Pharmacologic and Somatic Treatments Research Branch collaborative study of long-term maintenance drug therapy in affective illness. Presented at the 19th Annual Meeting of the American College of Neuropsychopharmacology. San Juan, 16–18 December.

Quitkin, F. M., Kane, J., Rifkin, A. et al. (1981). Prophylactic lithium with and without imipramine for bipolar I patients. *Archives of General Psychiatry* 38: 902–907.

Quitkin, F. M., Rabkin, J. G., Ross, D. et al. (1984). Duration of antidepressant drug treatment. *Archives of General Psychiatry* 41: 238–245.

Quitkin, F., Rifkin, A., and Klein, D. F. (1979). Monoamine oxidose inhibitors: review of effectiveness. *Archives of General Psychiatry* 36: 749–760.

Rabin, E. Z., Garston, R. G., Weir, R. G. et al. (1979). Persistent nephrogenic diabetes insipidus associated with long-term lithium carbonate treatment. *Canadian Medical Association Journal* 121: 194–198.

Rabkin, J. G., Klein, D. F., and Quitkin, F. M. (1983). Somatic treatment of acute depression. In *Schizophrenia and Affective Disorders*, ed. A. Rifkin, pp. 35–77. Boston: John Wright PSG, Inc.

Ramsey, T. A., and Mendels, J. (1981). Lithium ion as an antidepressant. In *Antidepressants: Neurochemical, Behavioral and Clinical Perspectives*. ed. S. J. Enna, J. B. Malick, E. Richelson, pp. 175–182. New York: Raven Press.

Ravaris, C. L., Nies, A., Robinson, D. S. et al. (1976). A multiple-dose, controlled study of phenelzine in depression-anxiety states. *Archives of General Psychiatry* 33: 347–350.

Riblet, L. A., and Taylor, D. P. (1981). Pharmacology and neurochemistry of trazadone. *Journal of Clinical Psychopharmacology* 1: 17S–22S.

Richelson, E. (1982). Pharmacology of antidepressants in use in the United States. *Journal of Clinical Psychiatry* 43: 4–11.

Robinson, D. S., Nies, A., Ravaris, C. L. et al. (1973). The monoamine oxidase inhibitor phenelzine in the treatment of depressive anxiety states. *Archives of General Psychiatry* 29: 407–413.

———— (1978a). Clinical psychopharmacology of phenelzine: MAO activity and clinical responses. In *Psychopharmacology: A Generation of Progress*. ed. M. A. Lipton, A. DiMascio, and K. F. Killam, pp. 961–973. New York: Raven Press.

———— (1978b). Clinical pharmacology of phenelzine. *Archives of General Psychiatry* 35: 629–635.

Roose, S. P., Glassman, A. H., Siris, S. G. et al. (1981). Comparison of imipramine- and nortriptyline-induced orthostatic hypotension: a meaningful difference. *Journal of Clinical Pharmacology* 1: 316–319.

Rosenblatt, J. E., Pert, C. B., Tallman, J. F. et al. (1979). The effect of imipramine and lithium on α- and β-receptor binding in rat brain. *Brain Research* 160: 186–191.

Rubin, R. T., and Marder, S. R. (1983). Biological markers in affective and schizophrenic disorders: a review of contemporary research. In *Affective and Schizophrenic Disorders: New Approaches to Diagnosis and Treatment*, ed. M. R. Zales, pp. 53–99. New York: Brunner/Mazel.

Rubin, R. T., Poland, R. E., Blodgett, A. L. N. et al. (1982). Endocrine responses to perturbation tests in primary endogenous depression: preliminary findings.

In *Proceedings of III World Congress in Biological Psychiatry*, ed. B. Jansson, C. Perris, and G. Struwe. Amsterdam: Elsevier-North Holland.

Rush, A. J., Schlesser, M. A., Roffwarg, H. P. et al. (1983). Relationships among the TRH, REM latency and dexamethasone suppression tests: preliminary findings. *Journal of Clinical Psychiatry* 44: 23–29.

Sabelli, H. C., Fawcell, J., Javaid, J. I. et al. (1983). The methylphenidate test for differentiating desipramine–responsive from northiptyline–responsive depression. *American Journal of Psychiatry* 140: 212–214.

Scher, M., Krieger, J. N., and Juergens, S. (1983). Trazadone and priapism. *American Journal of Psychiatry* 140: 1362–1363.

Schildkrant, J. J., Orsulak, P. J., Schatzberg, A. F. et al. (1983). Laboratory tests for discriminating subtypes of depressive disorders based on measurements of catecholamine metabolism. In *Affective and Schizophrenic Disorders: New Approaches to Diagnosis and Treatment*, ed. M. R. Zales, pp. 103–123. New York: Brunner/Mazel.

Schubert, J., Nycack, H., and Sedvall, G. (1970). Effect of antidepressant drugs in accumulation and disappearance of monoamines formed *in vivo*. *Journal of Pharmacology* 22: 136–138.

Sethy, V. H., and Hodges, D. H. (1982). Role of β-adrenergic receptors in the antidepressant activity of alprazolam. Presented at Benzodiazepine Symposium, National Institute of Health, 12–14 April.

Sheehan, D. V., Ballenger, J., and Jacobson, G. (1980). Treatment of endogenous anxiety with phobic, hysterical and hypochondriacal symptoms. *Archives of General Psychiatry* 37: 51–59.

Singh, A. N., Saxena, B., Gent, M. et al. (1976). Maprotiline (Ludiomil, Ciba 34276-BA) and imipramine in depressed outpatients: a double-blind clinical study. *Current Therapeutic Research, Clinical and Experimental* 19: 451–462.

Siris, S. G., and Rifkin, A. (1983). Side effects of drugs used in the treatment of affective disorders. In *Schizophrenic and Affective Disorders*, ed. Arthur Rifkin, pp. 117–138. Boston: John Wright PSG, Inc.

Small, J. G. (1980). Complications with electroconvulsive treatment combined with lithium. *Biological Psychiatry* 15: 103–112.

Stern, S. L., and Mendels, J. (1981). Drug combinations in the treatment of refractory depression: a review. *Journal of Clinical Psychiatry* 42: 368–373.

Strömgren, L. S. (1975). Therapeutic results in brief-interval unilateral ECT. *Acta Psychiatrica Scandinavica* 52: 246–255.

Thomsen, K., and Schou, M. (1975). Treatment of lithium poisoning. In *Lithium Research and Therapy*, ed. F. H. Johnson. London: Academic Press.

Tilkian, A. G., Schroeder, J. S., and Kao, J. (1976). Effect of lithium on cardiovascular performance: report on extended ambulatory monitoring and exercise testing before and during lithium therapy. *American Journal of Cardiology* 38: 701–708.

Tollefson, G. D. Monoamine oxidase inhibitors: a review. *Journal of Clinical Psychiatry* 44: 280–288.

Treiser, S. L., Cascio, C. S., O'Donohue, T. L. et al. (1981). Lithium increases serotonin release and decreases serotonin receptors in the hippocampus. *Science* 213: 1529–1531.

von Meduna, L. (1935). Die konvulsions therapie der schizophrenie. *Psychiatrisch-neurologische Wochenschrift* 37: 317–319.

Wang, R. Y., and Aghajanian, G. K. (1980). Enhanced sensitivity of amygdaloid neurons to serotonin and norepinephrine after chronic antidepressant treatment. *Communications in Psychopharmacology* 4: 83–90.

Wehr, T. A., and Goodwin, F. K. (1979). Rapid cycling in manic-depressives induced by tricyclic antidepressants. *Archives of General Psychiatry* 36: 555–559.

Wehr, T. A., Muscettola, G., and Goodwin, F. K. (1980). Urinary 3-methoxy-4-hydroxyphenylglycol circadian rhythm: early timing (phase-advance) in manic-depressives compared with normal subjects. *Archives of General Psychiatry* 37: 257–263.

West, E. D., and Dally, P. J. (1959). Effects of iproniazid in depressive syndromes. *British Medical Journal* 1: 1491–1494.

White, K., and Simpson, G. (1981). Combined MAOI-tricyclic antidepressant treatment: a reevaluation. *Journal of Clinical Psychopharmacology* 1: 264–282.

Williams, L. T., Lefkowitz, R. J., Watanabe, A. M. et al. (1979). Thyroid hormone regulation of β-adrenergic receptor number. *Journal of Biological Chemistry* 252: 2787–2789.

Winokur, A., Amsterdam, J. D., Oler, J. et al. (1983). Multiple hormonal responses to protireline (TRH) in depressed patients. *Archives of General Psychiatry* 40: 525–531.

Worral, E. P., Moody, W. P., Peet, M. et al. (1979). Controlled studies of the acute antidepressant effects of lithium. *British Journal of Psychiatry* 135: 255–262.

Yogi, H. (1977). Central nervous actions of carbamazepine. *Journal of the Yonago Medical Association* 28: 182–195.

Zall, H. (1971). Lithium carbonate and isocarboxazid — an effective drug approach in severe depressions. *American Journal of Psychiatry* 127: 1400–1403.

Zeller, E. A., Burksy, J., and Fouts, J. R. (1952). Influence of isonicotinic acid hydrazid (INH) and 1-isonicotinyl-2-isoproply hydrazid (IIH) on bacterial and mammalian enzymes. *Experientia* 8: 349–350.

INDEX